Economic Prehistory

Around 15,000 years ago, almost all humans lived in small mobile foraging bands. By about 5,000 years ago, the first city-states had appeared. This radical transformation in human society laid the foundations for the modern world. We use economic logic and archaeological evidence to explain six key elements in this revolution: sedentism, agriculture, inequality, warfare, cities, and states. In our approach the ultimate cause of these events was climate change. We show how shifts in climate interacted with geography to drive technological innovation and population growth. The accumulation of population at especially rich locations led to creation of group property rights over land, stratification into elite and commoner classes, and warfare over land among rival elites. This set the stage for urbanization based on manufacturing or military defense and for elite-controlled states based on taxation. Our closing chapter shows how these developments eventually resulted in contemporary global civilization.

Gregory K. Dow has published six articles on economic prehistory with Clyde Reed, including in the *Journal of Political Economy,* ranked among the top economics journals in the world. His other books include *Governing the Firm: Workers' Control in Theory and Practice* (2003) and *The Labor-Managed Firm: Theoretical Foundations* (2018), both published by Cambridge University Press.

Clyde G. Reed is an economic historian. His dissertation was supervised by Douglass North. Until recently, his main research interest has been Medieval European economic history. Working jointly with Greg Dow, Clyde's most recent research focus has been economic prehistory. In addition to academic pursuits, Clyde is a musician (double bass).

Economic Prehistory

Six Transitions That Shaped the World

GREGORY K. DOW
Simon Fraser University

CLYDE G. REED
Simon Fraser University

CAMBRIDGE
UNIVERSITY PRESS

CAMBRIDGE
UNIVERSITY PRESS

Shaftesbury Road, Cambridge CB2 8EA, United Kingdom

One Liberty Plaza, 20th Floor, New York, NY 10006, USA

477 Williamstown Road, Port Melbourne, VIC 3207, Australia

314–321, 3rd Floor, Plot 3, Splendor Forum, Jasola District Centre, New Delhi – 110025, India

103 Penang Road, #05–06/07, Visioncrest Commercial, Singapore 238467

Cambridge University Press is part of Cambridge University Press & Assessment, a department of the University of Cambridge.

We share the University's mission to contribute to society through the pursuit of education, learning and research at the highest international levels of excellence.

www.cambridge.org
Information on this title: www.cambridge.org/9781108839907
DOI: 10.1017/9781108878142

First published 2022

Printed in the United Kingdom by TJ Books Limited, Padstow Cornwall

A catalogue record for this publication is available from the British Library.

Library of Congress Cataloging-in-Publication Data
NAMES: Dow, Gregory K., 1954- author. | Reed, Clyde G., 1942- author.
TITLE: Economic prehistory : six transitions that shaped the world / Gregory K. Dow, Simon Fraser University, British Columbia, Clyde G. Reed, Simon Fraser University, British Columbia.
DESCRIPTION: 1 Edition. | New York, NY : Cambridge University Press, 2022. | Includes bibliographical references and index.
IDENTIFIERS: LCCN 2022007065 (print) | LCCN 2022007066 (ebook) |
ISBN 9781108839907 (hardback) | ISBN 9781108813815 (paperback) |
ISBN 9781108878142 (epub)
SUBJECTS: LCSH: Economic history. | Economic development. | Social stratification. | Cities and towns–Growth. | BISAC: BUSINESS & ECONOMICS / Development / Economic Development
CLASSIFICATION: LCC HC21 .D86 2022 (print) | LCC HC21 (ebook) | DDC 330.9–dc23/eng/20220214
LC record available at https://lccn.loc.gov/2022007065
LC ebook record available at https://lccn.loc.gov/2022007066

ISBN 978-1-108-83990-7 Hardback

For Margaret and Sherrill

Contents

Figures

Tables

Preface

This is a book about the origins of things: sedentism, agriculture, inequality, war, cities, and states. We begin with a few words about the origins of the book.

The proximate cause for Greg's interest in prehistory involved his effort to design a course on comparative economic institutions at Simon Fraser University during the late 1990s. This course was aimed at second- and third-year students who had seen some basic economics but had no math background beyond high school algebra. The goal was to use case studies of small-scale communities or societies to illustrate how economic reasoning can help to explain social behavior. A core element of this course was Johnson and Earle's book *The Evolution of Human Societies* (2000), which includes 19 case studies of anthropologically observed societies, ranging from mobile foraging bands to densely populated agrarian states. Greg's earliest attempts to model the emergence of agriculture and inequality began as lecture notes for this course.

Clyde became interested in long-run economic growth as a graduate student at the University of Washington. After passing a field exam in international trade, Clyde started searching for a dissertation topic that was not in international trade. In his search, he took a course in economic history from Douglass North, and the rest is history. At that time, the University of Washington was richly endowed with economic historians: Douglass North, Robert Thomas, Morris D. Morris, Kozo Yamamura, and Robert Higgs. There were frequent economic history lunches in addition to seminars. Regular visitors included Bob Fogel (Chicago) and Bill Parker (Yale). It was a very stimulating environment, to say the least.

Fast forward to Simon Fraser University early in the decade 2000–10. Clyde is teaching graduate courses on long-run economic and social change from the perspective of economic history. Greg is teaching undergraduate courses located at the intersection of economics and anthropology. In 2003 the two of us began to discuss the origins of agriculture, and whether economists had anything to add to the existing literature on this topic. We also discussed whether the arguments in Jared Diamond's classic book *Guns, Germs, and Steel* (1997) made economic sense. Our progress was initially slow because we needed to make investments in learning about the archaeological literature, surveying what other economists had said, and working out our own theoretical perspective. The resulting article on agriculture appeared in the *Journal of Economic Growth* in 2009.

At first we had no particular plan beyond addressing the Neolithic transition to agriculture. But one thing led to another, and we started to think about technological innovation during the Upper Paleolithic; specifically, the question of why technological progress took so long. With the main setup costs behind us, our own progress became more rapid, and we published five more prehistory articles between 2011 and 2017. In the course of these efforts, we developed a consistent theoretical approach that seemed helpful in understanding several prehistoric transitions, and a book became inevitable.

This book is meant to be accessible to archaeologists, anthropologists, and other interested social scientists, not just economists. At the same time we have included the kind of formal modeling that economists expect to see. To achieve both goals we made extensive modifications to our journal articles and added several chapters that have not previously been published. Four chapters have no math. The chapters that do have math include several sections where theoretical arguments are expressed in a clear verbal way.

Where relevant, we present mathematical material in a series of technical sections in the middle of a chapter. The proofs of mathematical propositions are available on the Cambridge University Press website. The technical sections should be accessible to any academic economist or graduate student with standard training in microeconomic theory. Readers without this background should be able to skip the math while still following the thread of the argument.

In Part I, Chapter 1 presents key theoretical principles. It also explains how our economic approach resembles and differs from various theoretical perspectives in archaeology and anthropology. Chapter 2 is a short introduction to the Malthusian theory of population dynamics, which will be used repeatedly later in the book. Part II (Chapters 3–5) focuses on technological matters, including innovation in societies of the Upper Paleolithic, the transition from mobile to sedentary foraging, and the transition from sedentary foraging to agriculture. Part III (Chapters 6–8) addresses institutional developments in pre-state societies, specifically the emergence of inequality, warfare over land between egalitarian groups, and warfare over land among elites in stratified societies. Part IV (Chapters 9–11) investigates the evolution of cities and states. We conclude in Part V, Chapter 12 by constructing theoretical and empirical bridges that link prehistory with the modern world.

A book-length treatment enables us to provide a continuous narrative and to put greater emphasis on the interdisciplinary nature of the subject. Our work has improved considerably through feedback from editors and referees at economics journals, and we are grateful for their efforts. But economics journals naturally want to publish articles aimed at professional economists, and they often want relatively short papers that focus crisply on formal models and technical results. More than once we had to make painful cuts to empirical discussions or literature reviews in order to meet tight page limits. We also sometimes had to reduce the space for topics we regarded as central in order to make room for topics we regarded as peripheral. This book tells our story in the ways we find congenial, free from the constraints often imposed by our home discipline.

Some readers may be curious about our division of labor and/or the nature of the process we use in reaching our conclusions. Because Greg is an applied microeconomic theorist and Clyde is an economic historian, it would be natural to imagine that Greg does the theory and Clyde does the empirics. This is too simplistic a description of our work habits. Each time we have started a new project (for example, the origins of inequality), our first task has been to read broadly in the relevant archaeological literature, seeking to find out what key facts need to be explained, what candidate explanations are currently in circulation, and what areas of the world have well-documented archaeological records for the phenomenon in question. Sometimes we read the same books and articles in order to have a shared grasp of the issues, but we also read different books and articles in order to cover more empirical terrain and challenge each other's interpretations of the facts. Over time we converge on a tentative view about the major causal forces at work.

Greg then starts to construct a formal model that captures these theoretical ideas. Clyde provides feedback on the modeling, identifying minor matters that can be deleted and major matters that were ignored. Greg argues that including some points Clyde sees as major would make the math intractable. Sometimes Clyde agrees that such points can be left to a verbal discussion, while at other times he (gently) suggests that Greg should try harder. Clyde also tries to keep Greg honest by emphasizing that the modeling must be constrained by respect for certain key facts. And so on. This iterative process leads to a formal model with which we are both comfortable, in the sense that (a) we believe it offers a reasonable explanation for most of the facts we originally wanted to explain and (b) we think further complications would yield sharply diminishing intellectual returns.

Because we each read subsets of the theoretical and empirical literature on a topic, some regional case studies were largely written by Clyde and others were largely written by Greg. Similarly, we each contribute parts of the literature review on a subject, with a division of labor reflecting who read what. However, many rounds of discussion ensure that these parts of the book are joint products.

We do not have archaeological training and we have not used shovels to dig for artifacts. Apart from our own reading, we have relied on a network of archaeologists to point us toward important sources of information, explain key ideas, and give feedback on early drafts. Naturally we have also consulted with a number of economists over the course of our research. The postscripts for the individual chapters acknowledge advice from these helpful colleagues. None of the people mentioned in the Acknowledgments or in the postscripts bears any responsibility for our errors or interpretations. On some issues their opinions may differ substantially from our own.

Acknowledgments

Our intellectual debts are vast and we will only single out a few people here. Among archaeologists we first thank some colleagues from the Department of Archaeology at Simon Fraser University: Mark Collard, David Burley, and Brian Hayden. We especially thank Mark Collard, who served as the director of the Human Evolutionary Studies Project (HESP) at SFU, a project that included Greg as one among seven co-principal investigators. Mark ran a research seminar for his graduate students and other members of HESP. These sessions provided us with invaluable exposure to the way archaeologists think. We sometimes presented our research to this group, which gave us important early feedback.

We also express our thanks to Stephen Shennan of the Institute of Archaeology at University College London (UCL). Stephen gave a keynote lecture at a conference on economic prehistory in Vancouver in 2009, and we have kept in touch since then. In 2019 we spent three months at UCL and enjoyed extensive conversations with Stephen, which included his comments on three seminar presentations. Our discussions with Stephen's colleagues at UCL were enormously helpful and came at a crucial time in the evolution of the book.

Another archaeologist who has had an important role in shaping the book is Tim Earle. As we mentioned earlier, our interest in prehistory was stimulated to a very large degree by Earle's book with Allen Johnson, *The Evolution of Human Societies* (2000). Over the years we have learned a lot from Tim's other publications. We thank Tim both for his inspiration and for generous comments on our previous work.

Two more archaeologists who were particularly helpful with Part IV of the book are Guillermo Algaze and Norman Yoffee. Guillermo repeatedly commented in detail on the material on southern Mesopotamia in Chapter 9. Norman read drafts of the material for Chapter 11 and offered guidance to the literature on early cities and states. Although he did not comment directly on this book, we want to extend our special gratitude to Ofer Bar-Yosef, who encouraged the early stages of our work on the origins of agriculture and exerted a strong intellectual influence from afar. We also want to highlight the influences of the anthropologist Robert Kelly (often cited in Parts II and III) and the political economist Carles Boix (often cited in Parts III and IV, as well as the Epilogue).

Among economists we start by thanking our colleague Arthur Robson from the Department of Economics at Simon Fraser University. Arthur works in a neighboring field – the biological evolution of human preferences. We have benefited from Arthur's insights through shared supervision of PhD students, his participation as a co-investigator in the HESP project described above, his invitations to other researchers to visit SFU, and his writings. We greatly value Arthur's friendship and encouragement.

Another economist with whom we have often shared ideas about prehistory is Sam Bowles. Readers will find that Sam's name comes up often in these pages. He has written extensively on the origins of agriculture, early inequality, and early warfare, and we will discuss Sam's work on these topics at some length. We thank Sam for feedback on preliminary versions of several chapters, especially Chapters 5–7.

Four more economists who have influenced our thinking are Matt Baker, Omer Moav, Ola Olsson, and Louis Putterman. All have made central contributions to the field of economic prehistory. Matt has published key articles on foraging societies, the origins of agriculture, and the origins of the state; Omer has a long list of influential articles on prehistory, including the origins of the state; and Ola and Louis have explored linkages between prehistory and modern economic growth. We received valuable comments from Louis on Chapters 9–12; from Omer on Chapter 9; and from Ola on Chapter 12.

During our writing we have enjoyed ongoing conversations with Nathan Nunn, particularly around the economics of culture. We thank Nathan Nunn and Melissa Dell for invitations to visit the Department of Economics at Harvard in the fall of 2018.

In addition to the people already named, we have received expert archaeological advice from Andrew Bevan, Sue Colledge, Rowan Flad, Dorian Fuller, Andrew Garrard, Jonathan Mark Kenoyer, Li Liu, Jeffrey Quilter, Jason Ur, and David Wengrow. Among economists, we have received helpful feedback from Richard Lipsey, Richard Harris, and James Kai-sing Kung. Another economist and friend, Cliff Bekar, has frequently offered insightful comments on our work.

We also thank our co-authors on previous publications, including Nancy Olewiler for an article on the origins of agriculture, Simon Woodcock for an article on exogamous and endogamous marriage, and Leanna Mitchell for an article on early warfare over land. As we explain in postscripts to the relevant chapters, our research with Nancy evolved into Chapter 5 of this book and our research with Leanna evolved into Chapter 7. Our research with Simon does not directly correspond to a chapter in this book, but he has contributed to our thinking about marriage institutions in small-scale societies, a subject that will arise in a number of chapters. We are grateful for the contributions of these co-authors, but we bear sole responsibility for the presentations appearing here.

We extend our very special thanks to Huiqian Song, who created the graphs and tables for this book, and to Vivian Gu, who has generously designed and maintained our websites for many years. Several past SFU graduate students in economics have added to our knowledge of prehistory and related areas: Mahsa Akbari, Duman Bahrami-Rad, Kevin Haiyun Chen, Colleen Cunningham, Giuseppe Danese, Liang Diao, Ideen Riahi, Nick Robalino, Scott Skjei, and Michael Straw. We have fond memories of our days at SFU with all of them.

Further thanks are extended to a large number of students at SFU who have taken Greg's courses in economic prehistory at both the undergraduate and graduate levels. In all of these courses Clyde has been a frequent guest, and together we have learned how to present archaeological information (and economic theory) to student groups with varying degrees of preparation in economics. We hope our exposition has improved as a result of these teaching experiences.

Several chairs in the Department of Economics at SFU (Gordon Myers, Nicolas Schmitt, David Jacks, and Brian Krauth) provided teaching releases, study leaves, and office space. Likewise, several deans of the Faculty of Arts and Social Sciences at SFU (John Pierce, Lesley Cormack, John Craig, and Jane Pulkingham) provided study leaves, research funding, and conference support; Jon Driver, a former Vice President-Academic at SFU, provided conference support; and the Office of Research Services of the Vice President-Research at SFU provided funding and administrative support. The Human Evolutionary Studies Project at SFU supplied teaching releases as well as funding for research assistants. Bev Neufeld in the FASS office at SFU helped to refine our grant applications on multiple occasions.

The Social Sciences and Humanities Research Council of Canada (SSHRCC) funded much of our research over the last two decades. We especially appreciate SSHRCC's willingness to support stays at Harvard University and University College London from September 2018 until March 2019, which improved the book in many ways. We also appreciate the excellent administrative support and pleasant surroundings offered by the Department of Economics at Harvard, the Standing Committee of Archaeology at Harvard directed by Rowan Flad, the Institute of Advanced Study at University College London directed by Tamar Garb, and the Institute of Archaeology at UCL.

Chris Harrison of Cambridge University Press showed great enthusiasm for this project and trusted our promises about it. We are extremely grateful for his support and flexibility. Rachel Blaifeder of CUP also supplied vital administrative help early in the editorial process. In addition, we thank Abigail Fiddes, Jessica Norman, Sable Gravesandy, Erica Walsh, Hemalatha Subramanian, Dhanuja Ragunathan, Sivaraman Madavan and Christine Ranft for their contributions in the final stages of publication.

In some chapters we rely on material from previously published journal articles. Springer Business+Science Media provided permission to use material from Gregory K. Dow, Clyde G. Reed, and Nancy Olewiler, 2009, Climate reversals and the transition to agriculture, *Journal of Economic Growth* 14(1), March, 27–53. Elsevier provided permission to use material from Gregory K. Dow and Clyde G. Reed, 2011, Stagnation and innovation before agriculture, *Journal of Economic Behavior and Organization* 77(3), March, 339–50; Gregory K. Dow and Clyde G. Reed, 2015, The origins of sedentism: Climate, population, and technology, *Journal of Economic Behavior and Organization* 119, November, 56–71; and Gregory K. Dow, Leanna Mitchell, and Clyde G. Reed, 2017, The economics of early warfare over land, *Journal of Development Economics* 127, July, 297–305. The University of Chicago Press gave permission to use material from Gregory K. Dow and Clyde G. Reed, 2013, The origins of inequality: Insiders, outsiders, elites, and commoners, *Journal of Political Economy* 121(3), June, 609–41.

Finally, we thank our readers. This book will make demands on their time and perhaps also their patience, but we hope they will conclude that it was time well spent.

Abbreviations

AHP	African humid period
AMHs	Anatomically modern humans
APL	Average product of labor
BP	Before present
BSR	Broad spectrum revolution
CE	Current era
IPCC	Intergovernmental panel on climate change
KYA	Thousand years ago
LGM	Last glacial maximum
LRE	Long-run equilibrium
MP	Middle Paleolithic
MPA	Monotone population adjustment
MPL	Marginal product of labor
NPP	Net primary productivity
PPNA	Pre-pottery Neolithic A
PPNB	Pre-pottery Neolithic B
SCCS	Standard cross-cultural sample
SRE	Short-run equilibrium
UP	Upper Paleolithic
VLRE	Very-long-run equilibrium
YD	Younger Dryas

PART I

PROLOGUE

I

Economics Meets Archaeology

Anatomically modern humans have existed for about 300,000 years. For almost all of that time, people lived in small mobile bands, obtained their food by hunting and gathering, had egalitarian social systems, and were free from external political control. These features of human society began to change around 15,000 years ago, as a more sedentary lifestyle with higher population densities took hold in some parts of the world. The most fundamental changes were associated with the shift to agriculture, which first arose in southwest Asia around 12,000 years ago and emerged independently in several other regions, including China, sub-Saharan Africa, Mesoamerica, and South America.

Before agriculture, food storage was limited and there were few opportunities for wealth accumulation. The entire world population was comparable to that of present-day New York City. Population density was very low, probably less than one person per square mile in the inhabited regions of the world. There were no towns, no governments, and no written records. There was probably considerable interpersonal violence, with no police, courts, or prisons to suppress this violence, though the evidence is mixed. Technological innovations took millennia to spread from one part of a continent to another.

After agriculture, the world changed. Many writers dislike the term "agricultural revolution" (or "Neolithic revolution") because the full transition from foraging to farming took thousands of years. But the agricultural revolution nevertheless transformed society. It reinforced tendencies toward inequality and warfare that had begun with the

3

emergence of sedentary foraging. It also provided the economic underpin-
nings for urbanization and state formation. It was a necessary condition
for the industrial revolution, which led to sustained growth in per capita
income of 1 percent per year or more (Clark, 2014).

The echoes of the Neolithic persist in other ways. Some economists
have found that contemporary economies have higher per capita incomes
or higher rates of economic growth if they are located in regions of the
world that had an early Neolithic transition to agriculture or the early
emergence of a state (Bockstette et al., 2002; Hibbs and Olsson, 2004;
Olsson and Hibbs, 2005; Putterman, 2008; Borcan et al., 2018). One can
question the causality, but the correlations are striking.

We find it intriguing that sedentism, agriculture, inequality, warfare,
cities, and states emerged independently in several regions of the world.
This strongly suggests that parallel causal mechanisms were at work; it
strains credulity to argue otherwise. At the same time, identifying these
mechanisms is challenging to say the least. Archaeological evidence
clearly indicates that no simple unilinear model is sufficient. Different
regions have followed different technological and institutional trajectories. And, as we explain later, cases of non-transition can be just as
informative as cases of transition.

Economic theory can help in understanding early social trajectories.
Throughout these transitions, individuals and groups were making economic decisions: where to live, what natural resources to exploit, what
production methods to use, how to assign property rights over scarce
resources, whether to hire other people, and whether to seize resources
from others through the use of force. Economics offers a powerful toolkit
for modeling these decisions and their consequences.

By combining economic theory with archaeological data, we attempt
to explain (1) the transition from mobile foraging to sedentary foraging;
(2) the transition from sedentary foraging to agriculture; (3) the origins of
inequality; (4) the origins of warfare; (5) the origins of cities; and (6) the
origins of states. We argue that these events were set in motion by climate
changes near the end of the Pleistocene between 21,000 and 11,000 years
ago, which led to growing populations and new technologies for food
production. These developments strengthened incentives for appropriation, defense, and conquest of valuable territories. In several parts of
the world, the eventual outcome was inequality, warfare, urbanization,
and state power.

We hope this book will be of interest to a wide audience, including
economists, archaeologists, anthropologists, political scientists, geographers,

other social scientists, and historians. The interests of these diverse scholars will naturally vary. For example, economists like formal models and expect them to satisfy certain professional norms. Readers from other disciplines may not share an economist's enthusiasm for mathematics at all, let alone the disciplinary norms that guide an economic theorist. We have included all the formal analysis an economist might want, but the mathematical presentations are self-contained and can be skipped by readers who prefer to dispense with them. The verbal portions of each chapter should make the central ideas widely accessible.

We also want to express some humility. There is no presumption that economic theory is the best or only way to understand prehistory. Rather, the book is meant to be an exploration of how much economics can contribute to that goal. Later in this chapter we will discuss how our approach is related to that of other economists, archaeologists, anthropologists, and the pioneering work of the geographer Jared Diamond (1997).

Our subject is bounded in several ways. First, we define economic prehistory as the study of economic activity in societies without written records. This distinguishes it from economic history, where written documents are available. We limit our attention to prehistory because the six transitions we will explore all had their earliest manifestations before the emergence of writing.

Second, we focus on pristine transitions rather than processes of diffusion. For example, the transition to agriculture in southwest Asia was pristine in the sense that it was not influenced by prior transitions in other regions. Agriculture later diffused from southwest Asia to Europe. To understand the origins of agriculture, we therefore focus on southwest Asia rather than Europe. This restriction is imposed partly to keep our task manageable and partly because the causal mechanisms that explain pristine origins may be quite different from those that explain diffusion.

We also distinguish our subject from human biological evolution (Robson, 2001). Thus we skip over the biological line of descent involving australopithecines and archaic members of the genus *Homo*, such as Neanderthals. Until very recently the accepted date for the presence of anatomically modern humans in Africa was around 190,000 years ago (McDougall et al., 2005). This has been pushed back to around 300,000 years ago based on new evidence from Morocco (Hublin et al., 2017).

We assume that the cognitive, social, and linguistic abilities of all contemporary human populations are identical. The date at which these abilities arose is unknown, and they may extend back hundreds of thousands of years. However, the six transitions that provide the subject matter for this book did not begin until about 15,000 years ago. The existence of behavioral modernity in this time frame is not controversial (Nowell, 2010).

We are not attempting here to provide a full chronological narrative of events in prehistory. We do use regional case studies extensively, so readers will see information about a wide variety of societies drawn from different points in space and time. But these regional examples are used primarily for the purpose of constructing economic models or discussing the potential application of such models, and thus the empirical presentation is guided by the theoretical questions we want to investigate. It should also be emphasized that we are not attempting to provide a comprehensive and impartial survey of economic (or other) theories about prehistory. We have a particular theoretical framework in mind, and our goal is to show how this framework can be used to construct causal explanations. The relationship of our approach to that of other economists will be discussed in Section 1.8 and in subsequent chapters as specific issues arise.

Readers who are unfamiliar with archaeological time scales may gain perspective from Figure 1.1, which indicates several major signposts along the long road to our own society. Archaeological and genetic evidence about human migrations across continents is accumulating rapidly (Reich, 2018), and the true dates may differ from those shown in Figure 1.1. The time line starts on the left side with the presence of anatomically modern humans in Africa around 300,000 years ago, or 300 KYA.

There is evidence that anatomically modern humans moved into southwest Asia by around 180 KYA (Hershkovitz et al., 2018), but these early migrations may not have had much lasting impact. Permanent large-scale migration of modern humans into Asia probably occurred by 70 KYA and perhaps substantially earlier (Bae et al., 2017), so we use the

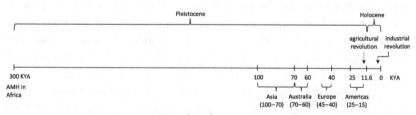

FIGURE 1.1. Time line for economic prehistory

interval 100–70 KYA in Figure 1.1. Modern humans reached Australia by 70–60 KYA (Clarkson et al., 2017). Migration to Europe occurred by 45–40 KYA (Hoffecker, 2009). The timing of the first migration into the Americas has been hotly debated, with genetic evidence suggesting 25–15 KYA (Moreno-Mayar et al., 2018). Recent research (Bennett et al., 2021) offers strong support for the presence of modern humans in North America between 23–21 KYA.

Ice Age conditions prevailed during most of this time, except for an interglacial period called the Eemian around 126–116 KYA (Woodward, 2014). Climate fluctuations occurred, technological innovations occasionally arose, and regional populations waxed and waned. But qualitatively new economic systems did not develop until the end of the Pleistocene and the start of our own interglacial period, the Holocene, around 11.6 KYA. Agriculture has been important for the last 10,000 years, and fossil-fuel-powered industry has been important for the last 250 years. Thus, anatomically modern humans have spent 96.7 percent of their time on Earth without a farming economy and 99.9 percent of their time without an industrial economy. From this perspective, our contemporary world civilization is very recent and very puzzling.

One key economic puzzle involves the long delay in the evolution of agriculture. If agriculture was an attractive way to obtain food, why did it take so long for people to adopt it? If agriculture was an unattractive way to obtain food, why did people adopt it at all? Figure 1.1 suggests a role for climate change: perhaps under cold Ice Age conditions farming was relatively unproductive, and the warmer conditions of the Holocene reversed that calculation. However, the story is more complicated than this. While we agree that climate change was the prime mover, it is significant that agriculture emerged in several areas of the world but not everywhere. Moreover, agriculture emerged at different times in different places. We will attempt to explain these variations across time and space.

Although our subject matter is prehistory, and therefore ends with the appearance of written documents in city-states, the time line in Figure 1.1 suggests another question: Why was there such a long lag between the evolution of pristine states more than 5,000 years ago and the industrial revolution starting around 250 years ago? If state societies were technologically progressive, why did the industrial revolution take so long to occur? If they were technologically stagnant, why did industrialization occur at all? These issues are central for economic historians, development economists, and growth theorists. We will return to them in our concluding chapter.

1.2 OUR QUESTIONS

Our goal is to explain the six transitions described above: sedentism, agriculture, inequality, warfare, cities, and states. What caused them? Why did the timing of a given transition differ across regions? Why did some parts of the world undergo all six of these transitions, while others experienced only a subset? Why did the order of the transitions sometimes vary across regions? Before we begin to address these questions, we need to consider what a candidate theory should look like.

At the most basic level, a theory of social evolution seeks to explain why certain societies transitioned from an initial condition A to a later condition B. For such a theory to be interesting, there must be a collection of societies that have made the transition. For such a theory to have some generality, it must abstract from variations within the set of societies characterized by A and variations within the set of societies characterized by B. Having suppressed these (one hopes) irrelevant distractions, the theorist proposes a causal mechanism through which A could have become B. A good theory will spell out the circumstances under which a transition from A to B is likely or unlikely to occur. These assertions need to line up with the available evidence. A good theory will also typically have other empirical implications that can be checked against current or future data.

Nothing in this exercise implies that there is a fixed series of stages through which all societies must pass, or that local conditions are irrelevant, or that chance plays no role. Frequently, however, theorists have classified societies into broad types corresponding to alleged evolutionary stages and have claimed that many or most individual societies tend to follow this uniform evolutionary trajectory. One common basis for such classification schemes has been to arrange evolutionary stages in order of increasing social complexity, defined in whatever way the individual writer finds most persuasive or convenient. This approach has intuitive appeal because it is hard to imagine how complex societies could have arisen at all except through some process of emergence from simpler predecessors.

Modern thinking along these lines derives from Service (1971), who classified societies as bands, tribes, chiefdoms, and states. We find this typology too constraining and do not use it here. Such terminology is widespread and impossible to avoid entirely, so there will be occasional references to foraging bands, pristine states, and the like. But for theoretical purposes, we treat technology and institutions as independent

Production Technology

Social Institutions	mobile foraging	sedentary foraging	agriculture	manufacturing
open access	A	B	C	
closed access (peace/war)		B'	D	
stratification (peace/war)		B"	E	E'
states (peace/war)			E"	F

FIGURE 1.2. Classification system for early social trajectories

dimensions in describing a society, which allows for a variety of developmental pathways.

Figure 1.2 displays a classification system we have found useful in organizing our own thoughts. This system has two dimensions: the nature of production technology and the nature of social institutions. Production technologies are listed in the columns, which correspond to mobile foraging, sedentary foraging, agriculture, and manufacturing. We will use the terms "forager" and "hunter-gatherer" interchangeably. It is best to picture new technologies being added as one moves from left to right, without old technologies being abandoned completely. For example, sedentary foragers sometimes go on hunting trips, farmers may gather wild plants, and societies with manufacturing sectors generally have farmers too. We also do not mean to imply that there is no manufacturing in foraging or agricultural societies. At a minimum, all the societies discussed in this book manufacture stone tools. The fourth column of Figure 1.2 refers to societies where manufacturing is a full-time occupation for some workers, who obtain their food from others. Pastoralism is omitted from Figure 1.2 but will be discussed where appropriate in later chapters.

The rows of Figure 1.2 describe social institutions. The top row for open access refers to those societies where population can flow relatively freely from one territory to another. Such flows tend to preserve economic equality across territories, because people can migrate from locations with low resources per capita to locations with high resources per capita. The second row for closed access refers to societies where population flows of this kind do not occur. Instead, insiders prevent outsiders from entering their territory. This creates economic inequality across territorially defined groups, but groups remain internally egalitarian. We will call this *insider–outsider* inequality. The third row for stratification continues to have closed access, but adds unequal access to land or other natural resources among the individual members of a territorially based group. We call this *elite–commoner* inequality. The fourth row for states continues to have closed access and stratification, but adds collection of taxes by the elite. When we say "closed access" without any further qualification, we are typically referring to the second row of Figure 1.2 (no stratification). When we say "stratification" without any further qualification, we are typically referring to the third row (no state).

In addition to territorial exclusivity across groups and stratification within groups, we will be concerned with warfare, because this is a common institutional mechanism for transferring resources from one group to another. We are especially interested in warfare aimed at seizing land from nearby groups, or gaining control over inhabitants of the land. We do not consider this type of warfare in the top row of Figure 1.2 because open access preserves freedom of movement for individuals, which tends to restrain the use of force among groups. But groups living under closed access may have reasons to engage in warfare with neighboring groups, and the elites in stratified societies often engage in warfare with the elites of neighboring societies.

Property rights need to be enforced, and there are technologies of coercion that can be used for this purpose, just as there are technologies of production. In general, we distinguish three kinds of coercive technology. The first is exclusion technology, where an organized group of insiders prevents unorganized outsiders from entering a territory. The second is military technology, where one organized group fights another organized group for control of a territory. The third is confiscation technology, where an organized elite seizes resources (food, labor time, manufactured goods, and so on) through taxation of individuals in the territory controlled by the elite.

The letters A, B, C, D, E, and F in Figure 1.2 highlight a series of transitions that we call the *main sequence*. This is the sequence we find most useful analytically and it is the sequence in which the book is organized. After a primer on Malthusian economics in Chapter 2, Part II examines the technological path leading from A to B to C. We consider mobile foragers (Chapter 3), sedentary foragers (Chapter 4), and farmers (Chapter 5). In these chapters we assume that social institutions permit flexible population flows across sites or territories, so the top row of Figure 1.2 applies.

Part III addresses the institutional pathway running from C to D to E, starting with the transitions from open to closed sites and from closed to stratified sites (Chapter 6). Next, we investigate the conditions affecting warfare over land among egalitarian groups (Chapter 7). Finally, we study issues of war and peace in stratified societies (Chapter 8). It is simplest to think about the institutional transitions in Part III while assuming that the production technology involves agriculture, indicated by the third column of Figure 1.2. However, exceptions sometimes arise, as will be discussed below.

Part IV concludes our study of the main sequence by addressing the transition from E to F: that is, from stratified agricultural societies to city-states having an urban manufacturing sector and an elite with the power to tax. We begin with archaeological data and hypotheses related to early state formation in southern Mesopotamia (Chapter 9). We follow this with an economic model designed to account for the data (Chapter 10), and a more general discussion regarding the origins of cities and states (Chapter 11). In Figure 1.2 the main sequence involves a diagonal jump from the third row and third column to the fourth row and fourth column, because in southern Mesopotamia urban manufacturing and the state emerged simultaneously.

We need to provide a few caveats to our concept of a main sequence. First, the notion of open access in the top row does not literally mean that anyone can move to any site at any time. We use simplifying assumptions along these lines in some of our formal modeling, but our interpretation is more nuanced. In mobile foraging societies, people typically marry partners outside their own band (exogamy), which establishes a kinship network linking social groups. Agents who want to move between groups can do so by exploiting these connections. As a result, population flows relatively easily from places with low resources per capita to places with high resources per capita. These migration flows tend to equalize the distribution of resources across individuals within a region.

A second caveat is that sedentary foragers do not necessarily have open access in the sense defined above. Instead, they usually have stronger group identities, leading to closed access and perhaps stratification (cells B′ and B″ in Figure 1.2) as well as warfare. In the anthropological literature, sedentism is often associated with social complexity of this kind (Kelly, 2013a). In the archaeological literature, there are examples of sequences from A to B′ and B″. As the term "main sequence" suggests, other sequences are possible (our framework is consistent with multilinear evolution; see Steward, 1955). While cell B of Figure 1.2 may be empirically rare, nevertheless we find it theoretically convenient to study the sequence ABC in thinking about sedentism and agriculture.

A third caveat is that we focus on the formation of city-states in Part III, which generally have urban manufacturing sectors as in cell F of Figure 1.2. But in principle there can be cities without states or states without cities. The former case could arise if a stratified society developed an urban manufacturing sector without the taxation needed to support a state. This would involve a horizontal move to the right in the third row of the figure, from E to E′. The latter case could arise if a state developed through the taxation of agriculture without any urbanization or manufacturing. This would involve a vertical move down in the third column of the figure, from E to E″. We will discuss these issues further in Chapter 11.

Another more hypothetical sequence emphasizes the role of tight territoriality and frequent warfare from the Upper Paleolithic onward. Service (1971) argues that warfare was important at the band level and may have been a primary driver behind the evolution of tribes and chiefdoms. More recent writers have also argued that warfare has very deep prehistoric roots (Bowles and Gintis, 2011). In the scheme of Figure 1.2, this means that mobile foragers in the first column either never had open access or shifted at a very early date from open to closed access. Closed access and warfare then persisted at each of the technological steps leading from mobile foraging to sedentism and then agriculture, with stratification emerging in the wake of sedentism or perhaps agriculture. We will discuss scenarios of this kind when they become relevant in particular chapters.

We can now reframe our key questions: what caused prehistoric societies to move from one cell to another in Figure 1.2 and why did societies in different parts of the world sometimes follow different paths? Sections 1.3–1.6 will describe the methods we use to investigate these questions, and Section 1.7 will outline our answers. Sections 1.8–1.10 will discuss how our approach fits into the literatures of economics and archaeology.

1.3 ECONOMIC VARIABLES

When studying economic prehistory, it makes sense to focus on geographically defined regions of the world such as southwest Asia, northern China, or Mesoamerica. The boundaries of these regions are often vague, but they can reasonably be treated as independent cases in the sense that the developmental trajectory of one region had little or no effect on the trajectories of the others. The economies of such regions are the key units for theoretical and empirical analysis throughout the book.

Simply put, an economy is a social system that allocates resources. A description of an economy must include at least the following elements: The population of the region, the natural resources available in the region, the technology that can be used to transform inputs into outputs, the preferences of individual agents, and the institutions that structure the interactions of the agents. This section briefly introduces each variable. Section 1.4 describes the archaeological data available for each variable, Section 1.5 defines several concepts from economic theory, and Section 1.6 explains the theoretical assumptions we make about each variable.

Population: When describing an economy, the first variable of interest is the size of the population in a relevant geographical region. Our formal models will assume each adult agent has one unit of labor time that can be allocated to activities of various kinds, so we regard the adult population and the supply of labor as equivalent. The length of a time period is one human generation (about 20 years). The adults of one generation produce the adults of the next generation.

Resources: A population has access to non-labor inputs given by nature. These are determined by climate, geography, and local ecosystems. Climate includes the mean temperature and precipitation for a given region, along with the variances of temperature and precipitation. Geography includes the availability of surface water from rivers, lakes, and marshes; the altitude and steepness of the terrain; soil quality; and so on. Ecosystems determine the availability of wild plant and animal species.

Technology: A viable society needs a technology that converts natural resources into food and other desired goods. Food technologies may involve gathering wild plants, hunting wild animals, harvesting marine resources, cultivating domesticated plants, or raising domesticated animals. In addition to direct acquisition of wild or domesticated resources, foods generally require processing and may be storable. Technology is also used for the production of fire, shelter, clothing, jewelry, and musical instruments.

Preferences: In most economic models, agents have preferences about the goods they obtain from natural resources through the use of technology. These preferences may involve the mix of goods consumed, consumption today versus consumption tomorrow, physical goods versus leisure, or attitudes toward risk, among other things. Our formal models make very simple preference assumptions. In most chapters there is one good: food. Each individual maximizes his or her food income, or expected food income, and uses food to produce surviving adult offspring. Our food variable can be interpreted as net energy capture or some other variable correlated with reproductive success.

Institutions: In any economy, there are social mechanisms that specify how the individual agents interact with one another. Food may be shared or not; access to land may be controlled by groups, individuals, or no one; wealth or social positions may be inherited or not; and so on. Among economists, the modern approach to understanding institutions and institutional change can be traced to the work of Douglass North (1971, 1978, 1981, 1990, 1994, 2005; North and Thomas, 1973; North et al., 2009). North viewed institutions as rules (constraints) determining how agents interact in competition and cooperation. For example, a government may enforce laws or an experimenter may set the rules of a game that laboratory subjects are asked to play. However, North used a wider concept of "rules of the game" that encompassed formal rules, informal rules, and norms of behavior (see our discussion of culture in Section 1.6). In general, institutions influence the payoffs received by agents and therefore shape their incentives.

In small stateless societies, it is unclear who creates or enforces the rules of the game. Such societies may not be subject to any external coercive power, and are held together by norms, conventions, ideologies, and personal and group identities. A more useful definition for such cases is that an institution is a stable pattern of social behavior that persists over time as individuals come and go. In this perspective, it is still true that institutions influence the incentives of individuals. Now, however, an institution is just a collective behavioral pattern from which most individual agents do not deviate.

1.4 ARCHAEOLOGICAL DATA

This section provides a short outline of data sources for the economic variables described in Section 1.3. The discussion is kept general because the individual chapters will delve more deeply into the evidence bearing upon specific issues and regions, with appropriate methodological caveats and citations to the literature. Here we simply want to reassure the reader that even in the absence of written documents, much can be known about prehistoric economies.

First, we sketch what we mean by archaeology and anthropology. Non-specialists might think that archaeology is the study of dead societies and anthropology is the study of living societies. But some anthropologists study skeletons millions of years old, while some archaeologists study garbage produced by societies alive today. To further confuse the matter, some writers treat archaeology as a subset of anthropology, while others treat them as separate disciplines.

Given our focus on prehistory, it is convenient to adopt the following convention: *archaeology* means the study of material remains left by early non-literate societies, and *anthropology* means the ethnographic study of recent or current non-literate societies. In this context, "early" refers to societies that existed thousands of years ago, while "recent" refers to societies from the last few centuries. Scholars in both fields also study literate societies, but that is not our concern here. Most of the evidence we discuss comes from archaeology in the sense defined above, because most of the transitions of interest in this volume occurred several millennia ago. However, anthropological data will sometimes play a supplemental role. Readers wanting more information about field and laboratory methods in archaeology can consult Balme and Paterson (2006) or the relevant chapters of introductory archaeology textbooks (e.g., Feder, 2019).

Population: Archaeologists can often estimate the size or density of population in a geographic region in a given time period. They can also often estimate the populations of specific sites or settlements. Data are obtained from excavations of caves, campsites, houses, and villages. Of course, methodological difficulties can make such inferences problematic. These include various types of selection bias, questions about the reliability and calibration of dates, the use of modern anthropological data as a source of analogies, and so on. In some cases, DNA can be used to infer the size of past populations in given regions or the scale of population movements from one region to another. Even when an archaeologist cannot estimate the absolute population level at a point in time with much precision, it may be possible to learn whether the population in a given region and time period was rising, falling, cyclic, or stationary.

Resources: A given region will typically provide resources ranging from water and food to raw materials for the production of tools, clothing, and the like. In much of the book we will concentrate on food sources, which depend on climate, geography, and ecosystems. Archaeologists sometimes have good information about past climates, both globally and for specific regions. Data sources include ice cores, ocean sediments, and a large number of proxy variables to be discussed later when relevant. Archaeologists also know quite a bit about geology, rivers, lakes, marshes, deserts, mountains, coastlines, and other physical features that influenced the resources of prehistoric societies. Climatic and geographic data can provide insight into past ecosystems. Also, plant pollen and animal bones frequently offer direct evidence about the species available for hunting, gathering, or domestication in a region. The genetic pathways from wild to domesticated species can sometimes be identified.

Technology: Archaeologists have good data on tools made of durable materials such as stone, bone, and antler, as well as pottery. Researchers can often determine how such tools were made, what they were used for, and where the raw materials came from. They also frequently have good information on methods of food processing and storage, as well as the specific foods consumed, and methods of house construction. Information is much scarcer for technologies involving non-durable plant or animal materials, such as clothing or wooden boats. Early societies can often be classified by their dominant food technology (mobile foragers, sedentary foragers, farmers, or pastoralists) and it is usually known what domesticated plants and animals were present (if any). Dates can frequently be assigned to prehistoric events through radiocarbon techniques or other methods.

Preferences: Archaeologists often try to infer the preferences and beliefs of the members of prehistoric cultures from the material remains of these cultures. Inferences of this sort are difficult and often controversial. Fortunately, our theoretical framework does not require highly nuanced information about preferences in ancient societies. But we will occasionally refer to such issues (e.g., religious beliefs) when they have a direct bearing on institutional matters with which we are concerned.

Institutions: Relatively uncontroversial archaeological evidence about prehistoric institutions can sometimes be obtained. For example, the degree of economic inequality can be inferred from skeletal data on diet or disease, unequal grave goods or house sizes, and how exotic materials are distributed within a site. Organized warfare can be inferred from skeletal evidence of violent deaths (particularly in the context of mass graves), from defensive fortifications or the use of easily defended sites, from weapons, and from visual depictions. Large cities tend to be highly visible in the archaeological record. State-level institutions can usually be inferred from multi-tiered settlement hierarchies, bureaucratic administrative systems, or monumental palaces and temples.

In addition to these key variables, archaeologists can provide evidence about a variety of other factors that will be of frequent interest throughout the book. Foremost among these is the standard of living, which can be inferred from evidence on nutrition, health status, and estimates of life expectancy. We will also be interested in migration patterns, trade patterns, and similar economic issues on which archaeology sheds light.

Anthropologists provide valuable evidence on recent or contemporary hunting and gathering societies, as well as small-scale agricultural societies (Johnson and Earle, 2000; Robson and Kaplan, 2006; Kelly, 2013a). It seems plausible that societies having similar natural resources, technologies, and population densities would tend to develop similar economic institutions. To the extent that this is true, ethnographic analogies can offer insights into how prehistoric societies might have dealt with risk, trade, property rights, warfare, inequality, or resource depletion problems. Such analogies may suggest hypotheses about how societies evolved over time.

However, it is always perilous to assume that similarities and differences among recent societies can be mapped onto past evolutionary trajectories. For example, the few remaining hunter-gatherer societies tend to be located in environments like rain forests, deserts, or the Arctic that are of little interest to modern farmers, while their prehistoric ancestors had access to rich and diverse ecosystems before farmers arrived on the scene. Moreover, the remaining small-scale societies of any kind, whether foraging or farming, have virtually all had contact with contemporary state-level societies and world markets. Considerable caution is therefore required when using anthropological evidence to draw inferences about the nature of prehistoric societies or their developmental pathways.

I.5 ECONOMIC THEORY

This section reviews several basic concepts from economic theory. These ideas will be used in all of our formal models and much of our verbal discussion.

We want to stress one point at the outset. When an economist says, "I assume X," this almost never means the economist believes X is the literal truth. What it could mean is, "I am going to suppose for the sake of argument that X is true and see where that idea takes me." Or, "I would find it too challenging to consider the possibility of not-X at the moment, given all the other complications I have to deal with." Or, "everyone knows X is false, but the difference between X and not-X may not matter very much for present purposes, so let's ignore not-X."

A related potential source of confusion involves a stylistic convention frequently used by economists. In professional writing, an economist may make what appear to be bold empirical claims. For example, the economist may say, "There are only two sites in this region where food can be obtained," or "At each site, there are diminishing returns to labor." A casual reader might wonder whether the economist really checked to make sure there are no other food production sites, or whether numerical data on inputs and outputs support the assertion about diminishing returns.

This would be a misinterpretation. Actually, the economist is not making direct empirical claims but rather stating the assumptions to be included in a theoretical model. For any complex model, it becomes tedious to say repeatedly, "I assume that . . . ." It is more convenient to make a series of crisp declarative statements summarizing what the reader needs to know about the structure of the model.

We hope contextual clues will indicate when we are genuinely making empirical claims (look for discussions about data sources and their reliability). Similarly, context should reveal when we are introducing theoretical assumptions or deducing implications of those assumptions (look for discussions of modeling issues). In ambiguous cases, we ask readers to give us the benefit of the doubt rather than assuming that we are ignorant (although of course we could be).

Optimization: Most economic models include agents who maximize an objective function subject to constraints. In our models, an agent generally maximizes his or her food consumption subject to the constraint that he or she has a fixed amount of time. A simple example is an agent who must decide where to obtain food and picks the location where the most food is available.

In Part II, we assume small groups of agents can jointly optimize. That is, they make collective decisions about how to allocate the total time of group members across various natural resources that could be exploited, or various production techniques that could be used, in a way that maximizes the total food output of the group. This food is then shared equally among the group members. In this context, the constraints include the total time of group members, the available resources, and the available technology.

In Part III, we study the establishment of property rights over land and warfare over land. We continue to assume that individual agents want to maximize their food consumption and that small groups can jointly optimize. However, large groups spread across multiple sites or territories do not operate as collective actors and do not jointly optimize at a regional level.

In Part IV, we move away from the simple objective of maximizing food intake and consider agents who care about both food and manufactured goods. In this case we need a way of describing the preferences of agents over bundles of goods. The standard tool for this purpose is a utility function, which ranks all possible consumption bundles. An agent then maximizes utility subject to budget and time constraints.

Equilibrium: Informally, an equilibrium is a state of rest for an economic system. When the system is already in equilibrium, it stays there, unless disturbed by an external shock of some kind. When the system is not in equilibrium, it tends to move toward an equilibrium state, provided that the equilibrium is stable. There may also be equilibria that are unstable, so the system tends to move away from them. Only stable equilibria will be observed, so these provide the basis for empirical predictions. In some cases, the economic system can have multiple equilibria (Chapters 3 and 7 will provide examples).

The specific way in which an equilibrium is defined depends on the context. In some models (see Chapters 6, 8, and 10), elite agents hire commoner agents at a wage, and no individual agent can influence the market wage through his or her own actions. The equilibrium wage is determined by the requirement that the supply and demand for labor be equal, so the labor market clears. Such price-taking behavior by the individual agents is associated with *competitive equilibrium*.

For our models, it can be shown that a competitive equilibrium wage in a labor market is equivalent to a competitive equilibrium rent in a land market, in the sense that the allocation of resources and the distribution of income would be identical under these two institutional arrangements.

The wage or rent can always be paid in the form of food. We never assume the existence of a money economy, although our conclusions would be unchanged if money happened to exist.

In Chapters 9 and 10 we consider the possibility that elite agents could collude to restrict the scale of urban manufacturing. In this case, the elite can use its market power to drive up the price of manufactured goods and drive down the wage. This provides an example of *monopolistic equilibrium*.

Three other kinds of equilibrium can be mentioned at this point. We will often be interested in situations where there is a balance between fertility and mortality so regional population remains in a steady state and neither rises nor falls. We call this a *Malthusian equilibrium* (see Chapter 2). To model warfare in Chapters 7 and 8, we adopt the game-theoretic idea of *dominant strategy equilibrium* to determine whether there is a war (one group attacks another) or peace (no one attacks). In Chapter 8 we also adopt the idea of *Nash equilibrium* to determine the sizes of the armies recruited by elites.

Exogenous and Endogenous Variables: This distinction is fundamental to the way in which economists think about causality. An *exogenous* variable is relevant to a model but its level is not determined within the model. The level of an *endogenous* variable is determined within the model, and is often something the modeler wants to explain. For example, in the model of Chapter 3 where a foraging group is allocating time across food-collection activities, the allocation of time is endogenous. Climate, which influences the availability of natural resources, is exogenous. Climate is one important determinant of how foragers use their time, but the model says nothing about what determines climate.

Whether a variable is exogenous or endogenous depends on the model. If all we care about is explaining time allocation, we might regard population and technology (in addition to climate) as exogenous. But if we want to explain the population density of a region, clearly we need a model where population is endogenous. Similarly, if we want to explain technological innovation in the Upper Paleolithic, we need a model where the foraging technology is endogenous.

Economists often vary the level of an exogenous variable and see what effect this has on the endogenous variables, according to the model. For example, one can consider a change in climate and study its causal effect on time allocation. This method is called *comparative statics*, because it involves three steps: (a) start from an initial equilibrium; (b) change an exogenous variable; (c) compare the levels of the endogenous variables in the new equilibrium with their levels in the old one. In this book we are concerned with the direction of the changes in the endogenous variables at step (c), not the magnitude of the changes (we are interested in qualitative effects rather than quantitative effects).

Time Scales: Whether a variable is exogenous or endogenous may depend on the time scale to which the model applies. Economics has a tradition of distinguishing the *short run* from the *long run*. The details depend upon the model, but the idea goes as follows. There are often some variables in a model that are fixed in the short run (they are exogenous over a short period of time), while these same variables change in ways that are explained by the model in the long run (they become endogenous over a longer period of time). This can be extended to include a *very long run* when it is convenient to distinguish a third time scale. For example, as will be explained in Section 1.6, we treat total regional population as exogenous in the short run and endogenous in the long run. We treat technology as exogenous in both the short and long runs but endogenous in the very long run. Some variables are exogenous in all runs (climate and geography), while others are endogenous in all runs (time allocation).

Economists do not typically use the language of proximate and ultimate causes, but other social scientists frequently do. For example, an anthropologist who wanted to explain the causes of warfare (C) in a given society might say that the proximate cause was the presence of aggressive men in leadership positions (B), but the ultimate cause was resource scarcity (A). The implied causal pathway is A → B → C. An economist would probably be tempted to translate this into assertions about the short and long runs. The economist might say that in the short run, resource scarcity and the characteristics of leaders are both exogenous while warfare is endogenous, so (A, B) → C. But in the long run, leader characteristics and warfare are both endogenous and only resource scarcity is exogenous, so A → (B, C).

We close this section with a few remarks on the advantages of economics as a way of thinking about prehistory. Most fundamentally, economics highlights rational human responses to the natural and social environment. Few if any economists would claim that all individuals make rational choices all the time (the rapidly growing field of behavioral economics has identified many exceptions to the premise of rational choice). But economists do find it very useful to generate predictions about aggregate behavior by assuming that this behavior arises from rational individual decisions made under material and institutional constraints. Economics has three additional strengths.

Generality: Economics encourages abstraction. This may seem like a bad thing, but from the standpoint of theory construction it is a good thing. If one abstracts from the details of particular cases, one is more likely to see general patterns. Although we would not want to generalize excessively about archaeologists (each is unique), we have found that they often tend to care more about the particular than the general. However, a tight focus on the individual trees tends to steer attention away from forests or ecosystems. In contrast, the first question an economist would ask about a formal model inspired by one empirical case is whether it generalizes to other empirical cases of a similar kind.

Causality: In our experience, archaeologists are sometimes more concerned with description than explanation, and some actively resist inquiries into causal relationships. Economics forces the theorist to think clearly about causality. It is almost impossible to construct a formal economic model without distinguishing exogenous from endogenous variables, individual from aggregate behavior, local from regional events, or the time scales on which different causal relationships play out.

Observability: We will advance many causal hypotheses in this book and some of them may turn out to be incorrect or unfruitful. But economics has the virtue of steering attention toward variables that are relatively easy to observe, such as climate, geography, technology, and population. For example, we often suggest that climate change was the trigger for particular prehistoric transitions. These suggestions may or may not be right, but hypotheses based on climate change are open to empirical investigation in ways that hypotheses based on changes in preferences, beliefs, or attitudes are not.

1.6 OUR METHODS

We begin this section with a preliminary discussion of our intellectual strategy. Next, we move on to substantive assumptions that are the building blocks for our formal models. These are maintained in all chapters and give theoretical unity to our approach. Next, we identify some variables not included in our models and comment on the reasons for their absence. Finally, we discuss the relationship between theory and evidence, and address potential criticisms of our methods.

Our general strategy is to adopt a few simple assumptions and use them to derive as much theoretical payoff as we can. Our purpose is to isolate the most powerful causal forces, while abstracting from less powerful forces. A bare-bones model is most useful for clarifying causal relationships between exogenous and endogenous variables, as well as the interactions among endogenous variables. We then consider complicating factors, which often reinforce the results obtained from the simpler model. One helpful analogy is that models are to reality what a road map is to a road. A road map ignores numerous details in order to highlight the features of the landscape that are most important for the intended journey. Some amount of detail is good, but a road map as complicated as the road itself would not be useful.

When we refer to simple models, we mean models having few causal channels and yielding clear analytic results. Clear results are important because our models are intended to make contact with archaeological evidence, so they need to say something unambiguous about the real world. But even seemingly simple modeling assumptions can lead to difficult mathematical challenges. Thus we do not mean that the implications of our assumptions are obvious. While working through the mathematics, we have often found that we initially overlooked a crucial conceptual issue or interaction effect. Math can be a vital tool for clarifying one's own thoughts.

Good theory should be constrained by known facts, and one must use judgment in deciding which facts are the most important or relevant. Such judgments are guided here by our interest in economic variables like those in Section 1.3. It is also necessary to use judgment in deciding whether certain alleged facts are reliable. Because our data come from archaeology, we seek to discern whether archaeologists have achieved a consensus on the relevant issues or whether active debates are still underway. In the latter case, we flag the issue for the reader and explain how it affects the model we are constructing.

Our main source of empirical information involves regional case studies. For a specific type of transition (e.g., the origins of agriculture or the origins of the state), our goal is to create a formal model that captures the most prominent and robust features of the archaeological narrative, avoids any glaring contradictions with other archaeological facts, and preserves consistency with the theoretical premises used elsewhere in the book. In many cases our models build upon hypotheses already advanced by archaeologists.

We also examine whether alternative theories can account for the same evidence. Even a modest amount of archaeological evidence can serve to disqualify some theories. This may occur because (a) the theory cites universal causes that do not explain observed variations across space and time, (b) the theory focuses on variables that are uncorrelated in space and time with the phenomenon of interest, or (c) the theory ignores variables that are clearly central to the archaeological record. We have found that these problems more often arise for theories advanced by economists than those advanced by archaeologists.

A good theory should account for instances of non-transition as well as transition. For example, when thinking about the origins of agriculture, we want to identify not only the regions where it evolved, but also the regions where it seemingly could have evolved but did not, and then explain these differences. A good theory should also account for the timing of transitions in places where they did occur. Why at this time? Why not earlier? Why not later? We will often argue that our theory explains or predicts the timing of the transition in question while rival theories do not.

We approach the issue of timing in the following way. For any particular kind of transition X, our model will identify a set of necessary conditions that must hold in order for X to occur. Together, these conditions will be sufficient. We use the term *trigger* in referring to the necessary condition that is chronologically the last to be satisfied. Once the triggering condition is satisfied X occurs. Or to put it another way, the trigger is the proximate cause of X.

From an economic standpoint, the role of the triggering variable is to move the system from a boundary equilibrium where the endogenous variable X is at a zero level to an interior equilibrium where X is at a positive level. Whenever we are explaining a technological innovation involving food production, the trigger moves the system from an equilibrium where some resource is not exploited or some technique is not used to an equilibrium where the resource is exploited or the technique is used. The same is true for institutional innovations. For example, when we explain the origin of stratification, the trigger will move the system from an equilibrium where all social groups are internally egalitarian to an equilibrium where some groups have elite–commoner inequality.

In principle, empirical researchers could test our predictions about the temporal proximity of the change in the trigger variable to the transition we want to explain. This requires *time series* data on the evolution of relevant variables over time within a region. By contrast, *cross-sectional* data provide information about differences in the levels of variables across sites or regions at a point in time. We usually focus on time series data in order to explore causal hypotheses about the timing of a transition in a given region.

The models in this book adopt a common set of substantive assumptions. These assumptions knit the models together to provide a unified theory of economic prehistory. We summarize the most important ones below.

Agents: All agents are identical in their preferences, endowments, abilities, and knowledge. They are myopic in the sense that they do not anticipate or care about what will happen in future generations, but they are otherwise rational. Each is endowed with one unit of labor time and wants to maximize food (or expected food) because this yields the maximum number of surviving children (or expected surviving children). Adults live for one period, obtain food, have children, and then die. Their surviving children become adults in the next period. In Part IV we include a second good (e.g. clothing) in the utility functions of the agents. Individual agents are of negligible size relative to the population at a production site, and do not believe they have any effect on total food output or group decisions at a site. For some caveats about the assumptions of self-interest and identical preferences, see the discussion of institutions below.

Non-economists may find our preference assumptions cartoonish. We find them useful. Given the great difficulty of learning anything about the details of preferences in prehistoric societies, and the difficulty of testing any hypotheses based on differences in preferences across regions or over time, we do not want to build an economic model on such foundations. Instead, we make simple and stark preference assumptions. With this machinery operating in the background, we put more readily observable variables in the foreground and ask them to do the bulk of the explanatory work.

Geography: A region consists of one or more sites (sometimes two, sometimes a continuum). In our usage, the term "site" refers to a parcel of land with associated natural resources where food can be obtained through labor time. Depending on the application, a site could have a very large land area (in such cases, the term "territory" is a synonym), or a very small land area (in a model with a continuum of sites, each individual site has a negligible area). Different sites could have different land areas. Distances between sites are not an important feature of our models (a pair of sites may be adjacent or not). This is all quite different from the way the same term is used by archaeologists, for whom a site tends to mean "a place where archaeologists dig things up." But unfortunately there is no convenient alternative word that captures what we have in mind.

In our models, geography influences the quality of each individual site within a region, where the quality of a site refers to its productivity as a source of food. Thus, for example, a site's quality could be enhanced by availability of surface water, proximity to animal migration routes, fertile soil, or a coastal location where marine resources can be collected. Although geographic features usually vary across the sites within a region, we typically assume that geography is constant over time (we ignore earthquakes, volcanoes, or changes in the courses of rivers). Because geography is constant, it never triggers a transition in the economic system, but it may be quite important in determining what is required for some other variable (like climate change) to trigger a transition. We assume an agent can move from one site to another in the same region, unless excluded by agents who are already there. Sometimes we assume migration is costless (Chapters 4 and 5) but at other times we assume it is costly (Chapter 7). Geography is always exogenous.

Climate: A climate consists of a given weather pattern that is common to all sites in the same region. Sometimes we treat the climate as a probability distribution defined over weather, and think of it as mean precipitation, mean temperature, and the variances of these variables (Chapter 4). However, usually we collapse it to a scalar. For example, we may define climate by annual rainfall and assume that within the relevant range more rainfall is better. The productivity of a given site is a function of the current climate for the region as a whole and the local geographic features specific to that site. The regional climate could vary over time, which generates temporal variation in resource availability. We often talk about climate "shocks," meaning an abrupt change in the prevailing climate conditions. Such a shock may be either good or bad. Climate is always exogenous.

Time Allocation: The small-scale foraging and farming groups in Part II jointly optimize. That is, in the short run they allocate their total labor time to maximize total food output, and share the resulting food equally. We relax this assumption in Parts III and IV when studying coercive technologies. Time allocation is always endogenous.

Population: The number of surviving children for an adult depends on the adult's food income (or in Part IV, utility). When adult agents become better off, fertility rises and child mortality falls, so the adult agents leave more surviving offspring. This leads to dynamics where a higher standard of living causes the population to grow more rapidly or decline less rapidly. Economists call such models *Malthusian* and we use that term here. Other social scientists may mean other things by the same term. To avoid confusion, we emphasize that when we use the adjective "Malthusian," we do not necessarily mean that members of society are on the brink of starvation, or that population is stabilized through high mortality rates rather than low fertility rates (for a further discussion, see Chapter 2). The total regional population is always exogenous in the short run and endogenous in the long run. However, agents may move from one site to another, so local populations can be endogenous in the short run even though the aggregate regional population is fixed.

Food Technology: Everyone in a region knows the current food technology. For a fixed technology, with land and other natural resources held constant, more labor yields more food output but at a decreasing rate (that is, the returns to labor are diminishing). The initial use of a novel technique leads to learning by doing and productivity growth until an upper bound on productivity is reached. Sometimes we treat this as a stochastic process (Chapter 3) but elsewhere we treat it as deterministic. Production technology is always exogenous in the short and long runs, but endogenous in the very long run.

Coercive Technology: In Part II we assume open access to all sites in a region, but in Parts III and IV we consider coercive technologies that can be used to regulate access to a site. As with production technologies, the coercive technologies are known to everyone in a region. If an organized group of insiders has sufficient population density per unit of land, it can collude to prevent entry to a site by unorganized outsiders. There may also be a military technology enabling an organized group at one site to seize land controlled by an organized group at another site. Insiders regulating access to a site may allow landless commoners to work at the site in exchange for food. In such cases we call the insiders an *elite*. An organized elite that taxes the agents at a site is called a *state*.

Institutions: We assume that small groups whose members live in close physical proximity can typically achieve collective goals without much trouble. Specifically, they can overcome coordination, free rider, and distributional problems in order to maximize total food consumption for the group as a whole. Such groups could be mobile foraging bands, local elites in stratified societies, and the like. However, larger or more dispersed groups often have more difficulty achieving collective goals. In theoretical discussions, we often think of the former groups as "organized" and the latter groups as "unorganized." The arguments in favor of this approach come from a number of sources: game theory, the new institutional economics, experimental economics, and ethnography.

There is an extensive theoretical literature examining the conditions under which cooperation can arise in repeated prisoners' dilemma games. Factors that tend to support cooperation include a small number of players, a long time horizon, frequent interaction, low discounting of future payoffs, and easy monitoring of past behavior by other players (for an introductory treatment, see Binmore, 2007, ch. 5). Economists have also studied other ways in which enlightened self-interest can promote collective welfare when legal enforcement of contracts is infeasible, including reputations, hostage capital, posting of bonds, and efficiency wages.

Writers in the new institutional economics have conducted field research into the conditions under which collectively beneficial institutions or norms will arise in modern communities. Ostrom (1990) finds that communities tend to evolve effective institutions for solving common pool resource problems when they have limited size, their members have similar interests, their membership is stable, and members do not strongly discount future payoffs. Ellickson (1994, ch. 10) argues that the content of social norms tends to promote total welfare for close-knit groups where informal power is broadly distributed and the information relevant for informal social control circulates easily.

Setting aside enlightened self-interest, *Homo sapiens* display an unusual capacity for cooperation among genetically unrelated individuals. Cooperation may be supported by a sense of fairness, a willingness to punish behavior seen as unfair even if punishing is costly and provides no tangible benefit, an ability to keep mental accounts of favors owed and received in social relationships, positive and negative reciprocity, a desire for social approval, and an inclination to classify others into "us" and "them." Experimentalists have found such tendencies in numerous societies (Bowles and Gintis, 2011, ch. 3; Putterman, 2012, ch. 6). However, some authors doubt the generality of these results across societies with differing histories and cultures (Schulz et al., 2018).

In our theory these motivations stay in the background, but they help justify our claim that small groups tend to cooperate easily. We are agnostic about the importance of social preferences relative to enlightened self-interest and repeated interaction as the foundation for this claim, and we do not formally model coordination or free rider games in such groups. We simply assume that within local groups having a few hundred people, aggregate labor is allocated to maximize aggregate food; knowledge and food are widely shared; and public goods such as collective defense are effectively supplied. These ideas seem consistent with ethno-graphic evidence (Johnson and Earle, 2000; Kelly, 2013a).

However, it is equally important that larger groups do not easily cooper-ate. If we assumed they did, we would be driven to a theory where all societies were characterized by economic efficiency. In this setting it would become very difficult to explain certain crucial institutional developments, such as inequality, warfare, and the state. We do not believe social preferences or enlightened self-interest are strong enough, at least within the institutional framework of prehistory, to warrant an assumption of joint optimization for large populations or large geographical regions. Readers familiar with the extensive literature on transaction costs (for example Coase, 1937, 1960; Williamson, 1985; Dow, 1987) can attribute failures of joint optimization to high information or bargaining costs, a lack of institutional mechanisms to support credible commitment, and similar factors.

A related observation about agent heterogeneity is in order. We do not doubt the findings from experimental economics suggesting that there is a good deal of preference heterogeneity within any population of humans. For example, some people are strongly self-interested while others are more willing to sacrifice their own interests for the sake of the group. Archaeologists and anthropologists often treat this sort of heterogeneity as a theoretical premise, referring to highly self-interested agents as "aggrandizers" or "aspiring elites" (Hayden, 1995). Heterogeneity of preferences or abilities is also of great interest to economists, who use it as the basis for models of screening, signaling, and reputation. Although we simplify here by assuming all agents are identical, if we were to introduce incomplete information about the "types" of agents, it would only reinforce our view that cooperation is difficult in large groups.

Culture: We recognize that cultural variations across regions of the world today are large and important, and we believe the same was true in the past. Though it will not often be in the spotlight, the concept of culture plays a significant background role in the book. We therefore want to clarify how it fits into our theoretical framework.

We follow Mokyr (2018, 8) in defining culture as "the set of beliefs, values, and preferences, capable of affecting behavior, that are socially (not genetically) transmitted and that are shared by some subset of society." Henrich (2016, 3) and Nunn (2021) provide related defin-itions but they go further. Along with many archaeologists and anthropologists, they include technology and institutions within the ambit of culture, in large part because they are passed from one generation to the next through learning. We will refer to this as "culture in the broad sense."

In this book we will find it useful to treat technology (like the methods people use for foraging, agriculture, or manufacturing) as a distinct analytic category. Similarly, we will treat institutions (like property rights, stratification, warfare, cities, and states) as a distinct analytic category. The remaining elements of culture (like beliefs, preferences, language, ethnicity, ideology, and religion) will be called "culture in the narrow sense." Because our goal is to explain transitions in technology and institutions, we are seeking to explain changes in culture in the broad sense, but not in the narrow sense.

These boundaries are admittedly fuzzy. For example, beliefs and technological knowledge have some overlap. We will construct a formal model of social learning when we discuss the evolution of technology in the Upper Paleolithic (see Chapter 3). There is also some overlap between beliefs and institutions. North, Wallis, and Weingast (2009, 15) define institutions as "formal rules, written laws, formal social conventions, informal norms of behavior, and shared beliefs about the world." Norms of behavior arguably are part of culture under Mokyr's definition, and shared beliefs clearly are.

We think of culture in the narrow sense as imposing a set of constraints on human choices that are collectively and/or individually constructed and enforced, and that are distinct from the constraints imposed by nature through geography, climate, and resource endowments. Social norms, which are behavioral rules enforced within a community, are a prime example of a cultural constraint, and may sometimes be grounded in religious beliefs and practices.

We do not rely on exogenous changes in cultural constraints in order to explain transitions in technology and institutions. Instead, our focus is on exogenous changes in the constraints imposed by nature. If pressed, we would say that culture in the narrower sense tends to adapt to nature, technology, and population in the long run. But even after controlling for these three variables, there is a great deal of residual variation in culture across societies. Culture in the narrower sense may also be rigid over periods of decades or centuries, which can limit adaptations to changes in nature, technology, or population.

Although we do not use cultural change as an explanatory variable, we often do assume that societies have certain cultural features relevant for our models. An example is the social norm of food sharing in mobile hunting and gathering societies (see Chapter 6). Any member of a group who violates this norm can be punished in a variety of ways including ridicule, shunning, expulsion from the community, and physical harm resulting in injury or death.

Another example involves social norms about marriage. Consider the distinction between exogamy (marriage between members of different communities) and endogamy (marriage between members of the same community). We view exogamy as a key factor promoting individual mobility across social groups, which is an important variable in our analysis of warfare (see Chapter 7).

In our earlier discussion of institutions, we argued for the view that members of small groups can cooperate easily while members of larger groups have more difficulty with collective action. Beyond the factors mentioned in this earlier discussion, we add that shared culture frequently facilitates cooperation within small and localized groups. In particular, shared social norms are core elements in reaching and enforcing collective choices. Culture tends to be less effective in promoting cooperation among the members of large, dispersed, or heterogeneous populations.

Next, we make a few comments about factors that often arise in discussions of prehistory but are omitted from our models. We disregard genetic changes in the human species over time and genetic variation in human populations across different regions of the world. Instead, we assume that all humans have had approximately the same genetic endowment for at least the last 15,000 years. Evolution by natural selection has clearly occurred within this time frame and likely continues, for example with respect to skin pigmentation, lactose tolerance, and resistance to malaria (Chiaroni et al., 2009; Reich, 2018). But we do not believe genetic change can explain the massive technological and institutional transitions of the last 15,000 years. Even so, our assumptions about agent preferences are meant to be consistent with the genetic programming humans probably received earlier in their biological evolution.

Our formal models also omit gender differences, risk aversion, leisure, physical capital, and resource depletion. Any of these factors could be added to our models at the cost of greater complexity. For now, we believe the marginal cost of adding them exceeds the marginal benefit in terms of enhanced understanding, but we could change our minds in response to theoretical arguments or empirical evidence.

There is a common tendency in many disciplines to demand greater "realism" in modeling. However, our goal is not to construct a model that explains the maximum number of facts (recall the analogy involving the road map and the road). A model that explains the main facts about a particular type of transition without adding unnecessary complications is a good thing. Such a model reveals that the further complications were not needed to explain the phenomenon of interest. This does not mean the complications are absent in reality, but it may mean they are less important than researchers previously thought. Of course, a theory based on alternative variables might also suffice to explain the phenomenon. But at least we will know that a relatively simple economic model is a serious contender, and we will have a clearer sense of what the contest between the rival theories looks like.

We now turn to a concern raised by some of our colleagues in economics: perhaps our sample sizes are too small to allow any meaningful inference about the merits of rival theories. For example, depending on how one defines a region, one could argue that pristine transitions from foraging to agriculture occurred in roughly ten regions of the world. Does this mean that the relevant sample size is ten? If so, there is not much hope of rejecting the null hypothesis about the origins of agriculture, whatever it may be.

We do not believe the outlook is so bleak. First, a theory that specifies necessary and sufficient conditions for an event X (such as the transition to agriculture) makes two kinds of predictions: (a) X should occur when Y is present and (b) X should not occur when Y is absent. Instances of non-X (the absence of a transition) are also observations and count as part of the overall data set.

A more important consideration is that a single case of transition does not count as just one observation. In general, we observe much more than the presence or absence of a transition. One can often observe or infer the time paths of climate, technology, and population within a region, and possibly other variables such as migration patterns or the standard of living. If a theory says something about the expected directions of change in these variables before, during, and after a transition, or about the sequence in which such changes are expected to occur, these implications can be compared with the evidence.

We cannot use statistical inference for hypothesis testing because our data are the narrative accounts provided by archaeologists. In place of econometrics, we proceed as follows. After constructing a model, we study its implications for sequences of events involving climate, technology, population, migration, standards of living, inequality, or other variables that happen to be relevant. Often the implications of the model are non-obvious and could potentially be disconfirmed by qualitative evidence on the timing or location of specific events, or the directions of change in observed variables. Then we compare model predictions with regional case histories drawn from the archaeological literature to see whether the model gives an accurate account of similar developmental trajectories in various regions of the world.

This procedure is unavoidably subjective. The reader may be concerned that the cases we emphasize are the ones most consistent with the models we wanted to present, and that we ignored other less consistent cases. We have various responses to concerns about selection bias of this sort.

First, it is important to consider how we chose our regional cases. Our interest in pristine transitions led us to avoid using multiple cases in the same chapter that plausibly had common technological or institutional origins due to cultural diffusion. Thus, we are not padding the data set by including causally related cases. Our central criterion for the selection of cases was the richness and reliability of available archaeological information, especially about the variables discussed in Sections 1.3 and 1.4. Of course, this creates a bias in favor of regions and periods heavily researched by archaeologists, and against any regions or periods that have not left equally prominent trails in the literature.

To provide guidance for the reader, we organize our discussions so the empirical information that motivated the construction of a formal model, or provided an important source of constraints on the model, is presented before the model itself. In some chapters this information consists of broad empirical generalizations, but in other chapters it may include one or more detailed regional histories. We then present the formal model and develop its logical implications. While strictly speaking one cannot use the same data to formulate a model and also test it, we hope readers will appreciate that creating a model consistent with a large number of facts about a complex regional case is no small matter, and will find our theoretical explanation for these initial facts to be somewhat persuasive (perhaps more persuasive than rival explanations previously offered in the literature).

After the model, we provide further empirical material. If we are trying to explain transitions of type X, this material may include more examples of X, important examples of non-X, or applications of the model to related empirical matters. The information in these sections was not used as a source of constraints for model construction and thus is analogous to "out of sample" testing in statistical analysis. Some of this information was found through literature searches carried out long after the structure of the formal model was fixed. We have not knowingly suppressed any well-documented regional cases that contradict our theoretical expectations.

In some situations, we argue that current evidence is too sketchy to render a clear verdict on our model. Wherever possible we describe future archaeological findings that could lead to modification or abandonment of our models, and we invite readers to seek out evidence of this kind. Nothing forces future archaeological discoveries to conform to our expectations. If such discoveries do happen to support our theory, this suggests that we were on the right track.

In any event, we hope readers of all disciplinary backgrounds will suspend their methodological disbelief until the book is well underway. Those outside economics will need to tolerate a degree of abstraction in order to grasp what we are doing with models. Those within economics will need to indulge our taste for regional histories because they are the most important data source for the questions we are asking.

1.7 OUR ANSWERS

This section sketches our explanations for the transitions in the main sequence of Figure 1.2. Chapter 3 begins with mobile foraging in the Upper Paleolithic. A foraging band can obtain food from an array of natural resources. At a given point in time, some of these resources are actively exploited while others are latent. We show that societies of this sort can get stuck in a "stagnation trap" where latent resources are not used due to inadequate techniques, but techniques do not improve because the resources are not used. A positive climate change (usually involving warmer and wetter conditions) can raise the standard of living in the short run, which generates population growth in the long run for Malthusian reasons. This causes agents to exploit previously latent resources, broadening the diet. Once new resources are in use, learning by doing raises productivity in the very long run, causing further population growth and so on, until a new equilibrium is reached with an increased population and wider diet. The expansion of technological knowledge creates a ratchet effect where a return to the original climate regime need not imply that population or diet breadth will return to their initial levels. This can explain how humans migrated into more severe environments over time. We argue that there is archaeological evidence of such dynamics for the Mediterranean area around 50–40 KYA, and stronger evidence for southwest Asia during the Epi-Paleolithic period around 21–13 KYA.

Chapter 4 uses a related model to explain how sedentism could have evolved in response to improving climate conditions. We consider a climate shift involving higher means and lower variances for temperature and rainfall. Sedentism is defined to mean a willingness of human populations to stay at the same site for multiple generations despite occasional poor weather conditions there (or other factors that temporarily reduce local productivity). The model identifies three causal channels leading to sedentism. First, there is a short-run channel where climate improvement leads agents to stay at sites even when the weather there is temporarily bad, because when conditions are harsh, they are less harsh than they were under the previous climate regime. Second, there is a long-run channel where better climate leads to higher regional population for Malthusian reasons. This causes some population to remain at sites where weather is temporarily bad rather than abandoning such sites entirely, because the sites with good weather are now more heavily occupied than they were before. Finally, there is a very-long-run channel where higher regional population leads to the use of previously latent resources. We argue that these mechanisms can help to explain the emergence of large sedentary communities in southwest Asia during the Epi-Paleolithic and in Japan during the early Holocene.

Sedentary foraging is not identical to agriculture, which involves the cultivation of plants and eventually their domestication. Chapter 5 argues that agriculture arose in southwest Asia during a large negative climate shock called the Younger Dryas (from about 12.8–11.6 KYA). After a prolonged period of warm and wet conditions during which the regional population reached a high level, an abrupt reversion to colder and drier conditions forced this large regional population into a few high-quality refuge sites where surface water was available from rivers, lakes, marshes, and springs. The resulting spike in local populations at these sites drove down the marginal product of labor in foraging and triggered reallocation of some labor toward cultivation. As cultivation got underway, learning by doing and the domestication of plants and animals enhanced its productivity, which reinforced incentives to engage in cultivation. Eventually climate improved in the Holocene, regional population grew, and agriculture spread. There is strong evidence for this explanation in the case of southwest Asia, and similar processes could have been at work for other cases of pristine agriculture (for example, China and sub-Saharan Africa).

In Part III, we turn to institutions. Chapter 6 begins with a theory about the origins of inequality. Our model involves a continuum of sites that have differing productivities with respect to food. Initially all sites are open, and free mobility of agents across sites tends to equalize food income even though the site qualities differ. An organized group that is large enough relative to the land area of a site can use a technology of exclusion to close a site; that is, prevent any other agents from entering. Such a group can also hire outsiders to work on its land if it wishes. We show that as population density rises due to improving climate or food production technology, fewer sites remain in the commons and more are closed. This generates what we call *insider–outsider* inequality, where different groups have different standards of living based on the qualities of the sites they control. Eventually the insiders located at the best sites find it profitable to hire some outsiders (either by paying them a wage or requiring them to pay land rent). This generates *elite–commoner* inequality, or *stratification*. We show how class positions become hereditary, and how technological progress can make commoners worse off because property rights over land respond endogenously to technological change. We argue that the predictions of the model are consistent with archaeological evidence from southwest Asia, Europe, Polynesia, and the Channel Islands of California.

Chapter 7 addresses the issue of early warfare. This subject is controversial, with some authors arguing that warfare has been prevalent throughout the biological evolution of human beings, and others arguing it is a relatively recent phenomenon. We focus on warfare over land among internally egalitarian groups, which were the norm for most of human existence. Archaeological evidence for Europe and southwest Asia reveals that warfare was rare in the Upper Paleolithic, common in the Mesolithic, and widespread in the Neolithic. This suggests an increase in the frequency of warfare along the trajectory from mobile to sedentary foraging, and from sedentary foraging to agriculture. We build a model where two groups occupy sites with possibly different productivities, and each group must decide whether to attack the other. If either group attacks, the probability of one group seizing the land of the other depends on the sizes of the two populations. If neither attacks, there is peace.

We show that if individual agents can migrate between sites before group decisions about warfare are made, a stable equilibrium with warfare is highly unlikely. However, a model with costly individual migration and Malthusian population dynamics can yield warfare, provided that there are climatic or technological shocks influencing the relative productivities of the sites. We argue that these results are broadly consistent with archaeological evidence.

Chapter 8 develops a theory about warfare in stratified societies. A large body of archaeological and anthropological research suggests that warfare is more common when societies are more stratified. This is true for societies based on either sedentary foraging or agriculture. Warfare in stratified societies does not require climatic or technological shocks and results from the competition among rival elites over land rent. In our model, elites recruit specialized warriors by offering the successful warriors elite status either in conquered territories or their home territories. The unsuccessful warriors die. The sizes of the armies are determined by the land rents available from the territories at stake. We show that war is absent when stratification is absent. The probability of warfare rises as the difference in living standards between elites and commoners grows, because if there is a large gap then elites can recruit warriors relatively cheaply.

Part III addresses the origins of city-states. Chapter 9 surveys various facts about the formation of city-states in southern Mesopotamia, along with existing archaeological hypotheses about the causes of this process. Chapter 10 builds a model where an initial society has mild stratification. A shift in climate toward increasing aridity causes people in outlying areas dependent on rainfall to move to elite-controlled areas where irrigation is based on river water. Greater aridity also motivates foraging and herding populations in the wetlands of southern Mesopotamia to enter the urban labor market. The falling standard of living for commoners eventually makes it profitable for elites to establish urban workshops producing textiles, pottery, metalwork, and other goods, even though the reallocation of labor toward cities reduces the land rent going to the elite. The latter loss is offset by the taxation of urban manufacturing activities, which enables the elite to enforce monopolistic output restrictions, driving up the price of manufactured goods and driving down the wage. We claim that this mechanism generates the tax revenue needed for state formation, and is consistent with the evidence presented in Chapter 9.

In Chapter 11, we review the broader literature on the origins of cities and states. We argue that purely agricultural societies are unlikely to have cities because population dispersal reduces travel costs for farmers and herders. But incentives for agglomeration could arise from the productivity of urban manufacturing, the need for collective defense under a threat of war, or other factors. We next discuss how formation of pristine states might be explained. We briefly survey several regional cases including Egypt, the Indus Valley, China, Mesoamerica, and the Andes. Some of these examples appear to involve manufacturing activities in a central way, while others appear mainly to involve warfare among rival elites in an agricultural setting. We conclude that the model from Chapter 10 based upon climate change and urbanization applies to some cases but not all. However, the broader idea that either negative climate shocks or warfare can drive rural populations toward refuge locations, and that the resulting cities serve as the nuclei for pristine states, may have relatively wide applicability. We also suggest that even when these factors are absent, rising agricultural productivity resulting in rising population and stratification can lead to declining commoner living standards, eventually inducing city-state formation.

Chapter 12 closes with a discussion of the ways in which prehistory still matters. First, there is a growing empirical literature in economics arguing that prehistoric events continue to affect economic development today. Specifically, some authors claim that regions where agriculture began early, or where state formation occurred early, tend to have either higher per capita income or more rapid economic growth in the present. We consider the evidence for these correlations and the causal forces that may explain them.

Second, recent centuries have seen dramatic institutional change, with the rise of democratic polities foremost among them. We will consider some factors that may have led from the elite-dominated states of prehistory to the more democratic states of today.

Third, prehistory forces us to reassess our view of economic progress. Because incomes have risen in most countries for the last century or so, there is an understandable tendency to extrapolate backwards and assume that earlier people must have been poorer. But the perspective of prehistory suggests something else: the first farmers were almost surely worse off than mobile foragers in terms of nutrition, health, and life expectancy, and commoners remained badly off for millennia afterward due to the combined effects of stratification and Malthusian population dynamics. Only in the very recent past has material life improved for the majority of the population.

Fourth, we argue throughout the book that climate change was the prime mover for technological and institutional innovation in prehistory. Now that we are confronting the specter of human-caused climate change, are there lessons from prehistory about what its effects will be, or how to cope with them? We have no crystal ball, but we will hazard some guesses about how the consequences of climate change in prehistory could compare with its consequences in the Anthropocene.

1.8 ECONOMIC LITERATURE

Economic prehistory is a small field relative to the discipline of economics as a whole, but the literature has been growing steadily over the last few decades. It attracts talented researchers and sometimes yields publications in leading economics journals. In this section we sketch some topics that have intrigued economists, without any attempt at completeness. Detailed discussions will be left for the relevant substantive chapters. We also comment on the relationship of our own approach to the work of other economists.

Two early contributions by economists came from Smith (1975) and North and Thomas (1977). Both articles raised the idea that a lack of private property rights among hunter-gatherers could have led to resource depletion through overharvesting, and argued that this could have led to more tightly defined property rights and/or agriculture. Over the next decade other writers continued to theorize about the origins of agriculture (Pryor, 1983, 1986; Locay, 1989). Themes in the 1990s included technological innovation and Malthusian population dynamics (Kremer, 1993; Locay, 1997). The interest in resource depletion and Malthusian dynamics came together in a prominent article by Brander and Taylor (1998) that sought to explain economic collapse on Easter Island.

Early in this century, development economists began to explore the relationship between prehistory and modern economic growth. The first research along these lines emphasized regional differences in the number of potentially domesticable plants and animals, which were argued to have had a major influence on differences in the timing of the Neolithic transition to agriculture across regions (see also our discussion of Diamond, 1997, in Section 1.10). A bit surprisingly, geographical and ecological conditions during the Neolithic turned out to be strong predictors of per capita income for modern nations (see the references cited in Section 1.1 as well as Olsson, 2005; Comin et al., 2010; Bleaney and Dimico, 2011).

The origin of agriculture has remained the key technological issue for economic prehistory in the last two decades (Olsson, 2001; Hibbs and Olsson, 2004; Pryor, 2004; Olsson and Hibbs, 2005; Weisdorf, 2005, 2009; Marceau and Myers, 2006; Baker, 2008; Dow et al., 2009; Robson, 2010; Rowthorn and Seabright, 2010; Bowles, 2011; Guzmán and Weisdorf, 2011; Bowles and Choi, 2013, 2019; Matranga, 2017; Riahi, 2020, 2021a, 2021b).

Institutional questions involving property rights, warfare, and inequality have also received recent attention (Baker, 2003; Choi and Bowles, 2007; Borgerhoff Mulder et al., 2009; Bowles, 2009, 2012; Steckel, 2010; Dow and Reed, 2013; Rowthorn et al., 2014; Dow et al., 2017; Bowles and Choi, 2019). Another popular subject among economists over the last two decades has been the origin of the state (Allen, 1997; Grossman, 2002; Acemoglu and Robinson, 2006, 2012; North et al., 2009; Baker and Bulte, 2010; Baker et al., 2010; Mayshar et al., 2017, 2022; Allen et al., 2020; Borcan et al., 2021).

Against this backdrop, we make a few remarks on how our approach fits into the economic literature. First, in contrast to much of growth theory (see for example Galor, 2005, 2011), we do not study the accumulation of physical or human capital through saving out of current income. The internal dynamics of our models are driven by the accumulation of technological knowledge and changes in regional population from one generation to the next. These internal dynamics can be modified by external shocks from climate change. Technological knowledge is freely available to everyone and is acquired through learning by doing, which does not require any sacrifice of current consumption. We abstract from intertemporal optimization problems within a single human lifespan.

Another way in which we depart from most of growth theory is in our skepticism about the idea that prehistoric societies displayed any kind of exponential growth, even at very low rates (see Chapter 3). However, we share the interest of growth theorists in the co-evolution of technology and population over time. In particular, we agree that higher productivity tends to yield higher population and vice versa (Kremer, 1993; Galor, 2005, 2011; Baker, 2008). Use of Malthusian models by economists concerned with prehistory is widespread and certainly not unique to us (Ashraf and Galor, 2011).

Some economists have placed considerable weight on genetic factors or processes of natural selection in attempting to explain the course of history or prehistory (Galor and Moav, 2002; Clark, 2007; Galor and Michalopoulos, 2012; Ashraf and Galor, 2013). As explained in Section 1.6, we do not pursue such ideas and tend to be skeptical about them.

We make frequent use of conventional economic concepts involving optimization, equilibrium, and comparative statics. This distinguishes us from other theorists for whom dynamics are determined by the laws of motion of the system, with only initial conditions treated as exogenous. One example is the model of Kremer (1993), where population and technology yield a positive feedback loop described by differential equations. Another is the model of Brander and Taylor (1998), where population and natural resources generate a cyclic time path, again described by differential equations.

In these examples, the dynamics are autonomous in the sense that external forces do not steer the system. Our framework differs by allowing exogenous shifts in climate to alter the system trajectory. The central analytic tool is the standard comparative static framework where we study the effects of climate change on equilibrium outcomes in the short, long, and very long runs. This enables us to explain the timing and location of key transitions by reference to climate shocks. Models with fully autonomous dynamics do not provide equally persuasive explanations for the timing of these transitions.

Despite our heavy use of comparative statics, we do include one important form of positive feedback in our theory. This involves learning by doing, where the use of a new technique leads to productivity growth. There are two effects: in the short run, rising productivity causes substitution of labor toward the new technique, and in the long run, rising productivity causes population growth. These effects push in the same direction, causing more use of the new technique, more learning by doing, and so on (see Chapters 3–5). We believe such autocatalytic processes were important for sedentism, agriculture, and manufacturing in early cities.

However, learning by doing has a corollary: groups tend not to get better at things they don't do. For an economist wanting to explain the shift from foraging to agriculture, this poses a problem: If no one is currently engaged in agriculture, no one can get better at it, so it is hard to see how technical change could account for the Neolithic revolution. We solve this puzzle by arguing that climate change made cultivation attractive even with existing techniques. Once people started to cultivate plants, those activities became more productive over time, reinforcing the original decision to engage in them.

Other economists have used modeling techniques that differ greatly from those we employ. For example, Bowles and Choi (2013) use simulation techniques based on evolutionary game theory to study the co-evolution of technology and property rights. We will compare their approach with our own in the relevant substantive chapters.

Our methodological attitude toward such matters is one of pluralism. In dealing with complicated problems like the origins of agriculture, inequality, or city-states, social science is more likely to progress when multiple scholars use multiple methods. We also believe in a division of labor; scholars should specialize in methods they find congenial. In the long run, those methods bearing the most fruit will be the most likely to spread.

1.9 ARCHAEOLOGICAL THEORY

The relevant literature from archaeology and anthropology is huge, and we do not attempt to provide a survey. Instead, individual chapters will discuss material from these disciplines as the need arises. However, we do want to make a few points about how our theoretical approach is related to these disciplines.

Archaeology has a tradition of distinguishing among low-, middle-, and high-level theory. This terminology can be confusing for outsiders because the terms "middle level" or "middle range" have various shades of meaning among archaeologists. Here we largely follow Trigger (2006, 30–38, 508–528). To avoid possible ambiguities surrounding the term "middle range," we replace it with "middle level" (see 2006, 508–519 for details).

Low-level theory is a body of empirical generalizations: for example, that certain types of artifacts tend to occur earlier or later than other types in a given region. Middle-level theory goes from these generalizations to inferences about the human behavior that produced the data. Put differently, such theory links present-day material evidence with past behaviors that could have generated this evidence (Johnson, 2010, ch. 4).

High-level theory involves abstract theoretical propositions that apply to major categories of phenomena. One example is the synthesis of genetics and Darwinism in biology. Within archaeology, examples include Marxism, cultural materialism, and cultural ecology. High-level theories guide the construction of middle-level theories. They cannot be directly falsified by evidence, but their credibility is influenced by the success or failure of the middle-level theories derived from them.

Our high-level theory is the mainstream microeconomic theory of the late twentieth and early twenty-first centuries. Textbook versions include Varian (2019) at the undergraduate level, Varian (1992) at the advanced undergraduate or first-year graduate level, and Mas-Colell, Whinston, and Green (1995) at the advanced graduate level. Our main deviation from this framework involves the model of technological learning by doing in Chapter 3, which owes more to theories of biological and cultural evolution than to economics. The use of formal economics as a source of archaeological theory is hardly new with us. For example, microeconomic theory provides foundations for optimal foraging models and central-place models (Yoffee, 2005, 187–188; Bettinger, 2009). The key novelty here is that we try to explain several important prehistoric transitions using a unified theoretical framework derived from economics.

Our formal models do not speak directly to the raw data pried from the ground by archaeologists, or to low-level empirical generalizations. Our models instead speak to the narrative accounts published by archaeologists, and thus represent a form of middle-level theory. Archaeologists have already engaged in several stages of theoretical processing in going from field data to published narratives about events in specific regions of space and time (LaMotta, 2012). By the time these "facts" arrive at our door, they are heavily theory-laden. Our models provide yet another stage of theoretical processing, in which we identify past economic activities that could have generated the narratives supplied by present-day archaeology.

Because we are not trained in the discipline, we cannot directly assess the quality of the narratives published by professional archaeologists. This leaves us vulnerable to two related dangers. The first is that we may mistakenly rely on evidence that is open to serious doubt among informed researchers. The second is that the middle-level theories of archaeologists could change and thus the interpretations placed on data could change. As a result, what appear to be facts today may cease to be accepted as facts tomorrow. There is little we can do about either problem except to point out that all theories run the risk of empirical contradiction from one direction or another.

In anthropological terminology, this book engages in "formalist" economics rather than "substantivist" economics. "Formalist" economics is simply what most economists do. It involves the study of human action using mathematical models with optimizing agents and one or more system-level equilibrium requirements. Mainstream economists tend to think that this modeling framework is highly flexible and can be applied to a wide range of social behaviors and institutions that at first glance do not appear to be "economic" in character. Indeed, economists are renowned (or notorious) for their imperialistic attitude toward other social sciences. The Nobel Prize winner Robert Mundell (1968) once called economics the "science of choice," a definition that does not leave much room for anyone else who might be interested in human social behavior. Unsurprisingly, scholars in other disciplines often harbor skepticism about the universal applicability of economic logic.

"Substantivist" economics (notice the unsubtle propaganda about which approach has more substantive value) had its source in the writing of Karl Polanyi (1957). Polanyi argued that through almost all of human history and prehistory, economic activities were embedded within or subordinated to other social institutions. In his view, it was not until the nineteenth century that autonomous markets for labor, land, and capital arose, and he regarded this development as a dire threat to social cohesion. Many anthropologists have embraced the idea that in small-scale societies economic behavior is not easily separated from other kinds of behavior, and that it is subject to various institutional constraints (see for example Sahlins, 1972). This has motivated doubt that abstract economic models are useful in understanding such societies, and strong suspicion in certain quarters that these models are mere reflections of neocolonial Western culture.

However that may be, we are unabashedly located on the "formalist" side of this fence. We certainly accept the importance of social institutions, norms, and conventions, whether in small mobile foraging bands or contemporary megacities. At the same time, we believe people in all societies make economic decisions, and that economic theory is useful for understanding these decisions. This remains true for societies without money or explicit markets for labor, land, and food. The proof of the pudding is of course in the eating. If the "substantivists" are right, our models will not shine any light on prehistoric events. If the "formalists" are right, they will provide substantial illumination.

We do, however, want to immunize our non-economist readers against a frequent misconception. It is not true that modern economics is just about modern capitalism, or that we are imposing a theory about capitalism on precapitalist societies. Contemporary economists study a wide range of institutional arrangements and often try to understand how one set of institutions emerged from another. In our own models, there is no capital apart from the technological knowledge that accumulates over time and is handed down from one generation to the next. We assume that this kind of "capital" is freely available to everyone in a given geographic region (there are no patent laws or trade secrets, and children become technologically competent by imitating their parents and other adults). We also often assume that food is shared equally within social groups, and that groups rather than individuals control access to land. In several models, we assume there is an open-access commons whose resources can be used by anyone. In short, we tailor our assumptions to the societies we study. Many of these assumptions would be completely out of place in a study of modern capitalism.

Researchers in social sciences other than economics often give great emphasis to the concept of human agency (Johnson, 2010). Although we do not study agency in the same sense, we do not deny the importance of purposive human action. Our models do include agents who pursue goals subject to constraints. Their goals are quite simple and their cognition is not complex enough to require analysis of beliefs or other mental states. But without individual human agents we would have no models. As an aside, we observe that many economists use models with more cognitively sophisticated agents, and closely examine the beliefs, expectations, and learning processes of human decision-makers.

Are we guilty of environmental, technological, or demographic determinism? We treat technology as an endogenous variable in Chapters 3–5 so we are clearly innocent of technological determinism in this part of the book. We treat population as an endogenous variable in all chapters so we are not demographic determinists either (though population is a crucial proximate cause for many of the phenomena we explore). The ultimate cause for the entire cascade of transitions studied here is climate change. Because this factor is the prime mover, we do not contest allegations of environmental determinism. However, the effects of a given climate change depend heavily on circumstances of time and place, including geography, existing technology, existing population, and existing institutions.

Our archaeological friends can best determine where we fit into their theoretical universe. However, a few remarks may be useful. We generally expect to be labeled as processualists and neo-evolutionists. We are processualists in the sense that we focus on physical, biological, and economic variables, and attempt to understand the processes that generated certain kinds of archaeological data. We are neo-evolutionists in the sense that we find social typologies like the one in Section 1.2 useful, and want to understand major prehistoric transformations in technology and institutions. Many non-economists have also theorized about social evolution on long time scales. For various perspectives and reviews of the literature, see Sahlins and Service (1960), Hallpike (1988), Sanderson (1990, 1999), Trigger (1998), Harris (2001), and Carneiro (2003).

Our use of the term "neo-evolutionism" refers only to social and cultural evolution rather than biological evolution. In particular, our framework is not an example of dual inheritance theory (Boyd and Richerson, 1985; Shennan, 2012) because we treat human genetic endowments as constant. However, our agents behave in ways that are entirely compatible with a Darwinian framework: they maximize their food income and then use this income to produce surviving adult children.

Our approach runs parallel to human behavioral ecology (HBE) in some ways (Bird and O'Connell, 2012). HBE emphasizes the adaptation of rational individual agents to their natural environment, as do we. There are some differences in terminology: for example, we prefer to talk about optimizing behavior rather than "functional" behavior, for reasons explained below. More substantively, we operate on a radically different time scale from most HBE models. The latter may involve minute-by-minute or day-by-day decisions to harvest particular resources, while our time frame involves human generations. Thus, although we are interested in some issues that overlap with HBE (such as diet breadth and "broad spectrum revolutions"), our formal models differ. We also focus more on system-level equilibrium conditions than would usually be true in the HBE literature.

To limit confusion, we avoid using the word "functional" to describe an agent's behavior. This runs too great a risk that we will be viewed as "functionalists" in an older sense that still resonates in archaeology, anthropology, and sociology. This school of thought claims that a society is a system of interacting elements in which each element contributes to the collective needs or survival of the society as a whole. Our theory might superficially appear to be of this type because we view economies as systems, we assume that agents interact, and we often talk about equilibrium at the system level.

Even so, we depart from functionalism in several ways. First, we do not base our theory on the physical or biological survival requirements of a society. It is trivially true that when societies fail to survive in their natural environments, they will not be observed at later dates. But this imposes very minimal constraints on the technology or institutions of surviving (and therefore observable) societies.

One could argue that societies compete with one another through warfare or by other means, and that this competition forces surviving societies to display at least some degree of technological and institutional competence (Diamond, 1997). However, such arguments only provide solid foundations for functionalism if the selection mechanisms that operate upon societies are somehow connected to the "needs" or "performance" of the society as a whole (rather than, say, the needs of an elite). We prefer to model warfare and other competitive processes explicitly, rather than simply assuming in advance that these processes force societies toward some collective optimum.

In our framework, equilibrium does not imply collective optimality or efficiency. An equilibrium is just an economic state that is not subject to disruption from processes internal to the system. Such a state need not be a good thing. For example, in Chapter 3 we argue that foraging societies can get stuck in equilibria with little or no technological innovation. We also show in Chapter 6 that equilibrium can involve substantial poverty or inequality, and that technological progress can make these problems worse. We try to explain how elites arise, but we do not argue that elites emerge because they are socially necessary. The same holds true for state institutions. In Chapter 11 we regard the state as reflecting the dominance of organized elites over unorganized commoners, not as a boon for society as a whole.

A final point is that functionalism has tended to motivate static (or synchronic) theoretical perspectives, while our interest is in the dynamic (or diachronic) processes responsible for major economic transitions. While we often use the idea of equilibrium as a temporary stopping point (in the short run, the long run, or the very long run), our main goal is to identify the forces that destabilize prevailing equilibria and lead to new technological or institutional arrangements.

1.10 GUNS, GERMS, AND STEEL REVISITED

No one can discuss the big questions of economic prehistory without addressing the book *Guns, Germs, and Steel* by Jared Diamond (1997). Because Diamond is neither an economist nor an archaeologist, and because his work has had exceptional influence, we discuss his ideas separately here.

Diamond attempts to explain the dramatic differences in technological, economic, and political outcomes across regions of the contemporary world. He especially wants to refute racist ideas that these differences arose because some people were more intelligent or energetic than others. His counter-argument is simple: people in some regions became richer and more powerful over time because they had better geographical starting points. In particular, areas like southwest Asia were well endowed with plants and animals that could readily be domesticated, which gave such regions a head start toward agriculture. Furthermore, the Eurasian land mass had a dominant east–west axis that enabled advances in agriculture to diffuse easily into neighboring areas having similar climates. It was also large and had relatively few barriers to the movement of people, goods, and ideas. All of this contrasts with the Americas, sub-Saharan Africa, and Australia, which had far fewer domesticable species, had dominant north–south axes that made it difficult for agricultural innovations to spread, or were isolated from developments elsewhere in the world.

Diamond goes on to say that an early start with respect to agriculture led to early population growth, technological innovation, and institutional innovation. This trajectory led to state organization, standing armies, and writing, among other things. At the same time, animal domestication and increased population densities promoted the evolution of epidemic diseases. The inhabitants of these societies developed a degree of immunity to these diseases, while inhabitants of other societies did not. When such societies collided, one result was a massive death toll among people having no previous exposure. The title "Guns, Germs, and Steel" refers to three proximate causes that led to European conquests after 1492. According to Diamond, these factors explain why Spain conquered the Incan Empire rather than the other way around.

Diamond has much to say about the emergence of agriculture, inequality, and the state. To this degree, his questions overlap with ours, and we will discuss his answers in the relevant chapters. However, Diamond's main goal is to explain the historical patterns of the last 500 years. By contrast, we are squarely focused on prehistory. Our goal is to explain why a series of crucial prehistoric transitions occurred in certain regions but not others, and at certain points in time but not others. Sedentism, agriculture, inequality, warfare, and city-states had great consequences for the modern world, but even without such consequences these developments would deserve study, much as the origins of the universe and the evolution of dinosaurs deserve study for their own sake.

A second difference is that we base our theory on economic logic, and we apply this logic consistently (some might say relentlessly). We also draw more heavily than Diamond on archaeological evidence. Although Diamond's work is full of illuminating examples, our systematic use of regional cases from archaeology is distinctive. Further, we have the advantage of being able to exploit new findings from the last two decades.

A third difference involves the nature of our proximate causes. During our time frame, guns and steel did not exist. Germs did exist and no doubt became more important as settlement sizes grew and domestic animals became widespread. While we sometimes refer to germs, we think the main causal factors driving the transitions in this book were different: they largely involved climate, geography, technology, and population.

Another point involves our concentration on the timing of events. Diamond very rarely cites triggering variables that explain the timing of the transitions discussed here. He uses geography as his fundamental exogenous variable, and he does get considerable mileage by using this variable to explain the differences in trajectories across regions of the world. But geography is largely static and does not answer the fundamental question of why a specific regional transition happened when it did, rather than earlier or later. In our framework, the main source of exogenous variation over time is climate change. We will argue that at least in some important regional cases, this variable can account for the timing of agriculture and city-states.

In the case of agriculture in southwest Asia, Diamond references climate change as a contributing factor in determining the timing of initial cultivation. We contrast his analysis with ours in Section 5.12. Unlike Diamond, we also regard climate change as a critical variable for understanding both technical change in the Upper Paleolithic and the emergence of sedentism. Finally, we view climate change and the processes of technical innovation it unleashed as key factors driving the growth of inequality and the increased frequency of warfare over land, as well as the eventual rise of city-states.

2

A Primer on Malthusian Economics

2.1 INTRODUCTION

This chapter describes basic Malthusian ideas about technology and population. It explains how and why we treat population as an endogenous variable over intervals of a century or more; that is, intervals of the kind that matter for prehistory. Later chapters build on the concepts developed here and extend them in many directions.

We want to emphasize that these ideas are not original with us, are routinely used by economists interested in prehistory, and are not controversial within economics. The intellectual framework has descended with modification from Malthus (1798), but we are only concerned with the way in which this framework is used by modern economists, not with what Malthus "really meant." We assume no prior familiarity with economics, rely mainly on graphs, and often simplify for the sake of clarity. For a lucid presentation of similar material by an anthropologist, see Wood (1998).

Section 2.2 introduces the production function and describes some of its standard properties. Section 2.3 explains how technological innovation is accommodated within the theory. In Section 2.4 we show why it makes sense to treat population as endogenous over multiple human generations. A variety of conceptual matters, including migration, carrying capacity, population density, and population pressure, are discussed in Section 2.5. Finally, Section 2.6 concludes by discussing the evidence in favor of a Malthusian perspective for pre-industrial societies.

We start with a remark on terminology. When archaeologists or anthropologists refer to "food production," they often mean agriculture rather than foraging. Economists would use the term "production" for both activities because both involve the conversion of natural resources and labor time into food. The framework in this chapter applies equally well to foraging or farming. For concreteness we assume food is obtained from foraging, but this is not essential.

2.2 THE PRODUCTION FUNCTION

Consider a population of N people living in a fixed geographic area with fixed natural resources. Each person is endowed with one unit of labor time, so N is also the supply of labor. There is a single consumption good called "food." Food can be obtained by using labor time to collect and process wild plants and animals. The maximum output of food Y that can be obtained from the labor input N is given by the *production function* Y(N), illustrated in the top panel of Figure 2.1. More labor yields more food (the curve is upward sloping), but at a decreasing rate (the slope of the curve is diminishing).

In the top panel of Figure 2.1, the *marginal product of labor* MP(N) is the slope of the production function Y(N) at a particular level of the input N; see the heavy tangent lines at the population levels N_0, N_1, and N_2. MP(N) is the rate at which output increases with a small increase in input, starting at the given value of N. The declining slope of the Y(N) curve results from the diminishing marginal productivity of labor when resources are fixed. For example, the first few units of labor time might be employed to pick low-hanging fruit, so at first output rises rapidly as labor increases. Further units of labor time might be used to pick higher-hanging fruit, so then output rises more slowly.

The *average product of labor* is AP(N) = Y(N)/N. This is food output per unit of labor input. In the top panel of Figure 2.1, AP(N) is the slope of a line from the origin to the corresponding point on the curve Y(N); see the dashed lines for population levels N_0, N_1, and N_2. Due to the curvature of the production function, the average product AP(N) falls as N rises, so food per person decreases as the population increases.

The bottom panel of Figure 2.1 shows the marginal product and average product curves as functions of the labor input N. Notice that MP and AP are not the same thing. Both decrease as N increases, but at a given positive level of N, AP is larger than MP (for any given N, the dashed line in the top panel is steeper than the heavy tangent line). The only exception is at N = 0. In later chapters we will need a finite MP at N = 0 in order to explain why some resources are used while others are

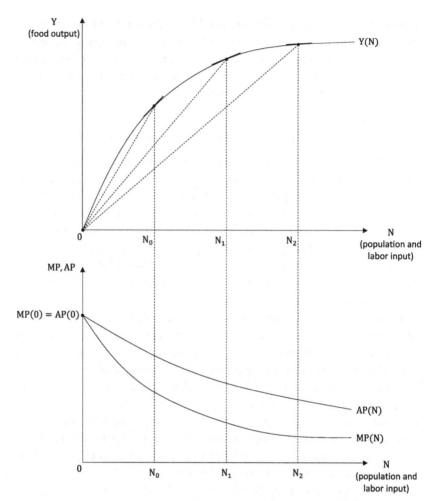

FIGURE 2.1. Production technology

not. Mathematically, this implies $MP(0) = AP(0)$ as shown in the graph. We generally assume MP and AP approach zero as N goes to infinity. We also assume foraging bands share food equally, so $AP(N)$ is the food consumption of each individual forager when the population size is N. The average product will often be written $y(N) = AP(N)$, reflecting the notational convention adopted throughout the book that Y refers to the aggregate output or consumption of food, while y refers to the consumption of an individual agent.

2.3 TECHNOLOGICAL INNOVATION

Figure 2.1 assumes that both natural resources and technology are held constant, so only the labor input and food output vary. But suppose the society finds a better way of hunting or gathering, and hence becomes more effective in harvesting local resources. An improved technology could involve new or better tools such as projectile points, nets, or sickles, but it could also take a less tangible form such as better understanding of local ecosystems, better scheduling of activities, or better modes of teamwork. In general, we think of technological innovation as reflecting an improvement in collective knowledge about production activities among the members of a social group.

Such an improvement shifts up the entire production function Y(N) in Figure 2.1 because now each level of the labor input N provides more food than before. It is crucial to distinguish clearly between movements along a given production function due to more labor input with knowledge held constant, and an upward shift of the entire Y(N) curve due to more knowledge with labor held constant. These ideas are often lumped together by archaeologists and anthropologists as forms of "intensification" (more food output per unit of land), but to an economist they are quite different.

The effect of improved technical knowledge on average product is clear: because AP(N) = Y(N)/N and better technology raises Y(N) at each N, food per capita must also rise at each N. We illustrate this in Figure 2.2, where the average product curve before the technical innovation is $y(N, K^\circ)$ and the average product curve after the innovation is $y(N, K^1)$. Technical knowledge is indexed by K where $0 < K^\circ < K^1$.

For a fixed technology K° and fixed natural resources, the average product curve $y(N, K^\circ)$ implies a tradeoff: one can have a low population with high food per capita or a high population with low food per capita. The $y(N, K^\circ)$ curve depicts a frontier beyond which both cannot be increased simultaneously with the prevailing technology K°. But the outward shift of the average product curve to $y(N, K^1)$ opens up new possibilities.

Suppose the society is initially at an arbitrary point A along the curve for K° and then technology improves to K^1. One possibility is that the society could move to point B where population stays at N_A while food per capita increases to y_B. Another possibility is a move to point C where food per capita remains at y_A while population increases to N_C. There

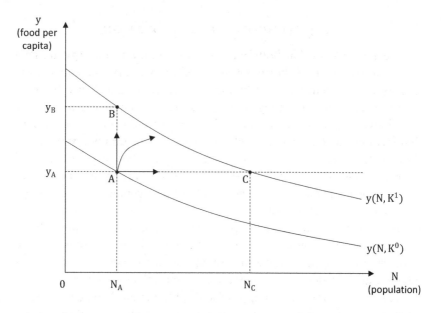

FIGURE 2.2. Improved technical knowledge

could also be some combination of growth in both population and food per capita, as indicated by the points along the $y(N, K^1)$ curve between B and C.

We need a convenient term for outward shifts in the average product curve due to improvements in technology with natural resources held constant. For lack of any better alternative, and because this usage is common in economics, we call such shifts technical progress. We hasten to add that this concept does not refer to political, social, or cultural "progress," whatever those terms may mean. In particular we want to distinguish our use of the word "progress" from phrases like "human progress" or "inevitable human progress," popular language in the early literature of archaeology (see the discussion in Fagan and Durrani, 2016, 47–65). Here we are using the term only in a narrow technological sense that is devoid of value judgments. More formally:

Definition 2.1

   Technical progress means an increase in the ability of a human population to obtain food within a given geographic area with given natural resources.

The qualification of given natural resources in D2.1 is important. The production function Y(N) from Figure 2.1 assumes that climate, geography, and ecosystems remain constant and only labor time varies. But in principle the average product curve in Figure 2.2 could shift up either because technology improves while natural resources stay constant, or because natural resources improve while technology stays constant. The main reason why plant or animal resources can become more abundant is a better climate. We return to this theme repeatedly in later chapters. Our definition in D2.1 excludes any shift due to nature, and only refers to shifts associated with better technical knowledge.

2.4 POPULATION DYNAMICS

To model population dynamics we treat N as the number of adults and assume only adults produce food. This simplification is reasonable given that in contemporary foraging societies, children do not typically produce enough food to support themselves until about the age of 18 (see Robson and Kaplan, 2006). We will also assume a closed population without migration (see the discussion of migration in Section 2.5).

Consider Figure 2.3 where the function $\rho(y)$ describes the average or expected number of surviving children for an individual adult with food income y. Note that we draw the graph so that $\rho(y) > 0$ for all $y > 0$. It might be objected that adults need some minimum amount of food $y_{min} > 0$ before $\rho(y)$ becomes positive. In particular, an adult must have enough

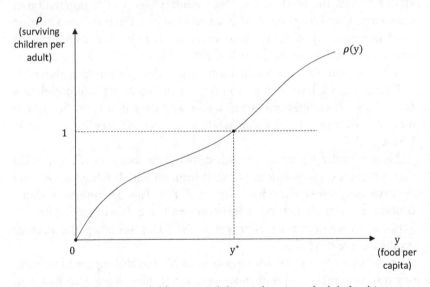

FIGURE 2.3. Surviving children per adult as a function of adult food income

food to survive before it becomes possible to have any children. For almost all of our formal modeling, we could add a threshold of this kind without altering any conclusions. However, occasionally we do use the assumption $\rho(y) > 0$ for all $y > 0$ in the proof of a formal proposition. This will be indicated explicitly where relevant.

During prehistory $\rho(y)$ was an increasing function over the relevant range. When food per adult rose, female fertility rose while child and adult mortality fell. Evidence for this assertion will be given in Section 2.6. In our formal modeling we assume adults live for one period or generation. They acquire food, have children, die, and are replaced by their surviving children at the start of the next period. Accordingly, we often ignore adult mortality and interpret $\rho(y)$ as being determined by female fertility and child mortality.

To have a viable society that can reproduce itself over multiple generations, there must be a feasible level of food income y such that $\rho(y) \geq 1$, so on average each adult is replaced by at least one surviving child. Assuming $\rho(y)$ is continuous as in Figure 2.3, there will be a unique y^* such that $\rho(y^*) = 1$ so the food income y^* is just sufficient to keep the population stationary, with neither growth nor decline across generations.

We can now combine Figures 2.2 and 2.3 to characterize a long-run equilibrium population level. Figure 2.4 shows the average product curve $y(N, K^{\circ})$ and the level of food per adult y^* at which population is stationary. Consider point A with population N^*. From the construction of y^* in Figure 2.3, if the population is already at N^* it does not change over time. If the population is below N^* in Figure 2.4, we have $y > y^*$ so $\rho(y) > 1$ in Figure 2.3 and population rises. If the population is above N^* in Figure 2.4, we have $y < y^*$ so $\rho(y) < 1$ in Figure 2.3 and population falls. Thus the equilibrium N^* is stable; any deviation from N^* sets in motion a dynamic process that tends to restore N^* (see the arrows in Figure 2.4).

Next consider Figure 2.5, which displays the long-run effect of technical progress on population. We start from an initial technology K° and the associated average product curve $y(N, K^{\circ})$. This determines an initial equilibrium population N° consistent with the food per capita y^*. Suppose technology then improves to K^1. This shifts up the average product curve to $y(N, K^1)$.

In the short run, population remains at N° and the improved technology results in higher food income per adult (a move from A to B and an increase in food from y^* to y_B). In the long run, however, population

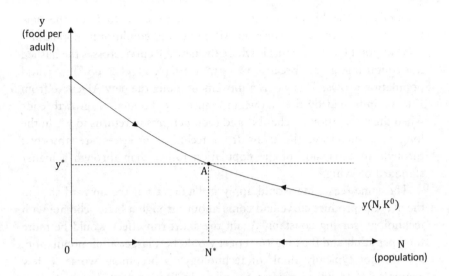

FIGURE 2.4. Stability of long-run equilibrium population

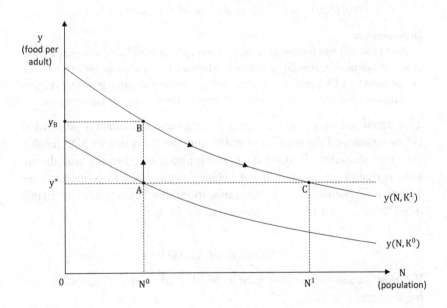

FIGURE 2.5. Short-run and long-run responses to technical progress with fixed natural resources

responds to the higher standard of living. Observe that for the new technology K^I and its associated AP curve, the equilibrium population is N^I at point C because this is where the new AP curve crosses the dashed horizontal line at y^*. Because $y_B > y^*$ we have $\rho(y_B) > \rho(y^*) = 1$ and population grows. This yields a movement along the new AP curve from B to C, indicated by the arrows in Figure 2.5. Population growth ends when the population reaches N^I and food per person returns to y^*. In the long run, therefore, the gains from technical progress are absorbed through an expansion of the population rather than through a higher standard of living.

The same reasoning would apply in Figure 2.5 if the upward shift in the average product curve had come about through a better climate with technology staying constant. Again the short-run effect would be more food per adult and the long-run effect would be a larger adult population. We do not typically think of technology as becoming worse (a few examples of technical regress are given in Section 3.9), but it is quite possible for climate to become worse (for instance, colder or drier). In this case the entire process is thrown into reverse. The short-run effect is a decrease in food per capita while the long-run effect is a decrease in population sufficient to restore y^*.

Economists usually call such processes *Malthusian*.

Definition 2.2

A *Malthusian equilibrium* consists of a food per capita y^* and a population N^* at which population remains stationary. *Malthusian population dynamics* refers to a process by which population approaches a new equilibrium level that restores the original food per capita y^* after a change in technology or natural resources.

This definition says nothing about whether the equilibrium population N^* is maintained through low fertility and low mortality or high fertility and high mortality. It also says nothing about whether the equilibrium food per capita y^* is high or low. Hence in the usage of economists the adjective "Malthusian" has no implications for the standard of living, other than the fact that it is constant in the long run.

2.5 CONCEPTUAL ISSUES

We now pause to consider how a number of related concepts fit into the theory.

Migration: In later chapters we define a region to be a geographic area for which there is no in- or out-migration. However, in many of our models we have multiple sites within a region and allow agents to migrate among these sites in the short run (possibly subject to social barriers or costs). As a result site-level populations are endogenous in the short run even though the regional population is exogenous in the same time frame.

Carrying Capacity: This is normally defined as the maximum population a given region can support with a given array of resources and a given technology (French, 2016, 173). The idea of the "maximum population" is often interpreted to mean "the population that can be supported when individuals are at their biological minimum for food intake." Thus one sometimes sees estimates of carrying capacity derived from assumptions about subsistence requirements (e.g., 2000 calories per day for an adult male engaged in work of a particular kind).

Our theory makes no use of subsistence concepts. Our concern is with the actual population supported in long-run equilibrium, not the maximum population that could be supported if everyone ate as little as possible. For reasons we will not go into here, we do not believe that Darwinian evolutionary logic implies that people must be on the brink of starvation in the long run. Therefore we do not assume that when a society is initially in Malthusian equilibrium and confronts a negative environmental shock, it will necessarily suffer an immediate and drastic increase in mortality through famine. Both the standard of living y^* and the rates at which populations adjust to positive or negative shocks are matters for empirical investigation.

Population Density: The standard definition of *population density* is the ratio of population to land area. Suppose we have two societies A and B, where the population density for A is higher than for B. Within a Malthusian framework, how might such an observation be explained?

One possibility is that A or B (or both) is far from a long-run equilibrium, perhaps due to some recent shift in environmental or technological conditions. But if we have no evidence for a recent shift of this sort, we might suppose each society is close to its long-run population level. In that case we would look for some persistent difference between the societies in their natural environment or technology, on the assumption that A has a permanent advantage in relation to B. For example, A might have more annual rainfall, greater access to useful plant or animal species, better terrain, or a coastal location. It might also have better technology for harvesting or processing wild species.

Another way to explain the difference in population density between A and B would be to question the implicit assumption that the equilibrium standard of living y^* is identical for the two societies. If the societies are similar in other ways, we would likely think that the underlying relationships of fertility and mortality to food consumption are similar, and thus that y* is similar. However, for societies that are sufficiently different in other ways, it could make sense to look for differences in y*. Chapters 4 and 5 will consider how y* might change as a result of the transitions to sedentism and agriculture.

Population Pressure: The conventional definition of *population pressure* is the ratio of population to food where each is measured in relation to a given geographic area. The inverse of population pressure is simply food per capita. The Malthusian framework of this chapter makes a crucial point: as long as y* does not vary, societies will not differ in their long-run levels of population pressure. By definition population pressure exists and is equal to 1/y*, but it has no causal significance.

At most, population pressure plays a causal role in the short run. For example, if there has been a recent negative climate shock and food has become less abundant, in the short run this increases population pressure by reducing food per person. One short-run response could be migration from sites where food per capita is low to sites where it is high. In the long run the increased population pressure will decrease fertility and raise mortality. If the region was in a Malthusian equilibrium before the shock and the adverse climate persists, population will decline until a new Malthusian equilibrium is reached at which population pressure returns to 1/y*.

These points are important because archaeologists, anthropologists, and others often appeal to population pressure as an explanation for social trajectories that unfolded over several centuries or millennia. We are skeptical about such stories, which generally treat population as an exogenous variable that rises over time without regard to feedback loops involving living standards. We believe such feedbacks tend to be important over a few generations and certainly over a few centuries. Thus population must be endogenous on these time scales.

Having said this, we do not dispute that population is often a proximate cause for important social transitions. It will frequently play this role in subsequent chapters. But in archaeological time, it cannot be an ultimate cause; population growth or decline must itself be explained. Such explanations should be sought in technical or climatic change.

2.6 EVIDENCE

There is a great deal of evidence supporting a Malthusian framework for the kinds of societies we are studying in this book. Sources include anthropological observation of foraging and farming societies, biological studies of female fertility, historical examples, econometric research on pre-industrial societies, and the findings from paleo-demography. Here we sketch evidence of the first four kinds. Paleodemography, which represents one especially crucial form of evidence, will be left for Section 3.3. For brevity we will focus most of the discussion on foragers, but the examples to be cited below involving the Enga of New Guinea, the Polynesian colonization of Pacific islands, and econometric research on the pre-industrial era all involve agricultural societies.

With regard to anthropological research, French (2016, 178) states, "it is widely accepted that hunter-gatherer population density is heavily determined by environmental factors, particularly as they relate to food availability." She notes that population density is highest in temperate and tropical coastal environments, and lowest in semi-desert and Arctic environments. There is also a positive correlation between population density and environmental productivity as measured by primary biomass. Baker (2008) finds that the best predictors of population density for hunter-gatherer societies are rainfall, number of frost months, land slope, and habitat diversity. These findings are all consistent with the Malthusian expectation that foraging populations will equilibrate in the long run and that equilibrium population levels will reflect the richness of the surrounding resources.

Although women in mobile foraging societies lack reliable forms of contraception or abortion, they probably have some conscious control over fertility. The main methods discussed in the literature are lengthy breastfeeding, which could suppress ovulation, and infanticide. Hill and Hurtado (1996, 309–311) discuss the evidence on breastfeeding. On the question of infanticide see Harris and Ross (1987), Hill and Hurtado (1996), Caldwell and Caldwell (2003), and Kelly (2013a, 186–193). There were also options of abstinence, sexual behaviors that did not result in conception, and efforts at birth control through the use of herbal remedies (see the discussion in Lipsey et al., 2005, 330–332). The efficacy of such remedies is controversial (for a skeptical view see Caldwell and Caldwell, 2003). Nevertheless, if women responded to food scarcity with more breastfeeding and/or more infanticide and/or greater use of other birth control methods, these behaviors could have contributed to pro-cesses of Malthusian population adjustment.

Aside from conscious controls, there are complex physiological mech-anisms that influence fertility (see Kelly, 2013a, 197–200). Nutrition and activity levels affect how much energy is stored in the body as fat, the current balance between energy inflows and outflows, and the rate at which energy both enters and leaves the body. Food abundance enhances energy storage and results in a more favorable energy balance, both of which promote fertility. A high rate of energy intake along with a high expenditure rate due to physical labor depresses fertility, but an environment of food abundance should decrease the need for intensive physical effort and thus promote fertility. For a review of evidence that female food intake is related to fertility, see Hill and Hurtado (1996, 312–314). For physiological mechanisms, see Vitzthum (2008).

Child mortality rates among observed foraging groups are high, with only 50–60% of children surviving to age 15 (Kelly, 2013a, 200–202). In most of the foraging societies examined by Kelly, child deaths from infectious and parasitic diseases are more common than deaths resulting from accidents or violence. However, there are exceptions such as the Ache (Hill and Hurtado, 1996, 158–165). It is unclear whether children in prehistoric foraging societies had levels of exposure to infectious diseases similar to those of recent foragers. In any event Wood (1998) cites evidence that good nutrition boosts immune function in children, so food abundance will tend to reduce child mortality.

A review of data on 20 hunter-gatherer societies by Volk and Atkinson (2013) reached similar conclusions. The mean infant mortality rate (likelihood of dying before age 1) was 26.8% and the mean child mortality rate (likelihood of dying before age 15) was 48.8%. The range for the former was 14–40% and the range for the latter was 22–56%. Child mortality rates for many historical societies, from ancient Rome to Imperial China to nineteenth–century France, resembled those for hunter-gatherer societies: about a quarter of infants died and nearly half of children died by age 15. These are stunningly high levels compared to those in modern developed countries, where such rates tend to be 1% or less. Volk and Atkinson cite several causes of child mortality, but one factor that tends to reduce it is an increase in the quality and quantity of food. For further references to the literature showing that food intake is causally related to child survival, see Hill and Hurtado (1996, 299–300).

We are less concerned with adult mortality, but intermittent famines could have had a substantial demographic impact in prehistoric foraging societies. We will address the connections between food availability and warfare in Chapter 7.

Hill and Hurtado (1996) have conducted a very careful and detailed demographic study of the Ache, a society of mobile foragers in eastern Paraguay. The data cover the century 1890–1990. We focus on the first

80 years, during which the Ache were forest dwellers prior to peaceful contact, and ignore the later contact and reservation periods.

During the time of observation, the Ache were very far from equilibrium. Their annual growth rate of 2.5% would have taken them from a population of two individuals to 106 billion in 1000 years. Hill and Hurtado suggest three reasons for the recent rapid growth: (a) the neighboring horticultural societies were devastated by slave trading in the seventeenth and eighteenth centuries, creating an empty niche into which the Ache could expand; (b) European oranges spread rapidly into Paraguayan forests and became a food source for prey animals favored by the Ache; and/or (c) long population growth phases could have been interrupted by occasional unobserved crashes (1996, 258).

For the period in which the Ache were forest dwellers, it is clear that individual-level resource differences influenced fertility and mortality. There is a highly significant relationship between male hunting skill and male fertility rate, although causality issues arise (for example, men who have more children may do more hunting). There is also a strongly significant positive relationship between paternal hunting skill and survivorship for children ages 5–9, with a less significant relationship for ages 1–4. This implies that better hunters have more surviving offspring. Female body size (a measure of resource availability) is positively but only weakly related to fertility. Seasonal variations in food availability are positively associated with variations in the probability of conception. No relationship was found between resource availability and adult mortality (for details on these findings, see Hill and Hurtado, 1996, ch. 10). While the effects of food income at the individual level could differ from the effects at the social level (especially for males, who may be competing for reproductive opportunities in a zero-sum way), the Ache data support the idea that resource availability is connected with fertility and child survival.

Anecdotal examples of Malthusian dynamics in small-scale societies are not hard to find. To take one case, the Polar Inuit of northwest Greenland were apparently struck by an epidemic in the 1820s that killed the older and more knowledgeable members of their society. Due to this loss of technical knowledge, they could not hunt caribou and had less capacity to hunt seals or fish for arctic char. Consequently, population declined between 1820–1862. However, when previously available tools were reintroduced from the Inuit of Baffin Island, they were immediately adopted and population grew (Boyd et al., 2011, 10920). Another case involves the introduction of the sweet potato to the Enga of New Guinea.

Following this improvement in food technology, the Enga population grew from 20,000 to 150,000 in about 220 years (Wiessner and Tumu, 1998, ch. 4).

There are many cases where small groups colonize pristine environments with abundant resources. The near-universal result is *logistic growth*: after a relatively slow start, population rises rapidly, but then stabilizes after several centuries as the limits of the natural environment and current technology are reached. This pattern is also called *density-dependent growth*. Chapter 6 will discuss such examples from Polynesia.

Econometric research likewise yields results consistent with Malthusian ideas. For example, before the Industrial Revolution societies that had better natural resources, better geography, or better technology tended to have higher population densities, but at most enjoyed only minor advantages with respect to living standards (Ashraf and Galor, 2011). For evidence of Malthusian dynamics in Britain during the period leading up to the Industrial Revolution, see Crafts and Mills (2009). Only after industrialization was there a systematic tendency for fertility to fall when incomes rose. This brought about the much-discussed demographic transition of the twentieth century (see Chapter 12).

PART II

SEDENTISM AND AGRICULTURE

3

The Upper Paleolithic

3.1 INTRODUCTION

This chapter has several goals. Among other things, we introduce terminology and facts about the Upper Paleolithic (UP); explain why conventional theories of economic growth do not adequately capture the dynamics of population and technology during this period; develop our own formal model of these matters; suggest that climate change was the driving force behind population growth and technological innovation in the Upper Paleolithic; and argue that our model can account for some empirical patterns identified by archaeologists. The ideas in this chapter provide foundations for our analysis of the transition to sedentism (Chapter 4) and the transition to agriculture (Chapter 5).

Following an overview in this section, we offer empirical information on climate, population, and technology in Sections 3.2–3.4. Section 3.4 argues that standard models of economic growth conflict with crucial facts about the Upper Paleolithic. In particular, any model predicting continuous expansion at an exponential or faster rate contradicts the observation that regional populations were commonly flat, cyclic, or subject to collapse.

This motivates our effort in the second part of the chapter to construct a formal model better suited to the archaeological evidence about the Upper Paleolithic. In our framework the equilibrium growth rate for population and technology is zero almost all of the time, with transitory periods of growth triggered by climate change. While some readers will not want to delve deeply into the mathematics in this part of the chapter, we urge all readers to look at the verbal portions, which often discuss important conceptual points. Proofs of all formal propositions are available at cambridge.org/economicprehistory.

Section 3.5 presents a model of technological innovation based on learning by doing. In our approach, technology is more likely to improve for food resources that are more intensively exploited, and it remains constant for any resources not currently in use. Section 3.6 studies the short-run allocation of labor time across individual food resources. Section 3.7 adopts a long-run framework in which population is endogenous and evolves according to Malthusian dynamics. Section 3.8 uses a very-long-run framework where technology is also endogenous and evolves according to the model of learning by doing in Section 3.5. There can be many equilibria in the very long run, and foraging societies can get stuck in what we call a "stagnation trap." In such situations, some resources are not used because they are unattractive with existing technical knowledge, but knowledge does not improve because the resources are not used. Section 3.9 shows that changes in climate can sometimes enable foraging societies to escape from stagnation traps, leading to episodic technological innovation and population growth.

In the rest of the chapter we resume a verbal presentation. Section 3.10 suggests that our model can explain two empirical patterns in the archaeological record. One of these is the broadening of the diet in the Upper Paleolithic (the so-called broad spectrum revolution). The other is the increasing ability of human groups to colonize harsh natural environments such as Siberia. Section 3.11 is a summary and Section 3.12 is a postscript.

We begin by explaining some terminology for the benefit of non-archaeologists. Newcomers to the literature will frequently encounter references to the Lower, Middle, and Upper Paleolithic, where the term Paleolithic means "old stone age." In all three of these periods, stone tools were used for hunting and gathering. The Neolithic period, or "new stone age," refers to the use of stone tools for agriculture (see Chapter 5).

The boundary between the Lower and Middle Paleolithic is traditionally dated to about 250 KYA. Until recently, the accepted date for the advent of anatomically modern humans (AMHs, or *Homo sapiens*) was around 200 KYA, so the Lower Paleolithic was associated only with archaic humans; that is, members of the genus *Homo*, but not *Homo sapiens*. The most famous of these is *Homo neanderthalensis*. However, new discoveries from Morocco have pushed the appearance of *Homo sapiens* back to 300 KYA or earlier (see Section 1.1), creating overlap between AMHs and the Lower Paleolithic. Because very little is known about the technology used by AMHs at such early dates, we ignore the Lower Paleolithic here.

The boundary between the Middle and Upper Paleolithic is more relevant for our purposes. We will address the question of dates for this boundary below. The distinction between the two periods is based on differences in the methods used to create stone tools. The Middle Paleolithic is generally associated with a relatively primitive technique called "flake technology" while the Upper Paleolithic exhibits a more advanced technique called "blade technology" (for a description of the latter, see Fagan and Durrani, 2019, ch. 5).

In blade technology, the tool producer (or knapper) starts with a prepared core of stone material, often flint. A punch stone and hammer stone are used to split fragments from the core, which are called blades. The blades are then shaped into a variety of tools including knives, scrapers, burins, and so on. The Upper Paleolithic toolkit represents an advance over the Middle Paleolithic in several ways: (a) raw materials such as flint are used more efficiently; (b) specialized tool types are made for specialized uses; (c) each tool type follows a standardized pattern; (d) stone tools are used to make further tools out of bone, antler, or ivory; and (e) composite tools can be created using multiple materials. The ability to carve bone or ivory made possible the creation of new tools like fishhooks and sewing needles. Composite techniques also widened the range of tools; for example, spears could involve a wood handle, a bone tip, and resin to attach the tip to the handle.

Later improvements in hunting methods included spear throwers as well as bows and arrows. Other markers of the Upper Paleolithic are grinding and pounding tools for processing wild plant foods; long-distance trade in raw materials; food storage facilities; structured hearths; specialized habitation areas for butchering, cooking, waste disposal, and sleeping; and artistic items such as ornaments, paintings, and musical instruments.

The traditional date for the boundary between the Middle and Upper Paleolithic is around 40–45 KYA, the period when AMHs were arriving in Europe. This amounts to a distinction between the technology used by Neanderthals already living in Europe and the technology brought to Europe by the first AMH immigrants. However, the technology of Upper Paleolithic Europe closely resembles technology used by AMHs in South Africa as early as 60–80 KYA (Mellars, 2007; Mourre et al., 2010; Nowell, 2010). Mellars argues that the pioneering blade technology of South Africa fueled the spread of AMHs to Asia and Europe, a view that remains debatable. In any event, 40–45 KYA may represent not so much a qualitative boundary in the technical progress of AMHs as a milestone in their geographic dispersal (see our discussion in Section 2.3 on what we mean and don't mean by the word "progress" in the context of technical change).

Archaeologists often refer to the Upper Paleolithic as a revolution in comparison with the Middle Paleolithic (Bar-Yosef, 2002a). The dramatic contrast in technological capabilities between the two periods warrants this label. From an economic perspective, however, the innovation process was remarkably slow. More than 200,000 years elapsed between the emergence of anatomically modern humans and the earliest widely accepted evidence of blade technology around 80 KYA. Tens of millennia more elapsed before the Neolithic transition to agriculture began around 12 KYA in southwest Asia. While spearthrowers and the bow and arrow were breakthroughs for the people who invented them, the average pace of technical progress in the Upper Paleolithic was negligible by comparison with early agricultural societies, let alone industrial societies.

Blade technology is a classic example of what economists would call a general-purpose technology (Lipsey et al., 2005). In this chapter we treat the existence of blade technology as given and do not attempt to explain the transition from the Middle to the Upper Paleolithic (for an intriguing demographic hypothesis about the rise and spread of UP culture see Powell et al., 2009, 2010). Our focus is on the development of techniques specific to individual food resources. For example, nets can be used to catch birds, snares can be used to catch hares, weirs can be used to catch fish, and sickles can be used to harvest wild grasses. Our model of learning by doing in Section 3.5 addresses resource-specific technologies of this kind.

There is no uniform end date for the Upper Paleolithic. In the European context, archaeologists sometimes treat the Upper Paleolithic as terminating with the onset of the Holocene climate regime around 11.6 KYA (see Figure 1.1 in Chapter 1). For Europe, the period between the start of the Holocene and the arrival of agriculture is often called the Mesolithic. Because agriculture arrived at different times in different subregions of Europe, the timing of the shift from the Mesolithic to the Neolithic varies with location.

In the context of the Levant or other parts of southwest Asia, archaeologists often refer to the period between the Last Glacial Maximum and the Holocene (about 21–11.6 KYA) as the "Epi-Paleolithic," meaning "Final Old Stone Age." This terminology works well for southwest Asia because the Neolithic transition to agriculture roughly coincided with the arrival of the Holocene around 11.6 KYA (see Chapter 5). The distinguishing technological features of the Epi-Paleolithic in southwest Asia include microblades and, by about 14.5–13.0 KYA, increasing sedentism (see Chapter 4).

These terminological schemes are not necessarily a good fit for other regions of the world such as Africa and China. In the New World, the period known as "Archaic" is sometimes regarded as paralleling the Upper Paleolithic of the Old World. However, in many parts of the world the Upper Paleolithic never led to indigenous agriculture or to indigenous metal tools. In much of Africa, Asia, and the Americas, and all of Australia and the Arctic, an Upper Paleolithic toolkit remained in use until contact with the global economy in the last few centuries.

Direct evidence on Upper Paleolithic social institutions is scarce, so ethnographic analogies are helpful in painting a picture. There is broad agreement that prior to the rise of sedentary communities, the basic social unit was the mobile foraging band. Bands observed by anthropologists generally have about 25 members, with 7–8 healthy adults who can search for food on a full-time basis (Kelly, 2013a, ch. 7; French, 2016, 176–179). These figures vary across societies, but they likely reflect a rough compromise between the insurance benefits from sharing food within the group and the fact that larger groups would deplete local resources too quickly, requiring more frequent residential moves (Kelly, 2013a, ch. 7). Such bands tend to make regular seasonal rounds within a familiar territory (see the description of traditional Shoshone society in Johnson and Earle, 2000, ch. 3). Several bands may come together annually at times and places of resource abundance or when stored food is available, offering opportunities to find mates, share information, trade exotic items, and engage in ritual activities.

Beyond the day-to-day benefits from food sharing within a band, the key strategy for coping with negative environmental shocks that are local and temporary is reciprocity among neighboring bands. This may involve sharing of food or access to territory (Kelly, 2013a, ch. 6). Storage technology is usually limited and tends to play a minor role in risk management. For negative shocks that are widespread and prolonged, the only practical response is a search for better resources in more distant territories.

Of course, small egalitarian bands of mobile foragers were not the only form of social organization in the Upper Paleolithic. Graeber and Wengrow (2021, 86–92) cite a few examples from the period of settlements that include stone temples, elaborate burials, and massive monuments. But these findings are rare and are not the focus of this chapter.

3.2 CLIMATE

Climate reconstruction (paleoclimatology) involves observations on polar ice, alpine glaciers, ocean and lake sediments, tree rings, calcite precipitated on the walls of caves, growth bands in corals, and the chemistry of marine shells. Polar ice cores have more than 40 distinct climate-related properties and provide data on temperature, rainfall, ice volume, and atmospheric CO_2 concentrations (EPICA, 2004; McManus, 2004). For an introductory review of Ice Age climate history, see Woodward (2014, chs. 8–9).

Figure 3.1 summarizes climate history for the last 420,000 years using data from the Vostok ice core in Antarctica. Notice that from a climatic standpoint this covers the Late Pleistocene and the Holocene. These terms should not be confused with the terms Paleolithic and Neolithic, which are defined by technology rather than climate. The data in Figure 3.1 were published by Petit et al. (1999) and the graph was taken from Creative Commons (2019). The top panel shows temperature variation in degrees Celsius relative to the Holocene, the middle panel shows atmospheric carbon dioxide in parts per million by volume, and the bottom panel shows atmospheric dust concentration. The latter is a proxy for aridity, so the bottom panel can be interpreted as the inverse of precipitation.

From other Antarctic ice cores it is known that the pattern of Ice Ages depicted in Figure 3.1 extends back at least 800,000 years (EPICA, 2004). The underlying cause is a complex set of cycles involving the Earth's orbit. Each cycle lasts about 100,000 years, with glacial periods lasting about 90,000 years separated by interglacial periods of about 10,000 years. During glacial periods, large volumes of water are locked up in ice sheets on the continents and sea levels are consequently low. In the past this has created bridges between land masses that are currently separated by ocean. The best known is Beringia, a former land bridge between Siberia and Alaska.

The three time series are not perfectly correlated, but glacial periods (or stadials) tend to have low temperatures, low CO_2, and low precipitation, while interglacial periods (interstadials) tend to have the opposite conditions. It is also evident from Figure 3.1 that there are major temperature fluctuations within each glacial period. By comparison with the Holocene,

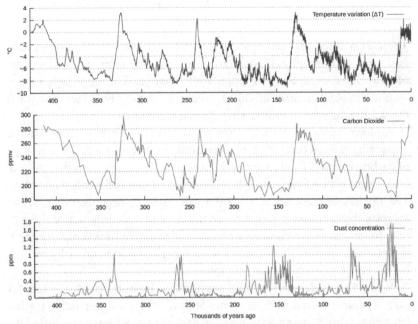

FIGURE 3.1. Glacial cycles from Antarctic ice core

the last Ice Age involved a decrease in global mean annual temperature of 5–10 degrees Celsius, a 30% reduction in atmospheric CO_2 concentration, and a drop in sea level of 125 meters (Cronin, 1999).

Several climate events that will be significant for later discussions are visible in Figure 3.1. The Eemian period of 126–116 KYA was the most recent interglacial before the Holocene and was slightly warmer at its peak. The temperature fell rapidly starting around 116 KYA, recovered during 100–80 KYA, and fell rapidly again until 65 KYA. This was followed by a moderate phase during 65–30 KYA. The Last Glacial Maximum (LGM) brought a low point around 21 KYA. Temperature recovered quickly beginning around 19 KYA. A temperature drop called the Younger Dryas (YD) can be seen around 13.0–11.6 KYA. Although this reversal appears brief on the scale of Figure 3.1, it lasted over 1000 years and had major demographic repercussions (see Section 3.3). The Holocene brought warmer, wetter, and more stable conditions beginning at 11.6 KYA. During the Holocene there have been various global and regional climate fluctuations, which will be discussed as they become relevant in later chapters.

3.3 POPULATION

There is a large archaeological literature dedicated to Pleistocene and Holocene demography. French (2016) reviews the many proxies archaeologists have used to infer population change. The approach in this section involves a method called "dates as data." First, we provide a quick introduction to radiocarbon dating techniques.

Archaeologists frequently estimate the age of organic materials by measuring the concentration of a naturally occurring radioactive isotope of carbon called ^{14}C relative to the more common stable isotopes ^{12}C and ^{13}C. Plants and animals absorb ^{14}C from their environments while alive, and this isotope decays at a known rate after an organism dies. Older samples therefore have lower concentrations of ^{14}C. In practice the true date for a sample is estimated with error. The extent of this uncertainty is sometimes expressed by a confidence interval, and sometimes by providing an entire probability distribution.

Radiocarbon dating has three limitations. First, it does not work for non-organic material such as stone. Second, dates are unreliable further back than about 40–50 KYA because earlier samples have too little ^{14}C. Third, the atmospheric concentration of ^{14}C varies over time, creating the need for calibration techniques that translate "radiocarbon years" into calendar years. All radiocarbon dates in this book are calibrated and can be treated as calendar years unless the contrary is explicitly stated. Additional information about radiocarbon dating methods is available in introductory archaeology textbooks.

The idea behind "dates as data" runs as follows. If the population in a geographic region in a given time period is large, it is likely to generate extensive material remains that can be discovered by archaeologists. Thus if a relatively large number of observed radiocarbon dates fall in a given time interval, one can infer the presence of a relatively large population during that interval, and conversely if there is a relatively small number of radiocarbon dates in a different time interval. This yields information about how the population changed over time in a region. Archaeologists sometimes use supplemental data to estimate absolute population levels.

Early research using "dates as data" placed individual estimated dates in temporal bins, and used the number of dates in each of the bins to generate a histogram indicating how population changed over time. The size of the bins was usually adjusted to reflect the degree of uncertainty in the dating process. For example, if a typical date had a 95% confidence interval of 1,000 years, the researcher might choose 1,000 years as the size of a bin. Since about 2010, many archaeologists have begun to exploit the entire probability distribution for each date, where the sum of the radiocarbon probabilities is treated as a proxy for population. Various sources of bias in this approach are discussed by French (2016), who also provides extensive references.

In this chapter we limit attention to regions for which data extend far back into the Pleistocene (Europe and Siberia), for which Upper Paleolithic technology continued into the Holocene (North and South America), or both (Australia). Other regions (including southwest Asia, Japan, and the Sahara) will be discussed when appropriate in Chapters 4 and 5. For brevity we focus on recent studies and often omit citations to earlier research on the same geographic region.

We begin with Europe during 30–13 KYA, a period that covers the growth and retreat of ice sheets associated with the Last Glacial Maximum. Tallavaara et al. (2015) derive population estimates in two ways. First, they use a "dates as data" approach of the kind described above, where 3,718 calibrated median dates from 895 archaeological sites are placed in bins with 1,000-year durations. They compare these results with population estimates obtained through climate modeling in conjunction with population densities for recent hunter-gatherer societies. Both techniques indicate a large contraction in human population size and range due to the LGM beginning around 27 KYA, with a minimum around 23 KYA and a rapid recovery during 19–13 KYA. The simulations indicate an initial European population of 330,000 at 30 KYA, a minimum of 130,000 at 23 KYA, and 410,000 at 13 KYA. The simulations also show that even in the depths of the LGM, human populations extended north as far as central France, southern Germany, and the southern parts of Ukraine and European Russia, with around 36% of Europe remaining habitable. Tallavaara et al. (2015, 8235) remark that "climatic conditions were crucial drivers of last glacial human population dynamics."

Fernández-López et al. (2019) have studied population dynamics in the Iberian peninsula for 16.6–8 KYA using summed probability distributions with 907 radiocarbon dates. The later part of this interval extends into the Holocene, but the Iberian population were still foragers at this time, so the results are relevant here. The authors found several statistically significant upward and downward deviations from a null exponential model. Three qualitative phases were apparent: (a) exponential growth in a period of improving climate called the Last Glacial Interstadial; (b) collapse followed by prolonged stagnation during the Younger Dryas and the first half of the Early Holocene; and (c) logistic growth in the second half of the Early Holocene. The population during phase (a) was positively correlated with temperature and precipitation. The population in phase (c) became stable as temperature and precipitation stabilized during the second half of the Early Holocene.

Population trends in Siberia have been studied by Kuzmin and Keates (2005) for 46–12 KYA using 437 dates (these authors do not discuss calibration issues, and their dates appear to be uncalibrated). They group radiocarbon dates at individual sites into "occupation episodes" of 1,000 years each. On this basis, they conclude that population density was low until 36 KYA, increased gradually during 36–16 KYA, and increased more rapidly from 16–12 KYA. They find that Siberia was not depopulated at the Last Glacial Maximum. Their conclusions for the LGM are controversial (see Section 3.10).

Australian population trends from 50 KYA to European contact are examined by Williams (2013), who uses 4,575 calibrated radiocarbon dates from 1,750 archaeological sites. The median dates are assigned to 200-year bins. Williams finds low populations through the late Pleistocene, with a drop of about 60% associated with the Last Glacial Maximum during 21–18 KYA. A slow stepwise increase begins around the time of the Holocene, near 12 KYA, with population recovering to pre-LGM levels by about 9.6 KYA. Williams suggests that high-amplitude environmental shocks may have kept the population low during the Late Pleistocene, with climate stabilization in the Holocene allowing population growth. The Holocene shows several population fluctuations that are probably driven by climatic variation, with a peak population in the Late Holocene. Williams suggests that a founding group of 1,000–3,000 people around 50 KYA and a maximum population of 1.2 million around 500 years ago would be consistent with the data. The average annual growth rate for the entire 50,000-year interval is about 0.01% with a range between 0.07 and -0.03.

Several recent articles have focused on North American paleodemography. Two points should be kept in mind in this regard. First, recent evidence indicates that human settlement occurred in North America by 23–21 KYA, but radiocarbon data usable for paleodemography are not available until around 15 KYA. Second, although much of the western portion of the continent was occupied by mobile foraging populations until European contact, sedentary foraging was important in the Pacific

Northwest and farming became important east of the Mississippi River as well as in the southwestern US. We focus on the findings for mobile foragers.

Peros et al. (2010) use 25,198 calibrated dates for all of North America, where the median probability value for each date is assigned to a 200-year bin. The dates run from about 15 KYA until European contact. The most rapid growth rate was shortly before 14 KYA. Population was low and relatively constant until roughly 6 KYA, when it began to increase. Because plant domestication is known to have occurred in the eastern half of the continent starting about 4 KYA (see Chapter 5), results after that date are not relevant here. The authors do not report any population decline associated with the Younger Dryas.

Anderson et al. (2011) use summed radiocarbon probabilities to investigate the possible effects in North America from the cold and arid period of the Younger Dryas, which occurred during 12.9–11.6 KYA. Their 682 calibrated radiocarbon dates run from 14–11 KYA. They find a large population increase before the YD followed by a rapid drop (perhaps up to 30–50%) in the first few centuries of this period. There is a gradual rebound over the next 900 years in the later stages of the YD, suggesting adaptation to the adverse climatic conditions. This pattern holds for all regions of the continent and is supported by evidence on projectile point frequencies as well as quarry use. Anderson et al. describe similar results using radiocarbon data for Europe, Asia (excluding the Middle East), and Africa. Interestingly, the Middle East does not display a significant population drop with the onset of the Younger Dryas, a point to which we will return in Chapter 5.

Kelly et al. (2013) explored the relationship between population and climate for foragers in the Bighorn Basin of Wyoming over the last 13,000 years, using the summed probabilities derived from several hundred radiocarbon dates. Fluctuations in population were complex, with several peaks and troughs where intervals of population growth were associated with cooler and wetter conditions. An increase in temperature of one degree Celsius led to a 45% decline in population, and a decrease in moisture of 50 mm led to a 26% decline in population after a lag of 300 years. However, the authors were unable to distinguish migratory effects from natural population growth or decline.

Zahid et al. (2016) studied forager populations in Wyoming and Colorado during the last 15,000 years using summed probabilities for 7,900 radiocarbon samples. Because this is a larger geographic area than that studied by Kelly et al. (2013), migration effects may be less of a concern. Following an early jump in population, Zahid et al. found an exponential trend for 13–6 KYA with an average annual growth rate of 0.04%, but with several large upward and downward deviations from this trend that lasted for centuries. Population leveled off and declined during 6–3 KYA. The authors attribute the earlier exponential trend to climate change or endogenous biological processes rather than technical innovation. They do not propose a specific explanation for the population decline following 6 KYA.

Our last stop is South America. Goldberg et al. (2016) use 5,464 radiocarbon dates from 1,147 sites to compute summed probabilities for 15–2 KYA. Dispersal by the original colonizers is not visible because the earliest dates are scattered throughout the continent. The authors find a rapid increase both in radiocarbon dates and occupied sites during 13–9 KYA, followed by oscillations around a constant mean during 9–5.5 KYA. They suggest that a peak around 11 KYA could reflect an overshoot associated with a megafaunal extinction. Growth resumed in the interval 5.5–2 KYA. The best fit was provided by a two-phase model with logistic growth until 5.5 KYA followed by an exponential growth trend thereafter. The authors note that the timing of exponential growth coincided with a shift toward agriculture across much of South America.

The main lessons we take away from this review of demographic research on five continents are that mobile foragers with Upper Paleolithic technology tended to converge on equilibrium populations for the environments they inhabited, and that there were often very strong climatic effects on population size. Some periods of slow population growth appear to be consistent with slow technological progress in a natural environment where resources were fluctuating around a constant mean. But steady exponential growth was certainly not the norm in the Pleistocene, and probably not in the Holocene either. Even when an exponential trend was sustained for a substantial period, large and statistically significant deviations were usually superimposed on the trend, and regional population contractions were not unusual.

3.4 TECHNOLOGY

If one wanted to argue that the Upper Paleolithic was a technically progressive period, one could. Direct archaeological evidence reveals considerable evolution in the design of stone tools, including the development of microblades. New hunting methods such as the spear thrower and bow and arrow were also developed. Two other empirical patterns are evident. First, people began to rely less on hunting large mammals and more on small prey like hares and birds, along with a wide array of plant foods. This process is known as the *broad spectrum revolution*. Second, people colonized harsh environments such as the Arctic, which required new hunting technologies as well as innovations with respect to clothing, shelter, and transport.

On the other hand, one could also argue that the Upper Paleolithic was technically stagnant. Tens of thousands of years elapsed between the beginnings of blade technology around 80 KYA and the beginnings of agriculture around 12 KYA. Precursors of modern society like metallurgy and writing are even more recent. Strikingly, much of the world continued to rely on stone-age foraging techniques until European contact in the last 500 years. This suggests that Upper Paleolithic technology was a stable way of life, and that unusual circumstances were needed to push societies toward other economic systems.

In our view, a theoretical framework that can reconcile these two perspectives will need to have the following features:

(a) Technology should be endogenous, with innovation being slow, sporadic, and frequently absent for long periods of time.
(b) Population should be endogenous, with Malthusian dynamics.
(c) Nature should be exogenous, with changes in climate, geography, and ecosystems serving as triggers for changes in technology and population.
(d) The theory should be consistent with the climate history in Section 3.2.
(e) The theory should be consistent with the population history in Section 3.3.
(f) The theory should account for the broad spectrum revolution and the expansion of human populations into harsh environments.

We will construct a model along these lines in Sections 3.5–3.9.

In this section, we review several previous efforts to endogenize technology. We begin with a model of economic growth by Kremer (1993). Although this is about three decades old, it is worth discussing because it is a pioneering application of growth theory to prehistory and because it crystallizes key issues in a relatively simple way. In fairness we should say that Kremer's central concern is the transition to modern economic growth, not economic prehistory, but he does claim that his model is relevant for pre-agricultural societies. Other efforts to construct comprehensive theories of economic growth having relevance for prehistory, such as Galor (2005, 2011), will be discussed in Chapter 12.

Kremer's starting point is a sequence of estimates for world population beginning a million years ago and ending with the twentieth century. The early figures in the series are crude and should not be taken seriously. Much more sophisticated estimates are available today (see Goldewijk et al., 2010), and we need not linger over measurement issues here. The more interesting questions are theoretical in nature.

Kremer's model rests on two causal relationships. First, he argues that the size of the world population is determined by technological productivity in a Malthusian manner. His model of population is a simplified version of the one in Chapter 2, where short-run adjustment processes are ignored and population is assumed always to equal its long-run equilibrium level given the current productivity level. Equivalently, the average product of labor is always equal to the fixed long-run standard of living y^* from Chapter 2.

Second, he argues that the rate of productivity growth is proportional to the level of world population. Note that this claim involves a linkage between a growth rate and a level, in contrast to the Malthusian part of the model that provides a linkage between the level of population and level of productivity. Kremer's argument for this second causal relationship is that a larger population implies a larger number of independent inventors, and therefore more useful inventions per unit of time. Although Kremer studies several ways of specifying the determinants of productivity growth, we focus on his basic linear model. The idea that a higher population level yields a higher productivity growth rate is common among economists (see Becker et al., 1999; Galor and Weil, 2000; Jones, 2001; Galor, 2005; Olsson and Hibbs, 2005; Aiyar et al., 2008).

Putting together the causal relationships from the two preceding paragraphs gives a simple prediction: the current population growth rate will be proportional to the current population level. Kremer argues (plausibly) that this provides a good fit to the data over the last several thousand years, except in the twentieth century when the Industrial Revolution and the associated demographic transition became important. For our purposes, the main points are that the model predicts continuous growth in both population and productivity, and that the growth process will be faster than exponential.

This is clearly inconsistent with our criteria for a satisfactory theory of Upper Paleolithic technology. First, it is incompatible with the fact that technical progress was usually sporadic or absent. Second, the prediction about population growth conflicts with findings that regional populations often exhibited stasis, cycles, or collapse. And finally, the model ignores the powerful demographic effects of the natural environment.

As Richerson et al. (2001) have pointed out, when tiny rates of technical change are compounded for tens of millennia, they have enormous consequences for population, the standard of living, or both. Even a small founding population could bring all of Asia to modern hunter-gatherer population densities within a few thousand years. Over the 50 millennia in which humans have occupied Australia, a tiny rate of population growth can take a founding population from the low thousands to the low billions (Williams, 2013). This is true even for a small constant rate of exponential growth. If the growth rate is an increasing function of the population level, as in Kremer (1993), the results are still more explosive. Because there is no sign of sustained population growth (or improving living standards, or greater social complexity) before the first known sedentary communities at about 15 KYA, the equilibrium growth rate must have been zero almost all of the time.

Another problem with the Kremer framework requires comment. In a Malthusian setting it is reasonable to hypothesize that observed population growth could be explained by unobserved technological progress. But the Kremer model ignores the possibility that population growth could have been stimulated by climate improvements with technology held constant (e.g., the recovery from the Last Glacial Maximum, or the shift from the Pleistocene to the Holocene). It also ignores the fact that the colonization of new land masses can yield world population growth with a constant technology. For inferences of unobserved technological progress to be persuasive, one must argue that population grew within a fixed geographic region with fixed natural resources, and that this increase was not driven by migration from external sources.

Archaeology and anthropology also have a literature linking population size to innovation, based on social learning and cultural transmission (Shennan, 2001; Bentley et al., 2004; Henrich, 2004; Powell et al., 2009, 2010; Boyd et al., 2011; Richerson, 2013; Crema and Lake, 2015). The usual (although not invariable) conclusion is that a higher population level leads to more rapid social learning and technical change. Eventually this yields greater cultural complexity, better adaptation to the environment, and/or enhanced biological fitness. These ideas have been applied in discussions of the Upper Paleolithic (Shennan, 2001; Powell et al., 2009, 2010).

The archaeological literature on social learning is consistent with the part of the Kremer model where the innovation rate is an increasing function of the population level. However, it omits the other part of the Kremer model where population is endogenized through Malthusian dynamics. If we were to add a Malthusian population equation, we would be back to the same positive feedback loop where technology and population can both grow explosively. We are not aware of any formal modeling in archaeology that tackles this issue, although the potential for positive feedback has been noted (Shennan, 2001, 14; Powell et al., 2009, 1301; 2010, 145). This problem could be mitigated by a concave relationship between the population level and the innovation rate, as is usually found in social learning models, rather than the linear relationship used in the simplest version of the Kremer model.

Anthropological data have been used to test the claim that technical innovation is an increasing function of population size. Some studies support this hypothesized link while others do not (Collard et al., 2013). We are not surprised by these mixed results. Virtually all such studies use (small) samples of recently observed foraging or farming societies. The hypothesis being tested treats population as exogenous and technology as endogenous. But on time scales where technology is endogenous (and perhaps at or near an equilibrium level), population will almost certainly also be endogenous for Malthusian reasons (and also at or near an equilibrium level). Regressing technology on population thus involves regressing one endogeneous variable on another, resulting in simultaneity bias. In a model where both technology and population are endogenous, the exogenous variables are those determined by nature (climate, geography, and ecosystems).

Our own story about technical change in the Upper Paleolithic is closely related to other theories about social learning that have been influential among archaeologists. For analytic convenience, our formal model adopts a very simple approach to social learning where learning is initiated through mistakes in copying, which can be regarded as a form of accidental experimentation. Directional learning occurs through comparisons among the accidentally generated techniques for harvesting a particular resource. However, our modeling framework could be extended to accommodate deliberate experimentation.

It is useful to compare our analysis with that in Henrich's (2016) highly influential book *The Secret of Our Success*. Henrich's treatment of collective learning is much more detailed than ours. It stresses the innate ability of humans to copy from each other and the importance of social norms for the transfer of new knowledge within a society and to future generations. We accept Henrich's richer view of collective learning and see it as complementary to our simplified account. However, we differ from Henrich in that our analysis is motivated by the observation that technological progress was dramatically uneven during the Upper Paleolithic. Why were there periods of technical improvement separated by long periods of apparent stagnation? Henrich does not address this question but elements of his analysis suggest a pathway to an answer.

Let social norms be the primary mechanism for knowledge transfer, as Henrich suggests. Strict adherence to social norms related to technology could theoretically shut down both experimentation and knowledge transfer. Under what conditions will norms be flexible enough to allow for technological change? Giuliano and Nunn (2021) find that tradition and cultural persistence are weaker in less stable environments. We can link this idea with Henrich's (2016, 301) view that climate fluctuations are a source of intensified pressure for social learning. Perhaps climate fluctuations simultaneously loosened the restrictive grip of social norms on new technologies. Our simpler approach yields a relationship between climate and technical innovation that is more easily tested, but it could potentially be expanded to include social norms as a mediating factor.

A brief comment on our relationship to the framework of Boserup (1965) is also in order. Boserup famously argued that population growth puts downward pressure on living standards, which stimulates techno-logical innovation (often called "intensification" by archaeologists and anthropologists). If population growth is viewed as an exogenous vari-able, we would reject this approach. However, Wood (1998) provides a synthesis of Boserupian and Malthusian ideas where population is treated as endogenous.

Even so, our theory diverges from Boserup. We do not treat falling standards of living (whether caused by a movement along a declining average product curve, or by a downward shift of the curve) as a causal stimulus for innovation. We do sometimes treat a negative climate shock as the trigger for technical change (see our models of agriculture and manufacturing in Chapters 5 and 10, respectively), but our causal mech-anisms differ from those of Boserup. Perhaps more importantly here, we also believe positive climate shocks, which raise living standards in the short run, were a key trigger for innovation in the Upper Paleolithic. Details will be given in Sections 3.9 and 3.10. We make similar arguments regarding positive climate change as a stimulus for sedentism in Chapter 4.

We suggest the following way of thinking about Upper Paleolithic technology. Nature provides many potential food resources that could be exploited if a society had suitable technical knowledge. In a static environment, foragers become very competent at exploiting some subset of these resources, but face long-run stagnation because (a) there is an upper bound on productivity for each resource, (b) latent resources remain unexploited due to the limitations of prevailing knowledge, and (c) knowledge cannot improve for resources that are never used.

To escape from such a trap, a foraging society must be exposed to shocks from nature. For example, an improved climate tends to increase population in the long run. If this Malthusian effect is large enough it may become attractive to exploit latent resources. Once this occurs, learning by doing will generate improvements in the techniques used to harvest, process, or store these new resources. If such knowledge gains are irreversible, a series of positive and negative climate shocks can yield a ratchet effect in technological capabilities, with occasional episodes of population growth and technical innovation.

We develop these ideas formally in Sections 3.5–3.9. Our theory can explain the prolonged periods of economic stagnation found in many pre-agricultural societies, both in the distant past and among recent hunter-gatherers. In Section 3.10 we suggest that our theory can also account for some macro-level patterns in the Upper Paleolithic, including the broad spectrum revolution and the colonization of extreme environments.

3.5 LEARNING BY DOING

The next several sections develop a formal model of Upper Paleolithic economic growth that conforms to the requirements (a)–(f) identified in Section 3.4. We begin with a model of technical innovation along lines similar to those of the social learning models used in archaeology and anthropology, where children learn techniques from adults. Our approach makes a number of simplifications. We assume children can imitate any adult, without special preferences for biological parents or prestigious role models; we assume children can compare techniques among themselves and adopt the best ones available, so there is no variation among the members of any given generation in the techniques used; and we study a limiting case where the number of imitation events goes to infinity while the mutation rate goes to zero. This yields directional learning over multiple generations, where techniques may improve or remain static but never deteriorate.

Consider a list of natural resources $r = 1..R$. These could include blueberries, rabbits, and so forth. Each resource can be converted into food through the use of labor. We treat food as a homogeneous output, ignoring distinctions among calories, protein, vitamins, and so on. The production function for converting resource r into food is

$$F_r(a_r, k_r, n_r) = a_r g_r(k_r) f_r(n_r) \qquad (3.1)$$

where a_r is the abundance of resource r (regarded as a flow provided by nature in a given time period); k_r is the technique used to harvest it; and n_r is the labor used for harvesting. The abundance of each resource is determined by climate, geography, and ecosystems. However, climate is the only determinant of resource abundance that will be varied in this chapter, so for convenience we often refer to $a = (a_1 .. a_R) > 0$ as "climate."

For fixed a_r and k_r, each production function in (3.1) has the same general shape as the production function from Chapter 2. We impose the following technical conditions.

Assumption 3.1
The functions f_r are twice continuously differentiable and satisfy $f_r(0) = 0$; $0 < f'_r(n_r) < \infty$ for all $n_r \geq 0$ with $f'_r(n_r) \to 0$ as $n_r \to \infty$; and $f''_r(n_r) < 0$ for all $n_r \geq 0$.

Each function has a positive and finite marginal product $f'_r(0)$ when labor input is zero. We will say that resource r is *active* if $n_r > 0$ and *latent* if $n_r = 0$. The finiteness of the marginal products at zero will be important when we discuss conditions under which a latent resource becomes active. As in Chapter 2, the function f_r exhibits diminishing marginal productivity (the second derivative is negative).

Dropping the r subscript momentarily, one example of a function satisfying the requirements in A3.1 is $f(n) = 1 - e^{-mn}$, where the marginal product at zero is $f'(0) = m > 0$. This functional form is consistent with an interpretation where a_r is the resource flow in nature, $g_r(k_r)$ is the fraction of a_r that is potentially accessible with the current technique k_r, and $f_r(n_r)$ is the fraction of $a_r g_r(k_r)$ that is actually harvested.

Techniques are modeled as binary strings of uniform length Q so $k_r = (k_{r1} .. k_{rQ}) \in \{0, 1\}^Q$. Let k_r^* be the best method for transforming resource r into food: $0 < g_r(k_r) < g_r(k_r^*)$ for all $k_r \neq k_r^*$. The function

$g_r(k_r)$ is increasing in the number of digits of k_r that match k_r^*. It does not matter which digits are matched. The number of matching digits indexes the level of technical knowledge regarding resource r.

Q is assumed to be large enough that an exhaustive search for the ideal strings is impractical. Instead, each generation inherits a repertoire of techniques from its parental generation. The repertoire available to the adults of generation t is $K^t = \{k_1^t..k_R^t\}$. This array summarizes the current state of technological knowledge for all natural resources, where this knowledge is freely available to all adults of generation t.

The repertoire K^{t+1} for the next generation is derived as follows. Let there be N^t adults in period t. Each adult is endowed with one unit of labor time. The society's labor allocation is $n^t = (n_1^t..n_R^t)$ where $\sum_r n_r^t = N^t$. All adults use the same time allocation, so each person devotes n_r^t/N^t time units to resource r.

A typical child in the period t has X opportunities to watch parents or other adults harvest resources, where X is a large number. Xn_r^t/N^t of these observations will involve resource r (there are no observations for latent resources with $n_r^t = o$). Every time a child i sees the exploitation of resource r, the string $k_r^t = \left(k_{r1}^t..k_{rQ}^t\right)$ is copied. For each of the Q positions on the string, with probability p an error is made in copying the current digit, and with probability 1-p the digit is copied accurately. Mutations are independent across loci, observations, and agents. A copy is denoted by k_{rix}^t where x indexes observations.

Whenever a copy of k_r^t is made, child i uses a negligible amount of labor $\varepsilon > o$ to determine the marginal product $a_r^t g_r(k_{rix}^t) f_r'(o)$. If the new copy achieves a higher value than the best previous copy, the child retains the new copy and discards any earlier copy. Otherwise, the best previous copy is retained and the new copy is discarded. At the end of this learning process, child i has a best string for resource r, which we denote by k_{ri}^{t+1}.

The number of children who survive to adulthood is N^{t+1}. When the parents from period t die and their children become adults, these new adults compare their strings for resource r and coordinate on (one of) the best available. The result for resource r is $k_r^{t+1} = \text{argmax}\left\{g_r(k_{ri}^{t+1}) \text{ for } i = 1..N^{t+1}\right\}$.

This process gives updated strings for the resources r having $n_r^t > o$. In most of this chapter, we will assume passive updating for latent resources: that is, $n_r^t = o$ implies $k_r^{t+1} = k_r^t$. We discuss alternative productivity assumptions for latent resources at the end of Section 3.9. The entire updated repertoire $K^{t+1} = \{k_1^{t+1}..k_R^{t+1}\}$ is freely available to all adults of generation t + 1.

Let q_r^t be the number of correct digits in the string $k_r^t \in K^t$. To model technical progress for active resources, we need to know the probability distribution over q_r^{t+1}.

Proposition 3.1 (learning by doing).

Assume $n_r^t > 0$ so resource r is active in period t. Define $\rho^t \equiv N^{t+1}/N^t$ to be the number of children who survive to adulthood in period $t+1$ per adult in period t. Let the number of observations per child (X) approach infinity and the mutation probability (p) approach zero with $\lambda \equiv Xp > 0$ held constant. In the limit,

$$\text{Prob}\left(q_r^{t+1} = q_r^t\right) = \exp\left[-\lambda n_r^t \rho^t (Q - q_r^t)\right] \quad \text{and}$$
$$\text{Prob}\left(q_r^{t+1} = q_r^t + 1\right) = 1 - \exp\left[-\lambda n_r^t \rho^t (Q - q_r^t)\right]$$

All other transition probabilities for q_r^{t+1} go to zero in the limit.

Proposition 3.1 shows that technical evolution for an active resource is directional. Either the number of correct digits in the string is unchanged and so is productivity, or there is a one-step improvement in the string for resource r with an associated productivity gain.

The intuition behind this result is not hard to grasp. In order to obtain technical regress for the string for resource r, it would be necessary for every observation of k_r^t to be worse than the status quo. In the limit as the number of observations goes to infinity, the probability of this outcome goes to zero. But technical progress only requires that at least one observation be better than the status quo. The probability of this outcome does not go to zero (though the probability of multiple productivity steps does). Proposition 3.1 does not require a large population. Each child only needs to have many opportunities to observe adult behavior, which could be true even in a small foraging band.

The probability of technical progress is an increasing function of the mutation rate, the labor input for the resource, the population growth rate, and the current distance from the ideal string. Other things equal, progress is more likely for resources involving larger labor inputs because children make more observations for these resources. It is also more likely when the population growth rate is higher because then there are more children who can compare notes on the copies they have made. Finally, progress is more likely when the distance from the ideal string is greater (the current technique is worse), because then there are more opportunities to learn something useful. One corollary of

Proposition 3.1 is that if the transition probabilities are continuous at $n_r^t = 0$, productivity for a latent resource is constant with certainty. This provides a theoretical rationale for the idea that strings for such resources are passively updated.

Notice that if we fix the fraction of total time devoted to each resource, a higher population N implies a higher labor input n_r for every active resource r, and therefore an increased probability of technical progress for every resource (as long as its current string remains imperfect). This is consistent with the idea that a larger population leads to more innovation. Moreover, the relationship between population and innovation is concave. A less standard result is that a higher rate of population growth (ρ) also stimulates technical progress. However, when a society is close to a Malthusian equilibrium this parameter is close to unity, so the population growth effect may not play a significant role in practice. We often refer to processes of technical change like those modeled in this section as *learning by doing*. The everyday sense of this phrase is that an individual person can become better at a task by doing it repeatedly, perhaps refining methods through trial and error or improving skills through practice. Our use of the phrase instead refers to social learning in which one generation's techniques are an improvement on the techniques of the preceding generation. The fundamental idea is that one generation must actively use a resource or technique in order for the next generation to attain higher productivity for that particular resource or technique.

3.6 SHORT-RUN EQUILIBRIUM

The next three sections develop increasingly inclusive equilibrium concepts. We start in the present section with the *short run*, in which time allocation is endogenous and population, technology, and climate are all exogenous. Section 3.7 goes to the *long run*, where we treat population as endogenous using Malthusian dynamics. Section 3.8 goes to the *very long run*, where we also treat technology as endogenous through the model of learning by doing developed in Section 3.5. At this point, the only remaining exogenous variable will be climate. Section 3.9 will show how climate change can induce changes in all of the other variables. The relationships among the short, long, and very long runs are summarized in Table 3.1.

At the moment we are only concerned with the allocation of time across various resources, and for this purpose it is useful to adopt more compact notation. Let $A_r(a_r, k_r) \equiv a_r g_r(k_r)$ be the productivity of resource r when its natural abundance is a_r and technique k_r is used. As mentioned earlier, $A_r(a_r, k_r)$ can be interpreted as the amount of resource

TABLE 3.1. *Endogenous and exogenous variables*

	Short Run	Long Run	Very Long Run
Endogenous	Time allocation	Time allocation	Time allocation
	Population	Population	Population
	Technology	Technology	Technology
Exogenous	Climate	Climate	Climate

r that is potentially accessible for harvesting under current technology. The corresponding vector of productivities will be written A(a, K). When a and K are being held constant, as in this section, we drop these arguments and write this vector as $A = (A_1 .. A_R)$.

In keeping with our general premise that a small group with frequently interacting members can resolve coordination, distribution, and free rider problems (see Chapter 1), we assume a foraging band allocates the total adult labor supply N across the individual resources to maximize total food, which is shared equally. The resulting time allocation will be called a short-run equilibrium (SRE).

Definition 3.1

A *short-run equilibrium* for the productivities $A > 0$ and population $N \geq 0$ is a labor allocation $n(A, N) = [n_1(A, N) .. n_R(A, N)]$ that achieves

$$H(A, N) \equiv \max \Sigma_r A_r f_r(n_r) \text{ subject to } n_r \geq 0 \text{ for all } r \text{ and } \Sigma_r n_r = N. \quad (3.2)$$

The next proposition characterizes the optimal time allocation.

Proposition 3.2 (short-run equilibrium).
The solution in (3.2) is unique and continuous in (A, N). Moreover:

(a) Scale effect. Fix $A > 0$ and suppose $0 < N' < N''$. If $0 < n_r(A, N')$ then $n_r(A, N') < n_r(A, N'')$.

(b) Substitution effect. Fix $N > 0$ and suppose $0 < A_r' < A_r''$ with $0 < A_s' = A_s''$ for all $s \neq r$. Also suppose $0 < n_r(A', N)$ and $0 < n_s(A', N)$ for some $s \neq r$. Then $n_r(A', N) < n_r(A'', N)$ and $n_s(A', N) > n_s(A'', N)$.

(c) $H(A, N)$ is strictly concave in N and $y(A, N) \equiv H(A, N)/N$ is decreasing in N.

(d) $\lim_{N \to \infty} H(A, N)/N = 0$.

(e) $\lim_{N \to 0} H(A, N)/N = H_N(A, 0) = \max\{A_r f_r'(0)\}$ where $H_N(A, N)$ is the derivative with respect to N.

The scale effect in part (a) says that if population increases, with all productivities held constant, more labor time will be devoted to every active resource. The substitution effect in part (b) says that if productivity increases for a particular active resource r, with all other productivities and population held constant, more labor time will be devoted to r and less time will be devoted to all other active resources. The remaining parts say that the food per person $y(A, N)$ falls when population rises, that food per person goes to zero as population goes to infinity, and that food per person has a finite upper bound equal to the largest marginal product among all of the resources, evaluated at zero labor time.

The model of this section shows why diet breadth might expand when population grows. Consider Figure 3.2, where the group population N is on the horizontal axis and the marginal products for two resources $(r = 1, 2)$ are on the vertical axis. The graph is drawn such that the marginal product for resource 1 always exceeds the marginal product for resource 2 when the same amount of labor time is devoted to each. In the language of diet breadth models (Bettinger, 2009), resource 1 is unambiguously more highly ranked.

If $N < N^a$ in Figure 3.2, it is optimal to allocate all labor to resource 1 because then $A_1 f_1'(N) > A_2 f_2'(0)$ and any attempt to transfer labor from resource 1 to resource 2 would result in less total food. This is what an economist would call a *corner solution* (or a *boundary solution*). However, when $N > N^a$ this is no longer the case. If all labor were to be used for resource 1, we would have $A_1 f_1'(N) < A_2 f_2'(0)$ and the marginal product for resource 1 would be lower than the marginal product for resource 2. This implies that if a small amount of labor were transferred from 1 to 2, the gain in food output from resource 2 would outweigh the loss in output from resource 1. In this case optimality requires that positive labor time be devoted to each resource (what an economist would call an *interior solution*). Furthermore, optimal time allocation requires equal marginal products; that is, $A_1 f_1'(n_1) = A_2 f_2'(n_2)$ where $n_1 > 0$, $n_2 > 0$, and $n_1 + n_2 = N$.

It may seem counterintuitive that even though one resource clearly dominates in Figure 3.2, a group might want to use both. But because resource 1 has a diminishing marginal product, if enough labor is used to harvest this resource, its marginal product will eventually become so low that it is worthwhile to exploit resource 2 as well. This provides an elementary theory about the linkage between population and diet breadth: as population rises, a group eventually shifts from exploiting one resource to exploiting two. It should be clear that the same logic

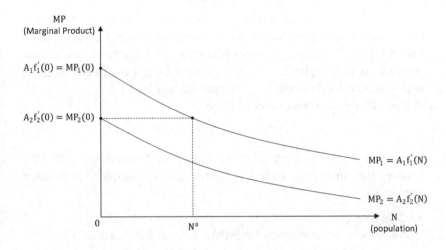

FIGURE 3.2. Population and marginal products for two resources

extends to three or more resources. We will return to this point in Section 3.10 in connection with the broad spectrum revolution.

3.7 LONG-RUN EQUILIBRIUM

This section extends the theory of Chapter 2 to determine the population N. We assume that the conditions for short-run equilibrium from Section 3.6 are satisfied in each time period, and we continue to treat technology and climate as exogenous. Accordingly, we continue to use the productivity notation $A = (A_1 .. A_R)$. For simplicity we consider a closed population where migration issues do not arise.

Let time periods be indexed by $t = 0, 1 ..$, where a time period is the length of a human generation (about 20 years). We assume adults live for one period. During this time, they produce food, have children, and then die. When the adults from period t die, they are replaced by their surviving children, who become the adults for period $t + 1$.

Suppose a typical adult has $\rho(y)$ children who survive to adulthood, where y is the adult's food income. We have already assumed that food is shared equally among adults, so y is the same for everyone. In a simple interpretation, each adult has the same number of surviving children. However, if there is random variation across adults in numbers of offspring, we can also think of $\rho(y)$ as the average number of children as long as there are enough adults that the random variation across individuals washes out. Integer problems involving the number of children are ignored. As in Chapter 2, $\rho(y)$ is a continuous and increasing function with a unique food income $y^* > 0$ such that $\rho(y^*) = 1$.

The population evolves according to

$$N^{t+1} = \rho[y(A^t, N^t)]N^t \qquad (3.3)$$

where $y(A, N)$ is food per adult as defined in Proposition 3.2(c). We impose the following technical restriction to simplify population dynamics.

Assumption 3.2

Monotone population adjustment (MPA). Suppose there is a population $N^* > 0$ such that $H(A, N^*)/N^* = y^*$. Keep A constant over time and consider any $N° > 0$. If $H(A, N°)/N° > y^*$ then $N^{t+1} > N^t$ for all $t \geq 0$. If $H(A, N°)/N° < y^*$ then $N^{t+1} < N^t$ for all $t \geq 0$. In either case $\lim_{t\to\infty} N^t = N^*$.

This says that if the initial population $N°$ yields an income above the equilibrium level y^*, so population tends to rise, it will rise steadily along the path leading to the equilibrium at N^*. By the same token, if $N°$ yields an income below y^*, so that population tends to fall, it will fall steadily along the path leading to N^*. Thus MPA rules out oscillations around N^* along the adjustment path. It holds when the direct positive effect of N^t on N^{t+1} in (3.3) outweighs the indirect negative effect of N^t through $y(A^t, N^t)$. Note that the latter indirect effect is negative because as N rises, y falls, and this dampens the rate of growth $\rho(y)$.

We can now give a formal definition of long-run equilibrium. The central idea is that we need a constant population $N(A)$ that solves (3.3) for a given productivity vector A. We also require that the time allocation for this population satisfy the requirements for a short-run equilibrium.

Definition 3.2

A *long-run equilibrium* (LRE) for the productivity vector A is a population level $N(A)$ such that $N(A) = \rho[y(A, N(A))]N(A)$, along with the associated SRE labor allocation $n[A, N(A)]$ obtained from (3.2).

If the population is zero in period t, it must also be zero in period $t + 1$, and this satisfies D3.2. Hence $N = 0$ is always an LRE. The more interesting question is whether there is a non-null LRE having $N(A) > 0$. If such an LRE exists, it must have $y[A, N(A)] \equiv y^*$ in order to have $\rho(y^*) = 1$. Proposition 3.3 determines when a non-null LRE can occur.

Proposition 3.3 (long-run equilibrium).

(a) When $\max \{A_r f_r'(0)\} > y^*$, there is a unique LRE with $N(A) > 0$ and $y[A, N(A)] = y^*$. There is also an LRE with $N = 0$.

(b) When $\max \{A_r f_r'(0)\} \leq y^*$, there is no LRE with $N(A) > 0$. The unique LRE has $N = 0$.

Part (a) shows that if at least one resource is productive enough, it is possible to support a positive population in the long run. Part (b) shows that it is impossible to have a positive population in the long run if no resource is productive enough to achieve food income y^*.

Remark: For brevity we omit a formal definition of stability for LRE. When Proposition 3.3(a) is relevant, the fact that $y(A, N)$ is decreasing in N, plus monotone population adjustment from A3.2, guarantees that the non-null LRE with $N(A) > 0$ is globally asymptotically stable and the null LRE with $N = 0$ is unstable. When Proposition 3.3(b) is relevant, the null LRE with $N = 0$ is globally asymptotically stable.

In every non-null LRE, per capita food consumption is y^*. As the vector A varies with climate or technology, the long-run population $N(A)$ will vary but the long-run living standard will not. This is the Malthusian feature of the model: an improvement in climate or technology increases food consumption per person in the short run but leads to a larger population with unchanged food per person in the long run.

Figure 3.3 illustrates the results from Proposition 3.3. When some natural resources are sufficiently abundant and/or technology is sufficiently productive, the curve $y(A, N)$ has a vertical intercept above y^* and a positive LRE population $N(A)$ exists. The arrows show directions of population adjustment and indicate the stability of $N(A)$. However, if resources are too scarce and/or technology is too unproductive, the vertical intercept for $y(A, N)$ is at or below y^* and the only LRE is the one with zero population.

A concept that will be useful later is the *habitation boundary*. Suppose there is just one food resource and just one technique for obtaining it. The productivity A is then a scalar rather than a vector. In general, there is a boundary productivity level A^b with the feature that $A \leq A^b$ implies a zero long run population and $A^b < A$ implies a positive long run

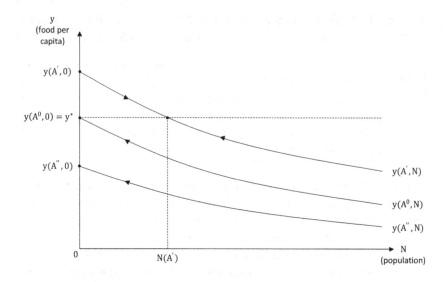

FIGURE 3.3. Population levels in long-run equilibrium

population. For a given technology, A^b determines a boundary between a geographic region where natural resources are sufficient to support a positive human population and an adjacent region where they are not. For example, there could be a latitude in northern Asia beyond which foragers cannot survive because natural resources are too scarce. The habitable geographic region will expand when technology improves, a point to which we return in Section 3.10 when discussing the colonization of harsh environments.

3.8 VERY-LONG-RUN EQUILIBRIUM

The models in Sections 3.6 and 3.7 showed how time allocation and population could be treated as endogenous variables. Here we continue down this path by making technology endogenous as well, leaving only climate as a source of exogenous shocks.

We begin with an informal interpretation of the model developed thus far. Let N^t be the number of adults at the start of period t and let K^t be their technology. The adults observe the climate $a^t = \left(a_I^t \ldots a_R^t\right)$. Together, K^t and a^t determine the productivities A^t. The adults then collectively choose a time allocation n^t that maximizes total food output. This also maximizes the per capita food income y^t. Early in the period, the adults form couples and the flow of food y^t determines the number of live births per couple. Later in the period, these children begin to observe the production activities of the adults. At the same time the flow of food y^t determines how many children survive to adulthood. When children become adults, their parents die and the period ends. The N^{t+1} surviving children become the adults of period $t + 1$. They compare techniques for harvesting each resource and choose the best possible repertoire K^{t+1}. The process then repeats.

We use the term "very-long-run equilibrium" (VLRE) for a situation in which the LRE requirements are satisfied and in addition, the prevailing technological repertoire K is transmitted to the next generation with probability one. Proposition 3.1 showed that for an active resource $(n_r > 0)$, there is a positive probability of technical progress whenever $k_r \neq k_r^*$. This implies that in a VLRE, the equilibrium repertoire K must include the ideal string k_r^* for every active resource, so that productivity for each of these resources is at its upper bound. Moreover, given prevailing technical knowledge, it must be optimal to assign a zero labor input to each latent resource $(n_r = 0)$.

This leads to the following formal definition.

Definition 3.3

A *very-long-run equilibrium* (VLRE) for the fixed climate vector $a > 0$ is an array (K, N, n) with the following features:

(a)   (stationary technology) $k_r = k_r^*$ for all r such that $n_r > 0$;
(b)   (stationary population) $N = N[A(a, K)]$ obeys Proposition 3.3;
(c)   (optimal time allocation) $n = n[A(a, K), N]$ solves (3.2).

We say that (K, N, n) is a *null VLRE* if $N = 0$ and a *non-null VLRE* if $N > 0$.

One interpretive remark is important here. The term "very long run" might suggest that technology evolves on a longer time scale than population does. This is not the case. In reality, technology and population evolve on the same time scale (one human generation at a time), according to the dynamic rules described in Sections 3.5 and 3.7. However, for analytic purposes it is often useful to hold technology constant while allowing population to evolve. This is the setting of the long-run model in Section 3.7. In the very long run, by contrast, both variables are allowed to evolve simultaneously (both are endogenous).

To characterize the set of VLREs, we need additional terminology and notation. Let $S \subseteq \{1 .. R\}$ be a non-empty set of resources. A VLRE is said to be of type S if $k_r = k_r^*$ for $r \in S$ and $k_r \neq k_r^*$ for $r \notin S$. All opportunities for technical progress have been exhausted for the resources in the set S but such opportunities remain available for the resources not in this set. If the ideal string k_r^* is available for resource r, we use the notation A_r^* for the associated productivity $a_r g_r(k_r^*)$.

Next we construct a specific repertoire of type S. Let k_r^{min} be the string having minimal productivity for resource r. Define the repertoire K^S by setting $k_r^S = k_r^*$ for $r \in S$ and $k_r^S = k_r^{min}$ for $r \notin S$. Thus, we assign the best possible technique to each resource in the set S and the worst possible technique to each resource not in S. The next proposition describes the conditions under which there is a non-trivial VLRE of type S with the specific repertoire K^S. It also shows that all of the other VLREs of type S are essentially identical, in the sense that they have the same population and time allocation.

Proposition 3.4 (very-long-run equilibrium).

Fix the climate vector $a > o$. Let A^S be the productivity vector associated with K^S, let $N^S = N(A^S)$ be the LRE population level for A^S, and let $n^S = n(A^S, N^S)$ be the SRE labor allocation for (A^S, N^S). The array (K^S, N^S, n^S) is a non-null VLRE of type S if

(a) $A_r^* f_r'(o) > y^*$ for some $r \in S$ and
(b) $H_N(A^S, N^S) \geq A_r(k_r^{min}) f_r'(o)$ for all $r \notin S$.

Every other non-null VLRE of type S has the same population $N^S > o$ and the same labor allocation n^S. If either (a) or (b) fails to hold, any VLRE of type S is null.

Part (a) says that there must be at least one resource for which the ideal string k_r^* is available, and the resource can support a positive population at the food income y^*. If the latter condition is not satisfied, the equilibrium population must be zero. Part (b) says that the marginal product of labor for the society as a whole (H_N) must be at or above the marginal product for every latent resource. If this were not true, one could increase food output by using some latent resource, so time allocation would not be optimal. The only differences among non-null VLREs of type S involve techniques for the latent resources $r \notin S$. These must be sufficiently unproductive but are otherwise indeterminate.

A resource that satisfies $A_r^* f_r'(o) > y^*$ as in condition (a) of Proposition 3.4 will be called a *staple*. Such a resource can support a positive population even in the absence of any other resource. Every non-null VLRE of type S must have at least one staple in the set S. It can be shown that every staple in S must be active. Any resources with $A_r^* f_r'(o) \leq y^*$ will be called *supplements*. The set S could include one or more supplements, and these resources may be either active or latent.

Every resource $r \notin S$ is latent, regardless of whether it is a staple or a supplement. Condition (b) from Proposition 3.4 requires that for each of these resources, there must be a harvesting method so unproductive that it would not be optimal to exploit the resource. It seems plausible that for each resource there is some highly unproductive technique of this kind. As a result, many different VLREs could exist, with different resources being active and latent (or more precisely, different specifications of the set S).

The following corollary to Proposition 3.4 provides a general test for the existence of a VLRE with positive population.

Corollary 3.1

Let K^* be the repertoire where the ideal string is available for every resource, with $N^* = N(A^*)$ being the associated population from LRE and $n^* = n(A^*, N^*)$ being the associated time allocation from SRE. If max $\{A_r^* f_r'(o)\} > y^*$ then (K^*, N^*, n^*) is a non-null VLRE. If max $\{A_r^* f_r'(o)\} \leq y^*$ then every VLRE is null.

The corollary says that whenever at least one staple exists, there is a non-null VLRE of the form (K^*, N^*, n^*). We call this the *maximal* VLRE because although other VLREs could exist, no VLRE can support a larger population, and any VLRE with fewer active resources will have a smaller population. A VLRE with population below the maximum associated with (K^*, N^*, n^*) will be called a *stagnation trap*, because a larger population could be supported if suitable technological knowledge were available. When no staple exists, even ideal technical knowledge is inadequate to maintain a viable population.

3.9 THE EFFECTS OF CLIMATE CHANGE

We are now ready to address a central theoretical question: What environmental conditions are most conducive to technical progress? In particular, can climate change help a society escape from a stagnation trap?

The first task is to show that the system converges to a VLRE from any initial state. This is done in Proposition 3.5. The second task is to study the impact of climate shocks on technology, population, and labor allocation. Proposition 3.6 provides such an analysis for neutral shocks that affect all resources in the same proportion. We show that in this case, positive shocks can stimulate progress while negative shocks cannot.

We then discuss biased shocks in a setting with two resources. Our analysis shows that negative shocks biased toward latent resources can generate progress, but this depends on the outcome of a race between rising productivity and declining population. Finally, we discuss the possibility of regress when active resources shut down.

Before defining convergence to a VLRE, we need to spell out how techniques and population are updated over time for a fixed array of resource abundances $a = (a_1 .. a_R) > 0$ called "climate." Let (K^t, N^t) be the state in period t. We obtain (K^{t+1}, N^{t+1}) as follows.

(a) K^t determines the productivities $A^t = [a_1 g_1(k_1^t) .. a_R g_R(k_R^t)]$.
(b) A^t and N^t determine SRE labor allocation n^t and food output $H(A^t, N^t)$ as in (3.2).
(c) N^t and $H(A^t, N^t)/N^t \equiv y(A^t, N^t)$ determine N^{t+1} as in (3.3).
(d) K^t, n^t, and N^{t+1} determine the probability distribution over K^{t+1} as in Proposition 3.1. This yields a new state (K^{t+1}, N^{t+1}).

Proposition 3.1 is expressed using q_r^t (the number of digits in k_r^t that match the ideal string k_r^*), but it generates a probability distribution for k_r^{t+1} conditional on k_r^t because there is an equal probability of mutation at every locus of k_r^t that does not already match k_r^*. We assume existing strings for latent resources are retained with probability one. The laws of motion in (a)–(d) above yield the following results.

Proposition 3.5 (convergence to very-long-run equilibrium).
Assume $\rho(y) > 0$ for all $y > 0$. Fix the climate $a > 0$ and consider any initial state (K^0, N^0) with $N^0 > 0$.

(a) Each sample path $\{K^t, N^t\}$ has some finite $T \geq 0$ and K' such that $K^t = K'$ for all $t \geq T$. Along a fixed sample path, $\{N^t\} \to N' = N(A')$ and $\{n^t\} \to n' = n(A', N')$. We will call K' the *terminal repertoire* for the sample path and $A' = A(K')$ the *terminal productivity vector*. We also say K' *generates* (K', N', n').
(b) With probability one, the *terminal array* (K', N', n') is a VLRE.
(c) If $N^0 < N[A(K^0)]$ then $\{N^t\}$ is increasing. If $N^0 = N[A(K^0)]$ then $\{N^t\}$ is non-decreasing. If $N^0 > N[A(K^0)]$ then $\{N^t\}$ may decrease for all $t \geq 0$, or it may decrease until some $T > 0$ and become non-decreasing for $t \geq T$.

Part (a) shows that the system always reaches a stationary technology in finite time. Once this occurs, population converges to the corresponding Malthusian level and the allocation of labor time converges to the corresponding optimum for this technology and population. Because regress is impossible for active resources and strings remain constant for latent resources, the productivity vector $\{A^\tau\}$ must be non-decreasing.

We know from part (b) that the system converges to some VLRE. However, it is difficult to say much about the probability of converging to any specific VLRE because this depends in a complex way on how mutations affect the productivities, which affect population dynamics, which feed back to the mutation probabilities as in Proposition 3.1.

Part (c) does provide some information about the population dynamics. There are three possibilities. If population is initially below the LRE level, it always rises, because Malthusian forces push population in this direction and could be reinforced by technical progress. If population is initially at the LRE level, it cannot decrease and may remain at a constant level (with no technical progress) or rise (if progress occurs). If population is initially above the LRE level, it may fall forever (for Malthusian reasons), or it may fall for some finite number of periods and then never fall again (because technical progress eventually outweighs Malthusian tendencies).

We next consider responses to climate shocks and associated changes in resource abundances. Recall that technical progress enables a society to support a larger long-run population with a given set of natural resources. This definition requires us to distinguish population growth due to technical change (holding climate constant) from population growth due to climate change (holding technology constant).

Our approach is based on the following thought experiment. Let the system be in a VLRE corresponding to some initial climate state a°. Suppose the climate jumps from the initial state a° to a new state a' and stays in the new state for a long time. The system will eventually converge to a VLRE for the new climate state. Finally, suppose climate jumps back to the original state a° and stays there for a long time. The system will now converge to a VLRE for the original climate. If the population in the final equilibrium is higher than in the initial equilibrium, this can only be due to technical progress along the adjustment path.

The next proposition carries out this thought experiment for a case where climate change influences all productivities in the same proportion. Hence the abundances of all plant and animal species move up or down together, so nature as a whole becomes either more generous (*positive shock*) or less generous (*negative shock*). In either situation, the shock is *neutral* because we are ruling out substitution effects among the resources.

Proposition 3.6 (neutral shocks).
   Let $(K^\circ, N^\circ, n^\circ)$ be a non-null VLRE for the climate $a^\circ > 0$. Define $A^\circ = A(a^\circ, K^\circ)$ and consider a permanent climate change $a' = \theta a^\circ$ where $\theta > 0$.

(a) <u>Negative shocks.</u> Suppose $\theta \in (0, 1)$. Assume $N(\theta A^\circ) > 0$ so a positive long-run population can be supported under the new climate without any technical change. The system converges to the new VLRE (K', N', n') with $K' = K^\circ$, $N' = N(\theta A^\circ) < N^\circ$, and $n' = n[\theta a^\circ, N(\theta A^\circ)]$. The active resources in n' are a subset of the active resources in n°. If the climate a° is permanently restored starting from (K', N', n'), the system converges to the original VLRE $(K^\circ, N^\circ, n^\circ)$.

(b) <u>Positive shocks.</u> Suppose $\theta > 1$. The system converges to a new VLRE (K', N', n') where $K' \neq K^\circ$ iff

(*) $n_r[\theta A^\circ, N(\theta A^\circ)] > 0$ for some r such that $k_r^\circ \neq k_r^*$.
   The new population satisfies $N' \geq N(\theta A^\circ) > N^\circ$, where $N' > N(\theta A^\circ)$ iff (*) holds. If a° is permanently restored starting from (K', N', n') and (*) does not hold, the system converges to the original VLRE $(K^\circ, N^\circ, n^\circ)$. If a° is permanently restored starting from (K', N', n') and (*) does hold, the system converges to some VLRE (K'', N'', n'') where $K'' = K' \neq K^\circ$ and $N' > N'' \geq N^\circ$. The last inequality is strict iff $n[A(a^\circ, K''), N^\circ] \neq n^\circ$. In this case, some resource with $n_r^\circ = 0$ has $n_r'' > 0$.

Proposition 3.6(a) shows that a negative neutral shock cannot stimulate technical progress, because it cannot change the repertoire K. Population falls and some of the previously active resources may become latent (the diet may narrow). Reversing the shock returns the system to the original VLRE and restores the previous population, as long as the society has not gone extinct in the meantime. Restoration of the status quo population reflects the absence of technical progress in response to the climate change.
   Proposition 3.6(b) shows that a positive neutral shock can stimulate permanent progress. A necessary and sufficient condition for this outcome is that the shock must lead to exploitation of a latent resource whose technique can be improved. This cannot occur in the short run through substitution effects because relative resource abundances are held

constant. Instead, the key causal channel is a scale effect involving population.

Without technical change, the improved climate would lead to a larger population $N(\theta A^\circ)$ in the long run. This population growth could make one or more latent resources active, as explained at the end of Section 3.6. If so, the technical repertoire K improves through learning by doing, and population expands beyond the level $N(\theta A^\circ)$ induced by the climate change alone. But if the scale effect is too small to activate a latent resource, or productivity is already at its upper bound for each newly active resource, technology remains static and population grows only to the extent that climate permits.

If the climate returns to its original state a° and technology has not improved in the meantime $(K' = K^\circ)$, clearly population must return to its original level N°. The same is true if technology improves as a result of the climate shock, but not by enough to alter the set of active resources used in the original climate a°. For progress to become visible in the population level $(N'' > N^\circ)$ after climate reverts back to a°, the string for at least one previously latent resource must improve to a point where the old labor allocation n° is no longer optimal at the old population level N°. In this case, at least one new resource will be used after the climate returns to a°. Simultaneously, some of the resources that were previously active at the climate a° may be abandoned due to substitution effects.

Provided that strings for latent resources are conserved, the new technical plateau will be permanent. Proposition 3.6(a) shows that subsequent negative shocks cannot force a technological retreat. The result is a ratchet effect in which technological knowledge gradually improves. But unlike conventional growth models, our framework predicts a punctuated process where intermittent productivity gains stimulated by positive climate shocks can be separated by long periods of stagnation during which technology does not change and the average population growth rate is zero. During these intervals population will fluctuate in response to climate, and individual resources may go in and out of use as a result, but there is no lasting improvement in technological capabilities.

Thus far we have made two key assumptions: that climate shocks are neutral and that strings for latent resources are conserved. In the rest of this section we consider the consequences of relaxing each assumption.

Shocks biased toward or against particular resources create short-run substitution effects that can activate latent resources even before population has time to adjust. It will be convenient to discuss these effects in the context of two resources $(R = 2)$. In all cases we start from an initial VLRE

$(K^\circ, N^\circ, n^\circ)$ associated with climate a° in which resource 1 is active and resource 2 is latent, and we assume the new climate is permanent. Because a negative shock to a latent resource cannot affect the system, we ignore this case.

A Positive Shock to the Latent Resource: There is an immediate substitution effect away from resource 1 toward resource 2 with N° constant. If the shock is large enough, $n_2^\circ > 0$ will occur (otherwise the shock is irrelevant). In the long run, population grows and the productivity A_2 rises. For both reasons, n_2^t increases. With probability one, the ideal string k_2^* is eventually identified and the ideal repertoire K^* is achieved.

A Positive Shock to the Active Resource: An immediate substitution effect keeps resource 1 active and reinforces the latency of resource 2. However, population grows in the long run and this scale effect may eventually outweigh the substitution effect to give $n_2^T > 0$ at some $T > 0$. If resource 2 ever becomes active, it remains so, and the analysis from that point on is identical to the preceding case.

A Negative Shock to the Active Resource: An immediate substitution effect favors resource 2 at the expense of resource 1. If the shock is large enough, $n_2^\circ > 0$ will occur. There are then two possibilities: (a) $n_2^t > 0$ for all $t \geq 0$ or (b) there is a $T > 0$ such that $n_2^t = 0$ for all $t \geq T$. Case (a) occurs when technical progress for resource 2 is rapid enough to outweigh the population decline resulting from the negative shock. In this scenario, population could eventually begin to grow and the ideal repertoire K^* could be achieved. Case (b) occurs when technical progress for resource 2 is too slow, so that this resource eventually shuts down due to the declining population. This aborts further progress and leads to a new VLRE in which resource 2 is again latent.

These conclusions are all tilted in favor of progress by our assumption that strings for latent resources remain intact. This assumption is appealing on grounds of tractability and because it is the limiting case of Proposition 3.1. However, techniques may deteriorate if they are passed down through oral traditions in the absence of any practical experience with the resource in question. Henrich (2004) cites Tasmania as a prominent example of technical regress. Among non-literate societies, Aiyar et al. (2008) mention Tasmania and Easter Island. Boyd et al. (2011) mention Tasmania, other Pacific islands, and the Polar Inuit of northwest Greenland. These cases all involve small population sizes and isolation from external reservoirs of technical knowledge. Such conditions could have been relatively common in the Upper Paleolithic.

An extreme way to introduce regress into our model would be to assume that if a resource shuts down, the associated string drops out of the technical repertoire. Then the only way to revive the resource would be to borrow a string already in use for an active resource. Using a two-resource framework, it can be shown that in this situation negative climate shocks can lead to regress and the population may not entirely recover when such shocks are reversed. A less extreme approach would allow random mutations leading to the deterioration of previous strings (for other modeling frameworks, see Henrich, 2004; Aiyar et al., 2008).

With these ideas in mind, we can identify a number of prerequisites for sustained technical progress. First, climate shocks must be large enough to trigger experimentation with new resources. Second, they should permit the preservation of existing knowledge. Strong substitution effects that flip a society's time allocation from one corner solution to another can interrupt the process of "remembering by doing." Third, a new climate state must persist long enough for new techniques to develop. If a shock is brief, there is little opportunity for productivity to rise for new resources, and the system will return to the previous equilibrium once the status quo is restored. As was shown in Proposition 3.1, productivity gains are accelerated if a society allocates a large amount of labor time to newly active resources. It is also helpful for population to grow quickly in response to positive shocks and not decline too rapidly in response to negative shocks.

We conjecture that in the Upper Paleolithic, technical innovation would have been more common in temperate regions that were more vulnerable to large climate shocks, as compared with tropical regions that were probably buffered from such shocks, at least to some degree. Future archaological research may shed light on this hypothesis.

3.10 ARCHAEOLOGICAL APPLICATIONS

The theoretical framework constructed in this chapter can shed light on instances of technological innovation in the archaeological record. We will consider two examples here: the broad spectrum revolution, and colonization of the Arctic.

The Broad Spectrum Revolution: The BSR refers to expansion in the set of animal and plant species used for food. First we consider animal prey. As shown in Figure 3.1, during about 64–32 KYA the world climate entered a milder phase within the prevailing glacial period. This led to population growth in southwest Asia between 60–44 KYA (Stiner et al., 2000). Stiner et al. (1999, 193) observe that "in western Asia ... human populations increased substantially before the remarkable and rapid technologic innovations (radiations) that mark the Upper and Epi-Paleolithic periods." The diet began to include birds in Italy around 35 KYA. Such prey were previously available but had not been exploited. Similarly the diet began to include birds in modern Israel around 28–26 KYA (Stiner et al., 2000). Stiner et al. link this dietary expansion to the diffusion and refinement of blade technology, and perhaps also population growth.

These events preceded the Last Glacial Maximum at about 21 KYA, a very large negative climate shock that depressed population in much of the world (see Sections 3.2–3.3). Climate recovery after the LGM led to substantial population growth in southwest Asia and Europe (Gamble et al., 2005). In southwest Asia the period after the LGM was warm and wet, with increased population density (Bar-Yosef, 2002b, 2002c).

By 19–17 KYA hares and rabbits had been added to the diet in Italy, and the same occurred by 13–11 KYA in southwest Asia (Stiner et al., 2000). As with birds, these prey species had previously been available but remained latent until the climate moderated and population grew. Stiner (2001, 6996) comments: "early indications of expanding diets in the eastern Mediterranean precede rather than follow the evolution of the kinds of tools (specialized projectile tips, nets, and other traps) needed to capture quick small animals efficiently." Fresh water aquatic foods (fish, mollusks, waterfowl) were exploited before the LGM, but in western Asia and southern Europe their use intensified after the LGM (Richards et al., 2001). By about 13 KYA, people in southwest Asia consumed a very wide range of animal prey (Savard et al., 2006).

As we explained at the end of Section 3.6 in connection with Figure 3.2, it is not hard to see how population growth can lead to a broader diet. The results of Section 3.9 add two things: the role of climate improvement as a stimulus for population growth, and the refinement of techniques after latent resources become active. To put the argument in a nutshell: A positive neutral climate shock, if sufficiently large and persistent, can start a causal cascade with (a) population growth, (b) broader diet, and (c) technical progress. The latter can feed back to population growth, generating further rounds of (a), (b), and (c) until the system settles into a new equilibrium. This does not require exact climate neutrality. All we need is for the abundance of resources to rise and fall in a correlated way, as one might expect for major climate shifts lasting thousands of years. It appears likely that this mechanism was operative at least twice for animal resources, once during the warm phase before the LGM and a second time during the recovery afterward.

Dietary breadth with respect to plant foods is more controversial. It is clear that at the LGM, inhabitants of southwest Asia relied heavily on small-seeded grasses (Weiss et al., 2004). As climate improved afterward, large-seeded grasses became more common (especially wild wheat, barley, and rye). According to a school of thought represented by Weiss et al., people increasingly specialized in large-seeded grasses, which smoothed the path to agriculture. Another school of thought represented by Savard et al. (2006) argues that a combination of climate change and population growth led to a gradual broadening of the diet to include more plant species. In this perspective large-seeded grasses were a minor part of the Epi-Paleolithic diet, despite their later centrality for agriculture.

In a re-analysis of data from sites in southwest Asia shortly before agriculture, Savard et al. (2006) find that the plant component of the diet was highly diverse at each site, and also that there was substantial diversity in the composition of the diet across sites. The increased abundance of large-seeded grasses after the LGM did not drive out consumption of the small-seeded grasses that were important at the LGM. The results for the region as a whole "fit with elements of ... the broad spectrum model" (Savard et al., 2006, 192). In a similar vein, Hillman et al. (2001) report that just before the start of cultivation, more than 100 species of edible seeds and fruits were used in southwest Asia. This broad pattern of plant exploitation was accompanied by considerable technological paraphernalia, such as querns, mortars, pestles, bowls, grinders, pounders, whetstones, choppers, and sickles. Again, this is consistent with our expectations from the model in Section 3.9. Recovery from the LGM led to population growth, use of previously latent plant resources, and improvements in the techniques used to exploit those resources.

The original BSR hypothesis from archaeology involved exogenous population pressure on ecologically marginal areas (Flannery, 1969). In our hypothesis the BSR is triggered by positive climate change and the resulting endogenous population growth is not "pressure." Rather, it is a response to temporarily higher living standards and leads to greater dietary breadth as people find it more attractive to exploit latent resources. This stimulates technological innovation, which allows more efficient harvesting of the new resources. By contrast with theories based on exogenous population growth, we would not expect any systematic decrease in living standards over long time scales. We could incorporate resource depletion into the model, but this is not an essential feature of our framework. One advantage of our approach in comparison with theories based upon exogenous population growth is that we can explain the timing of BSR episodes by tracing them to shifts in the prevailing climate regime.

Colonization of the Arctic: Occupation of the Eurasian steppe, Siberia, and the Americas required foragers to overcome severe resource constraints. Novel techniques had to be developed to keep warm, secure shelter, and hunt prey. For a vivid description of the technical problems confronting the Inuit of the Central Arctic and the sophisticated nature of their solutions, see Boyd et al. (2011). Here we focus on northeast Asia, which includes northern China, Mongolia, and Siberia.

The relevant period begins around 47 KYA and extends beyond the Last Glacial Maximum. Numerous climate fluctuations occurred over this time (data in this paragraph are from Brantingham et al., 2004). A cold-dry glacial event ended around 52–47 KYA, followed by a cool and wet period during 47–25 KYA. This in turn was followed by a second cold-dry glacial event, the LGM, from 24–20 KYA. The cool-wet intermediate period was associated with lake expansion, the partial replacement of deserts by steppe grasslands, and northward movement in the boundary between forest and tundra. These developments were reversed in the LGM. Also in the cool-wet phase from 47–25 KYA, there were millennial-scale oscillations, with warm events during 37–35 KYA and 28–27 KYA separated by a cold event centered around 32 KYA.

Southern Siberia was permanently occupied by at least 44 KYA. (Information in this paragraph is from Kuzmin and Keates, 2005. The radiocarbon dates given by these authors appear to be uncalibrated. To obtain dates comparable to those used elsewhere in this section, one should add about 2,000 years.) Northern Siberia was colonized around 34–27 KYA. According to Kuzmin and Keates, the number of occupation episodes for Siberia as a whole stayed roughly constant through the LGM, but then rose substantially during 16–12 KYA. Other authors argue that the LGM led to a large population decline in Siberia, as will be discussed below. Kuzmin and Keates reject the assertion that there were successive waves of colonization in Siberia and argue for steady population growth without noticeable minima or maxima, although at varying rates over time.

A transition from Middle to Initial Upper Paleolithic technology has been found at the site of Kara Bom in the Altai region of southern Siberia dating to about 43 KYA (data in this paragraph are from Brantingham et al., 2001, except as indicated). UP features did not completely replace those of the Middle Paleolithic (MP), but an increased emphasis on blade production is evident. Similar Upper Paleolithic technology has been found at two sites in Mongolia dated 33–27 KYA and in northern China around 25 KYA. The Initial UP technology in northeast Asia was associated with wider foraging areas and also the use of non-local raw materials. Upper Paleolithic technology was being used in the Siberian Arctic by around 32 KYA (Goebel et al., 2008).

Brantingham et al. (2004) note an apparent correlation between climate events and the numbers of radiocarbon dates assigned to temporal bins, with a peak in human activity around the warming at 34 KYA, a subsequent decline at the colder spell of 32 KYA, another peak just before the LGM, and a dramatic decline (suggesting a "severe population bottleneck") during the LGM. With respect to technology, they argue that classic Upper Paleolithic features including microblades, bone/antler/ivory technology, portable art, and indications of structures "emerged in a rapid, punctuated fashion" (270). This was especially true for microblades. The classic UP did not coalesce until 26 KYA, approximately 20,000 years after the initial steps in that direction, and only lasted from 26 to 22 KYA before being overtaken by the severe climate shock of the LGM.

Brantingham et al. (2004) find that traditional stone tools tend to cluster around 51° N. Microblades and the other advanced technologies of the preceding paragraph tend to cluster further north, around 53–55° N. Based on a sample of all types of technological artifacts, the authors estimate that human occupation expanded north into the sub-Arctic at a rate of 89 km per 1,000 radiocarbon years. Older types of stone tools expanded at a rate of 33–44 km per 1,000 years, while the bone-antler-ivory technology and portable art expanded at a rate of 56 km per 1,000 years. Microblades and structures expanded north at a very rapid rate shortly before the LGM.

To see how our theory can explain the colonization of extreme environments like Siberia, recall the concept of a habitation boundary introduced at the end of Section 3.7. Suppose initially there is only one food resource, and food becomes less abundant as one moves from south to north. With a given technology, there will be some latitude beyond which natural resources cannot support a positive population. But a superior technology can compensate for scarcity of resources, so if food acquisition methods improve while the environment remains unchanged, the habitation boundary will shift to the north.

Our theory is somewhat more complicated because in a very-long-run equilibrium each active resource must already be at its maximum productivity level. But if there are many distinct resources, with some active and the rest latent, the technological repertoire as a whole can improve. As we showed in Section 3.9, this can occur through a sequence of positive and negative climate shocks that generate a ratchet effect, whereby knowledge improves for each latent resource after it becomes active. This enables people to expand into latitudes that were too hostile with the previous repertoire. The northward expansion will open up Arctic food resources that were not available further south, these new latent resources can also become active, and again techniques can improve.

At present we cannot identify the particular food resources that shifted from latent to active status in the course of sub-Arctic and Arctic colonization. However, the climate fluctuations, population trends, and technological developments in northeast Asia appear to be consistent with our theoretical framework. Similar dynamics could have played out for migration into other challenging environments, such as deserts or tropical rainforests.

3.11 CONCLUSION

We have developed a theory to explain why technological progress was slow and sporadic during the Upper Paleolithic. The theory presented in Sections 3.5–3.9 satisfies the following criteria from Section 3.4.

(a) Technology is endogenous and the rate of productivity growth in very-long-run equilibrium is zero. However, occasional technical progress can occur.

(b) Population is endogenous and described by Malthusian dynamics.

(c) Climate change is the main driver of changes in technology and population.

(d) The model is consistent with the climate history in Section 3.2.

(e) The model is consistent with the population dynamics in Section 3.3.

(f) The model suggests explanations for the broad spectrum revolution and the gradual colonization of extreme environments.

In our framework, foragers exploit a subset of the resources provided by nature. Although they often reach high productivity levels for these resources, further advances require the use of latent resources, which is not attractive in light of existing knowledge. We call this a stagnation trap. Climate shocks can cause foragers to experiment with latent resources. This generates punctuated equilibria where foragers acquire enhanced technical capabilities and higher populations at successive plateaus. If a foraging society can retain enough knowledge of inactive techniques, it may benefit from a ratchet effect through which technology progresses over archaeological time. We will build on these ideas to explain the origins of sedentism and agriculture in Chapters 4 and 5.

3.12 POSTSCRIPT

This chapter is based on the article "Stagnation and innovation before agriculture" by Dow and Reed (2011) in the *Journal of Economic Behavior and Organization*. We received advice on drafts of the original article from Matthew Baker, Cliff Bekar, Mark Collard, Brian Hayden, Stephen Shennan, Lawrence Straus, an anonymous referee, and colleagues at Simon Fraser University, the University of Copenhagen, and the Canadian Network for Economic History. Scott Skjei assisted with the research, and the Social Sciences and Humanities Research Council of Canada provided financial support. As always, the opinions are those of the authors.

Sections 3.1–3.4 are new for this volume, as are the graphs. References to the archaeological literature have been updated and Section 3.10 has been entirely rewritten. The formal model is identical to the one in Dow and Reed (2011). When we constructed the original model, we were aware of the climate history in Section 3.2, some of the early findings from paleodemography (although none of the specific studies in Section 3.3), and the evidence on the broad spectrum revolution in Section 3.10. We were not aware of the information about Siberian climate, population, or technology.

4

The Transition to Sedentism

From the origins of anatomically modern humans until after the Last Glacial Maximum around 21,000 years ago, almost everyone lived in small, mobile foraging bands. Starting around 15,000 years ago, foragers in some regions such as southwest Asia and Japan began to develop permanent settlements. Sedentary foraging predated agriculture by several millennia and accelerated with the onset of the Holocene 11,600 years ago, which brought a warmer, wetter and more stable climate. The best evidence for early sedentism is from temperate zones. Among modern hunter-gatherer societies, those in tropical rainforests and the Arctic have remained the most mobile (Kelly, 2013a).

Sedentism can be defined in various ways and is a matter of degree, so we need to clarify our use of this term. First, it is important to recognize that mobile foraging groups do not just move at random across the landscape. A common pattern involves the use of seasonally shifting base camps over an annual cycle, with hunting and gathering on trips away from each base camp. When anthropologists and archaeologists refer to sedentism, they often mean settlements that are at least partially occupied year-round.

Evidence used by archaeologists to infer sedentism at a site includes the presence of plants and animals from all four seasons; the presence of species that flourish when in frequent contact with humans (e.g., mice, rats, and sparrows); substantial investments in dwellings, earthworks, ceremonial structures, or monuments; greater use of cemeteries; and site-specific investments in food processing and storage facilities.

Marshall (2006) cites the durability of dwellings and the size of settlements as the most crucial markers.

While we accept these indicators of sedentism, we require more than simply the year-round occupation of a site. A time period in our model is defined to be one human generation. We are therefore interested in the conditions under which adult children stay in the same location as their parents, even when facing multi-year environmental shocks that reduce the abundance of local food resources. We call a community *sedentary* if it is robust to such negative shocks over periods lasting decades or centuries. We sometimes refer to this phenomenon as *sustained sedentism* to differentiate it from more temporary or fragile forms of sedentism. A time interval lasting generations or centuries makes it possible for major structures to be built, for burial practices to develop, for the regional population to grow, and for new technologies and institutions to evolve.

Why was sustained sedentism an important transition, one that (as in the words of our subtitle) shaped the world? The development of large permanent communities was a massive social upheaval relative to the ancestral lifestyle of small mobile bands. We will unpack some of the implications in what follows.

Ethnographic data indicate that group sizes among sedentary foragers are much larger than for mobile foragers (Kelly, 2013a, 171–172). Sedentism is also correlated with other important variables. Using original data from Keeley (1988, 1991), Rowley-Conwy (2001, 40–44) shows that ethnographically known foragers fall into two distinct clusters. Those with low sedentism have low population relative to natural productivity, low use of food storage, and low stratification. Those with high sedentism have high levels on these other dimensions. A classic example of the latter kind is provided by the societies on the northwest coast of North America (Ames and Maschner, 1999). Such societies illustrate Kelly's point that sedentary foraging is correlated with "social hierarchies and hereditary leadership, political dominance, gender inequality, and unequal access to resources" (2013a, 104). Anthropological evidence strongly suggests that even if sedentary foraging had never led to agriculture, it would still have led to economic inequality, and it would probably have led to greater warfare over land. We pursue these ideas in Chapters 6–8.

The other (and larger) reason why sustained sedentary foraging shaped the world is that at least in some cases, it was a precursor to agriculture. We want to be careful in our comments on this matter because there is a long and unhelpful tradition of conflating sedentary foraging with agriculture. Sloppy language such as "the transition to sedentary agriculture" should therefore be avoided. It is essential to recognize that the transition to sedentary foraging was distinct from the transition to agriculture, and requires a distinct theoretical explanation (Marshall, 2006). Indeed, we will propose in this chapter that the transition to sedentism was largely driven by positive climate trends, while we argue in Chapter 5 that transitions to agriculture were often driven by negative climate shocks.

Sedentary foraging is clearly not a sufficient condition for a subsequent transition to agriculture. For example, millennia of sedentary foraging never led to indigenous agriculture in Japan or along the northwest coast of North America. When domesticates finally arrived, they were imported from elsewhere. We discuss the case of Japan further in Section 4.3. Nor is year-round sedentism a necessary precondition for agriculture. In the American Southwest, for example, imported domesticates like maize appear to have been integrated into a foraging system involving seasonal mobility, with truly sedentary villages arising a millennium or more later (Wills, 1988).

Nevertheless, we believe that sustained sedentism contributed to several pristine agricultural transitions. One leading example is southwest Asia (see Section 4.3). In this region, sedentism supported a large population and led to technological innovations that were pre-adapted for cultivation. For reasons to be explained in Chapter 5, both factors made a subsequent transition to agriculture more likely. Sedentism may also have led to institutional innovations with respect to property rights that increased the probability of an agricultural trajectory, as some economists have asserted (see Section 4.2). However, robust foraging communities arose 3,000 years before agriculture and were clearly not the proximate cause of this trajectory in southwest Asia. Although sedentism helped set the stage, we will argue that climate and geography took the leading roles. Our hypothesis about the agricultural transition in southwest Asia will be presented in Chapter 5.

This chapter assumes that people in a region can freely migrate from one location to another. Thus, as discussed in Section 1.2, we are studying a transition along the main sequence from cell A to cell B in Figure 1.2, where institutions allow open access for both mobile and sedentary foragers. To be sure, the sedentary foragers described by anthropologists often exercise group property rights over valuable locations, exhibit stratification, and engage in warfare. We take up these subjects in Chapters 6–8, where we explore sedentary foraging with closed access (cell B′ in Figure 1.2) or stratification (cell B″ in Figure 1.2). But when mobile foragers began their journey toward sedentism, their institutions probably did not yet involve rigid property rights or social stratification. These are more likely to be effects of sedentism rather than causes. Therefore, we would like to know whether an initial impetus toward sedentism can develop in a setting of free mobility. We will answer in the affirmative.

What caused mobile foragers to become sedentary foragers? A common answer involves direct effects of nature. The idea is that people are mobile when the location of food resources is constantly shifting, or when important resources are not available all in one place, or when local resources are rapidly depleted. People become sedentary when nature provides a rich, diverse, and reliable assortment of resources at a single location, and these resources are not easily depleted.

We don't doubt that this is part of the story, but it is far from the whole story. As we will see in Section 4.3, sedentism was not just a matter of people settling down in one place. It also involved new food sources, larger settlements, larger regional populations, and technological innovation. These changes often included more use of plant or aquatic foods as compared with prey animals; fixed investments in mortars, ovens, and storage facilities; and more durable housing (Kelly, 2013a, 122–128). How can we explain the recurrent pattern of greater dietary breadth, population growth, and technical change?

We develop a formal model that addresses these questions. We consider a region with many individual production sites, where the weather at each site can be good or bad. Good weather is associated with abundant food resources and bad weather is associated with scarce food resources. In our model, a *climate regime* is defined by the probability distribution over weather conditions (temperature, precipitation, etc.) at each site. For a given climate these random draws are independent across sites and time periods, so a site that is good in one period can be bad in the next. A *change in climate* refers to a change in the probability distribution for weather events. The *rate of sedentism* is the fraction of the local population that remains in place when a site switches from good to bad weather. This is our measure of how robust communities are to natural shocks.

The shift from the Last Glacial Maximum to the Holocene involved both better mean weather and decreased variance in weather (see Section 3.2; Richerson et al., 2001; Woodward, 2014, chs. 8–9). These trends were sometimes associated with sedentism well before the Holocene (see the discussion of southwest Asia in Section 4.3), although more often sedentism developed in the early Holocene. Climate shifts of this kind could have led to a positive rate of sedentism through three causal mechanisms.

First, let total regional population be constant in the short run. The lower variance shrinks the productivity gap between sites with good weather and sites with bad weather. To take the simplest case, imagine that the productivity of good sites does not change but bad sites become better. If the bad sites improve enough, diminishing returns at the good sites could make it attractive for some agents to start using bad sites. It follows that when a site switches from good weather to bad weather it will no longer be entirely abandoned.

Second, in the long run the better mean weather conditions result in population growth through Malthusian dynamics. Even if the decreased variance in weather is not sufficient to cause sedentism by itself, a higher regional population could lead to some use of sites with bad weather due to diminishing returns at sites with good weather. It can thus yield a positive rate of sedentism. Neither of these two mechanisms requires technical change, and each is reversible in the sense that if climate reverts to its earlier mean and variance, the rate of sedentism will eventually return to its original level.

The third causal mechanism involves technological innovation. We assume that agents can use two methods of food collection. We will refer to these metaphorically as "hunting" (a shorthand term for mobile methods) and "gathering" (shorthand for stationary methods). Suppose that a society initially uses only hunting, and suppose climate change leads to Malthusian population growth. This will reduce the marginal product of labor in hunting. At some point gathering may begin, with new food resources being targeted. If so, learning by doing could increase the productivity of gathering over time. The rising productivity of gathering will then reinforce the population growth generated by climate change. This trajectory can lead to sedentism even when climate change and population growth alone would not. Assuming that new knowledge about food acquisition methods is retained over time, this process creates a ratchet effect such that even if climate reverts to its original state, greater dietary breadth, increased population, and new techniques of gathering can persist. The sedentism rate can thus remain above its original level.

The rest of the chapter is organized as follows. Section 4.2 reviews a number of existing theories about the origins of sedentism from both anthropology and economics. Section 4.3 reviews archaeological evidence on sedentary foraging, including the leading cases of southwest Asia and Japan.

Sections 4.4–4.10 develop our formal model. We consider three different time spans: the short run, the long run, and the very long run. In the short run, the allocation of labor across sites and food procurement methods is endogenous, while the aggregate regional population, technology, and climate are exogenous. In the long run, the regional population becomes endogenous while technology and climate remain exogenous. In the very long run, technology becomes endogenous and only climate is still exogenous. This parallels the structure of our modeling efforts in Chapter 3.

Section 4.4 describes food acquisition at an individual site. Section 4.5 considers the regional economy, which has a continuum of production sites. The sites are exposed to idiosyncratic variations in food availability due to weather shocks. Property rights are characterized by open access. As explained above, this is a logical starting point for the development of sedentism, and we see it as a reasonable approximation when population density is low and the agents can move relatively easily from one site to another through kinship ties. A short-run equilibrium (SRE) is an allocation of regional population across production sites such that no individual agent can gain by changing sites.

Section 4.6 adopts the Malthusian assumption that the population growth rate is an increasing function of food per capita, as was discussed in Chapter 2 and Section 3.7. A long-run equilibrium (LRE) is an SRE such that the regional population stays constant over time. Section 4.7 adds technological innovation where the gathering technology can improve through learning by doing, along lines discussed in Section 3.5. A very-long-run equilibrium (VLRE) is an LRE such that technological capabilities remain constant over time, as was discussed in Section 3.8.

Section 4.8 constructs a baseline VLRE that captures central features of the Last Glacial Maximum. These include a climate where weather conditions have a low mean and high variance, a low population, the use of mobile food acquisition techniques, and complete abandonment of sites whenever natural resources become locally scarce. We then consider a permanent shift to a new climate regime with a higher mean and a lower variance. Section 4.9 studies three causal mechanisms by which climate amelioration can lead to sedentism. The first operates in the short run through the reduction of variance in weather conditions across sites. The second operates in the long run through Malthusian population growth, and the third combines population growth with technical innovation.

Section 4.10 examines the consequences of sedentism for demography and living standards. Assuming sedentism made children less costly, as is often said to be true, our theory predicts a shift toward increased fertility, increased child mortality, decreased food per capita, and increased regional population. Section 4.11 follows with some comments on how our model relates to theories based on resource depletion.

Section 4.12 reviews further archaeological evidence. Section 4.13 summarizes our conclusions and discusses a few extensions of the theory. Section 4.14 is a postscript. Proofs of the formal propositions are available at cambridge.org/economicprehistory.

4.2 THEORIES OF SEDENTISM

There are five main alternatives to our explanation for the origins of sedentism, three from anthropology and two from economics. Price and Brown (1985) describe two traditional theories from anthropology, which they label as "pull" and "push." According to the pull hypothesis sedentism arose due to resource abundance, which encouraged people to reduce their mobility. According to the push hypothesis foragers were forced to adopt sedentism by resource scarcity, which caused a shortage of food relative to population. This led to greater dietary breadth and more time devoted to harvesting and processing wild food resources, which in turn led to lower mobility. These theories have various empirical inadequacies (Kelly, 1992).

A third anthropological explanation is summarized by Kelly (2013a), who argues that sedentism was driven by regional population growth, which led to group packing and made it harder for groups to relocate when local resources were depleted. Sedentism by one group raised the cost of moving for other groups, and therefore sedentism tended to spread. Sedentism typically emerged in places where the local resource base was hard to deplete (e.g., on coasts or rivers where aquatic resources were available). Sedentism led to further population growth through increased fertility, so once the process was set in motion it became self-reinforcing. Technology evolved toward the use of lower-value but less-easily-depleted food resources.

We agree with Kelly that population growth and technical change were mutually reinforcing in the transition to sedentism. Our model does not include resource depletion because we want to show that the qualitative evidence on the transition to sedentism can be explained without appealing to this variable. Indeed, we will argue that sedentism was triggered by the greater resource abundance brought about by a better climate. We will, however, discuss resource depletion issues further in Section 4.11. Another contrast with Kelly is that we do not emphasize the group ownership of production sites in this chapter, although we discuss and model it extensively in Chapters 6–8. We also depart from Kelly by endogenizing population through Malthusian dynamics, and by emphasizing technical ratchet effects along the lines of Chapter 3.

Acemoglu and Robinson (2012, 137–143) offer an economic and political story about the origins of sedentism. Their account centers on Natufian society in southwest Asia, which we will discuss in Section 4.3. Acemoglu and Robinson note that the Natufians were sedentary foragers well before they began to domesticate plants and animals. They observe that mobility was costly for the young and old, made food storage difficult, and prevented use of productive but heavy implements such as grinding stones. However, "while it might be collectively desirable to become sedentary, this doesn't mean that it will necessarily happen. A mobile group of hunter-gatherers would have to agree to do this, or someone would have to force them" (139). "In order for sedentary life to emerge, it therefore seems plausible that hunter-gatherers would have had to be forced to settle down, and this would have to have been preceded by an institutional innovation concentrating power in the hands of a group that would become the political elite, enforce property rights, maintain order, and also benefit from their status by extracting resources from the rest of the society" (139). "The emergence of political elites most likely created the transition first to sedentary life and then to farming" (140). "Institutional changes occurred in societies quite a while before they made the transition to farming and were probably the cause both of the move to sedentarism [sic], which reinforced the institutional changes, and subsequently of the Neolithic Revolution" (141).

One can argue that there was mild inequality among the Natufians after sedentism and before agriculture, although some archaeologists call them egalitarian (Grosman and Munro, 2017, 704). There is also evidence for mild inequality in southwest Asia after the spread of agriculture during the Holocene. We will return to both points in Chapter 6. However, there is no evidence at all that the mobile foragers who preceded the sedentary Natufians had either political elites or stratification. In fact there is no evidence that any prehistoric or more recent society of mobile foragers has had a political elite or economic stratification. Acemoglu and Robinson appear to believe that an elite could have emerged prior to sedentism through random institutional drift, but they offer no further explanation as to how or why this could have happened. They also do not explain how an elite in a mobile band could have forced other band members to settle down, or what their motivation for this would have been. Chapter 6 will develop a theory about the origins of inequality that is more consistent with archaeological evidence. In this chapter, we ignore the alleged role of coercion as a causal factor in the transition to sedentary foraging.

Bowles and Choi (2013, 2019) view sedentism in the context of the transition to cultivation, which eventually led to farming communities dependent upon domesticated crops. They think sedentism initially arose at atypically rich production sites where wild resources were sufficiently concentrated to allow sedentary living, and to make defending the resources worthwhile. They also emphasize the reduction of climate volatility, which lessened the pressure for mobility.

Their causal sequence runs as follows. Initially production technology was based on mobile hunting and gathering. Climate change led to warmer and more stable weather conditions favorable to plant growth, which resulted in a few particularly well-endowed production sites. The existence of these sites motivated a transition to greater sedentism. Finally, sedentism created an environment where the coevolution of property rights and agriculture could occur. We will return to the ideas of Bowles and Choi when we discuss the origins of agriculture in Chapter 5.

4.3 SOME ARCHAEOLOGICAL EVIDENCE

This section provides background information about the rarity of sedentism at the Last Glacial Maximum and its emergence as climate conditions improved. We then take a closer look at two regions where early sedentism is well documented: southwest Asia and Japan. These cases offer guidance for our formal model. We conclude this section with some remarks on the relationship between sedentism and agriculture.

In the first three chapters, we used the notation "KYA" to abbreviate dates going back tens of thousands of years. In this chapter and those to come, it will be convenient to switch to the notation "BP," meaning years before the present. This naturally raises the question of what is meant by the present. In archaeological publications from the second half of the twentieth century, the present was usually defined by convention to be 1950 AD (or CE, meaning "current era"). However, in the twenty-first century some scholarly work has begun to treat the year 2000 CE as the definition of the present. For the time scales of this book a difference of

50 years is negligible, because 95% confidence intervals for radiocarbon dates are often ±100 years or more. Readers can therefore enjoy the simplicity of round numbers and treat 10,000 BP as 10,000 years before 2000. As always we use calibrated (calendar) years rather than uncalibrated (radiocarbon) years unless otherwise stated.

The Last Glacial Maximum (LGM) occurred around 21,000 BP in calendar years, or around 18,000 BP in uncalibrated radiocarbon years. The contributors to two volumes edited by Gamble and Soffer (1990) and Soffer and Gamble (1990) survey archaeological evidence from this period for 30 regions of the world. Many regions had settlement sizes ranging from small (probably temporary hunting camps or tool-making workshops) to medium (probably seasonal base camps) and large (probably residential camps with occasional population aggregation). Some foraging groups in areas of high ecological diversity may have collected food within relatively compact territories, and such groups probably had higher population densities than elsewhere.

Nevertheless, in the 600+ pages of the two volumes edited by Soffer and Gamble, only one author claims evidence for a sedentary lifestyle (involving permanent structures in Siberia; see Madeyska, 1990, 32). Archaeological evidence for sedentary communities at the time of the LGM may not have survived or may have been overlooked. But if there were such communities during this period, they were apparently rare and ephemeral.

Aside from southwest Asia and Japan, which will be discussed in detail below, sedentism arose early in the Holocene in Portugal, the Baltic region, and parts of Africa. For Portugal in the first 5,000 years of the Holocene, Straus (1996) reports the appearance of cemeteries, dugout structures, and large shell middens, with a highly diversified diet from hunting, fishing, other aquatic resources, and probably abundant nuts, berries, and tubers. Straus describes the settlements as "semi-sedentary." For Eastern Europe and the Baltic region, Dolukhanov (1996) doubts that year-round settlements existed in the late Pleistocene, but by the early Holocene climate change had led to "comparatively large settlements of permanent and semi-permanent character in Baltic lagoons and inland lacustrine depressions, with an economy based on the exploitation of a wide spectrum of wildlife resources" (168). Sedentary foraging arose in North Africa and East Africa around the same time (Barham and Mitchell, 2008, 351–355).

Such evidence for early sedentism is important, but it is necessary to emphasize that in other places there was no such transition. For example,

Hiscock (2008, 252–253) doubts that sedentary villages existed in Australia prior to European contact. The same was probably true for most tropical rain forests, deserts, and the Arctic.

Southwest Asia: We begin with a short summary of climate in the Levant, which is defined to include modern Israel, Palestine, Jordan, Lebanon, and Syria, plus areas of Turkey and the Sinai Peninsula. The information in this paragraph is from Robinson et al. (2006). Data from many proxies such as lake levels and sediments, palaeosols, fluvial sediments, palaeobotanical records, speleothems, mollusk chemistry, calcretes, and deep-sea cores tell the following story. From the Last Glacial Maximum (23–19,000 BP) until Heinrich event 1 (16,000 BP), the Levant was cool and dry. The Bølling-Allerød interval (15,000–13,000 BP) was warmer and wetter. The Younger Dryas (12,700–11,500 BP) reverted to cold and extremely arid conditions. The early Holocene (9500–7000 BP) was warm, and also the wettest phase over the last 25,000 years. This regional climate history is consistent with the climate history for the Northern Hemisphere revealed in Greenland ice cores. For more on climate in southwest Asia in this period, see Roberts et al. (2018).

The dates for initial sedentism in southwest Asia are still somewhat controversial. Some authors argue that sedentism evolved in a gradual way with foundations that trace back to the Last Glacial Maximum (Maher et al., 2012). Others are skeptical about any evidence for sedentism before farming economies emerged in the early Holocene (Boyd, 2006). But most experts believe a sedentary lifestyle developed in the Bølling-Allerød period and was associated with an archaeological culture called the Early Natufian.

Kuijt and Prentiss (2009) date the start of the Early Natufian to 14,900/14,600 BP in the Jordan Valley. Byrd (2005, 255–262) believes sedentism began in the resource-rich Mediterranean woodland. He comments that sites were located at junctions between two environmental zones, were close to springs, and may have had about 60 inhabitants. He stresses the heightened importance of plant foods, an elaborate array of ground stone tools, the use of baskets for storage, permanent stone architecture, and complex mortuary practices. Hunting of large mammals and birds, as well as freshwater fishing, were also important. Grosman and Munro (2017) cite evidence for permanent architecture, heavy non-mobile ground stone tools, and domestic mice, rats, and sparrows.

The Early Natufian period was accompanied by a ten-fold increase in settlement sizes (Bellwood, 2005) and a "fertility explosion" despite the absence of any cultivation (Bocquet-Appel and Bar-Yosef, 2008, 4–5). The central innovation with respect to lithic tools was the sickle blade, used for harvesting wild cereals (Grosman and Munro, 2017). The Natufian culture expanded northward out of its core area in Palestine/Israel through the Mediterranean forest zone at around 14,000 BP and subsequently into western Syria and Lebanon (Ibáñez et al., 2017).

Valla et al. (2017) provide detailed information for the site of Ain Mallaha, one of the main Natufian settlements in the Levant, which enjoyed a permanent spring, a rivulet, and marshes along the shore of a lake. Ain Mallaha is dated to 14,326 ± 266 BP. It was a hamlet with semi-buried buildings having circular walls and postholes. Several of the buildings have superimposed floors, suggesting that they were rebuilt in the same location. Graves were either under floors or in fills. The hypoplasia found on some skeletons indicates dietary deficiency or infectious diseases in childhood. Dental caries may be related to a diet rich in vegetal food. Traces of trauma on the bones are rare. The site had a broad-spectrum economy including large and small mammals, birds, reptiles, crustaceans, fish, and mollusks. Hares may have been trapped using novel techniques. Small-seeded grasses are more prominent than barley and wheat, perhaps because the latter had to be gathered 12–16 km away. The authors infer that the people of Ain Mallaha were sedentary based on the numerous graves, the use of heavy basalt pounding tools, and the wealth of resources in the surrounding area.

Using climate data from Greenland ice cores and archaeological data from the southern Levant, Maher et al. (2011, 16) express skepticism about the causal connection between the onset of the Bølling-Allerød and the start of the Early Natufian, suggesting that the latter began first. But they also comment that "populations may have increased and settlements became quite large during the Early Natufian, perhaps taking advantage of the Bølling-Allerød's higher precipitation and associated increases in available food resources, even if … the Early Natufian actually started somewhat earlier than the Bølling-Allerød" (21). They acknowledge that climate impacts may have varied across the Levant, and that the lithic artifacts used to date cultural periods may be imperfectly correlated with changes in settlement patterns or the economy (22). Grosman and Munro (2017) agree that Early Natufian culture began before the Bølling-Allerød, but assert that it mainly corresponded to this climate phase. Roberts et al. (2018, 62) argue that the rejection of causal linkages between climate phases and cultural periods by Maher et al. (2011) and Henry (2013) is unpersuasive given the limited temporal precision of the data.

With the onset of the Younger Dryas around 12,700 BP, climate became colder and drier for over 1,000 years. According to Kuijt and Prentiss (2009), this period was associated with more mobility, less elaborate architecture, smaller buildings, shallower cultural deposits, and fewer burials. Many people abandoned previous forms of food storage, adopted mobile hunting and gathering, and had smaller group sizes. At the same time, at least one favorable site in the northern Levant, Abu Hureyra, saw an increase in population (see Chapter 5). Likewise sites in the southern Levant with locally favorable conditions, such as locations in river valleys and on Mount Carmel, continued to support sedentary communities (Bocquet-Appel and Bar-Yosef, 2008, 6). Thus, it is difficult to generalize about the effect of the Younger Dryas on sedentism for the region as a whole.

Maher et al. (2011) again express skepticism about the causal connection between the Younger Dryas and the Late Natufian developments of the sort described by Kuijt and Prentiss (2009), but agree that these events occurred relatively closely in time. Grosman and Munro (2017) paint a more complex picture. In the Mediterranean zone, the shift from Early Natufian to Late Natufian culture occurs before the Younger Dryas, but in more arid regions, the Late Natufian coincides with the Younger Dryas. Late Natufian sites are sometimes mobile and seasonal, but in other cases Early Natufian sites continue in use during the Late Natufian. Sedentary or semi-sedentary sites with large structures were still being used in the Jordan Valley during this period, for example.

At the start of the Pre-Pottery Neolithic A (PPNA), which coincides with the start of the Holocene around 11,600 BP, climate changed drastically, becoming much warmer and wetter. This resulted in dramatically better growing conditions for plants. At about the same time groups showed greatly decreased residential mobility, the construction of buildings requiring more labor investment, and food storage. Economic practices were now centered on expanding communities of forager-collector-cultivators. Subsistence strategies continued to include hunting of wild game and collecting of wild plants, but agriculture spread widely across the region (Kuijt and Prentiss, 2009).

This chronology is supported by evidence from paleodemography. For southwest Asia as a whole, Roberts et al. (2018) found that population shows a downward deviation relative to a fitted exponential curve in the later part of the Bølling-Allerød and the early Younger Dryas. They found an upward deviation early in the Holocene. The latter event could have been driven partly by the spread of agriculture, although climate amelioration was almost certainly a contributing factor (see Section 5.9 for a more detailed discussion).

Several features of this case are worth highlighting. First, climate change was strongly correlated with shifts between mobile and sedentary lifestyles, and the climate effects involved changes in mean temperature and precipitation rather than merely lower variance. Second, lifestyle transitions went in both directions: when the regional climate deteriorated, sedentism tended to be abandoned, except at locations that were buffered from climate shocks. Third, climate change was associated with changes in population densities, reflected in settlement sizes. Finally, sedentism involved a distinct repertoire of techniques with respect to diet, food storage, and housing. These techniques began to develop more than 3,000 years before domesticated cereals emerged in the PPNA.

Japan: Another case of sedentary foraging involves the Jomon of Japan, a society that lasted over 10,000 years. Aikens and Akazama (1996) use tree pollen data to argue that a warmer climate in the late Pleistocene and early Holocene led to the spread of oak forests from south to north through the Japanese archipelago. The new oak forests were followed by a broad-spectrum diet with greater reliance on plant and aquatic foods, early development of pottery for cooking, storage facilities, and durable residences.

The remaining information on Jomon society in this section is taken from Habu (2004) except where noted. While some non-staple plants were probably domesticated, most of the Jomon diet consisted of wild animals, wild plants, and aquatic resources (see ch. 3 of Habu, 2004). The Jomon display no evidence of warfare or political complexity. There is little evidence of inequality and this is only found in the Late/Final periods.

The dating of Jomon periods is complicated by regional diversity and radiocarbon calibration problems (37–42), so the dates given below are approximate. The Incipient Jomon period began around 12,000 BP and was characterized by mobile foraging (246–247). The Initial Jomon period is dated from 11,000 to 6900 BP and corresponded to the transition "from the Final Pleistocene to the warmest part of the mid-postglacial period" (42). Most settlements in Honshu remained small (generally 3–5 pit dwellings) and there is little evidence for food storage, so it is likely that mobile foraging continued as the dominant food acquisition strategy. However, there is evidence for larger sedentary communities in Hokkaido and southern Kyushu.

The Early and Middle Jomon periods (roughly 6900–4000 BP) overlap with the "Climatic Optimum," the warmest part of the postglacial (Holocene) period. The Early Jomon had more sedentism, larger settlements, and food storage technologies. Aggregate population reached a maximum around the Middle period, and in some regions increased by a factor of 50 or more relative to previous levels (254). Likewise, site densities and settlement sizes reached a high point (133). One site had continuous occupation by 200–500 people for over 1,500 years (114). Such settlements had hundreds of labor-intensive pit dwellings.

The Late/Final Jomon, starting around 4,000 BP, was associated with a cooling trend. Over 600–700 years, population fell to levels prevailing before the Early/Middle growth phase (197, 254). The number of large settlements declined, along with site density, to levels similar to those of the Early Jomon, although this was not accompanied by a full return to mobile foraging. The Final Jomon dates to 3,300–2,100 BP. During the second half of this period, influences from the Korean peninsula led to rice cultivation.

Crema et al. (2016) study population dynamics between 7,000–3,000 BP for the Jomon. Relative to null hypotheses with uniform or exponential distributions, they find a sequence with rapid initial population growth, a high-density plateau, a decline, and then renewed growth. They suggest (but do not test) the hypothesis that these fluctuations were associated with climate change. In general, their results are consistent with what one might expect based on the relevant part of the narrative presented by Habu (2004).

As in southwest Asia, climate appears to have played a key role in determining the subsistence strategies of the Jomon. Favorable climate was closely associated with population growth, and a deteriorating climate was associated with population decline. Sedentism involved both an increased reliance on food storage and greater residential construction, with some communities lasting for many centuries. Another parallel with the case of southwest Asia is that sedentary foraging became widespread in Japan more than 3,000 years before the arrival of agriculture from Korea. Finally, we note that the lack of political complexity, warfare, and inequality in the early stages of sedentism is consistent with our modeling assumption of relatively free individual mobility.

Sedentism and Agriculture: This chapter is concerned with pristine transitions from mobile to sedentary foraging, where the term "pristine" means that the transition was not caused by a diffusion of sedentary lifestyles from other societies. Specifically, we are not addressing cases where sedentism was triggered by the diffusion of agriculture from a neighboring society.

A society that experiences a pristine transition to sedentary foraging may follow various subsequent trajectories: (a) after a potentially long lag it may undergo a pristine transition to agriculture, as in southwest Asia; (b) after a potentially long lag it may adopt agriculture through diffusion from outside sources, as in Japan; or (c) it may never adopt agriculture, as along the northwest coast of North America prior to European contact. A society of mobile foragers that does not undergo any transition to sedentary foraging may likewise follow various trajectories: (a) it may eventually adopt sedentism and agriculture simultaneously due to the diffusion of agricultural technology; (b) it may be displaced by farming populations, as in parts of Europe (Shennan, 2018) and southern Africa; or (c) it may engage in mobile foraging indefinitely, as in Australia prior to European contact.

The next several sections build a formal model of the conditions that could trigger a pristine transition from mobile to sedentary foraging. The conditions that could trigger a subsequent pristine transition to agriculture will be left for Chapter 5.

4.4 THE PRODUCTION SITE

We consider a site with L agents. Each agent is endowed with one unit of labor time, and each agent is of negligible size relative to the population at the site. The food produced at the site is shared equally among the agents, who allocate their labor time to maximize total food output. Our use of the term "site" will be flexible and may involve a relatively large geographic area within which mobile foragers search for food.

Food can be obtained by hunting or gathering. We use "hunting" as a generic label for mobile food procurement activities involving a portable toolkit, minimal processing, and quick consumption. Aside from literal hunting, this could include the collection of berries or other easily harvested wild plant foods. We use "gathering" as a generic label for stationary activities involving fixed assets, extensive processing, or storage. Fixed assets could include grinding stones, ovens, pottery, or storage pits. Further examples outside the literal definition of gathering include animal traps and fishing weirs.

Total food output (in calories) is given by

$$Y = \theta[f(L_f) + kg(L_g)] \qquad (4.1)$$

where f and g are the production functions for hunting and gathering respectively; θ is the weather; $L_f \geq 0$ is the labor input for hunting; $L_g \geq 0$ is the labor input for gathering; and $k > 0$ is the productivity of gathering. The parameter θ is neutral between the two activities and reflects the general abundance of food resources at the site.

The production functions have the following properties:

Assumption 4.1
$f(0) = g(0) = 0$; $f'(L) \in (0,\infty)$ for all $L \geq 0$; $g'(L) \in (0,\infty)$ for all $L \geq 0$; $f''(L) < 0$ for all $L \geq 0$; and $g''(L) < 0$ for all $L \geq 0$. The marginal products $f'(0)$ and $g'(0)$ are positive and finite at zero labor input. We also assume $f'(\infty) = g'(\infty) = 0$.

One example of such a production function is $f(L) = A(1-e^{-mL})$ where $m > 0$ and A can be interpreted as the natural supply of some wild food resource available for harvesting.

At a benchmark site where $\theta = 1$, the maximum food output is

$$H(L,k) \equiv \max\{f(L_f) + kg(L_g) \text{ subject to } L_f \geq 0, L_g \geq 0, \text{ and } L_f + L_g = L\} \qquad (4.2)$$

The solution in (4.2) is unique due to the strict concavity of the objective function. The optimal labor allocation and the function H have the following properties.

Proposition 4.1 (optimal labor allocation).
(a) Suppose $f'(0) > kg'(0)$. Define $x_f > 0$ by $f'(x_f) \equiv kg'(0)$.
   (i) For $0 \leq L \leq x_f$ the solution has $L_f = L$ and $L_g = 0$ with $f'(L) \geq kg'(0)$.
   (ii) For $x_f < L$ the solution has $L_f > 0$ and $L_g > 0$ with $f'(L_f) = kg'(L_g)$.
(b) Suppose $f'(0) < kg'(0)$. Define $x_g > 0$ by $f'(0) \equiv kg'(x_g)$.
   (i) For $0 \leq L \leq x_g$ the solution has $L_f = 0$ and $L_g = L$ with $f'(0) \leq kg'(L)$.
   (ii) For $x_g < L$ the solution has $L_f > 0$ and $L_g > 0$ with $f'(L_f) = kg'(L_g)$.
(c) Suppose $f'(0) = kg'(0)$. For all $L > 0$ the solution has $L_f > 0$ and $L_g > 0$ with $f'(L_f) = kg'(L_g)$.

(d) $H(L, k)$ is continuous, increasing, and strictly concave in L for any fixed $k > 0$.

(e) Food per capita $h(L, k) \equiv H(L, k)/L$ is decreasing in L for any fixed $k > 0$.

(f) (i) As $L \to 0$, $h(L, k) \to \max\{f'(0), kg'(0)\} \equiv h(0, k)$ for any fixed $k > 0$.

    (ii) As $L \to \infty$, $h(L, k) \to 0$ for any fixed $k > 0$.

Part (a) of Proposition 4.1 says that if gathering productivity (k) is small enough, only hunting is used at low levels of L and both activities are used at higher levels of L. Conversely, part (b) says that if k is large enough, only gathering is used at low levels of L and both activities are used at higher levels of L. Part (c) is a boundary case. Part (d) shows that the marginal product of labor is positive and decreasing. Part (e) shows that food per capita $h(L, k)$ decreases as labor input rises. Part (f) shows that food per capita is finite at $L = 0$ and goes to zero as L goes to infinity. For an unoccupied site, food per capita is defined to be $h(0, k) \equiv \max\{f'(0), kg'(0)\}$.

As in Chapters 2 and 3, for the production function $f(L_f)$ the marginal product of labor and the average product of labor are equal to the same finite constant at zero input. The production function $g(L_g)$ has the same feature. This extends to the function $H(L, k)$, which has $H_L(0, k) = h(0, k)$ where $H_L(0, k)$ is the marginal product of labor at zero and $h(0, k)$ is the average product of labor at zero, as in Proposition 4.1(f)(i).

4.5 SHORT-RUN EQUILIBRIUM

This is the first section of the book in which we need to distinguish between sites and regions. We think of a region as a contiguous geographic area for which there is no in- or out-migration. This may be true because the area is circumscribed by mountains, deserts, or oceans, or because heavily populated zones are far apart and it makes sense to ignore migration between such zones. In empirical discussions we often refer to regions like southwest Asia, sub-Saharan Africa, or Mesoamerica that correspond to areas studied by archaeological specialists. In such contexts we assume that events in separate regions evolved independently.

Within a region there are generally multiple production sites. In Chapters 4–5 we assume that individuals can move freely among these sites. For simplicity we ignore the costs associated with travel over intra-regional distances. We also assume there are no social barriers to movement among sites, either because population densities are too low to make exclusion feasible, or because kinship links enable population to flow relatively freely between sites when this is economically advantageous to the individuals involved. Property rights therefore involve open access. In Chapters 6–8 we consider physical and social barriers to mobility across sites.

The number of sites in a region depends on the model. In Chapters 4–6 it will be convenient to assume a continuum of sites. In Chapters 7–8 we will study models where a region has only two distinct sites or territories. Finally, in Chapter 10 we will consider a region with one large site and many small sites.

Now consider a continuum of production sites uniformly distributed on the unit interval and indexed by $s \in [0, 1]$. The weather at an individual site s is binary:

Assumption 4.2

$\theta_s \in \{\theta_A, \theta_B\}$ with $0 < \theta_B < \theta_A$. The probability that a site s has good weather (θ_A) is $\lambda \in (0, 1)$ and the probability that the site has bad weather (θ_B) is $1 - \lambda$. Weather is independent across sites. The fraction of sites with good weather is always λ and the fraction of sites with bad weather is always $1 - \lambda$.

We think of the regional economy as having a fixed total supply of food resources under a given climate regime. The weather in the current period determines how this supply is distributed across sites. There is no aggregate uncertainty.

We define the short run to be a time period over which regional population $N > 0$ does not change (one human generation, or about twenty years). Due to open access, it must be true in equilibrium that no agent can obtain a higher food income by changing sites. This motivates the following definition.

Definition 4.1

Fix the parameters $(\theta_A, \theta_B, \lambda, k)$ and the regional population $N > 0$. Let L_A (L_B) be total labor at a production site having weather $\theta_A (\theta_B)$, and let y be food per capita. The combination (L_A, L_B, y) is a *short-run equilibrium* (SRE) if

(a) $\theta_A h(L_A, k) = y$ with $L_A > 0$
(b) $\theta_B h(L_B, k) \leq y$ with equality if $L_B > 0$
(c) $\lambda L_A + (1 - \lambda)L_B = N$.

The logic behind this definition runs as follows. Due to $N > 0$, if we had $L_A = 0$ we would need to have $L_B > 0$. The resulting food per agent at a site of type B would be $\theta_B h(L_B, k)$, which is less than $\theta_A h(0, k)$, the food an agent could obtain by moving to an unoccupied site of type A. To prevent such incentives for movement, we must have $L_A > 0$ as in condition (a) of D4.1. The associated food income per agent is denoted by y.

If $L_B = 0$ then we must have $\theta_B h(0, k) \leq y$ to avoid the movement of agents from sites of type A to unoccupied sites of type B. If $L_B > 0$ then sites of type B must provide the same income as sites of type A, because otherwise agents would move from sites of one type to sites of the other. This gives condition (b) in D4.1. The local populations at the individual sites must add up to the regional population N, so we require $\int_0^1 L_s \, ds = \lambda L_A + (1-\lambda)L_B = N$ as in condition (c).

There is a unique SRE for each $N > 0$. To see why, let η be the inverse function h^{-1}, where we temporarily suppress the parameter k to simplify notation. This gives

$$L_A = \eta(y/\theta_A) \text{ where } \eta(y/\theta_A) \equiv 0 \text{ for } y/\theta_A \geq h(0) \qquad (4.3a)$$

$$L_B = \eta(y/\theta_B) \text{ where } \eta(y/\theta_B) \equiv 0 \text{ for } y/\theta_B \geq h(0) \qquad (4.3b)$$

The regional "demand" for labor is $D(y) \equiv \lambda\eta(y/\theta_A) + (1-\lambda)\eta(y/\theta_B)$. The equilibrium food income y must satisfy

$$D(y) \equiv \lambda\eta(y/\theta_A) + (1-\lambda)\eta(y/\theta_B) = N \qquad (4.3c)$$

The demand $D(y)$ is zero for $y \geq \theta_A h(0)$. It is continuous and increases as y decreases for $y \leq \theta_A h(0)$, with $D(y) \to \infty$ as $y \to 0$. This implies the existence of a unique food income $y(N)$ such that (4.3c) holds for the given $N > 0$. More formally:

Proposition 4.2 (short-run equilibrium).
Fix $(\theta_A, \theta_B, \lambda, k)$. Choose any $N > 0$.

(a) There is a unique $y(N)$ that solves (4.3c), with $0 < y(N) < \theta_A h(0)$.
(b) This value of y and the associated labor allocation from (4.3a) and (4.3b) with $L_A = \eta(y/\theta_A)$ and $L_B = \eta(y/\theta_B)$ constitute a unique SRE for N.
(c) $y(N)$ is continuous and decreasing in N, with $y(N) \to 0$ as $N \to \infty$.

In the rest of this section we show how the qualitative nature of SRE depends on the parameters N and k. It is easy to see from the definition of SRE that either $0 = L_B < L_A$ or alternatively $0 < L_B < L_A$. We assume throughout this section that $f'(0) > kg'(0)$, because we want to focus on situations where an initially low population density implies that only the hunting technique is employed. It follows from Proposition 4.1(a) that either $L_{Af} > 0$ and $L_{Ag} = 0$ (only hunting is used at sites of type A) or $L_{Af} > 0$ and $L_{Ag} > 0$ (both hunting and gathering are used at sites of type A). When sites of type B are active, $L_{Bg} > 0$ implies $L_{Ag} > 0$ due to the greater population at sites of type A. Thus if gathering is used anywhere, it must be used at sites of type A.

These considerations yield four possibilities for the structure of SRE:

(I) Only type A sites are active ($L_B = 0$) and only hunting is used ($L_{Ag} = 0$).

(II) All sites are active ($L_B > 0$) and only hunting is used ($L_{Ag} = 0$).

(III) Only type A sites are active ($L_B = 0$) and both techniques are used ($L_{Ag} > 0$).

(IV) All sites are active ($L_B > 0$) and both techniques are used ($L_{Ag} > 0$).

Figure 4.1 illustrates these four regions in (N, k) space for a fixed climate regime $(\theta_A, \theta_B, \lambda)$. Regions I and II where only hunting is used are associated with low values of the gathering productivity k, while regions III and IV where both hunting and gathering are used are associated with higher values of k. Regions I and III where sites of type B are inactive correspond to low values for the regional population N, while regions II and IV where all sites are active correspond to higher values of N.

The locations of the regions in Figure 4.1 depend only on the productivity ratio θ_B/θ_A and not the absolute productivity levels (θ_A, θ_B). The boundary for the use of the gathering technique (labeled $L_{Ag} = 0$ in Figure 4.1) is determined using Proposition 4.1(a). The relevant equation is

$$f'(L_A) = kg'(0) \tag{4.4}$$

When only sites of type A are active (regions I and III), the local population density $L_A = N/\lambda$ is obtained directly from condition (c) in the definition of SRE. Substitution into (4.4) gives the desired relationship between N and k. When all sites are active but gathering is not used, (a) and (b) in the definition of SRE imply $\theta_A f(L_A)/L_A = \theta_B f(L_B)/L_B$. This and (c) determine local populations $L_A(N)$ and $L_B(N)$. Substituting $L_A(N)$ into (4.4) gives the relationship between N and k corresponding to the boundary $L_{Ag} = 0$ in Figure 4.1.

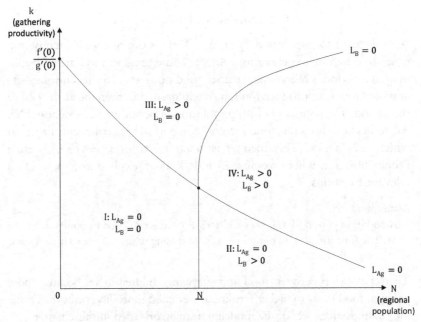

FIGURE 4.1. Short-run equilibrium as a function of regional population and gathering productivity for a fixed climate regime

The boundary for use of sites of type B (labeled $L_B = 0$ in Figure 4.1) is derived as follows. We use the notation $h(0, k)$ and $\eta(\cdot, k)$ to indicate that these functions depend on the gathering productivity k. Consider the population threshold

$$N(k) \equiv \lambda\eta[\theta_B h(0, k)/\theta_A, k] > 0 \qquad (4.5)$$

When $N \leq N(k)$ only sites of type A are active ($L_A > 0, L_B = 0$). When $N > N(k)$ all sites are active ($L_A > 0, L_B > 0$). This boundary is vertical at $\underline{N}$ in Figure 4.1 when gathering is not used, because then the parameter k is irrelevant and $N(k) = \underline{N}$ is a constant. When gathering is used at sites of type A, the boundary $L_B = 0$ slopes up as indicated in Figure 4.1. This occurs because higher gathering productivity drives a wedge between the A and B sites in a way that favors the type-A sites, which are already gathering. As we explain later, our concept of sedentism focuses on the question of whether bad sites are active, so a key task will be to determine how $N > N(k)$ can be achieved if it does not hold initially.

4.6 LONG-RUN EQUILIBRIUM

We turn next to population dynamics. Time is discrete with each period equal to one human generation. Agents come to adulthood at the beginning of a period, observe the weather conditions at each site, choose a site at which to work, produce food, have children, and then die at the end of the period. The regional (adult) population in period t will be denoted N^t. All adults have the same food income y^t in period t regardless of the site at which they work. This income is obtained from $y^t = y(N^t, k)$ using Proposition 4.2, where we now include k as an explicit argument in all relevant functions.

Assumption 4.3

An adult in period t has $\rho(y^t)$ children who survive to become adults in period $t + 1$. The function $\rho(y)$ is continuous and increasing with $\rho(0) = 0$. There is some $y^* > 0$ such that $\rho(y^*) = 1$.

The relationship between food and surviving children arises because more parental food leads to higher fertility, lower child mortality, or both. This is the Malthusian aspect of the modeling framework used in this chapter.

As in Chapter 3, population evolves according to

$$N^{t+1} = \rho[y(N^t, k)]N^t \quad t = 0, 1, . \tag{4.6}$$

This equation implies that a non-null stationary population $N > 0$ must yield $\rho[y(N, k)] = 1$ or equivalently $y(N, k) = y^*$. We formalize this idea in the following definition.

Definition 4.2

Fix the parameters $(\theta_A, \theta_B, \lambda, k)$. The combination (L_A, L_B, N) with $N > 0$ is a non-null *long-run equilibrium* (LRE) if (L_A, L_B) and y^* form a SRE for N.

In order to support a positive population in the long run, food income must achieve the level y^* needed for demographic replacement. This gives an existence result.

Proposition 4.3 (long-run equilibrium).
  Fix the parameters $(\theta_A, \theta_B, \lambda, k)$.

  (a) If $\theta_A h(0, k) > y^*$ then there is a unique non-null LRE population $N > 0$.
  (b) If $\theta_A h(0, k) \leq y^*$ then no non-null LRE exists.

The following monotone convergence assumption simplifies later analysis.

Assumption 4.4

Monotone population adjustment (MPA). Suppose there is a population $N^* > 0$ such that $y(N^*, k) = y^*$. Keep the parameters $(\theta_A, \theta_B, \lambda, k)$ constant over time and consider any $N^\circ > 0$. If $y(N^\circ, k) > y^*$ then $N^{t+1} > N^t$ for all $t \geq 0$. If $y(N^\circ, k) < y^*$ then $N^{t+1} < N^t$ for all $t \geq 0$. In either case $\lim_{t \to \infty} N^t = N^*$.

As with A3.2 in Section 3.7, this rules out oscillations around N^* along the adjustment path. MPA holds if the direct positive effect of N^t on N^{t+1} in (4.6) outweighs the indirect negative effect operating through $y(N^t, k)$.

Figure 4.1 can be used to determine how the structure of SRE changes along the adjustment path $\{N^t\}$. For example, imagine that a horizontal line associated with a fixed value of k crosses regions I, II, and IV because gathering productivity is low. Suppose the initial population N° from A4.4 is in region I and the LRE population N^* from A4.4 is in region IV. This implies that population will increase over time and the system will move horizontally from left to right in Figure 4.1. At first only sites of type A are active and only hunting is used; after a while, sites of type B become active but gathering is not yet used; and eventually both hunting and gathering are used, at least at the type-A sites. Other chronological sequences could occur depending on the productivity level k, the initial population N°, and the final population N^*.

4.7 VERY-LONG-RUN EQUILIBRIUM

This section is based on the model of learning by doing described in Section 3.5 and the concept of very-long-run equilibrium defined in Section 3.8. To avoid repetition, the discussion here will be kept brief. Suppose the resources for the hunting production function f have been exploited for many millennia, and there are no further opportunities to increase hunting productivity through learning by doing. On the other hand, resources associated with the gathering production function g have not previously been exploited. If gathering begins, learning by doing also begins, and in each period there is a positive probability that the productivity coefficient k will jump by a discrete amount. All such innovations are freely available throughout the region. This process can end in one of two ways: either (i) the gathered resources are no longer used, which terminates learning by doing and prevents k from rising any further or (ii) k reaches an upper bound k^* and there are no further opportunities for technical innovation in gathering.

These ideas lead to the following definition.

Definition 4.3

Fix the parameters $(\theta_A, \theta_B, \lambda)$ and let k^* be the maximum achievable value of k. The combination (L_A, L_B, N, k) with $N > 0$ is a non-null *very-long-run equilibrium* (VLRE) if

(a) (L_A, L_B, N) form an LRE for the given k; and
(b)   Either $L_{Ag} = L_{Bg} = 0$, or $k = k^*$, or both.

Condition (b) ensures that the productivity level k remains constant with probability one.

As in Chapter 3, "very long run" does not imply that population adjustments occur first (in the long run) and then technical adjustments occur second (in the very long run). The population and technology (N^t, k^t) adjust simultaneously. This terminology is meant simply to highlight that the productivity level k is exogenous in the definition of LRE but endogenous in the definition of VLRE.

***

Proposition 4.4 (very-long-run equilibrium).
Fix the parameters $(\theta_A, \theta_B, \lambda)$.

(a) For a given $k \in (0, k^*)$, there is a unique non-null VLRE iff $\theta_A f'(0) > y^*$ and the value of L_A such that $\theta_A f(L_A)/L_A = y^*$ gives $f'(L_A) \geq k g'(0)$. This determines the equilibrium value of $L_A > 0$. If $\theta_B f'(0) > y^*$ then $L_B > 0$ satisfies $\theta_B f(L_B)/L_B = y^*$; otherwise $L_B = 0$. Finally, $N = \lambda L_A + (1-\lambda)L_B > 0$.
(b) For $k = k^*$, there is a unique non-null VLRE iff $\theta_A h(0, k^*) > y^*$. In equilibrium $L_A > 0$ satisfies $\theta_A h(L_A, k^*) = y^*$. If $\theta_B h(0, k^*) > y^*$ then $L_B > 0$ satisfies $\theta_B h(L_B, k^*) = y^*$; otherwise $L_B = 0$. Finally, $N = \lambda L_A + (1-\lambda)L_B > 0$.

***

Part (a) deals with VLREs in which gathering productivity is below its maximum possible value. In order to avoid learning by doing that raises k with positive probability, we need $L_{Ag} = L_{Bg} = 0$ so the gathering technology is not used at any site. For the VLRE to be non-null $(N > 0)$, it must be possible to support a positive population L_A at the good sites with hunting alone. Bad sites may or may not be active, depending on their natural productivity θ_B. The requirements for a VLRE of this kind parallel those for an LRE in which hunting is the only technology, but with the additional requirement that the latent productivity k be low enough to ensure that gathering is not used. Chapter 3 referred to such a VLRE as a "stagnation trap"; gathering is not used because its productivity is too low, but its productivity cannot increase because gathering is never used.

Part (b) deals with VLREs where gathering productivity is at the maximum k^*. This removes the need for any restriction on the use of gathering. In general, VLRE may involve hunting, gathering, or some combination of the two. The condition for VLRE to be non-null $(N > 0)$ is identical to the condition for an LRE to be non-null with gathering productivity k^* (see Proposition 4.3(a)). When k^* is small enough, part (b) reduces to an equilibrium in which only hunting is used, as in part (a).

4.8 THE BASELINE EQUILIBRIUM

A site's natural productivity is θ_A with probability λ and θ_B with probability $1 - \lambda$. These draws are independent across sites and periods. Thus the mean productivity of a site is $M = \lambda\theta_A + (1 - \lambda)\theta_B$ and the variance is $V = \lambda(1-\lambda)(\theta_A-\theta_B)^2$. These equations give

$$\theta_A = M + [(1-\lambda)V/\lambda]^{1/2} \quad \text{and} \quad \theta_B = M-[\lambda V/(1-\lambda)]^{1/2} \quad (4.7)$$

In our analysis of climate change, we keep λ constant and only consider changes in the productivity levels θ_A and θ_B.

Between the Last Glacial Maximum and the Holocene, mean weather conditions improved and the variance of weather declined. We thus contrast two climates: an initial bad regime (M°, V°) and a subsequent good regime (M^*, V^*), where $0 < M^\circ < M^*$ and $0 < V^* < V^\circ$. From (4.7) this unambiguously raises θ_B and the ratio θ_B/θ_A. The productivity θ_A may go in either direction. Here we assume θ_A rises, because it is reasonable to think that the Holocene was beneficial at both good and bad sites. The ratio θ_B/θ_A must rise, so worse sites must improve in greater proportion.

Assumption 4.5
The climate amelioration from (M°, V°) to (M^*, V^*) yields $\theta_A^* > \theta_A^\circ$, $\theta_B^* > \theta_B^\circ$, and $\theta_B^*/\theta_A^* > \theta_B^\circ/\theta_A^\circ$. V is positive in both regimes so $0 < \theta_B^\circ < \theta_A^\circ$ and $0 < \theta_B^* < \theta_A^*$. We ignore possible changes in the fraction of good sites λ.

Our concept of sedentism is that agents remain at a location even when resources become scarce at that location. This contrasts with a fully mobile lifestyle where agents always move to the locations where resources are most abundant. To formalize this idea, recall that in a long-run equilibrium there is a constant regional population N with local populations (L_A, L_B) at the individual production sites. Suppose a site changes from A (abundant resources) in period t–1 to B (scarce resources) in period t. In LRE each adult has one child who survives to adulthood so the L_A adults at the site in period t–1 leave L_A surviving adult children at the site at the start of period t. Due to the diminished local abundance of resources in period t, there is an outflow of $L_A - L_B > 0$ agents in period t, with L_B agents remaining behind. When $L_B > 0$, a production site is always occupied by some agents even if weather conditions turn bad at that site.

We define the rate of sedentism to be

$$S = L_B/L_A \in [0, 1] \tag{4.8}$$

because this is the fraction of the local population that remains in place when there is an adverse weather shock. The sedentism rate is zero if sites are entirely abandoned when resources are locally scarce ($L_B = 0$). In a long-run equilibrium where type-B sites are active, we have $\theta_A h(L_A, k) \equiv y^*$ and $\theta_B h(L_B, k) \equiv y^*$. This implies that for a fixed value of θ_A, the sedentism rate $S = L_B/L_A$ is increasing in θ_B with $S \to 1$ as $\theta_B \to \theta_A$. In other words, the sedentism rate rises when the variance in weather conditions drops. Under our definition, sedentism can be positive even when only "hunting" (mobile food acquisition) is used, as long as sites are not fully abandoned when local weather worsens. "Gathering" (stationary food acquisition) is not a necessary condition for a positive sedentism rate.

Next consider a baseline VLRE reflecting the circumstances of the Last Glacial Maximum. We want a VLRE in which only sites of type A are active and only hunting is used. Whenever an individual site shifts from good to bad weather conditions, all agents move away from that site.

Proposition 4.5 (baseline VLRE).

 The parameters $(\theta_A^\circ, \theta_B^\circ, k^\circ)$ with $k^\circ < k^*$ yield a non-null VLRE in which (i) only sites of type A are active and (ii) only hunting is used iff

$$\theta_A^\circ f'(0) > y^* \tag{4.9a}$$

$$\theta_B^\circ f'(0) \leq y^* \tag{4.9b}$$

$$f'(L_A^\circ) \geq k^\circ g'(0) \qquad \text{where } L_A^\circ > 0 \text{ satisfies } \theta_A^\circ f(L_A^\circ)/L_A^\circ = y^*. \tag{4.9c}$$

Condition (4.9a) ensures that a site of type A can support a positive workforce L_A° at the food per capita y^*. Condition (4.9b) ensures that agents with access to income y* will not move to a site of type B. Condition (4.9c) ensures that gathering is unattractive when the work-force at a site is L_A^o. It is easy to see that such parameter values exist: choose a large enough value of θ_A^o to satisfy (4.9a), a small enough value of θ_B^o to satisfy (4.9b), and a small enough value of k^o to satisfy (4.9c).

4.9 THE EFFECTS OF CLIMATE CHANGE

Starting from the baseline equilibrium constructed in Section 4.8, suppose there is a permanent improvement in climate to (θ_A^*, θ_B^*) in period $t = 0$ as described in A4.5. In reality the shift from the LGM to the Holocene was lengthy, non-monotonic, and uneven across regions of the world, but the qualitative effects of climate change are most easily studied using this simple framework.

We are interested in causal mechanisms that yield $L_B > 0$ and thus a positive rate of sedentism. Three mechanisms are considered. The first, called "climate only," operates in the short run. The second, called "climate plus population," operates in the long run. The third, called "climate plus population and technology," operates in the very long run.

Proposition 4.6 (short run; climate only).
    Start from a baseline VLRE as in Proposition 4.5. Let the climate change described in A4.5 occur at the start of period $t = 0$.

(a) Gathering is not used at any site in period $t = 0$.
(b) Sites of type B become active in period $t = 0$ iff $\theta_A^* y^*/\theta_A^o < \theta_B^* f'(0)$.

Part (a) results from the following facts: (i) L_B is zero in the baseline equilibrium; (ii) the regional population is fixed in the short run at N^o; (iii) the new equilibrium must therefore have L_A no larger than its baseline level, and smaller if L_B becomes positive; (iv) there is a corner solution with no gathering at type-A sites in the baseline equilibrium and L_A does not increase, so the new SRE also has a corner solution for these sites; (v) if gathering is not used at type-A sites, it cannot be used at type-B sites either, because $L_B < L_A$ must hold in SRE. Part (b) is straightforward. In the short run, regional population is fixed at N^o. If the type-B sites improve enough relative to the type-A sites, some of this population will spread out into the B sites.

In the rest of this section we assume that the condition in Proposition 4.6(b) does *not* hold so sedentism does not arise immediately. We first want to show that even when climate change does not lead to sedentism directly, it can trigger a process of population growth that leads to sedentism indirectly. The key idea involves Malthusian population dynamics. In the short run, higher productivity at the type-A sites makes all agents better off. Because food per capita y° now exceeds y^*, the regional population increases.

Let the population adjustment path be $\{N^t\}$. The climate change is permanent so (θ_A^*, θ_B^*) remains in effect along this path. Temporarily we also assume that k° remains in effect, and ignore the learning by doing issues raised in Section 4.7. Due to A4.4, $\{N^t\}$ is increasing and converges to a new LRE population $N^* > N^\circ$ as $t \to \infty$. Food per capita $\{y^t\}$ is decreasing and converges to y^*.

Now consider Figure 4.2, where all of the curves reflect the new ratio θ_B^*/θ_A^*. The boundaries $L_B = 0$ and $L_{Ag} = 0$ intersect at $(\underline{N}, \underline{k})$, where $\underline{L}_A$, $\underline{N}$, and $\underline{k}$ must satisfy

$$\theta_A^* f(\underline{L}_A)/\underline{L}_A \equiv \theta_B^* f'(0)$$
$$\underline{N} \equiv \lambda \underline{L}_A \qquad\qquad (4.10)$$
$$\underline{k} \equiv f'(\underline{L}_A)/g'(0)$$

At the point $(\underline{N}, \underline{k})$ we have a SRE in which only type-A sites are active and only hunting is used. Agents are indifferent about moving to an unoccupied type-B site, and gathering would come into use at the type-A sites if there were any increase in its productivity.

One possibility is that the gathering productivity k° from the baseline equilibrium may be below $\underline{k}$. In this case we start from a point like P in region I. As population rises, the system moves to points like Q in region II, where type-B sites are active but gathering is still not used. With enough population growth, the system eventually moves to points like R in region IV, where type-B sites remain active and both hunting and gathering are used at the type-A sites.

Another possible sequence arises when latent gathering productivity k° is above $\underline{k}$. Now we start from a point like S in region I. Population growth first leads to points like T in region III where hunting and gathering are both used at the type-A sites, while type-B sites remain inactive. Further population growth moves the system to points like U in region IV where type-B sites become active.

Whether these transitions occur depends on the new long-run population level N^*, which is determined by the absolute level of the new climate parameters (θ_A^*, θ_B^*). We can hold the ratio θ_B^*/θ_A^* constant while scaling up the degree of climate improvement by multiplying the productivities of both

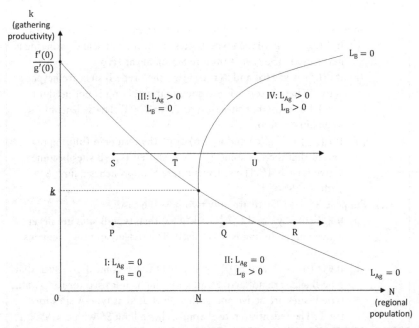

FIGURE 4.2. Possible trajectories resulting from Malthusian population growth after climate amelioration

A and B sites by an identical factor $\mu > 1$. This raises the LRE population N^* without altering the location of the regions in Figure 4.2.

The following proposition describes the range of potential outcomes.

Proposition 4.7 (long run; climate plus population).

Start from a baseline equilibrium as in Proposition 4.5. Let the climate change described in A4.5 occur at the start of period $t = 0$. Define $L_A^* > 0$ using $\theta_A^* h(L_A^*, k^\circ) \equiv y^*$. Assume that the inequality in Proposition 4.6(b) does *not* hold so sites of type B do not become active at $t = 0$. Let k° remain constant.

(a) Suppose $k^\circ < \underline{k}$. There are three possible cases.
    (i) If $\theta_B^* f'(0) \leq y^*$ then type-B sites are never active and gathering is never used. The sedentism rate S remains at zero.
    (ii) If $\theta_B^* f'(0) > y^*$ and $f'(L_A^*) \geq k^\circ g'(0)$ there is some $T > 0$ such that type-B sites are not active for $t < T$ but are active for $t \geq T$. Gathering is never used. The sedentism rate S^t approaches a limit S^* with $0 < S^* < 1$.
    (iii) If $\theta_B^* f'(0) > y^*$ and $f'(L_A^*) < k^\circ g'(0)$ the results in (a)(ii) apply, except that there is some $T' \geq T$ such that gathering is used at sites of type A for $t \geq T'$.

(b) Suppose $k° > \underline{k}$. There are three possible cases.

    (i) If $f'(L_A^*) \geq \underline{k}°g'(o)$ then type-B sites are never active and gathering is never used. The sedentism rate S remains at zero.

    (ii) If $f'(L_A^*) < k°g'(o)$ and $\theta_B^* f'(o) \leq y^*$ then type-B sites are never active. There is some $T > o$ such that gathering is not used for $t < T$ but is used at sites of type A for $t \geq T$. The sedentism rate S remains at zero.

    (iii) If $f'(L_A^*) < k°g'(o)$ and $\theta_B^* f'(o) > y^*$ the results in (b)(ii) apply, except that there is some $T' \geq T$ such that type-B sites become active for $t \geq T'$. The sedentism rate S^t approaches a limit S^* with $o < S^* < 1$.

(c) Suppose $k° = \underline{k}$. There are only two possible cases.

    (i) If $\theta_B^* f'(o) \leq y^*$ and $f'(L_A^*) \geq k°g'(o)$ then type-B sites are never active and gathering is never used. The sedentism rate S remains at zero.

    (ii) If $\theta_B^* f'(o) > y^*$ and $f'(L_A^*) < k°g'(o)$ there is some $T > o$ such that type-B sites are not active and gathering is not used for $t < T$, but type-B sites are active and gathering is used at type-A sites for $t \geq T$. The sedentism rate S^t approaches a limit S^* with $o < S^* < 1$.

Proposition 4.7 makes several points. First, when the climate amelioration is small, population does not grow enough to cause any qualitative change relative to the baseline VLRE. In the new LRE, there is still no sedentism and still no gathering. This is true for cases (a)(i), (b)(i), and (c)(i). Second, population growth can lead to sedentism while at the same time all food continues to be obtained from hunting. This occurs in case (a)(ii). Third, population growth may fail to generate sedentism because the type-B sites remain inactive, but there may be enough population growth to stimulate the use of gathering at the type-A sites. This occurs in case (b)(ii). Finally, when the climate amelioration is sufficiently large, Malthusian population growth eventually leads to both sedentism and gathering. This is true for cases (a)(iii), (b)(iii), and (c)(ii).

We conclude this section by showing that even if climate change plus population growth does not stimulate sedentism, these factors can trigger a process of technological innovation that does. The key idea is that population growth may not directly make sites of type B active, but it may cause agents at sites of type A to use gathering as well as hunting. Once gathering begins, learning by doing raises gathering productivity over time. This can eventually make the type-B sites active, thus yielding sedentism.

It is not hard to show that once gathering comes into use, it must remain in use. This is true for three reasons. First, even if gathering productivity remains constant, the fact that regional population is growing means that the local population at type-A sites is also growing. This scale effect implies that gathering continues to be used at these sites. Second, if learning by doing raises gathering productivity, there is a substitution effect that increases the incentive to use gathering at a given local population level. Third, the productivity growth leads to further regional population growth beyond what is caused by climate change alone. This reinforces the growth of local population at the type-A sites. Thus gathering cannot shut down at the type-A sites after it begins.

For this reason, the only way to reach a new very-long-run equilibrium is for the gathering productivity to reach a maximum value k^* at which opportunities for technical improvement are exhausted. It can be shown that as time goes to infinity, the probability of reaching the maximum gathering productivity k^* approaches one. The question we want to address here is whether type-B sites are active in the new VLRE associated with k^*. Proposition 4.8 resolves this issue.

Proposition 4.8 (very long run; climate plus population and technology).

Make the same assumptions as in Proposition 4.7, except that now the learning process from Section 4.7 begins whenever gathering is used, and therefore k is no longer constant. Assume case (a)(iii), (b)(ii), (b)(iii), or (c)(ii) from Proposition 4.7 applies, so population growth leads to gathering. In the cases (a)(iii), (b)(iii), and (c)(ii), sites of type B are active in VLRE. In case (b)(ii), sites of type B are active in VLRE if and only if $\theta_B^* k^* g'(o) > y^*$.

The results for cases (a)(iii), (b)(iii), and (c)(ii) are not surprising. We already saw in Proposition 4.7 that for these cases Malthusian population growth alone makes the type-B sites active, and therefore yields some sedentism even without technical change. The rise in gathering productivity induced by technical innovation reinforces this result.

What is more interesting is the result for case (b)(ii). From the definition of this case we have $\theta_B^* f'(o) \leq y^*$, so it is not possible to support a positive population at type-B sites by hunting alone. Thus population growth by itself, in the absence of technological change, cannot lead to sedentism. However, population growth does lead to gathering at the type-A sites. The resulting rise in gathering productivity (from k^o to k^*) can make the type-B sites active. This only occurs if $\theta_B^* k^* g'(o) > y^*$. The inequality indicates that it must become possible to support a positive population at type-B sites by gathering alone.

We can also make a definite prediction about the type-A sites that applies to all of the cases in Proposition 4.7. The following result holds regardless of whether or not there is any technological innovation with respect to gathering.

Proposition 4.9 (persistence of mobile activities).
Starting from the baseline VLRE defined as in Proposition 4.5, suppose the climate change described in A4.5 leads to a new VLRE. In the new VLRE, agents at the type-A sites must do some hunting.

One might imagine that if gathering became productive enough, the substitution effect would be so powerful that the type-A sites would abandon hunting completely and only gather. This argument is incorrect because it overlooks the fact that higher productivity for gathering also leads to a larger regional population in the long run, which increases the supply of labor at the type-A sites. This scale effect maintains the use of hunting at these sites, no matter how productive gathering may become.

4.10 DEMOGRAPHY AND LIVING STANDARDS

Many authors argue that sedentism raises fertility (Bocquet-Appel and Naji, 2006; Kelly, 2013a). In southwest Asia, sedentism was accompanied by a "fertility explosion"; and in both southwest Asia and Japan, sedentism was associated with larger settlements, higher site densities, and increased regional population (see Section 4.3). We show in this section that there are strong theoretical reasons why sedentary foraging will be associated with higher population levels than mobile foraging, other things being equal.

If we have higher fertility, clearly we must also have higher mortality in order for regional population to be constant in long-run equilibrium. It is often said that a lifestyle involving large permanent settlements increases mortality by causing greater exposure to infectious disease (see for example Scott, 2017, 96–113). While this is no doubt true, our theory predicts worse nutrition and shorter life expectancy even in the absence of disease.

Suppose that for any given level of food per capita, a sedentary lifestyle increases the number of surviving offspring per adult. This could result from less physical exertion by women, shorter periods of breastfeeding, greater paternal contributions in households, lower economic costs or higher economic benefits derived from offspring, or diminished infant mortality (Kelly, 2013a, 193–202, 209–213). Any of these factors would shift up the entire $\rho(y)$ function in Section 4.6 at each value of y.

As shown in Figure 4.3, this decreases the long run level of food per capita y^* at which the population is stationary ($\rho = 1$). Thus it lowers the long-run standard of living measured in food units, by comparison with a long-run equilibrium where foragers are more mobile. The intuition is that any factor apart from food income that raises fertility must be offset by a long-run reduction in food income in order to ensure the stationarity of the population. With technology and resources held constant, this reduction in food per capita requires a higher regional population by comparison with mobile foragers.

Further insights can be gained from a simple formal model (readers who prefer a verbal presentation can skip to the summary at the end of this section). For concreteness we focus on the cost of children. Suppose that women in mobile foraging groups find it difficult to carry two or more young children simultaneously, and try to limit these costs by engaging in prolonged breastfeeding or infanticide (see Section 2.6). A transition to sedentism might thus encourage women to have more children. Our model can also be interpreted in a context where the mechanisms are physiological and do not require any conscious choice about breastfeeding or infanticide, as we will discuss below.

We want to derive the function $\rho(y, v)$ where y is food income for an adult, v is the cost of a child to an adult, and ρ is the number of surviving offspring. Assume that an adult requires a $\geq$ 0 units of food to stay alive. If $y < a$, the adult dies and has no children. If $y \geq a$, the adult survives for one period with certainty. We only consider the latter case.

The adult must expend $v > 0$ units of food for each child. These are costs directly incurred by the adult, such as the calories used for carrying the child during infancy. The number of children is $q \geq 0$. After these expenses, the adult has the net food income $y - a - vq$, which is divided equally among the q children. Therefore the food intake per child is $z(q) = (y - a - vq)/q$.

Let $p(z)$ be the probability that a child having food intake z survives to adulthood, where $p(0) = 0$ and $p(\infty) = 1$ with $p'(z) > 0$ and $p''(z) < 0$ for all $z \geq 0$ so that the survival probability is increasing and strictly concave. We disregard any non-food-related reasons for childhood mortality. In one time period the adult collects food, has children, and dies. The

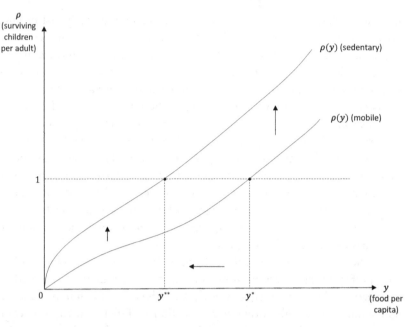

FIGURE 4.3. Effects of sedentism on long-run food income

children inherit their food bequests from the adult, and each child then survives with the probability $p(z)$ to become an adult in the next period.

Each child's survival is independent, conditional on food, so there is a binomial distribution for surviving children. The expected number of such children is $qp[z(q)]$. Ignoring integer problems, the adult chooses the quantity of children q to achieve

$$\rho(y, v) \equiv \max qp[z(q)] \text{ subject to } 0 \le q \le (y-a)/v \qquad (4.11)$$

where the upper bound on q comes from $z(q) \ge 0$ (children cannot have negative food).

Even if one does not believe that women in prehistory had significant conscious control over fertility (q), nature would have provided physiological mechanisms through which fertility responds to (y, v) in a manner that solves (4.11), because this maximizes the expected number of surviving offspring and would be favored by natural selection. Such mechanisms may include suppression of ovulation, a reduced probability of fertilization, and an increased rate of miscarriage when food is scarce and the cost of children is high.

In the case $y > a$, from $p(\infty) = 1$ we have $qp[z(q)] \to 0$ as $q \to 0$. Likewise from $p(0) = 0$ we have $qp[z(q)] = 0$ for $q = (y - a)/v$. Thus there is an interior solution $q(y, v) > 0$. The objective function is strictly concave in q so this solution is unique. We refer to $q(y, v)$ as the quantity of children and $p[z(q(y, v))]$ as the quality of children. We also sometimes call $q(y, v)$ fertility and $1 - p[z(q(y, v))]$ child mortality.

The first-order condition for (4.11) can be written as $p(z) = p'(z)(z + v)$. Treating this as an identity, it can be shown that z is an increasing function of v when food income (y) is held constant. Therefore when the cost per child (v) falls, as we expect with greater sedentism, the food intake per child (z) also falls. Hence $p(z)$ falls, and each child is less likely to survive. Because there is an inverse relationship between z and q, it follows that $q(y, v)$ must rise when the cost per child declines. Accordingly, sedentism causes adults to substitute in the direction of higher quantity and lower quality of children. As a result both fertility and child mortality increase at a fixed level of food income.

It can be shown that an increase in food income (y), holding the cost of children (v) constant, causes a linear increase in quantity but has no effect on quality. It can also be shown that the maximum value $\rho(y, v)$ is increasing in y and decreasing in v. From an economic standpoint $\rho(y, v)$ is just an indirect utility function that is increasing in income (y) and decreasing in price (v).

Continuing to assume that sedentism leads to a lower cost per child v, we want to know the consequences for long-run equilibrium. LRE requires $\rho(y^*, v) = 1$, where y^* is the level of food per adult that keeps population constant. In a comparison among such equilibria, the cost v and food income y^* must move in the same direction to maintain the expected number of surviving offspring constant at one per adult. Specifically, suppose a transition from mobile to sedentary foraging causes the cost per child to decrease from v_1 to $v_2 < v_1$. This shifts up the entire function $\rho(y, v)$ as shown in Figure 4.3, which implies that $y_2^* < y_1^*$ must hold in order to maintain $\rho(y_1^*, v_1) = \rho(y_2^*, v_2) = 1$. Therefore, in the long run, food income per adult also decreases. Other things equal, a lower y^* means that regional population N must be larger in order to obtain a lower average product of labor. Thus we predict a larger population when the cost per child is lower, as compared to a parallel situation where the cost per child does not change (that is, $v_1 = v_2$ so $y_1^* = y_2^*$).

We know from the first-order condition for (4.11) that if sedentism decreases v, it must also decrease z and $p(z)$. Because $qp(z) = 1$ holds for every LRE, this means that in the long run a transition from mobility to sedentism causes $q(y, v)$ to rise. In the notation of the preceding paragraph, $q(y_1^*, v_1) < q(y_2^*, v_2)$ so fertility is higher under sedentism.

Summary: We can now pull these conclusions together. Start from a reduction in the cost of children caused by sedentism. At any given food income, this raises fertility. In the long run the increase in fertility must be offset by a reduction in food income per adult because the number of surviving offspring per adult must stay fixed at one (this is the definition of long-run equilibrium). The decreased food income and lower cost per child cause adults to substitute toward more children with a lower survival probability for each child. This reduces life expectancy calculated at birth.

These effects are distinct from the health effects connected to more crowding and more transmission of infectious diseases in permanent settlements, although such effects could also occur. Indeed, the decreased food intake per child arising in our theory would weaken the immune systems of children and make them more vulnerable to disease.

A transition to sedentism may initially increase the rate of population growth but the *growth rate* falls to zero in LRE. However, sedentism does have a permanent effect on the *level* of population, because for any given technology and natural resources, the population must become larger in order for long-run food per capita to become smaller.

The model of this section is too simple to include effects of sedentism on adult diet and mortality (adult food consumption was fixed at a subsistence level and adults always lived for one period). In a more sophisticated model, sedentism could yield lower adult food consumption and higher adult mortality. Although a subsistence minimum is a helpful simplification for the purposes of this section, this notion is not part of our overall theoretical framework and will not be used in later chapters.

All of the effects described in this section are a matter of degree. A society could utilize a combination of mobile and sedentary food collection techniques, and in this case the cost per child (v) would depend on the average rate of sedentism.

4.11 RESOURCE DEPLETION

Archaeologists and anthropologists often use arguments about resource depletion to explain increases in dietary breadth, the transition to sedentism, and the transition to agriculture (see our discussion of Kelly, 2013a, in Section 4.2). A common story is that exogenous population growth leads to overharvesting of highly ranked prey such as large mammals. Eventually this leads to a focus on lower-ranked resources that are less easily depleted, such as rapidly reproducing smaller mammals, plants, or aquatic resources. For similar reasons, people might switch from mobile to stationary food resources, leading to greater sedentism, or from wild to cultivated plants, leading to agriculture.

There is an interesting symmetry between the resource depletion theories used in archaeology and our own Malthusian theory. Conventional archaeological theories treat population as exogenous, resource stocks as endogenous, and rely on exogenous changes in population to drive the depletion process, leading to social and technological change. Conversely, we treat resource availability as exogenous, population as endogenous, and rely on exogenous changes in resources to drive population dynamics, again leading to social and technological change.

In our view, the main problem with the traditional archaeological approach is the premise of exogenous population growth. The transitions with which we are concerned played out over centuries or millennia. On such time scales population must be treated as endogenous for the reasons discussed in Sections 2.6, 3.3, and elsewhere. We handle this problem through a Malthusian feedback loop where falling living standards lead to lower fertility and higher mortality, putting the brakes on population growth and leading to an equilibrium long-run population. These dynamics will tend to restrain the overharvesting of wild resources envisaged in the archaeological literature. There is no parallel problem for our theory because the effect of climate on resource abundance is clearly exogenous.

Before we consider the interaction between Malthusian population and resource depletion in more detail, it is important to be clear about the kind of depletion involved. First, in our theory we put great emphasis on exogenous changes in resource abundance due to climate change, so effects of this kind are included in our models. Second, to the extent that depletion effects are local and play out within one human generation, they are included through the diminishing marginal and average productivity of foraging labor. However, in our models the food resources grow back from one generation to the next. Therefore, depletion effects at the regional level or across generations are not included. Intergenerational resource depletion can lead to complex dynamics involving interactions between resource stocks and human populations. One influential example is the model of resource depletion on Easter Island constructed by Brander and Taylor (1998).

A reasonable economic model of a transition to sedentism or cultivation typically has the feature that local population (the number of people at a production site) must pass a threshold level in order to trigger the transition in question. In this context, depletion has two effects going in opposite directions: (a) a downward shift in the marginal product curve for the highly ranked resource, which tends to accelerate the transition by reducing the population threshold required for it to occur and (b) a lower long-run population due to the decreased productivity resulting from depletion, which makes it less likely that the population threshold will be crossed. The net effect is indeterminate, so it is difficult to obtain sharp predictions.

Agent-based simulation methods have recently been used to study the interactions among mobility, population density, and resource depletion (Gallagher et al., 2019). This framework endogenizes both population and resources. Not surprisingly, the authors find that when resources have high replenishment rates and low vulnerability to depletion, this tends to support more sedentism. They also find that sedentism is associated with lower mean food income, despite the absence from the model of the cost of children, crowding, or disease. The reason is that mobile foragers have more variance in their food incomes, and are at greater risk of falling below the subsistence level of food needed for survival. In equilibrium this is offset by a higher mean food income.

Although we agree that such interactions are of interest, we simplify our models by ignoring endogenous resource depletion and emphasizing the direct determination of resource abundance by nature. From a theoretical standpoint this enables us to show that resource depletion is not logically necessary to explain the transitions with which we are concerned. From an empirical standpoint we have not yet seen persuasive evidence that endogenous resource depletion was an important factor in the transitions to sedentism or cultivation. However, in our opinion the evidence favoring a causal role for exogenous climate change is quite convincing.

We do believe endogenous resource depletion was important for other phenomena in prehistory. For example, it seems likely that humans had a role in the mass extinctions of large mammals in Australia and the Americas (Riahi, 2020). It also seems quite likely that resource depletion contributed to numerous instances of social collapse.

We suggest a few ways in which empirical research might proceed. First, if an endogenous resource depletion process unfolds over centuries, traditional archaeological theory predicts that this should be accompanied by population growth because exogenous population growth drives the depletion. Our theory, on the other hand, predicts declining population or at least slower growth for Malthusian reasons, other factors held constant. Another distinction is that the traditional archaeological approach predicts falling living standards in the interval leading up to a transition involving sedentism or cultivation. By contrast, our Malthusian framework predicts that long-run living standards should remain roughly constant before such a transition, although living standards might fall afterward for the reasons we discussed in Section 4.10. We look forward to future archaeological findings that can disentangle these issues.

4.12 MORE ARCHAEOLOGICAL EVIDENCE

This section briefly summarizes what is known (or sometimes, not known) about non-agricultural sedentism in several regions beyond those discussed in Section 4.3. All of these cases will be discussed further in Chapter 5. After describing the evidence, we will offer a few thoughts on the implications for our theory.

Northern China: According to Shelach-Lavi (2015, 50–56), fewer than 20 very late (terminal) Pleistocene sites have been found in north China. Small stone tools, grinding stones, and ceramic vessels may have been part of a broad-spectrum hunter-gatherer strategy. The fact that ceramics are easily breakable and hard to transport suggests a "context of decreased mobility" (54). There are even fewer early Holocene sites in north China, and none is well documented.

Liu and Chen (2012, 46–51) believe that terminal Pleistocene sites show a high degree of hunter-gatherer mobility, with no evidence for storage facilities or residential structures. Based on site sizes, burials, and a range of technological features, they argue that early Holocene sites reflect a higher degree of sedentism (51–58).

Southern China: For the late Pleistocene, evidence of human occupation is found in caves (information in this paragraph is from Shelach-Lavi, 2015). Ceramic production dates back to 15,000–20,000 BP, the earliest in the world. The plant and animal species used were quite diverse. Open-air sites became common during the early Holocene, with some reflecting substantial expansion in community size. "House structures are found at most of the sites in the Yangzi River basin, together with formal burial pits, suggesting a transition to full-scale sedentism and the incipient development of village life" (59). There is an active debate about whether rice from these sites was domesticated (60).

Liu and Chen (2012, 61–64, 70–73) describe the early Holocene site of Shangshan in the Yangzi River region. They believe its "subsistence economy was characterized by the broad-spectrum strategy, relying on fishing, hunting, and collecting wild plants … [it was] a perhaps semi-sedentary or almost fully sedentary village" (72). They also state that technological innovations involving processing and storage for acorns and other nuts may have been prerequisites for a sedentary lifestyle. According to the authors, many of the features of this site parallel those of Jomon sites in Japan (see Section 4.3).

Saharan Africa: Manning and Timpson (2014) investigate population trends for the Sahara in the Holocene. The Sahara was much wetter between 12,000–6000 BP than today. This is known as the African Humid Period (AHP). In the early Holocene the region was occupied by mobile foragers, and in the mid-Holocene by pastoralists with domesticated cattle. The demographic trends include slow population growth before the AHP, a large increase shortly after 11,000 BP, a decline between 7600–6700 BP, a recovery during 6700–6300 BP, and a major collapse during 6300–5200 BP. The authors were unable to show a significant correlation between population and the available climate proxies, but argue that the synchronous nature of demographic change over a large geographic area indicates a causal role for climate.

Garcea (2006) provides details on subsistence technology for the central Sahara and upper Nile Valley. She asserts that in the early Holocene a combination of hunting, gathering, and fishing made it possible for foraging groups to develop settlements that were continually occupied and semi-permanent. This lifestyle evolved along perennial rivers (the Nile) or seasonal watercourses. Food included fish, plants, and land animals attracted to riverbanks by drinking water. Evidence for greater sedentism includes pits, house foundations, deep wells, and clusters of stone structures (western Egypt); pottery, large combustion structures, intra-site organization, and walled huts (southwest Libya); and thickness of deposits, frequency of burials, density of potsherds and animal bones, and the construction of huts (Sudan). "Late foragers in the Sahara and Sudan continually occupied the same sites for long periods of time throughout the year" (214). Greater sedentism facilitated pregnancy, birthing, nursing, and childcare, which caused population growth. This led to new technology (pottery by 9000 BP, ground stone tools by 6000 BP, and also bone harpoons and fish hooks). Grinding stones were used for processing wild grain, dried meat, and fish, as well as cracking nuts. In the 7th millennium BP, climate deteriorated and some Saharan groups moved to the Nile Valley. Around the beginning of the 6th millennium BP, some groups returned to the desert where they herded domestic animals. This transition to pastoralism occurred several millennia before farming of pearl millet developed in the southern Sahara and Sahel (see Chapter 5).

South America: The earliest stage of human occupation in the Americas is called the Paleo-Indian period and is associated with the hunting of now-extinct big game. The Archaic period comes after the Paleo-Indian period but before agriculture. Information in the next paragraph is from Moore (2014, ch. 4).

There is scattered evidence for Archaic sedentism in South America. At the end of the Pleistocene, people in southern Peru and northern Chile moved seasonally between the highlands and the coast, relying on fishing and mollusks from the latter. In the early Holocene, around 10,900–8900 BP, more permanent settlements emerged along the coast, indicated by post molds and a house floor. Travel into the sierra appears to have ceased. A group of 55 small sites emerged within one area, suggesting "more permanent coastal adaptations" (107). Similar settlements based on marine resources and sea birds arose elsewhere along the coast. At some coastal locations with freshwater sources in northern Chile, multiple lines of evidence indicate sedentism, including cemeteries with complex mummification practices. These traditions began around 7000 BP and lasted for nearly four millennia. Another well-watered location in southern Peru had three cemeteries, 75 terraced residential areas, and extensive shell middens. It was seasonally occupied in the Middle Archaic but became a permanent settlement in the Late Archaic. Moore does not mention any use of domesticated food sources at these sites.

Mesoamerica: The Archaic period in Mesoamerica (about 9000–4000 BP) has traditionally been seen as a transitional interval between Paleo-Indian big-game hunting and the emergence of pottery. The semi-arid highlands of central Mexico appear to have been occupied by mobile foragers throughout much of the Archaic (information is from Kennett, 2012). Although domesticated maize is not found in this area until the Late Archaic or after, domesticated squash may go back as far as 7900 BP. Similarly, in the Oaxaca Valley the main strategy seems to have been mobile foraging, despite dating of domesticated squash to 10,000 BP and domesticated maize to 6200 BP. These findings raise questions about the relationship between foraging and cultivation, although squash may have been used as a container rather than a food source. Matters are little clearer in the tropical lowlands, where many sites once located along the coast are now underwater. Some sites along the Pacific coast were used seasonally for mollusk harvesting, but these people may also have been swidden farmers. Because domesticated plants go back to the early Holocene (see Chapter 5), it is uncertain (at least to us) whether sedentary foraging without cultivation ever existed in Mesoamerica.

Eastern North America: The discussion here is based on Gibson (2006). A long tradition in the lower Mississippi Valley of building earthen mounds dates back to 7400–7300 BP. Most mounds could have been built by a few workers living in communities of a few dozen people. This practice peaked around 5600–5300 BP and then appears to have stopped for a long time. By far the largest such earthwork was built in 3700–3600 BP at Poverty Point in northeastern Louisiana. Construction is estimated to have taken at least a generation or two, and possibly a century or more. Over 2000 people, the Tamaroha, lived in the area, with more than four dozen villages and camps spread across 1800 square kilometers. No maize or other signs of cultivation have been found. Staple foods included fish and wild aquatic roots. Architectural evidence strongly suggests that the earthworks at Poverty Point were created by sedentary foragers who lived at the site year-round. The Tamaroha engaged in considerable techno-logical innovation, including a new cooking oven, redesigned hunting equipment, improved fishnets and hoes, and stationary facilities. The causes for the rise of the Tamaroha are unclear, but they provide a striking example of sedentism without agriculture.

Although the evidence is fragmentary, events in some of the regions described in this section are consistent with our theory. China, Saharan Africa, and South America all developed sedentary foraging in the early Holocene, perhaps in response to an improved climate. This process often appears to have been associated with population growth and techno-logical innovation. The situations for Mesoamerica and the Mississippi Valley are murkier. In all cases, we anticipate that archaeological research will supply new data that can be used to evaluate our theoretical framework.

4.13 CONCLUSION

We have defined sedentism to mean a willingness by some people to remain at a production site when weather conditions worsen. In our framework a time period is one human generation, so our theory is about the evolution of settlements that remain in use for decades or centuries, not merely years. Within a period we consider two kinds of sites, good and bad. Due to random weather shocks, sites that are good in one period may become bad in the next or vice versa. There are two methods of food collection, which for convenience we label "hunting" and "gathering." The former involves portable tools (whether aimed at plants or animals) and the latter involves stationary tools (again, whether aimed at plants or animals). In principle, sedentism as we define it is logically compatible with exclusive reliance on portable tools or "hunting."

We believe that climate change was the ultimate reason for increasing sedentism in the period leading up to the early Holocene. Our analysis starts from a climate where weather conditions have a low mean and high variance as at the Last Glacial Maximum. In the associated baseline equilibrium, only currently good sites are exploited and only "hunting" is used. Agents abandon a site whenever local weather conditions change from good to bad. We then consider an improvement in climate involving a higher mean and lower variance with respect to the distribution of weather conditions at individual sites.

Climate amelioration can lead to sedentism through three causal mechanisms. First, lower variance in weather conditions reduces the productivity gap between sites that are currently bad and sites that are currently good. Part of the regional population may therefore begin to use sites where the weather is currently bad. This implies that if the weather switches from good to bad at a particular site, some individuals will stay at that site, which fits our definition of sedentism. Second, in the long run a better climate yields population growth, which can lead directly to sedentism. Third, population growth can lead indirectly to sedentism through technological innovation.

The first two mechanisms are fully reversible, in the sense that if climate returns to its baseline state, this will set in motion an adjustment process that returns the system to the previous baseline equilibrium. This need not be true for the third mechanism that involves technical change. If innovations are always preserved once they are achieved, there is a ratchet effect where the productivity of gathering remains above its baseline value, population can remain above its baseline level, and sedentism can be preserved even if climate returns permanently to its baseline state.

Our theory is consistent with the fact that sedentism arose earliest and most often in temperate zones, where climate amelioration probably had the greatest proportional impact on natural productivity, rather than in tropical rain forests, deserts, or the Arctic. This would be expected for two reasons. First, the initial gap in productivity between good and bad sites was probably substantial in temperate areas. The subsequent large reduction in this gap would lead to sedentism through the first causal mechanism above. Second, the large proportional gain in mean productivity in temperate areas led to large responses in the form of Malthusian population growth. This provided more scope for our second and third causal mechanisms to operate. These implications seem consistent with the chronology of sedentism in southwest Asia and Japan set out in Section 4.3, and possibly with events in some of the regions discussed in Section 4.12.

We have addressed issues involving demography and living standards (in Section 4.10) and resource depletion (in Section 4.11). We close with a few comments on dietary breadth, property rights, investment, and site heterogeneity.

Dietary Breadth: The model has implications for dietary breadth among foragers. A transition to sedentism involving our short-run causal mechanism (direct improvement in the quality of previously poor sites) does not imply any change in the food resources being exploited. A transition involving our long-run mechanism (Malthusian population growth without technological change) likewise does not imply any change in the nature of food resources. However, in our analysis a transition with technological innovation is always associated with the exploitation of new food resources. Our model predicts that this will occur first at sites with good weather conditions, and that previously exploited resources will remain in use at these sites as technology improves. Thus dietary breadth increases at such sites. This is consistent with the frequent comments by archaeologists that sedentism is associated with broad-spectrum food acquisition strategies.

Property Rights: Reliable concentrations of natural resources tend to encourage both sedentism and the defense of property rights (Baker, 2003; Bowles and Choi, 2013, 2019). Allowing insiders to exclude outsiders from favorable sites would reinforce our conclusions, because agents trapped at sites where weather conditions have become bad will then face more difficulty in moving to a better site. Our definition of sedentism is based on the degree to which people remain at sites when weather conditions deteriorate, so closed access would tend to raise the rate of sedentism for the region as a whole. This is related to the idea of population packing in anthropology (see Kelly, 2013a). For more on the origins of group property rights over production sites, see Chapter 6.

Investment: Another factor that can reinforce a transition to sedentism is the role of investments in durable capital. Returning to our

metaphorical definition of "gathering" as a technology involving stationary assets, here we have treated such assets as automatic by-products of
technological knowledge about "gathering." In reality, labor time has to
be taken away from food collection in order to create durable equipment
and structures. The existence of secure property rights would encourage
these investments. In turn, reliance on stationary assets would encourage
agents to stay at a site despite weather shocks, thus reinforcing sedentism.

Site Heterogeneity: In this chapter we emphasized positive climate
trends as a basis for sedentism. However, suppose some of the sites within
a region are consistently better than others, perhaps due to more reliable
fresh water or more diverse ecosystems. A negative region-wide climate
shock could disproportionately decrease productivity at sites of lower
quality, causing migration from locations with poor permanent resources
to those with richer permanent resources (e.g., from arid zones to river
valleys). The short-run effect would be a local population spike at the
higher-quality sites. As in Section 4.9, this local population spike can
lower the marginal product of mobile food collection, lead to use of
new food resources, and promote innovation involving the new resources.
The result could be a tendency toward sedentism at the refuge sites. This is
consistent with our narrative for southwest Asia in Section 4.3, where the
cool and arid conditions of the Younger Dryas seem to have led simultaneously to more mobility for people in locations having few permanent
geographic or ecological advantages, but continued or expanded settlements in favorable locations. We suggest in Chapter 5 that a dynamic of
this kind can help explain the transition to agriculture in southwest Asia.

4.14 POSTSCRIPT

This chapter is based on an article entitled "The origins of sedentism:
Climate, population, and technology" in the *Journal of Economic
Behavior and Organization* (Dow and Reed, 2015). Funding was pro-
vided by the Social Sciences and Humanities Research Council of Canada
(SSHRCC) and the Human Evolutionary Studies Project (HESP) at Simon
Fraser University. We extend thanks to Peter Stahl and the audience at a
conference of the Canadian Economics Association for comments on the
original paper. The resulting opinions are our own.

Section 4.1 has been completely rewritten. Sections 4.2 and 4.3 include
updates on the relevant literatures. We are especially grateful to Andrew
Garrard of the Institute of Archaeology at University College London for

advice about the literature on southwest Asia discussed in Section 4.3. The model in Sections 4.4–4.9 is formally identical to the one in the *JEBO* article but the text has been lightly edited. Sections 4.10, 4.11, and 4.12 are entirely new. We were generally aware of the archaeological information in Section 4.3 when we constructed the model, although not all the details from recent publications. We did not know about the archaeological evidence in Section 4.12. The conclusion in Section 4.13 has been rewritten to reflect changes elsewhere in the chapter.

5

The Transition to Agriculture

5.1 INTRODUCTION

The importance of the transition to agriculture is almost impossible to overstate. Agriculture stimulated the spread of hereditary inequality and organized warfare, and was necessary for cities and states. Modern civilization could not exist without it. While the development of agricultural societies was slow, this process deserves the label "Neolithic Revolution" for the sheer scale of its impact.

The origin of agriculture is probably the most debated question in archaeology (Bellwood, 2005, 14–28). It has also become a central concern for economists studying economic growth in the very long run. Before agriculture, technological innovation and population growth were unusual. After agriculture, they became commonplace. Further, as we will discuss in Section 12.3, there are strong correlations between the timing of the Neolithic Revolution across regions of the world and the modern economic performance of the nations located in those regions. A substantial group of economists believes that these correlations reflect causal dynamics unfolding over many millennia.

There is wide agreement that the most influential domestications were wheat and barley in southwestern Asia, rice in southern China, and maize in Mesoamerica. Some authors identify around 8–10 independent centers of plant domestication (Balter, 2007); others identify as many as 24 (Purugganan and Fuller, 2009). We consider nine pristine centers: southwest Asia, northern China, southern China, Mesoamerica, South America, highland New Guinea, sub-Saharan Africa, eastern North America, and India.

From these pristine centers, agriculture diffused to most parts of the globe. We will not examine diffusion mechanisms here. For an archaeological study of the diffusion of agriculture from southwest Asia to Europe, see Shennan (2018). For economic studies of diffusion, see Ashraf and Michalopoulos (2015) and Matranga (2017).

Among pristine centers, southwest Asia has the most complete data documenting the transition from (a) gathering of wild plants to (b) cultivation to (c) domestication and finally to (d) fully agricultural societies. Cultivation refers to activities such as planting, weeding, and otherwise tending plants prior to harvest, rather than simply harvesting the plants supplied by nature. Domestication refers to genetic changes in plants caused by the practice of cultivation (Nesbitt, 2002; Tanno and Willcox, 2006; Weiss et al., 2006; Balter, 2007). Following Price and Bar-Yosef (2011, S165) we use the term "farming" to mean the utilization of domesticated plants and/or animals for food and other purposes. We use the term "agriculture" to mean that farming and/or herding predominate among the activities of a community and provide its main diet.

The overall process from (a) to (d) took many thousands of years. Domesticated plants and animals were frequently accompanied for millennia by continued hunting and gathering before a completely agricultural economy arose. Gathering wild plants was a necessary first step in this process. Once cultivation began, from an economic standpoint it is not hard to understand the rest of the events in the sequence: the productivity of plant and animal exploitation increased over time due to learning by doing and domestication, and habitat for wild plants and animals was gradually destroyed by farming. Eventually this led to the displacement of foraging activities by agriculture. The origin of cultivation is the critical puzzle to be solved and provides the focal point for this chapter.

How can one explain the long lag between the evolution of modern humans and the shift to cultivation? Consider southwest Asia, which had a significant population of modern humans by 50,000 BP. Numerous grass species, including cereals that were later domesticated, were being gathered for food by at least 23,000 BP (Weiss et al., 2004). It then took over 10,000 years to move from gathering to cultivation (see Section 5.3). The transition from cultivation to fully domesticated plants and animals may have taken one or two millennia, with the transition to farming and finally agriculture requiring another one or two millennia.

The southwest Asian transition, like several other agricultural transitions, dates to around the Pleistocene–Holocene boundary. This suggests a common cause, and indeed a number of authors have pointed to climate change as a leading suspect behind the origins of agriculture. Richerson et al. (2001) assert that agriculture was impossible in the most recent Ice Age because prevailing climate conditions (low temperatures and atmospheric CO_2 levels, extreme aridity, and large fluctuations on time scales of a decade or less to a millennium) severely limited returns on investments in agriculture. They argue that the warm, wet, and stable conditions of the Holocene encouraged cultural evolution toward reliance on specialized plant resources, leading ultimately to agriculture.

We agree that climate change was the trigger for cultivation in southwest Asia. However, we believe the role of climate was more complex than just a simple transition from poor conditions in the Pleistocene to good conditions in the Holocene. Following the Last Glacial Maximum, warmer and wetter conditions indeed led to abundant wild resources, population growth, and a sedentary lifestyle in southwest Asia as discussed in Section 4.3. This idyllic period ended around 13,000 years ago with an abrupt climate reversal, the Younger Dryas, in which colder and drier conditions returned. As we will discuss in Section 5.3, the timing of the first cultivation in southwest Asia is a matter for archaeological debate, but we believe that on balance the evidence supports initiation in the Younger Dryas.

Our causal explanation for the origins of cultivation during the Younger Dryas can be summarized as follows. Consider a region having many food production sites of varying quality, suppose there are many sedentary settlements in the region, and assume settlements are small enough to allow community decision-making with regard to food acquisition strategies. For simplicity let cereals be the only source of food and assume there are only two ways to obtain food: Gathering cereals or cultivating cereals. Because food is shared equally, the goal of each community is to maximize total food output.

Gathering and cultivation can be used in any combination by having some people engage in one and some in the other (or having individuals divide their time between the two). Each activity exhibits diminishing returns to labor: the additional food produced by an additional worker (the marginal product of labor) falls as more labor is devoted to that activity. Suppose that initially the marginal product of gathering exceeds the marginal product of cultivation. As long as this remains true, food output is maximized when all members of the community engage in gathering. But as more workers are added to the gathering activity, eventually the marginal product of gathering declines to a point where it is below the marginal product of the first worker who could potentially be employed in cultivation. Beyond that point, the maximization of total food output requires that some labor be used for cultivation.

For a graphical illustration of these ideas, see Figure 3.2 in Chapter 3, where we interpret the higher marginal product curve as gathering and the lower marginal product curve as cultivation, rather than interpreting the curves as referring to different resources. For any community size below the threshold N^a shown in Figure 3.2, all labor is allocated to gathering, and for any community size above this threshold, some (but not all) labor is allocated to cultivation.

The question is what caused the sizes of settlements to increase so that it became optimal for some people to engage in cultivation. In our framework this resulted from migration among communities, where the migration process was triggered by climate change. We argue that a long period of good climate with abundant rainfall supported a high regional population, although the sizes of individual settlements were not yet large enough to induce cultivation. A climate shock in the direction of decreased rainfall (the Younger Dryas) reduced productivity throughout the region, but by proportionally more at sites with limited access to surface water relative to sites with rivers, lakes, marshes, or springs. This caused migration toward the latter sites, which served as refuge locations. Because the large regional population was forced through a narrow geographic bottleneck due to the limited number of refuge sites, there was a spike in local labor supply at these sites. This pushed such settlements beyond the size threshold required for cultivation.

We also explore long-run dynamics. One might think that with a recovery from the Younger Dryas and higher rainfall during the Early Holocene, population would once again disperse across the region, refuge settlements would lose population through out-migration, and cultivation would be abandoned in favor of a renewed focus on gathering. But after cultivation began, learning by doing gradually raised its productivity relative to gathering and this process preserved incentives for cultivation. This technological factor was reinforced by regional population growth in the Holocene, which tended to keep the sizes of many settlements above the threshold for cultivation. The resulting trajectory in southwest Asia led to domestication and fully agricultural societies.

In our model of this process, climate and geography are the exogenous variables. Climate change serves as the trigger, and geography is import-ant because heterogeneity across production sites within a region is needed in order for climate change to generate migration effects.

Cultivation is a short-run response to these migration effects, while in the long run, population and technology respond endogenously to climate.

We do not claim that the mechanism outlined above applies in every case, even if one accepts the fundamental role of climate change. We showed in Chapters 3 and 4 that technological innovation could be triggered by climate shocks of various kinds, such as biased negative shocks, biased positive shocks, and neutral positive shocks. The process we suggest for the southwest Asian region combines a neutral negative climate shock at the regional level with a bias generated by migration effects at the local level.

Similar dynamics may help to explain agricultural origins in China, sub-Saharan Africa, and other regions (see Section 5.10). However, we do not argue that the Younger Dryas was the specific climate trigger in all cases. For example, pristine agriculture arose in sub-Saharan Africa many millennia later, and we suggest that this occurred in response to a different negative climate shock, although the causal processes leading to cultivation appear to resemble those that played out much earlier in southwest Asia. Furthermore, in certain regions the Holocene itself may have functioned as a large positive shock that led to population growth and local densities sufficiently high to trigger cultivation. While we view climate change in some form as the most likely exogenous trigger, the causal details may well have varied considerably from one region to another.

Whether one prefers causal explanations based on climate change or other factors, in our view an adequate theory of the agricultural transition should address the following questions. Why were there relatively few pristine transitions? Why were there no such transitions in previous interglacial periods, in the last glacial period, or during the initial warming that followed the Last Glacial Maximum? Why were pristine transitions rare in tropical rainforests? Why did agriculture not emerge in the Holocene in some promising regions with large sedentary populations, sophisticated technologies, and complex social organization? Why did agriculture begin in places where natural resources were locally abundant, rather than marginal areas? We argue that our theory offers coherent answers to these questions, while competing explanations often fail to do so (see Section 5.11).

The rest of the chapter is organized as follows. Section 5.2 reviews a number of proposed causal explanations for the origins of agriculture. Section 5.3 summarizes the archaeological evidence for southwest Asia. We begin the construction of our formal model in Section 5.4. Short-run and long-run equilibrium are studied in Sections 5.5 and 5.6. We use the model to study the dynamics of the southwest Asian case in Section 5.7. Following this, Sections 5.8 and 5.9 discuss how the model addresses population trends and living standards.

We survey other agricultural transitions in Section 5.10 and important examples of non-transition in Section 5.11. These cases provide evidence that can be used to assess competing theories. Section 5.12 addresses the role of biological endowments, a factor emphasized by Diamond (1997). Section 5.13 briefly summarizes our contributions. These include creating an empirically grounded explanation for pristine cultivation; showing that biased climate change, a frequent assumption in other work, is unnecessary and problematic; identifying heterogeneous production sites and migration as key causal factors; and endogenizing population and technology, which have often been treated as exogenous in previous theories. Section 5.14 is a short postscript. Proofs of the formal propositions are available at cambridge.org/economicprehistory.

5.2 THEORIES OF AGRICULTURE

Due to the vast scale of the literature, we will be highly selective in our review. We first consider theories from archaeology and then theories from economics.

Among archaeologists, one early advocate of a link between climate change and agriculture was V. Gordon Childe (1951, 67–72), who argued that reduced precipitation in arid sub-tropical regions forced animals, plants, and humans to retreat to springs and streams where water remained available. Childe believed that this process likely led to animal domestication. He thought that plant cultivation began earlier, perhaps in river valleys subject to annual flooding such as the Nile. Childe's approach fell out of favor because he lacked data on climate as well as the location and timing of early cultivation.

During the 1960s and 1970s, archaeological attention shifted to theories based on population pressure (for references, see Weisdorf, 2005; Price and Bar-Yosef, 2011). The "marginal zone" hypothesis suggested that population pressure would be felt first in areas with fewer foraging resources, and thus such areas would be the first to engage in agriculture. The "nuclear zone" hypothesis suggested the opposite: areas having a rich resource endowment would allow foragers leisure time to experiment with agriculture. Both arguments stressed the alleged effects of living standards on technical change.

From our standpoint, theories relying on population pressure as an exogenous variable are problematic for several reasons. First, in the short run people may migrate from areas with low food per capita to areas with high food per capita, and this tends to erode differences in living standards across sites. Second, in the long run, differences in living standards across sites tend to disappear due to Malthusian dynamics. Third, in the absence of external shocks, population stabilizes at an equilibrium level as in Chapters 2–4.

In recent decades numerous archaeologists have returned to climate explanations. Bar-Yosef and Meadow (1995) and Bar-Yosef (2011) argue that cold and dry conditions during the Younger Dryas caused yields from wild cereal stands to decrease in southwest Asia, which provided incentives for cultivation. Bar-Yosef (2011) extends this argument to explain the origin of cultivation in China. Similarly, Hillman et al. (2001) suggest that the Younger Dryas drove foraging populations to cultivate staples in southwest Asia.

A common climate story among archaeologists is that climate change caused the natural range of valuable wild plants to move away from existing settlements, leaving the inhabitants with an unpleasant choice between staying in place and giving up important staple foods, or moving to follow these foods while giving up other advantages of their current location (perhaps reliable fresh water in a river valley). An alternative solution was to stay in place and cultivate the desired plants through increased inputs of human labor, as a substitute for inputs such as generous rainfall previously supplied by nature.

From an economic standpoint, the problem with this story is that it assumes the marginal product of cultivation labor for the desired plants somehow increased, at least in comparison with the marginal product of foraging, because otherwise cultivation would not become attractive. However, climate change was taking away complementary inputs such as rainfall, and thus shifting down the entire marginal product curve for cultivation. To meet this objection, one could maintain that the marginal product curve for foraging shifted down even more. But arguments based on biased climate shocks of this kind run into other difficulties, as we will discuss later in this section and in Section 5.13.

Another strand in the literature involves human behavioral ecology (HBE). This school of thought borrows concepts like marginal valuation and opportunity cost from microeconomic theory. HBE has a close connection to dietary breadth models and sees agriculture as a rational response to changes in resource availability (Winterhalder and Kennett,

2006). Such changes could arise through climate shifts, population pressure, technological innovation, or resource depletion.

We share HBE's emphasis on constrained optimization by individual agents. Our approach differs primarily by devoting attention to longer time periods, social aggregates, and system-level dynamics. We sympathize with the view that archaeologists should make greater use of economic concepts such as risk, discounting, economies of scale, and transaction costs in understanding the development of agricultural societies (Winterhalder and Kennett, 2009), although our own model of initial cultivation does not employ these concepts. In particular, we assume agents are risk neutral, in contrast to a common focus on risk aversion among archaeologists (e.g., Bar-Yosef, 2011), largely because we want to construct tractable models and do not need risk aversion in order to obtain our results. We also want to avoid explanations based on unobservable risk preferences.

Some archaeologists highlight cultural or institutional factors, such as religion or status competition, as potential prime movers for agriculture. As Zeder and Smith (2009) point out, proposals along these lines have not garnered much support. Zeder and Smith, like many archaeologists, view all "single-factor models" or "universal causes" as dubious. They stress the unique features of particular regional transitions and prefer multivariable explanations that incorporate climate, demography, economics, biology, social structures, and cultural belief systems.

At this point we would remind readers of our arguments in Chapter 1 about the virtues of simple models. But we also note that our own framework is not a single-factor model, despite the prominent role we give to climate change as a trigger. It also includes geographic, technological, and demographic factors, and requires that multiple necessary conditions be satisfied in order for a pristine transition to occur (see Section 5.11).

We now turn to research by economists. The main ideas in this literature involve property rights and resource depletion, technological innovation, and climate change. For convenience we organize the discussion according to these categories. However, some of the hypotheses discussed below involve multiple factors. For surveys of earlier work by economists, see Locay (1989, 1997), Pryor (1983, 1986, 2004), and Weisdorf (2005).

Property Rights and Resource Depletion: Economists have sometimes argued that foraging societies suffered from overharvesting of wild resources due to an open access property regime, and that this tragedy of the commons was exacerbated by population growth. As a consequence, private property and agriculture became attractive (Smith, 1975; North and Thomas, 1977). Marceau and Myers (2006) develop a more elaborate resource depletion story. They suggest that modest foraging capabilities were compatible with the existence of a grand coalition that restrained overharvesting. After technology advanced to a certain point, the grand coalition collapsed, overharvesting prevailed, and it became attractive for smaller coalitions to abandon foraging in favor of agriculture.

Riahi (2020, 2021a, 2021b) focuses on domestication of animals rather than plants. He argues that the extinction rates for large mammals were tied to the timing of hominin dispersals across continents. The resulting coevolution of hominins and megafauna influenced the pristine emergence and diffusion of agriculture. In contrast to archaeological emphasis on the broad-spectrum revolution (Section 3.10) and resource depletion (Section 4.11), Riahi examines the suitability of the surviving megafauna for domestication. He also provides an econometric analysis of pristine agricultural transitions.

Bowles and Choi (2019) continue in the tradition of linking property rights with agriculture, although without resource depletion. They argue that the decreased climate variance of the Early Holocene led to greater sedentism, that some sedentary groups with highly productive and concentrated resources developed private property institutions, and that some sedentary groups with private property also adopted farming. Bowles and Choi use evolutionary game theory to model these processes and emphasize two factors. First, a critical mass of individuals had to adopt private property institutions; and second, there was a positive feedback loop between farming and private property. This loop emerged because private property raised the payoffs from farming investments, while the outputs from farming were more conducive to the definition and defense of property rights than the outputs from foraging.

We agree with Bowles and Choi on some matters and disagree on others. We accept their view that early cultivation was no more productive than foraging and thus that the transition to cultivation did not have a technological trigger. We also agree that cultivation was not triggered by regional population pressure. However, we do not see private property as a necessary condition for early agriculture, and our formal model in this chapter shows how it could have developed under open access. We also differ from Bowles and Choi in our interpretation of the empirical evidence surrounding cultivation in southwest Asia, as will be discussed in Section 5.3.

The game-theoretic framework used by Bowles and Choi leads to two questions. First, how would it be possible to have two stable equilibria, one with foraging/common property and the other with farming/private property? Second, given two such equilibria, what would trigger a transition from one to the other? In contrast we rely on optimization at the local level and have unique equilibria at the regional level. Our central question is how a climate shock could move the system from a corner solution without cultivation to an interior solution with it. Unlike Bowles and Choi, we endogenize local and regional population, and we model technological innovation through learning by doing.

Our approach yields sharper predictions about the times and places of agricultural transitions, including some triggered by climate events later in the Holocene that were not related to the Younger Dryas (see Section 5.10). It also adds predictive content regarding population and productivity. On the other hand, Bowles and Choi offer predictions about family-level property institutions while we do not. Our theory of property rights, where groups rather than individuals or families control land, will be presented in Chapter 6.

Technology: Agriculture is sometimes portrayed as a technological breakthrough analogous to the light bulb. In this view, agriculture was invented by an astute group of pioneers and diffused rapidly as others recognized its benefits. This scenario is no longer taken seriously for several reasons. First, anthropological research has made it clear that foragers are knowledgeable botanists and certainly grasp the feasibility of planting seeds in order to obtain a harvestable crop. Second, there are many examples of foragers who lived close to farmers or traded with them but did not embrace farming (Bellwood, 2005, 28–43). Third, the hypothesis does not explain why agriculture arose in specific places and times, or why many millennia were needed to invent it.

Nevertheless, one can argue that a gradual accumulation of technical knowledge eventually made cultivation productive enough that it became attractive by comparison with foraging. Olsson (2001) suggests that improvements in agricultural productivity could have arisen as a by-product of foraging. Hibbs and Olsson (2004) and Olsson and Hibbs (2005) develop a model of long-run growth in which the pace of innovation in a region is an increasing function of that region's biogeographic endowment, including its suite of potentially domesticable plants and animals.

Weisdorf (2003) combines exogenously improving food production with satiation in food consumption to model the emergence of a non-food-producing sector, which he identifies with the creation of food surpluses under agriculture. Weisdorf (2009) argues that rising agricultural productivity was the central reason for the adoption of agriculture, and Guzmán and Weisdorf (2011) assume explicitly that productivity for agriculture was higher than for foraging.

Baker (2008) presents a model where agricultural adoption depends on population density, technological sophistication, and natural resources. A key assumption is that the improvement of a general-purpose technology tends to increase total factor productivity more for agriculture than for foraging. Ashraf and Michalopoulos (2011, 2015) propose that mild climate stress led to changes in foraging techniques, causing more investment in tools, infrastructure, and habitat clearance. In turn, this caused the latent productivity of agriculture to rise until a threshold was crossed and agriculture was adopted.

We agree that foraging activities could yield knowledge that would be useful for agriculture (for example, the development of sickles to harvest wild cereals). But in a foraging society, learning by doing seems more likely to raise foraging productivity than agricultural productivity. We doubt that agricultural productivity in a given region would have risen significantly in relation to foraging before cultivation had begun in that region. Accordingly, we are skeptical about hypotheses where increases in the latent productivity of cultivation play a central role in triggering a transition.

Climate Change: As discussed earlier, archaeologists often treat climate change as a trigger for the Neolithic transition. However, such arguments can run into difficulty. If the climate improves, why doesn't productivity rise equally for foraging and cultivation? If the climate deteriorates, why doesn't productivity fall equally for both?

The model constructed by Olsson (2001) includes the possibility that changes in climate were biased toward agriculture or against foraging. In particular, Olsson favors the view that conditions in southwest Asia deteriorated less for agriculture than foraging. Observe, however, that if this is true, the climate recovery of the Holocene should have restored foraging, which it did not. Other hypotheses involving direct climate biases are vulnerable to similar objections, unless they incorporate some kind of path dependence. Ashraf and Michalopoulos (2011, 2015) rely on a different type of bias by arguing that mild climate stress promotes technological innovation biased toward cultivation. Given the lack of persuasive archaeological evidence for either direct or technically mediated climate biases, we remain doubtful about hypotheses of this sort.

Matranga (2017) emphasizes a different climate dimension: seasonality. He notes that Earth's orbital parameters lined up in the Early

Holocene in a way that tended to raise seasonal variation in temperature and precipitation across the Northern Hemisphere. The causal argument is that greater seasonality increased incentives for sedentism and storage, and that sedentism facilitated a transition to agriculture. He stresses that seven centers of pristine agriculture were all highly seasonal, and establishes that agriculture spread more quickly in areas where the weather had more pronounced seasonal patterns. A limitation of Matranga's approach is that he only offers a story about the shift from mobile foraging to sedentary foraging with food storage, not the full shift from sedentism to agriculture.

5.3 THE TRANSITION IN SOUTHWEST ASIA

Roberts et al. (2018) provide a detailed history of climate conditions in southwest Asia during 16,000–9000 BP (see also Robinson et al., 2006; Bar-Yosef, 2011; Maher et al., 2011; Henry, 2013, and Section 4.3). Roberts et al. synthesize lines of evidence such as stable isotope measurements from speleothems and lake and marine sediments, along with pollen and charcoal data for a variety of species.

There are four phases. The coldest and driest spans 16,000–15,000 BP, and is associated with the Heinrich I climate event. Archaeologically, this corresponds to the Kebaran culture. Climate became warmer and wetter in the Bølling/Allerød interstadial of 15,000–13,000 BP, which corresponds to early Natufian culture. The third phase is the Younger Dryas stadial, bringing a reversal to colder and drier conditions during 13,000–11,700 BP and corresponding to late Natufian culture. Finally, warm and wet conditions returned in the Early Holocene starting around 11,700 BP. Archaeologically, the period 11,700–10,500 BP is known as the Pre-Pottery Neolithic A (PPNA).

There is some debate about the exact timing of the Younger Dryas in the Levant. For example, according to Bar-Yosef (2011, S180), worsening conditions probably began around 12,600/12,500 BP rather than 13,000 BP (see also Rohling et al., 2002; Mayewski et al., 2004; Sima et al., 2004). The duration of the Younger Dryas in the Levant could thus have been shorter than what is indicated by ice cores from Greenland or Antarctica. Such ambiguities are unsurprising because the confidence intervals for regional climate proxies in southwest Asia are on the order of ±200–500 years (Roberts et al., 2018, 51).

Roberts et al. believe climate changes were synchronous across the region subject to uncertainties about dates. There were two major warming steps, one at approximately 14,500 BP and the other at approximately 11,700 BP. "These abrupt and sustained shifts in climate, with mean temperatures rising by up to 1°C per decade, had dramatic consequences for environmental resource availability and would have been felt directly within an individual human lifetime" (51).

Ohalo II, a site dating to 23,000 BP, provides the earliest evidence for extensive gathering of wild plants in southwest Asia. This site was submerged under the Sea of Galilee and discovered in 1989 after water levels dropped dramatically. The inhabitants gathered a broad range of grains (Weiss et al., 2004). A significant portion of their diet consisted of small-seeded grasses, far smaller than the wild cereals we associate with the origin of agriculture (which were utilized as well). At this time of extreme aridity, much of southwest Asia was thinly populated or unoccupied. People lived in small campsites in groups ranging from one to five families and pursued a nomadic lifestyle.

Early Natufian communities flourished in southwest Asia in the warm and wet Bølling/Allerød period (Bar-Yosef, 2002b, 2002c). Population grew substantially and some people became sedentary (see the references from Section 4.3). Food was plentiful and skeletal evidence shows few signs of trauma, suggesting little conflict among groups. Migration and settlement patterns closely followed changes in biomass, which in turn were largely determined by the amount and distribution of winter rains. This way of life lasted more than 1,500 years.

The formal model to be developed in Sections 5.4–5.7 is largely inspired by data from Abu Hureyra, a village located on the ecotone between the Euphrates River Valley and the woodland-steppe in what is today northeast Syria. Hillman et al. (2001, 383) date the start of the village to approximately 13,500 BP, although others have dated it to about 13,100 BP (Colledge and Conolly, 2010). In either case there is agreement that the initial occupation occurred during the late Bølling/Allerød. Thereafter Abu Hureyra provides a sequence of archaeological deposits extending through the Younger Dryas and into the Early Holocene, spanning more than 3,000 years. The information below is from Moore et al. (2000) and Hillman et al. (2001). We will review a number of debates about their arguments later in this section.

Excavation uncovered two superimposed settlements. Abu Hureyra 1 (AH1) was inhabited by sedentary foragers. The remains of food plants from 13,500 BP reflect a diverse diet typical of hunter-gatherer societies. There is no evidence for the cultivation of crops here or at any Natufian site before the Younger Dryas.

The use of several wild foods, including some caloric staples, fell rapidly in the early stages of the Younger Dryas. The order in which species declined was (i) drought-sensitive fruits and nuts, (ii) lentils and other large-seeded legumes, (iii) wheats and ryes, (iv) feather grasses, and (v) chenopods. This is consistent with advancing desiccation. Foods of types (i) and (ii) disappeared entirely while those of (iii), (iv), and (v) were used less heavily. Some staple foods from the river valley did not decline at all, probably due to regular over-bank flooding.

According to Moore et al. and Hillman et al., several lines of evidence indicate that cultivation began at Abu Hureyra 1 during the Younger Dryas. These include:

(a) *Weeds.* The decline in wild cereals was followed by the rapid rise of a weed flora typical of arid-zone cultivation involving substantial tillage. These weeds, which include small-seeded legumes, small-grained grasses, and dryland gromwells, are drought-sensitive and would not have replaced other plants without cultivation.

(b) *Cereals.* Wheats and ryes continued in use, albeit in smaller quantities, despite the YD having "almost certainly eliminated all wild stands from the area" (387). The authors argue that even under modern conditions no extensive stands of wild wheat or rye can grow within 60–70 km of Abu Hureyra. In the drier conditions of the YD, the nearest stands would have been even farther away.

(c) *Legumes.* Later in the YD lentils and other large-seeded legumes reappeared and increased in abundance, despite local absence for centuries and continuing aridity that would have prevented the natural re-establishment of wild stands.

The authors argue that cultivation of cereals and legumes would have been possible with clearance of competing scrub, soil tillage, and seeds obtained from distant wild stands. In their view, cultivation was precipitated by the decline in wild cereals and environmental stress was the trigger.

We note in passing that Hillman et al. (2001) advanced a claim for domesticated rye seeds at AH1 early in the YD. This alleged finding was eventually rejected due to a lack of corroborating evidence from sites elsewhere in the region, possible intrusion from higher levels of the excavation, doubts about the radiocarbon dating, and difficulties in distinguishing large wild seeds from domesticated seeds (Nesbitt, 2002; Balter, 2007; Colledge and Conolly, 2010). Accordingly, we will not comment further on this matter.

During the Younger Dryas, part of the Natufian population returned to a nomadic lifestyle (see Bar-Yosef and Meadow, 1995; Bar-Yosef, 2002b, 2002c). An alternative option was to migrate to sites in river valleys and on lake shores where water was nearby, and where expanses of fertile soils became available as rivers and lakes shrank due to aridity (Bar-Yosef, 2002b, 116; Mithen, 2003, 53). The migration of population to Abu Hureyra 1, implied by growth in its geographic size, is an example. The population of Abu Hureyra 1 rose to perhaps as many as 100–300 people at its maximum during the Younger Dryas. The absence of evidence for any violence or fortifications at Abu Hureyra 1 suggests that this migration process was peaceful.

Access to reliable water supplies and fertile soils also characterized the other sites in southwest Asia that had an early shift to agriculture (Smith, 1998). Bellwood (2005, 57) describes the sites in southwest Asia with the oldest potentially domesticated cereals as follows: "[A]ll were located near springs, lakes, or riverine water sources. Such sites include Jericho, Netiv Hagdud, Gilgal, Tell Aswad, Abu Hureyra, and Mureybet. Early agricultural sites elsewhere, such as Ali Kosh in Khusistan, had similar advantages."

Abu Hureyra 2 is dated from roughly 11,400 BP, that is, within the PPNA. The villagers were farmers who also collected wild plants and hunted game, but eventually became wholly dependent on domesticated plants and animals. The population increased rapidly to levels more than twenty times the population of Abu Hureyra 1 and surpassed almost all other contemporary sites in southwest Asia.

In the preceding narrative we outlined three central arguments for cultivation at Abu Hureyra during the Younger Dryas. We turn now to archaeological debates about these claims, especially controversies over the role of arable weeds as an indicator.

Colledge and Conolly (2010) suggest that some "weeds" identified by Hillman et al. (2001) at AH1 during the YD could actually have been food items obtained without cultivation. In particular, they suggest that small legumes and small-seeded grasses were low-ranked foods that replaced other increasingly scarce high-ranked foods. The former were common in steppe ecosystems and would have been available as climate worsened (along with feather grasses and chenopods). They maintain that this provides a more parsimonious explanation than invoking cultivation, although "[w]ithout discounting entirely the possibility of cultivation of wild cereals and legumes" (124–125).

We agree that dietary substitution toward small legumes and small-seeded grasses is a plausible explanation for the increasing frequency of such seed remains. But we note that Colledge and Conolly do not make a similar argument for the third weed category of dryland gromwells, which were "stony seeded" and inedible, as well as drought-sensitive and therefore unlikely to rise in frequency in the absence of cultivation. We also note that they do not dispute the assertions by Hillman et al. regarding the absence of uncultivated wild cereals within a reasonable distance of Abu Hureyra during the Younger Dryas, or the return of large-seeded legumes at a time when arid conditions persisted. Therefore these lines of evidence for cultivation at AH1 still stand.

Partly in response to Colledge and Conolly's argument that some of the "weeds" at AH1 could have been food items, Willcox (2012) identified 19 weed taxa that have been recognized as arable weeds at later Neolithic and Bronze Age agricultural sites, and have no known human use. He argues that "arable weeds are probably the best indicator of pre-domestic cultivation when the crops were morphologically indistinguishable from their wild ancestors" (163). His main results are as follows. The LGM site of Ohalo II had two weed taxa. The Natufian sites of AH1 and Dederiyeh each had six. A group of PPNA sites with no domestication had between 9 and 16, while a group of later Neolithic sites with domestication had between 12 and 17. Willcox asserts that the similarity in the counts for the latter two groups indicates cultivation at the PPNA sites. For the Natufian sites of Abu Hureyra and Dederiyeh, he comments that the weed frequencies "are low but nevertheless present. Because of this we should not totally discount the possibility of cultivation at Natufian sites" (166).

Bar-Yosef (2011) adds Tel Qaramel, Mureybet, and Jerf el-Ahmar to the list of Natufian villages where arable weeds suggest cultivation in the Younger Dryas. In the last decade, the weed taxa identified by Willcox (2012) have become widely accepted as a way of inferring cultivation prior to domestication (see the references from Weide et al., 2021, 2) and have been used to support claims of cultivation during the Younger Dryas.

However, Weide et al. (2021) have recently criticized the conclusions of Willcox (2012). They compare the weeds in modern cultivated fields with weeds in modern wild cereal stands, all located in the Levant. They show that the identification of weeds at the species level does allow one to distinguish statistically between the cultivated and wild stands. However, the Willcox taxa are at the broader genus level and fail to distinguish between the two types of habitat. Hence, knowing whether the Willcox weed taxa were present or absent at a site would not assist with inferences about the presence or absence of cultivation at that site.

The issue for us is whether this critique sheds any light on the presence or absence of cultivation during the Younger Dryas. In considering this issue, one should recognize that different authors are asking different questions. Moore et al. (2000) and Hillman et al. (2001), along with Colledge and Conolly (2010), are concerned with the changing plant frequencies at one site (AH1) and whether these dynamics support the hypothesis of cultivation at that location. Willcox (2012) does not address these dynamics and instead compares the numbers of weed taxa across different sites observed at different points in time, although he does suggest that cultivation at AH1 should not be discounted.

Weide et al. (2021) make cross-sectional comparisons of modern sites with and without cultivation. They find that Willcox's taxa are not helpful in drawing inferences about the presence of cultivation, which calls into question the recent archaeological use of these taxa to infer cultivation at various PPNA and Younger Dryas locations. Susan Colledge (private communication) points out that there is a mismatch between Weide et al. and Willcox in the data on which their results are based. Weide et al. use present-day ecological differences at the species level. But it is rarely possible at pre-Neolithic sites to identify wild taxa beyond the genus level because preservation is usually too poor. New data from older sites will be required to refute or confirm Willcox's work.

We do not know how archaeologists will resolve this issue. But whatever the resolution may be, the Weide et al. findings have no relevance for the changes in plant frequencies observed at AH1 over time. For reasons discussed above, we believe that three lines of evidence for cultivation advanced by Hillman et al. (2001) remain intact.

We now turn to two further issues: the timing of domestication, and the length of the lag between cultivation and domestication. For cereals, peas, lentils, bitter vetch, and chickpeas – the early domesticates in southwest Asia – a key difference from wild varieties is that domesticated crops cannot reseed themselves. Therefore, if domesticated seeds are found, this indicates the existence of cultivation because the seeds in question must have been both planted and harvested, not just harvested. Harlan (1995), Smith (1998), and Moore et al. (2000), provide details on the morphological markers of domestication. According to Willcox (2012), the first domestic cereals in southwest Asia date to about 10,500 BP. Roberts et al. (2018, 48) date the PPNA and PPNB to 11,700–10,500 and

10,500–9000 BP, respectively. Thus the first domesticated seeds appear at the boundary of the PPNA and PPNB.

As we discussed above, claims for cultivation in the PPNA or the Younger Dryas often rely upon arguments about arable weeds, crops found far from their natural habitats, or other circumstantial evidence. A separate line of argument involves the lag from cultivation to domestication. Artificial selection (which may be unintentional) takes time, so there is inevitably some interval between the point at which cultivation begins and the point at which it results in observable domestication. For cereal crops in southwest Asia, in the early 1990s this lag was estimated at no more than a few centuries, perhaps much less (Hillman and Davies, 1990). However, subsequent archaeological research and field experiments overturned this view, resulting in a new consensus that the lag was at least a millennium (Tanno and Willcox, 2006; Balter, 2007).

Allowing a time lag of 1000 years from cultivation to domestication places initial cultivation at 11,500 BP, within two centuries of the boundary between the PPNA and the Younger Dryas. If the lag was actually 1500 years then cultivation began at about 12,000 BP. Larson et al. (2014) estimate that for southwest Asia, "documented exploitation" or "necessary lead-time to domestication" began by 12,000 BP for wheat, barley, lentil, flax, sheep, goat, and pig, and by 11,500 BP for peas and cattle. The date of 12,000 BP falls squarely within the Younger Dryas.

Next we return to our earlier discussion of Bowles and Choi (2019) from Section 5.2. We agree with these authors that morphologically domesticated seeds do not appear in southwest Asia until about 10,500 BP. But as discussed above, recent scholars accept lengthy lags between cultivation and domestication. Bowles and Choi characterize the relevant lag as "a matter of centuries" and are only prepared to grant that cultivation may have begun "at the very end of the Younger Dryas in Southwest Asia" (2194), although they do not think this is likely. But the recent consensus puts the lag at a millennium or more, providing substantial evidence that cultivation began in the Younger Dryas.

Bowles and Choi (2019, 2215–2216) interpret Abu Hureyra as a case in which sedentism led to private property, which then led to farming. We are not aware of any evidence for the evolution of family-level property rights at AH1 within the relevant time frame. But there is strong evidence for a negative climate shock at AH1, and there is also evidence for local population growth, which is consistent with the model we will develop in the next several sections.

In their discussion of Dow et al. (2009), Bowles and Choi (2019, 2220) suggest that we do not need climate adversity to obtain the local population growth that triggers cultivation in our story. This is correct, and in Section 5.10 we suggest that some pristine transitions to agriculture may have resulted from long-run Malthusian population growth generated by positive climate trends. But taking the various lines of evidence as a whole, we think it is more likely than not that initial cultivation in southwest Asia was triggered by the Younger Dryas. We recognize that future archaeological research may lead to a different conclusion. Nevertheless, we think the evidence is strong enough to warrant the exploration of causal mechanisms through which a negative climate shock could have led to initial cultivation. Sections 5.4–5.7 study one such mechanism.

5.4 THE PRODUCTION SITE

Our goal in the next several sections is to construct an initial equilibrium in which there is no cultivation at any site, and identify conditions under which a new equilibrium emerges with positive labor time allocated to cultivation at some sites. This parallels the analytic approach taken in Chapters 3 and 4.

We treat a region as having a continuum of food production sites, where people and technological knowledge can flow freely across sites. Informally, two sites are in the same region if the cost of moving between them is relatively low, and different regions if the cost of moving between them is relatively high. These costs could involve physical distance; geographic barriers such as mountains, deserts, or oceans; social barriers such as territoriality, strong norms against intermarriage, or differences in culture or language; technological barriers involving an inability to exploit unfamiliar natural resources; or informational barriers involving a lack of knowledge about the features of remote sites.

When regions are defined in this way, exogenous shocks such as climate change may cause populations to move among the sites within a region but not between regions. Changes in the aggregate population of a region are therefore driven by natural increase or decrease, not migration. On the other hand, migration is crucial for determining the local populations at particular sites within a region. Although our formal modeling will simplify by allowing any individual agent to locate at any site in a region, in practice we do not need this stark assumption to obtain our qualitative results. It is sufficient to have local populations move freely between adjacent sites, so that from an economic point of view all sites in the region are "in the same market" and adjustments in local populations rapidly erode differences in food per capita across sites.

We do not regard cultural diffusion or trade as sufficient evidence that two sites are in the same region. Our migration arguments involve changes in the distribution of population across production sites, and transmission of culture or objects is not enough to establish that this occurred. Moreover, our model of technology from Chapter 3 involves learning through observation, so transmission of a technique to a new location generally requires the physical movement of knowledgeable individuals.

A region may have many different plant species that are available for cultivation. We will aggregate all such plant species and consider only two sources of food: foraging and cultivation. The food from these sources is identical in consumption. This clarifies the main causal mechanisms at work, but one could build a similar model in which each species has unique ecological and technological characteristics.

Each agent is endowed with one unit of labor time. The production function for foraging at an individual site is $F(n_f, c, s)$ and the production function for cultivation at a site is $G(n_g, c, s)$, where $n_f \geq 0$ is foraging labor, $n_g \geq 0$ is cultivation labor, $c \in [0, 1]$ is climate, and $s \in [0, 1]$ is site quality. Climate is identical for all sites in the region and refers to average temperature and precipitation. Site quality is a permanent feature of a particular location, perhaps reflecting access to fresh water or fertile soil.

Assumption 5.1

$F(n_f, c, s)$ and $G(n_g, c, s)$ are twice continuously differentiable. When any input is zero, output is zero. When all inputs are positive, each input has a positive first derivative and a negative second derivative.

The adult population $(n \geq 0)$ at a given site allocates labor time to maximize the total food obtained from the site, where we define the maximum food to be

$$H(n, c, s) \equiv \max \ F(n_f, c, s) + G(n_g, c, s) \tag{5.1}$$
$$\text{subject to } n_f \geq 0, n_g \geq 0, \text{and } n_f + n_g = n$$

Proposition 5.1 (optimal time allocation).

Fix $(c, s) > 0$. The optimization problem in (5.1) has a unique solution. H is continuous in (n, c, s) and strictly concave in n for any given $(c, s) > 0$. The optimal (n_f, n_g) and the maximum food H are differentiable functions of (n, c, s) except possibly at the boundary $n = n^a(c, s)$ defined in (5.2) below.

We assume that when the local population n is sufficiently small, the marginal product of foraging exceeds the marginal product of cultivation even when all labor is allocated to foraging. However, when the population of a site becomes large enough, the diminishing marginal product of foraging eventually makes it attractive to put some labor into cultivation. Assumptions of this sort are standard in the economic literature on the origins of agriculture (Weisdorf, 2005). Similar assumptions were used in Chapters 3 and 4 (see Section 3.6 and Figure 3.2). We formalize this idea as follows.

Assumption 5.2

Fix $(c, s) > 0$. $F_n(0, c, s) = \infty$ and $F_n(\infty, c, s) = 0$, where the subscript n denotes differentiation. $G_n(0, c, s)$ is positive and finite, with $G_n(\infty, c, s) = 0$.

Next define the population threshold $n^a(c, s) > 0$ by

$$F_n[n^a(c, s), c, s] \equiv G_n(0, c, s) \qquad (5.2)$$

A5.2 implies that for $0 \leq n \leq n^a(c, s)$ it is optimal to set $n_f = n$ and $n_g = 0$ (zero cultivation), but for $n > n^a(c, s)$ it is optimal to set $n_f > 0$ and $n_g > 0$ (positive cultivation).

As discussed in Section 5.2, archaeologists have sometimes relied on exogenous population growth to explain the origins of agriculture. This might seem to be an obvious way in which to attain a population beyond the threshold $n^a(c, s)$ and trigger cultivation. But as we argued in Chapters 2–4, explanations based on exogenous population growth are unsatisfying. Instead, we endogenize local population through migration among sites in the short run, and we endogenize regional population through Malthusian dynamics in the long run. Migration will provide the trigger needed to initiate cultivation.

We have established in Chapters 3 and 4 that climate changes need not be directly biased for or against particular resources or techniques in order to affect time allocation. Similarly, in the present context we do not want to claim that the negative shock of the Younger Dryas was directly biased in favor of cultivation relative to foraging. This is partly because there is insufficient archaeological evidence to support such a claim, and partly because we want to make the theoretical point that such biases are unnecessary to explain the transition to agriculture. An indirect causal channel where the climate shock leads to migration across sites can do the job.

We say that climate and site quality are *neutral* if n^a is a constant that does not depend on (c, s). This is true if the production functions have the following multiplicative form:

Assumption 5.3

$$F(n_f, c, s) = A(c, s)f(n_f) \quad \text{and} \quad G(n_g, c, s) = kA(c, s)g(n_g)$$

where $k > 0$ is a productivity parameter. A5.3 implies that the population threshold n^a is a decreasing function of the cultivation productivity k, so it is easier to cross this threshold when the latent productivity of cultivation is higher. A5.3 also implies that total output has the form $H(n, c, s) = A(c, s)h(n)$ and that the optimal labor allocation (n_f, n_g) for a given n is independent of (c, s).

Food output per capita with the climate quality $c > 0$ and site quality $s > 0$ is

$$y(n, c, s) \equiv H(n, c, s)/n \tag{5.3}$$

By the strict concavity of H, output per capita (y) is decreasing in local population (n).

Lemma 5.1

Suppose A5.1–A5.3 hold. For any fixed $(c, s) > 0$ we have

(a) $\lim_{n \to 0} y(n, c, s) = \infty$
(b) $\lim_{n \to \infty} y(n, c, s) = 0$

As we will explain in Section 5.6, this guarantees that it is possible to support a positive regional population in the long run. In contrast to Chapters 3 and 4, there is no need to consider cases where the equilibrium population is zero.

5.5 SHORT-RUN EQUILIBRIUM

Because the region as a whole has many individual sites, and agents can migrate freely among sites, the definition of short-run equilibrium must take into account both the optimal time allocation from (5.1) for each individual site and the idea that in equilibrium, no agent wants to move to a different site. Within a given time period t, events unfold in the following sequence.

(i) Let the initial number of agents at a typical site of quality s at the start of period t be n_{st}^0. All sites of the same quality level have the same number of agents.

(ii) The current climate c_t and the site qualities s are observed by all agents.

(iii) Each agent decides whether to stay at her current site or move elsewhere. These decisions determine final population levels for each site, denoted by n_{st}.

(iv) The agents at each site obtain food by allocating labor to foraging and cultivation as in equation (5.1). Food is shared equally at each site, yielding y_{st} per agent.

The location decisions at step (iii) are made by individual agents and involve a comparison of food per capita across all sites. If food per capita is unequal across sites, the agent goes where the most food is available. The agent is indifferent between sites that offer the same amount of food. The optimization decisions at step (iv) are made by local groups and involve a comparison of marginal products for foraging and cultivation at a given site with a given population. We assume that agents can anticipate their food income at step (iv) when making location decisions at step (iii). An individual agent is "small" relative to the population of a site. Therefore, she ignores her own influence on the group time allocation and the food per capita at a site when choosing among sites.

We assume an open access property rights regime where insiders cannot exclude outsiders. If there are no mobility costs and an individual agent treats the post-migration population at each site (n_{st}) as parametric, then in equilibrium food per agent (y_{st}) must be equal across sites. Otherwise, some agents would switch to different sites. Hence short-run equilibrium in period t requires a uniform food per capita $y_t = y_{st}$ for all $s \in [0, 1]$.

The open-access assumption is a convenient way to generate a positive short-run relationship between site quality and local population, as in Proposition 5.2(b) below, but a similar relationship could arise under more complex property rights systems that impede full food equalization. For example, foragers can frequently move to better locations by exploiting kinship networks, generating a tendency for population to concentrate at good sites (Kelly, 2013a). Our qualitative results survive as long as this tendency exists.

Let N_t be the overall population mass for the region as a whole in period t. This fixed population is distributed across sites to equalize food per capita. We will write the inverse of y(n, c, s) as n(y, c, s), where the latter function indicates the local population n that yields the food per capita y when climate and site quality are $(c, s) > 0$.

Definition 5.1

Fix the climate $c_t > 0$ and the regional population $N_t > 0$ for period t. The food per capita y_t and associated local populations $n(y_t, c_t, s)$ for $s \in [0, 1]$ are a *short-run equilibrium* (SRE) for period t if

$$N_t = \int_0^1 n(y_t, c_t, s)q(s)ds \qquad (5.4)$$

where q(s) is the density function for site quality (assumed positive everywhere).

The function q(s) gives the number of sites for each quality level s and is exogenously determined by the geography of the region. The equilibrium population densities $n_{st} = n(y_t, c_t, s)$ ensure that all agents throughout the region have the same food per capita y_t and therefore do not want to change sites. This gives the following results.

Proposition 5.2 (short-run equilibrium).

  Suppose A5.1–A5.3 hold.

  (a) For any $(N_t, c_t) > 0$, the SRE condition (5.4) has a unique solution $y_t = z(N_t, c_t)$ where y_t is decreasing in N_t and increasing in c_t.

  (b) Write $n_{st} = n[z(N_t, c_t), c_t, s]$. For a fixed regional population $N_t > 0$ and a fixed climate $c_t > 0$, the local population n_{st} is increasing in the site quality s.

Part (a) shows that in the short run, food per capita across the region is lower when the regional population is higher (due to diminishing returns to labor), and food per capita is higher when climate is better. Part (b) gives the intuitive result that when agents are free to move, the higher-quality sites have higher populations.

Recall that cultivation will occur at a site if and only if that site has a population exceeding the threshold n^a. Because the best sites (s = 1) have the highest populations in SRE, a necessary and sufficient condition for cultivation to arise somewhere in the region is $n(y_t, c_t, 1) > n^a$. If cultivation occurs at all, it must occur at the best sites.

We want a causal mechanism that links climate change with the local populations at the individual sites. For this purpose we think of the climate parameter (c) as indexing rainfall and the site quality parameter (s) as indexing surface water (springs, marshes, rivers, lakes). Under this interpretation, the climate quality c and site quality s should be good substitutes, because water from the sky is a good substitute for water on the ground. With this idea in mind, we impose more structure on the production technology.

Assumption 5.4

  The function A(c, s) from A5.3 has constant returns to scale and an elasticity of substitution greater than unity.

> **Proposition 5.3** (climate and migration in short-run equilibrium).
> Suppose A5.1–A5.4 hold and the regional population N > 0 is fixed. An increase in climate quality (c) decreases the local population n[z(N, c), c, 1] at the best sites (s = 1).

A5.4 is a technical way of saying that rainfall and surface water are close substitutes. If the climate shifts toward greater rainfall at all sites, this is more beneficial for poor sites that have little surface water than for good sites that have abundant surface water. Therefore, productivity rises proportionately more at the poor sites. In order to maintain a uniform food per capita across all sites in the region, it is necessary for some population to move away from the sites where the productivity increase was relatively small, and toward the sites where the productivity increase was relatively large. For this reason, population at the best sites (those with s = 1) must fall in the short run.

The converse is also true. If the region as a whole suffers from reduced rainfall, this reduces productivity everywhere, but productivity declines more in relative terms at inferior sites that were more dependent on rainfall. It declines less in relative terms at the best sites, which are buffered from the shock by their proximity to rivers, lakes, and other permanent water sources. To preserve equal food per person, some population must shift from the relatively poor sites to the relatively good ones. This is the mechanism we will use to link climate change with cultivation in Section 5.7.

5.6 LONG-RUN EQUILIBRIUM

The next step is to make the regional population N endogenous. We do this in the standard Malthusian way. As in earlier chapters, a time period is one human generation. The number of surviving adult children $\rho(y)$ for an individual adult agent is an increasing function of that agent's food income (y).

Assumption 5.5
$\rho(y)$ is continuous and increasing with $\rho(0) = 0$ and $\rho(+\infty) > 1$. There is a unique $y^* > 0$ with $\rho(y^*) = 1$.

Let the number of adults at a typical site of quality s at the start of period t be n_{st}°. The sequence of steps in each period is the same as in (i)–(iv) from Section 5.5, except that to model population dynamics we now add a fifth step:

(v) The current adults die at the end of period t. At the start of period t+1 the initial adult population at a typical site of quality s is $n_{s,t+1}^{\circ} = \rho(y_t)n_{st}$.

The food income y_t at step (v) is determined according to D5.1. Because all sites have the same food per capita and the same population growth rate, we can write

$$N_{t+1} = \rho[z(N_t, c_t)]N_t \qquad (5.5)$$

where $y_t = z(N_t, c_t)$ is food per capita in SRE for the population N_t and climate c_t.

We define long-run equilibrium as follows.

Definition 5.2

Fix the climate $c > o$. $N^*(c)$ is a *long-run equilibrium* (LRE) population for c if $N^*(c) = \rho[z(N^*(c), c)]N^*(c)$. The LRE is *non-null* if $N^*(c) > o$.

Proposition 5.4 (long-run equilibrium).

Suppose A5.1–A5.3 and A5.5 hold. The unique non-null LRE population for climate $c > o$ is

$$N^*(c) \equiv \int_0^1 n(y^*, c, s)q(s)ds > o \qquad (5.6)$$

where $N^*(c)$ is an increasing function of the climate quality c.

The intuition behind this result is simple. To have a stationary regional population, food per capita must be y^*. To compute the size of the stationary population, we must find the value for N that yields y^* in short-run equilibrium. We therefore substitute $y_t = y^*$ in the definition of SRE from D5.1, which determines what $N^*(c)$ must be in order to give y^*. It is clear from (5.6) that the solution for $N^*(c)$ is unique, and it is non-null when $c > o$. The fact that $N^*(c)$ is an increasing function comes as no surprise: a better climate raises food output, and by Malthusian reasoning this allows the region to support a larger population.

As in Chapters 3 and 4, we simplify by assuming that the population converges to LRE along a monotonic path. This will be useful for the graphical analysis in Section 5.7.

Assumption 5.6

Monotone Population Adjustment. Let $c > 0$ so $N^*(c) > 0$. Consider some initial period arbitrarily labeled $t = 0$ in which the regional population is $N_0 > 0$, where $N_0 \neq N^*(c)$. If the climate $c > 0$ prevails in period $t = 0$, the regional population moves in the direction of $N^*(c)$ in period $t = 1$. Hence if the initial population is below the LRE level, we have $N_0 < N_1 < N^*(c)$. If it is above the LRE level, we have $N^*(c) < N_1 < N_0$. If $c > 0$ is constant over time, the sequence $\{N_0, N_1 . .\}$ converges monotonically to $N^*(c)$ starting from any initial population $N_0 > 0$.

As long as the expression $\rho[z(N, c)]N$ from (5.5) is increasing in N (that is, the direct positive effect of N exceeds the indirect negative effect operating through z and ρ), population adjustments will be monotonic.

5.7 THE EFFECTS OF CLIMATE CHANGE

This section applies the formal model to the case of southwest Asia discussed in Section 5.3. We consider the temporal climate sequence $\{c_{IA}, c_{WA}, c_{YD}, c_{HO}\}$ where IA = Ice Age, WA = Initial Warming, YD = Younger Dryas, and HO = Holocene. The loose term "Ice Age" refers to the Last Glacial Maximum or the Heinrich I event, depending on how one chooses to use the model, and the shorthand term "Initial Warming" refers to the Bølling/Allerød (B/A) interstadial. In order of climate quality, the parameter values are ranked from worst to best as $c_{IA} < c_{YD} < c_{WA} < c_{HO}$.

For reasons discussed earlier, we are especially interested in changes in rainfall. Roberts et al. (2018) estimate that the Heinrich I phase (our "Ice Age") had mean monthly precipitation around 60% of the modern level, the B/A (our "Initial Warming") had mmp around 120% of the modern level, the Younger Dryas had mmp about 75% of the modern level, and the Early Holocene had mmp about 130% of the modern level. These estimates are consistent with the ranking we adopt for the four levels of our climate parameter.

We will use graphs to explain the qualitative features of the model. We simplify by treating climate changes as a series of abrupt jumps in the parameter $c \in [0, 1]$, with each jump followed by a period of stasis until the next jump. In reality, climate changes were considerably more complex and erratic. Even so, the speed of the warming events at 14,500 BP and 11,700 BP gives some justification for this stepwise approach (Roberts et al., 2018). The analysis in this section ignores effects on population caused by shifts from a mobile to a sedentary lifestyle, or vice versa. We discuss this issue and related demographic matters in Section 5.8.

Ice Age: Denote long-run regional population at the LGM by $N_{IA} = N^*(c_{IA})$. The absence of cultivation in the last Ice Age indicates that even at the best sites ($s = 1$), local population $n(y^*, c_{IA}, 1)$ was below the cultivation threshold n^a. We will use this long-run equilibrium as a starting point.

Initial Warming: In the short run, a climate improvement from c_{IA} to c_{WA} would increase food per capita at all sites according to the function $y = z(N_{IA}, c)$, with regional population fixed at N_{IA}. This results in a move from A to B in Figure 5.1. According to Proposition 5.3, cultivation cannot be a short-run response to this climate improvement, because the local population falls at the best sites:

$$n[z(N_{IA}, c_{WA}), c_{WA}, 1] < n[z(N_{IA}, c_{IA}), c_{IA}, 1] \equiv n(y^*, c_{IA}, 1) < n^a \quad (5.7)$$

If cultivation is not used at the best sites, it cannot be used at inferior sites either. The short-run loss in population for $s = 1$ is shown as a move from A to B in Figure 5.2.

If the climate c_{WA} had remained in effect permanently, in the long run population would have risen to a higher steady state $N_{WA} = N^*(c_{WA})$ and food per capita would have returned to y^* (a move from B to C in Figure 5.1). But even with population growth at the regional level, the

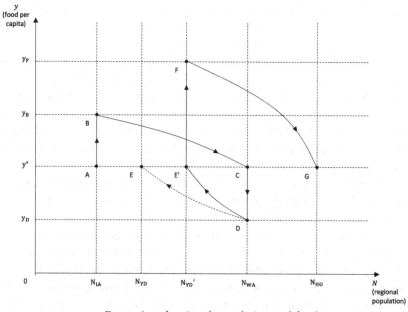

FIGURE 5.1. Dynamics of regional population and food per capita

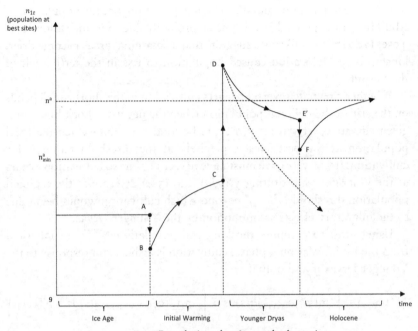

FIGURE 5.2. Population density at the best sites

local population at the best sites $n(y^*, c_{WA}, 1)$ was not enough to stimulate cultivation (see the move from B to C in Figure 5.2).

Younger Dryas: Now consider the deterioration in climate from c_{WA} to c_{YD} due to the Younger Dryas. In the short run, the regional population stays fixed at the level N_{WA} inherited from the Initial Warming. Food per capita diminishes (a move from C to D in Figure 5.1). More significantly, a migratory response causes local population to rise at the best sites (a move from C to D in Figure 5.2), crossing the n^a threshold and yielding initial cultivation. Algebraically, we have

$$n(y^*, c_{WA}, 1) \equiv n[z(N_{WA}, c_{WA}), c_{WA}, 1] < n^a < n[z(N_{WA}, c_{YD}), c_{YD}, 1]$$

$$(5.8)$$

The reasoning involves another application of Proposition 5.3. As precipitation declined, climate refugees fled sites that lacked permanent water sources and sought sanctuary at better locations. This is consistent with the fact that many sites were abandoned during the Younger Dryas, and also with the fact that the sites in continued use (such as Abu Hureyra) were less dependent on rainfall. As noted in Section 5.3, the population of Abu Hureyra expanded in this phase, probably due to in-migration. Bar-Yosef (2002b, 116) likewise suggests that as marginal areas became drier, kinship-based relocation caused population to rise in the fertile belt of the Levant.

Whether a climate reversal triggers cultivation in the short run depends on the size of the regional population when the negative shock hits. For a given climate c, let $y^a(c) \equiv y(n^a, c, 1)$ be food per capita when the local population at the best sites is precisely at the threshold required for cultivation. If $y < y^a(c)$, we must have $n(y, c, 1) > n^a$ so cultivation occurs at the best sites. Substituting $y^a(c_{YD})$ into (5.4) determines the regional population threshold $N^a(c_{YD})$ beyond which cultivation would begin due to the migratory effects set in motion by the Younger Dryas.

Using (5.6) to compute the long run population $N^*(c_{WA})$ inherited from the Initial Warming phase, cultivation is a short run response to the Younger Dryas if and only if

$$N^*(c_{WA}) \equiv \int_0^1 n(y^*, c_{WA}, s)q(s)ds > \int_0^1 n[y^a(c_{YD}), c_{YD}, s]q(s)ds \equiv N^a(c_{YD})$$

$$(5.9)$$

This inequality says that the regional population associated with the Initial Warming was large enough that when the Younger Dryas arrived, the population at refuge locations like Abu Hureyra grew sufficiently via migration to make cultivation attractive. Because the inequality (5.9) states a necessary and sufficient condition for the transition to cultivation, we pause to provide some interpretive details.

First, a larger pre-existing regional population makes a transition more likely, all other things being equal. This follows immediately from the appearance of $N^*(c_{WA})$ on the left-hand side of (5.9). Second, a more severe climate reversal is more likely to trigger an agricultural transition. This follows from the fact that the right-hand side is smaller when c_{YD} is smaller.

Such a transition is also more likely when the latent productivity of cultivation is higher, other things equal. Recall that the local population threshold n^a is a decreasing function of the cultivation productivity parameter k introduced in A5.3. This implies that $y^a(c_{YD})$ is increasing and $N^a(c_{YD})$ is decreasing in the parameter k, so (5.9) is more likely to hold when cultivation productivity is high.

If technical progress tends to raise the latent productivity of cultivation relative to the actual productivity of foraging (Ashraf and Michalopoulos, 2011, 2015), it becomes easier to satisfy (5.9). Conversely, if latent cultivation productivity had been low enough, even a large climate shock like the Younger Dryas would not have triggered a transition. A biological endowment favorable for cultivation (e.g., several species of large-seeded wild grasses; see Section 5.12) acts through the same causal channel. A more favorable endowment implies a higher productivity parameter k, implying a lower local population threshold n^a for cultivation. This makes it easier to satisfy inequality (5.9).

Finally, a transition is more likely when there are relatively few good sites and many poor ones, again holding other things equal. In this case a negative climate shock forces a large regional population through a few local bottlenecks, putting more pressure on the refuge sites and making it more likely that these sites will adopt cultivation. More formally, fix the existing population $N^*(c_{WA})$ on the left-hand side of (5.9) and consider the site density function $q(\cdot)$ on the right-hand side. The function $n[y^a(c_{YD}), c_{YD}, s]$ does not depend on $q(\cdot)$ and is increasing in s. Thus, a shift toward a less favorable site distribution in the sense of first-order dominance will lower the right-hand side and make it easier to satisfy inequality (5.9) for the given $N^*(c_{WA})$ on the left-hand side.

Until recently, received archaeological wisdom held that regional population fell during the Younger Dryas due to colder and drier conditions and resulting food scarcity. In the rest of this section, we explain how this scenario would play out within our model. In Section 5.8, we consider an alternative scenario where regional population rose during the Younger Dryas, along the lines suggested by Roberts et al. (2018).

Assuming regional population declined during the Younger Dryas, in the long run this would have alleviated migratory pressures on the refuge sites. If the climate reversal had been permanent and technology had been constant, eventually the population would have dropped to $N_{YD} = N^*(c_{YD})$ and food per capita would have returned to y^* (see the dashed curve from D to E in Figure 5.1). Because the long-run population in the Initial Warming was insufficient to support cultivation, the still lower long-run population of the Younger Dryas would also have failed to do so. Thus, cultivation would only have been a temporary stopgap along a path leading back to universal foraging (see the dashed curve in Figure 5.2).

In reality, however, the practice of cultivation in southwest Asia led to increases in productivity through better knowledge about important technological details: optimal times for planting and harvesting, optimal locations, correct spacing and depth of seeds, the best methods of weeding, fertilization, irrigation, etc. Eventually artificial selection on the genetic characteristics of plants culminated in full domestication. In our model, this productivity growth shows up as an increase in the parameter k defined in A5.3.

We assume that productivity gains were freely available to everyone in the region. The process of productivity improvement can be modeled in many ways (see Chapters 3 and 4), and only broad qualitative issues are pertinent here. Suppose before cultivation starts, its productivity is k_o. Let the regional population engaged in cultivation be

$$M \equiv \int_S^{I} n_g[z(N, c, k), c, k, s]q(s)ds \qquad (5.10)$$

where $S = S(N, c, k)$ is the marginal site quality for cultivation and n_g is the optimal input of cultivation labor given the local population $n[z(N, c, k), c, k, s]$. A simple and general model for productivity growth is

$$k_{t+I} = \phi(k_t, M_t) \qquad (5.11)$$

where ϕ is increasing in M_t and $k_{t+I} = k_t$ when $M_t = 0$. Thus, when cultivation is active its productivity rises, and this occurs more rapidly when aggregate labor input to cultivation is larger. When cultivation is inactive, its productivity remains constant. These ideas are consistent with the model of learning by doing in Chapter 3.

Whether cultivation persists during a climate reversal depends on the outcome of a race between population and technology. As the regional population falls, populations at individual sites also fall, decreasing the number of sites using cultivation as well as the amount of labor allocated to cultivation at each site. This restrains technical progress and could shut down cultivation entirely. On the other hand, as productivity improves, more sites adopt cultivation and more labor is allocated to it where it is already in use. These effects promote more technical progress and slow the loss of population by cushioning the blow to living standards.

The resulting dynamics are shown in Figure 5.3 (climate is held constant at c_{YD}). For each cultivation productivity level (k), the curve $N^a(k)$ gives the maximum regional population that is consistent with universal foraging. This is obtained by computing the cultivation threshold $n^a(k)$ as a function of k, finding the food per capita $y^a(k)$ such that the local population is exactly $n^a(k)$ at the best sites, and finally computing the regional population $N^a(k)$ that would be consistent with $y^a(k)$. The result is

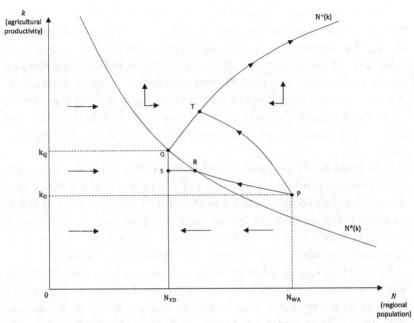

FIGURE 5.3. Dynamics of population and technology during a climate reversal

$$N^a(k) \equiv \int_0^1 n[y^a(k), c_{YD}, s]q(s)ds \qquad (5.12)$$

We omit k as a separate argument of n(y, c, s) because only foraging is relevant in (5.12). To the left of this curve, labor is allocated entirely to foraging at all sites and cultivation productivity stays constant. To the right of this curve, labor is allocated to cultivation at some sites and its productivity therefore rises over time.

The second curve $N^*(k)$ in Figure 5.3 depicts the long-run regional population corresponding to a given cultivation productivity k. This is derived by finding the local population for each site consistent with the food per capita y^*, given the productivity k, and then substituting these local populations into (5.6):

$$N^*(k) \equiv \int_0^1 n(y^*, c_{YD}, k, s)q(s)ds \qquad (5.13)$$

Below the $N^a(k)$ curve, $N^*(k)$ is a vertical line at N_{YD} because k is irrelevant if all labor is used for foraging. Above $N^a(k)$, cultivation occurs and $N^*(k)$ is increasing in k.

The starting point P involves the long-run population N_{WA} inherited from the Initial Warming phase and the latent cultivation productivity k_o. During the Younger Dryas, this combination was sufficient to induce cultivation at good sites, so P is above the locus $N^a(k)$. Depending on the rate of productivity growth, two possibilities arise. If learning by doing is relatively slow, the system trajectory hits the $N^a(k)$ curve below Q, at a point like R. Cultivation then shuts down and the system moves horizontally to the left, approaching a point like S with the population N_{YD}.

If learning by doing is fast enough, however, the trajectory eventually rises above the productivity level k_Q. In this case it is impossible to return to pure foraging because $N^a(k)$ is to the left of $N^*(k)$. Hence, cultivation becomes permanent and its productivity continues to rise. This growth process is limited only by the possibility of a ceiling k_{max} on cultivation productivity at which technological opportunities are exhausted.

The archaeological evidence suggests that this latter trajectory was followed in southwest Asia during the Younger Dryas. In Figures 5.1 and 5.2, we assume that k has an upper bound k_{max} and so n^a has a lower bound n^a_{min}. Improved cultivation technology implies a higher long run population in Figure 5.1 (point E′ rather than E with N_{YD}' rather than N_{YD}). In Figure 5.2, population density at the best sites remains above the threshold $n^a(k)$, which declines to n^a_{min} as k increases to k_{max}, resulting in a move from D to E′.

The Holocene: Finally, suppose the climate recovers. The short-run effect on food per capita is given by the upward jump from E′ to F in Figure 5.1. As with Initial Warming, the local populations drop at the best sites due to out-migration (the downward jump from E′ to F in Figure 5.2). This need not shut down cultivation because cultivation technology improved during the Younger Dryas, decreasing the threshold density n^a. The long-run result is a larger regional population N_{HO} than under any previous regime (from F to G in Figure 5.1) and higher populations at the best sites (the path starting from point F in Figure 5.2). The combination of better technology and higher population led to the spread of cultivation across the region.

5.8 DEMOGRAPHY

Few people doubt that agriculture led to population growth. Indeed this growth has acquired a name: the Neolithic Demographic Transition

(Bocquet-Appel and Naji, 2006; Bocquet-Appel, 2008a, 2008b, 2009, 2011; Bocquet-Appel and Bar-Yosef, 2008). Evidence is not hard to find. In most of the regional cases reviewed by Bellwood (2005), early agriculture was associated with more settlements, larger settlements, or both, often involving increases on the order of 10-fold to 50-fold. Bocquet-Appel uses the fraction of skeletons from ancient cemeteries that were 5–19 years old at death to infer population dynamics before, during, and after agriculture, defined by the date at which domesticates are first observed in the local area. Using data from Europe, North Africa, and North America, he finds that (a) population growth was positive but showed moderate slowing in the millennium before the transition and (b) population growth increased dramatically in the millennium after the transition. Notice that these population trends are defined in relation to the onset of domestication, not cultivation. If the gap between the two lasted for a millennium (see Section 5.3), it is quite possible that population growth could have slowed during the first millennium of cultivation as described in (a).

Bowles (2011) and Bowles and Choi (2019) argue that early cultivation was no more productive than foraging. Economic theory supports this assertion. Optimal time allocation implies that the marginal products of labor in foraging and cultivation will be equal when both activities are used. Also, when cultivation is just starting, the average and marginal products of cultivation are equal to each other, as well as to the marginal product of foraging. And finally, the average product of foraging exceeds its marginal product due to the concavity of the production function. Together these points imply that at an early stage of cultivation, the average product of foraging labor exceeds the average product of cultivation labor, as Bowles and Choi claim on empirical grounds.

This does not, however, imply anything about rates of population growth in early agricultural societies as compared with foraging societies. In general, the relative growth rates depend upon fluctuations in the natural environment, rates of productivity growth in cultivation and foraging, the economic costs and benefits of children in each society, and similar factors. Bettinger (2016) argues that as an empirical matter, population growth in early agricultural societies was no faster than in foraging societies. He points to evidence from paleodemography that annual growth rates for foragers in the Rocky Mountains and Australia (in each case, about 0.04%) were similar to growth rates for farmers in Europe and North America. Nevertheless, in the millennia following the Neolithic Revolution, technical innovations like domestication and metallurgy eventually led to demographic domination by agricultural societies in most areas of the world.

In what follows, we discuss population trends specific to southwest Asia. We will focus on the earliest stages of cultivation in an attempt to shine further light on the causal mechanisms behind the Neolithic transition.

Roberts et al. (2018) use summed calibrated radiocarbon probabilities to construct a proxy for population in southwest Asia during 16,000–9000 BP, with 1917 radiocarbon dates. The authors fit an exponential growth curve for this proxy and look for statistically significant deviations from the fitted curve to identify periods when the actual population was above or below the predicted level. This procedure reveals two important deviations from the trend. First, population is below expectations during 13,600–12,700 BP, which corresponds to the later part of the Bølling/Allerød and the start of the Younger Dryas. Population subsequently recovers to the expected range by 12,500 BP, well before the end of the Younger Dryas. Second, the population is above expectations from 11,700 BP (the end of the Younger Dryas) until 11,100 BP (the Early Holocene). The latter result is unsurprising given the major climate improvement associated with the Holocene.

Roberts et al. divide their data into three sub-regions: (a) the southern and central Levant, (b) the northern Levant and upper Mesopotamia, and (c) south-central Anatolia. All regions show significant departures from the pattern for southwest Asia as a whole. For the southern Levant, there is a significantly higher population during 14,500–13,500 BP, corresponding to the Bølling/Allerød climate period and the early Natufian cultural period (see Section 5.3). There appears to have been a brief period of population growth near the middle of the Younger Dryas, but this subsequently leveled off. Further growth had to await the close of the Younger Dryas and the onset of the Holocene.

Trends for the northern Levant/upper Mesopotamia region look quite different. Population was below the regional trend during 16,000–13,400 BP. This was followed by steady growth starting in the Bølling/Allerød and continuing through the Younger Dryas, with populations significantly above the regional expectation during 11,700–10,500 BP (the PPNA). The authors estimate that this sub-region had a roughly 20-fold population increase in the period 13,400–11,500 BP. They note that all sites in the area dating to the Younger Dryas were at intermediate elevations that include the "northern hilly flanks" of the Fertile Crescent.

Finally, south-central Anatolia had a period of about 500 years beginning around 15,200 BP in which population exceeded regional expectations. However, over 12,700–11,200 BP (most of the Younger Dryas and the first 500 years of the Holocene), this sub-region had a flat population that was consistently below predicted levels.

Before Roberts et al. (2018), many archaeologists specializing in southwest Asia thought that regional population probably fell during the Younger Dryas. Our own views were similar, as indicated in Figure 5.1. The findings summarized above are recent and it remains to be seen whether they will be widely accepted among specialists. However, we will take them at face value and ask how they could be interpreted in light of our model.

If we ignore sub-regions and return to the population proxy for southwest Asia as a whole, the main result to be explained is why the negative deviation from the trend line ended at about the middle of the Younger Dryas (12,500 BP), rather than continuing until the arrival of the Holocene. This does not appear to be a great puzzle in our framework. We have argued that cultivation began during the Younger Dryas. We have also argued that cultivation leads to learning by doing, with associated productivity gains. Assuming that cultivation began early in the Younger Dryas, these gains could have begun to offset the adverse climate by the middle of the Younger Dryas, resulting in population growth.

The trends for the southern Levant also seem consistent with our expectations. It is not surprising that population would have grown during the warm and wet conditions of the Bølling/Allerød. Indeed, this is consistent with our arguments about sedentism in Section 4.3. It is likewise unsurprising that population leveled off in the Younger Dryas.

It is more startling that population in the northern Levant and upper Mesopotamia exhibited sustained growth throughout the Younger Dryas when climate was poor. Some of this growth could reflect migration from the southern Levant or south-central Anatolia. This is suggested by the fact that in the former case population was largely flat during the Younger Dryas, while in the latter case it was below regional trends. It is also consistent with hints that the Younger Dryas may have been less severe in the northern Levant and upper Mesopotamia than elsewhere in southwest Asia (Roberts et al., 2018, 62–64). The migratory story is likewise consistent with the finding that for southwest Asia as a whole, population remained below the trend until 12,500 BP and did not exceed the trend for the rest of the Younger Dryas.

Having said this, we still need to explain why the region-wide population grew at all in the Younger Dryas. Two factors consistent with our Malthusian framework could have counteracted the negative climate effect: Increasing sedentism and the productivity gains from cultivation. We established in Section 4.10 that sedentism will generally lead to higher population levels than would otherwise occur. If a large fraction of the regional population responded to the Younger Dryas by switching from mobile to sedentary living due to a reliance on refuge sites, this could account for some of the population growth. If these refuge sites were also disproportionately located in the northern Levant and upper Mesopotamia, population growth due to increased sedentism would tend to occur largely in this sub-region. Unfortunately, we are unaware of any data that illuminate this issue.

Another way to account for population growth in the Younger Dryas is through the effects of cultivation. Three effects could be important: (a) cultivation could provide an additional incentive for sedentism; (b) cultivation could decrease the economic cost of children, leading to a higher population, as will be explained in Section 5.9; and/or (c) cultivation could start a process of learning by doing that would raise productivity and therefore also population. The concentration of population growth in the northern Levant during the Younger Dryas is consistent with Bar-Yosef's (2011) argument that cultivation began within this sub-region and then spread southward. If cultivation caused population growth during the Younger Dryas, it would have had to arise at a number of sites in order to generate an appreciable aggregate effect.

We should emphasize that we interpret the concept of "learning by doing" broadly in the context of early cultivation. This no doubt included narrow technical matters such as the timing of planting, the depth and spacing of planted seeds, and so on. But social and cultural processes were probably also involved, through participation in communal activities surrounding plant processing, detoxification, cooking, and storage (Asouti and Fuller, 2013). Cultural evolution of this sort probably enhanced the productivity of cultivation relative to hunting and gathering.

If one believes that cultivation did not begin until the Early Holocene, then the full burden of explaining population growth in the Younger Dryas falls upon increased sedentism. Although it is conceivable that sedentism alone could have been sufficient, in our opinion the evidence from Section 5.3 makes it more plausible that cultivation was a factor, and perhaps the primary factor, generating population growth despite the adverse climate regime. In general, the finding of population growth during the Younger Dryas, if accepted, strengthens the inference that cultivation began in this period.

5.9 LIVING STANDARDS

Most archaeologists believe that early farmers were worse off than their foraging ancestors in the sense that they had poorer nutrition, more disease, and shorter lives. The relevant evidence from teeth and skeletons is extensive (see Cohen, 2009; Lambert, 2009; and the references cited there). The literature is often unclear about whether the decrease in living standards was associated specifically with sedentism, cultivation, or agriculture. Furthermore, some researchers emphasize poor diet and a weaker immune system, while others emphasize greater exposure to infectious diseases when people are sedentary, live in large settlements, and/or have domesticated animals.

The first question raised by these findings is why people would voluntarily adopt a technology that made them worse off. Our theory suggests some answers. We believe that in the short run, cultivation was triggered by a negative climate shock and migration among sites in a region. Even if inhabitants at each site always respond optimally to the climate they currently face, people will become worse off when climate becomes worse (economists will recognize this as an application of the envelope theorem). Thus a short-run drop in living standards is to be expected.

In the long run, a simple Malthusian model predicts a return to the previous level of food per adult through a decrease in regional population. Food per adult will continue to remain constant in the long run regardless of further changes in climate or technology. To explain a long-run reduction in living standards, we require a change in the economic costs and benefits of children. If agricultural technology makes children less costly or more productive (perhaps because children can now add to food output through sowing, weeding, and harvesting), the same mechanisms as in Section 4.10 lead to lower long-run food per adult (lower y^*). This reinforces whatever long-run decline in living standards resulted from sedentism alone. If children become increasingly valuable in production as learning by doing and domestication proceed, equilibrium food per adult will continue to decline. This can yield a gradual decline in nutrition for both adults and children. If poor diet compromises immune function, it can also lead to more disease. These effects are in addition to disease effects resulting from larger communities and animal domestication.

A second question is how lower living standards can be reconciled with increased fertility and population growth (see Lambert, 2009). The model sketched in Section 4.10 also resolves this problem. We showed there that if the "price" of children to their parents drops (either due to lower costs or higher productivity benefits) the long-run consequence is higher fertility, higher child mortality, and lower life expectancy at birth. At the same time, regional population can grow, because in long-run equilibrium, lower food per adult is associated with higher population for any given climate and technology. Moreover, for the usual Malthusian reasons, increasing agricultural productivity over time implies rising regional population over time. Thus our theoretical framework can account for evidence that agricultural populations grew even as living standards fell.

Guzmán and Weisdorf (2011) cite evidence about the decline in living standards under agriculture, stress the greater productivity of children in agriculture as compared to foraging, and reach conclusions similar to those described above. Robson (2010) focuses on biological factors including disease in early Neolithic communities. In contrast to our interpretation, Rowthorn and Seabright (2010) attribute the reduction in living standards to costs associated with the defense of agricultural output (see Chapters 7 and 8).

5.10 OTHER TRANSITIONS

The task of this section is to review evidence about pristine transitions other than the one in southwest Asia. Although the particular climate episode of the Younger Dryas may have been relevant in certain other regions, some of the pristine transitions discussed in this section occurred much later. Thus our interest is less in the Younger Dryas per se, and more with the potential applicability of the general causal mechanism investigated in Sections 5.4–5.7, involving a large pre-existing regional population, heterogeneous sites, a negative climate shock, and migration to refuge locations. As we explain in more detail at the end of this section, we do not believe that a negative climate shock was the trigger in all cases and we are open to the possibility that positive climate trends in the Holocene may have led to pristine cultivation in some regions.

Our survey of regional cases proceeds in rough chronological order from earlier to later transitions. In all cases, it is essential to distinguish dates for initial cultivation from dates for full domestication. There is often a very long gap between the two. Larson et al. (2014) provide a broad overview of dates for initial cultivation across regions, along with dates for domestication. Purugganan and Fuller (2009) offer a similar overview for domestication dates. Even with such estimates in hand, uncertainties about the timing of climate change and initial cultivation make causal inferences very challenging. At most, some of the cases described below offer tentative support for our theory. We are unaware of any cases that directly contradict our theory.

Northern China: There were two main centers of pristine agriculture in China, one in the north around the Yellow River basin involving millet, and another in the south around the Yangzi River basin involving rice. Some archaeologists regard these as aspects of a single overarching transition process rather than as two distinct centers (Bellwood, 2005; Liu and Chen, 2012, 67; Shelach-Lavi, 2015, 66–67). We accept Cohen's (2011) view that cultural interactions between the north and south were extensive. However, we treat them as separate cases here because they involved the domestication of different plants in different natural environments. Hunting, gathering, and fishing remained important for several millennia in both the north and south before full dietary reliance on domesticates (Cohen, 2011; Liu and Chen, 2012; Shelach-Lavi, 2015).

Liu and Chen (2012, 34) comment that "The widespread monsoon maximum in north China ca. 9000 cal. BP provided favorable conditions for the flourishing of early Neolithic villages along the Liao and the middle and lower Yellow River valleys." To the north of the Yellow River, evidence for domesticated millet comes from the Cishan culture (8000–7700 BP). To the south of the river, the Peiligang culture also provides evidence of millet cultivation (8500–7500 BP). In all, there are five known early centers of millet farming in north China (Bettinger et al., 2010a). The early Neolithic villages in this region had a few hundred people each (Liu and Chen, 2012, 71).

Some authors assert that millet domestication occurred earlier than these dates would suggest. Larson et al. (2014) believe that foxtail millet was "exploited," although not domesticated, as early as 11,500 BP. Lu et al. (2009) provide phytolith evidence for domesticated broomcorn millet at Cishan by 10,300 BP. Crawford (2009) and Bettinger et al. (2010b) accept the claim for millet farming at Cishan near 10,300 BP. Zhao (2011) criticizes the methods used by Lu et al. (2009) but agrees that millet domestication might have begun by 10,000 BP. Cohen (2011) expresses caution and calls for further research.

Much depends on the lag between cultivation and domestication, because if the domestication date of 10,300 BP is accepted, then a lag of 1500 years or more puts initial cultivation in the Younger Dryas. This seems reasonable, given current views about the length of this lag (see Section 5.3). Indeed, Bar-Yosef (2011) proposes that the Younger Dryas led to millet cultivation by causing hunter-gatherers to retreat to favorable habitats such as river valleys, and generating "population pressure" at these locations.

A major problem for north China is that there are very few Early Holocene sites, and none has been extensively excavated or documented (Shelach-Lavi, 2015, 54–56). One (Nanzhuangtou) has been dated to ca. 12,000–10,000 BP, and another (Donghulin) has been dated to ca. 11,000–9000 BP. Shelach-Lavi states that there is a chronological gap of about one thousand years, as well as a geographic gap, between these sites and the earliest known Neolithic villages in north China. Yang et al. (2012) date the occupation of Nanzhuangtou to 11,500–11,000 BP and the early phase of occupation of Donghulin to 11,150–10,500 BP. For both sites, they use evidence involving starch grains found on tools to argue that domestication of millet had begun by these dates.

Another intriguing site is Dadiwan, in the western Loess Plateau near the valley of the Qing Shui River (a tributary of the upper Wei River). Bettinger et al. (2010a, 2010b) suggest that prior to the end of the Pleistocene, microlithic hunters were located in deserts along the upper Yellow River about 300–400 km north of Dadiwan. Around the time of the Younger Dryas (12,800–11,500 BP), cold and dry episodes caused the upper Yellow River environment to deteriorate, and these hunters were pushed further south toward the upper Wei River and the gallery forests of the western Loess Plateau. By 8000 BP, and possibly earlier, the inhabitants had begun to engage in millet cultivation. A key problem is the absence of radiocarbon dates at Dadiwan for 18,500–8000 BP (for a skeptical view, see Cohen, 2011). More generally, at present there is no definite connection between the Younger Dryas and initial cultivation in north China, but the question remains open.

Southern China: The crucial crop in the south was rice. No sites show the complete transition from foraging to agriculture. Molecular data is consistent with a single origin of domesticated rice between 13,500–8200 BP (Shelach-Lavi, 2015, 60). Zhao (2011) believes that rice cultivation began around 10,000 BP, and that the earliest site in China clearly exhibiting rice agriculture is Jiahu, located on the upper Huai River and dated to 9000–7800 BP. This is consistent with the date of 10,000 BP given for the earliest rice cultivation by Larson et al. (2014). By 8500 BP agricultural villages of 200–300 people were distributed across the middle and lower Yangzi valley, and in regions to the north (Shelach-Lavi, 2015, 50). These communities had permanent houses, public structures, and cemeteries. Rice agriculture gradually replaced hunting and gathering over several millennia (Zhao, 2011).

Rice phytoliths have been used to estimate the timing of domestication in the Yangzi valley (data in this paragraph come from Zuo et al., 2017). Phytoliths have been found in marine sediments dating to 13,900–13,000 BP, but their wild or domesticated status is unclear. Rice remains from the Shangshan site dated to about 11,000–8600 BP may reflect cultivation, but there has been controversy over whether these remains were wild or domesticated, as well as the reliability of previous dating methods. More recent dating indicates that Shangshan was occupied by about 9400 BP and the nearby site of Hehuashan by about 9000 BP. Zuo et al. report morphological evidence from phytoliths that rice domestication was underway by 9400 BP, and they suggest that this process can be linked to the climatic transition from the Pleistocene to the Holocene.

Mesoamerica: The information on this region is from Piperno and Smith (2012) except where stated. In addition to the crucial domestication of maize from wild teosinte, other domesticates included two squash species, common beans, lima beans, two pseudo-cereals, avocado, chili pepper, and some trees. Tomato and cacao were native to South America but were probably domesticated in Mexico. Based on genetic research, maize and one squash species were domesticated once within a circumscribed region. Some other species were domesticated on multiple occasions either within Mesoamerica, or both there as well as South and/or North America.

The earliest archaeological evidence of domestication in the lowlands is from the Central Balsas region of southwestern Mexico where the wild ancestors of maize and one type of squash are found. Starch grain and phytolith evidence indicate the domestication of both by 8700 BP. The context was a seasonally dry tropical forest (see the discussion of such forests in South America below). Matsuoka et al. (2002) infer from genetic data that maize was domesticated around 9000 BP. In the case of maize, Larson et al. (2014) offer an estimated date of 10,000 BP for "documented exploitation before domestication or posited as necessary lead-time to domestication." Larson et al. cite the same date for morphological evidence for the domestication of squash.

Evidence for domestication in highland areas comes mainly from five dry caves excavated between 1954 and 1966. Domestic bottle gourds from 10,000 BP have been found at Guila Naquitz in Oaxaca (Flannery, 1986; Marcus and Flannery, 1996; Smith, 2001). This species is a "container crop" rather than a food crop, and is thought to have a wild ancestor in East Asia (Piperno and Smith, 2012, 158). Another domesticated species of squash has been found at the same site. The earliest evidence for domestication of the common bean, which appears to have occurred in western Mexico, is not until 2300 BP, around the same time as the domestication of the turkey.

According to Piperno and Smith, "It is now clear that in both the highlands and tropical lowlands, plant cultivation and domestication emerged during the early Holocene period" (152). They see the chronology as similar to that of southwest Asia and China. Humans are known to have migrated into Mesoamerica around 15,000 years ago (Goebel et al., 2008). However, any connection of initial maize cultivation to the Younger Dryas is purely conjectural. We have no evidence about the timing of initial cultivation, and a scenario of this kind requires a lag of up to 3000 years from cultivation to domestication of maize, or earlier dates for domestication than are currently accepted.

South America: This case is complex, and the dates given by Larson et al. (2014) for cultivation and domestication vary widely by species. South America does not appear to have had a single center for agriculture. Piperno (2011) believes there may have been two or three independent centers and that the data suggest the development of cultivation in the Early Holocene (11,000–7600 BP). Plant domestication is evident by 7600 BP with a significant part of the diet coming from crop plants by this time. During 7600–7000 BP both site numbers and artifact densities increase, probably due to higher carrying capacity associated with horticulture and slash-and-burn cultivation.

The wild ancestors of domesticated plants were often native to seasonal tropical forests that had 4–7 months each year with little or no rainfall. Food production is often associated with rock shelters or small open-air occupations near secondary watercourses. Settlements were small and many were probably seasonal, but they tended to be in areas of resource abundance. Unlike the Near East and China, cultivation did not involve large permanent villages in major river valleys. Piperno believes that the Near East trajectory was "a product of ecological and demographic circumstances very different from those associated with the beginnings of Neotropical food production" (S462).

Piperno does say that "the shift from foraging to food production began within contexts of rapid and significant changes of climate, vegetation, and fauna occurring at the close of the Pleistocene" (S465). She believes the main factor was a change from savanna-like scrub to seasonal tropical forest. This lowered the efficiency of hunting and gathering, and led to greater diet breadth due to the prevalence of smaller animals as well as plants that required extensive processing. Hence, cultivation became a more attractive strategy relative to full-time hunting and gathering. Piperno believes the key period was 11,000–9000 BP and that this process was especially relevant to "highly seasonal types of tropical forest, where the end-Pleistocene environmental perturbations would have impacted foraging return rates most strongly" (S465).

There is a distinct literature on the origins of agriculture in the Andes. Dillehay et al. (2007) report evidence for horticultural economies in a dry forest valley in the Andes at 10,000 BP but their claim of domesticated squash, peanuts, and other plants has been questioned. Well-accepted evidence for sedentary settlements, pottery, and agriculture dates to around 5000 BP (Balter, 2007, 1833; Quilter, 2014, 64, 76–78). Domesticated crops included squash, achira, and beans, but not maize (Bellwood, 2005, 159–164).

El Niño-Southern Oscillation (ENSO) refers to oscillations in the Pacific Ocean between a warm tropical-water phase and a cold-water phase. The gradual onset of this cycle and a general increase in climate variability began around 5800 BP (Sandweiss et al., 1999). Archaeological evidence shows that in this period, major debris slides wiped out coastal foraging villages, and local fish populations disappeared due to migration to cooler water. Any causal connection with plant cultivation in the Andean highlands is uncertain (Bellwood, 2005, 149; Quilter, 2014, 30–31, 105–106), but coastal populations may have migrated inland, raising population densities there and inducing cultivation.

New Guinea: Highland New Guinea was an independent center of domestication for bananas and taro, and perhaps also yams and sugar cane (Bellwood, 2005, 142–145). Larson et al. (2014) use 10,000 BP as a date for "documented exploitation" or "necessary lead-time to domestication" for bananas, taro, and yams, with management or cultivation by 7000 BP but still without morphological indications of domestication.

The information below is taken from Denham (2011, S383–S387) except where indicated. Agriculture emerged out of foraging practices sometime in the Early Holocene but few sites dating to this period have been excavated. There are "questionable" claims for Pleistocene settlements in the highlands. However, most settlements postdate 4000 BP. Knowledge about the phenotypic or genotypic transformation from wild to domestic plants is weak, as is knowledge about the relationship between sedentism and agriculture. Pottery and domesticated animals are absent. The case for early agriculture rests mainly on evidence for agricultural technology and its environmental effects.

The most detailed data come from the Upper Wahgi Valley and relate to bananas, taro, and yams. Denham believes these plants were of lowland derivation and brought to the highlands by people, although they could have grown wild in the highlands during the Early Holocene. By 7000–6500 BP, mounded cultivation occurred on the wetland margin of Kuk Swamp. By 4000 BP, ditched fields and greater domestication existed. Denham hypothesizes that managed plants were translocated from lower altitudes to the floor of the Upper Wahgi Valley, where wild stands of the same species were rare or absent.

Bellwood (2005) points out that the domestication of bananas, taro, and yams was centered in highland valleys and that the same plants could have been domesticated in the lowland rainforests but were not. He suggests that this occurred because highland valleys were at the edge of the wild range for these plants, so foragers in the highlands were more exposed to environmental stresses than foragers in the tropical lowlands.

Sub-Saharan Africa: Northern Africa has shifted from a "green Sahara" in the Early Holocene to a large desert today (information in this paragraph is from Manning and Timpson, 2014; see also Section 4.12). The "African Humid Period" (AHP) began around 12,000 BP, with an initial occupation by hunter-gatherers and massive growth in population density starting shortly after 11,000 BP. Pastoralists with domestic livestock appear around 8000–7500 BP. The population density decreased during 7600–6700 BP but rebounded in 6700–6300 BP, reaching a Holocene maximum. A major population collapse followed during 6300–5200 BP at the end of the AHP.

Data from Lake Yoa in northern Chad show that increasing aridity began around 5600 BP, with windblown sand appearing by about 3700 BP and a true desert ecosystem by 2700 BP (Kröpelin et al., 2008). Annual rainfall was about 250 mm in 6000 BP, less than 150 mm by 4300 BP, and less than 50 mm by 2700 BP. Brooks (2006, 2013) offers comments on the cultural consequences of greater aridity in the Sahara after 6000 BP.

Africa differs from other examples of pristine agriculture in having domesticated animals, particularly cattle, long before the domestication of indigenous plants (Manning and Fuller, 2014). Plant domestication occurred in five geographic zones: three in West Africa (the Sahara/Sahel, grassy woodlands, and forest margins), and two further to the east (East Sudanic grasslands and Ethiopian uplands). Important crops included pearl millet, finger millet, African rice, cowpea, yam, sorghum, and tef, with domestication occurring around 4500 BP or later (Fuller and Hildebrand, 2013). We omit discussion of the estimated dates for cultivation from Larson et al. (2014) in this case due to an overly broad definition of the geographic region.

Domesticated pearl millet has been found in the Tilemsi Valley in northeast Mali (information is from Manning and Fuller, 2014). This valley "provided a fertile and accessible corridor into sub-Saharan Africa at a time of increasing aridification and southward displacement of Saharan populations" (73). The wild progenitors of this crop are found nearby in the Saharan zone of West Africa. Sites occupied during 4500–4000 BP offer evidence of domesticated pearl millet. Initial inhabitants of the Tilemsi Valley brought domesticated millet as well as livestock (cattle, sheep, and goats) from elsewhere. Manning and Fuller suggest a lag between cultivation and domestication of about 1000–2000 years and infer that cultivation began around 6000–5000 BP. They also suggest that pearl millet was suitable for cultivation by mobile pastoralists due to its minimal water requirements and high productivity over a short growing season.

Another important African crop, sorghum, had a wild progenitor located in the savannahs of what is presently the Sahara Desert (Fuller and Stevens, 2018). These wild stands retreated south as the Sahara dried and expanded, and this process may have been accompanied by southward migration. Fuller and Stevens suggest a protracted period of sorghum cultivation during 5500–3700 BP that eventually led to domestication. This was probably associated with a relatively sudden increase in settlement sizes after 5800 BP and a shift to a more sedentary lifestyle (Winchell et al., 2018). The inhabitants were harvesting mixed stands of wild and domestic sorghum by about 5500–5000 BP.

This is consistent with earlier archaeological views about climate change as a driver of domestication in sub-Saharan Africa. According to Smith (1998, 110), some researchers believe "the timing of initial domestication of millet and sorghum was tied to the southward expansion of the desert, which intensified about 4000 years ago, displacing people south." Smith goes on to state that African rice may also fit this model (112). Bellwood (2005, 103) describes a similar archaeological consensus. Smith observes that settlements in the savanna zone from 5000–3000 BP were located on the shores of lakes, that fish were an important food source, and that wild rice, millet, and sorghum were probably harvested at these sites. We infer that such locations may have played a refuge role in relation to increasing aridity.

Eastern North America: The dates for initial cultivation reported by Larson et al. (2014) are generally around 6000 BP. The information here is taken from Smith (2011). Domesticated seeds for four plants, including squash and sunflower, have been found in seven sites scattered across the oak-savannah and oak-hickory forests of North America. Three of the plants are dated to 5000–4400 BP. The fourth is dated to 3800 BP but Smith believes that further research will likely push this back to the earlier interval. Three more plants were probably cultivated but evidence for domestication is lacking. This occurred alongside hunting and gathering. Wild food resources included white-tailed deer, small mammals, and turkeys; oak, hickory, and walnuts; and fish, bivalves, and waterfowl.

Around 6500–6000 BP, many river systems developed meandering patterns with oxbow lakes, backswamps, and shoals. This increased the abundance and diversity of floodplain resources, both plant and animal; "at the same time an apparent decrease in effective precipitation resulted in a deterioration of upland resources" (S477). This led to intensified human occupation of river and stream corridors. Domestication probably occurred first in resource-rich river valleys associated with small secondary or tertiary tributaries of the Mississippi River. Three of the four species involved are floodplain weeds that colonize disturbed soil exposed by spring floods. The fourth (sunflower) is found in the same setting but also thrives in other environments.

Smith believes the cultural context involved river valley base camps that were permanent or semi-permanent and reoccupied annually by a half dozen or more extended families. When these camps flooded, extended families would move to the uplands for shorter-term occupations. There is no evidence of ascribed status differentiation or any organization beyond the level of the extended family.

In Smith's opinion, domestication cannot be explained by population pressure or resource depletion, greater territoriality and competition, or an environmental downturn. However, he does not offer an explicit causal story that would account for the transition. The hint that lower rainfall caused population to shift from uplands to river valleys, and that this led to domestication, seems consistent with our theory.

India: The case of the Indian subcontinent is complex. A number of indigenous plants were domesticated there, but some domesticates arrived from outside the region, and some indigenous plants may have been domesticated in response to these external influences. Sites showing the transition from hunting and gathering to cultivation have not yet been found. When sedentary villages are observed, dependence upon cultivation already exists. Most of the hard evidence for cultivation and domestication dates from about 5000 BP onward. Due to space constraints and the absence of direct relevance for the theoretical issues with which we are concerned, we omit a detailed review here. The interested reader can consult Fuller (2011).

It should be clear from this brief survey that there is no smoking gun among the pristine transitions outside southwest Asia. However, environmental stresses appear to be plausibly connected with the origins of agriculture in several regions. Our theory may have some application to northern China and sub-Saharan Africa, where refuge locations could have been important. Initial cultivation in southern China and Mesoamerica could be connected with the Pleistocene–Holocene transition but clear evidence is lacking. The role of seasonally dry tropical forests in South America could be consistent with a biased climate shift that depressed the returns to foraging and made cultivation relatively more attractive, even without migration to refuge locations. The development of agriculture in highland New Guinea rather than the tropical lowlands could reflect greater vulnerability to climate shocks in the highlands. We find only a vague suggestion that our framework might apply to eastern North America and no apparent application to India.

We close this section by emphasizing that we do not see a negative climate shock as being necessary for the start of cultivation in all cases. There is at least one other way for cultivation to begin that is consistent with our model: A positive climate trend leading to region-wide Malthusian population growth, which could eventually cause populations at the local level to exceed the threshold needed for cultivation. This mechanism is quite similar to the impacts of climate amelioration discussed in Chapters 3 and 4, which led to technical innovation and sedentism through long-run population growth. In this chapter we have focused on the scenario of a negative shock and resulting migration among sites because we believe this scenario best fits the currently known facts about southwest Asia. But it is certainly possible that in other parts of the world, the Holocene served as a large and protracted positive shock, and induced population growth that led to cultivation.

The main difference in the two causal channels is that a negative shock relies on short-run migration to generate local population spikes, while a positive shock generates more gradual local population growth due to long-run natural growth for the region as a whole. Accordingly, transitions involving negative shocks are likely to have sharper correlations with the timing of initial cultivation. Another distinction is that negative shocks tend to initiate cultivation at a small set of refuge sites, while climate amelioration and long-run population growth tend to initiate cultivation across a broader subset of sites (although the best sites in the region will lead the way in either case). Further empirical research may make it possible to distinguish between these two mechanisms.

5.11 NON-TRANSITIONS

A general theory of agricultural origins should not only be consistent with known transitions. It should also be consistent with cases where no transition occurred. Ideally, as we suggested in Section 5.1, it should address the following questions.

Why a small number of pristine cases?

Consider the conditions that must hold in order for the model of Sections 5.4–5.7 to predict initial cultivation. A period of "good" climate must last long enough for a large regional population to accumulate, diet must be strongly dependent on wild plants vulnerable to climate change, a negative climate shock must be sudden enough that gradual population decline through lower fertility does not solve the problem, a few sites must remain habitable while others are abandoned when the climate turns "bad," migration flows must be sufficiently free, and the productivity of cultivation must rise quickly enough once it begins. Multiplying the probabilities of the numerous necessary conditions together yields a low probability of agriculture, which is consistent with the small number of pristine cases in the archaeological record.

Why no agriculture in earlier interglacials?

The last interglacial period comparable to our own, the Eemian, occurred between about 126,000–116,000 BP, with glacial conditions gradually intensifying during 116,000–78,000 BP. Anatomically modern humans did not live outside Africa in large numbers until around 50,000–70,000 BP, and we do not know to what degree Africa would have been affected by climate shocks around the time of the Eemian. We also do not know whether anatomically modern humans from 100,000 years ago had the cognitive or technological capabilities needed for agriculture.

Why no agriculture during the last Ice Age?

There is no doubt that modern cognitive abilities existed by 40,000–13,000 BP. Richerson et al. (2001) attribute the absence of agriculture at this time to the low mean and high variance of weather during the last Ice Age, which deterred investments in agriculture. This may have played a role, but our approach suggests a further factor: climate instability ruled out long mild periods during which large regional populations could accumulate. There was no precedent for the 1,500–2,000 years of warm and moist climate during which Natufian society arose in southwest Asia. Without this large pre-existing population, a climate reversal would not have caused a sufficient spike in local populations at the best sites, and the cultivation threshold would not have been crossed.

Why no agriculture in the initial warming after the Last Glacial Maximum?

The climate reversal of the Younger Dryas was apparently a necessary condition for initial cultivation. The Natufians failed to embrace cultivation despite 1,500 years of favorable conditions prior to this negative shock, and might never have done so in the absence of such a shock. We attribute this to the insufficiency of local population densities arising through long-run Malthusian growth alone.

Why no pristine agriculture in tropical rainforests?

Bellwood (2005) observes that pristine agriculture never emerged in the rainforests of Africa (or for that matter, anywhere south of the equator in Africa), or in southeast Asia. Higham (1995) takes a similar view of southeast Asia. Pristine agriculture also failed to arise in lowland New Guinea or tropical Australia. Piperno (2011) makes a strong case for domestication in tropical South America, but she stresses the prominent role of forested areas subject to prolonged seasonal droughts. From our perspective, the obvious reason for the rarity of pristine agricultural transitions in tropical rainforests is that such areas are buffered from climate shocks involving periods of aridity lasting for a generation or more. Our theory requires protracted aridity in a populous region with production sites of varying quality. This was probably a rare conjunction in rainforest environments.

Why no pristine agriculture in Japan or on the northwest coast of North America?

These two cases drive home the point that a rich natural setting, a sedentary lifestyle, a high level of technological sophistication, and a complex society are insufficient to bring about an agricultural economy.

Furthermore, both had severe Younger Dryas events and experienced the cooling of 8200 BP, making them especially good points of comparison. For these reasons, we will discuss each case in some detail.

The Jomon period in Japan is dated from about 16,000 BP (see Section 4.3). It is characterized by very early pottery, relatively early sedentism, and a rather late transition to full-scale rice farming (around 2500 BP). When cultivation finally arrived it appears to have been borrowed, along with other cultural characteristics, from the Mumun culture of Korea. It is uncertain whether this involved major population flows from Korea. Rice cultivation could easily have been borrowed from China or Korea at much earlier dates but was not (Bellwood, 2005, 114)

The coastal inhabitants of the Pacific Northwest in North America are often used as the textbook example of a complex society not based on agriculture (see Johnson and Earle, 2000, 204–217). Fish were a key food source, especially the rich seasonal runs of salmon and eulachon. Many other wild foods were used, such as shellfish, waterfowl, marine and land mammals, roots, and berries, but by 8000 BP salmon was the dominant food. Despite a promising environment with mild temperatures and ample precipitation, agriculture never became a core component of the economy (Deur, 1999, 2002).

Our explanation for the non-transition to agriculture in both of these societies is that they were cushioned from negative climate shocks by the availability of fresh water and marine dietary resources. This averted a shift to cultivation despite high population densities (according to Habu, 2004, this is a standard archaeological explanation for the failure of the Jomon to adopt agriculture). Moreover, differences in site qualities might have been less extreme as compared to southwest Asia (or China, or sub-Saharan Africa), so climate fluctuations would have affected most sites in a parallel way. This would have restrained any migratory responses to such shocks, dampening the local population spikes needed to trigger cultivation.

These two cases highlight the fact that our model requires more than just a large climate reversal. If the reversal does not have a major impact on staple foods, or does not occur in a geographic setting with large differences in site qualities, it will not stimulate a transition. The Jomon and Northwest Coast examples had large pre-existing populations and were exposed to significant climate shocks, but lacked these other necessary factors.

5.12 BIOLOGICAL ENDOWMENTS

Diamond (1997) argues that agriculture began in regions having wild plant and animal species that were easy to domesticate. The leading case is southwest Asia, which had an outstanding array of grasses, legumes, and animals that were excellent candidates for domestication. China also had a favorable biological endowment. By contrast, New Guinea and eastern North America had substantially less favorable endowments. Some regions that have high agricultural productivity today, such as California, southwestern and southeastern Australia, southern Africa, and Chile and Argentina, were disqualified from pristine transitions because they had little or nothing to domesticate. As a result, agriculture had to diffuse to such locations from other parts of the world. These ideas have been influential among economists (see Sections 1.10 and 12.3).

When Diamond seeks to explain the timing of the Neolithic in southwest Asia, he appeals to an assortment of factors including resource depletion, increasing availability of domesticable wild plants, technological innovation, and population growth. He says that prior to 8500 BC (10,500 BP), these factors had not yet come into play. Climate is only mentioned in the context of an argument that the transition from the Pleistocene to the Holocene expanded the geographic range for domesticable wild cereals (1997, ch. 6).

Our general view is that Diamond's story may help to explain *where* agricultural transitions occurred, but says little about *when* they occurred. Having a good biological endowment does not by itself shed any light on the question of whether cultivation would begin at 12,000 BP or 8000 BP or 4000 BP. Another problem with Diamond's theory is that it focuses on ease of domestication. In our view, the key question is why cultivation began at all, so what matters most is the marginal productivity of cultivating wild plants relative to the marginal productivity of foraging. The ease of domestication is important in determining the rate at which agricultural productivity rises after cultivation begins, but that is a separate issue.

Despite these objections, there is some empirical support for Diamond's thesis. Olsson and Hibbs (2005) and Bleaney and Dimico (2011) find that regions with more potentially domesticable plant and animal species tended to have earlier transitions to agriculture. However, most of the observations in their data sets involve the diffusion of agriculture, rather than the pristine transitions with which we are concerned. For a study of pristine transitions, albeit with a different focus from Diamond, see Riahi (2020).

We think of Diamond (1997) as providing the "supply side" for a theory about the origins of agriculture, but lacking the "demand side" that would account for the timing of decisions to cultivate. In our approach the supply side consists of the latent productivity of cultivation before it begins and the rate of productivity growth after it gets underway. The demand side involves climate shocks, migration to refuge sites, and the diminishing marginal product of foraging. These factors determine the timing of pristine cultivation. Our model from Sections 5.4–5.7 has both supply and demand components.

To see why biological endowments do not provide a full explanation, consider the failure of the wild-rice-eating people of tropical southeastern Asia to initiate agriculture, in contrast to the people of southern China who did. These two populations had similar biological endowments, but a pristine transition only occurred in the area that was more exposed to climate shocks and had more heterogeneous sites. A similar example is the contrast between lowland (tropical) New Guinea with no transition, and highland (non-tropical) New Guinea where domestication of bananas, taro, and yams occurred. This can be explained by the greater vulnerability of the highlands to climate shocks and the tendency of tropical climates to mute variations in site quality. Although one can argue that Japan and northwest North America lacked good candidates for domestication (the supply-side story), they also had abundant foraging opportunities that were relatively insensitive to climate shocks (the demand-side story).

We close this section by emphasizing that our theory is open to refutation. If future research shows that pristine agriculture evolved in a region where important staple foods were not vulnerable to climate shocks or where the initial cultivation of staples did not coincide with a climate reversal, the version of our theory involving negative climate shocks and migratory responses would not apply, so other explanations would have to be sought. A similar verdict would follow if pristine agriculture occurred in a region with a low initial population density or many high-quality sites, if it occurred first at the lower-quality sites, or if it was not accompanied by migration from poor sites to good ones.

Our survey of pristine transitions in Section 5.10 suggests that our theory is likely to be more relevant for some regions than others. We also suggested that some regional cases might be better explained by positive climate change accompanied by Malthusian population growth in the long run. We leave it for future researchers to decide whether these ideas provide useful insights in particular cases.

5.13 CONCLUSION

We have developed a formal model to explain the origins of agriculture, and we have provided empirical support for our theory. This chapter contributes to the economic literature on the Neolithic Revolution in three main ways: by showing that biased climate change was not necessary for the transition, by highlighting the importance of migration among heterogeneous local sites, and by making population and technology endogenous. We briefly summarize each point.

Biased Climate Change: Much of the literature assumes that agriculture arose due to climate changes that favored cultivation over foraging (see Section 5.2). While this could be true in certain cases, economists rarely provide any evidence that such biases actually existed. If a positive climate shock occurred, why would foragers want to start cultivating rather than enjoying rich foraging opportunities? If a negative climate shock occurred, why would foragers start cultivating at a time when cultivation productivity probably fell? Arguments appealing directly to climate biases raise further puzzles. If a good climate leads to cultivation, why didn't cultivation start in southwest Asia during the Bølling/Allerød period? If a bad climate leads to cultivation, why didn't cultivation start during the Last Glacial Maximum, and why didn't cultivation end in the Early Holocene?

Our formal analysis was carried out on the assumption that climate changes are neutral with respect to the choice between foraging and cultivation. The migration effect from a negative climate shock removes the need for a direct bias, and provides additional empirical content by predicting that the best sites within a region should start cultivating first. Our theory gets the timing right because it is not a specific climate state that causes agriculture. Rather, it is the entire sequence of climate events. The model in this chapter can be extended to accommodate biased shocks if future archaeological research shows that such shocks were important in particular regions.

Heterogeneity and Migration: Theories about the agricultural transition often do not distinguish between processes occurring at the regional and local levels. In our view, this distinction is critical. It is entirely possible that population could be increasing at the regional level while decreasing at some individual sites or vice versa. Models that fail to take this point into account will overlook the role of scarce refuge sites as agricultural incubators. To see the importance of this factor, consider a counterfactual. If all of the sites in southwest Asia had been identical, the Younger Dryas would not have triggered any migration among sites, there would have been no short-run spike in local population anywhere, and there would have been no reason to allocate any labor to cultivation.

Population and Technology: Many economists and archaeologists have debated the relative importance of climate, geography, population, and technology as factors in the origins of agriculture. We view climate and geography as the underlying exogenous variables, with climate change functioning as the trigger that accounts for the timing of initial cultivation, and geography contributing the necessary condition of heterogeneous sites. However, population and technology cannot be ignored. Without a large regional population, a climate reversal cannot generate local population levels sufficient to trigger cultivation. Without rapid technical change once cultivation gets underway, a declining regional population during the reversal could take a society back to foraging rather than forward to a farming economy. By endogenizing population and technology, our model helps to clarify these crucial interactions.

5.14 POSTSCRIPT

This chapter is based on the journal article "Climate reversals and the transition to agriculture" published in the *Journal of Economic Growth* (Dow, Reed, and Olewiler, 2009). Our co-author Nancy Olewiler, an environmental economist at the School of Public Policy at Simon Fraser University, contributed to early drafts of that article. Doug Allen, Matthew Baker, Ofer Bar-Yosef, Cliff Bekar, Sam Bowles, Sue Colledge, Patrick Francois, Oded Galor, Brian Hayden, Hillard Kaplan, Gordon Myers, Arthur Robson, and four anonymous referees gave helpful comments on drafts of the original article. We are also grateful to audiences at Simon Fraser University, the University of British Columbia, the 2005 SSHA conference, the 2006 AEA conference, the 2006 SFU workshop on the Neolithic transition, and the 2006 Conference on Early Economic Developments at the University of Copenhagen. The Social

Sciences and Humanities Research Council of Canada provided financial support. All are absolved of responsibility.

This chapter benefited from feedback at a 2019 seminar given at the Institute of Archaeology, University College London. We are very grateful to Stephen Shennan for hosting our visit to UCL and to Andrew Bevan, Sue Colledge, Dorian Fuller, and Andy Garrard for their expert advice. We also thank Rowan Flad of Harvard for his guidance with regard to China. Sam Bowles, Sue Colledge, and Stephen Shennan commented on a preliminary draft of this chapter. All are likewise absolved of responsibility.

Sections 5.1 and 5.2 have been largely rewritten, with updating in 5.2 to reflect developments in the economic literature since 2009. We have also updated the evidence on southwest Asia in Section 5.3. The model in Sections 5.4–5.7 is unchanged from the original journal article but the text has been revised to clarify various conceptual points. Sections 5.8 and 5.9 are new. Section 5.10 on other transitions has been updated and expanded. Sections 5.11–5.13 have been substantially rewritten.

The formal model in Sections 5.4–5.7 was based almost entirely on data for Abu Hureyra in Moore et al. (2000) and Hillman et al. (2001). When writing the *JEG* article, we had a general awareness of the Neolithic transition in regions such as China and sub-Saharan Africa, roughly at the level of Bellwood (2005), but the archaeological evidence from outside southwest Asia contributed almost nothing to the construction of the model. We had no knowledge of the sources from 2009 and later discussed in Sections 5.8–5.10.

PART III

INEQUALITY AND WARFARE

6

The Transition to Inequality

6.1 INTRODUCTION

Beginning with this chapter we shift from a focus on technological developments to a focus on institutions. Chapters 6–8 explore the origins of inequality and warfare in a pre-state setting. Chapters 9–11 study the origins of cities and states.

These chapters go beyond the food production technologies of Chapters 3–5. In the rest of the book food production will still matter, but we will also have to consider technologies for coercion; that is, the technologies used by one social group against another social group. Chapter 6 introduces a simple technology through which organized insiders can exclude unorganized outsiders from a production site. We show that under suitable conditions, such a technology leads to endogenous group property rights and inequality. Chapters 7–8 consider technologies for conflict between organized groups, leading to an exploration of the conditions for war and peace. Chapters 9–11 study technologies of confiscation, where an organized elite can seize goods, land, or labor from unorganized commoners. This will lead to a theory of taxation and the state.

Economists and archaeologists use terms like "equal" and "egalitarian" in various ways, so we need to be careful about definitions. First, it should be noted that inequality could be social, political, or economic in nature. These types of inequality are positively but imperfectly correlated. Our concern here is only with economic inequality. Second, economic inequality could be defined in terms of wealth, income, or consumption. The theoretical framework of this chapter focuses on consumption.

We use the term "equality" in a modeling context where all of the individuals in a group or region consume the same amount of food, which is the only consumption good in the formal model of this chapter. When inequality arises in our model it is a matter of degree, and we will explain later how inequality can be quantified (see the discussion of Gini coefficients in Section 6.3). Of course, food varies both in quality and quantity, and people value additional consumption goods such as housing and clothing. For modeling purposes we will ignore these complications.

We use the term "egalitarian" (following archaeologists and anthropologists) when referring to situations where agents have equal access to subsistence resources, but some may consume more food than others due to special skills, hard work, or other forms of personal achievement (see Mattison et al., 2016, 185). We are not concerned with such inequalities because we want to explain inequalities across sites or across the economic classes at a site, not among the individuals who make up these groups. When reporting on empirical evidence from archaeology or anthropology we interpret "highly egalitarian" to mean something approaching equal consumption among the members of a group.

We use the term "inegalitarian" when differences in food consumption arise from structural differences in access to subsistence resources such as the exclusion of outsiders from a site or control over land by an elite. This is consistent with common usage among archaeologists. For example, Mattison et al. (2016) call a society "inegalitarian" when access to subsistence resources is unequal due to inheritance or ascribed roles, so that inequality is persistent and institutionalized.

Archaeologists agree that almost every society was egalitarian before 10,000 BP, and that most societies have become inegalitarian in the last 10,000 years (Kohler and Smith, 2018). There are exceptions (for example, southwest Asia shows some signs of inequality well before 10,000 BP, as we will discuss in Section 6.11), but they are rare. This is consistent with evidence from ethnography, which indicates that mobile foraging groups are highly egalitarian. Such societies have been studied in the Kalahari Desert, Australia, Southeast Asia, Amazonia, and the Arctic (Kelly, 2013a). In these societies strong social norms support food sharing and oppose self-aggrandizement (see Boix, 2015, 46–51, and the sources cited there). There may be some differences in work tasks associated with age, sex, and ability, but food consumption is evened out by sharing, and gender-based inequality is frequently muted (Leacock, 1992; Endicott, 1999). Hereditary class distinctions are absent.

Several reasons are often given for why mobile foraging groups tend to be highly egalitarian: (a) production technology is simple and available to everyone; (b) individuals have access to similar natural resources; (c) mobility limits the accumulation of material assets; (d) food storage technology is frequently minimal; (e) the technology for the use of violence is simple and widely available; (f) hunting often involves teamwork; and (g) there are large gains from risk sharing. Anthropologists particularly emphasize the value of food sharing as a form of insurance against bad luck, illness, or injury (Kelly, 2013a).

Sedentary foraging societies are more diverse. Some are relatively egalitarian, but others display considerable inequality both across and within communities. As we discussed in Section 4.1, group sizes for sedentary foragers are larger than for mobile foragers (Kelly, 2013a, 171–172). Compared to mobile foragers, sedentary foragers also have higher populations relative to natural productivity, more food storage, and greater inequality (Rowley-Conwy, 2001, 40–44). Some societies of this kind have hereditary elites, as along the northwest coast of North America (Ames and Maschner, 1999).

More generally, sedentary foraging is correlated with "social hierarchies and hereditary leadership, political dominance, gender inequality, and unequal access to resources" (Kelly, 2013a, 104). To illustrate Kelly's point about gender inequality, we refer again to Abu Hureyra (see Sections 4.3 and 5.3). This village along the Euphrates River was based on sedentary foraging during 13,500–13,000 BP and began to cultivate cereals in subsequent centuries. Molleson (2000, 311–317) reports that women suffered from severe skeletal deformation due to repetitive dehusking and grinding tasks. The specialization of male and female activities was clearly causing systematic and lifelong physical injuries to women.

Ethnography suggests that in agricultural economies all forms of inequality tend to become more pronounced, and class structures are often based upon elite control over land (Johnson and Earle, 2000). However, as with sedentary foraging, there is diversity among agricultural societies. Bogaard et al. (2019) argue that labor-constrained (and chronologically earlier) forms of agriculture tended to exhibit less inequality than land-constrained (and chronologically later) forms. We return to these issues in Section 6.3.

We argued in Chapter 5 that cultivation triggered a long process of learning by doing that raised productivity. Over the course of one or two millennia, cultivation often led to domestication, with additional productivity gains. Here we treat this productivity growth as exogenous and explore its implications for population, property rights, and inequality, which are endogenous. Specifically, we explain the associations among (a) rising productivity, (b) rising population, and (c) rising inequality. The link between (a) and (b) results from Malthusian dynamics while the link between (b) and (c) results from endogenous property rights.

Our starting point is a region in which many identical agents have free mobility across many food acquisition sites. These sites vary in quality due to water availability, soil fertility, and other factors. In a world of open access, food consumption is equal across sites (and individuals) because if it were not, agents would move from sites with low consumption to sites with high consumption. As in Chapter 5, equilibrium implies that local populations must be highest at the best sites.

The new element in this chapter is a technology of exclusion, which underpins the formation of group property rights over production sites. When the number of agents at a site exceeds a critical mass, as it eventually will due to Malthusian population growth, the insiders can drive away or kill outsiders who try to enter. This prevents any further entry and converts open-access land into an exclusive resource.

The insiders at a closed site continue to share food equally. They are better off than outsiders who remain in the commons, and insiders at higher-quality sites are better off than insiders at lower-quality sites. We call this situation *insider–outsider* inequality. Additional growth in productivity and population leads to the enclosure of lower-quality sites. Regional inequality increases in the long run, and the agents still in the commons become increasingly impoverished.

When productivity and population are sufficiently high, stratification emerges at the best sites and then spreads across the region. At stratified sites, insiders control land and employ outside labor at a wage equal to food per person in the commons, generating inequalities within sites rather than just across sites. The marginal product of labor in the stratified sector is equal to its average product in the open sector. Members of the elite at a stratified site receive both land rent and an implicit wage. We call this *elite–commoner* inequality. Our theory predicts that insider–outsider inequality will arise first, with elite–commoner inequality following later if regional population density and settlement sizes become large enough.

Although in our formal modeling we assume that elites hire commoners by paying wages, one can easily reformulate the model to have commoners pay land rents to elites. Our conclusions are not affected by the institutional distinction between a labor market and a land market. Elites and commoners could also adopt sharecropping arrangements. In any of these cases we assume commoners have freedom of movement. This includes movement among open sites in the commons, as well as between open and closed sites (assuming a willingness to work at the terms offered by the insiders at a closed site).

For brevity we omit consideration of slave societies. We think of slavery as the type of commoner labor that occurs when it is easy to monitor and enforce work effort, and to prevent exit from a site. Prehistoric slavery tended to arise through the taking of prisoners in raiding or other forms of warfare. When the technology of coercion makes slavery viable, it is not hard to understand how inequality can emerge. However, in this chapter we will show that inequality can develop even without direct control over labor.

We need to be clear about the distinction between the absolute population at a site and the population density at the site. We assume that members of an insider group help each other repel intruders, and their ability to do so is a function of the physical distances among the insiders. There are no specialized guards or warriors. A site becomes closed when an organized group of insiders becomes sufficiently numerous relative to the land area of the site it is defending. Thus there is a minimum local population density that is necessary in order for insider–outsider inequality to occur.

In the formal model of this chapter, we assume all sites have the same land area. Thus the distinction between local population levels and local population densities will not be important. But in later chapters we sometimes use formal models where the sites have differing land areas and in such cases the proper theoretical concept is local density. We generally simplify by assuming that the required insider density is a parameter that is invariant across sites and over time. But in practice this threshold could depend upon the terrain, the efficiency of the technology used to repel outsiders, the value of the resources at the site, or external events that may encourage entry attempts by outsiders.

A central simplifying assumption is that insiders are organized while outsiders are not. This means that intruders only need to be deterred or repelled one at a time. We will study conflicts over land between organized groups in Chapters 7 and 8, which deal with warfare when the contending groups have internal equality and inequality, respectively.

Another simplifying assumption is that the number of children for a given adult is proportional to that adult's food income, and that all adults convert food into children at an identical rate. This implies that aggregate population growth or decline depends only on aggregate food output, not the way in which food income is distributed among agents. Redistributing income would simply lower the number of children for some agents while raising the number for others by an equal amount, without affecting regional population.

Our theory has implications for upward and downward economic mobility. In long-run equilibrium, aggregate population is stationary, so in each generation parents have just enough children to replace themselves. However, elite agents at stratified sites have more children than are needed for replacement, and the same is true for the insiders at high-quality closed sites without stratification. Conversely, commoners have fewer children than are needed for replacement, and the same is true for the insiders at lower-quality closed sites. To maintain a stationary class structure over time, there must be a mechanism to ensure some downward mobility among children of rich parents. There must also be a process for replenishing the membership of poor insider groups at low-quality closed sites, as well as the membership of the commoner class.

We handle these issues by assuming that in each generation, the children of the previous insiders at a site form a new insider group based, for example, on birth order. After the critical mass needed for exclusion is reached, other offspring are expelled from the site. As a result, all elite agents at a stratified site have elite parents, so elite status is hereditary. However, not all children of elite parents stay in the elite. The same is true for insider groups at high-quality closed sites. On the other hand, when insider parents have too few children to maintain exclusion at a site, all of their children retain insider status. In addition, some commoners will enter until exclusion is restored.

Our theory focuses on the development of corporate landowning groups based on kinship or common descent, rather than property rights at the level of individuals, nuclear families, or households. Agents inherit land by inheriting membership in these corporate groups. We do not rule out more individualistic types of landownership after corporate groups have formed. But the central concept is that insider groups operate as collective actors with respect to the appropriation of land, and we think of them as being the early arrivers at a site. We assume individual members of corporate landowning groups share resources and food equally. In general, we are only concerned with inequalities emerging across classes of insiders, outsiders, elites, and commoners, not with inequalities internal to such classes.

This point requires emphasis because a number of researchers instead focus on inequality across individuals or households (see Sections 6.2 and 6.3). Our perspective leads us to expect bimodal distributions of consumption, income, or wealth at stratified sites, rather than continuous distributions like those of a normal or log normal type. This expectation carries over to diet, health, stature, housing, grave goods, life expectancy, and similar measures of well-being. We do not deny that ranking or inequality occurs within elites or other social classes, but our theory deals with the structural economic inequality across classes.

The reader may recall from Section 1.2 that our "main sequence" went from mobile foraging with open access to sedentary foraging with open access, and then to agriculture with open access, closed access, and stratification. In Chapters 3–5 this sequence enabled us to model the technological trajectory leading to agriculture without the complication of distinguishing between open and closed production sites. However, in practice sedentary foragers can sometimes reach population densities sufficiently high to yield closed access and possibly stratification, which gives an alternative sequence in Figure 1.2. The formal model in this chapter applies equally well to foraging and agricultural societies.

We pause for a moment to consider possible objections from non-economists. It should be clear from the preceding discussion that our theory is highly stylized. To take just one example: the motivations of the agents are extraordinarily simple. We assume they care only about food consumption, and are attracted to food sources like moths to a flame. Readers may ask why our agents do not sacrifice some food income for the sake of proximity to their families and friends, the enjoyment of beautiful landscapes, or an emotional attachment to their places of birth.

As we discussed in Chapter 1, we do not claim to account for the full richness of human psychology. We only claim that simple models can yield interesting insights. It would be impossible to understand the interactions among our variables without adopting various strategic simplifications. The test is not whether our theory is true in the sense of being descriptively accurate, but whether it does a better job of explaining a certain set of empirical facts than other currently available theories.

The rest of the chapter is organized as follows. Section 6.2 discusses conceptual issues and surveys theoretical ideas from archaeologists, economists, and others about the origins of prehistoric inequality. Section 6.3 describes several empirical generalizations from archaeology and anthropology. In Section 6.4 we deviate briefly from prehistory to discuss the California gold rush. This example suggests how group property rights over valuable production sites can be established in the absence of a state.

Section 6.5 develops a short-run model in which a given regional population is distributed across sites, and property rights are endogenously determined at each site. Section 6.6 introduces an aggregate production function for the region as a whole and identifies the distortions associated with property rights issues. Section 6.7 combines the aggregate production function with Malthusian population dynamics to define long-run equilibrium and characterize the adjustment path leading to equilibrium.

Sections 6.8, 6.9, and 6.10 give formal results regarding poverty, inequality, and demography. These sections show that when some sites are closed, higher productivity makes commoners poorer and increases inequality for the region. When stratification exists, some elite children move down into the commoner class in each generation.

Section 6.11 presents archaeologically-based narratives describing the emergence of inequality in four regions: Southwest Asia, Europe, Polynesia, and the Channel Islands off the coast of California. For each of these cases we argue that the sequence of events is consistent with our theory. Section 6.12 summarizes our results and Section 6.13 is a postscript. Proofs of all formal propositions are available at cambridge.org/economicprehistory.

6.2 THEORIES OF INEQUALITY

In one perspective, the egalitarianism of mobile foraging groups represents the natural human condition, and inequality is an anomaly that requires an explanation. In another perspective (common among modern anthropologists and archaeologists), most egalitarian societies harbor "aggrandizers" or "aspiring elites," and the capacity of these societies to restrain incipient inequality is what requires an explanation.

We assume that individuals and small groups routinely engage in self-interested behavior. However, we are also impressed by the fact that for most of human existence, egalitarianism prevailed. At a general level our goal is to explain variations across time and space in the degree of inequality, and we want to identify causal mechanisms linking inequality with the natural environment, technology, and population. But the key item on our agenda is to explain how societies became inegalitarian.

We begin with a conceptual point. Economic inequality (e.g., with respect to food consumption) can involve differences across communities or differences within communities. The archaeological and anthropological literature focuses heavily on the emergence of elite and commoner classes within communities. Much less attention has been paid to inequality across sites, settlements, or communities, each of which may be internally egalitarian. A complete theory of early inequality needs to explain inequality both across the sites within a region (*insider–outsider* inequality) and within individual sites (*elite–commoner* inequality).

Inequality across social groups is likely to arise whenever groups are sedentary, control natural resources of unequal value, are physically able to prevent outsiders from accessing their resources, and can overcome the free-rider problems associated with the defense of a site or territory. There are strong incentives for local groups to solve such problems in order to ensure that entry by outsiders does not reduce food per capita for those already present. When they succeed in creating property rights of this kind, local groups have permanently better standards of living than outsiders who must obtain their food in the remaining open locations. This disables the mechanism that brought about equal food per capita across sites in Chapters 4–5, because now individual agents cannot migrate from sites with low food per capita to sites with high food per capita. However, it does not necessarily imply any departure from egalitarianism within groups.

Another conceptual issue involves the role of biology. Many writers assume that inequality emerges when technology becomes productive enough to provide more food than the biological minimum needed by a society. This generates a surplus that can be distributed unequally, in some cases to support a non-food-producing elite. Such ideas are widespread in the literatures of archaeology and anthropology, and are occasionally adopted by economists as well (for example, Milanovic et al., 2011).

We do not believe commoners' living standards are fixed biologically, for several reasons. First, nutrition, health, and life expectancy are continuous variables and respond to food intake in a continuous way. Second, ethnographic data indicate that under normal conditions, foragers do not devote extraordinary labor time to food acquisition, contrary to what might be expected if they were on the brink of starvation (see table 1.1 in Kelly, 1995). Third, living standards within egalitarian societies evidently declined during the transition from mobile to sedentary foraging as discussed in Section 4.10, and during the transition from sedentary foraging to agriculture as discussed in Section 5.9. Fourth, if commoners in a stratified society have insufficient food to replace themselves demographically, they can be replaced through downward mobility from the elite, as we argued above and will show in Section 6.10. And finally, archaeological evidence suggests that standards of living for commoners in stratified societies have varied across time and space. For example, there is substantial debate over whether early states made commoners better off or worse off, a topic to be discussed in Chapters 9–11. These points support the view that the standard of living among commoners is an economic variable, not a biological constant, even when one adopts a Malthusian perspective.

We do not treat "surplus" as a concept defined by technical productivity in relation to subsistence requirements, and we do not say that rising productivity directly increases "surplus" in some mechanical way. In our theory, the gap in food consumption between elite and commoner agents is traceable to the rent an elite appropriates from the land it controls. Rising productivity in food technology does indeed lead to inequality, but this occurs indirectly by causing regional population density to rise for Malthusian reasons. As a result local populations also rise, and insiders at the most valuable sites eventually become numerous enough to exclude outsiders. The endogenous emergence of property rights enables insiders to capture land rent, and can lead eventually to stratification. As this process unfolds, the rich get richer and the poor get poorer. This contrasts with the prediction that living standards for the poor remain constant at a biological minimum.

In the rest of this section, we survey a range of theoretical perspectives. We start with authors who emphasize natural resources, technology, and population. Next, we go to authors who assign a larger role to coercion. This is followed by a review of ideas on property rights, and finally some comments on culture. As will no doubt become clear, these categories are artificial, and individual authors often cite multiple causal factors. We omit a history of archaeological thought on the subject, but see Price and Feinman (1995, 2012) for references to earlier literature.

Mattison et al. (2016) have proposed a synthesis of archaeological ideas about the transition to inequality (see also the review by Kohler and Smith, 2018, ch. 1). Mattison et al. argue that the Holocene shift to a more stable climate was a necessary condition for the emergence of persistent institutionalized inequality, because the mobile foraging strategies associated with climate instability in the Pleistocene were incompatible with wealth accumulation. However, this climate change was not sufficient (many foraging societies remained egalitarian in the Holocene). A second necessary condition was the presence of dense and predictable resource patches where the benefits of group defense exceeded the costs. A third necessary condition was a role for material assets, such as land or livestock, whose ownership could be readily passed from parents to children. Together these three conditions were sufficient for the emergence of systematic and persistent economic inequality.

Mattison et al. are skeptical about the role of population as a causal factor behind the growth of inequality. They observe that according to some archaeologists, inequality arises when resources are scarce relative to population, while according to others it arises when resources are abundant relative to population. Mattison et al. also tend to see early inequality as emerging from prestige and resulting in broad social benefits. They grant a significant role to coercion only in larger-scale chiefdoms and states.

We agree with Mattison et al. about the importance of high-value sites that can be readily defended. In our model, we assume that regional geography generates a resource gradient from low to high quality sites. We adopt a simple technology for site defense: if the current insider group is too small, it cannot stop further entry, but if it is large enough, it can. The valuable resource in our framework is land. Rights to land can be transmitted from parents to children but only through the inheritance of membership in a social group that collectively controls access to a site.

We do not see population pressure (people relative to resources) as an important factor. Instead, what matters in our theory is population density (people relative to land). It is only at high population densities that an insider group will achieve the size needed to exclude outsiders from a site or territory. In this sense our view is closer to Kelly (2007, ch. 8), who believes population density is the key proximate cause of inequality among hunter-gatherers. In our framework the ultimate causes are nature and technology, which determine population density in the long run through Malthusian dynamics. When nature becomes more benign or technology improves, population rises and inequality increases.

Kennett et al. (2009) offer an explanation for the emergence of stratification that stresses the role of heterogeneous production sites, demographic change, constraints on mobility, and competition over scarce resources. Kennett et al. see increasing population density as a source of social stress that allows dominant individuals to shape institutions in ways favorable to stratification. They argue that this is more likely when productivity differences across sites are large and geographic or social barriers inhibit migration. We agree about the importance of heterogeneous sites and demographic factors. However, by contrast with Kennett et al., we emphasize the endogenous nature of population, the causal dependence of mobility constraints on endogenous property rights, and the idea that insider–outsider inequality is a necessary precursor to stratification.

Johnson and Earle (2000) develop a broad theory of human social evolution from foraging bands to local groups, chiefdoms, and agrarian states. Using many ethnographic studies, they argue that population growth and technological innovation led to subsistence intensification, which generated a series of problems involving risk, conflict, investment, and trade. The solutions to these problems typically implied greater political integration and social stratification.

In the Johnson and Earle framework, population and technology serve as prime movers. Other writers endogenize these variables. For example, Kirch (2010, 190–201) combines an agricultural production function with Malthusian population dynamics to explain the evolution of inequality in Hawaii. His focus on resources, technology, and population is very much in the spirit of our approach.

Henrich and Boyd (2008) endogenize technology. They assume that people acquire economic strategies through imitation, learning, and teaching, and that cultural variants spread if they enhance economic success. There are benefits from specialization and exchange across groups, with unequal productivity gains over time through learning by doing. Poorer groups cannot easily imitate the techniques used by richer groups, so the resulting inequalities become permanent. Henrich and Boyd argue that their model can explain stratification without coercion, deception, or exogenous group differences.

We agree that cultural learning tends to make food technology more productive over time (see Chapters 3–5), especially in the context of cultivation and domestication. However, our model differs by treating technological innovations as common knowledge throughout a region. Another difference is that we require a technology of exclusion by which group property rights over land can be enforced. To this extent, we do include a role for coercion, but only insofar as insiders threaten outsiders with violence in order to deter unauthorized entry at a site. The relationships between elite and commoner agents within stratified sites are voluntary in the sense that the commoners receive wages equal to the food income they could obtain by exiting to one of the remaining open sites.

We turn next to authors who give a larger role to coercion. Gilman (1981) argues that stratification in Bronze-Age Europe resulted from site-specific capital investments, high exit costs, and the use of force by "protectors" who exacted tribute from other agents at the site. Webster (1990) maintains instead that stratification in prehistoric Europe was caused by incipient control over labor through patron–client relationships, rather than by control over non-human wealth or natural resources such as land. Arnold (1993, 1995) surveys a wide range of anthropological explanations for the emergence of inequality in hunter-gatherer societies. Her primary argument is that aspiring elites gain control over household labor in times of environmental or social stress, but she provides few details.

Jared Diamond (1997) has proposed a theory about the origin of inequality that combines increasing productivity with a political economy constraint involving social cohesion. According to Diamond, early foraging bands were kinship-based groups of no more than a few dozen people. With the development of a sedentary lifestyle, tribes of perhaps a few hundred people arose. Diamond sees tribes as egalitarian units within which social cohesion was maintained through kinship ties. He argues that inequality emerged with the formation of chiefdoms whose populations were in the thousands. At high population densities, conflicts between individuals and groups could no longer be resolved through kinship ties alone. The continued existence of such societies required the transfer of coercive power to a "chief" and this concentrated power led to inequality.

The political economist Boix (2015) argues that among simple foragers, social norms prevent predatory behavior. As technology advances, inequality begins to develop because some people are better innovators and some control resources complementary to the innovations. Growing inequality eventually destabilizes the cooperative equilibrium and causes agents to specialize in production or predation according to their comparative advantage. Two possible trajectories can occur: one where coalitions of producers try to keep order and another where predators become rulers. The former path usually leads to less inequality than the latter.

Borgerhoff Mulder et al. (2009) have provided an influential view of inequality in 21 small-scale societies studied by ethnographers. We discuss their empirical findings in Section 6.3, but it is useful to discuss their theoretical perspective here. They define four types of societies based on food technology: hunter-gatherer, horticultural, agricultural, and pastoral. In this classification, horticultural societies have domesticated plants but not plows. They are constrained by labor but not land, and have no land markets.

Borgerhoff Mulder et al. present an equation, applying to all four types of society, in which the wealth of an individual household is a weighted average of wealth inherited from parents and the average wealth of the society, plus an exogenous shock associated with accidents, illnesses, theft, and other random events that are independent across households. They show that in a steady state, the variance of wealth for the society as a whole depends positively on the variance of shocks and also positively on the transmissibility of wealth from parent to child. While random shocks to households will create some initial inequality, the inequality can become permanent over time through inheritance.

There are three general kinds of assets that children can inherit from their parents. The first is embodied wealth (skill, strength, health, intelligence, personality traits). The second is material wealth (land, cattle, tools, houses, resource locations). The third is relational wealth (friendships, kinship connections, positions in social networks). The authors argue that material assets are most easily transmitted from parent to child, while embodied and relational assets are less easily transmitted.

Different types of society tend to have different levels of inequality because their food technologies depend more or less heavily on the various asset types. As we discuss in Section 6.3 below, Borgerhoff Mulder et al. find that hunter-gatherer and horticultural societies tend to have relatively low inequality, while agricultural and pastoral societies tend to have higher levels of inequality. They attribute this to the reliance of the former on embodied and relational assets with low levels of heritability, and the reliance of the latter on material assets such as land or animal herds with greater heritability.

This approach has a number of limitations. First, it focuses heavily on random shocks at the level of the household, rather than structural features of the economy as a whole. Second, it does not explain how property rights over material assets such as land were created and instead simply assumes the inheritability of these assets. Third, it does not provide a theory about the origins of inequality except in the sense that technological developments caused food producers to make greater use of material assets. The model facilitates cross-sectional comparisons among societies of different types, but says little about the causal mechanisms that increased inequality over time within a given society.

Because our story for the origin of inequality stresses the creation of endogenous property rights over land, it is useful to contrast our analysis with that of other economists who have theorized about the evolution of property rights to land in prehistoric societies. North and Thomas (1977), for example, argue that foragers had open access to natural resources that were subject to depletion by over-harvesting. Population growth made this problem more severe and motivated the development of communal property rights over land, which in turn made agriculture attractive.

De Meza and Gould (1992) assume that agents choose whether or not to enforce private ownership claims on resource sites. Our model resembles theirs in having many resource sites with costless mobility among sites. However, they assume that there is a fixed cost of enclosing a site, while we assume that group property rights are a costless byproduct of food acquisition when insiders are sufficiently numerous.

Baker (2003) seeks to explain why foraging societies have varying land tenure institutions. The explanatory variables include resource density and predictability, as well as production and conflict technology. The model involves strategic interactions between insiders and outsiders, where groups must decide how much of their endowed territory to defend and whether they will intrude on territories defended by others.

Rowthorn and Seabright (2010) develop a model of property rights that applies to agriculturalists during the Neolithic transition. They cite evidence showing that increased productivity in early farming was associated with lower levels of nutrition and health. In their model this is explained by an increase in resources allocated to the defense of crops and land from outside groups.

Bowles and Choi (2019) study the co-evolution of agriculture and property rights. In their view, mobile foraging bands had communal control over land. With the arrival of the Holocene, a few sedentary groups with unusually productive and easily defended resources developed private property institutions. A subset of these groups then adopted agriculture. This led to a positive feedback loop in which agriculture reinforced private property rights, and private property rights encouraged agriculture (see Section 5.2).

Our theory differs from North and Thomas (1977), de Meza and Gould (1992), Baker (2003), Rowthorn and Seabright (2010), and Bowles and Choi (2019) in several ways. First, these authors study the creation of group or individual property rights over land but not the emergence of inequality across or within social groups. Second, Baker (2003) limits attention to foraging societies, North and Thomas (1977) and Bowles and Choi (2019) study the co-evolution of property rights and agriculture, and Rowthorn and Seabright (2010) assume an agricultural transition. Our theory applies to both foraging and agricultural societies, while explaining why inequality increases as agricultural societies develop. Finally, unlike these authors we treat population as endogenous.

We end this section with some remarks on the book *The Creation of Inequality* by Flannery and Marcus (2012), who assign a central role to culture. Their book provides a vast array of case studies, ranging from mobile foragers to kingdoms and empires. One key transition is from societies where inequality is based on achievement to those where it is based on hereditary rank. Other transitions involve stratification and monarchy.

Flannery and Marcus often provide rich and insightful cultural descriptions, but their causal stories about transitions from one social structure to another are sometimes frustratingly vague. The following statement about causality is representative.

[I]nequality results from people's efforts to be thought of and treated as superior. Whatever the supporting role of factors such as population growth, intensive agriculture, and a beneficent environment, hereditary inequality does not occur without active manipulation of social logic by human agents ... We suspect that prehistory is full of cases where one segment of society manipulated itself into a position of superiority; the problem for archaeologists is finding a way to document the process.

(191)

Our problem with this approach is that in virtually every society, some people seek to be treated as superior, and seek to manipulate prevailing social norms in their favor. If this were sufficient to create inequality, then inequality would be universal. It is essential to identify the objective conditions under which such strategies are likely to succeed or fail. The relevant conditions almost certainly involve population, technology, and the natural environment. Unfortunately, Flannery and Marcus pay little attention to these variables, and often dismiss them or minimize their importance, although they do concede near the end of the book that population growth, intensive agriculture, and climatic improvement "could create a favorable environment for inequality" (553).

In our theory culture does not instigate major economic transitions, but it is an enabling factor that operates in the background to facilitate collective decision-making and learning by doing. Our foreground factors for explaining the origins of inequality, as in previous chapters, are the natural environment, technology, and population.

6.3 EVIDENCE ON INEQUALITY

This section surveys broad empirical generalizations about prehistoric inequality in order to provide a backdrop for the formal model we will develop in Sections 6.5–6.10. The ideal data for testing our theory would involve evidence on the emergence of insider–outsider and elite–commoner inequality within a geographic region over time. A number of archaeological narratives of this sort will be presented in Section 6.11. Here we focus mainly on cross-sectional data at the level of individuals or households, although a few time-series findings will also be discussed.

Archaeologists have several sources of information on inequality in prehistoric societies, including house sizes, artifact distributions, burials, and health status inferred from bones and teeth. Each source has its advantages and disadvantages. For example, house size may vary with family size over the life cycle rather than reflecting permanent inequalities in wealth. Grave goods may reflect prestige rather than the tangible wealth owned by a person in life. Nevertheless, evidence of each kind offers valuable insights.

Archaeological measures of inequality typically involve stocks of wealth such as housing or jewelry. On the other hand, our formal models refer to flows per unit of time (food income and food consumption). An individual with permanently high food income is likely to have high wealth because food resources can be exchanged for labor services such as house construction, or for the jewelry placed in burials. Thus in practice there is likely to be a strong association between stock and flow measures of inequality.

The most commonly used quantitative index of inequality within a population is the Gini coefficient. The construction of this index will be explained using Figure 6.1. One first ranks the individual members of a population on the dimension of interest (e.g., house size). One then creates a graph where the horizontal axis indicates the poorest 10% of the population, the poorest 20%, and so on, up to the poorest 100%. By definition the latter is the entire population. On the vertical axis, one plots the percentage of the total wealth (e.g., total housing space) owned by the corresponding subset of the population. For example, the poorest 10% might own 3% of the total housing space, the poorest 20% might own 8%, and so on, up to the poorest 100%, who necessarily own 100% of the total housing space.

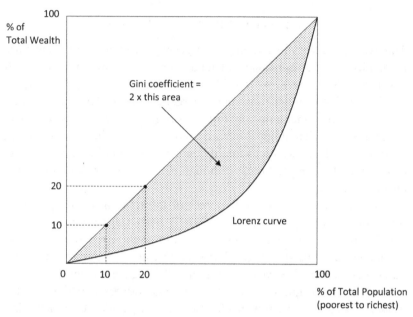

FIGURE 6.1. Lorenz curve and Gini coefficient

The resulting curve is called a Lorenz curve. In a society with perfect equality the Lorenz curve would be the straight diagonal line from the lower left to the upper right in Figure 6.1 (the "bottom" 10% would have 10% of the total housing space, and so on). The curve bows outward below this diagonal line if there is some inequality. In the extreme case where one person owns all of the wealth in question, the Lorenz curve is identical to the horizontal axis except for a jump to 100% along the right side of the graph because the richest person is included in the poorest 100% of the population.

The Gini coefficient is defined to be twice the area between the diagonal line of perfect equality and the actual Lorenz curve. This yields a numerical value between zero (complete equality) and one (extreme inequality). The same methods can be applied to other forms of wealth, such as inequality in grave goods. Assuming the availability of data, a Gini coefficient can also be used as a summary measure for inequality in income or consumption. Moreover, the units of observation need not be individuals; they could be households or other subunits within a larger social group.

The Gini coefficient has limitations. For example, suppose a site is stratified and there is a bimodal distribution where a small elite is quite wealthy and a large majority is very poor. Although the resulting Gini value will be high, it will not reveal the existence of the underlying class structure. For this, one needs the entire Lorenz curve. The shape of the Lorenz curve predicted by our theory of stratification will be discussed in Section 6.9. Partly for these reasons, archaeological narratives like those in Section 6.11 provide an important supplement to Gini coefficients and other numerical indexes of inequality.

More broadly, archaeological applications of the Gini coefficient frequently have problems of non-comparability, bias, and lack of precision. Fochesato et al. (2019) find that the statistical adjustments needed to deal with grave goods, slaves, and exclusion of households without property are often substantial. On the other hand, the adjustments to deal with differing populations and sample sizes are generally minor.

Kohler et al. (2018) offer the most comprehensive overview of prehistoric Gini coefficients with respect to housing inequality. The authors draw upon archaeological data from 62 societies running the gamut from foraging groups to state-level societies such as Old Babylonia and Pompeii. Foraging societies generally have the lowest inequality, with Gini coefficients that vary within a narrow band below 0.2. Horticultural societies, which have domesticated plants, move frequently, face minimal land constraints, and use some foraged resources, typically have higher Gini coefficients for housing than foragers, as well as a greater range of variation. Agriculturalists have the highest levels of housing inequality and also the greatest range of variation, with some overlap in the distributions for agriculturalists and horticulturalists.

The same authors explore relationships between settlement sizes and inequality. They define a *village* as a settlement of fewer than a thousand residents lacking a central feature; a *town* as a settlement of more than a thousand residents without a central feature or more than two hundred with a small or moderately sized central feature; and a *city* as a settlement with more than a thousand residents and a large central feature. They find that Gini coefficients tend to be larger as one moves from villages to towns to cities, although there is substantial overlap in the distributions of Ginis for each category.

Kohler et al. find no relationship between regional population size and the Gini coefficient for housing. This is perhaps not surprising, given that regions can differ in their geographic scale. A more relevant measure is population density. For the 11 Old World cases where data exist, they find a strong positive relationship between population density and inequality. No such relationship is found for the 28 New World cases. They also find a positive relationship between population at a local site and inequality. This relationship is stronger in the Old World than in the New World.

In both hemispheres, Ginis start low and rise as cultivation begins. The authors associate this with rising productivity, greater residential stability, and increasing size of social groups (309). For the first two millennia after cultigens are observed, the Ginis are similar in the two hemispheres. The Ginis then flatten out in the New World. But in the Old World there is a pause about three millennia after the appearance of cultigens, which is followed by resumption in the growth of Ginis. Fochesato et al. (2019, 867) comment that "no plausible adjustments ... would change the result that post-Neolithic wealth inequality in Eurasia tended to be higher than inequality in the Western hemisphere."

Kohler et al. consider various explanations for this difference. One possibility is a difference in the nature of state institutions. However, the difference in Gini coefficients across hemispheres becomes evident prior to state formation (by about 6000 BP). Their preferred explanation is that Old World societies had greater access to large domesticated animals. This could have increased inequality through several causal channels: enhanced agricultural productivity through plowing, inequality in the ownership and inheritance of animals, the use of horses and camels for military conquest, and so on. For more on this topic, see Kohler et al. (2017).

Bogaard et al. (2019) distinguish between labor-limited and land-limited farming technologies. The ratio of the marginal product of labor to the marginal product of land is higher in societies of the former type than societies of the latter type. Intuitively, when agriculture is labor-limited the society treats labor as scarce and land as abundant. When agriculture is land-limited the society instead treats labor as abundant and land as scarce.

Bogaard et al. draw on evidence from western Eurasia to argue that Neolithic agriculture was labor-limited and had levels of inequality similar to foraging societies. Over time, land scarcity tended to increase due to changes in the underlying production technology, such as the use of oxen for plowing. This was associated with rising Gini coefficients. The authors attribute increasing inequality partly to opportunities for the unequal ownership and inheritance of valuable land (as well as animals). Some of their data comes from societies with states and written texts but the general pattern is clearly visible among pre-state farming societies.

Prehistoric inequality can also be assessed using grave sizes or grave goods. We will provide some qualitative information of this sort in

Section 6.11 when we present our regional narratives. Yu et al. (2019) employ quantitative methods to study two Neolithic Chinese settlements, each of which had strong class stratification.

The Dawenkou archaeological site was a central settlement in North China. A total of 133 graves were excavated. Most were small (less than 5 m²), but a few were huge (around 14 m²). The latter were filled with ceramic vessels along with jade, bone, and antler implements. The early phase of occupation (6000–5500 BP) gives a Gini for grave areas of 0.23; the middle phase (5500–5000 BP) a Gini of 0.34; and the late phase (5000–4500 BP) a Gini of 0.65. The differences are strongly statistically significant and reveal "gradually increasing social inequality" (4953). Yu et al. suggest that this may help to explain an escalation of violent conflict and social turmoil in the late phase.

Liangzhu was a central settlement in East China during the late Neolithic period. A total of 80 graves were excavated, again with a clear class distinction. Most graves were less than 3 m² and commonly contained pottery. A few elite graves were 5–7 m² and had jade, silk, ivory, and lacquer artifacts. In the early phase (5500–5000 BP), the Gini for grave sizes is estimated to be 0.43. During the middle phase (5000–4500 BP), this falls to 0.19, and in the late phase (4500–4000 BP) it is 0.20. The decline is strongly significant, indicating that elite–commoner inequality can sometimes drop substantially.

Another way to assess prehistoric inequality is through variation in the heights of individuals inferred from skeletal data (Boix and Rosenbluth, 2014; Boix, 2015). While much of this variation (perhaps 80%) is due to genetic factors, some (perhaps 20%) is due to environmental conditions. In particular, short stature tends to be associated with a lack of food during childhood and adolescent growth spurts. There are methodological issues surrounding such inferences (see Boix and Rosenbluth, 2014, 4–6), but skeletal remains do provide an interesting additional perspective on inequality.

Boix and Rosenbluth describe intriguing time-series findings for Japan. The early Jomon, a largely sedentary hunter-gatherer population (see Section 4.3), had a coefficient of variation for male height of 2.70. By contrast, the agricultural Yayoi who supplanted the Jomon had a male coefficient of variation of 3.56. The authors say this is "suggestive but not conclusive evidence" that agriculture resulted in more male inequality (14). They argue that male height dispersion increased further, again indicating greater inequality, as agriculture became more labor intensive and warfare became more widespread.

Ethnography offers further information about inequality in small-scale societies. As usual, one should be cautious about extrapolating back from recent societies to those of the distant past. However, some empirical generalizations seem very robust and it is difficult to imagine that they would not also have applied in prehistory.

As we observed in Section 4.1 and reiterated in Section 6.1, mobile and sedentary foragers tend to differ along several dimensions. Sedentary foraging societies generally have highly predictable natural resources, large settlement sizes, perimeter defense, and tightly controlled resource ownership. There is often, although not always, a hierarchical class structure based upon descent (Kelly, 2007, ch. 8). In some situations, technological innovation and climate change have led to transitions from mobile to sedentary strategies, resulting in the development of closed settlements and stratification (see the discussions of northwest Alaska and the northwest coast of North America by Boix, 2015, 96–101). Thus it can be misleading to lump all hunter-gatherers together. However, in the work of Borgerhoff Mulder et al. discussed below, the sedentary hunter-gatherer societies tend to be near the egalitarian end of the spectrum, which mitigates this problem.

Borgerhoff Mulder et al. (2009) have estimated Gini coefficients for 21 societies studied by ethnographers, classified into four broad types: hunter-gatherer, horticultural, agricultural, and pastoral. We discussed the theoretical framework used by these authors in Section 6.2. In their model, the welfare of a household is determined by its embodied, material, and relational capital, with weights on these three kinds of capital that can vary across societies. These weights come from estimates by experts who have studied each society and indicate the percentage increase in welfare that would occur in response to a 1% increase in each type of wealth. The authors estimate heritability measures for each type of capital in each society using regression techniques.

The central results can be summarized as follows. First, material wealth (such as land or animals) is highly heritable for agricultural and pastoral societies. It is not highly heritable for hunter-gatherers or horticulturalists, probably because material wealth in the latter cases tends to take a different form (for example, in a hunter-gatherer society it may include tools made from non-durable materials). Second, material wealth is much more important as a determinant of household welfare in agricultural and pastoral societies by comparison with hunter-gatherer and horticultural societies. Third, the societies in which wealth is more hereditable have more inequality measured by Gini coefficients. Hunter-gatherers have the lowest Ginis while horticulturalists have somewhat higher Ginis. The Ginis for agriculturalists and pastoralists are much higher, with pastoralists at the top.

For hunter-gatherer and horticultural societies, parents in the top wealth decile are three times more likely to have children in the top wealth decile as compared to parents in the bottom decile. For agricultural societies, this becomes eleven times more likely, and for pastoral societies, it is twenty times more likely. If we aggregate hunter-gatherer and horticultural societies into one group and agriculturalists and pastoralists into another group, 45% of the difference in inequality between the two groups is due to technology (differences in the relative importance of various assets) and 55% is due to institutions (differences in the hereditability of assets).

In our view, the general similarity of hunter-gatherer and horticultural societies suggests that it is not the availability of domesticated plants that matters for inequality. Rather, it is the degree to which good land is a scarce resource relative to population or labor supply. For details, see Gurven et al. (2010). Related articles appear in a special issue of *Current Anthropology* (Symposium, 2010).

Boix (2015, 37–44) uses data on 1,100 foraging and non-foraging societies from the Ethnographic Atlas. He finds a strong association between production technologies and settlement sizes. Among simple foragers, only 6.2% of societies have settlements of more than 200 people. For complex foragers (often those having aquatic food resources), this figure is 7.4%. Among societies with extensive or shifting agriculture (often called horticulturalists), the fraction rises to 44.1%, and for intensive agriculturalists it is 78.7%. No foraging societies in the sample had settlements larger than 1,000 residents, while 10% of horticulturalists and 51.5% of agriculturalists had such settlements.

For the same four categories defined by production technology, the percentage of societies having some inheritance rules about land is 8.3% among simple foragers, 24.7% for complex foragers, 87.1% for horticulturalists, and 96.5% for intensive agriculturalists. Importantly for us, the percentage of societies having an elite or other class structure is 1.9% among simple foragers, 25.6% for complex foragers, 28.7% for horticulturalists, and 55.4% for intensive agriculturalists. Boix carries out ordered probit regressions and finds that these differences are statistically significant at conventional levels (see also the results for settlement patterns and stratification in table 5.1 of Boix, 2015, 182–184).

Taking the evidence from this section as a whole, it seems indisputable that there are strong correlations between food production technology and inequality, with farming and pastoralism leading to greater differences in housing, stronger inheritance processes, and more stratification into elite and commoner classes. These patterns are visible from both prehistory and ethnography. There are also suggestions that the link between food production technology and economic inequality might be mediated by variables such as regional population density, settlement size, or both. We address these connections later in the chapter. First, however, we need another piece of the puzzle: the creation of group property rights over valuable production sites. For an illuminating recent case we turn to the California gold rush of the nineteenth century.

6.4 THE CALIFORNIA GOLD RUSH

When the California gold rush started in 1848, mineral rights were held by the US government (all information is from Umbeck, 1981). However, enforcement proved impossible due to high rates of desertion from the military. From 1848 to 1866 open access prevailed, except at sites where property rights were created endogenously.

Miners foraged for gold using simple technologies involving little human capital. The exclusion technology was based only on numbers of miners. Miners would wait a short period after a discovery at a site had been made public before allocating gold land. At that point, a majority vote would be held and early arrivers would be allowed to stay, while late arrivers would be compelled to leave. The values of the claims of the insiders were then equalized.

To maintain their exclusive mining rights, miners were required to be present at the mining site and to work their claims a specified number of days per week. Miners were collectively required to enforce each other's mining rights. Failure to comply with these rules led to expulsion from the site. Although all miners were well armed, there is little evidence of violence in the gold fields. There is also no evidence that specialized gunfighters were hired, or that unusual abilities in the use of violence were important.

The population of miners was perhaps 800 in May 1848 and had grown to over 100,000 one year later. Early in this process, there is no evidence that any sites were closed. Individuals or small teams worked under open access conditions. Population densities were higher at better sites (often those closest to water supplies).

By 1849, contracts between miners show that exclusive mining rights had arisen at some sites. These contracts describe explicit responsibilities for group enforcement of property rights. The inequality in the gold fields through 1866 was insider–outsider, in the sense that some groups of miners had more valuable sites and thus higher per capita incomes. It never involved stratification among miners at an individual site, except in a few instances where miners hired local Native Americans to search for gold. In 1866 the US Congress passed legislation that ended the need for self-enforcement by the miners.

This narrative captures several features of our formal model, including (a) many sites of heterogeneous quality within a region; (b) initial conditions of open access; (c) creation of group property rights when local population densities became high enough; (d) a low cost of property right enforcement after a critical mass of agents was reached; (e) little difficulty with free-rider problems among insiders at a site; (f) no specialization with respect to violence; and (g) roughly equal endowments of human and physical capital among the agents. The main difference from our framework is that we treat population growth as a Malthusian response to rising productivity, while in the gold fields population grew rapidly through in-migration.

Putting the latter point aside, we believe that small groups of hunter-gatherers or agriculturalists would most likely have cooperated to defend territories using generally available weapons (clubs, spears, bows and arrows) much as the gold miners did using rifles, and that the number of insiders would have been the key variable in deterring potential intruders. While our model does not deal with coalitions of intruders (that is, warfare), it should be noted that coalitions of gold miners did not engage in warfare over mining sites.

6.5 SHORT-RUN EQUILIBRIUM

At an individual production site, food output (in calories) is $\theta s L^{\alpha}$ where $\theta > 0$ reflects region-wide climate, resources, and technology; $s > 0$ is the quality of the site; $L \geq 0$ is labor used for food production; and $0 < \alpha < 1$. The input of land is normalized at unity. Variations in site quality reflect local geographic factors such as terrain, soil, or availability of fresh water. Labor has diminishing returns due to the fixed land input.

Each individual agent is negligible relative to the number of agents at the site as a whole. An agent is endowed with a unit of time, which is used for food production. We ignore leisure. Any agent at the site can migrate to another site and obtain a quantity of food w. There is an infinitely elastic supply of outsiders who will enter the site if they are not excluded and can obtain more than w by doing so.

A group of $d > 0$ or more food producers can cooperate to prevent outsiders from appropriating land at the site. This is an automatic by-product of food production and does not have an opportunity cost (exclusion involves deterrence rather than building a fence or patrolling a perimeter). The weapons used to defend a site are readily available to all. Deterrence fails whenever there are fewer than d agents at the site, and in this case outsiders will enter if they can enhance their food consumption by doing so.

Let n be the number of agents born at the site. There are two ways in which a group of size d may arise. If $n \geq d$, a subset of size d is determined by birth order. This core group, called *insiders*, appropriates all of the land at the site. The other n-d agents become *outsiders* and have no land endowment. Alternatively, if $n < d$, those born at the site fall short of the number needed for exclusion. But if enough outsiders are attracted to the site, exclusion occurs after the first d-n agents have arrived from other sites.

Next consider a region with a continuum of production sites. Physical mobility among sites is costless but the agents cannot leave the region due to natural barriers such as deserts, mountains, or ocean. Site qualities are distributed uniformly on the interval $s \in [0, 1]$. Let n(s) be the number of people born at a site of quality s. Define the short run to be a period in which the total regional population $N \equiv \int_0^1 n(s) \, ds$ does not change. We interpret this as one human generation.

In the short run, labor is allocated across sites as follows.

Definition 6.1

Fix the productivity $\theta > 0$ and the population $N > 0$. A *short-run equilibrium* (SRE) is a wage $w > 0$ and a density function $L(\cdot)$ with $N = \int_0^1 L(s) \, ds$ such that

    (a) If $L(s) < d$ then $w = \theta s L(s)^{\alpha-1}$ (open sites)

    (b) If $L(s) \geq d$ then   (closed sites)

         (i) $L(s)$ maximizes $\theta s L^\alpha - w(L - d)$ subject to $L \geq d$, and

        (ii) $r(s) \equiv \theta s L(s)^\alpha - w L(s) \geq 0$.

Part (a) states that all sites where exclusion is impossible must have the same food per capita w, which is equal to the average product of labor. Because mobility is costless these sites must be equally attractive in equilibrium. We call such sites *open* and refer to the set of all open sites as the *commons*.

Part (b) describes sites where insiders can exclude outsiders. We call such sites *closed*. At these sites the d insider agents choose some number of outsiders L – d ≥ 0 who are admitted to the site and allowed to produce food there. We assume that the methods used to exclude outsiders can also be used to prevent them from appropriating land after they are admitted. Any outsiders allowed to produce food at the site receive the wage w.

When L = d so that no outsiders are admitted, we say that the site is closed but *unstratified*. When L > d, the site is both closed and *stratified*. In the latter situation, we distinguish between the *elite* (the insiders who control access to land) and the *commoners* (the hired outsiders who have no land claim and receive the wage w). Commoner labor does not contribute to entry deterrence.

Condition (b)(i) in the definition of SRE requires that when a site is closed, the number of hired agents is chosen to maximize the net food income of the insider group. The resulting food is shared equally among the d landowners, so that each receives $w + [\theta sL(s)^\alpha - wL(s)]/d$. Condition (b)(ii) requires that the land rent $r(s) \equiv \theta sL(s)^\alpha - wL(s)$ obtained at a closed site be non-negative. Otherwise the insiders would be better off abandoning the site and moving to the commons themselves.

Landowners in the stratified sector maximize profit, and thus at every site in this sector the marginal product of labor is equal to the wage. The wage, in turn, is equal to the average product of labor in the commons. At a site that is closed but unstratified, the marginal product of labor at the site is below the average product in the commons, so it is unprofitable for insiders to employ outsiders.

We prove the existence and uniqueness of SRE in three steps. First, we consider an arbitrary wage w and characterize the property rights and labor inputs that must occur at each site in an SRE. This is done in Lemma 6.1 below. The main result is that there are quality bounds s^a and s^b with $0 < s^a < s^b$ such that sites with qualities below s^a are open, sites of intermediate quality are closed but unstratified, and sites with qualities above s^b are both closed and stratified. Lemma 6.2 establishes that if a wage and a labor allocation satisfy the conditions of Lemma 6.1 and also clear the labor market, then a SRE occurs.

Finally, Proposition 6.1 shows that equating labor demand with the labor supply N yields a unique equilibrium wage. This wage determines a unique set of property rights through Lemma 6.1. Because the definition of SRE only involves the ratio $x \equiv w/\theta$ rather than w and θ separately, in this section we fix θ and work with the normalized wage x.

Lemma 6.1

Fix the normalized wage $x \equiv w/\theta > 0$. Let $L(\cdot, x)$ be a density function that satisfies (a) and (b) in D6.1 for the given x. Define $s^a(x) \equiv xd^{1-\alpha}$ and $s^b(x) \equiv (x/\alpha)d^{1-\alpha}$.

(a) If $s < s^a(x)$ then $L(s,x) = (s/x)^{1/(1-\alpha)} < d$ (open sites)
(b) If $s^a(x) \leq s \leq s^b(x)$ then $L(s,x) = d$ (unstratified sites)
(c) If $s^b(x) < s$ then $L(s,x) = (\alpha s/x)^{1/(1-\alpha)} > d$ (stratified sites)

Lemma 6.1 shows that for any wage level, a commons must exist. If x is high enough that $1 < s^a(x)$, all sites are in the commons. At intermediate wage levels we have $0 < s^a(x) \leq 1 \leq s^b(x)$, where at least one of the latter inequalities is strict. Inferior sites are open and superior sites are closed, but no sites are stratified. If the wage is low enough that $0 < s^a(x) < s^b(x) < 1$, all three sectors exist, with the best sites both closed and stratified.

The latter case is illustrated in Figure 6.2. The density $L(\cdot, x)$ showing labor input as a function of site quality is rising in the open sector, flat on the interval where insiders do not use hired labor, and rising again in the stratified sector. The areas $D_O(x)$, $D_I(x)$, $D_E(x)$, and $D_C(x)$ under the density curve show the total labor input (i) at open access sites; (ii) by insiders at unstratified sites; (iii) by elites at stratified sites; and (iv) by commoners at stratified sites, respectively.

Lemma 6.2

Fix the population $N > 0$. A normalized wage x and a density function $L(\cdot, x)$ that satisfy (a), (b), and (c) in Lemma 6.1 form a SRE if and only if $N = \int_0^1 L(s,x)\, ds$.

Lemma 6.2 shows that an equilibrium can be found by associating each normalized wage with the corresponding density function from Lemma 6.1, computing the area under this density as in Figure 6.2, and then varying the wage until the total area under the density curve is equal to the regional population N. This procedure gives the following results.

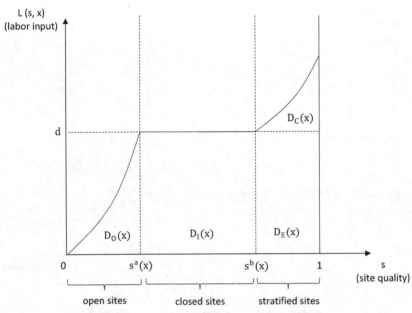

FIGURE 6.2. Labor input as a function of site quality for a fixed normalized wage

---

Proposition 6.1 (short-run equilibrium).

Define $Q \equiv (1 - \alpha)/(2 - \alpha)$, $N^a \equiv Qd$, $N^b \equiv 2Qd$, $x^a \equiv d^{\alpha-1}$, and $x^b \equiv \alpha d^{\alpha-1}$. Let the labor demand function be $D(x) \equiv \int_0^1 L(s, x)\, ds$ where $L(s, x)$ is obtained from **Lemma 6.1**.

(a) $N < N^a$ implies $x^a < x$ and $D(x) = Qx^{-1/(1-\alpha)}$

(b) $N^a \leq N \leq N^b$ implies $x^b \leq x \leq x^a$ and $D(x) = d-xd^{2-\alpha}/(2-\alpha)$

(c) $N^b < N$ implies $x < x^b$ and $D(x) = Q\left[xd^{2-\alpha}/\alpha + (\alpha/x)^{1/(1-\alpha)}\right]$

(d) The labor demand function $D(x)$ is continuously differentiable with $D'(x) < 0$ for all $x > 0$. Also, $\lim_{x \to 0} D(x) = \infty$ and $\lim_{x \to \infty} D(x) = 0$.

(e) For each $N > 0$, there is a unique $x > 0$ such that $D(x) = N$. The combination of this normalized wage and the associated labor allocation $L(\cdot, x)$ from Lemma 6.1 form a unique SRE for the given N. The equilibrium wage $x(N)$ is continuously differentiable with $x'(N) < 0$, $\lim_{N \to 0} x(N) = \infty$, and $\lim_{N \to \infty} x(N) = 0$.

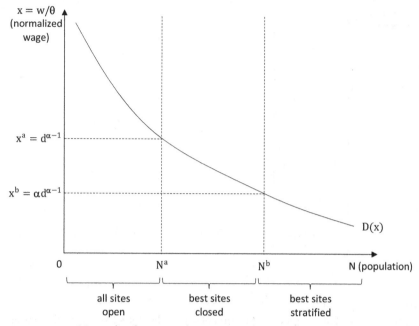

FIGURE 6.3. Normalized wage and property rights as a function of regional population

Figure 6.3 shows the relationships among the regional population N, the wage, and property rights. The downward sloping labor demand curve $D(x)$ is obtained from Proposition 6.1, and the regional population N gives a vertical supply curve for labor. At low population levels, the wage is high and all sites are open, because even the best sites fail to reach the threshold d. Population growth leads to a falling wage. Beyond N^a, the best sites become closed. Further population growth leads to more enclosures in order of decreasing site quality. Beyond N^b, the best sites are both closed and stratified.

6.6 THE AGGREGATE PRODUCTION FUNCTION

Before considering long-run equilibrium, we need to develop some ideas about aggregate output. First, suppose that all sites are open. Due to the constant elasticity of output, equalizing the average product of labor across sites is the same as equalizing the marginal product of labor (MPL = αAPL). Therefore labor is allocated efficiently. But if some sites are closed, a distortion occurs because labor input is constant on [$s^a(x)$, $s^b(x)$] while site qualities are not, so marginal products are unequal. If some sites are stratified, a second distortion arises because the marginal product of labor at such sites is equal to the average product at open sites. Here we study the implications for regional output.

Total food output for the region is

$$Y = \int_0^1 \theta s L(s, x)^\alpha ds \qquad (6.1)$$

where the labor allocation $L(\cdot, x)$ satisfies Lemma 6.1 and the equilibrium wage is derived from $D(x) = N$ in Proposition 6.1. Thus the aggregate production function becomes

$$Y(N) = \int_0^1 \theta s L[s, x(N)]^\alpha ds \qquad (6.2)$$

or

$$Y(N) = \phi[x(N)] \qquad \text{where} \qquad \phi(x) = \int_0^1 \theta s L(s, x)^\alpha ds \qquad (6.3)$$

Proposition 6.2 (aggregate production function).

As in Proposition 6.1, let $Q \equiv (1-\alpha)/(2-\alpha)$, $N^a \equiv Qd$, $N^b \equiv 2Qd$, $x^a \equiv d^{\alpha-1}$, and $x^b \equiv \alpha d^{\alpha-1}$.

(a) $N < N^a$ implies $x^a < x$ and $\phi(x) = \theta Q x^{-\alpha/(1-\alpha)}$
(b) $N^a \leq N \leq N^b$ implies $x^b \leq x \leq x^a$ and $\phi(x) = \theta[x^2 d^{2-\alpha}(Q - 1/2) + d^\alpha/2]$
(c) $N^b < N$ implies $x < x^b$ and $\phi(x) = \theta Q[x^2 d^{2-\alpha}(1+\alpha)/2\alpha + (\alpha/x)^{\alpha/(1-\alpha)}]$

The function $\phi(x)$ is continuously differentiable with $\phi'(x) < 0$ for all $x > 0$. The function $Y(N) = \phi[x(N)]$ is continuously differentiable with $Y'(N) > 0$ for all $N > 0$.

Corollary to Proposition 6.2

(a) $N < N^a$ implies $Y(N) = \theta N^\alpha Q^{1-\alpha}$
(b) $N^a \leq N \leq N^b$ implies $Y(N) = (\theta d^\alpha/2)[1 - \alpha(2-\alpha)(1 - N/d)^2]$
(c)   There is a population level $N^c > N^b$ such that (i) $Y''(N) > 0$ for $N^b < N < N^c$, (ii) $Y''(N^c) = 0$, and (iii) $Y''(N) < 0$ for $N^c < N$.
(d)   For any fixed $\theta > 0$, $Y(N)/N$ is continuously differentiable and decreasing, with $\lim_{N \to 0} Y(N)/N = \infty$ and $\lim_{N \to \infty} Y(N)/N = 0$.

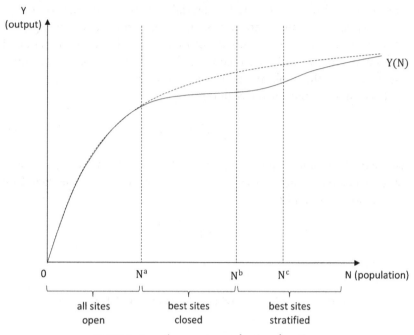

FIGURE 6.4. Aggregate production function

Figure 6.4 shows the production function Y(N). This function is increasing with a continuous marginal product, but its second derivative is discontinuous at N^a and N^b. In the population interval $N < N^a$, all sites are open and there are no distortions. Output has a Cobb–Douglas form as in part (a) of the Corollary, where Q can be interpreted as the endowment of quality-adjusted land for the region as a whole. In the range $N^a < N < N^b$, higher-quality sites are closed and labor input is constant at d across these sites. In this interval Y(N) is below the dashed continuation of the Cobb–Douglas function from (a).

When $N^b < N$, the highest-quality sites become stratified. This creates a further distortion because the marginal product of labor is not equalized between the open and stratified sectors. As shown in Figure 6.4, for population levels near N^b the production function is convex. The rising marginal product results from the shifting property rights boundaries between the open and closed sectors as well as the unstratified and stratified sectors. Y(N) has an inflection point at N^c and then returns to concavity. At very high population levels almost all sites are stratified, marginal products are equal at almost all sites, and Y(N) approaches the dashed Cobb–Douglas curve in Figure 6.4.

Aggregate per capita food Y(N)/N is globally decreasing in total population N, as indicated in part (d) of the Corollary. This occurs because the usual tendency for average product to decline at each individual site outweighs the property rights effects responsible for the non-concave portion of Y(N).

6.7 LONG-RUN EQUILIBRIUM

Population is endogenous in the long run. Each adult in period t has children who survive to become adults in period t+1. Adults from period t die at the end of that period. The number of children for an individual is equal to the parent's food income multiplied by a constant $\rho > 0$. This relationship arises because fertility is an increasing function of food, childhood mortality is a decreasing function of food, or both.

We assume that ρ is identical for all adults, so the aggregate number of new adults in period t+1 is ρY^t where Y^t is regional food output in period t. Let N^t be the population of adults in period t for the region as a whole. The dynamics for the region are given by $N^{t+1} = \rho Y(N^t; \theta)$ where $Y(N; \theta)$ is the aggregate production function in Section 6.6 with the productivity parameter θ included as an explicit argument. In a long-run equilibrium we always have $Y(N; \theta)/N = 1/\rho$. This is the Malthusian feature of the model: as long as the demographic parameter ρ is constant, every long-run equilibrium yields the same food per capita at the regional level. A permanent increase in productivity (θ) is thus absorbed in the long run through higher population rather than higher food per person.

Definition 6.2

Fix the productivity $\theta > 0$. A *long-run equilibrium* (LRE) is a population $N > 0$, a normalized wage $x \equiv w/\theta > 0$, and a density function $L(\cdot)$ with $N = \int_0^1 L(s)\,ds$ such that the conditions for SRE in D6.1 are satisfied, and also $Y(N; \theta)/N = 1/\rho$.

Proposition 6.3 (long-run equilibrium).

(a) For each $\theta > 0$ there is a unique LRE population $N(\theta) > 0$.

(b) $N(\theta)$ is continuously differentiable and increasing, with $\lim_{\theta \to 0} N(\theta) = 0$ and $\lim_{\theta \to \infty} N(\theta) = \infty$.

(c) There are productivity levels $0 < \theta^a < \theta^b$ such that
   (i) $0 < \theta < \theta^a$ implies $0 < N(\theta) < N^a$. All sites are open.

(ii) $\theta^a \le \theta \le \theta^b$ implies $N^a \le N(\theta) \le N^b$. There is a threshold $s^a(\theta) \in (0, 1]$ such that all sites with $s \in [0, s^a(\theta))$ are open and all sites with $s \in [s^a(\theta), 1]$ are closed. No sites are stratified.

(iii) $\theta^b < \theta$ implies $N^b < N(\theta)$. There is a threshold $s^a(\theta) \in (0, 1)$ such that all sites with $s \in [0, s^a(\theta))$ are open and all sites with $s \in [s^a(\theta), 1]$ are closed. There is also a second threshold $s^b(\theta) \in (s^a(\theta), 1)$ such that all sites with $s \in (s^b(\theta), 1]$ are stratified. The boundaries $s^a(\theta)$ and $s^b(\theta)$ are continuously differentiable and decreasing with $\lim_{\theta \to \infty} s^a(\theta) = 0$ and $\lim_{\theta \to \infty} s^b(\theta) = 0$.

(d) The non-normalized LRE wage $w(\theta)$ is continuously differentiable. For all $\theta \le \theta^a$, $w(\theta) = 1/\rho$. For all $\theta > \theta^a$, $w(\theta)$ is decreasing with $w(\theta) < 1/\rho$.

The results in Proposition 6.3 are shown in Figures 6.5(a), 6.5(b), and 6.5(c). The ray from the origin with slope $1/\rho$ is identical in all three graphs. The only distinction involves the productivity parameter θ, which is low in Figure 6.5(a), intermediate in Figure 6.5(b), and high in Figure 6.5(c). The values of N^a and N^b are independent of θ. In each case the LRE is unique because the aggregate average product of labor $Y(N; \theta)/N$ is globally decreasing in N (see part (d) of the Corollary to Proposition 6.2).

Figure 6.5(a) shows the case where $0 < \theta < \theta^a$ and $0 < N(\theta) < N^a$. The ray from the origin with slope $1/\rho$ intersects the production function $Y(N; \theta)$ at a population less than N^a. All sites are open because $N(\theta) < N^a$. Figure 6.5(b) shows the case where $\theta^a < \theta < \theta^b$ and $N^a < N(\theta) < N^b$. Because the production function $Y(N; \theta)$ has now shifted up, the ray from the origin and $Y(N; \theta)$ intersect at a higher value of N. Due to the larger population the best sites are closed, although none are stratified. Finally, Figure 6.5(c) shows the case where $\theta^b < \theta$ and $N^b < N(\theta)$. Here the productivity θ is high enough to support a long-run population above N^b and accordingly the best sites are stratified.

We conclude this section with a brief description of the process through which the system converges to long-run equilibrium for a fixed θ. This is shown in Figure 6.6. We start from an initial population N^0 with a corresponding output Y^0. Suppose N^0 is below the long-run population N^*. The output Y^0 determines the adult population N^1 in the next generation through $N^1 = \rho Y^0$. This implies that the point (N^1, Y^0) lies on the ray from the origin with slope $1/\rho$. N^1 yields the output Y^1 through the production function, and so on. The arrows show the process

(a)

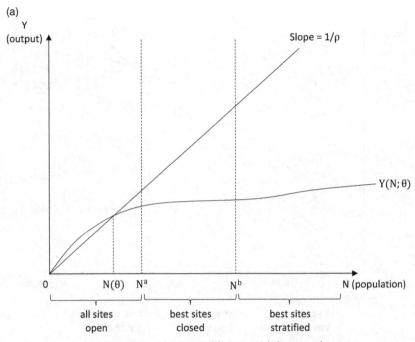

FIGURE 6.5.(a) Long-run equilibrium with low productivity

(b)

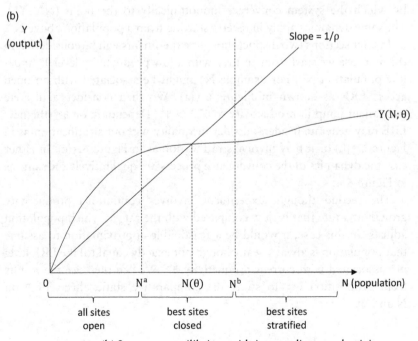

FIGURE 6.5.(b) Long-run equilibrium with intermediate productivity

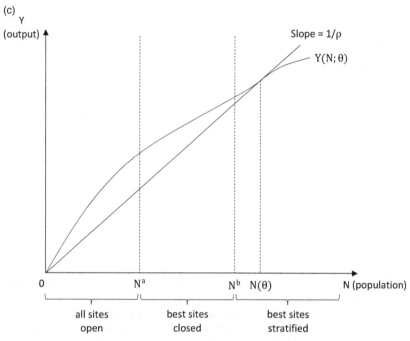

FIGURE 6.5.(c) Long-run equilibrium with high productivity

by which the system converges monotonically to the point (N^*, Y^*). The same dynamics apply in reverse starting from a population above N^*.

In later sections two distinct thought experiments will be considered. In the first case we start from an LRE with a low productivity level θ^* and a low population N^*. For example N^* might be associated with an open access LRE as shown in Figure 6.5(a). We then consider a discrete permanent jump in productivity to $\theta^{**} > \theta^*$. Depending on θ^{**} the new LRE may generate insider–outsider inequality without stratification as in Figure 6.5(b) or it may involve stratification as in Figure 6.5(c). In either case the dynamics of the convergence process are qualitatively the same as in Figure 6.6.

The second thought experiment involves continuous productivity growth at a rate that is slow compared with the rate at which population adjusts. In this case, it would be a reasonable approximation to assume that population is always near (though not exactly equal to) the LRE level N^* associated with current productivity θ^*. We can then use the results from Proposition 6.3 to study the comparative static effects of θ on N and w.

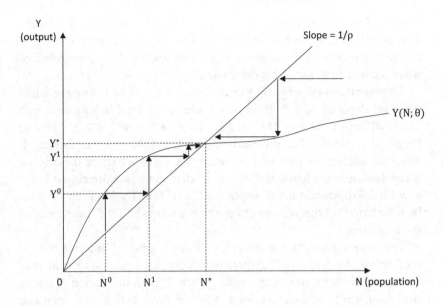

FIGURE 6.6. Monotonic convergence to a long-run equilibrium

6.8 POVERTY

The least well-off agents are those receiving the wage w, either in the commons or at stratified sites (if any). The dynamics of poverty can be investigated using the thought experiments described at the end of Section 6.7. We start in each case from a LRE with the productivity θ^*, population $N^* = N(\theta^*)$, and non-normalized wage $w^* = w(\theta^*)$.

First consider a permanent productivity increase to $\theta^{**} > \theta^*$ in period 0. We want to examine the dynamics of the wage along the adjustment path leading to the new LRE (θ^{**}, N^{**}). The immediate effect of the productivity shock is to raise the short-run equilibrium wage w° to a level such that $w^\circ/\theta^{**} = w^*/\theta^*$. This follows from the fact that the ratio $x \equiv w/\theta$ is determined solely by N in the short run, and the initial population N^* remains in place. The result is $w^\circ > w^*$, so the short run effect of a positive productivity shock is always to alleviate poverty by making commoners better off.

Along the adjustment path, we have an increasing population $(N^\circ, N^1, ..)$ where $N^\circ = N^*$ and the sequence converges to N^{**}.

Because population is rising, the ratio $x = w/\theta^{**}$ is falling due to the downward sloping labor demand curve. The new productivity level θ^{**} is constant throughout the adjustment process and so the non-normalized wage sequence $(w^0, w^1, ..)$ is decreasing.

Whether the final wage w^{**} in the new LRE is at or below the initial wage w^* depends on θ^{**}. If the new productivity level is consistent with universal open access $(\theta^{**} < \theta^a)$, then $w^* = w^{**} = 1/\rho$ due to Proposition 6.3(d). The productivity shock makes everyone better off along the adjustment path with eventual convergence back to the original wage. On the other hand, if $\theta^{**} > \theta^a$ so that some sites are closed in the new LRE, Proposition 6.3(d) implies $w^* > w^{**}$. In the long run the poor become worse off through the closure of more sites and the contraction of the commons.

The second thought experiment involves a gradual improvement in productivity from θ^* to θ^{**}, where we ignore short-run adjustments and focus on the long-run wage $w(\theta)$. Again Proposition 6.3(d) gives a straightforward verdict. As long as θ is low enough to maintain universal open access, the wage remains constant at $w(\theta) = 1/\rho$. However, once $\theta > \theta^a$ so that some sites are closed, further productivity growth reduces the wage and leads to worsening absolute poverty.

One implication of these results involves the distinction drawn by Bogaard et al. (2019) between labor-limited and land-limited agriculture. As explained in Section 6.3, these concepts are defined by the ratio of the marginal products for labor and land. Our food technology in Section 6.5 does not explicitly include land but in Section 8.4 we will extend it to include both inputs. With this extension, and the assumption that each site has one unit of land, it is easy to show that as the wage (w) declines, the stratified sites become relatively less labor-limited and more land-limited. This occurs even though in our model productivity growth is neutral between labor and land (the result stems from endogenous property rights to land). In the long run this strengthens incentives for elites to adopt innovations that enable them to substitute abundant labor for scarce land.

6.9 INEQUALITY

Here we address two separate issues: Inequality within a given site, and inequality for the region as a whole. First consider an individual stratified site. The total number of agents is L, where L - d are commoners and d are members of the elite. Each commoner receives the wage w and each elite agent receives w + r(s)/d where r(s) > o is land rent at a site of quality s. The Lorenz curve consists of two line segments, one for each class of agents (see the discussion of Lorenz curves and Gini coefficients from Section 6.3). The Gini coefficient for an individual stratified site is G = (1 - α)[1 - d/L(s, x)] where L(s, x) is the optimal labor input from Lemma 6.1(c) and α and d are fixed parameters.

In a short-run equilibrium, one can compare the Gini coefficients across stratified sites. Because L(s, x) is an increasing function of s, the better sites have more inequality. One can also compare the same site across short-run equilibria with different values of x. In the SRE where x is lower, or equivalently population N is higher, a given site has more inequality because the elite hires more commoners. As N approaches infinity and x goes to zero, L(s, x) goes to infinity for any fixed site quality s. Therefore the Gini at the site approaches 1 - α. This is the share of food output captured by landowners in a perfectly competitive equilibrium, as we will explain in connection with Proposition 6.4 below.

We now turn to the effect of population on regional inequality. When N < Nᵃ so that all sites are open, there is no inequality. In what follows, we assume N > Nᵃ so that some sites are closed. A Lorenz curve y(z) for this case is presented in Figure 6.7. The horizontal axis z indicates the

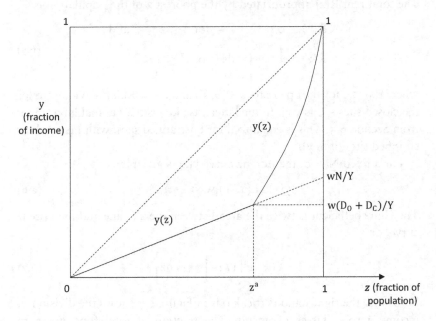

FIGURE 6.7. Lorenz curve y(z) for a fixed population when some sites are closed

fraction of the regional population (ordered from poorest to richest) whose food income falls below some given level, and the vertical axis y indicates the fraction of regional food income received by this subset of agents.

The Lorenz curve has two segments. First there is a linear portion involving the worst-off agents, who receive the wage w either in the commons or through employment at stratified sites. This group makes up a fraction $z^a \equiv (D_O + D_C)/N$ of the population and determines the Lorenz curve on the interval $[0, z^a]$. The slope of this segment is wN/Y, which is direct plus imputed labor cost as a fraction of total food output. The non-linear segment of the Lorenz curve beyond z^a involves agents who receive land rent. This part of the curve is derived as follows.

An insider or elite agent at a site of quality s receives the income w + r(s)/d where w is the imputed value of the agent's time, r(s) is land rent, and d is the number of insider agents. For any income level above w, there is some fraction of the population $z > z^a$ receiving that income or less. This group includes all commoners, as well as insiders who occupy sites at or below a quality cutoff s(z) given by

$$s(z) = 1 - (1-z)N/d \qquad \text{for } z^a \leq z \leq 1. \qquad (6.4)$$

The total rent R(z) appropriated by the poorest z of the population is

$$R(z) \equiv 0 \qquad \text{for } 0 \leq z \leq z^a \text{ and}$$
$$R(z) = \int_0^{s(z)} r(s)\, ds \quad \text{for } z^a \leq z \leq 1 \qquad (6.5)$$

where $r(s) \equiv 0$ for the open sites $s \in [0, s^a)$ and $r(s) = \theta s L(s)^\alpha - wL(s) \geq 0$ for the closed sites $s \in [s^a, 1]$. In the latter case L(s) is the optimal labor input from Section 6.5. This is equal to d for unstratified sites, with L(s) > d for stratified sites (if any).

For a fixed N > 0, the Lorenz curve y(z) is given by

$$y(z) = (1/Y)[wNz + R(z)] \qquad (6.6)$$

The Gini coefficient is twice the area between the 45° line and the Lorenz curve, or

$$G = 2 \left[1/2 - \int_0^1 y(z)\, dz \right] \qquad (6.7)$$

For z = 1, the right-hand vertical axis in Figure 6.7 shows the division of income across classes of agents. The fraction of total food going to commoners is $w(D_O + D_C)/Y$, the fraction going to insiders and elites as imputed wages is $w(D_I + D_E)/Y$, and the fraction going to the latter two groups as land rent is $1 - wN/Y$.

Proposition 6.4 (inequality).

Consider the short-run equilibria for populations N_1 and N_2. Let $N^a < N_1 \leq N^b$ so that N_1 generates insider–outsider inequality. Let $N_1 < N_2$ where N_2 may generate either insider–outsider ($N_2 \leq N^b$) or elite–commoner ($N^b < N_2$) inequality.

(a) The Lorenz curves satisfy $y_1(z) > y_2(z)$ for all $0 < z < 1$ and the Gini coefficients satisfy $G_1 < G_2$.

(b) Let $G(N)$ be the Gini for the population N. $G(N^b) = (2 - \alpha)(1 - \alpha^2) / 3(2 + \alpha + \alpha^2)$ is the upper bound for insider–outsider inequality and the lower bound for elite–commoner inequality. Furthermore $G(\infty) = 1 - \alpha$.

Part (a) shows that starting from insider–outsider inequality, population growth always leads to a higher Gini. Indeed we have Lorenz curve dominance: when N rises, the fraction of income $y(z)$ for the worst-off z of the population falls at every $0 < z < 1$. This is true whether the society remains in an insider–outsider regime or shifts to an elite–commoner regime. Although the Gini is not necessarily increasing in N throughout the elite–commoner range, it must increase within the insider–outsider range.

The absolute productivity θ drops out of the Gini coefficient and is irrelevant for Proposition 6.4. The only parameters that influence inequality are the elasticity α and the exclusion threshold d. Part (b) shows that any elite–commoner equilibrium has greater inequality than any insider–outsider equilibrium. The boundary value $G(N^b)$ is inversely related to α because when food output is more responsive to labor, commoners are paid more and land rents become less significant as a source of inequality.

The limit result for $G(\infty)$ follows from the fact that when the population is large, almost all agents are commoners, and almost all commoners are employed at stratified sites. The property rights distortions discussed in Section 6.6 become negligible, and the aggregate production function is approximately described by part (a) of the Corollary to Proposition 6.2. As a result, the slope of the linear part of the Lorenz curve in Figure 6.7 is approximately the labor share α arising in a competitive economy. Because the boundary z^a in Figure 6.7 approaches one, the area under the Lorenz curve approaches $\alpha/2$ and (6.7) gives a Gini of $1 - \alpha$. Hence in a large elite–commoner society, the Gini coefficient is the output share that would go to landowners in a perfectly competitive economy.

No assumptions about the long run are used in Proposition 6.4. However, suppose a society starts from long-run equilibrium with insider–outsider inequality. If better climate or improved food production technology stimulates population growth, this must increase inequality both along the adjustment path and in the new LRE. Higher productivity does not directly cause higher inequality; the two variables are linked only through the channel of Malthusian population growth and endogenous property rights.

6.10 DEMOGRAPHY

The definition of long-run equilibrium in Section 6.7 ensures that at the regional level, each generation produces exactly enough children to replace itself. But agents with high incomes produce more children than are needed to replace themselves, while agents with low incomes produce fewer children than are needed. The following proposition relates site quality to reproduction.

Proposition 6.5 (demography).

Consider a long-run equilibrium with $\theta^a < \theta$ so that some sites are closed. Commoners produce too few offspring to replace themselves. The site quality determined by $s^r \equiv d^{1-\alpha}/\theta\rho$ satisfies $s^a < s^r < \min\{1, s^b\}$. Insiders with $s \in [s^a, s^r)$ do not fully replace themselves; insiders with $s = s^r$ exactly replace themselves; and insiders with $s \in (s^r, 1]$ more than replace themselves.

Whenever there is inequality, the commoners have an income too low to permit demographic replacement. Insiders at sites with quality near s^a have land rents near zero and must also fail to replace themselves. On the other hand, insiders at the best sites ($s = 1$) must more than replace themselves in order to maintain a steady-state population for the economy as a whole. Since land rent is an increasing function of site quality, there is an intermediate value s^r at which the insiders are in demographic equilibrium.

Recall from Section 6.5 that when the number of agents born at a site (n) exceeds the number needed to close the site (d), the latter group is selected by birth order while the remaining n-d agents are excluded.

Proposition 6.5 shows that all stratified sites have downward mobility in the sense that some children of the elite are excluded from elite status. These agents go to an open site or are hired at a stratified site.

There is also downward mobility at high-quality unstratified sites (those with $s^r < s \leq s^b$) because some children of insiders do not become insiders themselves. However, at lower-quality unstratified sites (those with $s^a \leq s < s^r$) the number of children n born to insiders is less than d. As discussed in Section 6.5, in this case d-n commoners enter the site, and at that point the insiders become sufficiently numerous to block further entry.

<h2 style="text-align:center">6.11 REGIONAL CASES</h2>

During the Upper Paleolithic, foraging groups were small, mobile, and exploited large territories at low population densities (see Chapter 3). Our theory predicts minimal inequality under such conditions because almost all sites would have been open.

In some parts of the world foragers became sedentary during the recovery from the Last Glacial Maximum or shortly after the onset of the Holocene. We believe these transitions were caused by positive climate change and led to higher population densities (see Chapter 4). Our theory predicts that this process could have led to insider–outsider inequality and perhaps even elite–commoner inequality at the best sites.

Shortly before the Holocene a negative climate shock (the Younger Dryas) led to initial cultivation in southwest Asia and perhaps elsewhere. The effect of the Younger Dryas on sedentism is unclear (see Section 5.8), but learning by doing and the domestication of plants and animals raised productivity. This and the benign Holocene climate resulted in population growth along the trajectory leading to full agriculture, often resulting in settlements much larger than those of sedentary foragers (see Chapter 5). Our theory predicts that these trends would have intensified both insider–outsider and elite–commoner inequality.

This broad portrait is consistent with the empirical generalizations from Section 6.3. The evidence reviewed there indicates that inequality has tended to rise with the transitions from mobile to sedentary foraging and from sedentary foraging to agriculture. These trends are visible in archaeological data on housing and burials. Ethnography also supports these generalizations, and strongly suggests that population plays an important mediating role between productivity and inequality. It also suggests that class structures and inheritance are more common in agricultural societies than those based on foraging.

Here we present a series of regional case histories for Southwest Asia, Europe, Polynesia, and the Channel Islands of California. These examples are chosen mainly because they have been intensively studied by archaeologists, and reflect a variety of food acquisition strategies including foraging, fishing, and farming.

Southwest Asia: This region is of special interest as one of the first in which a sedentary lifestyle emerged after the Last Glacial Maximum (see Section 4.3), and also the first in which agriculture arose (see Section 5.3). We focus on the Levant, defined to be the area bounded by the Taurus Mountains to the north, the Mediterranean Sea to the west, the Syro-Arabian desert to the east, and the Sinai desert to the south. The southern and northern Levant will be discussed separately in what follows.

First, consider the southern Levant. Fochesato and Bowles (2017) report a Gini coefficient of 0.28 for the site of Ohalo II at the Last Glacial Maximum around 23,000 BP. This figure is based upon dwelling sizes and is within the expected range for hunter-gatherer societies (Borgerhoff Mulder et al., 2009), indicating a low level of inequality.

Following the recovery from the LGM, temperatures became milder and rainfall became more plentiful during the Bølling-Allerød period that lasted for about 1,500 years and ended about 13,000 BP. This corresponds to Early Natufian culture, a society that is generally believed to have consisted of both mobile and sedentary foragers (see Section 4.3). This culture developed in the south and later spread to the north (see Section 5.8).

For this period, Price and Bar-Yosef (2012, 151) report some evidence for "the existence of corporate groups that controlled important resources." Specifically, intra-site cemetery areas indicate territorial ownership (Bar-Yosef, 2011, S180). This suggests insider–outsider inequality. Evidence from mortuary practices also suggests some elite–commoner inequality (Kuijt and Prentiss, 2009; Price and Bar-Yosef, 2012).

Around 13,000 years ago, climate change throughout the northern hemisphere brought a temporary return to Ice Age conditions known as the Younger Dryas, which lasted over 1,000 years. There is some debate about the exact timing of this event in the Levant, with Bar-Yosef (2011) and others suggesting a later onset around 12,600/500 BP. According to Smith (1991), during the Younger Dryas many settlements were abandoned, sedentism was often replaced by mobile foraging, and skeletal data indicate a decline in nutritional levels, health status, and population.

Our Malthusian framework leads us to expect a decline in regional population in the Younger Dryas, assuming decreased sedentism and an absence of cultivation in the south. This is consistent with the traditional views from Smith (1991) and many others. However, there is some uncertainty about regional population trends, with Roberts et al. (2018) recently providing evidence that population remained largely flat in the southern Levant during the Younger Dryas. It is unclear whether this finding will be accepted. If it is, we would be inclined to regard it as evidence that sedentism at a small set of refuge sites and/or learning by doing associated with cultivation were offsetting the negative environmental shock (see Section 5.8).

The view that a large portion of the population became more mobile, except for those occupying a few favorable locations (Bar-Yosef, 2011), suggests that more sites had open access, and thus that the commons expanded. We cannot completely rule out the continuation of insider–outsider inequality at some high-quality sites, but we are not aware of any evidence for this. Bar-Yosef (2011) remarks that at this time the dead were rarely buried with adornments, and mortuary practices during the Younger Dryas show a complete absence of stratification (Kuijt and Prentiss, 2009).

When climate recovered after the Younger Dryas, cultivation became widespread and population grew rapidly (information is from Price and Bar-Yosef, 2012, except as indicated). Over the next millennium or two, as plant and animal domestication evolved, evidence for insider–outsider inequality includes uneven distribution of exotic materials across sites (155). Evidence for elite–commoner inequality includes unequal house sizes within communities (155), as well as unequal distribution of grave goods (158–159). But skeletal evidence on nutrition does not indicate inequality across or within settlements (Smith and Horwitz, 2007), and there is no convincing evidence for hereditary elites in the Pre-Pottery Neolithic (Kuijt and Goring-Morris, 2002).

We turn next to the northern Levant. According to Roberts et al. (2018), the northern Levant and upper Mesopotamia saw substantial population growth during the Younger Dryas. Again, this is a recent and somewhat surprising finding, so we treat it with caution. We argued in Section 5.8 that population growth in this region despite the poor climate of the Younger Dryas may have reflected a combination of migration from the south, greater sedentism, and learning by doing with respect to cultivation.

We will focus here on the site of Abu Hureyra in the northern Levant, which was discussed in Section 5.3. Information is from Moore et al. (2000, esp. 277–294). The dates that follow are taken from Moore et al. with an adjustment to be consistent with calibration used in the current literature. The first settlement (Abu Hureyra 1 [AH1]) spanned roughly 13,500–12,100 BP, with a maximum population of 100–300 (489). This was followed by an intermediate period, perhaps with population falling, from 12,100–11,400 BP. A subsequent settlement (Abu Hureyra 2 [AH2]) spanned roughly 11,400–8800 BP, with a maximum population of 5000–6000 (494).

Before the Younger Dryas, the inhabitants of AH1 were sedentary foragers. With the onset of the Younger Dryas, the local population rose, probably due to the role of Abu Hureyra as a refuge site, and evidence of cultivation is found (see Section 5.3). During AH1, human remains are scarce, despite around 1,500 years of occupation. This leads to an inference that most of the dead were buried elsewhere. No grave goods were found.

The starting date for Abu Hureyra 2 (around 11,400 BP) comes after the Younger Dryas and shortly after the start of the Pre-Pottery Neolithic A. At AH2, nearly 40% of burials were accompanied by small quantities of grave goods, mostly for adult females. These consist of small beads, small tools of flint and bone, and some animal bones, but no precious metals or stones and no elaborate works of art. Most burials are in houses or shallow pits in yards outside. The ratio of female to male burials is about 2:1, suggesting that many males were buried elsewhere. Only one male was buried with beads, part of a couple with especially high quality beads. Thus the grave goods may be associated with both gender and social status, but it is unclear whether they have economic significance.

We have no evidence on insider–outsider inequality in the northern Levant, either during or after the Younger Dryas. However, Fochesato and Bowles (2017) report a very low Gini coefficient of 0.15 based on house plans for Jerf al Ahmar (11,500–10,700 BP) in northern Mesopotamia. In related work Bogaard et al. (2019) have found that wealth disparities in Neolithic farming communities were small so the apparent egalitarianism of Abu Hureyra may not have been exceptional.

These authors relate this finding to the idea that Neolithic farming was labor-limited rather than land-limited (see Section 6.3).

We summarize this regional case as follows. It appears likely that group property rights over production sites emerged among the sedentary early Natufians of the southern Levant. There is some evidence for both insider–outsider and elite–commoner inequality, although the extent of the inequality was modest and the evidence is not overwhelming. The negative environmental shock of the Younger Dryas eliminated any such inequality across and within sites in the southern Levant, due both to greater mobility and (perhaps) a decline in regional population. Later, in the PPNA and PPNB, the south shows signs of renewed inequality, again of a modest nature. This is consistent with our theory, which leads us to expect that a favorable natural environment and high population density will be correlated with group property rights and inequality.

For the northern Levant, we are not aware of evidence for inequality either before or during the Younger Dryas. Evidence for stratification in the PPNA/B is ambiguous at best. The improved Holocene climate and the rising productivity of agriculture resulted in substantial regional population growth (with a local population of several thousand at Abu Hureyra), so the lack of clear evidence for inequality in the north during the PPN is puzzling. However, this may reflect institutional or cultural constraints. As we explain in Chapter 7 (see Sections 7.3 and 7.8), there is little or no skeletal evidence for violence in the southern Levant over a span of about 10,000 years. This suggests the existence of strong institutional or cultural forces that limited violent conflict in the south. Similarly, institutions or culture could have limited the degree of inequality in the north.

In the next three cases the development of stratification is more dramatic.

Europe: Domesticated plants and animals spread across the European continent from pristine origins in southwest Asia (all information is from Shennan, 2008). Before the arrival of agriculture, hunter-gatherer population densities were very low throughout Europe except for coastal or riverine areas with rich aquatic resources. The first farming in central Europe was associated with the "Linear Pottery Culture," or LBK in its German acronym. LBK culture arose around 7600–7500 BP near modern Hungary and Austria, and spread rapidly westward. Population increased quickly to new plateaus in Germany, Poland, and Denmark as this process unfolded. Agricultural colonization proceeded in a patchwork fashion where the best locations were settled first.

Shennan argues that "the growth in population should have led to a growth of inequality between territory-holding units as successively poorer settlement sites were occupied" (323). In our terminology, this represents insider–outsider inequality. The evidence that this did in fact occur comes from data on differences in house sizes, tools, and domestic animal bones. There is also evidence that inequality within settlements (what we would call elite–commoner inequality) increased, as indicated by a growing frequency of small houses relative to large ones. The fact that houses of the same types were rebuilt in the same places suggests that socio-economic status was inherited.

Cemetery data indicate that the earliest LBK settlements "present a picture of relatively egalitarian societies" (323). However, later cemeteries have a few graves, including some child graves, with markedly richer burials than others. Shennan argues that the cemeteries represented "an ancestral claim to territory in the face of increasing competition" (324). Other evidence suggests the emergence of patrilineal corporate groups that controlled prime locations, and whose senior members had larger houses.

The connections to our theory are fairly straightforward. Agricultural technology provided an abrupt productivity increase, which then triggered an upward adjustment of population in the regions where farming was introduced. One complication is that much of this population growth may have come from LBK migrants rather than expansion by hunter-gatherer groups who adopted agriculture (Shennan, 2018). In our framework the arrival of people with agricultural technology would only accelerate the adjustment to a new long-run equilibrium without changing the outcome. The sequence of relatively egalitarian LBK societies followed by insider–outsider and elite–commoner inequality, along with evidence for hereditary elite status, closely fits our theoretical expectations.

Polynesia: The islands of Polynesia differ widely in size, climate, topography, soil fertility, and ecosystems. All Polynesian societies are descended from a common ancestral culture based upon domesticated plants and animals, hunting, foraging, and fishing. A diverse set of societies evolved in the millennia before European contact. On small atolls with land areas less than 10 square kilometers and populations below 1,000 individuals, groups typically had weak chiefs and an egalitarian ethic.

On large volcanic islands with higher populations, inequality was often quite pronounced (Younger, 2008).

The island chains with the sharpest divisions between landowning elites and landless commoners prior to European contact are generally agreed to include Hawaii, Tonga, and the Society Islands, with Hawaii as the most extreme case. Sahlins (1958, 11–12) adds Samoa to this list, while Goldman (1970, 20–21) adds Mangareva. Of the ten island chains for which data are available, the four with the highest population densities per unit of arable land are Hawaii, Tonga, the Society Islands, and Samoa (Kirch, 1984, 37, 98). These are also the island chains with the best endowments of natural resources (Sahlins, 1958, 126–130; Kirch, 1984). These cross-sectional observations on productivity, population, and inequality are broadly consistent with our expectations. We turn next to the dynamics of inequality for the cases of Tonga and Hawaii.

For Tonga, the first phase of human occupation occurred during 950–700 BC and probably involved intensive foraging activity (all information is from Burley, 2007). The population may have reached 600–700 by the end of this period. A second phase, which occurred between 700 BC and 400 AD involved wider dispersal of population over the landscape. In this period, marginal islands were occupied and small hamlets were replaced by village-sized complexes. Burley says that this shift was associated with a "fundamental transformation in economy" (193) involving intensive dryland farming, which may have resulted from depletion of indigenous birds, iguana, shellfish, and other species. Burley estimates that with dryland agriculture, a theoretical carrying capacity of about 34,000 people would have been reasonable (185). He also estimates that by 400 AD, population had reached about half this level (196), or roughly 17,000 people.

The third phase of Tongan social evolution starts around 400 AD but observations are scarce until about 950 AD, when a dynastic chiefdom appeared. This chiefdom arose on the island with the most arable land and highest population. By 1200 AD this dynasty had gained full control of its home island, and by 1450 AD it was waging a campaign for unified control of the entire Tongan chain. Burley comments: "what is important from a demographic perspective is the emergence of this integrated polity as a theoretical response to and probable correlate of population pressure as carrying capacity limits were being reached" (197). Under this new political and economic structure, earlier hamlets and villages disappeared, and commoners worked on estates owned by chiefly lineages.

Hawaii's founding population has been estimated at fewer than 100 people, who arrived sometime during 800–1000 AD (Kirch, 2010, 126–129). The initial settlements occurred in a few ecologically favorable locations, primarily on the islands of Oahu and Kauai. During 1100–1500 AD the population doubled about every 1–2 generations. This growth was focused first in areas suitable for irrigated taro pond-fields (Oahu, Kauai, and Molokai) between 1200–1400 AD. In this phase "[i]rrigation works were developing in lockstep with the exponential rise in population" (145). A later growth phase involved intensive dryland sweet potato farming (Maui and Hawaii). This agricultural system became widespread circa 1400 AD. Around 1500 AD, the rate of population growth slowed dramatically. Kirch suggests that the expansion of dryland farming into areas that were marginal for rainfall increased mortality. The transition to a slowly growing or stable population occurred over about one century (139).

By the late 1400s, "virtually all of the agriculturally suitable landscapes across the archipelago [were] settled and territorially divided" (174). Kirch believes that a ruler on the island of Oahu dating to about 1490 AD was the first to institute "a formal system of hierarchical land divisions" and a regularized collection of tribute (92). Dryland agriculture on Maui and Hawaii took longer to develop, but led to "highly formalized garden plots and territorial boundaries" by 1600–1650 AD (153). Archaic states had arisen by this time and continued through European contact in 1778 AD. At the latter date, the population of the island chain was roughly 400,000 (130).

Late Hawaiian society was not based on continuous gradations of rank defined by kinship, but instead involved "distinct named, endogamous classes of persons" (34). The elite were internally ranked by descent, while the commoners were forbidden to keep genealogical records beyond the level of grandparents (72–73). The elite controlled land and gave commoners access to it in exchange for tribute and labor services. In one area, about half of all food output went to the elite (68).

In both the Hawaiian and Tongan cases, a small founding population eventually achieved a period of rapid population growth, followed by convergence to demographic equilibrium. In general, locations were settled in order of their ecological favorability, and stratified social institutions first appeared in high-quality areas. The availability of good agricultural land led to a high pre-contact population density, and the result was a high degree of inequality between elite and commoner classes. This is consistent with our analysis in Section 6.8 of the adjustment path from a low initial population with open access to a high equilibrium population with closed sites and inequality.

The Channel Islands: The northern Channel Islands include three main islands (Santa Cruz, Santa Rosa, and San Miguel) located off the coast of southern California (information in this section is taken from overlapping research in Kennett, 2005; Kennett et al., 2009; and Winterhalder et al., 2010, except where noted). The first residents were hunter-gatherers who depended heavily on the rich marine environment for food. Site quality varied with terrain, the presence of kelp zones, and watershed size. The qualities of potential coastal village locations have been ranked using a geographic information system, with site rankings based solely on environmental variables and independent of archaeological findings. Each island has multiple sites of varying quality.

The single-piece fishhook made from shell was developed between 2500–2100 BP. Prior to 1500 BP, communities expanded slowly. First- and second-ranked habitats were filled in during this period, with sites settled in order of quality. The bow and arrow was introduced between 1500–1300 BP. After 1500 BP the population grew rapidly and local densities increased as people nucleated into villages. Between 1500–1300 BP, third- and fourth-ranked habitats came into use, resulting in the occupation of all viable locations. This period marked the end of open access at the best sites, which was replaced by competition among communities and unequal control of local resources. By 1300 BP there was an increase in lethal violence involving projectile points. It is likely that defense was a public good fostering corporate group formation.

Insider–outsider inequality in the period after 1500 BP can be inferred from the skeletal evidence of Lambert and Walker (1991). *Cribra orbitalia* is a condition that develops as part of a child's response to anemia. Comparing contemporaneous skeletal remains, the frequency of *cribra orbitalia* was lowest on the California mainland, below 30% on Santa Cruz (largest of the northern Channel Islands and rich in diverse plants and animals), noticeably higher on Santa Rosa (an island of intermediate size), and over 70% on San Miguel (a small isolated island with a shortage of fresh water and terrestrial resources). Because movement among the islands was not physically difficult, these substantial health differences suggest that residents of lower-quality sites did not enjoy free access to higher-quality sites.

After 1300 BP there were advances in fishing technology related to tackle, plank canoes, and toggling harpoons. Fish bones from mid-water, deep-ocean, and open-ocean habitats became more common in faunal assemblages. Plank canoes also facilitated the exploitation of comparative advantage between the islands and the mainland. After 1300 BP there is evidence of large-scale craft specialization on the islands and also significant trading of groundstone from the islands for goods such as acorns from the mainland. In the period 1300–650 BP the population continued to grow, apparently because the new technologies and trading opportunities outweighed the effects of adverse climate events such as droughts (see Kennett et al., 2009, 310, and Winterhalder et al., 2010, 471).

Clear social inequality, inferred from burial practices, emerged by around 650 BP. At the time of first contact with Europeans two centuries later, there were around 3000 people on the Channel Islands living in at least 22 villages, which varied in their size and sociopolitical importance. The society was ranked and included hereditary chiefs whose kinship system was patrilineal and patrilocal, and who often married into chiefly families on the mainland. The majority of people had a matrilineal and matrilocal kinship system.

This history is consistent with our theory. Prior to 1500 BP regional population was low relative to the availability of good sites, there were no restrictions on entry into high-quality sites, and thus there is no evidence of inequality. As population increased during 1500–1300 BP, marginal sites were occupied, entry to the best sites was restricted, and insider–outsider inequality becomes archaeologically visible. During 1300–650 BP productivity advances involving fishing, hunting, and trade supported further population growth, which led to elite–commoner inequality with hereditary elite positions.

Arnold (1993, 1995) argues that a negative climate shock around 700–800 BP in the Channel Islands led to greater importation of food from the mainland, and enabled elites to gain control over the production of canoes as well as beads needed for export. More generally, she argues that aspiring elites can gain control over household labor in times of environmental or social stress. But as we noted above, population continued to increase in the Channel Islands during this period, suggesting that adverse climate events were more than offset by technological progress and expanding trade opportunities. Our explanation, in which ongoing population growth caused site closures and stratification within sites, avoids reference to mechanisms of monopoly power and labor control that are difficult to observe archaeologically.

6.12 CONCLUSION

We have developed a theory that links rising technical productivity with rising population density and inequality. Our approach attributes inequality to the creation of group property rights over land. Rising productivity does not lead to growing inequality directly, but rather indirectly via Malthusian population growth and endogenous property rights. The model applies equally well to foragers and farmers. It accounts both for the emergence of inequality within a society and variation of inequality across societies. In Section 6.11 we argued that several regional narratives from archaeology are supportive.

Our theory highlights the formation of corporate groups that collectively control access to valuable sites or territories. We do not examine landownership by individuals or households, but this could develop once sites are closed. In long-run equilibrium with stratification, elite agents inherit membership in these corporate landowning groups from their parents, although some offspring of the elite will suffer downward mobility into the commoner class. The same is true for insiders at high-quality unstratified sites. Insiders at lower-quality unstratified sites must accept some new outsiders in each generation to preserve their property rights. Commoners do not replace themselves demographically, so this class is maintained partly by downward mobility from elite and insider groups.

The aggregate production function shows how property rights affect allocative efficiency as population rises. Due to our Cobb–Douglas functional form, open access yields an efficient allocation of labor. When some sites are closed, output is below its theoretical maximum because marginal products of labor are not equated across closed sites. When population crosses into the elite–commoner range, another distortion arises because the marginal product of labor at stratified sites is equal to the average product in the commons. At very high population levels, almost all sites are stratified and almost all labor is paid its marginal product. As a result, aggregate output approaches its theoretical upper bound, and the Gini coefficient approaches the output share that would go to landowners in a perfectly competitive economy.

Our theory has numerous testable implications. Assume that climate and/or food production technology improves over time, and that regional population therefore grows over time. In this setting our predictions include the following.

(a) Insider–outsider inequality will arise first at the best sites in the region and then spread to sites of lower quality.

(b) Elite–commoner inequality will arise after insider–outsider inequality. It will also begin at the best sites and then spread to sites of lower quality.

(c) The commons will shrink and the average quality of open sites will decline.

(d) The distribution of food consumption within stratified sites will be bimodal.

(e) Inequality within stratified sites will be greater at the higher-quality sites.

(f) Once there is insider–outsider inequality, commoners will become increasingly impoverished over time.

(g) Once there is insider–outsider inequality, the regional Gini coefficient will rise over time (although not necessarily after stratification has begun to emerge).

(h) All elite individuals at a stratified site will have elite parents, but some children of elite individuals will become commoners.

Future archaeological research could refute these (or other) implications of our theory. In that case we would need to modify the model or look for alternative explanations.

6.13 POSTSCRIPT

This chapter is based on our article "The origins of inequality: Insiders, outsiders, elites, and commoners" published in the *Journal of Political Economy* (Dow and Reed, 2013). Leanna Mitchell provided exceptional research assistance for the original article. We are grateful for comments from colleagues at Simon Fraser University, participants at the Workshop on the Emergence of Hierarchy and Inequality hosted by the Santa Fe Institute in February 2009, and participants at the SFU Conference on Early Economic Developments in July 2009. We also thank two anonymous referees and two editors at the *Journal of Political Economy* for detailed comments on earlier drafts. The Human Evolutionary Studies Program at SFU and the Social Sciences and Humanities Research Council of Canada provided funding. We received valuable feedback on an earlier draft of this chapter from Samuel Bowles, Richard Lipsey, John

Chant, Jon Kesselman, Craig Riddell, Herbert Grubel, and Richard Harris. All opinions are those of the authors.

Sections 6.1 and 6.2 have been extended and updated for this volume, and Section 6.3 is entirely new. The descriptions of the gold rush in Section 6.4 and the formal model in Sections 6.5–6.10 are lightly edited versions of their counterparts from the *JPE* article. All formal propositions are identical. New material has been added at the start of Section 6.11 and we have rewritten the archaeological narrative for southwest Asia, but the other regional narratives are essentially unchanged. Section 6.12 has been rewritten. When the formal model from Sections 6.5–6.10 was constructed, we were not aware of the empirical findings reported in Section 6.3 with publication dates of 2014 or later.

7

Warfare between Egalitarian Groups

7.1 INTRODUCTION

Chapter 6 addressed the transition to inequality. In this chapter and the next, we address the transition to organized warfare over land. We regard these as the two most significant institutional developments before cities and states. This chapter explores the incidence of warfare among foragers and early farmers in a setting where the rival groups are egalitarian. This will be followed in Chapter 8 by an examination of warfare among elites in stratified societies.

In our theoretical framework inequality and warfare both involve technologies of coercion. We showed in Chapter 6 that inequality can emerge through a technology of *exclusion*, where a group of organized insiders prevents entry to a site by unorganized outsiders. For the purposes of Chapters 7 and 8 we introduce a technology of *combat*, where one organized group fights another organized group for control of a site.

Warfare has been defined in a variety of ways. For example, LeBlanc (2020, 40) takes it to mean "collective action by one group against another, without there being a larger overarching political entity, the membership of which includes both groups." In Chapters 7 and 8 we assume the absence of an overarching political entity and simply define warfare to be lethal conflict between organized groups.

Our focus is specifically on conflict between groups over land. This differs from other forms of lethal violence motivated by revenge, feuding, status competition, or theft. Violence has numerous proximate causes but it will be convenient to distinguish *raiding*, *displacement*, and *conquest*. Raiding means the theft of moveable wealth or kidnapping of humans.

It does not involve a transfer of land from one group to another. We are not proposing a theory of raiding. Whenever we use the term "war" without qualification, we mean "warfare over land."

Displacement means permanently taking over the territory of an opposing group and driving away or killing the previous inhabitants, with the intention of using the new territory as a source of food. Conquest means seizure of territory from a rival elite while keeping commoners in place to produce food and pay land rent. This chapter will focus on displacement and Chapter 8 will focus on conquest.

Our goal is not to resolve empirical disputes about the prevalence of warfare in prehistory. There has been intense debate over this issue, as will be seen in Section 7.2. Instead, we study a theoretical question: under what conditions are groups more likely or less likely to engage in warfare over land? However, we will argue that the evidence is consistent with the formal model we develop.

The central message of this chapter is that when groups are internally egalitarian and individual agents can migrate easily between groups, warfare over land is unlikely. The reason is that both individual migration and Malthusian population dynamics tend to generate a positive correlation between site quality and group size. This prevents war. A small group with a poor site might like to take over land controlled by a large group with a rich site, but a military victory over the larger group is unlikely. Hence the smaller and poorer group refrains from attacking. Conversely the larger and richer group has a high probability of military success, but gains little by taking over the site of the poorer group. We do not entirely rule out warfare among egalitarian groups but this occurs only under narrow conditions involving shocks from nature or technology. The story will be very different in Chapter 8, which will show that elites in stratified societies routinely engage in warfare with other elites, or use threats of force to bully their opponents into fleeing.

In both chapters groups consist of individuals who maximize their expected food consumption. There is a production technology where food is obtained from labor and land, and a military technology where the probability of a successful attack on another group depends on the relative size of the two groups. There are two sites or territories where food can be obtained and their productivities may differ.

In this chapter we assume that groups are internally egalitarian in the sense that they share food equally and reach unanimous collective decisions. Attacks are motivated by a group's attempt to increase the quantity and/or quality of land it controls. In order to focus on situations in which wars are actually fought, we assume a group defends its land when it is attacked, because fleeing to another location is even less attractive. Chapter 8 will instead consider three strategies: attack, defend, and flee.

Time periods are the length of a human generation. At the beginning of a period each site has a population inherited from the past. Individual agents can move between sites, although this is generally costly. Once the final group sizes are determined, each group decides whether to attack the other. Finally production takes place, agents have children, and fertility-driven Malthusian dynamics generate a new initial population for each site in the next period. The process then repeats.

As mentioned above, in this framework war is generally deterred by the positive correlation between site qualities and group sizes resulting from individual migration and Malthusian dynamics. There are two necessary conditions for warfare among egalitarian groups: an exogenous productivity shock from nature or technology to serve as a trigger, and costly individual mobility. Exogenous shocks that change the relative productivities of sites or territories can create a temporary imbalance between site qualities and group sizes while costly individual mobility makes it difficult to undo these imbalances through migration. Under our assumptions warfare tends to be self-limiting because it reallocates population toward better sites. Therefore a series of wars requires a series of shocks.

Our analysis suggests that warfare over land would have been rare among mobile foraging bands with exogamous marriage, where agents could respond to negative local shocks by exploiting kinship networks to join more prosperous groups. The analysis also suggests that warfare over land would have become more common after the emergence of sedentary foraging or farming groups with endogamous marriage and rigid membership criteria. Even in this case, exogenous shocks that changed the relative productivities of sites or territories would also have been necessary.

We make numerous simplifying assumptions in our formal model. For example, we employ a military technology where the winners suffer no casualties while the losers are exterminated. We also ignore potential advantages accruing to the role of defender, such as the ability to build fortifications. Some readers may be uncomfortable with these assumptions. Such readers should note that our assumptions about military technology usually stack the deck in favor of aggression. This only strengthens our conclusion that early warfare over land was rare, because more reasonable assumptions would make war even less likely than we claim. This issue will be discussed in more detail in Section 7.8.

In the formal model of this chapter we assume there are two sites or territories, with a group of agents at each location. We ignore the larger regional setting of Chapter 6 with many sites that are open, closed, or stratified. The model here can be interpreted as a simple region with only two sites rather than a continuum of sites. Accordingly, we do not utilize a technology of exclusion involving a critical mass of insiders who prevent entry by unorganized outsiders (there is no equivalent to the parameter "d" used in Chapter 6). Instead, we consider a technology of combat where insiders try to prevent entry by an organized coalition of outsiders. Section 7.9 discusses relationships between the models of Chapters 6 and 7.

Section 7.2 reviews the literature on the subject, and Section 7.3 surveys some archaeological and anthropological evidence about warfare in small-scale foraging and farming societies. Sections 7.4, 7.5, and 7.6 develop the formal model through a process of backward induction. Section 7.4 treats group sizes and site qualities as exogenous and derives conditions where war and peace occur. Section 7.5 moves back to the individual migration stage and characterizes locational equilibrium where no individual agent wants to change sites. Section 7.6 introduces our Malthusian fertility assumption and presents necessary and sufficient conditions for warfare. Non-economists may want to skip over the formal modeling in Sections 7.4–7.6. However, we recommend reading the opening paragraphs in these sections, which provide non-technical summaries of the results and create a pathway through the theory for those who prefer a verbal presentation.

Section 7.7 discusses how our theory can account for the evidence from Section 7.3. Section 7.8 examines a number of modeling assumptions that could be altered, and Section 7.9 links the models from Chapters 6 and 7. Section 7.10 is a postscript. Proofs of the formal propositions are available at cambridge.org/economicprehistory.

7.2 THEORIES OF EARLY WARFARE

There is a consensus that warfare is common among elites in stratified societies (see Chapter 8), but the frequency and intensity of warfare among internally egalitarian groups is more variable. Here we seek to shed light on the question of whether warfare over land had an origin, and more generally, how one might explain variation across small-scale foraging and farming societies in the incidence of warfare.

A number of scholars (Keeley, 1996; LeBlanc, 1999, 2007, 2020; LeBlanc and Register, 2003; Gat, 2006; Pinker, 2011) argue that humans are a violent and aggressive species, and from the beginning have lived in a state of frequent warfare. This has led to a literature that views war as a biological selection mechanism for other human traits (see Ferguson, 2013a, for a discussion and references). For example, Bowles and colleagues argue that warfare provides an evolutionary explanation for the co-existence of altruism within human groups and hostility across groups (Bowles, 2006, 2009, 2012; Choi and Bowles, 2007; Bowles and Gintis, 2011).

Claims of pervasive warfare in prehistory have been vigorously contested (Fry, 2006, 2012, 2013; Fry and Soderberg, 2013; Ferguson, 2018). While the "war" school argues that 15 to 25 percent of adult males died in warfare in prehistory (LeBlanc, 2020, 42), the "peace" school argues that the cases advanced as examples of early warfare are often not convincing and, in any case, are not representative of a reality in which warfare was rare. LeBlanc (2020, 50) argues that the "peace" school ignores bias in the evidence allegedly favoring a lack of warfare in contemporary ethnographic studies, and that this bias renders claims for the prevalence of peaceful societies "virtually worthless."

We contribute to this debate by studying the theoretical conditions under which early warfare could have occurred. As noted in Section 7.1, our focus is specifically on group conflict over land rather than other forms of lethal group violence such as raiding. These other types of violence may have predated warfare over land. The preponderance of the evidence for early warfare among foragers is associated with raiding (Gat, 2006, 184; LeBlanc, 2020, 42).

We are not concerned here with the question of whether a propensity toward war is part of human nature. If one believes that the relevant part of the human genome has been stable for the last 15,000 years or so, and if one wishes to explain variations in the incidence of warfare across societies during that period, then an explanation rooted in biology would be an explanation of a variable by a constant. We agree with Gat (2006, chs. 3–5) that war may or may not promote the deeper biological goals of survival and reproduction, depending on the circumstances. We will consider the biological subgoal of food acquisition, and study the roles of natural resources, technology, and population as causal factors in the prevalence of warfare.

Boix (2015) argues that cooperation within small foraging bands was destabilized by the inequality resulting from technical advances. In this scenario individuals specialized into roles as producers or predators, depending on their comparative advantages. Two trajectories tended to arise: Either the producers banded together to defend themselves against the predators, or the predators banded together to exploit the producers. Boix (2015, ch. 4) describes innovations in military technology and resulting changes in political structure. These innovations include metal weapons, horse domestication, and gunpowder, which are generally not relevant for the societies of interest in this chapter. However, we will return to ideas from Boix in Chapters 8, 11, and 12.

There is a small economic literature on conflict in prehistory. Baker (2003) constructs a model where groups compete for access to land. In equilibrium there is no actual warfare. North et al. (2009) and Rowthorn and Seabright (2010) study the effects of early warfare on the development of institutions and agriculture respectively. Bowles and co-authors, as mentioned above, study the effects of early warfare on the evolution of cooperation within social groups.

More generally, a number of economists and political scientists have developed theoretical models of conflict over resources. In economics it is common to have a first stage where the distribution of power is determined by the choices made by leaders, and a second stage determining whether war or peace occurs (Garfinkel and Skaperdas, 2007; Acemoglu et al., 2012; Bhattacharya et al., 2015). In political science the distribution of power is usually exogenous and the focus is on the issue of whether bargaining can avert costly warfare (Fearon, 1995; Powell, 1996, 2006). Theorists from both disciplines agree that if complete contingent contracts were feasible, peace would prevail. Fearon (1995) argues that such contracts can be impossible to negotiate or enforce due to asymmetric information, indivisibilities, or a lack of commitment devices.

Relationships among pre-state groups of foragers or farmers are "anarchic" in much the same way that relationships among states in the modern world are anarchic. Thus similar commitment problems arise. As Fearon (1995, 402) points out, repeated game effects cannot deter defections that will result in the death of one player. When a concession does not alter the prizes at stake or the probabilities of winning, groups will be tempted to renege after the concession is sunk. At best a territorial concession by a weak group might reduce the benefit of an attack to a strong group and thus forestall it. However, compact sites with highly valued resources create indivisibility problems that are difficult to resolve in this way.

We will show that even in this unpromising setting, powerful forces favor peace. In particular, we endogenize the probability of winning a conflict by having it depend on group sizes. The group sizes are determined in the short run by the migration decisions of individual agents, and in the long run by the effect of food income on fertility. Both mechanisms promote peace without any need for bargaining.

We also show that when individual mobility is costly enough, exogenous shocks can lead to warfare. Other authors have made related points. Powell (2006) finds that a rapid change in the distribution of power can result in warfare. In contrast to Powell, we highlight shocks to the value of the prizes at stake rather than to the power of each side to secure a prize. Chassang and Miguel (2009) present a model of civil war and show that a transient negative shock to labor productivity can lead to warfare by reducing the current opportunity cost of fighting relative to the future value of the assets seized in war. Roche et al. (2020) generalize and extend this model. We explore a different causal channel that involves shocks to site-specific productivities, rather than aggregate shocks and resulting inter-temporal tradeoffs.

7.3 EVIDENCE ON EARLY WARFARE

The model in this chapter assumes that groups are egalitarian with respect to consumption and decision-making. Small-scale foraging and farming societies often fit this description. As we discussed in Chapter 6, mobile foragers are normally egalitarian apart from gender and age distinctions. Sedentary foragers are sometimes stratified but not inevitably so (Kelly, 2013a, ch. 9). Johnson and Earle (2000) provide ethnographic examples of foraging and farming groups with up to a few hundred members that lack stratification. Some but not all engage in warfare, including warfare over land.

Two archaeological markers are widely used to infer early warfare: skeletons showing signs of deadly force, and defensive structures or settlements in easily defended locations. Other markers include specialized weapons and artistic depictions. The latter are more relevant for chiefdoms or states than for small egalitarian groups (see Haas and Piscitelli, 2013, 178–181, for a discussion of the severe problems in identifying warfare images in early rock art). In an archaeological context it can be very difficult to separate warfare over land from warfare having other motivations, and readers should bear this in mind throughout the rest of this section.

Even when skeletons show obvious evidence of violence, it can be difficult to distinguish warfare from individual homicide, execution, religious sacrifices, and non-warfare-related cannibalism. Uncertainties in the dating of skeletons can also make it difficult to distinguish cases where many deaths occurred simultaneously (a massacre) from cases where deaths occurred over a span of decades or centuries (a cemetery).

Defensive structures and defensively located settlements, while evidence of the threat of warfare, are not evidence of actual warfare. They tend to deter groups that may be considering an attack. Such investments could have been undertaken in the belief that they would prevent war or reduce its likelihood. They could also have been motivated by a belief that in the event of an attack, the defenders would be more likely to prevail.

The best-documented example of early large-scale violence is from the cemetery of Jebel Sahaba, which is located in the Nile valley in southern Egypt and has been dated between 18,600–13,400 BP (Crevecoeur et al., 2021). Of the 61 individuals examined, 41 had at least one healed or unhealed lesion, 38 had indications of trauma, and 25 had clear projectile impact marks. There is no patterning of trauma or projectile impacts by age or sex. Some individuals had experienced multiple episodes of violence in their lives. An assortment of weapons was used, including light arrows, heavier arrows, and spears.

Crevecoeur et al. reject the notion of a single catastrophic event at Jebel Sahaba and do not believe the evidence supports face-to-face battles. They favor the view that the community was a target for small recurrent attacks such as raids or ambushes over a short time scale. Large cemetery areas suggest some degree of sedentism and variation in lithic industries indicates differing cultural traditions. The authors conclude that climate change between the Last Glacial Maximum and the African Humid Period was probably responsible for triggering violent competition among culturally distinct groups of semi-sedentary hunter-fisher-gatherers.

Another case of inter-group violence has been documented for the early Holocene (10,500–9500 BP) at Nataruk, near what would then have been a lagoon on Lake Turkana in Kenya (Lahr et al., 2016). Details are available for twelve skeletons found *in situ*. Ten had lethal lesions, including five with sharp-force trauma probably involving arrows and five with blunt-force trauma to the head. The area was a fertile lakeshore that supported a substantial population of hunter-gatherers. The use of pottery may indicate storage and a reduction in mobility. The authors suggest that the massacre could have been part of a raid for resources (territory, women, children, or stored food).

Ferguson (2013b) reviews archaeological data on prehistoric warfare for Europe and the Near East. For Europe, the Upper Paleolithic shows negligible evidence of war, and barely any evidence of interpersonal violence. In the Mesolithic, from the onset of the Holocene around 11,600 BP until the arrival of agriculture, warfare is "scattered and episodic." This period is associated with increasing sedentism, more food storage, more distinctive group identities, and greater inequality. Approximately 500–1,000 years after the Neolithic transition to agriculture, warfare becomes widespread, and in the Copper, Bronze, and Iron Ages, warfare is the norm. Crevecoeur et al. (2021) likewise believe that fatal trauma became more frequent in Europe during the Mesolithic.

For the Near East, Ferguson (2013b) begins with early Natufian society around 15,000 BP, which was pre-agricultural and similar to the European Mesolithic. There is no skeletal evidence of war in the southern Levant for the next 10,000 years. Likewise there is no evidence of fortifications in this period. Peace came to an end in the southern Levant in the early Bronze Age around 5200 BP, a time that coincided with the formation of the Egyptian state. The apparent absence of war over this long span is remarkable in light of the intensive archaeological study the region has received; its history of climate shocks, technological innovation, and population fluctuation (see Sections 4.3 and 5.3); and the possibility of social stratification during some periods (see Section 6.11).

Ferguson reviews a substantial body of evidence indicating warfare in other parts of the Near East, including Anatolia and the northern Tigris area, at least as early as the Pottery Neolithic beginning around 8400 BP. At some sites warfare probably goes back to the Pre-Pottery Neolithic A during 11,600–10,500 BP when agriculture was beginning to spread in southwest Asia. Warfare continued through the Copper and Bronze Ages.

Using data on 16,820 hunter-gatherer burials at 329 archaeological sites in central California for 1530–230 BP, Allen et al. (2016) find that sharp-force trauma is correlated with resource scarcity measured by net primary productivity (NPP). These traumas were probably contributing factors for death in 95% of the cases where they occurred. There was no similar correlation for blunt-force traumas, which were much less likely to be the cause of death. The authors note that if populations were distributed over the landscape to equalize resources per person, differences in violence would not be caused directly by differences in scarcity. However, groups in areas with lower NPP (net primary productivity) might have had larger and more poorly defined territories, leading to greater conflict with neighboring groups. The NPP data are modern and do not provide information about past climate shocks.

The ethnographic literature provides direct evidence on warfare among hunter-gatherers. Modern hunter-gatherers may differ in important ways from those who lived thousands of years ago. Contemporary hunter-gatherers live in extreme environments, and behavior in these societies has been influenced significantly by the outside world (Lee and Daly, 1999). Thus caution must be exercised when extrapolating back from modern examples to the frequency of warfare (whether over land or not) in prehistory.

The Standard Cross Cultural Sample or SCCS is a representative sample of 186 well-documented and culturally independent pre-modern societies (Murdock and White, 1969, 2006). Two results from this data set stand out (Kelly, 2013a, 2013b). The first is that while there is evidence for warfare in all types of societies, the incidence of warfare is lower for egalitarian nomadic foragers than it is for non-egalitarian sedentary foragers. The second (first reported in Keeley, 1996) is that warfare is correlated with population pressure but not with population density, where population pressure refers to the ratio of population to total food, and population density refers to the ratio of population to total land. Keeley (1996) argues that the losers in early warfare are frequently driven off or killed, a finding that is consistent with the formal model we will develop later.

Fry and Soderberg (2013) use the SCCS to study 148 episodes of lethal violence in 21 mobile forager bands. They conclude that "most incidents of lethal aggression may be classified as homicides, a few others as feuds, and a minority as war" (270). Kelly (2000, ch. 2) observes that in a sample of 25 foraging societies drawn from the SCCS, war is strongly associated with segmented social structures that generate group identities. Ember and Ember (1992) use the SCCS to study the effect of ecological variables on war. They find that by far the best predictor of warfare is a history of natural disasters and that chronic scarcity has no independent effect on warfare.

Kelly (2013a) makes some additional observations about foraging societies that are particularly relevant to warfare over land. All such societies have ways of assigning individuals to specific tracts of land and allowing them to secure access to others (154–161). In some instances individuals can move flexibly across social groups. There is a widespread but not universal pattern among foragers in which "connections to land are social and permeable rather than geographic and rigid" (156). Perimeter defense is rare, but the need to ask permission to use another group's territory is common (it is normally granted). When foragers become sedentary, however, population is usually so high that residential movement is not possible without displacing another group; "war appears when mobility is not an option" (205).

A growing historical literature supports the idea that environmental shocks can trigger war. Zhang et al. (2006, 2007) find a positive association between abnormally cold periods and domestic rebellions in China during 1000–1911 AD. They argue that the causal mechanism involves Malthusian population growth during warm periods followed by reduced food output in cold periods. Tol and Wagner (2010) find a similar pattern for most of Europe during 1000–1990 AD, where unusually cold periods are associated with more violent conflict. Bai and Kung (2011) find that droughts are correlated with nomadic invasions of China between 220 BC and 1839 AD. They argue that drought had larger effects on food supply for pastoralists than for farmers in central China. In a meta-analysis of econometric research involving modern (post-1950) data, Burke et al. (2015) estimate that a one-standard deviation increase in temperature raises intergroup conflict by 11.3%, with smaller but still substantial effects for drought or extreme rainfall.

7.4 PRODUCTION AND WARFARE

The formal model has only two sites or territories, in contrast to the model from Chapter 6 that had a continuum of sites. We ignore the technology of exclusion used by insiders to prevent entry by individual outsiders and focus instead on the technology of combat between two organized groups. Connections to the formal model in Chapter 6 will be addressed in Section 7.9.

This section treats site qualities and group sizes as exogenous and examines the conditions under which war or peace will occur. The main results are as follows. First, war and peace are determined only by the ratio of the site productivities and the ratio of the group sizes. The absolute levels of these variables do not matter. Second, for a given productivity ratio peace occurs when the regional population is distributed across sites in a way that makes food per capita similar across sites. Extreme population distributions lead to large differences in living standards across the sites and result in war, where the attacker is the group with the larger size and lower food per capita.

Consider two sites i = A, B. Each agent is risk neutral and maximizes expected food consumption. Agents regard death as equivalent to being alive without food, where both yield zero utility (but see Section 7.8). Each agent is endowed with one unit of labor time. Individual agents are of negligible size relative to the total population at a site.

The production function for food is

$$Y_i = s_i n_i^\alpha \quad \text{with } 0 < \alpha < 1 \quad i = A, B \quad (7.1)$$

where $s_i > 0$ is the quality or productivity of site i and n_i is the population of site i at the time of production. Site qualities are determined by permanent geographic features such as lakes, rivers, good soil, and diverse local ecosystems, as well as transient factors such as weather. Equation (7.1) can be obtained from a Cobb–Douglas production function with constant returns to scale in labor and land. Here the land area for each site is normalized at unity. The full production function will be used in Chapter 8.

The agents at a site share food equally, so in the absence of warfare each agent at site i receives the average product

$$y_i = s_i n_i^{\alpha-1} \quad i = A, B \quad (7.2)$$

The two sites together form a region with total population $n_A + n_B = N > 0$.

We will develop a model with the following steps in each period: (i) Malthusian dynamics determine an initial population for each site, (ii) individual agents can migrate between sites, and (iii) the resulting groups decide whether or not to attack. We proceed by backward induction. This section gives the results at step (iii), treating the group sizes (n_A, n_B) and site qualities (s_A, s_B) as exogenous. Section 7.5 studies the location decisions at step (ii), and Section 7.6 describes the population dynamics at step (i).

At step (iii) a war occurs if at least one group chooses to attack. Given that a war takes place, the probability that group i wins is

$$p_i = n_i/(n_A + n_B) \quad \text{or} \quad p_i = n_i/N \quad i = A, B \quad (7.3)$$

The probability of victory for a group is equal to its share in total population. This seems plausible for small-scale societies without specialized warriors or weapons. The military technology in (7.3) assigns no advantage to the attackers or defenders. Our functional form is the simplest of those considered by Garfinkel and Skaperdas (2007).

We make several other simplifying assumptions (see Section 7.8 for the effects of relaxing these assumptions). Payoffs are "winner take all" in the sense that the winning group keeps its own site and gains the site of the opposing group. The winners suffer no casualties and spread their population across the two sites to maximize total food output. The losing group is killed or driven away and receives a zero payoff.

When group i with population n_i wins the contest, its total food output is

$$H(n_i) = \max \left\{ s_A L_A^\alpha + s_B L_B^\alpha \text{ subject to } L_A \geq 0, L_B \geq 0, L_A + L_B = n_i \right\}$$

(7.4)

This requires a few comments. Given that only the victorious group survives, this group gains control over both sites. Thus the winners can distribute their population across the two sites in order to maximize the food output of the group as a whole, which is shared in an egalitarian way. The simplifying assumption that winners suffer no casualties implies that the total labor supply available for allocation between the two sites is n_i.

Due to the nature of the production function in (7.1), it is never optimal to abandon the old site and locate the entire group at the new one. This follows from the fact that the marginal product of labor at a site approaches infinity whenever the labor input at the site approaches zero (this is true regardless of the productivity s_i for the site). Therefore, the winning group always chooses an interior solution with a positive population at each site, and equalizes the marginal products of labor across sites. A different production function might yield a boundary solution where only one site is used (presumably the new one).

Another feature of the production function in (7.1) is that whenever the marginal products are equalized across sites, the average products are automatically equalized as well. This implies that a member of the winning group is indifferent between site A and site B in the aftermath of a war. A different production function might not result in the equalization of the average products, implying a need for side payments across sites to equalize food consumption among the victors.

We can express the function H using the following notation. Let σ be the ratio of the site productivities as in (7.5a) below and let ϕ be the function of the site productivities defined in (7.5b) below. Then the total food output $H(n_i)$ can be written as in (7.5c) and the optimal labor allocation is described by (7.5d):

$$\sigma \equiv s_A/s_B \in (0, \infty)$$

(7.5a)

$$\phi(s_A, s_B) \equiv s_A / \left[1 + \sigma^{-1/(1-\alpha)} \right]^\alpha + s_B / \left[1 + \sigma^{1/(1-\alpha)} \right]^\alpha$$

(7.5b)

$$H(n_i) = \phi(s_A, s_B) n_i^\alpha$$

(7.5c)

$$L_A(n_i; \sigma) = n_i / \left[1 + \sigma^{-1/(1-\alpha)} \right] \quad \text{and} \quad L_B(n_i; \sigma) = n_i / \left[1 + \sigma^{1/(1-\alpha)} \right]$$

(7.5d)

The aggregate food output in (7.5c) has the same structure as the production function in (7.1) but the individual site productivity is replaced by the aggregate productivity $\phi(s_A, s_B)$. In (7.5d), the optimal labor allocation for the winning group has properties one would expect: the higher the productivity of site A relative to site B, and thus the larger the ratio σ, the more labor the winning group allocates to site A, and conversely. Equation (7.5c) gives an expression for per capita food consumption among the winning group, which we write as

$$h(n_i) = H(n_i)/n_i = \phi(s_A, s_B)n_i^{\alpha-1} \tag{7.6}$$

War occurs when group A attacks, when group B attacks, or when both attack. If group $j \neq i$ attacks, group i is indifferent between attacking or not because a war occurs in either case. If group j does not attack, it is optimal for group i to attack whenever $p_i h(n_i) > s_i n_i^{\alpha-1}$ where the left side is the expected food per person from a war and the right side is the food per person from peace. Thus whenever this inequality holds it is a dominant strategy for i to attack. Assuming a group does not attack in situations of indifference, we obtain the following result:

peace occurs if and only if $\quad p_i h(n_i) \leq s_i n_i^{\alpha-1} \quad$ for $i = A, B$ $\quad$ (7.7)

We next consider how war and peace are determined by the group sizes (n_A, n_B) and site qualities (s_A, s_B). Using (7.6) and (7.7), the functions in (7.8) provide lower bounds on the probability of victory p_A or p_B that would motivate an attack by A or B respectively.

$$x_A(\sigma) \equiv s_A/\phi(s_A, s_B) \in (0, 1)$$
$$x_B(\sigma) \equiv s_B/\phi(s_A, s_B) \in (0, 1) \tag{7.8}$$

These functions depend only on the ratio $\sigma \equiv s_A/s_B$.

Lemma 7.1
The functions x_A and x_B have the following properties.

$$x_A(\sigma) + x_B(\sigma) > 1 \text{ for all } \sigma > 0 \tag{7.9a}$$

$$x_A'(\sigma) > 0 \text{ and } x_B'(\sigma) < 0 \text{ for all } \sigma > 0 \tag{7.9b}$$

$$x_A(0) = 0 \text{ and } x_A(\infty) = 1 \tag{7.9c}$$

$$x_B(0) = 1 \text{ and } x_B(\infty) = 0 \tag{7.9d}$$

Our first proposition uses Lemma 7.1 to show that the occurrence of war or peace depends only on the ratio of the site qualities and the ratio of the group sizes.

Proposition 7.1 (war and peace).

Fix $s_A/s_B \equiv \sigma \in (0, \infty)$ and $n_A/n_B \in (0, \infty)$.

(a)   If $0 < n_A/N < 1 - x_B(\sigma)$ then group B attacks and there is war.
(b)   If $1 - x_B(\sigma) \leq n_A/N \leq$ then neither group attacks and there is
       $x_A(\sigma)$ peace.
(c)   If $x_A(\sigma) < n_A/N < 1$ then group A attacks and there is war.

Groups A and B never attack simultaneously. When average products are equal across sites (that is, $s_A n_A^{\alpha-1} = s_B n_B^{\alpha-1}$), case (b) holds with strict inequalities and there is peace.

These results are illustrated in Figure 7.1. The productivity ratio σ is on the horizontal axis. Group A's population share n_A/N, which gives the probability p_A that A wins a war if one occurs, is on the vertical axis. For a fixed productivity ratio σ, a war occurs if either A or B has a large enough population share. The boundary cases $n_A/N = 0$ and $n_A/N = 1$ lead to war

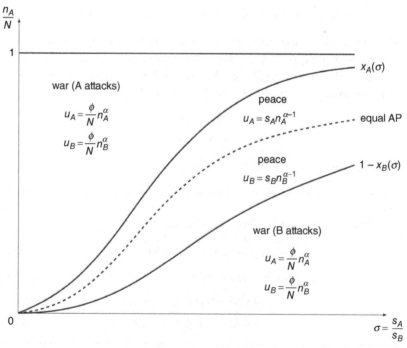

FIGURE 7.1. War and peace determined by the ratio of site productivities and the ratio of group sizes

only in the trivial sense that the grand coalition consisting of all agents in the region attacks an empty site and wins with certainty.

We adopt the term *trivial war* in referring to boundary cases of this sort, because graphically such points are in the warfare region of Figure 7.1. However, in trivial wars no land is transferred between groups and no one dies. The only result is an allocation of labor across sites to maximize total food as in (7.4). We refer to *non-trivial war* when we are discussing conflicts between two groups of positive size. In these cases one group dies and the other group takes its land. Only non-trivial wars are empirically relevant.

Peace occurs for intermediate population allocations. The dashed curve indicates the locus where average products are equal across sites, which is always in the interior of the peace region. Any population allocation that comes sufficiently close to equalizing the average products, and therefore the standards of living across sites in terms of food per capita, will ensure that peace prevails.

The utility functions of the individual agents are

war: $u_A(n_A,n_B) = [\phi(s_A,s_B)/N]n_A^\alpha$ and $u_B(n_A,n_B) = [\phi(s_A,s_B)/N]n_B^\alpha$
peace: $u_A(n_A,n_B) = s_A n_A^{\alpha-1}$ and $u_B(n_A,n_B) = s_B n_B^{\alpha-1}$

$$(7.10)$$

In wartime an agent prefers to be in a larger group because this increases the probability of victory. In peacetime an agent prefers to be in a smaller group because this increases the average product of labor and therefore raises food consumption per capita.

7.5 INDIVIDUAL MOBILITY

We now move back to the migration stage and examine the location decisions of the individual agents. This section is complex but the main results can be summarized as follows. Given the productivities of the sites and the distribution of regional population across them, an individual agent can form expectations about whether there will be war or peace based upon the results from Section 7.4. An agent must then choose a location. We will be interested in situations where no individual agent wants to switch sites given their (correct) expectations with regard to war or peace.

Suppose that an initial distribution of population across sites is inherited from the past (in Section 7.6 this will be determined by Malthusian dynamics). We will show that individual migration, if it occurs, will either push the system toward a boundary solution with trivial war (agents move to the site of the group that is expected to win) or toward a peaceful outcome (agents move to the site with higher food per capita). This shows that non-trivial wars cannot occur if migration occurs. Thus, non-trivial wars require mobility costs high enough to block migration, so agents do not flee from an impending conflict.

We assume an initial population allocation $m = (m_A, m_B) \geq 0$ with $m_A + m_B = N$. We want to know how individual migration determines a final allocation $n = (n_A, n_B) \geq 0$, which then leads to group decisions about war or peace as in Section 7.4. The individual agents observe the site qualities (s_A, s_B) and ignore their own influence on the sizes of the groups at each site. Each agent takes the locations of all other agents as given.

An agent initially located at site i who moves to site $j \neq i$ only receives a fraction $\eta \in (0, 1]$ of the utility u_j available to non-movers at $j \neq i$. The penalty 1-η may reflect a preference to live near family and friends, or to remain in a group with familiar customs and beliefs. It may also reflect a stigma imposed on outsiders by members of the other group. We use a multiplicative migration cost because under this assumption, only the relative group sizes will be important in our Malthusian model in Section 7.6.

Equilibrium is defined so that no agent wants to change sites.

Definition 7.1

Fix $\sigma > 0$ and $N > 0$. Consider allocations $n = (n_A, n_B) \geq 0$ with $n_A + n_B = N$. We call n a *locational equilibrium* (LE) in any of the following cases: $n = (N, 0)$; $n = (0, N)$; or $n > 0$ with

$$u_A(n) \geq \eta u_B(n) \quad \text{and} \quad u_B(n) \geq \eta u_A(n) \qquad (7.11)$$

The boundary cases $(N, 0)$ and $(0, N)$ are always equilibria because an agent who moves to an empty site is attacked by all other agents and loses with certainty, resulting in zero utility. In these boundary cases only one of the inequalities in (7.11) holds because utility is positive at one site and zero at the other. In interior cases both inequalities must hold.

The next task is to identify population distributions that lead to particular war or peace outcomes (as in Proposition 7.1) while simultaneously forestalling migration (as in D7.1). For example, suppose we seek an allocation leading to a war in which B attacks A, while ensuring that no individual agents flee their current locations. This is clearly true for $n = (0, N)$, which yields a trivial war and is also a locational equilibrium.

The interesting cases involve interior allocations. Now to have a war in which B attacks, we must satisfy both Proposition 7.1(a) and (7.11). For a given productivity ratio σ Proposition 7.1(a) requires $n_A/n_B < (1 - x_B)/x_B$. We obtain the utility levels for warfare from (7.10) and substitute these into (7.11) to obtain $\eta^{1/\alpha} \leq n_A/n_B \leq (1/\eta)^{1/\alpha}$. Combining these, we require $\eta^{1/\alpha} \leq n_A/n_B \leq \min \{(1/\eta)^{1/\alpha}, (1 - x_B)/x_B\}$, where n_A/n_B must be strictly less than $(1 - x_B)/x_B$. More generally we obtain the following restrictions on the ratio n_A/n_B.

Proposition 7.2 (interior locational equilibria).

Fix $\sigma > 0$ and $N > 0$. An allocation $n > 0$ is an LE if and only if it satisfies one of the following (mutually exclusive) conditions.

(a) B attacks: $n_A/n_B \in LE_B \equiv [\eta^{1/\alpha}, \min \{(1/\eta)^{1/\alpha}, (1 - x_B)/x_B\}]$

(b) peace: $n_A/n_B \in LE_P$
$$\equiv [\max \{(\sigma\eta)^{1/(1-\alpha)}, (1 - x_B)/x_B\}, \min \{(\sigma/\eta)^{1/(1-\alpha)}, x_A/(1 - x_A)\}]$$

(c) A attacks: $n_A/n_B \in LE_A \equiv [\max \{\eta^{1/\alpha}, x_A/(1 - x_A)\}, (1/\eta)^{1/\alpha}]$

We require $n_A/n_B < (1 - x_B)/x_B$ strictly in (a) and $n_A/n_B > x_A/(1 - x_A)$ strictly in (c).

The sets LE_B and LE_A in Proposition 7.2 may be empty or non-empty. We will discuss the relevant conditions for each case below.

Figure 7.2 shows a case where LE_B exists and LE_A does not (the interpretation of the arrows will be discussed later). Group size ratios n_A/n_B in the interval $(0, (1 - x_B)/x_B)$ lead to an attack by B due to Proposition 7.1(a). To keep agents at A from fleeing to B or vice versa, we also require $\eta^{1/\alpha} \leq n_A/n_B \leq (1/\eta)^{1/\alpha}$. In Figure 7.2 the upper bound on LE_B is given by $(1/\eta)^{1/\alpha}$ but in other situations it could be given by $(1 - x_B)/x_B$ instead.

The peace interval LE_P in Proposition 7.2(b) is always non-empty. When $\eta = 1$ so there is no mobility cost, LE_P contains the single point $n_A/n_B = \sigma^{1/(1-\alpha)}$ where the average products are equal across sites. As η falls and mobility costs rise, the interval LE_P grows (see Figure 7.2). When η is close to zero, every peaceful allocation in Proposition 7.1(b) is an LE and the interval LE_P in Figure 7.2 becomes $[(1 - x_B)/x_B, x_A/(1 - x_A)]$.

From Proposition 7.2(a) the interval LE_B is non-empty if and only if $\eta^{1/\alpha} < (1 - x_B)/x_B$. Using the properties of $x_B(\sigma)$ from (7.9) this requires a sufficiently large σ, so site A is a sufficiently valuable prize for group B. When $\eta = 1$ so there is no mobility cost, this reduces to $x_B(\sigma) < 1/2$. Similarly Proposition 7.2(c) implies that LE_A is non-empty if and only if

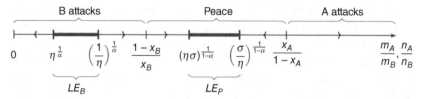

FIGURE 7.2. Migration and locational equilibrium

$x_A/(1-x_A) < (1/\eta)^{1/\alpha}$. This requires a sufficiently small σ, so site B is a sufficiently valuable prize for group A. When $\eta = 1$ this reduces to $x_A(\sigma) < 1/2$.

Given a fixed value of σ and assuming the relevant intervals exist, LE_B and LE_A both expand as mobility costs rise. This occurs simply because when migration is more expensive, agents are less inclined to move despite an impending war. When the warfare intervals exist they may either be adjacent to the peace interval or separated from it by an interval of non-LE allocations. However, the ratios n_A/n_B in the warfare interval LE_B are always less than those in the peace interval LE_P because group B must be strong enough to make an attack worthwhile. Likewise the ratios in LE_A always exceed those in LE_P.

Now consider a given initial (pre-migration) allocation $m \geq 0$. We want to know how the decisions of individual agents lead to a final (post-migration) allocation $n \geq 0$. When $m = (N, 0)$ or $(0, N)$ we already have a locational equilibrium by D7.1 and none of the agents wants to change sites. The same is true for any interior allocation $m > 0$ such that m_A/m_B is in one of the three LE intervals described in Proposition 7.2.

We therefore focus on cases where m is interior but not an LE. This implies that one of the conditions in (7.11) must be violated. Because the other condition in (7.11) must be satisfied, agents can only move in one direction. For example, if $u_B(m) < \eta u_A(m)$ then agents migrate from B to A and no agents migrate from A to B. In this situation we study allocations $n = (n_A, n_B) \geq 0$ with $n_A + n_B = N$ such that $n_A \geq m_A$. Migration stops when the system reaches an allocation where $u_B(n) = \eta u_A(n)$. This implies that $u_A(n) \geq \eta u_B(n)$ also holds, so we have an LE. If there is no interior $n_A \geq m_A$ at which this occurs then all agents go to site A, and the final allocation is $n_A = N$ and $n_B = 0$. If the initial allocation has $u_A(m) < \eta u_B(m)$ the same logic applies but with the roles of A and B reversed. This reasoning leads to the following definition.

Definition 7.2

Fix $\sigma > 0$ and $N > 0$. Also fix an initial (pre-migration) allocation $m \geq 0$. The final (post-migration) allocation n is as follows.

(a) If m is an LE then $n = m$. Otherwise:
(b) If $u_B(m) < \eta u_A(m)$ then n is the allocation with the smallest $n_A \geq m_A$ such that $u_B(n) = \eta u_A(n)$. When this condition cannot be satisfied we set $n = (N, 0)$.
(c) If $u_A(m) < \eta u_B(m)$ then n is the allocation with the smallest $n_B \geq m_B$ such that $u_A(n) = \eta u_B(n)$. When this condition cannot be satisfied we set $n = (0, N)$.

The intuition behind D7.2 can be clarified by considering the directions in which the agents flow. Suppose the system is not yet in locational equilibrium. When war is expected the utility functions are those for war in (7.10), and agents flow toward the site with the larger current population. This process is self-reinforcing and can only end with a boundary equilibrium or a transition to the peace interval. When peace is expected the utility functions are those for the peace case in (7.10), and agents flow toward the site with the higher average product. This reduces the difference in average products between the sites, and migration stops when this gap is small enough relative to the mobility cost. If the average product is initially higher at site A, migration stops at the lower bound of the peace interval LE_P in Proposition 7.2, and if the average product is initially higher at site B, migration stops at the upper bound of the peace interval LE_P.

For completeness we need to consider the cases where LE_B is empty or not, and where LE_A is empty or not. The formal results are as follows.

Proposition 7.3 (migration).

Fix $\sigma > 0$ and $N > 0$. Choose an arbitrary initial allocation $m \geq 0$. The final allocation n is well defined and exactly one of the following cases applies.

(a) If $m = (0, N)$, $m = (N, 0)$, $m_A/m_B \in LE_B$, $m_A/m_B \in LE_P$, or $m_A/m_B \in LE_A$, then $n = m$. In the rest of the proposition, we limit attention to interior allocations $m > 0$.
(b) Suppose LE_B is empty. If m_A/m_B is below $(1 - x_B)/x_B$ then $n = (0, N)$. If m_A/m_B is at least $(1-x_B)/x_B$ and below the lower bound of LE_P then n_A/n_B is equal to the lower bound of LE_P.
(c) Suppose LE_B is non-empty. If m_A/m_B is below the lower bound of LE_B then $n = (0, N)$. If m_A/m_B is strictly between the upper bound of LE_B and the lower bound of LE_P then n_A/n_B is equal to the lower bound of LE_P.

(d) Suppose LE_A is empty. If m_A/m_B is above $x_A/(1 - x_A)$ then $n = (N, 0)$. If m_A/m_B is above the upper bound of LE_P and does not exceed $x_A/(1 - x_A)$ then n_A/n_B is equal to the upper bound of LE_P.

(e) Suppose LE_A is non-empty. If m_A/m_B is above the upper bound of LE_A then $n = (N, 0)$. If m_A/m_B is strictly between the upper bound of LE_P and the lower bound of LE_A then n_A/n_B is equal to the upper bound of LE_P.

Figure 7.2 shows the migration process for the case where LE_B exists and LE_A does not, where the arrows indicate the direction of migration. If m_A/m_B is below LE_B, group B will attack, we have $u_A(m) < \eta u_B(m)$, and agents flow from site A to site B. From the war utilities in (7.10) this migration process raises u_B and lowers u_A, reinforcing the initial inequality. Population continues to flow in the same direction until all agents are at site B and we have $n = (0, N)$.

Next suppose m_A/m_B is between LE_B and LE_P. If $m_A/m_B < (1-x_B)/x_B$ so group B will attack, we use the war utilities from (7.10). The fact that m_A/m_B is above LE_B implies $u_B(m) < \eta u_A(m)$, so agents flow from B to A. As long as B will attack, migration raises u_A and lowers u_B so the preceding inequality continues to hold. Once the system reaches $n_A/n_B = (1-x_B)/x_B$ we use the peace utilities from (7.10). Now migration from site B to site A lowers u_A and raises u_B. This continues until $u_B(n) = \eta u_A(n)$ at the lower bound of LE_P. Migration then stops and we have a peaceful LE.

Finally suppose m_A/m_B is above LE_P. When peace is expected, population flows toward B and migration ends at the upper bound of LE_P. When A is expected to attack, population flows toward A until all agents are at site A and we have $n = (N, 0)$.

Several implications follow from Proposition 7.3. First, if the initial allocation m is not an LE, the system must move to one of four final allocations: $(N, 0)$, $(0, N)$, the lower bound of LE_P, or the upper bound of LE_P. None is consistent with non-trivial war. Thus, non-trivial warfare can only arise if the system starts from an initial population allocation m that is already in LE_B or LE_A, and mobility costs keep all agents at their initial sites. If the initial allocation m yields peace but is not an LE, the final allocation also yields peace and migration reduces the gap in average products across the sites.

The interval LE_P is stable in the sense that a small deviation to a point that is not an LE causes migration flows that bring the system back to

LE_P. The same is true for the boundary cases (N, o) and (o, N). But if the warfare intervals LE_A and LE_B exist they are unstable, in the sense that a small deviation to a point that is not an LE will lead either to a boundary case or an allocation in the peace interval LE_P. Points in the interior of LE_B or LE_A are neutrally stable because a small deviation leaves the system in LE_B or LE_A.

When mobility cost is zero ($\eta = 1$) three locational equilibria always exist: the boundary cases with trivial war, and the peaceful allocation with equal average products. If $x_B(\sigma) < 1/2$ then LE_B contains the single point $n_A = n_B = N/2$ and it is empty otherwise. A symmetric result holds for LE_A. At most one of these two interior warfare equilibria can exist. If either one does, it is unstable. Thus a positive mobility cost is a necessary condition for a stable equilibrium with non-trivial warfare.

We now pause to summarize the results so far. For an exogenously fixed ratio of site productivities $\sigma = s_A/s_B$, Proposition 7.1 derived the group size ratios n_A/n_B that lead to an attack by B, peaceful coexistence, or an attack by A. We then added the requirement that individual agents who foresee these outcomes not change sites. The group size ratios n_A/n_B consistent with this individual rationality requirement were given by the intervals LE_B, LE_P, and LE_A in Proposition 7.2.

Next we examined migration when the initial population allocation is not in one of these intervals. Proposition 7.3 showed that if the system is not already at a locational equilibrium with non-trivial warfare (LE_B or LE_A), then individual migration cannot take the system to such an equilibrium. Instead it either pushes the system to a boundary case with trivial warfare, or to the boundary of the peace interval LE_P. In Section 7.6 we will study how migration costs and productivity shocks can interact to yield non-trivial wars.

7.6 MALTHUSIAN DYNAMICS

This section embeds the model of Sections 7.4 and 7.5 in a Malthusian framework where population growth depends on food income. Chapter 6 used a similar framework to study inequality in small-scale societies.

The role of Malthusian mechanisms in the present model is to use the population levels from the two sites at the end of one period to generate new population levels at the beginning of the next. The latter populations provide the starting point for the migration process in Section 7.5, which then leads to the combat decisions in Section 7.4. Under the assumptions of this section, the group size ratio in one period along with the sequence of productivity ratios for the current period and all future periods suffices to determine all of the future group size ratios. This information also suffices to determine whether there is war or peace in each period.

We show that there are two necessary conditions for warfare over land. First it is necessary that there be no individual migration in response to the population allocation determined by Malthusian processes. This condition is required because we have shown in Section 7.5 that when migration occurs, it leads either to a boundary outcome where no actual fighting happens (trivial war) or to peace. The second condition is that there must be a sufficiently large exogenous shock to the ratio of the site productivities, either due to a change in nature or a change in food technology. Without this, Malthusian mechanisms will maintain the group size ratio within the interval needed for peace. A corollary is that a series of wars requires a series of shocks because in the aftermath of a war, population is reallocated across sites in a way that restores peace. The two necessary conditions are jointly sufficient; if both are satisfied then the model predicts that a war will occur.

Denote periods by $t = 0, 1, . .$ where a period is one human generation. For an individual agent let ρy be the number of that agent's children who survive to be adults, where y is the agent's food income and $\rho > 0$ is a constant. This captures the idea that adults with more food income are more fertile, have healthier children, or both. Adults in period t produce food, have children, and then die at the end of the period. The children become adults in period $t+1$ at the site where their parents produced food.

Let there be some sequence of productivity ratios $\sigma^t = s_A^t / s_B^t$ for $t = 0, 1, . .$ These are given exogenously by technological and environmental factors. Each period starts with an initial allocation of agents $m^t = (m_A^t, m_B^t)$ inherited from the past. The agents can then move from their birth site to the other site as in Section 7.5. These moves (if any) lead to the final allocation $n^t = (n_A^t, n_B^t)$. Once the final allocation has been determined, the two groups decide whether to attack and payoffs are obtained as in Section 7.4.

Suppose first that peace occurs in period t. This can happen only when the final allocation $n^t > 0$ is interior. The food income of an agent at site A is $y_A^t = s_A^t (n_A^t)^{\alpha-1}$ and the food income of an agent at site B is $y_B^t = s_B^t (n_B^t)^{\alpha-1}$. The Malthusian linkage between food and surviving children gives $m_A^{t+1} = \rho y_A^t n_A^t$ and $m_B^{t+1} = \rho y_B^t n_B^t$. Thus

$$\text{peace in period t yields} \quad m_A^{t+1}/m_B^{t+1} = \sigma^t (n_A^t/n_B^t)^\alpha \quad (7.12)$$

This result shows that in peacetime the ratio of the group sizes at the start of period t+1 is a strictly concave function of the ratio prevailing at the end of period t.

Now suppose instead that a war occurs in period t and the winner is $W \in \{A, B\}$. Group W allocates its population n_W^t across sites to maximize total food output as in (7.4) while the opposing group disappears. Let the resulting number of agents at each site be L_A^t and L_B^t where $L_A^t + L_B^t = n_W^t$. Due to the fact that the production function from (7.1) has constant output elasticity, the equalization of marginal products across sites implies equalization of average products. Thus every member of W has the same food income $y^t = H(n_W^t; s_A^t, s_B^t)/n_W^t$. Using $m_A^{t+1} = \rho y^t L_A^t$ and $m_B^{t+1} = \rho y^t L_B^t$ with (7.5d) implies that

$$\text{war in period t yields} \qquad m_A^{t+1}/m_B^{t+1} = (\sigma^t)^{1/(1-\alpha)} \qquad (7.13)$$

This result shows that in wartime the ratio of the group sizes at the start of period t+1 is a constant determined solely by the relative productivities of the sites. Because the winners distribute their period-t population across sites to maximize total food, the effect of group size ratios from earlier periods is erased and population adjustments restart from scratch. Notice that (7.13) applies both when $n^t > 0$ so the war is non-trivial, and also when the war is trivial because $n^t = (N^t, 0)$ or $(0, N^t)$.

Lemma 7.2

Fix $\sigma^t \in (0, \infty)$ and choose any interior allocation $m^t > 0$. The pair $(\sigma^t, m_A^t/m_B^t)$ suffices to determine the final allocation n_t, whether war or peace occurs in period t, and the group size ratio m_A^{t+1}/m_B^{t+1} where $m^{t+1} > 0$ is interior.

Lemma 7.2 shows that the initial group size ratio m_A^0/m_B^0 and the sequence of productivity ratios $\{\sigma^t\}$ determine the subsequent group size ratios m_A^t/m_B^t for all $t \geq 1$. This information also suffices to determine whether war or peace occurs in each period. Accordingly, our results do not depend on the absolute productivity levels (s_A^t, s_B^t), the absolute population levels N^t, or the identities of the winners in particular conflicts.

Now suppose we are given σ^t and m_A^t/m_B^t for period t. As in Lemma 7.2, we can compute m_A^{t+1}/m_B^{t+1}. We want to know the conditions under which a non-trivial war will occur in period t+1. This question is readily answered using Proposition 7.3. Such a war occurs if and only if the ratio

m_A^{t+1}/m_B^{t+1} is in the set LE_B or LE_A. If neither is true then either the ratio is in LE_P or m^{t+1} is not an LE. In the former case we have peace. In the latter case migration leads to peace or to formation of the grand coalition followed by a trivial war. The following proposition formalizes these ideas.

Proposition 7.4 (war and peace with Malthusian dynamics).

Fix $\sigma^t \in (0, \infty)$ and $m_A^t/m_B^t \in (0, \infty)$. Compute $m_A^{t+1}/m_B^{t+1} \in (0, \infty)$ as in Lemma 7.2. There is a non-trivial war in period $t+1$ if and only if the following two conditions are satisfied:

(a) $\eta^{1/\alpha} \leq m_A^{t+1}/m_B^{t+1} \leq (1/\eta)^{1/\alpha}$ and

(b) $\sigma^{t+1} \notin \left[\sigma_A^{t+1}, \sigma_B^{t+1} \right]$

where the bounds σ_A^{t+1} and σ_B^{t+1} are determined using m_A^{t+1}/m_B^{t+1} to compute m_A^{t+1}/N^{t+1}, and implicitly defining σ_A^{t+1} and σ_B^{t+1} using $m_A^{t+1}/N^{t+1} \equiv x_A(\sigma_A^{t+1}) \equiv 1 - x_B(\sigma_B^{t+1})$. These ratios have the property $\sigma_A^{t+1} < \sigma^t < \sigma_B^{t+1}$.

The necessity of (a) is straightforward. We have already shown that any time individual agents migrate from one site to another, a non-trivial war is impossible. Thus we are limited to cases in which no migration occurs in period $t+1$. If a war is expected the utility functions are obtained from (7.10). The absence of migration implies that these utilities must satisfy (7.11). Putting these conditions together, the initial population ratio in period $t+1$ (which is also the final population ratio) must satisfy Proposition 7.4(a). In this situation the mobility costs incorporated in the parameter η are large enough to prevent migration despite an impending war.

The necessity of (b) has the following intuition. If we use Malthusian dynamics to compute m_A^{t+1}/m_B^{t+1} and take this ratio as given, we know the initial population share m_A^{t+1}/N^{t+1} for group A. Because we have ruled out migration as explained in connection with Proposition 7.4(a), this must also be the final population share n_A^{t+1}/N_A. As shown in Figure 7.3, this fixes a horizontal line that determines an interval of productivity ratios σ^{t+1} consistent with peace. The latter is the interval $\left[\sigma_A^{t+1}, \sigma_B^{t+1} \right]$ in Proposition 7.4(b). To have a war the productivity ratio σ^{t+1} must be outside this interval so $\sigma^{t+1} \notin \left[\sigma_A^{t+1}, \sigma_B^{t+1} \right]$.

The key ideas from Proposition 7.4 can now be summarized. Malthusian dynamics generate a population allocation at the beginning of period $t+1$. If warfare over land is to occur, this allocation cannot be altered by migration. Moreover, given the probabilities of winning determined by the population shares, the productivity ratio between sites must be high or low enough that an attack is attractive for one group or the

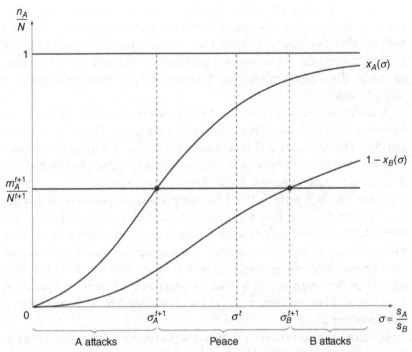

FIGURE 7.3. Productivity ratios for war and peace in period t+1 given initial group sizes

other. The conditions in Proposition 7.4 are sufficient because for given initial group sizes, a war will occur when migration is costly enough and the productivity ratio is extreme enough.

Proposition 7.4 has the following important implication.

Corollary to Proposition 7.4
If $\sigma^{t+1} = \sigma^t$ then there is peace in period t+1 regardless of whether there was war or peace in period t.

This follows from the fact that the productivity ratio σ^t is an interior point of the interval $\left[\sigma_A^{t+1}, \sigma_B^{t+1}\right]$ as indicated in Figure 7.3. In order for war to occur σ^{t+1} must involve a large enough shock relative to σ^t. When $\sigma^{t+1} = \sigma^t$ Proposition 7.4 already rules out a non-trivial war. The corollary also excludes trivial wars in the sense defined in Section 7.4.

The corollary shows that when the productivity ratio is constant over some time interval, there can be at most one war in this interval and it must occur at the start of the interval. Peace prevails thereafter. The reason is that war will equalize average products across sites and hence will equalize population growth rates across sites. This maintains the existing group size ratio, which maintains the equality of the average products. Thus peace continues. A series of wars therefore requires a series of shocks.

A useful thought experiment is to shut down individual migration by having η close to zero. This guarantees that (a) in Proposition 7.4 is satisfied. However, (b) is also necessary for war. In a stationary productivity environment Malthusian fertility effects ensure that (b) never holds. Even without migration this is enough to preserve peace.

Any exogenous variable that can alter the relative productivities of the sites can serve as a trigger for warfare. One such variable is production technology. Another is climate. Such shocks can easily change the relative productivities of sites or territories. For example, reduced rainfall may lower productivity substantially at sites far from lakes or rivers but only slightly at sites with access to surface water (see Chapter 5). Historical correlations between climate shocks and warfare are well documented (see Section 7.2).

We close this section with some remarks on the relationship between our theory and that of Malthus (1798 [2004]). Our framework is "Malthusian" only in the sense that we rely on a positive linkage between food per capita and fertility (or a negative linkage with child mortality). This is the operative check on population growth. We do not rely on mortality from warfare as a check on population. In fact our model predicts that in a stationary productivity environment, regional population will converge to an equilibrium level without warfare.

Some anthropologists argue that warfare will occur in a demographic steady state. For example, Harris (1977, 60) suggests that reproductive pressure leads to both warfare and female infanticide, and that infanticide is "a savage but uniquely effective solution to the Malthusian dilemma." In contrast, we believe fertility effects can restrain population growth even without any mortality effects derived from warfare or infanticide.

7.7 EMPIRICAL IMPLICATIONS

Three mechanisms tend to promote peace in our model: mobility between groups, Malthusian fertility effects, and reallocation of population after a war. All three assign larger populations to better sites. The resulting positive association between group size and site quality tends to deter attacks. A productivity shock can trigger a war by creating a temporary imbalance between group size and site quality, provided that the imbalance is not undone through individual migration. We remind the reader again that whenever we use the term "war" in this section, we are referring specifically to warfare over land.

Our theory helps explain Ferguson's (2013b) finding that in Europe warfare was rare or non-existent in the Upper Paleolithic, sporadic in the Mesolithic, and common in the Neolithic and later. The small foraging bands of the Upper Paleolithic probably had fluid social boundaries, with easy individual mobility across groups through exogamous marriage and kinship networks. At low population densities it would also have been hard to exclude outsiders from a territory, yielding open access and rough equality of average products of labor (see Chapter 6). The bands of the Upper Paleolithic almost surely had Malthusian fertility dynamics. Together these factors make warfare over land unlikely.

The shift to the Mesolithic and the Neolithic was associated with rising sedentism (see Chapter 4) and social segmentation (Kelly, 2000, ch. 4). This would make it harder for individuals to circulate among groups. In addition, community sizes were growing. Research on recent small-scale societies suggests that this probably made endogamous marriage more common (Dow et al., 2016), reducing kinship linkages across groups and increasing mobility costs for individuals. In combination with the shocks resulting from technological and environmental change, this would have made warfare more common. A possible source of such shocks was the diffusion of agriculture across Europe, which was accompanied by increased warfare (see Section 7.3).

Our results are also consistent with patterns detected in anthropology. The model accounts for the empirical finding that warfare is a function not of population density but rather of pressure on food resources. Population density can be high at good sites due to individual migration or Malthusian dynamics without leading to warfare. However, war may well occur when shifts in productivity mean that a group has many mouths to feed and few resources with which to feed them. The model correctly predicts that warfare will be more common when shocks from natural disasters or climate change are larger and more frequent. And finally, our prediction that costlier individual mobility makes warfare more likely is consistent with ethnographic evidence that warfare occurs more often in societies with strictly enforced group identities.

We conclude this section with an ethnographic case based on oral histories from the Enga people of highland New Guinea (Wiessner and

Tumu, 1998, ch. 5). The Enga are divided into many tribes, clans, and subclans. All such groups are egalitarian with no one in a position of authority other than "big men." These groups engage in foraging and farming in varying proportions. The Enga have a history of warfare in recent centuries, with the winning groups frequently pushing the losers off their land. The losers then had to move elsewhere. Although the proximate causes of conflict were often trivial, warfare resulted in major land redistributions among groups.

Two related questions are why warfare occurred at all, and whether it had been going on forever or had a recent origin. One place to look for an explanation would be climate shocks, and indeed Wiessner and Tumu note that there were occasional shocks due to frost or drought. These could have served as triggers for war. But perhaps more importantly, the system was far from equilibrium because the arrival of the sweet potato led to substantial regional population growth (see Weissner and Tumu, 1998, ch. 4, and Section 2.6 of this book). This caused considerable conflict. In particular, some people were pushed out of land at higher elevations that had previously been good for hunting and gathering but now became useful for farming. We suspect that this was a case where a large technological shock altered the relative productivities of sites and that our model of egalitarian warfare may apply. Unfortunately, however, we lack archaeological data on the frequency of warfare before and after the arrival of the new food technology.

7.8 EXTENSIONS OF THE MODEL

We have made a number of assumptions about warfare that could be questioned. In many cases, altering our assumptions would make war less likely. For example, one could assume that winning groups suffer injuries or deaths, that winning groups may not gain full control over the losing group's land, that attackers are risk averse rather than risk neutral, that groups preparing an attack incur an opportunity cost in the form of lost food output, that defenders have advantages due to their knowledge of local geography, that defenders can construct fortifications, that potential attackers have kinship connections with defenders, and so on. Because the assumptions used in our formal modeling tend to bias the analysis toward warfare, modifying these assumptions would tend to strengthen our conclusion that war was generally rare among small egalitarian groups in prehistory.

Another assumption that could be modified involves the utility function. We treat death as equivalent to being alive without food. But having no food may be better than death (perhaps more food will arrive tomorrow and one has a chance of surviving until then). This "happy to be alive" utility function makes the prospect of death seem worse in relative terms and would tend to discourage warfare, much as risk aversion would.

On the other hand, one can argue that a minimum amount of food is necessary for life, so a positive amount of food below this subsistence threshold would be useless. This "nothing to lose" utility function would make a group more inclined to attack a rival group when a food shortage looms, much as risk seeking would.

The question is whether these ideas have empirical implications. For example the "happy to be alive" case may apply when agents can smooth consumption through storage or pooling mechanisms while the "nothing to lose" case may apply when mean food output is low, variance is high, and smoothing is infeasible. The influence of such variables on the incidence of early warfare should be open to empirical testing.

In principle, our framework applies both to foragers and farmers. But farmers make greater site-specific investments in land clearance, irrigation systems, terracing, tree planting, and so on, and therefore are more inclined to defend their sites rather than flee from an attack. At the same time improved sites become more attractive to potential attackers, especially those whose own sites suffer from declining productivity due to soil erosion or exhaustion. The combination of endogenous investment and local resource depletion may tend to generate warfare cycles in egalitarian farming societies, especially if there are also barriers to individual movement among groups (see the examples of the Yanomamo, the Tsembaga Maring, and the Central Enga in Johnson and Earle, 2000).

We conclude this section with a remark on institutions. As discussed in Section 7.3, the southern Levant enjoyed about 10,000 years during which evidence for warfare is almost non-existent. From the perspective of our theory this may be surprising, given the numerous environmental and technological shocks affecting the region during this period, including an early transition to agriculture. War was clearly not restrained through state suppression of violence because no state existed at the time.

Our theory suggests an alternative: perhaps institutions of a more decentralized kind helped to transfer population across communities in response to shocks. Examples could include exogamous marriage, shared language, shared religion, or shared norms. Regional networking among local elites could also have facilitated individual migration when relative productivities changed. This is a possibility even for an agrarian society where warfare might otherwise have been expected. More generally, we believe good institutions can help to promote peace even when third party enforcement is absent.

7.9 INEQUALITY AND WARFARE

The model of this chapter may appear complicated in some ways but it is simple in one way: It only involves two sites located within an isolated region. Chapter 6 had a much richer setting with a continuum of sites and a range of property rights institutions, including sites that were open, sites that were closed but unstratified, and sites that were closed and stratified. The latter two cases generated insider–outsider inequality and elite–commoner inequality respectively. In this section we build various bridges between the results of Chapters 6 and 7.

The food technologies in the two models are identical (compare Sections 6.5 and 7.4). In both cases we use a Cobb–Douglas production function with inputs of labor and land, and we normalize the land input at unity. Chapter 6 decomposes site productivity into a regional effect from climate and/or technology and a local effect from geography, while Chapter 7 collapses these effects into a single parameter, but this is unimportant. The two models also assume identical Malthusian dynamics where an agent's surviving offspring are proportional to the agent's food income (compare Sections 6.7 and 7.6).

In Chapter 6 we assumed free mobility among sites within the commons, which equalized food per capita across all open sites. This equalization of average products is precisely the condition that ensures peace in Section 7.4. Therefore groups at open sites in Chapter 6 will not engage in warfare. This conclusion might need to be modified, of course, if there are costs of individual mobility across the sites in the commons, which could be physical, social, or informational in nature.

For sites that are closed but unstratified the issues are more subtle. In the model of Chapter 6 these sites were internally egalitarian but insiders blocked further entry by individual outsiders. This required that insider groups have a minimum size, which we called "d" in Chapter 6. Because closed sites had a range of productivities but the same group size, their food per capita varied from relatively low to relatively high.

A tempting approach in thinking about such sites runs as follows. Because all of the closed but unstratified sites have the same group size, they have equal military power, so in a conflict between two such groups each has an equal probability of winning. Then the question is whether differences in site qualities are large enough to induce the poorer group to attack the richer group. The technology of exclusion used by insiders prevents migration across groups, so individual mobility will not limit the incentives for war.

The problem with this reasoning is that in the model of Chapter 7 we assumed the victorious group would control both sites. In a world with just two sites and no outsiders this makes sense. But in the context of Chapter 6 there are many individual agents who might like to enter a site, and a group that hopes to gain control of a new site will need to exclude these outsiders after it wins the war. If the group intends to use both the old and new sites, as we assumed in Section 7.4, then it does not merely need a critical mass of "d" at its old site; it also needs "d" at its new site. This raises the question of how the winners find the necessary personnel to control and exploit both sites without suffering any entry by outsiders at one place or the other.

One possible answer is that this personnel constraint makes it impossible for the winners to control both sites, so they move all of their members to the new and better site while abandoning the old one. The downside for the winners is that by putting all of their labor input into one site, they obtain a lower food per capita than what they would get by spreading the same labor input across the two sites. This is true not just for the particular production function adopted in Section 7.4 but for the entire class of production functions where the marginal product of labor approaches infinity as labor input approaches zero, so interior solutions are optimal. Therefore if the personnel constraint binds, the gain to the winners of a war is smaller than it would otherwise be and warfare is less likely than the model of Chapter 7 suggests.

Both for this reason and in order to gain additional military strength in a world where warfare is common, an insider group may prefer to have more members than the minimum (d) needed to exclude unorganized outsiders. Ethnographic evidence suggests that in egalitarian societies with frequent warfare, local groups often recruit outsiders to enhance their military prospects. If an insider group chooses to have a membership size of at least 2d rather than d, the personnel constraint disappears, because if the group wins a war it will be able to control both sites. But there are still tradeoffs: a larger group may be beneficial in wartime but it lowers food per capita in peacetime. In principle, it would be possible to solve the latter problem by requiring new group members to pay entry fees to the old group members, but in practice this may not be feasible.

A further wrinkle involves Malthusian population dynamics. In Chapter 6 we showed that within the set of closed but unstratified sites, differences in food per capita would lead to population growth at higher quality sites and population decline at lower quality sites. We suggested in Chapter 6 that in the former case this would cause some children of the insiders to face downward mobility into the commons, while in the latter case it would cause insiders to recruit new commoners until group property rights were restored. An institutional environment with warfare opens up further possibilities.

Rather than departing for the commons, the surplus children of the insiders at rich sites may remain available to assist with military activity and may provide the personnel needed to control sites gained through warfare. The implications for insiders at poor sites who suffer population losses depend upon the sequence of events. If decisions about war take place before such groups can be replenished through recruitment from the commons, these groups will be militarily weak and vulnerable to attack (although their sites are not very valuable prizes). Under such conditions the Malthusian model of Section 7.6 may apply and individual mobility costs combined with productivity shocks may lead to war.

Another direction in which the model could be extended is to give up the idea of sites being indivisible units. We can instead think of each site as having some total land area (which was normalized to unity in Section 7.4). Instead of thinking of the parameter "d" from Chapter 6 as a minimum number of agents needed to close an entire site, we can think of it as the minimum density of organized insiders per unit of land that would have to be present in order to exclude unorganized outsiders. With these modifications we can treat the sites as divisible territories rather than indivisible units, and model warfare over fractional slices of territory. This eliminates the discrete nature of the "d" versus "2d" issue discussed above, and (depending on other details of the model) might lead to wars where groups with modest military advantages try to shift territorial boundaries in their favor.

In addition to sites that are open, or closed but unstratified, Chapter 6 developed a theory to explain the emergence of stratified sites with elite–commoner inequality. The next item on the agenda is to consider warfare in societies with stratification. Chapter 8 creates a formal model to describe wars of conquest among rival elites. There we argue that elite warfare tends to be chronic, even without mobility costs or productivity shocks.

7.10 POSTSCRIPT

This chapter is based on "The economics of early warfare over land" published in the *Journal of Development Economics* (Dow et al., 2017). Leanna Mitchell played an equal role in writing the version of this paper that was originally submitted to *JDE*. Dow and Reed rewrote the paper at the request of the *JDE* editor and are responsible for this chapter. Leanna received her PhD from the Department of Economics at Simon Fraser University in 2021.

Comments on the original article were provided by Cliff Bekar, Sam Bowles, David Burley, Timothy Earle, Curt Eaton, Mukesh Eswaran, Brian Ferguson, Lawrence Keeley, Patrick Kirch, Ian Kuijt, James Kaising Kung, Patricia Lambert, Gerard Padró i Miquel, Omer Moav, Peter Richerson, Stephen Shennan, Bruce Winterhalder, and two anonymous referees. We also thank participants at the 2014 meeting of the Canadian Economics Association and the 2015 symposium "Warfare in Interdisciplinary Perspective" organized by the Human Evolutionary Studies Program at Simon Fraser University. HESP, the Department of Economics at SFU, and the Social Sciences and Humanities Research Council of Canada provided financial support, and Ideen Riahi and Haiyun Kevin Chen supplied outstanding research assistance. We received valuable feedback on an earlier draft of this chapter from Samuel Bowles, Richard Lipsey, John Chant, Jon Kesselman, Craig Riddell, Herbert Grubel, and Richard Harris. Carles Boix gave us insightful comments on our analysis of warfare in both Chapters 7 and 8. All opinions are those of the authors.

We have expanded Section 7.1 substantially in order to create linkages with the other chapters in Part III of the book. Sections 7.2 and 7.3 are largely unchanged relative to the original journal article, although the discussion of the literature has been updated. The formal model in Sections 7.4–7.6 is unchanged but we have added intuition for the benefit of non-economists. Sections 7.7 and 7.8 have been lightly edited except for the discussion of the Enga at the end of Section 7.7, which is new. We were unaware of this case when the model was constructed. All of Section 7.9 on the connections with Chapter 6 is new.

8

Warfare between Elite Groups

8.1 INTRODUCTION

The preceding chapter studied warfare over land among egalitarian groups. Here we extend our study of warfare to elite groups in stratified societies. The formal model in this chapter, although similar to the one in Chapter 7 with respect to the production and military technologies, gives very different results. We will argue that elites are likely to engage in chronic warfare over land and have a strong bias toward territorial expansion. Our investigation of the origins of the state in Part IV (especially Chapter 11) will make use of these ideas, but for now we are only concerned with warfare in stratified non-state or pre-state societies.

In Chapter 7 we distinguished three kinds of warfare in early societies: *raiding*, *displacement*, and *conquest*. Raiding involves theft of moveable property or the capture of humans. It usually puts a premium on surprise, speed, and rapid escape. This is quite different from the military technology used to transfer land ownership permanently from one group to another. We want to reiterate that we are not offering a theory of raiding.

Displacement involves the seizure of land from a rival group while driving off or killing the previous occupants. Our model in Chapter 7 examined wars of displacement among internally egalitarian groups. In this chapter we will consider conquest, which we define to be the seizure of land from an opposing elite, where the previous elite is driven off or killed but commoners are left in place to pay land rent to the new elite.

We base our approach on the model of stratification developed in Chapter 6. In that model an elite begins as an organized insider group that achieves the threshold size needed to exclude unorganized outsiders from a specific site. Stratification occurs when these insider groups find it profitable to hire commoner labor to work their land. An elite enjoys land rent due to its collective ownership of the site, where the rent is equal to food output at the site minus elite expenditures on labor inputs. The wage paid to a commoner is equal to the food income that agent could get at an open site located in the commons.

We remind the reader that as in Chapter 6, when we use the terms "wage" or "labor market," we mean that elites provide food in exchange for labor services, not that there is a monetary payment in the modern sense. Our theoretical results would be identical with an alternative set of institutions where commoners pay "rent" to elites in a "land market," by which we mean that workers make food payments to elites in exchange for access to land. In this chapter we extend the idea of a "labor market" to include warriors who receive food payments from the elite in exchange for military services.

Here we ask whether elites will find it profitable to engage in organized warfare with neighboring elites in order to capture additional land rent. The short answer is yes. The incentives for warfare among egalitarian groups are limited by two main factors: the presence of diminishing returns to land for a fixed labor input, and the fact that a group's military power is limited by its size (for detailed discussions see Section 7.9 in Chapter 7 and Section 8.8 below). Both of these constraints are absent in the case of elite warfare.

The first factor restraining warfare in egalitarian societies is that groups have limited labor inputs, and as a result face diminishing returns to the accumulation of land. In contrast, elite groups can hire unlimited commoner labor at a parametric wage, which means they can scale up labor and land simultaneously if they acquire more land through warfare. Assuming the old and new land have equal quality, an elite's total land rent is proportional to the land area it controls. The fact that land has diminishing returns when the labor input is fixed becomes irrelevant because labor is not fixed. Variations in land quality do not affect the substance of this argument, because it is still true that an elite's total land rent is simply the sum of the land rents obtained from its individual territories. There is no tendency for the value of incremental land acquisitions to decline as an elite accumulates more land.

The second factor restraining warfare in egalitarian societies is that groups have limited military power because they have fixed sizes. Elite warfare differs because an elite can recruit an army of potentially unlimited size by hiring warriors at a parametric wage. As we will explain later, the warriors must be offered booty if they win a war to compensate them for the prospect of death if they lose. In some cases, the land rents that would be obtained by a victorious elite are insufficient to finance the required booty. But generally speaking, when the sizes of the rival combatant groups are determined by profit maximization rather than individual migration or Malthusian dynamics, the guardrail of limited military power is removed.

For these reasons our formal model leads to a stark conclusion: a pair of elites will not pursue policies of peaceful coexistence. Instead the elites either attack or flee. If both elites attack, there is a war. If one attacks while the other flees, the winner grabs the territory of the loser without a fight. We call this "winning through intimidation." What we do not obtain is a stable equilibrium in which each elite chooses an army size that successfully deters an attack by the opposing elite.

When the degree of inequality between elites and commoners is low, so the total land rent at stake in a conflict between rival elites is small relative to the cost of an army, open war may be avoided because intimidation causes one side to flee with certainty. But there are also equilibria in which open warfare and intimidation each occur with positive probability. When the degree of inequality between elites and commoners is sufficiently high, these become the only possible equilibria, so open warfare must sometimes occur. Army sizes for such equilibria are larger than when intimidation succeeds with certainty, and military expenditures dissipate the entire land rent of the elites, so war is maximally wasteful. Open war and intimidation both put territories under unified control, enabling the successful elite to engage in geographic expansion.

These rather extreme conclusions can be qualified in a number of ways. Two constraints on elite warfare are provided by (a) limitations on elite personnel needed to administer new territories and (b) limitations on the fiscal capacity of an elite to recruit warriors. We also discuss restraints on elite conflict involving preferences, geography, defensive technology, institutions, and culture (see Section 8.9). Although these factors may sometimes offer paths to peaceful coexistence, the key message from the model is that elites have strong incentives to conquer more territory, either through overt war or covert intimidation, so any restraints on aggressive behavior need to be equally strong.

Section 8.2 reviews theories of elite warfare and Section 8.3 surveys empirical evidence. We already discussed the literature on early warfare in Chapter 7 so we will keep these sections short and emphasize issues specific to stratified societies.

The next four sections develop the formal model. Section 8.4 intro-duces basic ideas. The main results are in Sections 8.5 and 8.6. Events unfold in two stages. First rival elites choose army sizes (what we call the *recruitment stage*). Once the army sizes have been determined and observed by each elite, there is a second stage at which each elite decides whether to attack, defend, or flee (what we call the *combat stage*). It is analytically convenient to start by treating army sizes as exogenous and examining the decisions made at the combat stage, which we do in Section 8.5. We then move back to the recruitment stage in Section 8.6 and study how army sizes are chosen, assuming that each elite under-stands how army sizes will influence outcomes at the combat stage.

Section 8.5 shows that there are no peaceful equilibria at the combat stage where both elites choose to defend. For most army sizes, either one elite or the other prefers to attack. There is a particular ratio of army sizes where each elite is indifferent between attacking and defending. But even in this situation there is an advantage to attacking, because the opposing elite might flee and it would then become possible to seize the other elite's land without a fight. This breaks the tie in favor of aggression.

Section 8.6 shows that open warfare of a deterministic kind is not an equilibrium at the recruitment stage, because each elite has an incentive to shift to a larger army size in order to win by intimidation. However, open warfare does arise probabilistically when armies are large enough. Section 8.7 addresses the role of fiscal constraints on warfare. Such constraints can limit warfare if elite–commoner inequality is very high, but do not prevent probabilistic warfare at low to moderate levels of inequality. One might expect that richer elites would have a greater ability to finance wars but in our model this is not true, because booty is paid out of the total rent appropriated by the victorious elite rather than being paid up front using an elite's current (smaller) land rent. Readers who want to skip most of the math should at least scan Section 8.4 to understand the general structure of the model, but can omit Sections 8.5–8.7 if they like.

Section 8.8 compares the warfare models in Chapters 7 and 8, and comments on applications of the formal model from Chapter 8 to arch-aeological evidence. Section 8.9 discusses factors omitted from the formal model that could limit elite warfare in practice. We will return to elite warfare in the context of state formation, so we will defer further discus-sion of regional cases until Chapter 11. Section 8.10 concludes with an overview of the theory of pre-state institutional development we have constructed in Chapters 6–8. Proofs of all formal propositions can be found at cambridge.org/economicprehistory.

8.2 THEORIES OF ELITE WARFARE

We are aware of relatively few theoretical contributions from either economists or archaeologists that focus specifically on warfare among societies having stratification but lacking states. The literature on warfare among state-level societies is huge, but does not speak to the issues we are addressing here.

As we discussed in Section 7.2, there has been intense debate between writers (sometimes called "hawks") who regard warfare as a constant feature of prehistory and writers (sometimes called "doves") who believe it was rare or non-existent among early egalitarian societies, and only became commonplace with the proliferation of stratified societies in the early Neolithic. The hawks often rely on genetic arguments to explain constant warfare and have trouble explaining variations in the incidence of war across time and space in the last 10,000–15,000 years. The doves often rely on ideas about non-observed institutions that are said to have maintained peace through most of prehistory.

While there is strong disagreement between hawks and doves over the incidence of early warfare and its causes, there are also several areas of agreement reflected in two recent publications by major figures in the debate (Ferguson, 2018; LeBlanc, 2020). The areas of agreement include the following:

(a) Warfare is defined as lethal organized conflict between groups.
(b) The earliest examples of warfare involve raiding, not set battles over territory.
(c) Archaeological evidence for very early warfare is weak and difficult to interpret (i.e., evidence for warfare and evidence for peace are both hard to find in the pre-Neolithic).
(d) There is strong evidence that stratified societies are prone to constant warfare.
(e) There are dangers of sample selection biases in using ethnographic data to infer warfare in prehistory.
(f) Climate change played an important role as a trigger for warfare.
(g) Raiding and warfare over land can be included in the same analysis.

We accept points (a)–(f) but believe it is important to provide separate theories of raiding and warfare over land, because the relevant military technologies differ substantially.

LeBlanc (2020) believes that the causal channel runs from a human genetic predisposition to violence, to constant warfare, to stratification. However, he treats the genetic predisposition as a hypothesis, not a fact (2020, 47–48). He explains the lack of warfare data in early egalitarian societies by the fact that populations were smaller and the time period was earlier compared to stratified societies. He does not see this lack of evidence for warfare as a reason to think there was actually less warfare. Rather, it is evidence that the markers of warfare are less visible to us today.

Ferguson (2018) believes that constant warfare resulted from the transition to complexity and stratification. He lists several conditions that promote war, including sedentism, regional population growth, livestock or other valuable resources, social complexity and hierarchy, trade, group boundaries and collective identities, and severe environmental changes. He also lists several conditions that promote peace, including cross-group linkages of kinship and marriage, cooperation in food production and food sharing, flexible social arrangements, norms that value peace, and recognized means for conflict resolution. We view these correlations as suggestive of causal connections, but explicit theory is required to make the case convincing.

In contrast to these authors we separate raiding from warfare over land. We offer a theory of stratification (see Chapter 6) that does not depend on warfare. We show that there is little economic incentive for warfare in egalitarian societies except during periods of sudden environmental or technological change (see Chapter 7). And we show in this chapter that in stratified societies there is an economic incentive for constant warfare that is independent of genetic predispositions for violence, population change, environmental shocks, and the other items on Ferguson's list of warfare-inducing conditions. While we do not rule out the possibility that good institutions (or other factors) might restrain such warfare, it seems clear from the data that potential solutions of this kind often fail.

Rowthorn et al. (2014) note that most theories of pre-modern stratified societies share three common elements: a class distinction between warriors and peasants, a food surplus generated by peasants that supports the warriors, and hereditary social positions. They use the microeconomic tool of rational individual choice to model such societies.

At the regional level the authors assume exogenous numbers of egalitarian and stratified societies. In egalitarian societies producers defend themselves using readily available weapons. In stratified societies a class of warriors defends the society using specialized weapons that others do not possess. Malthusian dynamics determine the sizes of the warrior and peasant classes in the long run, and the greater cost of warrior children leads to economic inequality in favor of the warriors. The relative military powers of the individual societies determine the land available for food production in each society.

Our model differs in several ways. First, we distinguish between an elite class of landowners and the warriors they employ. The elite guard their land against intrusion by individual outsiders and use the resulting land rent to recruit warriors for combat against the warriors employed by rival elites. Second, in our theory the size of the warrior class is determined by profit maximization on the part of the landowning elite, not directly by Malthusian mechanisms. Third, in the model of Rowthorn et al. warriors give peasants land to farm. By contrast in our model the elite recruits warriors to enhance its land rent and warriors provide no benefit to commoners. Fourth, the direction of causality differs. Rowthorn et al. take warfare for granted and explain the degree of inequality, while we take inequality for granted and explain the prevalence of warfare.

Rowthorn et al. argue that their theory can explain instances where changes in military technology led to changes in the relative numbers of warriors and peasants, and the degree of economic inequality between them. Most of their examples involve state-level (although pre-modern) societies, while our focus is on pre-state institutions.

Boix (2015, ch. 4) similarly argues for a causal channel running from warfare to inequality. He asserts that changes in military technology have led to dramatic changes in political and social institutions, including the degree of inequality between economic classes. Important innovations in military technology have included developments with respect to metallurgy (copper, bronze, carburized iron); horses (chariots, stirrups); and gunpowder (firearms, cannons). We agree that military technology has had far-reaching effects on political, social, and economic institutions. However, we make two points.

First, most of the military technologies discussed by Boix are not relevant for the societies studied here. The societies we consider did not have bronze weapons, let alone iron or steel. They certainly did not have domesticated horses or gunpowder. If we take prehistory to be defined by the absence of written records, our overlap with Boix mainly involves the use of copper weapons in southern Mesopotamia, a case to be discussed in Chapters 9 and 10. The emergence of the Mesopotamian city-states, accompanied by the first written records, substantially predates their eventual political unification by Sargon, which Boix attributes in part to the development of bronze weapons (2015, 132–133).

The second point is more theoretical. We start from the stratification model in Chapter 6 and consider the incentives for warfare between two neighboring elites. Our theory about the origins of stratification does not involve warfare. It simply requires a technology of exclusion through which organized insiders can establish property rights over valuable sites by repelling unorganized outsiders. In our approach the existence of elites leads to warfare, not the other way around.

We do not want to dismiss the argument by Boix that causality could also flow in the opposite direction, where warfare leads to inequality or stratification. Indeed we will see in Chapter 11 that many archaeologists believe warfare created a trajectory leading to pristine state formation. But in this chapter we hold military technology constant, change the institutional structure from egalitarian to stratified, and look at the effects on warfare, rather than changing military technology and looking at the effects on institutions. We will return to Boix (2015) in Chapter 12 when we discuss the transition from prehistory to the modern world.

Pandit et al. (2017) develop a theory of warfare in small-scale societies based on biological fitness. Individuals join attacking coalitions voluntarily if this enhances their fitness. The probability that a coalition wins a war depends on the difference in summed fighting abilities of the attacking and defending sides. After a war, surviving individuals have ranks in the fused society that reflect their fighting abilities.

A key question involves the impact of inequality with respect to fighting ability within each group, which determines access to economic resources and is correlated with reproductive success. The authors conclude that other things being equal, egalitarian groups have a military advantage relative to despotic ones. The reason is that when inequality is high, lower-ranking individuals are less likely to benefit from a successful war than those of higher rank, so elites have trouble recruiting coalition members. The authors point out that skew in intrinsic fighting ability is unlikely to vary much across societies, but actual fighting ability may depend upon training, weapons, or wealth. They also note that large complex societies typically overwhelm their small and less complex neighbors, so in such cases aggregate military power clearly outweighs the effects of skew within groups.

The theory of Pandit et al. resembles ours in some ways. For example, it assumes the use of simple weapons, and rules out state-level phenomena such as the imposition of coercive taxes on conquered societies. On the other hand, Pandit et al. also rule out the employment of mercenary warriors by elites, which we permit, and highlight differences in fighting ability across individuals, which we ignore. We assume individual agents are motivated by food rather than directly by fitness, although of course one is a means to the other. More generally, we differ from Pandit et al. in stressing the economic implications of stratification and warfare rather than direct biological implications.

8.3 EVIDENCE ON ELITE WARFARE

By contrast with warfare between egalitarian groups, where there is a serious dispute over the frequency and dating of warfare (see Section 7.3), there is a consensus that warfare between stratified groups was widespread in prehistory.

Kyriacou (2020, 44–45) studies the association of warfare and stratification using ethnographic data for the societies in the Standard Cross Cultural Sample. He estimates four regressions using ordinary least squares, with two alternative dependent variables (social stratification and class stratification) and two alternative independent variables (frequency of warfare or fighting, and casualty rate among the combatants). Population density is controlled in all four regressions, which have either 79 or 133 observations according to data availability. All of the coefficients display the expected positive sign, with the frequency of warfare significant at the 10% level (social stratification) or the 5% level (class stratification), and the casualty rate significant at the 1% level for both of the stratification measures. As discussed in Section 8.2, the direction of the causal arrow can be debated, but a positive correlation clearly exists in the ethnographic data.

Gat (2006) reports on the features of warfare in pre-state, pre-urban agricultural societies where stratification is common. He calls these groupings "tribal societies." They are much larger (typically about 2,000 people) than simple hunting and gathering or early agricultural groups (typically about 500 people; 2006, 176). Both, however, were based on kinship circles. They also shared similar armaments that were privately owned and generally of poor quality: spears, axes, clubs, knives, bows and arrows, shields, and occasional leather armor (185–186). Early stratification involved the selection of a chief who had limited authority, was often elected, and was often the war leader. Another form of early leadership was the "big man." In these stratified societies, food producers did not play an important role in warfare (298–299). The maximum size of the warrior group was around 200 (228). Open battles became more common over time as the element of surprise became more difficult to achieve in raiding expeditions. These open battles were increasingly fought over land (186). Our model incorporates a number of these features, although we do not address the leadership structure within the elite class.

Before presenting the formal model we briefly mention some regional cases that have both stratification and warfare in order to give a flavor of their varying relationship. Most were discussed in earlier chapters so we forego detailed descriptions here. Further cases will be discussed in Chapter 11 in the context of state formation.

The Northwest Coast of North America: These sedentary foraging societies relied on aquatic resources, especially salmon (see Ames, 1995; Ames and Maschner, 1999; and Johnson and Earle, 2000, 204–217). Communities usually had a few hundred people with a ranked hereditary elite and a class of free commoners as well as slaves captured in war. Chiefs regulated access to territories and food resources. Ames (1995) suggests that the emergence of warfare in the northern part of the region coincided with the emergence of stratification. Although there was a good deal of raiding, especially for slaves, there was also warfare over land involving displacement of rival groups. Johnson and Earle (2000, 207) quote Drucker: "true warfare, aimed at driving out or exterminating another lineage or family in order to acquire its lands and goods, was a well-established practice in the North ... The traditions are replete with accounts of groups driven out of their homes and lands, and of the hardships suffered before they found new homes." In areas where war was frequent, chiefs maintained a retinue of warriors. We are not aware of conquests in which commoners served a new elite. The long distances between sites and the limited transport technology would have made such conquests quite difficult.

Polynesia: As discussed in Section 6.11, Polynesian societies used a combination of marine resources and agriculture. There are strong correlations across island chains in the quality of natural resources, population density per unit of arable land, and the degree of stratification. Island chains having high levels of these variables, such as Tonga and Hawaii, had intense warfare, while those with lower levels were more peaceful (Younger, 2008). For Tonga and Hawaii, increased stratification over time was accompanied by increased warfare. Earle (1997) argues that the Hawaiian warfare involved competition among chiefs for control over productive land. These were wars of conquest where the commoners were left in place and had to pay land rent to the victorious elite.

Neolithic Europe: As discussed in Section 6.11, early farming in central Europe led to population growth, along with a transition from egalitarianism to insider–outsider inequality and then elite–commoner inequality. According to Ferguson (2013b), warfare became widespread in Europe about 500–1000 years after the arrival of agriculture (see Section 7.3). The temporal association between stratification and warfare suggests the possibility of a causal relationship.

Southwest Asia: We discussed the evidence for stratification in southwest Asia in Section 6.11, both in the context of sedentary foraging before the Younger Dryas and in the context of agriculture afterward. Ferguson (2013b) asserts that warfare in Anatolia and the northern Tigris goes back at least to the Pottery Neolithic period (which started around 8400 BP) and perhaps the Pre-Pottery Neolithic A (11,600-10,500 BP) when agriculture was first arising. These observations are similar to those for the arrival of Neolithic agricultural technology in central Europe.

For the southern Levant, Ferguson finds no skeletal evidence of warfare and no evidence of fortifications in the period spanning 15,000–5200 BP, where the latter date is in the early Bronze Age and coincides with the rise of the Egyptian state. This apparent absence of warfare in the southern Levant is puzzling but as we discussed in Section 6.11, any stratification in this region was probably modest. Some authors see no evidence for hereditary elites in the Pre-Pottery Neolithic, and it is unclear when such elites emerged. Institutions or other factors may have restrained warfare in this area even if stratification existed. We will discuss a variety of potential restraining factors in Section 8.9.

8.4 THE FORMAL MODEL

Consider two stratified sites $i = A, B$. We continue to use our standard term "sites" to distinguish geographically separate food production locations, although in the present context they can equally well be called "territories." As in the model of Chapter 6, at each site an organized elite prevents unorganized outsiders from entering. The elite also hires commoners to work the land. In contrast to the model of Chapter 6, we simplify here by assuming that the elite agents supply no labor to food production. In peacetime an elite merely guards its territory, employs commoners, and enjoys land rent. All agents (elite and commoner) are risk neutral and maximize expected food consumption.

Food is produced from inputs of labor and land using a Cobb–Douglas function with constant returns to scale:

$$Y_i = \theta_i L_i{}^{\alpha} Z_i{}^{1-\alpha} \qquad i = A, B \qquad (8.1)$$

where Y_i is food, θ_i is the productivity of site i, L_i is commoner labor, and $Z_i > 0$ is land. The productivity $\theta_i > 0$ is determined by nature and technology. As usual $0 < \alpha < 1$.

The minimum density of elite agents per unit of land needed to exclude outsiders and maintain property rights over a territory is $e > 0$. The corresponding parameter value in Chapter 6 was d. We adopt the new notation in order to highlight our new assumption that elites do not produce food and instead only guard land.

In order for elite property rights to be secure we require $e_i / Z_i \geq e$ where e_i is the size of elite i. When each elite is of the minimum necessary size, $e_i = e Z_i$ for $i = A, B$. But for reasons to be explained later in this section, it will be useful to consider situations where the elites have excess capacity in the sense that $e_i > e Z_i$. The sizes of the elites are exogenous throughout.

The stratified sites are embedded within a regional economy that includes a large commons with open access as described in Chapter 6. The food income of agents in the commons is $w > 0$. The elites at sites A and B treat w as parametric and hire commoners at this wage rate to work on their land. The resulting land rents are

$$r_i = \max \{\theta_i L_i{}^{\alpha} Z_i{}^{1-\alpha} - w L_i \text{ subject to } L_i \geq 0\} \qquad i = A, B \qquad (8.2)$$

Due to the Cobb–Douglas technology these land rents are strictly positive. It can also be shown that the rent from site i is proportional to the land area associated with the site, so $r_i = \beta_i Z_i$ where $\beta_i > 0$ is a constant determined by the exogenous parameters θ_i, α, and w. The sites (or territories) may have differing rents due to differences in their productivity or land area. We denote aggregate land rent by $R = r_A + r_B$.

For a given land area Z_i and elite size e_i we say that elite i is *economically viable* if its land rent r_i exceeds its opportunity cost $w e_i$. The latter is what the elite agents could obtain by abandoning their site, moving to the commons, and producing food there. We assume the productivity θ_i of each site is high enough to guarantee $w e_i < r_i$ for $i = A, B$ so there is an economic benefit from being in the elite, at least in peacetime. The members of the elite divide their land rent equally so each individual member receives r_i / e_i.

The degree of stratification in the society will be indexed by R/w, which is total rent normalized by the commoner wage. The lower bound for normalized rent is

$$e_A + e_B < R/w \qquad (8.3)$$

This must be true if both elites are economically viable in the sense defined above.

Each elite can recruit an army, which can be used to attack the rival elite. Elite i hires a number of warriors $m_i \geq 0$ from the commoner class where each warrior is paid an expected food income equal to w. Combat involves generally available weapons and the members of an army produce no food.

In Sections 8.5 and 8.6 we will construct a two-stage model. At the first stage the elites recruit their armies simultaneously. At the second stage the army sizes $(m_A, m_B) \geq 0$ are fixed and observed by both elites. The issue at the second stage is whether either of the elites wishes to attack the other. If neither elite wants to attack, there is peace. If one or both elites chooses to attack, there is war. We also allow a third option: elite i can flee to the commons and accept the reservation utility we_i available at open sites.

We proceed by backward induction. In Section 8.5 we examine the *combat stage* where (m_A, m_B) has already been determined and the elites make decisions about whether or not to attack. In Section 8.6 we move back to the *recruitment stage* where each elite hires its army (correctly anticipating the decisions to be made at the combat stage), and study Nash equilibria with respect to the choice of army sizes. This yields results about whether war or peace will prevail, and how these outcomes are related to the degree of stratification summarized by R/w.

In wartime the probability that elite i = A, B wins against $j \neq i$ is

$$p_i = m_i/(m_i + m_j) = m_i/M \qquad \text{where} \qquad M \equiv m_A + m_B \qquad (8.4)$$

The probability that elite i wins is independent of who attacked whom. This combat technology is identical to the one used in Chapter 7. As in that chapter, the probability of winning is determined by the relative sizes of the combatant groups. The only difference is that here the size of each combatant group is chosen by its sponsoring elite rather than being determined by individual migration or Malthusian dynamics.

If elite i wins, it retains the rent r_i from its existing site, appropriates the rent r_j from the site $j \neq i$, and compensates its warriors in a manner to be described below. If elite i loses, both the elite and its army die, resulting in zero payoffs (see the remarks on utility functions in Section 7.8). The commoners who engage in food production do not participate in combat, face no risk of death, and are indifferent toward the identity of the winning elite.

At this point we flag an issue about property rights over the conquered territory. We will assume that if elite i wins a war it gains the prize $R = r_i + r_j = r_A + r_B$ where this aggregate land rent is a constant that is independent of the sizes of the armies involved. The armies only affect the probability of victory, not the prize at stake. But how does elite i extend its property rights to the newly conquered territory at site j? If we have $e_i = eZ_i$ so elite i has the minimum density needed to control its home territory, any transfer of elite agents from site i to site j makes it impossible for elite i to fully guard its original territory, leading to entry by unauthorized outsiders and erosion of the home rent r_i.

The simplest way to address this problem is to assume that each elite has excess capacity so $e_i \geq e(Z_A + Z_B)$ for i = A, B. In this scenario the victorious elite can always spare enough personnel to occupy the other territory and establish property rights over it. For example, the agents placed in charge of the new territory may be offspring of the elite who would otherwise have moved down into the commoner class (see Section 6.10). For this excess capacity solution to work we need $e(Z_A + Z_B) < r_i/w$ for i = A, B so each elite can still cover its own opportunity cost we_i as discussed earlier. This will be true as long as the productivities θ_i in (8.1) are high enough relative to the wage w.

Next consider the payments to warriors from a sponsoring elite. If there is peace, warriors are paid their opportunity cost w, which is what they can obtain in the commons. We assume that warriors are "on call" and do not produce food because they must be ready to defend against a possible attack (or launch one). We ignore leisure, training costs, or the social status associated with the role of being a warrior. This gives elite i the payoff

$$\text{peace}: \quad r_i - wm_i \qquad i = A, B \qquad (8.5)$$

If a war occurs, an individual warrior faces a positive probability of being killed and receiving zero. We assume that warriors are not forced to fight; joining the army is a voluntary transaction. To compensate for the prospect of death a warrior must be offered a food income in the event of victory that exceeds the peacetime wage w. We refer to the wartime wage b_i as "booty." The booty must satisfy the participation constraint

$p_i b_i = w$ so expected food income per warrior is equal to what warriors could obtain in the commons. The payoff to elite i from war is therefore

$$\text{war} : p_i(R - b_i m_i) = p_i R - wm_i = \left[m_i / (m_i + m_j) \right] R - wm_i \quad i = A, B \quad (8.6)$$

There is an infinitely elastic supply of commoners willing to become warriors if they are offered an expected income of w, and all of the candidate warriors are perfect substitutes for military purposes. The elite offers the minimum booty needed to attract an army and captures all the *ex ante* surplus from warfare.

Under our "excess capacity" assumption about the elite's ability to take over any newly conquered territory, when elite i is victorious it gains the aggregate rent R. This can be used to finance the booty owed to its army. The warrior participation constraint gives $b_i = w/p_i = wM/m_i$ so the total payment owed to a victorious army is $b_i m_i = wM$. Because the winning elite i appropriates the total rent R, it can pay its army as long as

$$w(m_A + m_B) \leq r_A + r_B \quad \text{or} \quad M \leq R/w \quad (8.7)$$

This fiscal constraint involves both m_A and m_B because a warrior's willingness to fight depends on the probability of death, which depends on the sizes of both armies. There is no subscript $i = A, B$ in the condition $M \leq R/w$. When (8.7) holds, the winning elite will be able to pay its own troops their promised booty, whichever elite that may be. When (8.7) does not hold, neither elite will be able to do so even if it proves to be the winner. As a result neither will be able to recruit an army of the desired size, because all prospective warriors will correctly foresee a failure to deliver adequate booty in the event of victory. We will show in Section 8.7 that this fiscal constraint can sometimes limit the ability of elites to engage in open warfare.

Even if financial solvency is not an issue, one might question why the victorious elite would actually pay its warriors their promised wages *ex post*. Clearly in prehistory there were no legally binding contracts about such matters. One possible answer is that such games were played repeatedly and the elite wanted to build a reputation for paying its warriors. Another possible answer is that unhappy warriors, having been organized as an army, could take control of the elite's home territory and/or newly conquered territory. We will not delve into such details here and simply assume that elites honor promises to their warriors as long as their budget constraints allow them to do so.

8.5 THE COMBAT STAGE

In this section we treat army sizes $(m_A, m_B) \geq 0$ as exogenous and investigate elite decisions regarding warfare. The only restriction placed on army size is that when we are interested in decisions by elite i, we assume $m_j > 0$ so elite i's probability of victory in (8.4) is well defined even when $m_i = 0$. The case $m_A = m_B = 0$ will be addressed in Section 8.6.

We assume $0 < r_i/w-e_i$ for $i = A, B$ so in peacetime each elite is economically viable and enjoys a standard of living above that of commoners. This section ignores the fiscal constraint $M \leq R/w$ from (8.7) but we will return to it in Section 8.7.

Each elite $i = A, B$ has three options: attack, defend, or flee. We abbreviate these by A, D, and F in contexts where it is clear that A refers to a strategy rather than a site. If one elite attacks while the other either attacks or defends, then a war occurs with payoffs from (8.6). If both elites defend, there is peace with payoffs from (8.5).

If elite i flees, it joins the commoner class and receives the reservation payoff we_i regardless of the strategy of the other elite. When this occurs, elite i's army disbands and its individual warriors return to the commons to obtain w, so they are no worse off from having volunteered in the first place. If elite i flees while $j \neq i$ attacks, elite j can grab the site of elite i without overt conflict. We interpret this as "winning through intimidation." The resulting payoff to the grabber j is $R - wm_j$ because this elite gets the rent from both sites with certainty. If elite i flees while j defends, then j keeps its home site but does not occupy i's site and receives the peaceful payoff $r_j - wm_j$. If both elites flee, both receive their reservation payoffs (we_i, we_j) from the commons.

There are several reasons for including the strategy "flee." First, negative utility levels have no meaning here. Giving each player a unilateral option to take the positive payoff we_i guarantees that negative payoffs never arise. Second, when elites are making decisions about war and peace they can be expected to take into account that they have an opportunity cost, namely the payoff available in the commons. Finally, we want to study whether territorial expansion can be achieved by threats of violence rather than open war.

Before going to the formal analysis we review some terminology for readers who may not be familiar with game theory (these readers may want to consult Binmore, 2007, or an introductory game theory textbook). We express strategy combinations in the form XY where X is the strategy of elite i and Y is the strategy of elite j ≠ i. A strategy X for elite i is called a *best reply* to Y if, given the fixed choice of Y by elite j, elite i cannot obtain a higher payoff by deviating to any alternative strategy X′ ≠ X. Best replies need not be unique. For example X and X′ may give i the same payoff, while both are better than any alternative strategy X″. In such cases we say {X, X′} are best replies to Y.

The strategy combination XY is called a *Nash equilibrium* (NE) when X is a best reply to Y for elite i and Y is a best reply to X for elite j. The games considered here will always have at least one NE. In some situations there could be multiple Nash equilibria (two distinct strategy combinations XY and X′Y′ may both satisfy the definition of NE).

X is called a *dominant strategy* for elite i if it satisfies two conditions. First, X must be a best reply to each of the feasible strategies available to elite j (Y, Y′, Y″, and so on). For some choices by elite j, elite i could be indifferent between X and an alternative strategy (that is, elite i may have multiple best replies). Second, X must be a unique best reply (strictly better for elite i than any other strategy) for at least one feasible strategy Y available to j. In short: X is dominant for elite i if (a) for each feasible strategy choice by elite j, X maximizes the payoff of elite i; and (b) there is at least one feasible strategy for elite j such that X uniquely maximizes the payoff of elite i.

A player may or may not have a dominant strategy depending on the structure of the game. However, we make the following assumption.

Assumption 8.1
Whenever an elite has a dominant strategy at the combat stage, it will be used.

The strategy combination XY is a *dominant strategy equilibrium* (DSE) if X is dominant for i and Y is dominant for j. A DSE may not exist because one or both players may lack a dominant strategy. When a DSE exists it is unique because a player cannot have more than one dominant strategy. If there is no DSE we fall back on the more general concept of Nash equilibrium (NE). Any DSE is automatically a NE but a NE need not be a DSE.

The 3×3 payoff matrix describing the combat game is shown in Table 8.1. There are nine cells in the matrix corresponding to the nine strategy combinations. However, there are only four distinct payoff levels for each elite, which are associated with the four possible outcomes for that player: grabbing, war, peace, and flight.

According to Table 8.1, if an elite can grab an opponent's land it is strictly better off than it would be with war or peace. Elite i strictly prefers

TABLE 8.1. *Payoff matrix at the combat stage*

		Elite j		
		Attack (A)	Defend (D)	Flee (F)
Elite i	Attack (A)	(war) p_jR-wm_j p_iR-wm_i (war)	(war) p_jR-wm_j p_iR-wm_i (war)	(flight) we_j $R-wm_i$ (grabbing)
	Defend (D)	(war) p_jR-wm_j p_iR-wm_i (war)	(peace) r_j-wm_j r_i-wm_i (peace)	(flight) we_j r_i-wm_i (peace)
	Flee (F)	(grabbing) $R-wm_j$ we_i (flight)	(peace) r_j-wm_j we_i (flight)	(flight) we_j we_i (flight)

grabbing to peace because $r_i < R$. Elite i strictly prefers grabbing to war whenever the opposing elite j has an army of positive size ($m_j > 0$), because $p_i < 1$ for all $m_j \geq 0$ and elite i is better off grabbing site j for sure rather than fighting a war it might lose.

For these reasons there are only two outcomes that could be ranked highest by an elite: grabbing or flight. We begin with cases where flight is at least as good as grabbing for one or both elites. We then examine the case where grabbing is strictly preferred to flight by both elites.

> **Lemma 8.1**
> This lemma gives conditions for the dominance of flight. Consider elite
> i = A, B, let j ≠ i, and assume $m_j > 0$.
>
> (a) Flee (F) is a dominant strategy for elite i iff $m_i \geq R/w - e_i$ so elite i
>   prefers flight to grabbing, at least weakly.
> (b) Suppose F is chosen by j ≠ i. F is a best reply to F for elite i iff
>   F is dominant for elite i as in part (a). A is a best reply to F for elite
>   i iff $m_i \leq R/w - e_i$. D is never a best reply to F for elite i.

Lemma 8.1(a) can be understood from Figure 8.1. The vertical line at $m_i = R/w - e_i$ shows the points where elite i is indifferent between flight and grabbing. We call the line IC_i^{FG} to indicate that it is an indifference

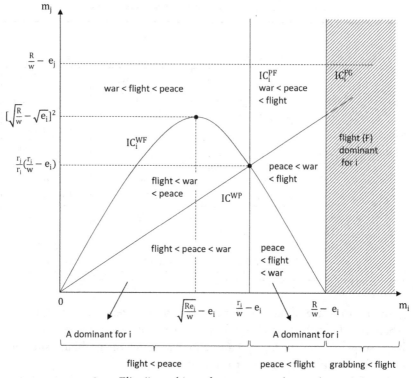

FIGURE 8.1. Elite i's ranking of outcomes at the combat stage

curve for elite i. In the shaded region along or to the right of IC_i^{FG}, F is a best reply to F for elite i. Even if elite $j \neq i$ flees, elite i is still at least as well off fleeing rather than grabbing because the total rent R is not big enough to justify the cost of elite i's army. Since grabbing is strictly better than war or peace, this makes F a dominant strategy. The other features of Figure 8.1 will be explained below.

Lemma 8.1(b) considers best replies to an elite using F, whether or not this happens to be a dominant strategy. The key point is that D can never be a best reply to F because D gives the peace payoff $r_i - wm_i$ while a deviation to A gives the larger grabbing payoff $R - wm_i$. This rules out DF or FD as Nash equilibria, whatever the other payoffs may be.

In the next several paragraphs we assume $m_i < R/w - e_i$ so that grabbing is strictly better than flight for elite i. The relevant points in Figure 8.1 are located in the unshaded region to the left of IC_i^{FG}. In this region elite i's best outcome is always to grab (when it can) but we need to examine elite i's ranking of the remaining outcomes: war, peace, and flight. Accordingly, we construct three more indifference curves for elite i, one for each possible pairwise comparison among these three outcomes.

The indifference curve IC_i^{PF} for peace/flight is the vertical line in Figure 8.1 at

$$m_i = r_i/w - e_i \qquad i = A, B \qquad (8.8)$$

To the left of this line elite i strictly prefers peace to flight. To the right elite i strictly prefers flight to peace. The interpretation is that when i's army is sufficiently small, the home rent r_i from peace can cover the direct cost of i's army plus i's opportunity cost we_i. But when i's army size exceeds the bound in (8.8), elite i prefers flight to the commons in order to shed its financial obligation to its warriors.

The indifference curve IC^{WP} for war/peace is the upward-sloping ray from the origin in Figure 8.1. We omit the i subscript here because, as will be explained later, the same indifference curve applies to $j \neq i$. From Table 8.1 elite i is indifferent between war and peace when $r_i = p_i R$ or

$$m_j = r_j m_i / r_i \qquad j \neq i \qquad i = A, B \qquad (8.9)$$

The slope of the war/peace indifference line in Figure 8.1 is therefore r_j/r_i, the ratio of the land rents. Above and to the left of this line, where m_j is larger than in (8.9), elite i strictly prefers peace, while below and to the right of this line, where m_j is smaller than in (8.9), elite i strictly prefers war.

Two interpretations of this condition may provide useful intuition. Elite i strictly prefers war if $m_i/m_j > r_i/r_j$ so that elite i's relative army size exceeds its relative land rent. This resembles the relationship between the ratio of group sizes and the ratio of the site productivities in Chapter 7. Another interpretation is obtained by dividing $m_j < r_j m_i/r_i$ by M to get $p_i r_i < p_i r_j$. This says that elite i wants war if the expected benefit from seizing more land rent exceeds the expected cost from losing its existing land rent.

The last indifference curve in Figure 8.1 is for war/flight. From Table 8.1 elite i is indifferent between these outcomes when $p_i R - wm_i = we_i$. This can be rewritten as

$$m_j = \phi_i(m_i) \equiv (R/w)[m_i/(m_i + e_i)] - m_i \qquad j \neq i \qquad i = A, B \quad (8.10)$$

The function $\phi_i(m_i)$ is strictly concave with $\phi_i(0) = \phi_i(R/w - e_i) = 0$. We have $\phi_i(m_i) > 0$ for $0 < m_i < R/w - e_i$ where $\phi_i(m_i)$ is maximized (uniquely) at $m_i = (Re_i/w)^{1/2} - e_i$. The maximized value of $\phi_i(m_i)$ is $[(R/w)^{1/2} - (e_i)^{1/2}]^2$ as in Figure 8.1. Elite i prefers war to flight when m_j

is below the level described by (8.10) and prefers flight to war when m_j is above this level.

Each indifference curve is affected by land rent in a different way. The location of the peace/flight boundary depends on the home rent r_i while the war/peace boundary depends on the ratio of the rents r_j/r_i and the war/flight boundary depends on the total rent R. The war/flight indifference curve in (8.10) passes through the intersection point for the peace/flight and war/peace indifference curves as shown in Figure 8.1. This intersection point may be either to the left or the right of the point where the war/flight curve has its maximum, depending on parameters.

The indifference curves divide up the unshaded area in Figure 8.1 into six regions, corresponding to the six ways in which elite i could rank the outcomes of war, peace, and flight. These rankings are indicated in Figure 8.1 and are useful in identifying conditions under which attack (A) is a dominant strategy for elite i. This is true for the two regions at the bottom of Figure 8.1 below both the war/peace and war/flight indifference curves, where the payoff to elite i from war exceeds the payoffs from both peace and flight.

Lemma 8.2

This lemma gives conditions for the dominance of attack. Consider elite i = A, B, let $j \neq i$, and assume $m_j > 0$. Suppose $m_i < R/w - e_i$ so by Lemma 8.1(a), flee (F) is not a dominant strategy for elite i.

(a) Attack (A) is a dominant strategy for elite i iff max $\{we_i, r_i - wm_i\} \leq p_i R - wm_i$.

(b) Suppose A is chosen by $j \neq i$. If $we_i > p_i R - wm_i$ then elite i's unique best reply is F. If equality holds then elite i is indifferent among the replies $\{A, D, F\}$. If the inequality is reversed then elite i is indifferent between the replies $\{A, D\}$ and both are strictly preferred to F.

Lemma 8.2 comes directly from the payoffs in Table 8.1. To grasp part (a), suppose $j \neq i$ chooses A or D. If the condition in (a) holds, elite i's warfare payoff, obtainable through attack (A), is at least as high as the payoff from peace or flight. Thus A is a best reply to A or D for elite i. Now suppose instead $j \neq i$ chooses F. In this case A gives the grabbing outcome for elite i, which is strictly better than any other outcome. Hence A is dominant for elite i even if the equality holds in part (a).

We adopt the following formal definition for equilibrium at the combat stage.

Definition 8.1

Fix the army sizes $(m_A, m_B) > 0$. Let $i \in \{A, B\}$ with $j \neq i$. Write a strategy pair in the form XY where $X \in \{A, D, F\}$ is the strategy of elite i and $Y \in \{A, D, F\}$ is the strategy of elite j. Use the payoffs from Table 8.1. A *combat equilibrium* is a Nash equilibrium strategy pair such that dominant strategies are used when they exist, as required by A8.1.

Combat equilibria can be studied using Figure 8.2. The IC_i^{WF} and IC_j^{WF} curves show loci for war/flight indifference for the elites i and j. The war/flight curve for elite j has a similar shape to the one for elite i in Figure 8.1 when viewed from the vertical axis. These curves have a unique positive intersection at a point along the ray $m_j/m_i = e_j/e_i$ (not shown in the graph to limit clutter). The intersection point of the war/flight curves is

$$m_i = \left[e_i/(e_i + e_j)\right](R/w - e_i - e_j) \quad \text{and} \quad m_j = \left[e_j/(e_i + e_j)\right](R/w - e_i - e_j)$$
$$(8.11)$$

Both army sizes in (8.11) are positive from (8.3). Figure 8.2 also shows the ray IC^{WP} with slope r_j/r_i for war/peace indifference from Figure 8.1. Elite i prefers war to peace below the ray and peace to war above it, while elite $j \neq i$ has the opposite preferences. Both of the elites are indifferent between war and peace at points along IC^{WP}.

We have arbitrarily drawn the graph so that the war/peace line passes above the intersection point in (8.11) for the war/flight curves. This will be true when $r_j/r_i > e_j/e_i$ or equivalently $r_j/e_j > r_i/e_i$ so that elite j is initially richer per capita. However, the reverse could also be true and this inequality has no bearing on any subsequent conclusions.

We also note that the maximum m_j value along the war/flight indifference curve IC_i^{WF} for elite i can exceed the horizontal line $m_j = R/w - e_j$ above which flight becomes dominant for elite j. The same is true for the maximum m_i value along IC_j^{WF} in relation to the vertical line $m_i = R/w - e_i$ where flight becomes dominant for elite i. Whether or not this occurs depends on the degree of asymmetry in the sizes of the elite groups.

Remark 8.1

When $e_A + e_B < R/w$ as in (8.3) and also $1/3 \leq e_A/e_B \leq 3$, IC_i^{WF} remains strictly below $m_j = R/w - e_j$ and IC_j^{WF} remains strictly below $m_i = R/w - e_i$.

We assume throughout that the elite sizes are similar enough to satisfy this condition.

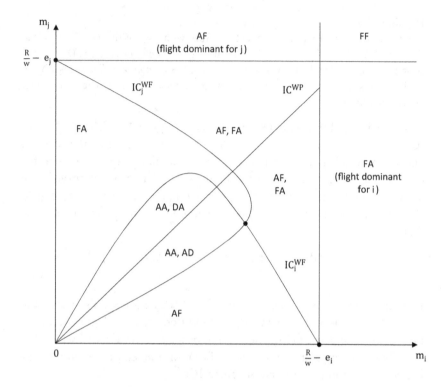

FIGURE 8.2. Nash equilibria at the combat stage

If the bounds on the army sizes in Lemma 8.1(a) are exceeded for both elites as in the upper right corner of Figure 8.2, we have the dominant strategy equilibrium FF where both elites flee to the commons because the cost of each elite's army exceeds the benefit from grabbing the total rent R. When one elite's army equals or exceeds the bound from Lemma 8.1(a) but the other elite's army falls below this bound, the first elite uses F while the second uses A. The attacker grabs the rival elite's territory without a war. This yields the outer Nash equilibria AF, FF, and FA indicated in Figure 8.2. These equilibria are all unique aside from the boundary cases where one elite is indifferent. The pattern of Nash equilibria for the inner rectangle of Figure 8.2 arises as follows.

AA is a Nash equilibrium if and only if both elites prefer war to flight, at least weakly. This corresponds to the region of Figure 8.2 consisting of points on or below both IC_i^{WF} and IC_j^{WF}. AD is an equilibrium in the subset of the AA region on or below IC^{WP} and DA is an equilibrium in the subset of the AA region on or above IC^{WP}.

DD is a Nash equilibrium for points along the war/peace indifference curve IC^{WP} that also satisfy the restrictions $m_i \leq r_i/w - e_i$ and $m_j \leq r_j/w - e_j$ so that both elites (weakly) prefer peace to flight. Such points do exist. However, DD is eliminated by A8.1 because at all such points A is a dominant strategy for at least one of the elites. We return to this issue later. DF and FD are never Nash equilibria because D is never a best reply to F.

AF is a Nash equilibrium if and only if grabbing is (weakly) preferred to flight by elite i and flight is (weakly) preferred to war by elite j. The first requirement is satisfied automatically for points in the rectangle we are considering. The second is satisfied on or to the right of IC_j^{WF} in Figure 8.2. Parallel logic shows that FA is a Nash equilibrium for all points on or above IC_i^{WF}. In some regions of (m_i, m_j) space only one of these strategy combinations is a Nash equilibrium while in other regions both are.

A key question in this chapter is whether two elites can enjoy a peace equilibrium where neither attacks and neither flees. The answer is no. To see why not, we consider the strategy combination DD in more detail. DD is only a candidate for Nash equilibrium at points along the war/peace indifference line IC^{WP} in Figure 8.2, because anywhere else one elite prefers war to peace and deviates by attacking. Table 8.1 also imposes another constraint: for DD to be a Nash equilibrium, both elites must prefer peace to flight, at least weakly. This requirement is satisfied for points on the war/peace indifference curve close enough to the origin, where both armies are relatively small. Thus there are points in Figure 8.2 at which DD is a Nash equilibrium.

However, even when DD is a Nash equilibrium, it is weak in the sense that both elites are indifferent between peace and war, and either could deviate to A without loss. Moreover, each elite strictly prefers A in the event that its rival chooses F, because then the elite can grab and this gives the highest possible payoff. Accordingly, whenever DD is a Nash equilibrium, A is a dominant strategy for one or both elites because grabbing could occur. From A8.1 this breaks the tie and rules out DD.

The results for the combat stage reveal that relationships between rival elites are inherently unstable. There are only two possibilities: either open warfare (AA, AD, DA) or winning through intimidation (AF, FA). Both lead to consolidation of territory under the control of a single elite. These conclusions are quite different from those of Chapter 7. We will provide a systematic comparison of the two models in Section 8.8 and discuss several factors that could restrain territorial expansion by elites in Section 8.9.

We close with a summary of formal results from this section for future reference. This gives an exhaustive characterization of outcomes at the combat stage for all possible army sizes $(m_A, m_B) \geq 0$ other than the special case $m_A = m_B = 0$.

Proposition 8.1 (the combat stage).

Let XY refer to the strategy combination in which elite i uses X and elite j uses Y. We adopt A8.1 so dominant strategies are used when they exist. Throughout the Proposition the roles of $i = A, B$ and $j \neq i$ can be interchanged.

(a) If $m_i \geq R/w - e_i$ for both $i = A, B$, then F is a dominant strategy for both elites and FF is a dominant strategy equilibrium.

(b) If $m_i \geq R/w - e_i$ for one of $i = A, B$ and $m_j < R/w - e_i$ for $j \neq i$, then F is a dominant strategy for elite i but not for elite $j \neq i$, and FA is the only Nash equilibrium.

In the rest of the Proposition let $m_i < R/w - e_i$ for both $i = A, B$ so that F is not a dominant strategy for either elite.

(c) If max $\{we_i, r_i - wm_i\} \leq p_i R - wm_i$ for both $i = A, B$ then A is a dominant strategy for both elites and AA is a dominant strategy equilibrium.

(d) If max $\{we_i, r_i - wm_i\} \leq p_i R - wm_i$ for one of $i = A, B$ and max $\{we_j, r_j - wm_j\} > p_j R - wm_j$ for $j \neq i$, then A is a dominant strategy for elite i but not for elite $j \neq i$. There are three possibilities.
   (i) If $we_j < p_j R - wm_j$ for $j \neq i$, the only Nash equilibria are {AA, AD}.
   (ii) If $we_j = p_j R - wm_j$ for $j \neq i$, the only Nash equilibria are {AA, AD, AF}.
   (iii) If $we_j > p_j R - wm_j$ for $j \neq i$, the only Nash equilibrium is AF.

In the rest of the Proposition let max $\{we_i, r_i - wm_i\} > p_i R - wm_i$ for both $i = A, B$ so that A is not a dominant strategy for either elite. There are only two possibilities.

(e) If $we_i < p_i R - wm_i$ for one of $i = A, B$ but $we_j \geq p_j R - wm_j$ for $j \neq i$, the only Nash equilibrium is AF.

(f) If $we_i \geq p_i R - wm_i$ for both $i = A, B$, the only Nash equilibria are {AF, FA}.

DF and FD are never Nash equilibria. DD is excluded by A8.1.

8.6 THE RECRUITMENT STAGE

We now move back one stage and consider decisions by elites about army sizes. We assume the elites correctly anticipate how the army sizes $(m_A, m_B) \geq 0$ selected at the recruitment stage influence each side's choices among attack (A), defend (D), and flee (F) at the combat stage. Army sizes are chosen simultaneously at the recruitment stage.

Before proceeding, we need to do some housekeeping with respect to multiple equilibria at the combat stage. Several issues arise. First, there are situations where the combat equilibria are {AA, AD} or {AA, DA}. Second, we have boundary cases where one elite is indifferent between two equilibria but the other is not. Third, there are cases with two combat equilibria {AF, FA}. We adopt a series of simplifying assumptions to address these situations.

When the combat equilibria are {AA, AD} or {AA, DA} as shown in Figure 8.2, we simply ignore the AD and DA equilibria. Neither of these exists except in situations where AA also exists. Moreover, each of AD and DA results in the same payoffs as AA because each yields war. Both elites are indifferent between such pairs of equilibria.

Assumption 8.2

If the pair (m_A, m_B) generates the combat equilibria {AA, AD} or {AA, DA}, the equilibrium AA is selected.

Other cases with multiple equilibria occur along the boundaries between the areas shown in Figure 8.2. For example, on elite i's indifference curve IC_i^{WF} for war and flight there are points where the set of equilibria is {AA, FA} because A is a best reply for elite $j \neq i$ in each case, but elite i is indifferent between A and F when j uses A. In such cases, elite $j \neq i$ strictly prefers FA because then elite j can grab i's site, which is better for j than a war, but elite i is indifferent between AA and FA. We show later that this issue can be resolved through dominance arguments in a smaller version of the game where each elite chooses between the strategies A and F.

A third situation with multiple equilibria involves {AF, FA}, again as depicted in Figure 8.2. These two combat equilibria cannot be Pareto ranked; in one case i grabs and j flees, while in the other case the roles are reversed. There is no obvious reason to select one outcome over the other. When both AF and FA are combat equilibria, we replace the two pure strategy Nash equilibria with a Nash equilibrium involving mixed strategies.

Lemma 8.3

This lemma characterizes mixed equilibria at the combat stage. Consider any $(m_i, m_j) > 0$. AF and FA are both Nash equilibria at the combat stage iff the following four conditions hold:

(a) $m_i \leq R/w - e_i$
(b) $m_j \leq R/w - e_j$
(c) $we_i \geq p_iR - wm_i$
(d) $we_j \geq p_jR - wm_j$

Conditions (a) and (b) hold at all points on or interior to the rectangle in Figure 8.2, (c) holds on or above IC_i^{WF}, and (d) holds on or above IC_j^{WF}. Whenever all four conditions hold, there is also a unique mixed strategy Nash equilibrium at the combat stage in which elite i attacks with probability $\lambda_i \geq 0$ but flees with probability $1-\lambda_i \geq 0$, while $j \neq i$ attacks with probability $\lambda_j \geq 0$ but flees with probability $1-\lambda_j \geq 0$. This equilibrium has

$$\lambda_i = \left(R/w - e_i - m_j\right)/(R/w)p_i \qquad \text{where } p_i = m_i/\left(m_i + m_j\right) \qquad (8.12)$$

and similarly for $j \neq i$ with an interchange of the subscripts. Each of the elites attacks with positive probability if there are strict inequalities in (a) and (b), as will be assumed throughout this section. Elite i flees with positive probability if there is strict inequality in (c) so (m_i, m_j) is located above IC_i^{WF} and elite j flees with positive probability if there is strict inequality in (d) so (m_i, m_j) is located above IC_j^{WF}. In any mixed equilibrium of this kind the expected payoffs for the two elites are (we_i, we_j).

For the mixed equilibrium in Lemma 8.3, there is war (AA) with probability $\lambda_i\lambda_j$, grabbing by i (AF) with probability $\lambda_i(1-\lambda_j)$, grabbing by j (FA) with probability $(1-\lambda_i)\lambda_j$, and flight to the commons by both (FF) with probability $(1-\lambda_i)(1-\lambda_j)$. In such equilibria elite i is indifferent between A and F given λ_j and similarly elite j is indifferent between A and F given λ_i. Because elite i always gets we_i when it uses F, it must be true in the mixed equilibrium that i's expected payoff is we_i and similarly for elite j. In an *ex post* sense elite i does worse than we_i when open war occurs, but *ex ante* this is offset by a probability that it will do better than we_i by grabbing when its rival $j \neq i$ flees. We will call this *dissipative warfare* because the total rent R is exhausted through elite military expenditures, and elite agents therefore have the same net food income as commoners.

Assumption 8.3

If the pair (m_i, m_j) generates the two combat equilibria AF and FA, we replace these pure Nash equilibria by the mixed Nash equilibrium from Lemma 8.3.

This selection rule has the advantage of simplicity because the payoffs from such equilibria are the same as for simultaneous flight by both elites. The disadvantage is that the mixed equilibrium is Pareto inferior to AF as well as FA (in the latter cases, one elite grabs while the other flees, which is Pareto superior to having both flee). Nevertheless, we use A8.3 because we believe that distributional conflict could lead to inefficiency, and that dissipative warfare could be an empirically significant phenomenon. Furthermore, A8.3 establishes a causal pathway from the degree of stratification R/w to the frequency of open warfare, as we will discuss in Section 8.8. Dissipative warfare also raises interesting issues of reverse causality by creating a mechanism through which warfare among elites could dampen the inequality between elites and commoners.

Because the defensive strategy D has no substantive role in the combat equilibria from Section 8.5, we drop it here and use a simpler 2×2 version of the game where each elite chooses between the two strategies "attack" (A) and "flee" (F) as shown in Table 8.2. The payoffs are otherwise identical to Table 8.1.

We use the following definition.

Definition 8.2

Consider army sizes such that $0 \le m_A < R/w - e_A$ and $0 \le m_B < R/w - e_B$. Define a *combat equilibrium* as in D8.1, except that $X \in \{A, F\}$ for elite i and $Y \in \{A, F\}$ for elite j with the payoffs from Table 8.2. A *recruitment equilibrium* is a pair of army sizes (m_A, m_B) that form a Nash equilibrium, where each elite recognizes the effect of its own army size on the resulting combat equilibrium.

We study the existence and properties of recruitment equilibrium using graphical methods. The next several pages are likely to be challenging for

TABLE 8.2. *Payoffs for reduced game at the combat stage*

		Elite j	
		Attack (A)	Flee (F)
Elite i	Attack (A)	(war) $p_j R - w m_j$ $p_i R - w m_i$ (war)	(flight) $w e_j$ $R - w m_i$ (grabbing)
	Flee (F)	(grabbing) $R - w m_j$ $w e_i$ (flight)	(flight) $w e_j$ $w e_i$ (flight)

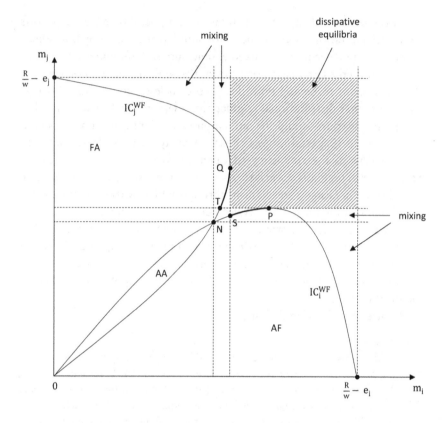

FIGURE 8.3. Recruitment equilibria for low values of R/w

readers unfamiliar with game theory, and such readers may prefer to skip down to the verbal overview following Proposition 8.2.

Figure 8.3 is derived from Table 8.2 and distinguishes four regions of (m_i, m_j) space depending on whether the relevant combat equilibrium is AA, AF, FA, or a mixing equilibrium as in Lemma 8.3. As before the curves IC_i^{WF} and IC_j^{WF} show where each elite is indifferent between open war and flight. This figure assumes that IC_i^{WF} and IC_j^{WF} are both rising when they intersect, a matter to which we will return below.

At any point on IC_i^{WF} elite i is indifferent between A and F when elite j chooses A. However, throughout the interior of the large dashed rectangle in Figure 8.3 where $m_i < R/w - e_i$ and $m_j < R/w - e_j$, elite i strictly prefers A when elite j chooses F, because then elite i can grab site j without a war and this is always better than fleeing (see Table 8.2). Therefore A is a dominant strategy for elite i at any point on IC_j^{WF}. Our assumption A8.1

that dominant strategies are used if they are available implies that elite i always chooses A along IC_i^{WF}. The same is true at points below IC_i^{WF} because elite i strictly prefers A to F when elite j attacks. The same argument applies when the roles are reversed, so elite j will always choose A at points on or below the indifference curve IC_j^{WF}.

The implication of these results is that AA occurs at all points on or below both of the indifference curves, AF occurs at all points on or below IC_j^{WF} but above IC_i^{WF}, FA occurs at all points on or below IC_i^{WF} but above IC_j^{WF}, and a mixed equilibrium occurs at all points above both of the indifference curves.

No Nash equilibrium can occur along the axes at the recruitment stage. Suppose $m_i = m_j = 0$ leads to peace, a reasonable assumption when no armies exist. By recruiting a very small army one elite could appropriate the entire rent R with certainty, a profitable deviation. At any point on the horizontal axis with $0 < m_i < R/w - e_i$ and $m_j = 0$, an attack gives elite i the grabbing payoff $R - wm_i$ with certainty regardless of what elite j does (the strategy A is dominant for i). This cannot be a Nash equilibrium because elite i can get the same result using a slightly smaller army, which is cheaper. A similar argument rules out a Nash equilibrium along the vertical axis. For these reasons, we confine attention to strictly positive army sizes $(m_i, m_j) > 0$ in the rest of this section.

We next observe that no recruitment equilibria can arise in the interior of the AA region. For brevity we will not discuss the details here, but the key idea is that any such equilibrium would need to be located at the intersection of the reaction functions for the two elites, where these reaction functions are based on the warfare payoff functions. But starting from such a point it is always true that one elite can deviate to a larger army size that takes (m_i, m_j) just outside the AA region, leading to an AF or FA outcome where the opposing elite flees rather than fighting a war. Despite the cost of the larger army needed for this intimidation tactic to work, seizing the entire rent R without fighting a war makes the deviation profitable.

Lemma 8.4

A necessary condition to have a recruitment equilibrium with open warfare in the interior of the AA region is $(m_A, m_B) = (R/4w, R/4w)$. This point is actually located in the interior of the AA region when $R/4w > e_i$ for $i = A$, B. But even when this is true, $(R/4w, R/4w)$ is not a recruitment equilibrium due to the existence of a profitable deviation that yields the grabbing outcome AF or FA outside the AA region.

The rest of this section is organized as follows. In Figure 8.3 the indifference curves are both rising at their intersection point. Depending on parameter values, these curves could also both be falling, or one could be rising while the other is falling. Lemma 8.5 classifies the possible cases (boundary cases are ignored for simplicity). The Nash equilibria for each case will be characterized graphically.

Lemma 8.5

Consider the unique positive intersection point for the indifference curves IC_i^{WF} and IC_j^{WF} from equation (8.11).

(a) <u>Low stratification.</u> If $R/w < (e_i + e_j)^2/(\max\{e_i, e_j\})$ then IC_i^{WF} and IC_j^{WF} are both increasing at the intersection point. The lower bound $e_i + e_j$ for R/w from (8.3) is strictly less than $(e_i + e_j)^2/(\max\{e_i, e_j\})$ so the relevant R/w interval is non-empty.

(b) <u>Intermediate stratification.</u> Suppose $e_j < e_i$. If $(e_i + e_j)^2/e_i < R/w < (e_i + e_j)^2/e_j$ then IC_j^{WF} is increasing and IC_i^{WF} is decreasing at the intersection point. The roles of i and j are interchanged when $e_i < e_j$.

(c) <u>High stratification.</u> If $(e_i + e_j)^2/(\min\{e_i, e_j\}) < R/w$ then IC_i^{WF} and IC_j^{WF} are both decreasing at the intersection point.

We begin with Figure 8.3, which corresponds to the situation from Lemma 8.5(a) where stratification R/w is low and both of the indifference curves are rising when they intersect. We confine attention to the rectangle in Figure 8.3 where $m_i < R/w - e_i$ and $m_j < R/w - e_j$. As was explained in Section 8.5, the points outside this rectangle have flight as a dominant strategy for one or both elites and are uninteresting here. Point N shows the intersection of the indifference curves, while P indicates the peak of the indifference curve for elite i and Q indicates the corresponding peak for elite j. Using the conditions from Remark 8.1 in Section 8.5, points P and Q are in the interior of the rectangle.

The first observation about Figure 8.3 is that elite i is indifferent among all points above the dashed horizontal line through P, because all such points yield the reservation payoff we_i either through a mixed equilibrium or a grabbing equilibrium FA. Likewise elite j is indifferent among all points to the right of the dashed vertical line through Q, because all such points give the payoff we_j either by a mixed equilibrium or a grabbing equilibrium AF. Any point in the interior of the shaded rectangle formed by these two dashed lines is a Nash equilibrium due to the absence of a profitable deviation for either elite. For all such equilibria the outcome is dissipative warfare.

There are other potential recruitment equilibria indicated by the heavy segment SP (excluding S) along IC_i^{WF} and the heavy segment TQ (excluding T) along IC_j^{WF}. Both kinds of equilibria exist if Q is above the horizontal line through P and P is to the right of the vertical line through Q as shown in Figure 8.3. Along SP we have an AF outcome in which elite i grabs and elite j flees. Given the size of elite j's army m_j, elite i is using the smallest possible army to grab and does not benefit from any horizontal deviation, which either raises the cost of grabbing or yields the payoff we_i through mixing or FA. Elite j gets we_j but any vertical deviation results in the same payoff through mixing or AF. The reasoning is similar for TQ with the roles of the elites reversed.

There are no other recruitment equilibria. At other points in the mixing region, either elite i can deviate to a point in the AF region or elite j can deviate to a point in the FA region. Either kind of deviation is profitable. At points in AF other than the segment NP, elite i can gain by reducing its army size slightly while continuing to grab (note that the boundary between AA and AF is part of AA, not AF). Points on the subsegment NS are ruled out because elite j would deviate up to a point in FA. The arguments ruling out points in FA other than the segment TQ are similar. No point on the boundary of AA can be an equilibrium. Along the lower boundary of AA, elite i can exploit a discontinuity in its payoff by using a slight increase in army size to capture a discrete jump in payoff via a move from AA to AF. Along the upper boundary of AA, elite j can similarly move from AA to FA. There is no equilibrium in the interior of AA due to Lemma 8.4.

Remark 8.2

Restrict attention to values of R/w consistent with Lemma 8.5(a).

(i) If $e_j \geq e_i$ then for all relevant values of R/w, point Q is strictly to the left of point P as shown in Figure 8.3. Thus when elite j is at least as large as elite i, the points along the non-empty segment SP (excluding S) are recruitment equilibria.

(ii) If $e_i \geq e_j$ then for all relevant values of R/w, point P is strictly lower than point Q as shown in Figure 8.3. Thus when elite i is at least as large as elite j, the points along the non-empty segment TQ (excluding T) are recruitment equilibria.

(iii) If $9/16 < e_i/e_j < 16/9$ and R/w is close enough to its lower bound $e_i + e_j$, then Q is strictly to the left of P and P is strictly lower than Q as shown in Figure 8.3. Thus when the sizes of the elites are similar enough and

> stratification is limited enough, the segments SP and TQ both exist and the points along each segment (excluding S and T) are recruitment equilibria. Therefore either elite may grab.

This completes the discussion of Figure 8.3 and Lemma 8.5(a).

In Figure 8.4, which corresponds to Lemma 8.5(b), IC_j^{WF} is rising at the intersection point N but IC_i^{WF} is falling at N. We are assuming $e_j < e_i$ in this case, so elite j has fewer members than elite i. However, the results for the converse case can be obtained through an interchange of the subscripts. As in Figure 8.3 the points in the interior of the shaded rectangle above the dashed line through P and to the right of the dashed line through Q are Nash equilibria with dissipative warfare. The points in the heavy lower boundary of this set are also included.

When point Q is above the dashed horizontal line through point P, there are more recruitment equilibria associated with the segment TQ

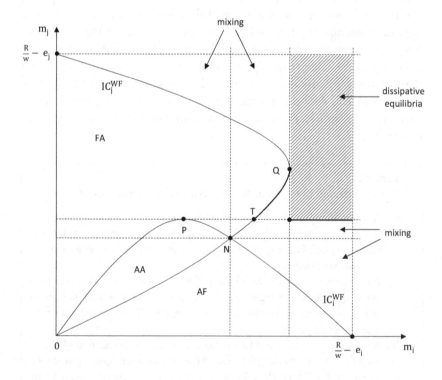

FIGURE 8.4. Recruitment equilibria for intermediate values of R/w

along IC_j^{WF}. At such points elite j grabs and elite i flees. Elite j does not deviate because a vertical movement would either increase the cost of grabbing or lead to we_j through mixing or AF. Elite i cannot gain by a horizontal deviation because this continues to give we_i through mixing or FA (or in the case of point P, through AA). Points along the segment NT (other than T itself) are not equilibria because elite i can deviate to an interior point in the AA region with a payoff greater than we_i. When Q is on the same horizontal line as P the segment TQ shrinks to the single point Q, and when Q is below this horizontal line such equilibria disappear.

There are no other recruitment equilibria. Arguments like those used for Figure 8.3 rule out other points in the mixing region, other points in the FA region, and all of the points in the AF region. No point along the boundary of the AA region is an equilibrium because either elite i can deviate slightly to the right and get a discrete payoff jump by moving from AA to AF, or elite j can deviate slightly upward and get a payoff jump by moving from AA to FA. The interior of the AA region is again ruled out by Lemma 8.4.

Remark 8.3

We have been studying the intermediate interval of R/w values from Lemma 8.5(b) using the assumption $e_j < e_i$. It can be shown mathematically that there is a value of R/w in the interior of the interval where Q is on the same horizontal line as P. Below this R/w level equilibria of the form TQ exist as depicted in Figure 8.4, but above it there are no such equilibria.

This completes our discussion of Figure 8.4 and Lemma 8.5(b).

The last scenario is shown in Figure 8.5, which corresponds to Lemma 8.5(c). Here both indifference curves are falling when they intersect at N. The usual dissipative Nash equilibria arise in the upper right corner, but now both of the heavy boundaries at the left and bottom of the shaded area are included.

There are no other recruitment equilibria. Arguments like those used previously rule out other points in the mixing region, all points in the FA region, and all points in the AF region. No point along the boundary of the AA region other than N is an equilibrium because either elite i can deviate slightly to the right and get a discrete payoff jump by moving from AA to AF, or elite j can deviate slightly upward and get a payoff jump by moving from AA to FA. Point N is ruled out because elite i can deviate left

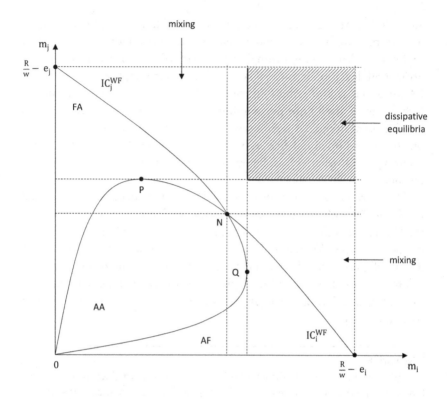

FIGURE 8.5. Recruitment equilibria for high values of R/w

to a point in the interior of AA with a payoff above we_i and elite j can deviate down to a point in the interior of AA with a payoff above we_j. The interior of AA is again ruled out by Lemma 8.4. This completes our discussion of Figure 8.5 and Lemma 8.5(c).

The results of this section can now be summarized formally.

Proposition 8.2 (the recruitment stage).

Confine attention to the points $(m_i, m_j) > 0$ such that $m_i < R/w - e_i$ and $m_j < R/w - e_j$. The latter two inequalities imply that grabbing is strictly preferred to flight. We adopt A8.1, A8.2, and A8.3, along with the conditions in Remark 8.1 ensuring that point P is below $R/w - e_j$ and point Q is to the left of $R/w - e_i$.

In all cases there are dissipative equilibria where open warfare and grabbing (by either elite) occur with positive probabilities. There are no recruitment equilibria other than these dissipative equilibria and the additional equilibria listed below.

(a) Low stratification. Suppose $R/w < (e_i + e_j)^2/(\max \{e_i, e_j\})$ so IC_i^{WF} and IC_j^{WF} are both rising when they intersect (Figure 8.3). The set of recruitment equilibria also includes at least one and possibly both of the following:
  (i) A non-empty interval SP (excluding S) on the rising part of IC_i^{WF} above the intersection point N.
  (ii) A non-empty interval TQ (excluding T) on the rising part of IC_j^{WF} above the intersection point N.
  The equilibria of type (i) have AF where elite i grabs and j flees.
  The equilibria of type (ii) have FA where elite j grabs and i flees.
  See Remark 8.2 for information on the conditions under which each case occurs.

(b) Intermediate stratification. Suppose $e_j < e_i$ with $(e_i + e_j)^2/e_i < R/w < (e_i + e_j)^2/e_j$ so IC_i^{WF} is rising and IC_j^{WF} is falling when they intersect (Figure 8.4). There are two possibilities:
  (i) If Q is above the horizontal line through P, there is a non-empty interval TQ along the rising part of IC_j^{WF} having recruitment equilibria of the FA type where elite j grabs and i flees. If Q is on the horizontal line through P then this interval shrinks to the single point Q.
  (ii) If the point Q is below the horizontal line through point P, there are no recruitment equilibria other than those of the dissipative kind.
  See Remark 8.3 for information on the conditions under which each case occurs.

(c) High stratification. Suppose $(e_i + e_j)^2/(\min \{e_i, e_j\}) < R/w$ so IC_i^{WF} and IC_j^{WF} are both falling when they intersect (Figure 8.5). There are no equilibria other than those of the dissipative kind.

We conclude this section with an overview of our results. First, there are never any recruitment equilibria yielding open warfare in a deterministic way (that is, within the AA region). Warfare only occurs probabilistically through dissipative equilibria.

Second, there can be recruitment equilibria where one elite intimidates the other into fleeing in a deterministic way (that is, within the AF or FA regions). This is most likely when the stratification level R/w is low relative to the sizes of the elite groups. For sufficiently low R/w values, either elite can potentially be the aggressor. The identity of the aggressor is not affected by asymmetries involving the status quo land rents because conflict is "all or nothing;" an elite either wins and gets the rent R or dies and gets zero.

At intermediate stratification levels R/w, the elite having fewer members is more likely to be aggressive. This may seem surprising, but it is important to recall that elites do not fight; they only employ warriors. The intuition is that a smaller elite has a lower opportunity cost because it gets less total food by fleeing to the commons. Therefore it behaves more aggressively in competing for land rents. When R/w is near the lower end of the intermediate R/w range the smaller elite can win through intimidation, but near the upper end this is no longer possible. At high stratification levels, recruitment equilibria where one elite intimidates the other in a deterministic way do not exist.

Equilibria involving dissipative warfare exist for all stratification levels R/w. In such cases each elite has positive probabilities of both attacking and fleeing. All four of the possible outcomes (open war, grabbing by one elite, grabbing by the other, and both fleeing) therefore occur with positive probabilities. Such equilibria involve larger armies than those where one elite wins through intimidation. They are also maximally wasteful in the sense that every elite agent is driven down to an expected food income equal to the commoner wage. All land rent is sacrificed to support warriors who produce no food but do receive the commoner wage (in an *ex ante* sense; see Section 8.7 for details).

Because all agents have the expected food income w in a dissipative equilibrium, it is easy to embed such warfare situations in a Malthusian framework. One only has to impose the requirement that the aggregate population N generate the uniform standard of living w consistent with demographic stationarity. This yields a long run equilibrium at the regional level as in the models of Chapters 3–6.

Whether there is overt war or covert intimidation, our formal model predicts that elites will be expansionist in the sense that both territories end up under the control of a single elite (other than in the dissipative outcome where both flee). Strikingly, we never predict peaceful coexistence between rivals. Section 8.9 will discuss a number of factors that could temper this stark conclusion.

8.7 FISCAL CONSTRAINTS

In Section 8.4 we argued that elites need to offer warriors an amount above their reservation utility w contingent upon the event that warfare occurs and the warriors win, because if the warriors lose they die and receive zero utility. We called such payments "booty." This led to the fiscal constraint $M \leq R/w$ in (8.7). When this inequality holds, the winning elite will have enough land rent available to compensate warriors in a way that gives an expected income of w and hence satisfies their *ex ante* participation constraint. When the inequality is violated, elites are unable to attract warriors because the promise to provide sufficient booty is non-credible. This is true for both of the elites (there is no "i" subscript in the condition $M \leq R/w$). Thus warfare becomes impossible.

This issue does not arise when peace prevails because in this case warriors can be paid their opportunity cost w directly. The same is true when an elite flees from its rival. In the latter case both the elite agents and their warriors go to the commons and get the food income w. The need for booty and the resulting fiscal constraint are only relevant when there is open warfare and a genuine chance of death.

Sections 8.5 and 8.6 ignored the question of whether elites can finance required payments of booty *ex post*. This section establishes that for an interval of stratification levels R/w, there are dissipative equilibria that do satisfy the fiscal constraint. Our theory of warfare from Sections 8.5 and 8.6 is therefore compatible with the limits on elite fiscal capacity described in Section 8.4.

Consider the army sizes $m_i = R/w - e_i$ and $m_j = R/w - e_j$ associated with the upper right corner of the large rectangle in Figures 8.3–8.5. These are the largest armies of theoretical interest (any elite with a larger army has "flee" as a dominant strategy by Lemma 8.1). To avoid a violation of the fiscal constraint we need $M = 2R/w - e_i - e_j \leq R/w$. This reduces to $R/w - e_i - e_j \leq 0$, which contradicts our earlier assumption that each elite can more than cover its opportunity cost in peacetime: $r_i > we_i$ for i = A, B and thus $R/w > e_i + e_j$ as in (8.3). However, such army sizes give a dissipative equilibrium with $\lambda_i = \lambda_j = 0$ in Lemma 8.3, meaning that each elite attacks with probability zero. As a result the inability of elites to offer adequate booty does not influence the outcome, which is that each elite (and its army) leaves the field of battle.

More interesting results are obtained when we examine the smallest army sizes consistent with dissipative equilibrium. In Figures 8.3, 8.4, and 8.5, these army sizes are located just above the dashed horizontal line through point P and just to the right of the dashed vertical line through point Q. From these points we obtain the lower bounds $m_i > \left[(R/w)^{1/2} - e_j^{1/2} \right]^2$ and $m_j > \left[(R/w)^{1/2} - e_i^{1/2} \right]^2$.

The goal is to discover whether army sizes at these lower bounds could satisfy the fiscal constraint $M < R/w$ with inequality. If this is true then there are army sizes in the interior of the dissipative region that also satisfy the fiscal constraint. By Lemma 8.3 such army sizes yield a positive probability of open warfare. On the other hand, if $M \geq R/w$ holds for the lower bounds listed above, the same must be true for all larger army sizes. In this case the fiscal constraint will not be compatible with any dissipative equilibrium of the kind discussed in Section 8.6.

Some algebra shows that $M < R/w$ holds for the lower bounds if and only if

$$R/w - 2(R/w)^{1/2}\left(e_i^{1/2} + e_j^{1/2}\right) + e_i + e_j < 0 \qquad (8.13)$$

This is a quadratic in $(R/w)^{1/2}$ with a minimum at $(R/w)^{1/2} = e_i^{1/2} + e_j^{1/2}$. Evaluating the left-hand side of (8.13) at this minimizer gives a strictly negative expression. This shows that there is a non-empty interval of R/w values where $M < R/w$.

Within this interval of R/w values, there exist dissipative equilibria near the lower bounds for the army sizes such that (a) the winning warriors can be offered enough booty to satisfy their *ex ante* participation constraints with equality; (b) when these payments to warriors are taken into account, elites have expected payoffs equal to what they could get in the commons, so their *ex ante* participation constraints are also satisfied with equality; and (c) open warfare occurs with positive probability.

We can now link inequality (8.13) with the specific R/w intervals in Proposition 8.2. This inequality always holds at $R/w = e_i + e_j$, which is the lower bound on aggregate rent. It also always holds at $R/w = (e_i + e_j)^2 /$ max $\{e_i, e_j\}$. This implies that all values of R/w associated with "low" stratification in Proposition 8.2(a) satisfy (8.13). When the stratification level falls in this range there are dissipative equilibria that satisfy the fiscal constraint and have positive probabilities of open war, as long as the army sizes are not too large. The fact that (8.13) holds with inequality at the upper boundary of the "low" stratification range in Proposition 8.2(a) implies that the same conclusions hold for some values of R/w in the lower part of the "intermediate" stratification range in Proposition 8.2(b).

The boundary between "intermediate" and "high" stratification levels in Proposition 8.2 occurs at $R/w = (e_i + e_j)^2 /$ min $\{e_i, e_j\}$. It can be shown that inequality (8.13) holds here if either $e_i \leq e_j < 4e_i$ or $e_j \leq e_i < 4e_j$. In these cases where the elite sizes do not differ too much, all values of R/w in the "intermediate" stratification range can generate dissipative equilibria that satisfy the fiscal constraint and have positive probabilities of open war, as long as the army sizes are not too large. The same will be true for values of R/w near the lower end of the "high" stratification range in Proposition 8.2(c). However, for high enough R/w values inequality (8.13) must be violated and there are no such equilibria.

If there is too much asymmetry in the elite sizes, inequality (8.13) will be reversed at $R/w = (e_i + e_j)^2 / \min \{e_i, e_j\}$. In this case there are no dissipative equilibria that satisfy the fiscal constraint near the upper end of the "intermediate" range from Proposition 8.2(b) or anywhere in the "high" range from Proposition 8.2(c).

The message from these results is twofold. First, limits on elite fiscal capacity do have some bite, and at sufficiently high stratification levels will rule out the kind of open warfare that would otherwise occur in dissipative equilibria. The reason for this result is that as stratification increases, the minimum army sizes needed for dissipative equilibria increase more rapidly than the rent available to satisfy warrior participation constraints. Eventually this makes it impossible for elites to recruit armies of the required size.

Second, limits on elite fiscal capacity do not have so much bite that they eliminate open warfare entirely. For all stratification levels R/w in the low range of Proposition 8.2, and some in the intermediate range, equilibria with warfare continue to exist. If the elite sizes are not too asymmetric, this is true throughout the intermediate range and even for some stratification levels in the high range. In all cases, however, fiscal difficulties rule out open warfare at very high stratification levels.

8.8 STRATIFICATION AND WARFARE

This section steps back from the details of the formal model to discuss broader issues surrounding the relationship between stratification and warfare. In particular we will clarify the similarities and differences between Chapters 7 and 8. We also comment on some nuances of the theory relevant for the interpretation of archaeological evidence.

The predictions of Chapters 7 and 8 differ sharply. In our model of egalitarian groups in Chapter 7, war required migration costs for individuals and exogenous shocks from nature or technology. A series of wars required a series of shocks. The model of elite warfare in Chapter 8, by contrast, predicts chronic conflict between rival elites even without shocks, along with a tendency toward territorial expansion. Why the difference?

It is important first to notice that certain factors do not account for this difference. In each case food is obtained through a Cobb–Douglas production function using inputs of labor and land. The role of the land input was not made explicit in Chapter 7 but the production function in Section 7.4 can be derived from the one in Section 8.4 by setting the input of land (Z_i in Section 8.4) equal to unity for each site. This convention about how units of land are measured does not explain why warfare is rare in one model but common in the other.

Furthermore, we used precisely the same combat technology in the two chapters. In each case a group's probability of victory was determined by the size ratio for the two combatant groups (compare equation (7.3) in Section 7.4 with equation (8.4) in Section 8.4). Whatever one may think about the descriptive realism of our assumptions in this regard, the differences in the conclusions do not stem from any difference in military technology. We visualize similar kinds of warfare in the two chapters: combatant groups use widely available weapons and the larger group tends to win.

We also stress that there is no difference between the chapters in preferences. In both chapters all agents are risk neutral and maximize expected food consumption. Also in both chapters being alive with zero food is equivalent to being dead. One may quarrel with these assumptions, but they are uniform across the two models.

One modeling difference is that in Chapter 6 the elites supplied production labor, and in Chapter 7 the same was true for the insiders in egalitarian groups. By contrast, in Chapter 8 the elite groups did not contribute any production labor. This simplification in Chapter 8 only affects the number of commoners the elite hires for food production, and has no implications for army sizes or the probability of warfare.

As we mentioned in Section 8.1, one factor that does help account for the differing predictions is that there are diminishing returns to land when labor is held constant. This matters for an egalitarian group, which has a fixed supply of labor determined by the size of the group and seeks to augment the group's supply of land by seizing another group's site. As described in Chapter 7, the victorious group distributes its labor across the old and new sites in a way that maximizes total food output. The group becomes richer on a per capita basis because it now has more land per unit of labor. If the group is militarily strong enough, this economic gain can provide a motive for war.

However, the fixed labor input of the group implies that living standards do not scale up linearly with land. To see how this works in the model of Chapter 7, suppose for simplicity that all land is of equal quality ($s_A = s_B$). A group that seizes a second site and thus doubles its land input will only increase food per person by the smaller factor of $2^{1-\alpha}$ where $1-\alpha$ is the exponent on the land input from the Cobb–Douglas production function. This limits the incentive for groups to seek more land through war. The result in Chapter 7 was an interval of group size ratios where neither group attacked and peace prevailed. The same argument extends to situations where the natural productivities of the two sites differ ($s_A \neq s_B$) so the amount of land controlled by a group is calculated in quality-adjusted units.

This argument is quite general but a few subtleties deserve attention. First, given the Cobb–Douglas food technology from Chapter 7, the winning group always allocates a positive number of people to each site in such a way that the marginal product of labor is equalized across sites. The winners do not simply abandon the old site and move to the new one. This would lead to an infinite marginal product of labor at the abandoned site and could not be optimal, even if the new site has better land. A different functional form could give different results by allowing boundary solutions with zero population at one of the sites. But even if only one site is used, any reasonable production function will have diminishing returns to land for a fixed labor input and therefore similar issues will arise.

Another caveat to the idea that the winners occupy both sites involves personnel constraints. As was explained in Section 7.9, a group that is too small to enforce property rights at both sites might have to abandon its old site in order to establish property rights over the new one. Such personnel constraints reduce the potential gain from warfare in egalitarian societies. By ignoring this constraint and assuming that a winning group can maintain property rights over both sites simultaneously, we are confining attention to the case where the incentive for warfare between egalitarian groups is strongest. Our point is that even in this case, diminishing returns to land will dampen the incentive for war.

The situation is different for warfare between elites, who are concerned about the total land rent they appropriate. In the model of Chapter 8 the fact that elites have fixed group sizes is irrelevant for the determination of labor inputs. An elite can always obtain more labor by hiring workers from the commons at a fixed wage. Although the returns to land are still diminishing for a fixed labor input, the input of commoner labor is not fixed. As we explained in Section 8.4, this implies that land rent scales up linearly with the land area an elite controls. Even when territories have differing natural productivities, which we allowed in the model of this chapter, land rents are additive across territories, with no tendency for marginal returns to fall as an elite accumulates more land. Thus elites have stronger incentives to seize additional territory than egalitarian groups.

A second difference between the models of Chapters 7 and 8 also contributes to their differing predictions. Elites do not just hire commoners to work their fields; they also hire warriors to fight their battles. In Chapter 7 the sizes of the combatant groups were determined in the short run by individual migration across sites and in the long run by Malthusian population dynamics. Each mechanism generated a positive correlation between site quality and group size, which tended to deter attack. Chapter 7 showed that under these conditions, war required both costly individual migration and an exogenous productivity shock.

Neither of these factors was relevant for Chapter 8. In the latter model an elite maximized expected food income by choosing its army size to maximize expected land rent. Much as egalitarian groups are constrained in the sizes of their labor inputs while elites are not, egalitarian groups are constrained in the sizes of their combat forces while elites are not. Again this gives elites stronger incentives to engage in warfare.

For these reasons we expect more frequent warfare in stratified societies than in egalitarian ones. Indeed, we expect elites in stratified societies to engage in chronic war even in the absence of exogenous shocks from nature or technology. This follows from our conclusion in Section 8.6 that stratification leads to dissipative equilibria where open war occurs with positive probability.

Although stratification leads to warfare, we have also shown that warfare makes elite–commoner inequality less extreme by dissipating elite land rent on military conflict. This is compatible with the view of Bowles (2012) that warfare has a leveling influence with respect to inequality. However, it differs from the view of Boix (2015) that warfare tends to cause inequality rather than the other way around.

Despite the wasteful nature of military expenditures, elites have a strong tendency to expand their territory. In the model of Sections 8.4–8.7 elite conflict generally led to the consolidation of territorial control in the hands of a single elite. The only exception was the theoretical possibility that both elites might flee simultaneously, opening up an opportunity for a new elite to emerge and gain control over an abandoned site. But we noted two possible constraints on territorial expansion: an elite could lack the personnel required to manage a larger territory or it could lack the fiscal capacity to recruit warriors by offering adequate booty in the event of victory. We return to these and other limits on territorial aggrandizement in Section 8.9.

First, however, we want to mention some nuances of the model that might affect the interpretation of archaeological evidence. In particular, the results in Section 8.6 do not just say "stratification leads to warfare." A more precise statement is that stratified societies always have equilibria where warfare occurs with positive probability. But we also established that there are sometimes additional equilibria where an elite wins through intimidation without actually fighting a war. Instead, the stronger elite threatens to attack and induces its opponent to flee. Such intimidation tactics result in territorial expansion but will not leave behind mass graves or other archaeological evidence for open warfare.

However, as stratification increases (measured by aggregate land rent relative to the commoner wage), the equilibria with deterministic forms of intimidation tend to drop away, leaving only equilibria where overt war and covert intimidation both have positive probabilities. The economic intuition is that higher stratification raises the stakes for the elites relative to the cost of recruiting an army and thus makes it more difficult to acquire an adversary's territory through threats alone.

We also want to stress that when assessing our theory using data, care is required in measuring the degree of stratification. What matters is the land rent and the degree of inequality that would exist between elites and commoners *before* military expenditures are deducted, because the theory predicts that *after* military expenditures are deducted, the inequality in food consumption between elites and commoners could be negligible.

Another nuance involves overlap between the roles of elites and warriors. It is analytically convenient to separate these two roles by having the elites use a technology of exclusion to establish property rights over sites, while the warriors use a technology of combat to fight against warriors sponsored by rival elites. In the real world, however, the same elite agents who exclude unorganized outsiders and enjoy land rents also frequently lead warriors in battle (see the discussion of Gat, 2006, in Section 8.3). When some or all members of the elite are also warriors, this will reduce the number of warriors who have to be hired externally. But as long as there is a horizontal supply curve where additional warriors can be hired at a fixed wage *ex ante*, and it is optimal for the elite to hire at least some warriors in this way, our qualitative conclusions will be unchanged.

8.9 EXTENSIONS OF THE MODEL

One could argue that our theory in Chapter 7 understated the importance of war in egalitarian societies. After all, such societies sometimes have warfare even without any obvious external shocks. In Section 7.8 we discussed ways in which our assumptions could be relaxed, and argued that in most cases relaxing our assumptions would make war less likely rather than more likely.

By the same token one could argue that our theory in Chapter 8 overstates the prevalence of war in stratified societies. For example, one might be concerned that in Section 8.5 we ruled out peaceful coexistence with neither side attacking or fleeing. One might also question our prediction that elites have expansionist tendencies. No doubt one could find empirical counterexamples to both claims.

There are clearly factors absent from our model that could tend to restrain open warfare and territorial expansion in stratified societies. This section discusses a number of such possibilities.

Preferences: The members of the elite or prospective warriors may be risk averse rather than risk neutral. Other things being equal this would make warfare less likely. It would also make threats of war less credible, weakening the effectiveness of intimidation tactics. A related point is that agents might regard being alive without food as preferable to being dead. This "happy to be alive" utility function has implications similar to those of risk aversion (see Section 7.8). One could also include a positive probability of survival among the losers, or a positive probability of injury or death among the winners.

Geography: The model of this chapter allowed territories to have differing land areas and natural productivities. These factors, as well as the initial distribution of land rents between elites, were irrelevant because the elites were engaged in an all or nothing conflict over an aggregate prize (total land rent). However, other geographical variables could affect our conclusions. For example, the rival elites may be separated by physical distance or by barriers such as deserts, mountains, rivers, or seas. This raises the cost of communication and transport, making successful attacks less likely. To take an extreme example: Kamehameha I achieved unified control over the Hawaiian Islands but would have had great difficulty crossing a large expanse of the Pacific Ocean to conquer Tonga.

Defensive Technology: Our military technology made no distinction between the roles of attacker and defender. But elites concerned about the dangers of being attacked could choose easily defended locations or create fortifications. Archaeological research on stratified societies often reveals investments of this sort even when evidence for open warfare is absent. More generally, military technology could give other advantages to the defending side such as local knowledge. Defenders may also have more durable alliances than attackers due to shared experiences among alliance partners with a common set of threats. On the other hand, attackers often have the advantage of surprise.

Personnel Constraints: The theory of stratification in Chapter 6 was based on the premise that a local group of insiders could defend a site or territory against unorganized outsiders and thereby establish shared property rights over it. This gave the insiders the ability to capture land rent. In Chapters 7 and 8 we extended this idea to include defense of land rent, or the acquisition of more rent, in conflicts with other organized groups.

In Chapter 6 we assumed that sites became closed to further entry as soon as the number of insiders reached the critical mass needed to exclude individual outsiders one at a time. These groups became elites when it became profitable for them to hire commoner labor. However, once warfare with organized external groups is a possibility, there could be advantages to an elite in having more members than are needed just to repel individual outsiders. In particular, an elite seeking to conquer a neighboring territory must be large enough to guard both its old and new territories against intrusion by outsiders, so it can collect land rents in both places.

In some cases surplus offspring from elite parents may play this role (see Chapter 6 on downward mobility from the elite to the commoner class). In other cases warriors who have conquered a territory may be accepted into the elite and allowed to administer conquered land as part of their booty from victory. Through repeated iterations this may lead to a hierarchical regional system where lower-level elites pay tribute to higher-level elites. If these sources of personnel are not sufficient, the elite may have to offer upward mobility to some commoners. This would limit the gains from conquest.

Fiscal Constraints: In Section 8.4 we made the point that elites have to offer booty to their warriors in the event of victory, and this booty has to exceed the commoner wage in order to compensate *ex ante* for the possibility of death in battle. We pursued this idea in Section 8.7 and concluded that elites are sometimes unable to recruit the armies needed for dissipative warfare because military expenditures would exceed the land rents used to finance them. This issue tended to arise at high stratification levels. Budget constraints do not eliminate the positive linkage between stratification and warfare but do temper it.

In our formal model we assumed that warriors would fight to the death and that an elite would only be killed if its army were also killed. But the need for generous booty is less pressing if warriors on the losing side have a reasonable prospect of avoiding death. For example, it may become

obvious that one army is going to lose and this army could run away to
the commons to produce food, leaving its sponsoring elite to its fate. Such
behavior is presumably not desirable from the standpoint of the losing
elite, but it does reduce the booty an elite must offer in order to recruit
warriors in the first place.

We assumed throughout this chapter that warriors were voluntary
participants in war, and had to be offered a compensation package with
the same expected value as the commoner wage. An elite seeking to
reduce its military expenditures might instead rely on slaves as soldiers.
We are doubtful about the effectiveness of unfree soldiers relative to free
ones, but the prevalence of this practice is a matter for empirical
investigation.

One natural way to think about financial constraints is that richer elites
can hire larger armies, which gives them a higher probability of victory,
makes them even richer in the event of victory, allows them to hire even
larger armies, and so on. Although this dynamic could frequently be
important in real cases, it does not arise in the model of this chapter
because armies are not financed out of current land rents. Instead elites
recruit armies by promising to pay booty out of future land rents if a war
is successful. Because the victorious elite will control the aggregate rent of
the two territories, it is this rent, not the current rent from an individual
territory, that is relevant in financing an army. But if elite promises along
these lines lack credibility (see the discussion of institutions below), the
currently available rent could become more important than the projected
future rent.

The positive feedback loop described in the preceding paragraph may
suggest a role for economies of scale in military technology. We have not
included this idea in our model and want to emphasize that it is not
necessary in order for elites to have powerful incentives for warfare.
Our results show that even with constant returns to scale in food technology and decreasing returns in military technology (the probability of
victory is a strictly concave function of army size, given the army size of
the opposing elite), elites do not embrace peaceful coexistence. As we
discussed earlier, in our model land rent is additive across territories and
this is enough. Economies of scale would exacerbate elite warfare and
territorial expansion but are not essential to the story.

Institutions: In our model warfare is inefficient. Both elites would be
better off if they could enjoy their land rents in peace rather than wasting
the rents by hiring armies to fight battles or pursue intimidation tactics.
Unfortunately the elites cannot make binding commitments to refrain

from hiring armies or attacking their opponents, and peace is not an equilibrium outcome. But several institutional factors might limit warfare in practice.

Even if it has adequate land rent and a reasonable prospect of acquiring more, an elite may be unable to recruit warriors due to doubts about the reliability of its promises to pay booty after a victory. Reputational and repeated game effects may be too weak to resolve these incentive problems, and this may make territorial expansion more difficult. Conversely if such effects are very strong, they may facilitate non-aggression pacts with rival elites that forestall war. Hostage exchanges or valuable trading relationships could offer further inducements for elites to pursue policies of peaceful coexistence.

We did not include asymmetric information in our model but some writers see it as one reason for war (Fearon, 1995; Powell, 1996, 2006). To the extent that this is true, signaling mechanisms could offer a way to avoid warfare by clarifying the true strengths of the potential combatant groups. For example, the large feasts called potlatches on the northwest coast of North America may have conveyed useful information both to allies and enemies about the wealth or military power of each chief (Johnson and Earle, 2000).

Readers familiar with game theory no doubt saw similarities between our model in Section 8.6 and the famous hawk–dove game, where pairs of animals or humans are in conflict over a valuable resource and must choose whether to behave in an aggressive or peaceful way. Such games have two pure-strategy Nash equilibria (like our AF and FA outcomes) as well as a mixed-strategy Nash equilibrium (like the one in Lemma 8.3).

In biological settings it is common for the first arriver to defend the prize (a food item, a site, a mate) while the second arriver departs. This strategy is called "bourgeois." Some writers have suggested that bourgeois strategies may explain how ancestral human groups established collective property rights over valuable sites (e.g., Putterman, 2012, 166–168). It is therefore natural to ask whether similar institutional arrangements could be used to avoid open warfare in stratified societies.

We tend to be skeptical, partly because the evolutionary processes underpinning bourgeois strategies in animal populations are probably not relevant, and partly because the identity of the first arriver in a conflict among elites over land is not always obvious. In any event our model shows that there can be strong temptations for elites to fight or to intimidate each other. Any social convention surrounding elite entitlements to particular territories would need to be at least as strong in order to restrain these temptations to use or threaten force.

Culture: Some societies have norms that restrain warfare or intimidation among rival elites. One source of such norms might be intermarriage, although this could also be used as a deliberate tactic to build and maintain alliances. More generally, a shared history, language, ethnicity, or religion might provide a basis for peaceful coexistence.

8.10 CONCLUSION

This completes our study of pre-state institutional developments in Part III of the book. We have sought to construct a unified theoretical framework for thinking about early inequality and warfare. At this point we will take stock of what we have learned from Chapters 6–8 and make a few general remarks on the nature of our theory.

Chapter 6 showed that inequality can emerge through a technology of exclusion, where organized insiders bar entry to valuable sites by unorganized outsiders. This led to the creation of collective property rights, to insider–outsider inequality, and eventually to elite–commoner inequality. The process was driven by regional population growth that resulted from the better Holocene climate and improvements in agricultural technology.

Our theory of warfare is layered on top of our theory of stratification. Warfare involves a technology of combat between organized groups, which is different from the technology of exclusion undergirding property rights. In Chapter 7 we considered a pair of internally egalitarian groups. We concluded that if individual agents are free to move between sites, the resulting groups are unlikely to go to war, because population tends to pile up at the better site and this deters attack from the smaller group at the worse site. In the framework of Chapter 6, this rules out warfare among groups in the commons.

We also concluded in Chapter 7 that even when individual mobility among sites is restricted, long-run Malthusian dynamics still tend to forestall warfare. Again the reason is that better sites have larger populations and this deters attack. But exogenous shocks from nature or technology can lead to imbalances between site qualities and group sizes that trigger episodes of warfare. We argued that the transition from mobile to sedentary foraging probably created greater barriers to individual migration across groups, partly due to more endogamous marriage, and that this led to increased warfare over land.

In Chapter 8 we shifted the focus from internally egalitarian groups (those in the commons or with insider–outsider inequality) to stratified groups. We argued that elites have strong economic incentives to engage in warfare or at least the intimidation of their rivals. There are two main reasons: elites can employ unlimited numbers of commoners to produce food and they can recruit unlimited numbers of warriors to fight their battles. The first factor implies that the land rent enjoyed by an elite scales up linearly with land area and the second creates an arms race where rival elites have incentives to waste their resources on military expenditures. Either through overt warfare or covert intimidation, successful elites tend to expand their territory.

We offered empirical evidence in Chapters 6–8 to establish that this theoretical framework is consistent with what we know from archaeology about the ways in which inequality and warfare have varied across pre-state or non-state societies. While we do not have space to summarize this evidence here, we hope the reader has been convinced by its breadth and depth.

Archaeologists and anthropologists sometimes distinguish between integration theory and conflict theory as alternative ways of explaining social complexity. For an integration theorist, elites arise because they solve broad social problems. For example, they may provide insurance, organize defense, invest in public works, or facilitate trade (Johnson and Earle, 2000). For a conflict theorist, elites pursue their joint self-interest through coercive means, generally at the expense of commoners.

The theory we developed in Part III does not attribute any socially useful function to elites. Although we investigate the determinants of warfare, we emphasize that elites do not provide the public good of "defense" to commoners because the commoners do not participate in warfare and do not care which elite requires them to pay land rent. Instead elites employ coercion to establish local property rights and extend their territorial scale. We do not deny that once they are established, elites may sometimes do socially useful things. However, we would argue that when they do, their motives are self-interested, and that these useful activities are not the reason why the elites arose in the first place.

We close by highlighting the difference between technologies of production and coercion. The literature on prehistory includes many claims to the effect that inequality, warfare, and even the state emerge because food technology becomes productive enough to create a surplus, which can be used to support landowners, warriors, or kings. We do agree that innovations in food production technology are important, mainly because they lead to Malthusian population growth that has institutional consequences. However, we strongly dispute the notion that "surplus" is generated directly by production technology.

For a given food production technology, the surplus captured by a pre-state elite comes from land rent. The level of land rent relative to the commoner wage depends on institutions. In turn these institutions rest ultimately upon technologies of coercion. A major advantage of our theory is that it clarifies how such technologies of coercion can account for variations in the living standards of elites and commoners across time and space. Another major advantage is that it can account for variations in warfare across time and space. Part IV will extend these ideas to the emergence of cities and states.

PART IV

CITIES AND STATES

9

Mesopotamian City-States

Data and Hypotheses

9.1 INTRODUCTION

In Part IV of the book we will explore the last two transitions on our list of six: the emergence of cities and states. We will not linger on the question of whether these developments were important. Everyone knows that cities and states are foundational components of the modern world. It is challenging to imagine what our lives would be like without them. But as with the four previous transitions we have studied, cities and states had origins, and we will attempt to explain how they arose.

Early states involved government of, by, and for elites. The elites achieved better standards of living than commoners in many ways, and the resulting levels of inequality varied from one society to another. The mechanisms of elite control included taxation; the ownership of agricultural land or other natural resources; the monopolization of trade, mining, or manufacturing; the plunder of neighboring societies; corvée labor; and slavery. But early states also offered benefits to commoners such as public order, suppression of local warfare, infrastructure, insurance against natural disasters, and the like. Archaeologists and economists share an interest in the question of whether early states made commoners better off or worse off on balance. We will return to this issue later.

Our concern is only with "pristine" or "primary" states. We ignore situations where states developed in response to influences from other preexisting states or through cycles of collapse and reintegration. Pristine states emerged independently, or nearly so, in several parts of the world. The classic list includes Mesopotamia, Egypt, the Indus River valley,

China, Mesoamerica, and South America. However, other probable or definite examples can be found in Africa, Southeast Asia, Europe, and North America.

Chapter 9 surveys the archaeological evidence about the emergence of city-states in southern Mesopotamia and outlines a number of causal hypotheses about this process. Chapter 10 builds a formal economic model of our own hypothesis, which we argue can explain several prominent features of the regional narrative from Chapter 9. In Chapter 11 we compare the Mesopotamian example with those of Egypt, the Indus Valley, China, Mesoamerica, and South America. We will argue that these six cases exhibit recurring patterns, including the universality of stratification in early state societies (Feinman and Marcus, 1998), and frequent connections between urbanization and state formation. We will also argue that a small set of causal mechanisms can account for these patterns. The rest of this section frames the key issues and provides conceptual background.

The first item on the agenda is to define a state. Scholars have proposed many definitions, and we will postpone a detailed discussion until Section 11.3. But in brief, we define a *state* to be an organized elite with significant powers of taxation in a well-defined geographic area. When further nuance is needed, we add the requirement that taxation is institutionalized in the sense that (a) it is carried out regularly by a permanent set of specialists, and (b) the resulting resources are transferred to a central elite group for allocation. The rationale for our definition is that if a state is to function as a collective actor, the elite must possess a centralized fiscal system so that it can collect and expend resources in a coherent way. We are not alone in seeing taxation as integral to the state. Most economic historians stress the importance of fiscal centralization (see the literature review in Acemoglu and Robinson, 2016).

Although we require a sufficient degree of internal organization within the elite, we do not require a king or some other supreme leader. A council of elite landowners, merchants, or priests might well collect taxes and allocate state resources according to a coherent preference ordering. At the other end of the spectrum, we would not view a set of fiscally autonomous landlords as constituting a state, even if they jointly monopolized the use of force, in the absence of centralized institutions for resource allocation.

Economists often take it for granted that states supply public goods such as law and order. While this is plausible, we do not require it here. In fact one implication of our formal model in Chapter 10 is that a state can arise because it enhances private elite consumption. Thus we view taxation, but not public goods supply, as a defining feature of the state. Of course, in practice most pristine states did make investments in temples, monuments, irrigation canals, and other public goods of interest to the elite.

Chapter 6 introduced a *technology of exclusion* to explain early inequality, and Chapters 7–8 introduced a *technology of combat* to explain early warfare over land. Part IV requires a *technology of confiscation* in order to explain the emergence of early states. This term refers to techniques through which an elite extracts resources from the agents who live within its territory.

Our definition of taxation includes all cases where an elite collectively confiscates resources (food, labor, urban outputs, raw materials, and so on). This includes the corvée labor often used for construction projects in early states. It also includes slavery, which appears to have been widespread in some early states. The labor time of slaves could be appropriated by elite individuals or households rather than the state itself, although state power might be deployed if a slave tried to escape.

Tax collection could involve the threat or use of physical force, but it need not. Depending on the circumstances, recalcitrant taxpayers might face the threat of losing social ties with other elite agents, or the threat that deities will withdraw their protection. As Liverani (2006, 25) observes, elites often prefer ideological forms of coercion where producers are convinced to give up substantial resources for religious reasons. See also Steinkeller (2015a, 15–17) on the probable role of deities in mobilizing the resources used to supply public goods in ancient Mesopotamia.

For concreteness, suppose the technology of confiscation involves the taxation of food output produced from agriculture. Many factors will influence the ease or difficulty of tax collection. These include:

(a) Whether tax collectors must travel long distances;
(b) Whether output is easily transported and stored;
(c) Whether output is easily hidden from tax collectors;
(d) Whether output is easily estimated by tax collectors;
(e) Whether potential taxpayers can run away.

The reader can no doubt think of additional factors that might be relevant.

These considerations are not limited to agriculture. Sedentary foragers are a poor target for taxation in several ways. Such societies often have patchy resources, and good sites may be far apart. Foragers also tend to harvest many different species of plants and animals, with some being difficult to store and others being easily hidden. Labor effort is usually unobservable, unlike the case of collective work on cultivated fields. Finally, the food income of foragers is difficult to estimate due to the diversity of harvesting activities and the many random variables that can influence outputs from hunting and gathering.

Agricultural societies are a mixed bag. Crops harvested in large quantities on a seasonal cycle at a limited number of sites could present an attractive target, but not all crops have these features. Some crops are readily stored while others are not (see Scott, 2017, on the differences between cereals and tubers). In some cases it is easy to estimate the output of farmers and tax them accordingly, but in other cases it is not. For example, it was easy to infer output from the height of the Nile flood in Egypt, but harder to make similar inferences in southern Mesopotamia (see our discussion of Egypt in Section 11.6 and our discussion of Mayshar et al., 2017, in Section 9.8).

We will also consider taxation of the output from urban manufacturing, which we think was a particularly tempting target. Such manufacturing occurred in compact areas; outputs of textiles, metal items, and pottery were easily counted, stored, and transported; and it would have been difficult to conceal workshops or warehouses. These factors tend to strengthen the linkage between early urbanization and early state formation.

We will not include all of the issues discussed here in our formal model (Chapter 10). However, for the reasons given above, we presume that technologies of confiscation were largely ineffective for sedentary foragers, had variable effectiveness for agriculture, and tended to be highly effective for urban manufacturing. Of course, environmental and technological details are important, and it matters what is being taxed. But the key point is that for an early state to have robust fiscal foundations, productive agriculture by itself is not enough. An effective technology of confiscation is also required (on this point, see also Mayshar et al., 2022).

We draw an important distinction between land rent and taxation. Simply put, land rents arise from a technology of exclusion, while taxes arise from a technology of confiscation. These are different things. In Chapter 6 we showed that a local elite can use an exclusion technology to prevent outsiders from accessing land at a particular site. This does not involve taxation but rather the closure of geographic areas that were once available to all. After such property rights have been created, markets for land or labor enable elite agents to collect land rents from commoners, leading to class stratification.

Recall from Chapter 6 that when we use the term "wage" we simply mean a food payment from an elite agent to a commoner in exchange for labor time. In this context, "land rent" means the food output retained by the elite agent after paying the "wage." This is the labor market way of telling the story. We can also have the commoner pay direct "land rent" (again in the form of food) to the elite agent in exchange for the right to work on a parcel of land, where the commoner keeps the output left over after paying the land rent. This is the land market way of telling the story.

In all of our formal models these two descriptions are equivalent, but we find it more convenient to use the description in terms of wages and labor markets, with land rent treated as a residual for the elite. We also note that in our analysis it does not matter whether wages or rents are fixed payments or shares in output. For urban manufacturing, what we call wages are sometimes called "rations."

Archaeologists and anthropologists often apply the label "tributary economy" to a system involving either direct taxes or land rents generated through market mechanisms, without specifying which of the two is being discussed (however, Earle, 1987, 294–295, has a cogent discussion of land rent in the context of chiefdoms). Writers in these fields do distinguish staple finance (e.g., transfers of grain or animal herds from commoners to the elite, usually with central storage facilities) from wealth finance (e.g., the payment of taxes in specialized craft goods or exotic materials such as metals). Both are consistent with centralized fiscal authority in a state. We will assume staple finance for simplicity, but nothing essential hinges on this assumption.

As we showed in Chapter 6, pre-state stratification can be based entirely on land rent without any reliance on taxation. In contrast, many economists concerned with state origins focus on technologies of confiscation where bandits, predators, gangs, or the state appropriate some portion of the output generated by producers. The primary issue in this literature is whether unorganized bandits will be replaced by an organized state that taxes the producers (see Section 11.4). This is an interesting question, but it is distinct from the question of whether an elite collects land rent.

To grasp this distinction, consider the following possibilities. In an agricultural setting it might be easy for a local elite to identify and punish trespassers (technology of exclusion), but difficult to seize output produced by commoners because food is easy to hide (technology of confiscation). This leads to land rent without taxation. On the other hand, it might be easy for roving bandits to seize food stores (confiscation), but hard for them to maintain permanent ownership rights over fixed land parcels (exclusion). This leads to taxation without land rent.

Our formal model in Chapter 10 begins with an agricultural economy where the elite controls land and collects rent but does not engage in taxation (perhaps because it is easy to hide food or long distances make the monitoring of agricultural activities costly). We will assume that urban manufacturing is readily taxed once it exists (perhaps because workshops are highly visible and cities are physically compact). In this setting we show that the elite confronts a tradeoff involving the land rent from agriculture versus the tax revenue from manufacturing. The challenge will be to identify conditions under which the balance tips toward the latter, in which case the elite establishes a city-state.

Most writers believe agriculture was a necessary condition for the existence of a state, and economists have examined the length of the lag between agriculture and state formation. Borcan et al. (2021) estimate the average lag to have been about 3,400 years for six pristine states (the same six we will discuss in Chapter 11). Their method of dating the transition to agriculture is to use the "approximate year in which a substantial population in some part of a country relied mainly on cultivated crops and domesticated animals for their subsistence" (10). They use two definitions of the state. Paramount chiefdoms that include multiple individually substantial chiefdoms count as proto-states, but specialized administration and soldiery are required for a full state. Much of their research deals with nonpristine state formation, which we will not address here.

Two common arguments about the necessity of agriculture for a state appear in the literature: (a) agriculture is needed in order to obtain food surpluses that can support state personnel (or urban populations); and (b) agriculture is needed in order to provide a sufficient tax base to finance state activities. Each argument has difficulties. A problem with (a) is that food surpluses are often defined in a purely technological way, as output relative to biological subsistence requirements. However, we argued in Section 6.2 that commoner food intake is not biologically fixed in stratified societies. Another issue is that agriculture is not the only possible source of food (see our discussion of wetlands in Mesopotamia in later sections). A problem with (b) is that this argument ignores issues with the technology of confiscation. As we suggested above, not all crops are equally useful for taxation purposes, and in some cases it may be considerably easier to tax urban manufacturing than rural agriculture.

Nevertheless, we believe that agriculture did play a crucial indirect role in pristine state formation. Our causal argument runs as follows: rising agricultural productivity led to rising population densities through Malthusian dynamics, and the rising population densities led to the formation of elite and commoner classes through the endogeneity of property rights (Chapter 6). Once stratification existed, several paths could lead to state formation, but this development was not inevitable, and different mechanisms appear to have been relevant in different regions. We postpone the details until Chapter 11 but we think pristine states had three main proximate causes: (i) a long run decline in commoner wages resulting from population growth and endogenous property rights that eventually led to urban manufacturing; (ii) chronic elite warfare that led to territorial expansion and defensive agglomeration; and (iii) climate changes that triggered migration toward refuge areas (often river valleys), again leading to declining wages and urban manufacturing.

Although sedentary foragers could and often did develop stratified societies, they lacked the technological dynamism resulting from domestication and learning by doing in agriculture, and therefore tended not to have persistently rising population densities over time. Moreover, as we discussed earlier, sedentary foraging is generally not an attractive target for tax collectors and is therefore an unpromising fiscal basis for a state.

In our view, the archaeological literature on pristine states supports the following qualified generalizations.

(a) Agriculture was a necessary condition for pristine states, but in some cases food obtained through foraging continued to be a significant component of the diet.
(b) Stratification was a necessary condition for pristine states, but a stratified core was often surrounded by an open-access periphery.

Note that agriculture may not have been a necessary condition purely for caloric reasons but also for its role in promoting stratification and providing a secure fiscal basis for the state. This chapter and Chapter 11 provide regional examples that illustrate these points.

Borcan et al. (2021) find statistical support for the idea that both agriculture and stratification played important roles in prehistoric political development. They use data from the Atlas of Cultural Evolution, which provides information on prehistoric societies defined by archaeological traditions. These are populations that had similar subsistence practices, technology, and sociopolitical organization; were spatially contiguous over a large area; and endured for a long time. Political integration, the dependent variable, was defined to be 1 for societies with integration above the community level and 0 otherwise (note that this includes simple and complex chiefdoms in addition to states). The authors regressed this variable on agriculture, stratification, population density, and urbanization in the year 4000 BP using observations on 74 societies.

Agriculture and stratification were both highly significant predictors of political integration, with a negative interaction between the two suggesting some substitutability between them. The other variables were less important. Although these cross-sectional findings do not shed any direct light on the causal dynamics central to our approach, and the definition of political integration is much broader than our definition of a state, we regard the results as consistent with our theoretical framework.

We begin our study of pristine states with southern Mesopotamia. Section 9.2 gives preliminary information. Sections 9.3–9.7 provide a chronological narrative for this region, including the pre-'Ubaid period (9.4), the 'Ubaid period (9.5), the Uruk period (9.6), and the post-Uruk period (9.7). In Section 9.8 we discuss several hypotheses about Mesopotamian city-state formation proposed by archaeologists and economists. Section 9.9 describes our own hypothesis, which will be formalized in Chapter 10. Section 9.10 is a brief conclusion. We defer acknowledgments of advice and financial support for this part of the book until the end of Chapter 11.

9.2 SOUTHERN MESOPOTAMIA

The city-states that emerged in southern Mesopotamia (also known as Sumer) by at least 5200 BP (calendar years before present) offer a sensible starting point for several reasons. They are often described as the first states; they have been subjected to intense archaeological study, especially the city-state of Uruk; and they had a major historical impact. Even so, debates on their origins continue, and economic reasoning may shed light on the issues at stake. We will start with a brief sketch of this transition. Empirical nuances and controversies are ignored in this section but will be addressed in detail later.

Southern Mesopotamia corresponds to modern southern Iraq. We structure the narrative using four time periods: the pre-'Ubaid, the 'Ubaid, the Uruk, and the post-Uruk. Authorities in the field assign different dates to these periods that sometimes vary widely. The beginning of the 'Ubaid period is dated in the range 8000–7500 BP, the beginning of the Uruk period is dated in the range 6300–5900 BP, and the beginning of the post-Uruk period is dated in the range 5100–4900 BP. We arbitrarily select the earliest date in each case in order to impose consistency throughout the chapter. Therefore in our scheme the 'Ubaid period runs from 8000–6300 BP, the Uruk period runs from 6300–5100 BP, and the post-Uruk period runs from 5100–4350 BP. These conventions about time periods have no substantive implications for our arguments.

We report dates in calendar years before present (BP) throughout. Some writers use dates BCE (before current era) and we have added 2,000 years in these cases. Thus if the original source reports that an event occurred in the 4th millennium BCE (4000–3000 BCE), we translate this as the 6th millennium BP (6000–5000 before present).

While it is generally agreed that city-states existed in southern Mesopotamia by 5200 BP, there is ambiguity over the date at which the first city-states appeared. In the Early Uruk period there was increasing immigration into Sumerian cities, but firm data on the extent of urbanization is unavailable. In roughly the same time period excavations reveal the existence of Tell Brak in northern Mesopotamia. Brak was a substantial city of 55 hectares, much larger than neighboring cities in the north but smaller than the southern city of Uruk (Ur et al., 2007). There is controversy over which location, Uruk or Brak, was the first to witness large-scale urbanization (see Pournelle and Algaze, 2014, 9–13). There is no controversy, however, in terms of relative historical importance. Tell Brak was largely abandoned in the 6th millennium BP. But the Sumerian cities, of which Uruk was by far the largest, continued to expand well into the 5th millennium BP, and as noted above are frequently described as the first states.

In the 'Ubaid period (8000–6300 BP), southern Mesopotamia developed a few towns of about 1000–2000 people and many smaller villages. This has sometimes been described as a system of "simple chiefdoms," with the larger settlements having temples and elite residences. Food was obtained from hunting, gathering, fishing, and farming.

During the Uruk period (6300–5100 BP), large-scale urbanization occurred. This culminated in a population of 20,000–50,000 for the city of Uruk and populations in the tens of thousands for nearby cities. Many authorities believe the urbanization process was triggered by adverse climatic changes, especially reduced rainfall. This encouraged migration toward southern Mesopotamia, where wetlands and river irrigation made food production less vulnerable to increasing aridity. These migratory responses could have caused spikes in local population at a few especially attractive sites in the south.

Urbanization was associated with the development of manufacturing, especially textiles, but also pottery, metallurgy, and stonework. Such activities had previously been carried out in smaller villages, but became more specialized and larger-scale in the new centers like Uruk. The evidence suggests that urban manufacturing had scale economies external to the individual workshop but internal to each city. There is an archaeological consensus that Uruk satisfied standard criteria for a city-state by 5200 BP if not earlier, including a large urban population, monumental architecture, specialized bureaucracy, a multitiered settlement hierarchy, colonial expansion, and in the final phase of the Uruk period, specialized commodity production and writing.

Next we provide a brief preview of our hypothesis about the economic sources of this transition (for a detailed verbal description see Section 9.9, and for a formal model see Chapter 10). We believe regional climate change in the form of increasing aridity reduced agricultural productivity in outlying areas including northern Mesopotamia. The result was a drop in the demand for commoner labor and a region-wide decrease in living standards for commoners. Simultaneously commoners migrated toward the south, where food production was less dependent on rainfall. Local elites in the south could pay lower wages in the form of rations to commoners, which made urban manufacturing attractive. We believe that manufacturing activities were more easily taxed than agriculture and that this provided the early fiscal foundations for the city-states of southern Mesopotamia.

Many other authors have proposed alternative hypotheses. We will review a number of them later in the chapter. But any credible hypothesis has to explain three main points. First, it needs to say why the population of southern Mesopotamia grew to a point at which large cities were possible. Second, it needs to say why such cities actually developed and were accompanied by large-scale manufacturing. Third, it needs to say why these were city-states; that is, why cities led to states in a region that previously had neither. Our theory accounts for each of these points.

9.3 ARCHAEOLOGICAL BACKGROUND

Our chronology involves a synthesis of facts, opinions, and interpretations from a number of archaeologists. Most statements reflect a wide consensus among the experts, to the extent that an outsider can judge. Where some issue is uncertain or controversial, we flag that issue for the reader. The archaeological literature includes debates not only about facts, but also about the causal mechanisms responsible for the emergence of the earliest city-states. We review these arguments in Section 9.8 along with related causal arguments from economists.

Problems associated with the lack of data or the interpretation of data are discussed by Algaze (2008, 2013), Nissen and Heine (2009), Brisch (2013), Pournelle (2013), Wilkinson (2013), and Pournelle and Algaze (2014), among others. In particular, Brisch (2013, 112) remarks that radiocarbon dating for ancient Mesopotamia is imprecise and difficult to link with historical events. In the absence of carbon dating, chronological analysis is based on ceramics. Ur (2013, 135) gives an example where a site with Uruk-period pottery was dated to the fourth millennium BCE (the sixth millennium BP). Also see Ur (2013, 132–136) for a summary of issues and methods pertaining to Mesopotamian settlement surveys.

Evidence for the period before 5200 BP comes entirely from archaeological findings (including seals, which pre-date writing). After this date written texts and tablets become available, but the earliest of these are difficult to interpret and offer no historical information.

9.4 THE PRE-'UBAID PERIOD: BEFORE 8000 BP

The source for information on this period is Kennett and Kennett (2006) except where indicated, but also see Brooks (2006, 2013) for a further discussion of geography and climate. At around 15,000 BP the global sea level was 100 m below today's level. Marine transgression into the Persian Gulf, associated with deglaciation, was just starting. The modern delta was absent. The Ur-Schatt river, carrying large volumes of sediments from the Tigris, Euphrates, and Karun rivers, flowed in an incised canyon. Climate was characterized by extreme aridity. Rapid sea level rise in the Persian Gulf occurred from 12,000 to 11,500 BP and 9500 to 8500 BP. Seasonal rainfall rose across the Arabian Peninsula and southern Mesopotamia between 10,000 and 6000 BP.

A transition from mobile hunting and gathering to sedentary agriculture occurred in southwest Asia between 12,000 and 8000 BP (see Chapters 4 and 5). Early villages in northern Mesopotamia had a few hundred people. Rainfall levels were often sufficient to support crop cultivation in northern and eastern Mesopotamia, but not sufficient in the south and west (Nissen and Heine, 2009, 2).

In the south, rivers created an immense alluvial plain that was nearly flat, such that small differences in elevation could result in large differences in the flow of water. The marine transgression reached the present-day northern Gulf area between 9000 and 8000 BP. From 9000 BP onward the rate of sea level increase slowed, and sea level may have reached a Holocene maximum at 6000 BP. At this point the Persian Gulf extended 200–250 km north of the current coastline, reaching the hinterlands of the settlements that would later become Ur and Uruk (Ur, 2013, 132). The area between the southern alluvial plain and the Persian Gulf was filled with marshes and lagoons. Estuaries extended north, following the Tigris–Euphrates–Karun River canyons, and formed a variety of productive wetland habitats throughout this region.

9.5 THE ʿUBAID PERIOD: 8000–6300 BP

The first evidence of permanent human settlement in southern Mesopotamia goes back to 8000 BP, the beginning of the ʿUbaid period. Early settlements were located on slight rises (turtlebacks) within aquatic habitats resulting from seasonal rains, or in the wetlands at the head of the Persian Gulf (Kennett and Kennett, 2006). These turtlebacks were the remains of river terraces cut during the Pleistocene. Over time the areas around the terraces were filled by river sediment and other early settlements are probably buried beneath silt deposits (Oates, 2014, 1480).

Algaze (2001, 2008, ch. 4) emphasizes several natural advantages of the region. Geography led to low transport costs through the use of rivers, the seacoast, and canals in flat terrain (the role of canals is controversial, as will be discussed below). Diverse local ecosystems included productive agricultural land due to river floods, nearby land suitable for grazing animals, and riverine, coastal, or marine areas where aquatic resources such as fish were available. Algaze (2008, 42) believes that these factors, along with favorable climate conditions including high winter rainfall and the possibility of some summer rain, supported a high population density at the mid-Holocene climatic optimum that prevailed during the ʿUbaid.

Throughout the ʿUbaid, human populations increased and nucleated into small towns and villages. By the middle ʿUbaid some communities in southern Mesopotamia had grown larger than their neighbors, including Eridu, ʾOuelli, Ur, and Tell al-ʾUbaid. However, these communities were still small, averaging about one hectare in area with estimated populations seldom exceeding 1000 people. They were also widely dispersed and lacked the linear distribution typical of settlements dependent on irrigation canals (Adams, 1981, 59).

In southern Mesopotamia and the Susiana Plain the number of known settlements increased, both due to greater archaeological visibility (larger sites are visible above the alluvium) as well as a larger regional population. A significant population expansion appears to have occurred in southern Mesopotamia during the 'Ubaid to Uruk transition around 6300 BP, but some areas such as the northern alluvium saw population decline as settlements became more concentrated in the south (Adams, 1981, 60–61).

According to Pollock (1999, 78–84), the primary food sources were wheat, barley, lentil, flax, caprids, cattle, pigs, fish, and hunting. Pollock believes that farmers paid land rent in goods or labor and made offerings to temples, but that production was not directly managed by elites (1999, 79–80). The distribution of wealth items within 'Ubaid sites is suggestive of economic inequality (Stein, 1994). There was mild inequality in housing, but there were no dramatic differences in grave goods and depictions of rulers were rare (Stein, 1994; Pollock, 1999, 86–92, 176–177, 199–204). Stone (2018) reports a "moderate" Gini coefficient for grave goods at Eridu, with all later Gini coefficients being higher.

A hierarchical distribution of settlements becomes visible in the middle 'Ubaid (Wright, 1981; Kennett and Kennett, 2006). Stein (1994) describes these as simple chiefdoms with a two-tier settlement hierarchy, where larger sites had temples. Stone tools, pottery, and cloth were made locally but metal ores and specialized stones such as obsidian would have been imported. Stein (1994) asserts that good agricultural land with easy irrigation was a scarce commodity to which access could be denied, and that this was the basis for chiefly power (but see the debate about irrigation below).

Temples played a prominent role in the 'Ubaid period. They were rectangular, oriented to the cardinal directions, and contained altars and offering tables. The temples were located at focal settlements throughout the region, a pattern that remained stable for 1500 years (Stein, 1994). The evidence from Eridu indicates that such temples tended to become larger and more elaborate over the course of the 'Ubaid. Stein (1994) argues that the 'Ubaid temple complex was used to legitimize differential access to resources including water, land, and labor, as agricultural production was intensified to sustain larger populations in the region. He also argues that temples mobilized food surpluses for storage and insurance purposes.

In Pollock's (1999) view, the 'Ubaid had some trade, probably no slavery, and probably no warfare except perhaps near the very end of the 'Ubaid. Stein (1994) sees no evidence for trade in exotic materials, and he agrees that warfare and political instability were absent. He also sees little evidence for elite control of long distance exchange or centralized control of high-status craft production. Kennett and Kennett (2006)

likewise agree that there is little evidence of warfare in southern
Mesopotamia until the end of the 'Ubaid. Settlements were unfortified
and 'Ubaid seals do not depict warfare. In contrast, there is evidence of
warfare in northern Mesopotamia during this period.

During the 'Ubaid southern Mesopotamia was linked to the surrounding region by social networks, and similarities in artifacts indicate widespread exchange of goods and knowledge. For example, 'Ubaid period
ceramics from the south appear in settlements in northern Mesopotamia
and along the eastern coast of the Arabian Peninsula (Kennett and
Kennett, 2006, 81; Oates, 2014, 1481). Such observations can be interpreted as evidence for cultural replication, migration, or political integration. Nissen (2015, 124) employs data from surface surveys to argue that
small 'Ubaid settlements were separated by large enough distances that
"they were not part of a regulated or central system." We follow what we
take to be the majority opinion in the literature that there were regional
markets for utilitarian goods, but without any political unification
beyond the two-tier system of a town and its associated villages or
hamlets.

There is a lively debate about the role of irrigation in the 'Ubaid and
subsequent Uruk periods. Many authors take it for granted that southern
Mesopotamia already had irrigation canals in the 'Ubaid. For example,
Kennett and Kennett (2006, 81) argue that reduced rainfall and a high
water table stimulated early experimentation with irrigated crops, and
Stein (1994) argues that the power of 'Ubaid chiefs was based on control
over irrigated land. Oates (2014, 1483–1484) distinguishes "the more
productive irrigation-based economy of the south versus the rain-fed
economy of the north."

However, Pournelle (2007, 2013) maintains that the wetlands provided abundant food even without irrigation or reliance on cereal crops.
Her sources include high quality satellite images, aerial surveys, hydro-
logical history, ancient sediments and watercourses, climate history, and
archaeological remains. She concludes that wetlands offered easy access
to fish, dates, birds, and turtles; fodder for domesticated goats, sheep, and
pigs; reeds for housing and watercraft; edible plants such as club rush,
cattails, and bulrush; and small mammals as well as migrating gazelles.
From this standpoint early cities can be imagined as "islands imbedded in
a marshy plain, situated on the borders and in the heart of vast deltaic
marshlands" (Pournelle, 2013, 28).

Wilkinson (2013, 35–40) accepts that wetlands were an important
source of food in the 'Ubaid, but uses evidence from charred plant

remains to argue that irrigated cereal cultivation also took place. He concludes that with the available data, it is not possible to determine which food source, cereal cultivation or wetland foraging, was more important to the 'Ubaid economy.

The relationship between irrigation and cereal cultivation follows from the pattern of seasonal flooding (information in this paragraph is from Wilkinson, 2013, 38–42). In southern Mesopotamia cultivated cereal crops were dependent on the use of river water due to the lack of rainfall. However, the timing of seasonal flooding in the Tigris and Euphrates caused problems. Flooding peaked in April and May as a result of winter rainfall and spring snowmelt in the mountains of Anatolia, Iran, and Iraq. Crops were endangered just as they were about to be harvested. Conversely, river levels were at their lowest in the fall when seedlings were most in need of water. Irrigation canals could be used to store excess water during the spring floods and then discharge it in the fall. Another problem was that hydromorphic soils, common in the flood basins and lower levee slopes of southern Mesopotamia, could become saline when the water table was high, leading to crop losses. This resulted in the extensive use of salt resistant barley as opposed to wheat.

9.6 THE URUK PERIOD: 6300–5100 BP

This section surveys information on urban population, specialized bureaucracy, settlement hierarchy, colonial expansion, and excavations of monumental architecture. All are normally treated in the literature as indicators of state-level organization.

In the Uruk period, the city of Uruk, the largest Sumerian city by far, achieved a population of 20,000–50,000, and several other substantial cities of smaller size came into existence (Yoffee, 2005, 43; Algaze, 2008, 103). Uruk covered an area of 250 ha with an urban core of 100 ha (Nissen, 1988; Kennett and Kennett, 2006; Nissen and Heine, 2009). For the early Uruk period, estimates of the share of the population living in relatively large towns (10 or more hectares) are in the range of 50–80% (Pollock, 2001; Algaze, 2013). By the end of the Uruk period, the city of Uruk plus its hinterland and offshoots had a total population estimated at 80–90,000 people (Algaze, 2013, 74).

Recently these population estimates have become controversial. While there is general agreement about the geographical size of Uruk around 5200 BP, the population estimate depends on density, which is more difficult to measure. Steinkeller (2018, 47), in comments on Algaze

(2018), argues that large unoccupied spaces existed within Uruk, reducing the total population estimate considerably. In private correspondence (2020), Algaze agrees with Steinkeller that Uruk was characterized by large open areas, which were recently documented in magnetometry surveys (Fassbinder et al., 2018). However, citing the excavation work of Postgate (1994) and his collaborators at Abu Salabikh and the remote sensing work of Stone (2017) at a variety of southern Mesopotamian urban sites, Algaze continues to believe that an estimate of 100 persons per occupied hectare is a reasonable, if somewhat minimal, conversion factor for demographic calculations of ancient southern Mesopotamian settlements. Such an estimate would yield a population around 25,000 for the city of Uruk in the Late Uruk period.

The presence of organizational complexity is inferred from lists of specialized administrative positions inscribed on clay tablets (Brisch, 2013). However, Algaze (2013, 72) points out that because most of the tablets were found in secondary contexts and date to the end of the Uruk period after city-state formation had already occurred, they "shed no light whatsoever on the beginnings of the urban revolution."

Another commonly used indicator of administrative specialization in state-level polities is a four-tier settlement pattern with cities, towns, villages, and hamlets (Adams, 1981). 'Ubaid settlement distributions were bi-modal, indicating a chiefdom level of organization (Nissen, 1988; Stein, 1994). According to Algaze (2008), survey evidence suggests that multimodal patterns typical of states were in place throughout the entire Uruk period.

In categorizing Uruk as a state, Algaze (2013, 82–85) gives particular weight to colonial expansion in the Middle and Late Uruk periods. He argues that such "massive, quickly erected and well planned enclaves ... could only have been built by state institutions capable of levying, commanding, and deploying substantial resources and labor" (85).

For most of the nineteenth and twentieth centuries, the excavations at Uruk were exclusively concerned with uncovering and analyzing monumental buildings (for details see Nissen, 1988, 96–100; Nissen and Heine, 2009, 22-26; Algaze, 2013, 75-79). As a result, the excavations revealed little else. Ur (2014, 14) notes that, "not a single non-monumental Uruk structure has been excavated on the southern Mesopotamian plain." Nissen and Heine (2009, 21) refer to the interval from the end of the 'Ubaid to 5200 BP as being "among the worst documented times of the history of the ancient Near East."

Algaze (2013, 71–72) summarizes the excavations as follows. First, excavations focused only on elite quarters of the city, not commoner residences or industrial areas. Except for a few deep soundings, most of the materials and buildings excavated date to the very end of the Uruk period after the city-state had already formed. There has been almost no systematic exploration of second-tier regional centers, villages, or hamlets. Nevertheless, estimates of the immense mobilization of labor and materials required to construct the buildings thus far exposed at the core of the site imply state-level control over labor as well as resource procurement and allocation.

There is general agreement that Uruk began as two settlements facing each other on opposite sides of a major channel of the ancient Euphrates. At an uncertain date the river shifted to a new course around the city, leaving the area between these two sites available for further settlement (Oates, 2014, 1484; Nissen, 2015, 116–117). The fact that Uruk was built with mud bricks confirms that it was on dry ground, but it was in close proximity to lowlands with a marshy environment. River water may have been used for irrigation on dry land located between the city and the surrounding wetlands.

There is likewise broad agreement that high levels of migration into southern Mesopotamia occurred in the Uruk period (Kennett and Kennett, 2006; Algaze, 2008, 2013, 2018; Nissen and Heine, 2009). Nissen (2015, 118, 126) describes an "enormous population increase" in the interval 6000–5500 BP, with the number of settlements in the hinterland of Uruk rising from 11 to more than 100, many of which were larger than the earlier settlements. Nissen believes this increase occurred within a short period of time, was more than could be accounted for by natural population growth, was associated with in-migration, and was linked to a drier climate that may have created new habitable land. To support the hypothesis of in-migration, Algaze cites Kouchuokos and Wilkinson (2007) for evidence of declining populations in northern Mesopotamia and southwestern Iran that appear roughly contemporaneous with population increase in the alluvium (see also Nissen and Heine, 2009, 40).

Because of the richness of the wetlands, archaeologists also stress the likelihood of high levels of migration to the wetlands prior to and during the Uruk period. Many of these immigrants would have become marsh dwelling herders and foragers. Pournelle and Algaze (2014, 13–20) use data sources from the last century to document a deltaic productive system that offers a picture of what rural life in the wetlands might have been like in prehistoric and ancient times. Potential confirming evidence from those times is hidden under deep layers of silt and in the impermanence of reed-constructed dwellings.

Climate change during the Uruk period is a key variable in several explanations of the origins of Uruk as a city-state, including our explanation. The climate phenomenon most relevant to the Uruk case is increasing aridity starting around 6000 BP. Kennett and Kennett (2006) report evidence from the Red Sea area indicating a marked trend toward greater aridity between 7000 and 5000 BP, which ultimately extended to Arabia and sub-Saharan Africa. After about 5500 BP, weakening monsoons led to more aridity over the Arabian Peninsula, with increasing dust transport in the Arabian Sea after 5300 BP. Aeolian deposits in deltaic sediments were most pronounced in southern Mesopotamia between 5000 and 4000 BP, and indicate severe aridity during this interval. Brooks (2006, 2013) links this overall climate trend to urbanization in southern Mesopotamia. He also views increasing aridity in Mesopotamia as part of a global climate transition related to solar radiation and the angle of the earth to the sun. For more on this global perspective, see the literature review in Roland et al. (2015, 209–210).

Direct evidence of the effect of increased aridity on cereal crops in northern Mesopotamia is provided in Riehl et al. (2014). The authors use carbon 13 measurements from ancient barley seeds sampled from northern Mesopotamia and the Levant to infer drought stress. Their study covers the period from 7500 BP to 2900 BP. The results show that favorable conditions prevailed from 7500 BP to 6000 BP. Then a downward trend began that reached a level of severe drought stress around 5500 BP and maximum drought stress at 5200 BP.

In the wetlands of southern Mesopotamia, Nissen and Heine (2009, 39) observe a relatively sudden shift to cooler and drier conditions starting about 5500 BP and associate it with less river flow than in previous millennia, fewer disastrous floods, more exposed land, and a dramatic increase in settlements in the hinterland of Uruk.

Crawford (2004, chs. 8–9; 2013) provides a useful summary of manufacturing and trade. Urban manufacturing included textile production, pottery making, metalworking, and stoneworking. Metals and stone were not available locally and had to be imported, along with precious stones and high quality timber for roofing (but also see Algaze, 2018, 36, on pine trees grown in the marshes a millennium later). Exports likely consisted of manufactured goods, primarily woolen textiles of varying quality. Cereals did not play a major role in cross-cultural long-distance trade. Trade flows increased significantly in the Uruk period. Following McCorriston (1997), Algaze (2008, 2013, 2018) emphasizes the transition from linen to wool textiles, and sees textiles as the most important of the urban manufacturing industries in terms of economic growth.

Presuming that the manufacture and export of textiles in the 6th millennium BP did not substantially diverge from later historically well-understood patterns dated to the 5th and 4th millennia BP, Algaze (2008, ch. 5) describes large urban workshops, which apparently adopted an extensive division of labor. Workshops were probably operated by state institutions, competing temples, and wealthy households. The existence of multiple workshops suggests that scale economies may have been partly internal to the production units and partly external. The degree of specialization among towns is unclear.

Precise estimates of the percentage of urban residents in the Uruk period who were employed in manufacturing are not available. Algaze (2018, 48) acknowledges that most were engaged in subsistence-related activities. But he also points out that "it is not always possible to sort ancient Mesopotamian productive activities into self-contained agrarian versus industrial categories owing to the substantial overlaps that existed between the two categories in terms of labor (seasonal workers), raw materials (e.g., wool, flax, skins, wood, and sesame oil), and energy sources (wood charcoal)."

There is little direct archaeological evidence for any form of taxation before written documents. However, Steinkeller (2015a, 17) believes corvée labor was used in the late Uruk period for harvest work, major building construction, maintenance of irrigation systems, and military service. Such work was of limited duration and owed to the state by all free citizens. Elites could substitute a payment in place of labor (see Steinkeller, 2015b, 138–153, for a detailed discussion of corvée). Under our definition, mandatory labor contributions involve confiscatory technology and constitute a form of taxation, as do mandatory payments by individual elite agents.

We also infer the presence of taxation in city-states from the existence of massive public architecture and multilevel administration. However, apart from corvée labor it is difficult to determine which sectors were taxed (agriculture, manufacturing, local trade, or external trade), or how taxes were levied (on income, wealth, sales, profits, imports, or exports). Liverani (2006, ch. 3) gives examples of taxes on cereals, manufacturing, trade, and raw materials, but the time period of these taxes is unclear, especially with respect to the question of whether they apply to the period of city-state formation before 5200 BP.

Because data from burial sites are not available for the Uruk period, there is no evidence from this source regarding the degree of stratification.

However, stratification with respect to housing does become more pronounced (Pollock, 1999, 204–205), and elites apparently had better access to meat than commoners (Pollock, 1999, 112). Based upon satellite imagery, Stone (2018) computes Gini coefficients for housing during the Uruk and subsequent Jemdet Nasr periods (see Section 9.7). Her estimates range from a low of 0.32 to a high of 0.57. According to Stone, housing data "suggest that the initial phase of social complexity in ancient Mesopotamia was associated with significant inequality" (249). Elite residents living close to temples enjoyed more spacious housing than those living in crowded residential areas elsewhere.

Another aspect of inequality in the Uruk period involves the relative political power of elites and commoners. On this, Graeber and Wengrow (2021, 297–302) point to three observations suggesting that elite rule was at least somewhat constrained: (1) monarchy was absent until the Early Dynastic period; (2) taxes in the form of corvée were paid by both elites and commoners; (3) there may have been popular councils and citizen assemblies (though these are more typically associated with the Early Dynastic period). In our view these observations do not contradict the evidence for increasing inequality in the Uruk and Jemdet Nasr periods, but they do suggest that oppression of the commoners was not absolute.

Slave labor was clearly used in the Uruk period (Englund, 2009). This may have involved prisoners of war (although see our remarks on warfare below) or farmers who became unfree when they were unable to pay off their debts. The proportions of free and slave labor in the urban and rural sectors are unknown.

Another indicator of the quality of life in prehistoric Uruk is life expectancy. Algaze (2018, 26) argues that mortality rates in Uruk would have been high due to poor sanitation and disease. He lists the following candidates for life threatening illnesses affecting dense urban populations in southern Mesopotamia: several types of malaria; hemorrhagic fevers of unknown origin; smallpox, chickenpox, and/or measles; early variants of bubonic plague; and tuberculosis, pneumonia, and/or pertussis. Chronic diseases included typhoid, cholera/dysentery, and hepatitis. He notes that these chronic diseases would have been particularly virulent among the young.

The standard indicators of warfare in prehistory are skeletal remains showing violence, city walls, settlements situated in locations that afforded defensive advantages, and visual depictions. For the Uruk period these indicators are largely lacking. Human skeletons were not analyzed or saved in the excavations. The construction of city walls is generally acknowledged to have occurred later in the Early Dynastic period.

Defensive locations are not obvious. In sum, our reading suggests that the extent of warfare within southern Mesopotamia in the Uruk period is largely unknown.

9.7 THE POST-URUK PERIOD: 5100–4350 BP

This section briefly sketches some developments after 5100 BP. Although we are mainly interested in the city-state formation process during the Uruk period, the next 750 years are of interest because written records are more informative, and one can observe the subsequent trajectory followed by city-states like Uruk, Kish, Nippur, Shuruppak, Isin, Lagash, Umma, and Ur, among others. Archaeological evidence supports the view that all of Sumer had a similar culture with minimal local variation during this time. For example, written scripts were similar across the region (Nissen and Heine, 2009, 42).

The Jemdet Nasr period starts around 5100 BP and is largely a continuation of the later Uruk. Wool supplanted linen in textile production, with linen comprising perhaps only 10% of total Sumerian output after 5000 BP (Wright, 2013, 397). Writing evolved in ways that allowed greater nuance, complexity, and speed. There were improvements in pottery technology that facilitated mass production, a trend starting in the middle Uruk period (Nissen and Heine, 2009, 42–43). The latter authors cite evidence of a city wall around Uruk and the beginning of large-scale canal and irrigation systems (46–48). Pournelle (2007, 2013) raises questions about the existence of a city wall at this time and contends that the observed straight alignment of watercourses indicates ancient transport routes rather than irrigation canals. Wilkinson (2013, 36) says, "Because the channels in the lower plain have a tendency towards straightness rather than being meandering, it is difficult to distinguish between natural and artificial channels." In contrast to the Uruk period, burials now become archaeologically visible, with extensive inequality in grave goods (Pollock, 1999, 206).

The Early Dynastic period runs from about 4900 BP to 4350 BP. There were written lists of kings, palaces gradually became architecturally distinct from temples and other large elite residences (Pollock, 1999, 48–51), and inequality of grave goods became more extreme (Pollock, 1999, 213–217). However, Stone (2018) computes lower figures for Gini coefficients on housing in the Early Dynastic relative to previous periods and she notes that kings described themselves as protectors of the weak from the strong. There is some possibility that popular assemblies existed side by side with kings.

The economy was dominated by large self-sufficient households centered around temples, palaces, and wealthy estates, where elite corporate groups owned both farm land and urban workshops (Pollock, 1999, 117–123, 147–148). The elites managed production directly and workers received rations of food and clothing. Some workforces were kin-based but other large workforces involved non-kin. Women and children were the main workers in large-scale cloth manufacturing. Slave labor was common and included prisoners of war. Uruk was a walled city-state.

During the Early Dynastic, the number of watercourses decreased with continued aridity (the information in this paragraph is from Nissen and Heine, 2009, 46–47). Some patches of land lost their access to naturally flowing water. Agricultural areas evolved into a system of "irrigation oases," each fed by a main canal that in turn was fed by river water. Populations in smaller settlements that were now without water tended to move into larger settlements, and by 4500 BP most of the population lived in cities. In some marginal areas, labor shifted toward herding, a semi-nomadic lifestyle.

Pournelle (2013, 24) agrees that during the Early Dynastic period, "aggregate site area increased even as the number of settlements fell." She attributes this to a migration of population from surrounding drying wetlands. Nevertheless, texts show the continuing importance of marsh resources like reeds, fish, fowl, pigs, and trees, as well as marsh-based products such as bitumen, boats, mats, and standardized fish baskets.

Warfare between cities is documented after 4600 BP and was motivated by conflict over food–producing areas. One example is a war between Lagash and Umma over the boundary between their rural hinterlands (Van de Mieroop, 1997, 33–34; Pollock, 1999, 181–84; Yoffee, 2005, 57). Kennett and Kennett (2006) and Algaze (2013) propose a causal link from warfare to the size of the urban population, with rural populations falling as people moved into the cities for protection. The first political unification of multiple city-states occurred through a series of conquests by Sargon around 4350 BP. This brought the Early Dynastic period to an end. The city of Uruk "remained occupied or was resettled at an urban scale for almost five thousand years" (Ur, 2013, 151).

9.8 EXISTING CAUSAL HYPOTHESES

This section reviews existing hypotheses about the development of city-states in southern Mesopotamia. These ideas provide context for the presentation of our theory in Section 9.9 and Chapter 10. We classify hypotheses into groups concerned mainly with (a) food supply; (b) climate and migration; (c) taxation of cereals; (d) manufacturing and trade; (e) warfare; and (f) religion. In each case we sketch the relevant ideas and identify a few problems or questions.

There appears to be a broad consensus that the climate of southern Mesopotamia was becoming more arid in the Uruk period, reflecting trends across the region. There is also a consensus that reduced rainfall outside the southern alluvium led to migration into the south where food availability was much less dependent on precipitation. Beyond this, individual authors begin to diverge in the stories they tell.

Food Supply: Pournelle (2007, 2013) and Pournelle and Algaze (2014) believe that due to abundant food resources in the wetlands, there is less need to conceptualize irrigation as being essential for the early cities in the alluvial lowlands. In their view this continued to be true after the Uruk period and perhaps into the Early Dynastic. Our sense is that Pournelle sees the productivity of wetlands as a permissive condition, allowing a transition to city-states but not compelling it. Pournelle does not explain how the use of wetlands for food was compatible with stratification in the ʿUbaid, or why urbanization occurred. She also does not explain why urbanization resulted in state organization. In response to Pournelle and Algaze (2014), Gibson (2014, 191–192) agrees that marshlands were important, but he stops short of concluding that marshes were the "mother" of cities. He writes, "That cities depended on marshes as much as on irrigation is clear from early cuneiform records, but I would question that they were the primary factor."

Climate and Migration: Nissen and Heine (2009) argue that drier conditions led to lower river levels and caused people to congregate at places with better water supplies. At first the availability of more dry land may have attracted population into the former wetlands and encouraged urbanization. Fewer disastrous floods may also have attracted larger populations to such centers. But eventually rising aridity required large irrigation systems to support the urban populations. In their view large-scale irrigation was more a result of urbanization than a cause. These authors identify Uruk as a state based upon its political and economic dominance over the surrounding area as well as its structured city government, but do not specify a causal link between urbanization and state institutions.

Kennett and Kennett (2006) agree that climate change triggered a migration into the cities of the south, probably due to declining labor productivity elsewhere relative to southern Mesopotamia. They believe that wetlands were an important food source but that irrigation was also important. They share the Nissen and Heine view that drying wetlands led to greater land area and at the same time led to congregation, urbanization, and taxation based on cereals. The latter point about taxation puts them into alignment with Mayshar et al. and Scott on state formation, as we will discuss below. With regard to urbanization, Kennett and Kennett (2006, 90–91) suggest that growing aridity between the end of the 'Ubaid and 5000 BP led to more competition for land and water resources, the concentration of the population in centers close to rivers and estuaries, and greater reliance on irrigation. They also suggest that the threat of war motivated migration from hinterlands to urban centers (90).

We make the following observations about Nissen and Heine (NH) and Kennett and Kennett (KK). In order for their stories to line up correctly with the timing of city-state emergence, the marshlands would have to dry out substantially earlier (i.e., in the Uruk period, not the Early Dynastic) from what Pournelle and Algaze appear to envisage. Another problem is that neither NH nor KK provide a detailed explanation for the urban agglomeration of the Uruk period. It is one thing to say that increasing aridity and lower river flow caused population to congregate in well–watered areas, but quite another thing to say that this led to cities of 20,000 or more people. Why did foragers or farmers agglomerate in a city? Why not spread out across the landscape to be close to food sources? If some people in the city were not producing food, what were they doing?

Taxation of Cereals: Mayshar et al. (2017, 630–631) consider ancient states in southern Mesopotamia as one case in a broader analysis of early states. Their general point is that when farming is transparent, for instance due to observable inputs such as available water for irrigation or homogeneity of the land, it is easier for elites to estimate output and thus to generate significant revenues through taxation. Although the focus in their 2017 article is not specifically on cereals, it is easy to imagine seasonal grains as a strong candidate for taxation because these are more transparent than other crops. The problem for tax collection and state formation in southern Mesopotamia, according to Mayshar et al. (2017), is that cereal outputs in that region were not especially transparent due to details of the irrigation process that would have made it hard for external observers (e.g., tax collectors) to estimate the true output of an individual elite estate and compare outputs across estates. While the elite estate managers knew their own outputs, they had an incentive not to reveal output and instead free ride on the financing of state formation.

In Mayshar et al. (2022) the focus is directly on cereal production. They include other aspects of appropriability in addition to transparency and measurement, especially durability and storage. Cereals, unlike other food sources such as tubers, can be stored for relatively long periods of time. Storage makes it easier for elites to appropriate grain output. They support their argument with extensive statistical analysis showing a strong empirical association between complex hierarchies (with states being a prime example) and cereal dependency. Land productivity has no effect after controlling for cereals.

Scott (2017), like Mayshar et al. (2022), argues that extensive cereal production was an essential source of tax revenue for emerging states. He then combines taxation with the climate change argument in Nissen and Heine (2009) to nail down the timing of state formation at Uruk. More specifically, Scott argues (120–122) that increasing aridity in the Uruk period caused a reduction in river levels, forcing the population to congregate in well-watered places and to become more urban. Another effect of increasing aridity was to diminish the productivity of wetland foraging, which reinforced the concentration of the population. The result was greater investment in irrigation canals in order to feed the increasingly urbanized population. Taxes on the newly expanded cereal output allowed city-states to form (128–136).

Allen et al. (2020) see state formation in southern Mesopotamia as a response to a series of river shifts that increased the demand for irrigation canals to replace river irrigation. Their hypothesis is that this collective action problem was solved by a social contract embodied in state formation. Statistical analysis supports the correlation of river shifts with city-state creation.

The hypotheses in this group, like others reviewed earlier, lack a clear reason for the formation of large cities, apart from a general tendency of population to concentrate in well-watered areas. Cereal taxation can potentially explain state formation, but it is unclear why the resulting states would not have been largely rural rather than urban.

Another difficulty for Mayshar et al., Scott, and Allen et al. involves timing. Small-scale cereal irrigation probably existed in the 'Ubaid period and probably generated land rent for the local elites, but no one argues that taxation of cereals in the 'Ubaid could have supported a state. Strong evidence for large-scale irrigation allowing high levels of cereal cultivation does not appear until the Jemdet Nasr or Early Dynastic period (Nissen and Heine, 2009; Wilkinson, 2013). This leaves a long gap during the Uruk period, when city-states with monumental architecture and other markers of state organization actually emerged. It is unclear how cereal taxation could have filled this chronological gap.

One possibility is a major improvement in the technology of food production in the centuries before large-scale irrigation becomes archaeologically visible. Liverani (2006, 15–19) and Mayshar et al. (2017, 630) stress technological innovation in agriculture. We will propose instead that the gap was filled by taxation of urban manufacturing. We note in this regard that the statistical analysis from Mayshar et al. (2022) does not control for urban manufacturing. Moreover, our theory provides a pathway to state formation that circumvents the taxation problem identified by Mayshar et al. (2017), namely the lack of transparency in Mesopotamian cereal cultivation. We return to these issues near the end of Section 9.9.

Manufacturing and Trade: Algaze (2001, 2008, 2013) adopts a quite different theoretical framework from the authors we have discussed so far. He focuses primarily on manufacturing, trade, and urbanization, with little discussion of climate or food production. The central idea for Algaze (2013) is that Smithian growth involving labor specialization raises productivity, and may temporarily outrun Malthusian population growth, leading to rising income per capita. However, population responds positively to productivity over time. Population growth encourages further specialization, yielding a virtuous circle. This central dynamic supports various related trends: increasing imports of raw materials to the south for processing; more exports of finished textiles to pay for imports; a general expansion in economic scale, along with import substitution; and a flow of captive labor to the south, both skilled and unskilled.

To our knowledge, Algaze is alone in the literature in arguing that manufacturing provided a reason for urbanization. But there are several puzzles in Algaze's account. One involves timing: there is no clear trigger that explains the development of city-states during 5500–5000 BP rather than some other time period.

A second puzzle is that while Algaze emphasizes the abrupt change in settlement patterns at the 'Ubaid/Uruk boundary, it is unclear why manufacturing or trade patterns would have shifted abruptly at this time in a manner that can account for the change in settlements. To be fair, Algaze (2018) clearly states that changes in manufacturing were not the initial cause of urbanization. But if not, then what was?

Most importantly, although Algaze maintains that productivity growth led to the expansion of trade and the formation of cities, he does not say why this led to a state. In Section 9.9 we will argue that our analysis offers answers to all three of these puzzles.

Warfare: We are not aware of any specialists in the field who believe that warfare was the central factor in the formation of southern Mesopotamian city-states. However, we make two points. First, as discussed in Section 9.5, some scholars believe there may have been warfare near the end of the 'Ubaid period. This would not be surprising given the climate deterioration at this time (see Chapter 7 for a model of climate shocks and early warfare). Second, both Kennett and Kennett (2006) and Algaze (2013) argue that much later in the Uruk period, warfare could have caused rural populations to flee to the cities for protection, which may have contributed to the size of the cities.

Religion: Algaze (2013, 75), inspired by Jacobsen (1976), suggests that cities arose from "the ideological attractions of living in centers where the gods themselves were thought to reside." The problem is that such religious ideas either go back to the 'Ubaid period and thus cannot serve as a trigger for urbanization in the Uruk period, or are an exogenous cultural mutation that coincides with city-state formation.

We do note, however, that our own theory about city-state formation will stress a falling wage for commoners, which we believe triggered the rise of urban manufacturing. In our approach the decrease in the wage is driven by climate change. But if people have non-economic reasons for wanting to be in a city, such as the threat of war or ideological convictions, this could expand the supply of urban labor and reduce wages beyond what we describe in Section 9.9, reinforcing the climate effect. However, the timing of these other effects did not necessarily coincide with urban manufacturing. Arguments of this kind also require a distinct urban labor market with a lower wage than in rural areas. In our model we will ignore such issues and assume a single wage for the entire region.

We conclude with a final point. The hypotheses reviewed in this section do not speak in any direct way to issues of stratification or inequality. They do not explain why 'Ubaid society had moderate inequality of grave goods (at Eridu) while later periods had uniformly higher Gini coefficients for grave goods (Section 9.5); why levels of housing inequality rose during the Uruk and Jemdet Nasr periods (Section 9.6); or why inequality of grave goods increased in the Early Dynastic (Section 9.7). Our theory in Section 9.9 and Chapter 10 accounts for such observations by showing how elites became better off and commoners became worse off in the early stages of city-state formation.

9.9 OUR CAUSAL HYPOTHESIS

A formal model of our own hypothesis about the Mesopotamian case is presented in Chapter 10. Here we provide a detailed verbal exposition. Our story borrows liberally from hypotheses reviewed in Section 9.8. In particular, we synthesize ideas about aridity and migration with Algaze's arguments about urban manufacturing. We agree with Scott (2017, 129, 135) and Mayshar et al. (2022, 3) that taxing wetland hunting and gathering would have been difficult due to a lack of transparency and appropriability. But we also argue, again using criteria of transparency and appropriability, that urban manufacturing was probably an easier target for taxation than rural agriculture in southern Mesopotamia (see Mayshar et al., 2017, 630–631), due to geographically compact production, visible workshop employment, and durable and storable outputs.

Our economic model for the rise of Mesopotamian city-states has the following structure. First consider an agricultural/foraging economy prior to urbanization. This can be interpreted as the 'Ubaid period. Food can be obtained from two areas: an open-access commons and a closed site controlled by a local elite. The results would be similar if we included multiple elite-controlled sites in the model but for simplicity we have only one. However, we do assume that individual elite agents have individual land parcels, which collectively add up to the fixed land area of the closed site. We sometimes use the term "estates" when referring to the land parcels owned by these individual agents.

The commons includes many small sites with diverse natural resources and food production techniques (such as farming, pastoralism, hunting, gathering, and/or fishing). There is a fixed regional population of commoners who are free to move anywhere in the commons. Alternatively, they could choose to work at the elite-controlled site.

Due to open access, in equilibrium all agents in the commons receive the same food per person. This is also the level of food per person that individual elite agents must pay in order to attract commoners to work on their estates at the closed site. Depending on context, we sometimes refer to food income per commoner as the commoner standard of living, the average product of food labor in the commons, the marginal product of food labor on elite estates, or simply "the wage." We emphasize that equality of food incomes among commoners is just a theoretical simplification. In reality we expect migration to respond to differences in living standards across the region and reduce these differences, without necessarily eliminating them completely.

The region-wide supply curve for labor is vertical in the short run due to a fixed population of commoners. The demand for labor has two sources: a demand curve from the river–irrigated elite site in the south, and a "demand curve" for labor in the commons. The latter is derived by computing the number of commoners who work in the commons at a given level of food income. We could add a third source of labor demand from elite-controlled but rain-dependent farms in the north. This would not alter our conclusions.

Both demand curves slope down because labor has diminishing returns when land and other natural resources are fixed. Summing these demands and equating aggregate demand with supply yields an equilibrium wage for the region as a whole. As mentioned in Section 9.1, while it is helpful for expositional purposes to assume that elite agents hire commoners in a labor market, our conclusions would be unchanged if commoners instead rented land from elite agents in a land market.

Now suppose some or all sites in the commons are vulnerable to aridity, so when rainfall starts to decline in the early Uruk period, output at such sites falls at a given level of labor input. Thus the "demand" for labor at the rainfall-dependent commons sites will drop. For the commons sites located in the wetlands of the south, the dominant view is that this process does not become severe until after the Uruk period, but eventually the wetlands dry out and become less productive, intensifying the decline in aggregate labor demand. Meanwhile the demand for labor at the elite site in the south is less affected by aridity due to local irrigation opportunities based on river water.

Increasing aridity causes a decline in the regional wage, and this causes the elite in the south to hire more commoners on their agricultural land. Thus commoners migrate from rainfall-dependent locations toward elite estates in the south and (initially) also foraging opportunities in the wetlands. This accounts for the evidence that the climate shift was accompanied by migration from the north to the south. It also accounts for the evidence of greater elite–commoner inequality, because land rents at the elite site were rising while wages were falling (keeping in mind that in our model, the total land area controlled by the elite is fixed).

In addition to food production, the regional economy had a latent manufacturing sector. When manufacturing became active, it exhibited aggregate increasing returns to scale, as long as the individual workshops were in close spatial proximity. In the model in Chapter 10, we attribute increasing returns to static Smithian forces of specialization and division of labor, although we believe dynamic processes of learning by doing and micro-invention were probably more important in the long run. These forces led to urban agglomeration.

We assume that manufactured goods were sold on a competitive regional market to all agents (both elite and commoner) at all sites. Manufacturing began when the wage became low enough relative to the productivity of manufacturing labor and the consumer demand for manufactured goods. As described above, the wage declined when climate deteriorated. Thus increasing aridity stimulated the formation of a manufacturing sector at the elite-controlled site.

As a benchmark we consider a free-entry equilibrium where any elite agent can establish an urban workshop when it is profitable to do so. The demand for labor now has three sources: the commons, elite agricultural estates, and manufacturing. The wage is determined by labor market clearing, the price of manufactured goods is determined by product market clearing, and the scale of urban manufacturing is determined by a zero-profit condition. We derive a threshold level for our climate parameter such that when commons productivity drops below this level, the manufacturing sector becomes active and urbanization occurs.

We next suppose that the elite at the closed site is organized enough to collect taxes from workshops based on the number of commoners they employ. We show in Chapter 10 that taxation of the workers themselves would give identical results. Though individual elite entrepreneurs are price takers, the elite as a whole has both monopoly and monopsony power. Specifically the elite can use the tax rate to limit the size of the urban sector, both driving up the output price and driving down the wage. The resulting profit is appropriated through the tax system and rebated to individual elite agents. In short, the elite taxes its members in order to enforce a cartel agreement. In our model tax revenue is used for private elite consumption, but in reality it was also used for public goods such as temples and to support state personnel.

In this framework the elite faces a tradeoff between land rent and manufacturing profit. For moderate climate deterioration, yielding a moderate decline in the commoner wage, the elite prefers to enjoy higher land rents and suppresses manufacturing. But for more severe climate deterioration and a correspondingly lower wage, the elite sets a tax rate at which manufacturing occurs. This yields a city-state with both urbanization and taxation. We show in Chapter 10 that elites became better off and commoners became worse off early in this process.

We close with some points of comparison between our hypothesis and those from Section 9.8. As with many other authors, we regard increasing aridity as the prime mover leading to city-state formation. We also believe the climate deterioration accounts for the evidence of migration to the south from other areas (northern Mesopotamia, southwestern Iran, and so on). One distinctive feature of our framework is that we link the exogenous climate shift to an endogenous decline in the commoner standard of living and increased use of commoner labor on elite agricultural estates. We also link the decline in the wage to elite incentives to promote urban manufacturing. We connect urbanization with state formation by arguing that urban manufacturing was an easier target for taxation than rural agriculture. And finally, we show that the elite may want to engage in taxation simply to enhance their own private consumption, even if they lack interest in public goods.

Because there has been much debate about the relative importance of food from the wetlands and food from agriculture, we stress that the qualitative implications of our theory do not depend on the initial richness of the wetlands or the rate at which they dried out. If there had been no wetlands at all, we would have defined the commons to be a set of open sites used for farming or pastoralism. If the wetlands were initially rich and dried out at the same rate as other sites in the commons, we would include wetland sites in our definition of the commons without changing our story. If the wetlands were initially rich and dried out more slowly, then migration from commons sites that were more vulnerable to aridity would still drive down the average product of labor at the wetland sites, and the wage paid by elites to commoners would still fall. At most, the role of the wetlands as a buffer would increase the size of the climate shift needed for city-state formation.

Our theory emphasizes wage reduction as the crucial stimulus to manufacturing, and in our model the land area controlled by the elite is fixed. However, some authors argue that increased aridity led to lower river levels and decreased flooding in the Uruk period. The resulting new land area available for settlement could have provided further incentives for manufacturing, which required contiguous land for worker residences and the exploitation of scale economies. We will return to this issue in Section 10.7.

In Section 9.8 we commented that the emphasis by Mayshar et al. (2017, 2022), Scott (2017), and Allen et al. (2020) on cereal taxation does not explain how the city-states were financed in the Uruk period, before large-scale irrigation projects appeared in the Jemdet Nasr and Early Dynastic periods. We propose that taxation of manufacturing filled this gap, and in our formal modeling we make the stark claim that this source of tax revenue was necessary and sufficient for city-states. Our story does not require technical innovation in the food production sector, which would have tended to increase the wage rather than decreasing it, making it harder to explain why urban manufacturing became profitable and why inequality between elites and commoners rose.

We would agree that in practice cereal taxation could have contributed something to the city-states of the Uruk period, but two factors probably limited revenues from this source. As Mayshar et al. (2017) mention, irrigated agriculture in southern Mesopotamia would not have been completely transparent for tax collectors. Moreover, the availability of wetland foods could have restrained demand for irrigated cereals and thus the potential tax revenues from such crops, until the wetlands eventually began to dry out.

We are doubtful that other revenue sources could have financed a state during the Uruk period. In particular, the lack of city walls suggests that little attempt was made to tax goods obtained in the surrounding wetlands or to tax trade directly (rather than taxing manufactured goods, some of which were exported and some of which were sold locally).

Although we agree with Algaze about the centrality of urban manufacturing, his story and ours have some important differences. Algaze asserts that productivity growth due to Smithian specialization, along with internal and external gains from trade, pulled labor into the cities. In contrast, we see climate-led reductions in the productivity of the commons as pushing labor into cities. One advantage of our approach is that it accounts for the timing of urbanization, and another is that it is consistent with evidence for rising elite–commoner inequality. Furthermore, we tend to think that learning by doing was an important source of urban productivity growth and it is hard to see how this process could have taken off without some initial trigger for manufacturing. Our climate story provides that trigger.

Pulling all of these elements together, we offer explanations for the following:

(a) The timing of city-state formation (increasing aridity due to climate change).
(b) Population growth in the south (migration due to declining productivity of food labor elsewhere in the region).
(c) Increasing inequality (falling wages and rising land rents).
(d) Urbanization (aggregate increasing returns to scale in manufacturing).
(e) State formation (taxation of urban manufacturing).

9.10 CONCLUSION

The next two chapters will elaborate on the ideas developed here. The first task is to build a formal model that captures the causal logic of Section 9.9, which we undertake in Chapter 10. The second task is to investigate whether our hypothesis about city-state formation in southern Mesopotamia can be generalized to other regions of the world. We address this question in Chapter 11. We will argue that although the climate mechanism has wider applicability, it is not universally relevant, and two other mechanisms are also important: one based on the model of property rights from Chapter 6, and another based on the model of elite warfare from Chapter 8.

10

Mesopotamian City-States

A Formal Model

10.1 INTRODUCTION

The preceding chapter provided a case study of city-state formation in southern Mesopotamia. We used archaeological evidence to construct a detailed chronology of events, and toward the end of the chapter we reviewed several attempts to explain these events. Specifically, we want to understand the transition from a set of relatively small and dispersed settlements to a few large cities with all the trappings of state power.

This chapter constructs a formal economic model embodying our own hypothesis about the transition to city-states in southern Mesopotamia. Like other economic models it is schematic, and is not meant to capture every archaeological fact from Chapter 9. We use economic logic to fill in gaps when the archaeological record does not speak directly to certain issues. As a result our hypothesis involves a degree of speculation, although of course the same is true for hypotheses advanced by other authors.

Having said that, we believe the theory presented in this chapter is consistent with the key facts, captures the key causal factors, and suggests questions that archaeologists could investigate in the future. We also ask the reader to consider the merits of our story not in isolation but in comparison with the alternative stories from Section 9.8. As we will argue later (Section 10.7), our theory often explains observations that other theories do not. We already gave a detailed verbal exposition of our story in Section 9.9 and will not repeat that discussion here. The rest of this introduction outlines the structure of the present chapter.

Section 10.2 introduces basic assumptions and describes an initial equilibrium for an agricultural society. Food can be produced in a commons where sites are open to all, and at a single closed site controlled by a local elite. In this setting we derive the effects of climate change on the wage and the allocation of labor between open and closed sites.

Section 10.3 describes the manufacturing sector and characterizes the conditions under which such a sector would emerge, assuming no taxation and free entry by firms controlled by individual elite agents who are price-takers in the markets for labor, food, and manufactured output. Due to aggregate increasing returns to scale, manufacturing develops at a single site (the one that is under elite control). We interpret the resulting agglomeration of population as an urbanization process.

Section 10.4 extends the model to include taxation of the manufacturing sector by the elite, where we assume the elite as a whole behaves collusively and uses taxation as a cartel enforcement device. By limiting employment in the manufacturing sector, taxation drives down the wage paid to commoners and drives up the price at which manufactured goods are sold. In place of the zero-profit equilibrium arising under free entry, the elite now captures positive profit in the form of tax revenue, which is rebated to the individual elite agents and enhances their private consumption. A large negative climate shock can lead to the emergence of a manufacturing sector. Given our definition of the state as an organized elite that can collect taxes, these theoretical results provide an explanation for the formation of city-states in southern Mesopotamia.

The next two sections develop further implications of the model. Section 10.5 is devoted to the effects of the transition on elite and commoner welfare. We show that in the early stages of city-state formation elites always become better off and commoners always become worse off. However, when the manufacturing sector is large the impact on commoners becomes ambiguous. Section 10.6 explores the question of whether long-run Malthusian population dynamics would undo the conclusions derived from our short run framework. We show that with certain assumptions about parameter values, our key results continue to hold in a long-run setting with endogenous population.

The remaining three sections are verbal. Section 10.7 discusses how the model accounts for the archaeological facts described in Chapter 9 and compares our framework with the alternative hypotheses in Section 9.8. Section 10.8 offers closing thoughts and Section 10.9 is a very brief postscript (we postpone acknowledgments of assistance until the postscript in Chapter 11). We do try to provide some intuition for non-economists in Sections 10.2–10.6 but these are unavoidably mathematical. Readers not interested in the math can skip sections 10.2–10.6 and proceed directly to Section 10.7. Proofs of all formal propositions are available at cambridge.org/economicprehistory.

10.2 STRATIFICATION

We begin with a model of the 'Ubaid period prior to urbanization. The only consumption good is food, which is produced using inputs of labor and land. Food production takes place at two locations: an open-access commons dependent on rainfall and a special closed site called U. The commons includes many small sites with varying land areas. Site U is an 'Ubaid town and the future city of Uruk. Food production at site U makes use of river-based irrigation. Thus production in the commons is vulnerable to drought but production at site U is not. A local elite controls access to the land at site U while the commons is beyond elite control.

Geographically the commons may include areas of northern Mesopotamia, areas of southwestern Iran, or wetlands in the south. These areas were not all equally exposed to drought, and the effects of aridity arrived at different times in different places. For example, wetland foraging was probably not initially vulnerable to reduced rainfall, but eventually the wetlands began to contract. We suppress these details and assume in the model that aridity affected all sites in the commons simultaneously.

In our approach the formation of a city-state does not require interaction with any other incipient city-state, so we simplify by having a single site of this kind. Section 10.8 will discuss how the theory would change if we had multiple sites controlled by distinct local elites, leading to the formation of multiple city-states.

We refer to all food production generically as "agriculture," although pastoralism and foraging may also have been important in the commons and herding may have been important at the closed site U. We assume site U has a fixed total land area and access to irrigation. It is divided equally into land parcels controlled by individual elite landlords. We refer to these individual land parcels as "estates."

There is a fixed population of commoners who can use any site in the commons. We ignore the costs of moving from one site to another. Commoners may also work on elite-controlled agricultural land. Due to open access, all agents throughout the commons have the same food income, and this is also the amount of food the individual elite agents must offer in order to attract commoners to work on their estates. We call this the wage. As mentioned in Section 9.1, our conclusions would be the same if commoners instead handed over some of their food output to elite landlords as a rental payment.

The assumption of zero mobility costs across sites implies that we have a regional "labor market" encompassing all open sites, whether located in the north or in the southern wetlands, as well as the closed site controlled by the southern elite. Importantly, we do not have separate labor markets with separate wages in different parts of Mesopotamia. For simplicity, we ignore any potential role for elites located in northern Mesopotamia. The existence of such elites would not affect our qualitative conclusions.

Each agent is endowed with one unit of time and maximizes food consumption. As in Chapters 6–8 we use a Cobb–Douglas production function for food. First consider the commons, which has total population C and total land area Z. The total food output from the commons is

$$Y_c = \theta C^\alpha Z^{1-\alpha} \qquad \text{with } 0 < \alpha < 1 \qquad (10.1)$$

The parameter θ captures the effect of rainfall on food output in the commons. At some points we consider the case $\theta = 0$, which is equivalent to a situation where no commons exists, but $0 < \theta < 1$ will be assumed unless otherwise stated.

Equation (10.1) is an aggregate production function. We think of the commons as including many small sites, each with the same Cobb–Douglas technology but possibly with different land areas. Due to free mobility, the population C is distributed in a way that equalizes the average product of labor across sites. The Cobb–Douglas assumption implies that the marginal product of labor is also equalized, so total food is maximized for the commons population C. This yields (10.1). Food per person in the commons is

$$w = \theta(Z/C)^{1-\alpha} \qquad (10.2)$$

Site U has the farming population F and one unit of land. Its food output is

$$Y_u = F^\alpha \qquad \text{with } 0 < \alpha < 1 \qquad (10.3)$$

Land at site U is irrigated using river water, so rainfall is irrelevant. We impose $0 \leq \theta \leq 1$ so the commons is less productive. Irrigated sites may also have had some problems with aridity due to lower river flows and shifting river channels, but we ignore this and assume irrigation systems could be expanded when needed to cope with these problems. Another wrinkle is that aridity led to some drying of the marshes and a corresponding increase in the land area available for elite-controlled agriculture. We do not include this change in land endowments in the formal model but will discuss the likely effects in Section 10.7.

To study inequality we assume that if an organized group occupies a site, has a density of $e > o$ agents per unit of land as in Chapter 8, and uses all of its time to exclude other agents, it enjoys collective property rights over the land at that site. Such a group will be called an *elite*. When a non-elite agent threatens the property rights of an elite agent, the latter can call upon other nearby landlords for help in repelling the intruder. In principle this could occur not only at site U but also at the sites in the commons, if those sites have enough elite agents per unit of land. The parameter e might vary as a function of geography (it may be easier to defend property rights over land on a flat alluvial plain than in wetlands or mountains) but here we assume it is identical for all sites.

Non-elite agents will be called *commoners* regardless of whether they work at a site in the commons or on elite land at site U. Commoners are unorganized in the sense that landlords only need to repel or deter them one at a time in order to maintain control over land. This resembles our model of inequality from Chapter 6. By contrast with the model from Chapter 6 but like the model in Chapter 8, we ignore farm labor supplied by the elite agents. We also ignore warfare, which involves conflict between two organized groups (Chapters 7 and 8). The commoners at site U are free to exit to the commons if they wish (they are not slaves). There is good evidence that slavery existed at Uruk but our model still applies as long as there was also a sufficiently large free labor force.

The regional population N is divided into classes of size (C, F, e) such that

$$C + F + e = N \tag{10.4}$$

$N > e$ is assumed throughout so there is a positive number of commoners $C + F$. Total population N is exogenous in Sections 10.2–10.5 but endogenous in Section 10.6.

Landlords treat the food per person w from (10.2) as a parametric wage because the standard of living in the commons determines what must be offered to attract and retain farm labor at site U. These wages are paid in the form of food. As in Chapter 8, the rent to the landlord is the output of food net of such wage payments.

An individual elite agent has an estate with $1/e$ land units and hires n commoners to maximize $n^{\alpha}(1/e)^{1-\alpha} - wn$. This results in the individual labor demand $n = (\alpha/w)^{1/(1-\alpha)}/e$. Multiplying by the number of elite agents gives the total demand for farm labor at site U:

$$F(w) = (\alpha/w)^{1/(1-\alpha)} \qquad (10.5)$$

Total land rent for the elite is

$$R(w) = F(w)^\alpha - wF(w) \qquad (10.6)$$
$$= (1-\alpha)(\alpha/w)^{\alpha/(1-\alpha)}$$

Food per elite agent is $R(w)/e$.

It will often be convenient to aggregate agricultural output from the commons and site U. Let $Y_a = Y_c + Y_u$ be total food output and let $A = C + F$ be total agricultural labor. Using (10.1) and (10.3) and the fact that the marginal product of labor at site U is equal to the average product of labor in the commons, we obtain

$$C = AZ\theta^{1/(1-\alpha)}/\beta(\theta) \qquad (10.7)$$
$$F = A\alpha^{1/(1-\alpha)}/\beta(\theta) \qquad \text{where } \beta(\theta) \equiv \alpha^{1/(1-\alpha)} + Z\theta^{1/(1-\alpha)}$$

Total food Y_a as a function of total agricultural labor A is

$$Y_a = Y(A, \theta) = \gamma(\theta)A^\alpha \qquad \text{where } \gamma(\theta) \equiv \left[\alpha^{\alpha/(1-\alpha)} + Z\theta^{1/(1-\alpha)}\right]/\beta(\theta)^\alpha$$
$$(10.8)$$

Because the marginal products of labor are not equated between the commons and site U, this aggregate output is below the theoretical maximum.

Equations (10.2) and (10.5) give a relationship between the wage and the total demand for agricultural labor at all sites in the region (the commons and site U together):

$$A(w, \theta) = \beta(\theta)/w^{1/(1-\alpha)} \qquad (10.9)$$

In a purely agricultural economy the equilibrium wage equates this total labor demand to the total supply of commoners N - e.

Definition 10.1

The wage $w(\theta)$ is an *agricultural equilibrium* associated with the commons productivity θ when $A[w(\theta), \theta] = N-e$ or equivalently $w(\theta) = [\beta(\theta)/(N-e)]^{1-\alpha}$.

In an equilibrium of this kind (10.7) gives $C = (N-e)Z\theta^{1/(1-\alpha)}/\beta$ and $F = (N-e)\alpha^{1/(1-\alpha)}/\beta$.

Two restrictions ensure open access in the commons and stratification at site U.

Definition 10.2

An agricultural equilibrium satisfies the *stratification constraints* when

(a) $C/Z < e$ so commons population density is too low to support elites, and

(b) $R(w)/e \geq w$ so elite agents at site U are at least as well off as commoners.

Proposition 10.1 (stratification).

A necessary condition for an agricultural equilibrium to satisfy both stratification constraints is

$$\theta < \alpha^\alpha (1 - \alpha)^{1-\alpha} \equiv \theta_{\max} \qquad (10.10)$$

When (10.10) holds, both stratification constraints are satisfied if and only if

$$e\beta(\theta)/(1-\alpha)\alpha^{\alpha/(1-\alpha)} \leq N - e < e\beta(\theta)/\theta^{1/(1-\alpha)} \qquad (10.11)$$

where the set of N values from (10.11) is non-empty. The lower bound in (10.11) is an increasing function of θ and the upper bound in (10.11) is a decreasing function of θ.

Condition (10.10) says that the productivity of the commons must be low enough relative to the productivity of site U (normalized at unity). If the sites in the commons are highly productive, two things happen. First, agents migrate into the commons, which can propel the population density there beyond the threshold e, resulting in the formation of elites. Second, a highly productive commons implies a high wage, which can make it unprofitable to be a member of the elite at U. When (10.10) is violated, at least one of these outcomes must occur. When (10.10) holds, there are commoner population levels N–e that satisfy both stratification constraints. The set of (N–e, θ) points for which this is true is shown in Figure 10.1.

When rainfall declines in the commons, θ falls while productivity at site U is left unchanged. The wage from D10.1 decreases, yielding less food per capita in the commons. Labor is reallocated away from the commons (C falls and F rises) because landlords hire more commoners at the lower wage. As a result total land rent R(w) rises. It is easy to see from Figure 10.1 that for a fixed population N, if both stratification constraints

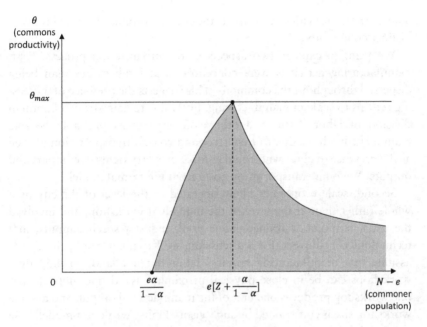

FIGURE 10.1. Stratification constraints

were satisfied initially then the same must be true after θ decreases due to lower rainfall.

Section 10.3 will show that a wage reduction of this kind can lead to urbanization at site U. One might think that similar results could occur if the agricultural productivity of site U rose for technological or environmental reasons. This would pull labor into site U rather than pushing it out of the commons. However, higher agricultural productivity at U would cause elite landlords to bid up the wage, which would not provide the same stimulus to manufacturing as a wage reduction caused by a drought in the commons.

10.3 URBANIZATION

Here we build on the model of Section 10.2 to show how urbanization could have occurred in the Uruk period. Rather than having just one consumption good we will have two: food (y) and manufactured goods (m). Prior to urbanization, manufactured goods such as textiles, pottery, and metal objects were produced by local specialists or farmers. We ignore these activities and treat the goods produced in cities as a distinct commodity.

We want to capture two aspects of the urbanization process. First, manufacturing activities were concentrated at Uruk rather than being dispersed throughout the commons. This suggests the presence of increasing returns to scale in manufacturing, likely due to gains from a Smithian division of labor. Uruk and other southern towns probably became manufacturing hubs due to easy river and coastal transportation as well as the presence of elites who could enforce property rights over inputs and outputs. We omit transportation costs from the formal model.

Second, scale economies likely operated at the level of the city as a whole rather than at the level of the individual workshop, and involved the usual suspects: a trained labor pool, industry-specific inputs, and technological spillovers (for a discussion, see Krugman, 1991, ch. 2). We assume that manufacturing requires labor but not land, so individual workshops can be in close physical proximity. We define units so that one workshop produces one unit of the manufactured output, and assume workshop size is constrained by supervisory limits. We do not model these managerial constraints and ignore the discrete nature of individual workshops.

We want to study the transition from a boundary solution with no manufacturing to an interior solution with positive manufacturing. Similar issues arose in Chapters 3–5, where we started with zero levels for the use of certain natural resources, for sedentary technology, or for agricultural technology, and derived the conditions under which these levels would become positive. The Cobb–Douglas functional form is not suitable for this purpose because the marginal product of labor approaches infinity as the quantity of labor approaches zero. Therefore we characterize the manufacturing sector using exponential functions for demand and cost that imply finite vertical intercepts at zero. For simplicity as well as consistency with the technological assumptions of Chapters 6–8 we continue to use the Cobb–Douglas functional form for agriculture, where boundary solutions will play no role in our analysis.

Consider the demand for manufactured goods. Each agent (elite and commoner) has the identical quasi-linear utility function

$$u(m, y) = b(m) + y \quad \text{where } b(m) = 1 - e^{-qm} \quad \text{with } q > 0 \quad (10.12)$$

This functional form has $b(0) = 0$ with $b'(m) > 0$ and $b''(m) < 0$ for all $m \geq 0$. It also has finite marginal utility $b'(0) = q$ at zero consumption, so boundary equilibria without any manufacturing can occur. The price of the manufactured good is p, the price of food is unity, and income is x, so the budget constraint associated with (10.12) is pm + y = x. The non-negativity constraint y ≥ 0 is ignored because this requirement is satisfied for all of the equilibria studied in this section.

There is a regional market for the m good so the price p applies both at site U and in the commons. All agents are price-takers. Let M be the aggregate market demand for the manufacturing sector. Because agents have identical preferences and the distribution of income can be ignored due to quasi-linearity, M satisfies

$$M = 0 \quad \text{for } p \geq b'(0) = q \quad \text{and} \qquad (10.13)$$
$$b'(M/N) = p \quad \text{for } p \leq b'(0) = q$$

Next consider the supply side. Labor is the only input for manufacturing. Let L be the workforce in this sector. The total output of the manufactured good at site U is

$$M(L) = e^{rL} - 1 \quad \text{with } r > 0 \qquad (10.14)$$

This functional form has $M(0) = 0$ with $M'(L) > 0$ and $M''(L) > 0$ for all $L \geq 0$. The sign of the second derivative yields aggregate increasing returns. The marginal product $M'(0) = r$ at zero input is positive and finite.

Due to increasing returns, we replace the standard supply curve with a zero-profit condition

$$pM(L) = wL \qquad (10.15)$$

Zero profit is maintained through free entry and exit by manufacturing workshops, where the individual elite entrepreneurs at site U are price-takers for both inputs and outputs.

We now extend the definition of equilibrium from D10.1 to include manufacturing.

Definition 10.3
The array (p°, w°, A°, L°) is a *zero-profit equilibrium* associated with the commons productivity θ when the following conditions hold.

(a)	consumer optimization:	$p° = b'[M(L°)/N]$	if $L° > 0$ or
		$p° \geq b'(0)$	if $L° = 0$
(b)	manufacturing equilibrium:	$w° = p°M(L°)/L°$	if $L° > 0$ or
		$w° \geq p°M'(0)$	if $L° = 0$
(c)	agricultural equilibrium:	$A° = A(w°, θ)$	
(d)	labor market equilibrium:	$A° + L° + e = N.$	

Condition (a) requires that consumer demand for manufactured goods at the price $p°$ add up to the amount $M(L°)$ produced by firms. If no manufactured goods are produced, we allow any price $p°$ that is sufficiently high to choke off demand. Condition (b) requires that if the manufacturing sector is active, firms receive zero profit. When $L° = o$, we set the average product of labor equal to the marginal product, and allow any wage $w°$ at or above the value of this average product. Thus profit is non-positive and there is no entry into manufacturing. Condition (c) requires that farm labor in the commons and on elite estates add up to total agricultural labor at the wage $w°$. This always implies that $A° > o$. Finally, condition (d) requires that total labor by commoners add up to the supply $N-e$. The food market clears automatically due to Walras's Law.

An equilibrium with positive manufactured goods $(L° > o)$ requires

$$b'[M(L°)/N]M(L°)/L° = w° \quad \text{and} \tag{10.16}$$
$$[\beta(\theta)/(N-e-L°)]^{1-\alpha} = w°$$

where the first equation comes from (a) and (b) in D10.3 and the second equation comes from (c) and (d) in D10.3. Together these yield

$$\beta(\theta)^{1-\alpha} = (N-e-L°)^{1-\alpha}b'[M(L°)/N] \, M(L°)/L°$$
$$\text{where } \beta(\theta) \equiv \alpha^{1/(1-\alpha)} + Z\theta^{1/(1-\alpha)} \tag{10.17}$$

To avoid complications involving multiple equilibria for a given value of θ, we want to guarantee that the right side of (10.17) is decreasing in L. The term involving the supply of agricultural labor $A = N-e-L$ is clearly decreasing in L. Thus it is sufficient for the average value product $b'[M(L)/N] \, M(L)/L$ to be non-increasing in L. Condition A10.1 ensures that this is true.

Assumption 10.1
   $q/N \geq 1/2$

Lemma 10.1
   Define $\phi(L) \equiv b'[M(L)/N] \, M(L)/L$. We have $\phi(o) = qr$ and $\phi(L) \to o$ as $L \to \infty$. If A10.1 holds, $\phi(L)$ is decreasing for all $L > o$. If A10.1 does not hold, there is some $L_c > o$ such that $\phi(L)$ is increasing for $L < L_c$ and decreasing for $L > L_c$.

A10.1 does not involve r so this parameter is irrelevant. We only need enough concavity in the utility function relative to the population N.

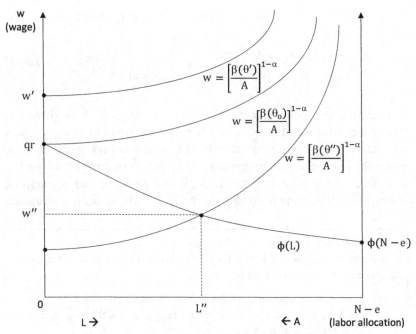

FIGURE 10.2. Labor allocation in zero-profit equilibrium

A zero-profit equilibrium as in D10.3 with $(A^\circ, L^\circ) > 0$ is stable in the sense that if the prices p and w adjust rapidly to a given labor allocation $(A, L) > 0$, profit will be positive when $L < L^\circ$ so new workshops enter, while profit will be negative when $L > L^\circ$ so some existing workshops exit.

Assuming A10.1 holds, the nature of zero-profit equilibrium is shown in Figure 10.2. The horizontal axis shows manufacturing labor L from left to right and agricultural labor A from right to left. These must sum to N−e to clear the labor market. The vertical axis shows the wage. At a high enough value θ' for the commons productivity, the demand curve for agricultural labor from (10.9) does not intersect $\phi(L)$ and we have an agricultural equilibrium where $L^\circ = 0$ as in Section 10.2. In this situation the wage w' that clears the labor market is too high to make manufacturing attractive. At the productivity level θ_0 the wage is qr and again $L^\circ = 0$. But if productivity falls to $\theta'' < \theta_0$ the system moves to an interior equilibrium with the manufacturing labor $L^\circ = L'' > 0$ and the wage w''. This marks the start of urbanization. Under present assumptions the level of manufacturing labor is a continuous function of θ so the transition does not involve any abrupt jumps.

To formalize these ideas we derive the boundary productivity θ_0 by setting $L^\circ = 0$ in (10.17). This yields

$$\beta(\theta_0)^{1-\alpha} = qr(N-e)^{1-\alpha} \qquad \text{or} \qquad (10.18)$$

$$\theta_0 \equiv \left\{ \left[(qr)^{1/(1-\alpha)}(N-e) - \alpha^{1/(1-\alpha)} \right] / Z \right\}^{1-\alpha}$$

Note that $\theta_0 > 0$ holds if and only if $N - e > (\alpha/qr)^{1/(1-\alpha)}$ so there is a large enough supply of commoner labor. If there are too few commoners then demand for agricultural labor by elite estates always keeps the wage above the level needed to trigger manufacturing, even if the commons has zero productivity (so in effect there is no commons). In such a situation, the causal link running from climate change to urbanization is disabled.

Proposition 10.2 (zero-profit equilibrium).
  Assume A10.1 holds. If $\theta_0 \leq 0$ then only part (a) below applies. If $\theta_0 > 0$ then both parts (a) and (b) apply.

  (a) A zero-profit equilibrium with $L^\circ = 0$ exists if and only if $\theta_0 \leq \theta$. For any such θ the wage w° is the same as in the agricultural equilibrium from D10.1 in Section 10.2.
  (b) A zero-profit equilibrium with $L^\circ > 0$ exists if and only if $0 \leq \theta < \theta_0$. For any such θ the associated equilibrium is unique. On this interval
    (i) The equilibrium values $(p^\circ, w^\circ, A^\circ, L^\circ)$ are differentiable functions of θ.
    (ii) The variables $(p^\circ, w^\circ, A^\circ)$ move in the same direction as θ. The variable L° moves in the opposite direction from θ.
    (iii) As $\theta \to \theta_0$ from below, we have $p^\circ \to q$, $w^\circ \to qr$, $A^\circ \to N-e$, and $L^\circ \to 0$. The equilibrium values of these variables are continuous at θ_0.
    (iv) For $\theta = 0$ we have $(p^\circ, w^\circ, A^\circ, L^\circ) > 0$

These results show that a drop in commons productivity from the interval in (a) to the interval in (b) leads to positive manufacturing output. This can only occur when the boundary value θ_0 is strictly positive. Taking the commoner labor supply $N-e$ as given, this requirement places a lower bound on qr (the average value product of manufacturing labor evaluated at zero input) through (10.18). When qr is too small, the elite's demand for farm labor always keeps the wage too high to make urban workshops profitable.

For an interesting model we need $\theta_0 < \theta_{max}$ where the upper bound comes from (10.10). Otherwise it would be impossible to have an agricultural equilibrium satisfying the stratification constraints from Section 10.2. It can be shown that if these constraints are satisfied in an agricultural equilibrium with $\theta_0 \leq \theta < \theta_{max}$, they remain satisfied when $\theta < \theta_0$ so manufacturing occurs. Thus open access persists in the commons and elite control persists at site U.

10.4 TAXATION

The model in Section 10.3 showed that climate change could trigger urbanization, but not why the resulting cities would also be states. Here we extend the model to show why the emergence of a city coincided with the emergence of a centralized fiscal system. We assume the elite at Uruk was organized enough to tax its own members and punish individuals who did not comply. The punishments could have involved physical force, social ostracism up to and including expulsion from the elite, or supernatural sanctions. The question is whether the elite as a whole would have gained from such taxation. We suggest that one motivation for a tax system would have been its usefulness as a cartel enforcement device.

Individual elite agents are wage takers in the labor market and price takers in the product market because they are small relative to the size of each market. However, as a group the elite confronts an upward sloping labor supply curve and a downward sloping product demand curve for manufacturing. The elite understands that if it can collectively restrict labor input (and thus output) in this sector, it can drive down the wage and drive up the output price. Starting from a zero-profit equilibrium this yields positive profit.

In our model tax revenue is rebated to individual elite agents and used for private consumption. This revenue is identical to the profit of the manufacturing sector. It is not important whether taxes nominally fell on elites or commoners, or whether workshops were taxed based on their inputs or outputs. We adopt the convenient assumption that a tax was levied on each elite workshop based on the number of commoners it employed.

For readers accustomed to the idea that elites exploit commoners, our assumption that the elite taxes itself may be counterintuitive. Such readers should bear in mind that the elite is using taxation to solve a collective action problem involving collusion against commoners. We show below that this can be done equally well by taxing the individual elite agents who hire commoners or the individual commoners who work for elite agents. As long as the tax revenue flows to the elite in each case, the results are the same.

It does matter that only manufacturing was taxed. If taxation of agriculture had been profitable, a state would have emerged prior to urbanization. This contradicts the idea that the Mesopotamian city-states were in fact pristine states. Most scholars date the earliest Mesopotamian states to the mid- or late-Uruk period, when cities were forming or had recently formed. We infer that agriculture by itself did not provide an adequate basis for centralized taxation, probably because its dispersed activities made rural output and/or workers costlier to monitor than urban output and/or workers.

The crucial question is whether the elite wants to tax manufacturing when doing so has no administrative cost in the form of hired tax collectors, fixed costs from setting up the tax system, and the like. Clearly a necessary condition for taxation to arise is that it must offer net benefits to the elite when it can be done costlessly. If this is true, it may also be profitable to create a tax system having fixed or variable administrative costs, as long as these costs are not excessive relative to the revenue obtained.

Suppose the elite levies a tax $t \geq 0$ per manufacturing worker, where tax revenue is collected by a central agency that redistributes it equally among the elite agents. The previous zero profit condition from (10.15) now becomes

$$pM = (w + t)L \tag{10.19}$$

Total tax revenue is $tL = pM - wL$, which is also the total profit from manufacturing.

Figure 10.3 illustrates these ideas. The average value product for manufacturing is given by the locus $\phi(L)$, which is downward sloping under condition A10.1 from Section 10.3. The supply curve for manufacturing labor is given by $w(L, \theta)$ reading from left to right, which is identical to the demand curve for agricultural labor in Figure 10.2 reading from right to left. This supply curve is always upward sloping.

The equilibrium (L°, w°) with zero taxation $(t = 0)$ occurs at point A. When the tax rate on manufacturing labor is positive $(t > 0)$, tax revenue and manufacturing profit are given by the area of the rectangle in Figure 10.3 defined by the average value product at point B and the wage at point C. The gap between B and C is $w^B - w^C = t$, the tax rate per worker. A higher tax rate implies a lower manufacturing workforce L. For any tax rate $t \geq 0$ there is a unique equilibrium level of L and vice

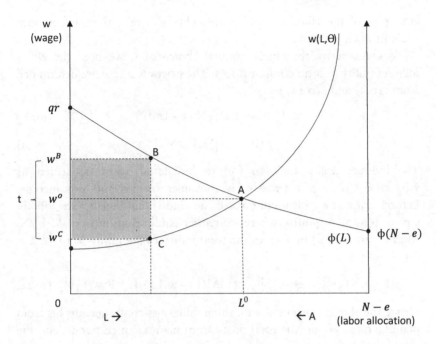

FIGURE 10.3. Taxation of manufacturing labor

versa, as long as L lies between zero and its equilibrium level L° > 0 with zero tax. In what follows it is simplest to have the elite choose L directly and collect the resulting manufacturing profit using whatever tax rate t ≥ 0 is needed to induce the desired L.

We can now show why taxation of elite employers and commoner employees has the same result. Suppose each urban worker pays the tax t > 0 from Figure 10.3. Such workers must receive the wage w^B from their employers in order to be recruited into the manufacturing sector, because the net wage is w^C after the worker pays the tax and w^C is available in the commons. The wage w^B is the average value product in manufacturing, which leaves zero profit for workshop owners. Again the elite collects its profit through the tax system, not directly in the markets for goods and labor. The level of profit is the same for a given tax rate t > 0 whether it is employers or employees who nominally pay.

A positive tax t > 0 has several effects relative to the zero-profit equilibrium with no taxation. First, taxation decreases urban employment L and manufactured output M. Second, the price p for manufactured goods rises. Third, the wage w falls. Finally, the lower wage raises the land rent of the elite. A sophisticated elite will take these effects into account in choosing L.

To characterize the elite's optimal choice of L we need the elite's indirect utility as a function of prices. The prices w and p are determined from (10.9) and (10.13) by

$$w(L, \theta) = [\beta(\theta)/(N - e - L)]^{1-\alpha} \qquad (10.20)$$

$$p(L) = b'[M(L)/N] \qquad (10.21)$$

The indirect utility function for an individual agent is written as $v(p, x) = s(p) + x$ where $s(p)$ is consumer surplus and x is income. Letting $m(p)$ be consumption for an individual agent, we obtain $s(p) = b[m(p)] - pm(p)$, where in market equilibrium $m(p) = M(L)/N$. Multiplying $v(p, x)$ by e gives the total indirect elite utility $V^E(p, X^E) = es(p) + X^E$ or

$$V^E[p(L), X^E(L, \theta)] = es[p(L)] + p(L)M(L) - w(L, \theta)L + R[w(L, \theta)] \quad (10.22)$$

Hence the elite is concerned with three things: its consumer surplus from manufactured goods, the total profit from manufactured goods, and the total land rent.

We now define an equilibrium with optimal elite taxation, where the scale of the manufacturing sector is chosen to maximize the total utility of the elite agents.

Definition 10.4

The array (p^E, w^E, A^E, L^E) is an *elite taxation equilibrium* associated with the commons productivity θ if

(a)	L^E maximizes $V^E[p(L), X^E(L, \theta)]$	for $0 \leq L \leq L^\circ(\theta)$
(b)	$p^E = p(L^E) = b'[M(L^E)/N]$	from (10.21)
(c)	$w^E = w(L^E, \theta) = [\beta(\theta)/(N - e - L^E)]^{1-\alpha}$	from (10.20)
(d)	$A^E + L^E + e = N$	from (10.4)

In condition (a) of the definition, L is constrained not to exceed $L^\circ(\theta)$ because this is the labor input for manufacturing when the tax rate is zero and we are only considering $t \geq 0$. A solution to the optimization problem exists because V is continuous and the feasible set is non-empty and compact. The other conditions are straightforward. The constraint that commoners have non-negative food consumption is discussed in the proofs of the formal propositions.

To characterize an elite taxation equilibrium, we need to differentiate the indirect utility function $V^E[p(L), X^E(L, \theta)]$ from (10.22) with respect to L. The derivative can be broken into two parts, corresponding to two channels through which L affects the other components of the model. The first channel acts through the product market and affects M, p, manufacturing revenue, and consumer surplus, where the key parameters are q and r. The second channel acts through the labor market and affects w, A, manufacturing cost, and land rent, where the key parameters are θ, Z, and α.

The derivative of elite utility with respect to manufacturing labor is

$$dV^E[p(L), X^E(L, \theta)]/dL =$$

$$\mu(L) + \lambda(L, \beta) \qquad\qquad \text{where}$$

$$\mu(L) = qre^{rL - qM/N}[1 - (1 - e/N)qM/N] \quad \text{with } M = M(L) \text{ from } (10.14)$$

$$\lambda(L, \beta) = -(N - e - L)^{\alpha-2}\left[\beta^{1-\alpha}(N - e - \alpha L) + \beta^{-\alpha}(1-\alpha)\alpha^{1/(1-\alpha)}(N - e - L)\right]$$

$$\text{with } \beta \equiv \alpha^{1/(1-\alpha)} + Z\theta^{1/(1-\alpha)} \text{ from } (10.7) \qquad\qquad (10.23)$$

The function $\mu(L)$ captures the product market channel and has an ambiguous sign. The function $\lambda(L, \beta)$ captures the labor market channel and is strictly negative for all $L < N - e$ and all β. The elite will always choose $L < N - e$ because $L \to N - e$ implies $A \to 0$, so the marginal product of agricultural labor goes to infinity, as does the wage.

Define $L_{max} > 0$ by $\mu(L_{max}) \equiv 0$, or equivalently $M(L_{max}) = N/q(1 - e/N)$. No labor input with $L \geq L_{max}$ can be optimal because then $\mu(L) \leq 0$ and $\lambda(L, \beta) < 0$ imply $dV^E/dL < 0$. In a situation of this kind, the elite would reduce L. Therefore the relevant interval in the optimization problem D10.4(a) is $0 \leq L < \min\{L_{max}, N - e\}$.

Because θ is non-negative the minimum value of β is $\alpha^{1/(1-\alpha)}$. For β greater than or equal to this level, $\lambda(L, \beta)$ is strictly decreasing in β and thus strictly decreasing in θ. This implies that a higher θ makes $\lambda[L, \beta(\theta)]$ more negative at any fixed value of L, so the elite is less inclined to expand manufacturing when commons productivity is higher.

It can be shown that $\partial\lambda/\partial L < 0$ always holds. However, in general $\partial\mu/\partial L$ has an ambiguous sign. Condition A10.2 below ensures that $\partial\mu/\partial L < 0$ holds on the interval $0 \leq L < \min\{L_{max}, N - e\}$.

Assumption 10.2

   $q/N \geq 1$

A10.2 gives $d^2V^E/dL^2 < 0$ for $0 \leq L < \min\{L_{max}, N - e\}$, so the objective $V^E[p(L), X^E(L, \theta)]$ from (10.22) is strictly concave in L on this interval. This is true for any productivity $\theta \geq 0$. A10.2 guarantees the uniqueness of the solution to the elite's optimization problem in D10.4(a).

   In non-trivial situations where $L^\circ > 0$ so some manufacturing is feasible in D10.4(a), there are three possible cases. First, there could be a boundary solution having $L^E = 0$ so the tax rate is high enough to prevent any manufacturing. This requires $\mu(0) + \lambda[0, \beta(\theta)] \leq 0$. Second, there could be an interior solution with $0 < L^E < L^\circ$ so manufacturing occurs but with a positive tax rate. This requires $\mu(L^E) + \lambda[L^E, \beta(\theta)] = 0$. Third, there could be a boundary solution with $L^E = L^\circ$ so the level of manufacturing is the same as in a zero-profit equilibrium and the tax rate is zero. This requires $\mu(L^\circ) + \lambda[L^\circ, \beta(\theta)] \geq 0$. Later we use a sufficient condition that rules out the last case, so a solution either involves no manufacturing or positive manufacturing at a scale below the zero-profit level.

   First we consider boundary solutions with $L^E = 0$ so manufacturing is absent.

Lemma 10.2

   Define θ_e implicitly by $\mu(0) + \lambda[0, \beta(\theta_e)] \equiv 0$. There are two cases.

   (a) If $qr(N-e)^{1-\alpha} < \alpha(2-\alpha)$ there is no such $\theta_e \geq 0$. In this case, the derivative in (10.23) is negative at $L = 0$ for all $\theta \geq 0$. Thus the elite always chooses $L^E(\theta) = 0$.

   (b) If $\alpha(2-\alpha) \leq qr(N-e)^{1-\alpha}$ there is a unique $\theta_e \geq 0$. The equality implies $\theta_e = 0$ and the inequality implies $\theta_e > 0$. In this case the derivative in (10.23) is positive at $L = 0$ for $0 \leq \theta < \theta_e$, zero at $L = 0$ for $\theta = \theta_e$, and negative at $L = 0$ for $\theta_e < \theta$. Thus the elite chooses $L^E(\theta) > 0$ for $0 \leq \theta < \theta_e$ and $L^E(\theta) = 0$ for $\theta_e \leq \theta$.

Part (a) shows that if qr and N–e are small enough, the elite never wants manufacturing $(L^E = 0)$. Part (b) shows that when qr and N–e are large enough and θ is small enough, the elite wants positive manufacturing $(L^E > 0)$.

   Next we rule out boundary solutions of the form $0 < L^E = L^\circ(\theta)$. Condition A10.3 (together with A10.2) is sufficient for this purpose.

Assumption 10.3

$e/N \leq 1/2$

This condition says that commoners represent at least half of the total population, and it limits the size of consumer surplus effects relative to income effects for the elite.

Lemma 10.3

Suppose $L^\circ(\theta) > 0$ in D10.4(a) so that a positive labor input is feasible. Assume A10.2 and A10.3 both hold. The derivative in (10.23) is always negative at $L = L^\circ(\theta)$. Therefore the elite always chooses $L^E(\theta) < L^\circ(\theta)$.

The last possibility is an interior solution with $0 < L^E < L^\circ(\theta)$. Suppose Lemma 10.2(b) applies and $0 \leq \theta < \theta_e$ so the elite's optimal labor input is positive. Let $L(\theta)$ be the input level defined implicitly by the first order condition

$$\mu[L(\theta)] + \lambda[L(\theta), \beta(\theta)] \equiv 0 \tag{10.24}$$

This yields

$$L'(\theta) = -\beta'(\theta)[\partial\lambda/\partial\beta]/[\partial\mu/\partial L + \partial\lambda/\partial L] \tag{10.25}$$

Due to $\beta'(\theta) > 0$ and $\partial\lambda/\partial\beta < 0$ in the relevant range for β, the numerator is positive. As mentioned above, $\partial\lambda/\partial L < 0$ always holds, and $\partial\mu/\partial L < 0$ holds in the relevant interval if A10.2 holds. Under these conditions $L'(\theta) < 0$ holds in (10.25), so a lower productivity in the commons leads to a larger manufacturing sector. We use $M^E(\theta) \equiv M[L^E(\theta)]$ to denote the elite's optimal output choice, and $M^\circ(\theta) \equiv M[L^\circ(\theta)]$ to denote output with free entry and zero taxation as in Section 10.3.

Lemma 10.4

Suppose Lemma 10.2(b) applies, and A10.2 and A10.3 hold. Consider the interval $0 \leq \theta \leq \theta_e$ where θ_e is defined in Lemma 10.2. We have $\theta_e < \theta_o$ where the zero-profit boundary θ_o is defined in (10.18). The elite's optimal output $M^E(\theta)$ is unique with $M^E(\theta_e) = 0$ and $0 < M^E(\theta) < M^\circ(\theta)$ for $0 \leq \theta < \theta_e$. $M^E(\theta)$ is decreasing on this interval and continuous at θ_e.

Lemma 10.4 shows that when $0 \leq \theta < \theta_e$ three things are true: (i) a zero-profit equilibrium of the kind described in Section 10.3 would lead to positive manufacturing; (ii) the elite will impose a positive tax on manufacturing; and (iii) the tax is not so high that manufacturing is entirely suppressed.

We now state our main results on elite taxation and its relationship to the zero-profit equilibria studied in Section 10.3.

Proposition 10.3 (elite taxation equilibrium).

Let θ_o be the zero-profit boundary in (10.18) and let θ_e be the elite taxation boundary in Lemma 10.2. Assume A10.2 and A10.3 hold.

(a) If $qr(N-e)^{1-\alpha} \leq \alpha$ then $\theta_o \leq 0$ and Lemma 10.2(a) applies so there is no solution for θ_e. For all $\theta \geq 0$, zero-profit equilibrium gives $M = 0$ without taxation.

(b) If $\alpha < qr(N-e)^{1-\alpha} \leq \alpha(2-\alpha)$ then $0 < \theta_o$ and either Lemma 10.2(a) applies so there is no solution for θ_e or Lemma 10.2(b) applies with $\theta_e = 0$.

   (i) For $0 \leq \theta < \theta_o$, zero-profit equilibrium would give $M > 0$ but the elite enforces $M = 0$ through high taxes.

   (ii) For $\theta_o \leq \theta$, zero-profit equilibrium gives $M = 0$ without taxation.

(c) If $\alpha(2-\alpha) < qr(N-e)^{1-\alpha}$ then Lemma 10.2(b) applies and $0 < \theta_e < \theta_o$.

   (i) For $0 \leq \theta < \theta_e$, the elite imposes positive taxes but allows $M > 0$.

   (ii) For $\theta_e \leq \theta < \theta_o$, zero-profit equilibrium would give $M > 0$ but the elite enforces $M = 0$ through high taxes.

   (iii) For $\theta_o \leq \theta$, zero-profit equilibrium gives $M = 0$ without taxation.

Proposition 10.3 shows that when qr, the average value product at $M = 0$, is small, as in (a) and (b), a manufacturing sector does not emerge for any commons productivity θ. This is true either because entry is unprofitable even without taxation, or because entry would occur but the elite prevents it in order to maintain land rents. The only situation where the elite allows manufacturing is (c), where this sector is profitable enough that the elite taxes it moderately. Even in this case it is also necessary to have a low commons productivity θ as in (c)(i), which pushes the wage down to a point where the gains from manufacturing outweigh the losses in land rent. These results are depicted in Figure 10.4, which shows case (c) where manufacturing is permitted when θ is sufficiently low. The intercept θ_s and the function $M^S(\theta)$ associated with a social planner will be discussed in Section 10.5 and can be ignored for now.

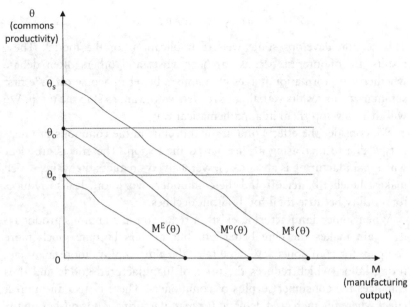

FIGURE 10.4. Manufacturing output as a function of commons productivity

A key implication is that a well-organized elite with the capacity to tax its own members may not want to form a state, even if manufacturing would be profitable and even if taxation has no administrative cost. The elite must also consider the opportunity cost in terms of the land rent it collects from farming. If manufacturing would place too much upward pressure on the wage rate, and therefore too much land rent would have to be sacrificed, the elite prefers to suppress manufacturing.

However, a well-organized elite with low administrative costs will allow a city-state if there is high demand for manufactured goods, high productivity in manufacturing, a large supply of commoner labor, and low productivity in outlying areas beyond elite control (or some combination of these factors, allowing for tradeoffs among them). If these requirements are met, urbanization and taxation arise together. The collection of taxes is driven by the elite's desire to enforce a monopolistic restriction on output from urban workshops, which increases total elite utility.

10.5 WELFARE

This section develops some welfare implications of the model. These results are of interest because archaeologists and others often debate whether state formation makes commoners better or worse off. We first summarize our results verbally for readers who want to skip the math. We will then develop them in a mathematical way.

We consider the effects of a gradual decline in the commons productivity θ due to increasing aridity across the region. The effects are clear when manufacturing is absent. A lower θ always reduces the wage, which makes the elite better off and the commoners worse off. It also reduces total utility because total food output declines.

When some manufacturing exists, a reduction in commons productivity again makes the elite better off, but matters become much more complex for commoners. When θ falls, the elite employs more manufacturing labor, which reduces the price of manufactured goods and thus enhances the consumer surplus of commoners. There is also an indirect effect where the increased demand for manufacturing labor pushes up the wage. On the other hand, the direct effect of lower commons productivity is to decrease the wage. In early stages of urbanization when the manufacturing sector is small, the consumer surplus effect is negligible and the direct effect on the wage dominates the indirect effect. Therefore commoners become worse off early in the transition to a city-state.

The impact on total utility early in the transition depends on parameter values. It may seem strange that a reduction in a productivity parameter could increase total utility. However, there are distortions in the pricing of manufactured goods that could yield this result. Due to increasing returns, marginal cost is lower than average cost. A first-best allocation requires marginal cost pricing, while a zero-profit equilibrium with no taxation requires average cost pricing, and an equilibrium with positive taxes requires price above average cost. Because the elite restricts output, lower productivity in the commons can lead to a social gain through greater manufacturing despite lower food production. This is not a Pareto improvement because the commoners become worse off.

As urbanization proceeds, commoner utility may eventually rise for two reasons: consumer surplus effects become more important and rising demand for labor may drive up the wage. However, if the initial productivity in the commons was sufficiently high, commoners never fully regain the welfare level they enjoyed before climate deterioration began, and total utility must be lower in a city-state than in the agricultural economy that preceded it (the loss to the commoners always outweighs the gain to the elite).

The rest of this section derives these results mathematically. We assume $M > 0$ throughout. Total utility for the elite class has already been computed in (10.22), which we repeat here for easy reference:

$$V^E\big[p(L), X^E(L, \theta)\big] = es[p(L)] + p(L)M(L) - w(L, \theta)L + R[w(L, \theta)] \quad (10.26)$$

Total utility for the commoner class is

$$V^C\big[p(L), X^C(L, \theta)\big] = (N{-}e)s[p(L)] + (N{-}e)w(L, \theta) \qquad (10.27)$$

where the total commoner income is $X^C(L, \theta) = (N{-}e)w(L, \theta) = (C + F + L)w(L, \theta)$. Summing (10.26) and (10.27) gives total utility for the entire region, which we denote by a superscript S. This is the objective a benevolent social planner would maximize.

$$V^S\big[p(L), X^S(L,\theta)\big] = V^E\big[p(L), X^E(L,\theta)\big] + V^C\big[p(L), X^C(L,\theta)\big] \qquad (10.28)$$
$$= Ns[p(L)] + p(L)M(L) + F[w(L,\theta)]^\alpha + Cw(L,\theta)$$

The first two terms in the second line of (10.28) give total utility from manufactured goods. $F[w(L, \theta)]$ is the elite's demand for farm labor at the wage $w(L, \theta)$ and $Cw(L, \theta)$ is food produced in the commons. Together the last two terms in the second line represent total food output (and also consumption because the market for food clears by Walras's Law).

Lemmas 10.5–10.7 derive the effects of θ on V^E, V^C, and V^S respectively. In all cases L is treated as a function of θ from elite taxation equilibrium, and the assumptions used in Section 10.4 are maintained.

Lemma 10.5
$dV^E\big[p(L(\theta)), X^E(L(\theta), \theta)\big]/d\theta = -(F + L)\partial w/\partial\theta < 0$

This result follows from the envelope theorem. V^E is already maximized with respect to L, so indirect effects through L can be ignored. The same is true for indirect effects on land rent through F. This leaves the direct effect of θ on the wage ($\partial w/\partial\theta$) through (10.20) times the total labor hired by the elite, which is $F + L > 0$. The wage is increasing in θ, so the elite always gains from lower commons productivity.

Lemma 10.6
$$dV^C\left[p(L(\theta)), X^C(L(\theta), \theta)\right]/d\theta$$
$$= (N-e)\{[-(M/N)\partial p/\partial L + \partial w/\partial L]L'(\theta) + \partial w/\partial\theta\}$$

The envelope theorem is of less use in this case, although one can exploit the fact that commoners maximize utility in choosing their consumption level for the m good. As a result the derivative of consumer surplus with respect to price p reduces to $-m = -M/N$. For both p and w we have indirect effects of θ acting through the elite's optimal labor input $L(\theta)$. There is also a direct effect of θ on the wage captured by $\partial w/\partial\theta$.

The derivative in Lemma 10.6 is hard to sign. Given positive manufactured output, a reduction in θ increases L. This lowers p and raises consumer surplus, which is good for commoners. The indirect effect through L also raises the wage from (10.20), which is again good for commoners. But the direct effect of θ on the wage in (10.20) implies that lower productivity yields a lower wage, which is bad for commoners. Even if we limit attention to the early stages of urbanization where M is small and thus consumer surplus effects are negligible, the direct and indirect effects of θ on the wage go in opposite directions. We will return to this issue below.

Lemma 10.7
$$dV^S\left[p(L(\theta)), X^S(L(\theta), \theta)\right]/d\theta$$
$$= (N-e)[-(M/N)\partial p/\partial L + \partial w/\partial L]L'(\theta) + (\partial w/\partial\theta)C$$

This is similar to Lemma 10.6 except that here the direct wage effect $\partial w/\partial\theta$ only multiplies the commons labor C rather than the entire commoner labor supply $N-e = C + F + L$. The reason is that when we sum to obtain $V^S = V^E + V^C$, wage transactions between the elite and commoners cancel out. However, the elite does not pay for labor in the commons, and the food produced there is important from a social standpoint. Notice also that elite consumer surplus plays no role in Lemma 10.7 because it vanished in Lemma 10.5 due to the envelope theorem (the elite already internalizes the effect of L on its own surplus).

The following proposition exploits these lemmas to characterize welfare effects when θ is near θ_e so the manufacturing sector is small. These can be regarded as effects arising in the early stages of city-state formation. After presenting the technical results, we provide some economic intuition.

Mesopotamian City-States: A Formal Model 417

Proposition 10.4 (local welfare effects).

Adopt the assumptions used for Proposition 10.3(c)(i) so $\theta_e > 0$. Abbreviate $\beta(\theta_e) \equiv \beta_e$. Consider the interval $0 \leq \theta < \theta_e$ where $L(\theta) > 0$ and let $\theta \to \theta_e$ from below, which gives $L(\theta) \to 0$ and $M^E(\theta) \to 0$. Let $D < 0$ be the limit of the denominator in (10.25). As $\theta \to \theta_e$ from below, the derivatives from Lemmas 10.5–10.7 have the following features.

(a) $dV^E/d\theta \to -(1-\alpha)\alpha^{1/(1-\alpha)}(N-e)^{\alpha}\beta_e^{-\alpha-1}\beta'(\theta_e)$ $\qquad < 0$

(b) $dV^C/d\theta \to (1/D)(1-\alpha)(N-e)^{\alpha}\beta_e^{-\alpha}\beta'(\theta_e) \bullet$

$\left\{ qr^2[1-(q/N)(2-e/N)]-(1-\alpha)(N-e)^{\alpha-2}\left[\beta_e^{1-\alpha} + \alpha^{1/(1-\alpha)}\beta_e^{-\alpha}\right] \right\} \quad > 0$

(c) $dV^S/d\theta \to (1/D)(1-\alpha)(N-e)^{\alpha}\beta_e^{-\alpha}\beta'(\theta_e) \bullet$

$\left\{ -\alpha^{1/(1-\alpha)}\beta_e^{-1}D + qr^2[1-(q/N)(2-e/N)]-(1-\alpha)(N-e)^{\alpha-2}\left[\beta_e^{1-\alpha}+\alpha^{1/(1-\alpha)}\beta_e^{-\alpha}\right] \right\}$

Part (a) is trivial because we already know from Lemma 10.5 that the derivative for the elite is negative. However, we state the limit result in terms of underlying parameters in order to facilitate comparisons with parts (b) and (c).

Part (b) indicates that commoners are always made worse off by a small decrease in the commons productivity θ if M is sufficiently small. More technically we can find a neighborhood $(\theta_e - \delta, \theta_e)$ with $\delta > 0$ on which this is true. There are two ideas involved. First, when M is small the effect of θ on consumer surplus can be ignored. Second, a drop in θ has direct and indirect effects on the wage. The direct effect lowers the wage, while the indirect effect raises it by encouraging the elite to hire manufacturing labor. Close to θ_e the direct effect dominates so the commoners are worse off. The sign in part (b) is obtained by noting that $D < 0$, the other factors in the first line are positive, and the second line is negative because A10.2 from Section 10.4 implies $1-(q/N)(2-e/N) < 0$.

The outcome in part (c) depends in a complex way on the parameter values. It can be shown that either sign is possible. The proof involves fixing a suitable value for β_e, setting $q = N$ and $e = N/2$ so A10.2 and A10.3 hold with equality, and adjusting r to keep β_e constant while varying the level of N. For a small population N, total utility moves in the same direction as commons productivity, but for a large value of N, total utility moves in the opposite direction to commons productivity.

The results in Proposition 10.4 are local (they apply only in some neighborhood of the transition point θ_e), and do not provide a global verdict on the welfare effects of city-state formation for all possible values of θ. Some progress on the global effects of θ can be made by imagining that a social planner allocates labor between the agricultural and manufacturing sectors to maximize total utility for all agents, both elite and commoner. Thus the planner maximizes

$$\gamma(\theta)(N\!-\!e\!-\!L)^{\alpha} + Nb[M(L)/N] \quad \text{subject to } 0 \le L \le N\!-\!e \qquad (10.29)$$

where $\gamma(\theta) \equiv [\alpha^{\alpha/(1-\alpha)} + Z\theta^{1/(1-\alpha)}]/\beta(\theta)^{\alpha}$ as in (10.8) and b(m) comes from (10.12). The first term in (10.29) is total food and the second is total utility from manufacturing. The planner must respect the constraint that within the agricultural sector, the average product of labor in the commons is equal to the marginal product of labor on elite estates. This constraint is embedded in the productivity coefficient $\gamma(\theta)$. The planner also respects the constraint that individual agents consume equal amounts of the manufactured good, as they would in market equilibrium, so welfare differences between elites and commoners are driven by differences in their levels of food consumption.

The term in (10.29) involving manufactured output is strictly concave when A10.2 holds from Section 10.4. Strict concavity guarantees a unique solution for L at each $\theta \ge 0$. We denote the solution in (10.29) by $L^S(\theta)$ and the resulting manufactured output by $M^S(\theta) \equiv M[L^S(\theta)]$. In Lemma 10.8 below we will use θ_s to denote the commons productivity level separating boundary solutions $L^S(\theta) = 0$ from interior solutions $L^S(\theta) > 0$. There are no boundary solutions of the form $L = N - e$, so this case will be ignored.

Lemma 10.8

Assume A10.2 and A10.3 hold. Define $\theta_s \ge 0$ (uniquely) by $\alpha\gamma(\theta_s) \equiv qr(N - e)^{1-\alpha}$ when such a value of θ exists.

(a) If $qr(N - e)^{1-\alpha} < \alpha$ then no such θ_s exists and $M^S(\theta) = 0$ for all $\theta \ge 0$.
(b) If $qr(N - e)^{1-\alpha} = \alpha$ then $\theta_s = 0$ and $M^S(\theta) = 0$ for all $\theta \ge 0$.
(c) If $qr(N - e)^{1-\alpha} > \alpha$ then $\theta_s > 0$. In this case
    (i) $M^S(\theta) > 0$ on the interval $0 \le \theta < \theta_s$ and $M^S(\theta) = 0$ for $\theta_s \le \theta$
    (ii) $dM^S(\theta)/d\theta < 0$ on the interval $0 \le \theta < \theta_s$ and $M^S(\theta)$ is continuous at θ_s
    (iii) $M^{\circ}(\theta) < M^S(\theta)$ on the interval $0 \le \theta < \theta_s$
    (iv) If Lemma 10.2(b) applies then $0 \le \theta_c < \theta_o < \theta_s$

The implications of Lemma 10.8 are shown in Figure 10.4. If $\theta \geq \theta_s$ so the planner chooses $M = 0$, we also have $M = 0$ in a zero-profit equilibrium and an elite taxation equilibrium. When the planner chooses $M > 0$, this output is larger than the zero-profit output, which may be zero or positive. If the zero-profit output is positive, then the zero-profit output is larger than the elite taxation output, which may be zero or positive. These relationships arise because a planner is not constrained to break even in the manufacturing sector. By comparison with zero-profit equilibrium, the elite wants to restrict output while the social planner wants to expand it.

Lemma 10.8 leads to the following global welfare results.

Proposition 10.5 (global welfare effects).

Assume A10.2 and A10.3 hold. Suppose $0 < \theta_e < \theta_s < \theta_{max}$ where θ_{max} is the upper bound defined in (10.10). Compare any agricultural equilibrium with $\theta \in (\theta_s, \theta_{max})$ against any manufacturing equilibrium with $\theta \in (0, \theta_e)$. Relative to the initial agricultural equilibrium, the commoners are worse off in the manufacturing equilibrium while the elite are better off. Total utility is lower in the manufacturing equilibrium.

A quick sketch of the proof runs as follows. First notice that the planner always uses positive labor for agriculture. This implies that the total utility of the planner is an increasing function of θ because when θ increases, the planner always has the option of maintaining the previous labor allocation and obtaining higher total utility. Whenever $\theta \in (\theta_s, \theta_{max})$, the social planner and the elite choose identical allocations with $L = 0$ and $A = N-e$. Thus total utility for the social planner is the same as in the initial agricultural equilibrium favored by the elite. For $\theta \in (0, \theta_e)$, the social planner has lower total utility than for $\theta \in (\theta_s, \theta_{max})$. Furthermore, the elite's allocation for $\theta \in (0, \theta_e)$ cannot yield a higher total utility than the planner would obtain at the same θ. Hence total utility in the manufacturing equilibrium is lower than in the agricultural equilibrium. From Lemma 10.5 the elite are better off in the manufacturing equilibrium. Because total utility decreases, the commoners must be worse off in the manufacturing equilibrium. It can be shown that there are parameter values for which the conditions of Proposition 10.5 hold.

10.6 POPULATION

The model from Sections 10.2–10.5 has an important limitation. Although we considered migration from rural to urban areas, we held the total regional population N constant. In reality the Uruk transition unfolded over centuries, and population would probably not have stayed constant through a large climate shift and an ensuing economic upheaval. This gap can be filled using Malthusian population dynamics. We will show that a combination of Malthusian dynamics and learning by doing in the manufacturing sector yields results consistent with our claim that climate change was the trigger for city-state formation. The next several paragraphs provide a summary for readers who want to skip most of the math. Afterward we will present the technical details.

The population model runs as follows. Time is discrete and a period is the length of a human generation (about twenty years). An individual adult who is alive in period t engages in economic activities and generates utility u^t. This adult has $n^{t+1} = \rho u^t$ surviving adult children in period $t+1$, where the period-t adults die at the start of period $t+1$. The coefficient $\rho > 0$ captures the idea that a higher level of parental utility increases fertility and decreases child mortality. This parallels our framework in Chapters 6 and 7 except that we include utility from both manufactured goods and food. For example, children are more likely to survive if they receive warm clothing as well as nutritious bread. The demographic parameter ρ is identical for all agents and stays constant over time. Events occurring within a single period constitute the *short run* while events spanning multiple periods constitute the *long run*.

Aggregating utility across agents (both elite and commoner) generates a time path for aggregate population. For a given level of productivity θ in the commons, we define long-run equilibrium (LRE) as a population N and a level of manufacturing labor L^E such that (a) L^E is optimal for the elite given (N, θ), and (b) the total utility $U(L^E, N, \theta)$ keeps the aggregate population N constant over time. We compare LREs for alternative values of θ and ignore the path along which N^t approaches a new equilibrium when θ changes. This is a reasonable simplification for processes operating on a time scale of centuries.

In an LRE associated with a given productivity θ, elites and commoners will have different incomes and different utilities. As a result, they will have different numbers of surviving children. To keep the populations of the two classes stationary, there must be some downward mobility from the elite to the commoner class, perhaps based upon birth order (see Section 6.10).

The main results are as follows. Suppose we start with an initial LRE with a high commons productivity θ and (due to Malthus) a correspondingly high regional population N, but no manufacturing. We know that in the short run with N held constant, a negative climate shock can reduce θ and trigger $L^E > 0$ so that manufacturing becomes active. But in the long run lower commons productivity tends to reduce population and the supply of labor, which could return the system to a purely agricultural economy.

However, a shock giving $L^E > 0$ in the short run is likely to raise the productivity of manufacturing in the long run, using our standard arguments about learning by doing for a previously unexploited technology or resource (see Chapters 3–5). If the increase in manufacturing productivity is large enough, this can rule out a new long-run equilibrium based on agriculture alone. Instead the economy shifts permanently to an equilibrium in which some commoner labor is devoted to urban manufacturing.

We now proceed to the mathematics. Aggregating utility across agents (both elite and commoner) generates a time path for aggregate population according to

$$N^{t+1} = \rho U[L(N^t, \theta^t), N^t, \theta^t] \qquad (10.30)$$

where $L(N^t, \theta^t)$ is manufacturing labor in period t when the regional population is N^t and commons productivity is θ^t. Because all agents have the same ρ, aggregate population in period t+1 depends only on aggregate utility in period t. As in (10.29) the utility function is

$$U(L, N, \theta) \equiv \gamma(\theta)(N - e - L)^\alpha + Nb[M(L)/N] \quad \text{where } 0 \leq L \leq N - e \quad (10.31)$$

The first term in (10.31) is the total output of food and the second is the total utility derived from manufactured goods. We use the notation U to indicate the aggregate direct utility function based on quantities of goods, as contrasted with the notation V used in Section 10.5 for the aggregate indirect utility function based on prices.

Definition 10.5

Fix the parameters $(\alpha, Z, e, q, r, \rho)$. Let $L^E(N, \theta)$ be the labor optimally allocated to manufacturing by the elite from D10.4. The pair (L, N) is a *long-run equilibrium* (LRE) associated with the commons productivity θ if

(a) $L = L^E(N, \theta)$
(b) $N = \rho U(L, N, \theta)$

Condition (a) says that L is a *short run equilibrium* (SRE) at the prevailing population and productivity, in the sense that this is the labor allocation the elite would choose in such circumstances. Condition (b) says that N remains constant over time, given elite optimization and the prevailing level of commons productivity.

First we study a purely agricultural economy where we impose the constraint $L \equiv 0$. We will show that there is a unique stable stationary population N for each commons productivity level $\theta \geq 0$ if and only if the size of the elite (e) is small enough in relation to other parameters. An upper bound on the elite size is required because the elite produces no food but must be replaced demographically in every period. Stability requires that the regional population rise (fall) when N is slightly below (above) the equilibrium level.

Figure 10.5 illustrates these issues. With the constraint $L \equiv 0$ the total utility from (10.31) is $U(0, N, \theta) \equiv \gamma(\theta)(N - e)^{\alpha}$. For N to be stationary, the utility function must intersect the ray N/ρ. As shown in the graph this typically occurs at two points (the possibility of a tangency point is ignored because the associated population would be unstable). Such intersection points can only occur when the elite is small enough.

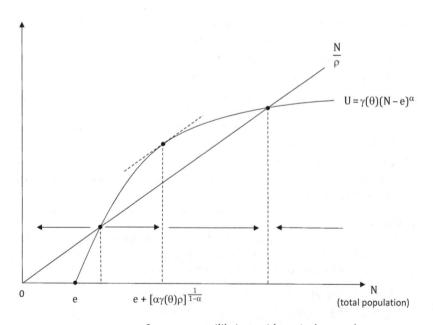

FIGURE 10.5. Long-run equilibrium with agriculture only

> **Lemma 10.9**
> In an agricultural economy with $L \equiv 0$, there is a (unique) stable stationary population iff $e < (1-\alpha)\alpha^{\alpha/(1-\alpha)}(\rho\gamma)^{1/(1-\alpha)}$. This population is increasing in γ.

When the inequality in Lemma 10.9 holds, the intersection point from Figure 10.5 with the lower population is an unstable steady state and the one with the higher population is a stable steady state (directions of population change are shown by the arrows). We will ignore the former throughout and focus on the latter.

Recall that $\theta = 0$ implies $\gamma = 1$. In this case there is no commons and all labor is used on elite agricultural estates. If the condition in Lemma 10.9 holds for this case, as will be true when the elite size e is small enough relative to the demographic parameter ρ, it holds automatically for all $\theta \geq 0$.

Now consider an arbitrary regional population $N^\circ > e$. We want to characterize the parameter values that would support N° as a stable LRE with agriculture alone ($L^E = 0$). N° must be a steady state population as in D10.5, which implies

$$(\rho\gamma)^\circ = N^\circ/(N^\circ - e)^\alpha \qquad (10.33)$$

This only determines the product $(\rho\gamma)^\circ$, not the individual factors ρ and γ. Equation (10.33) does not guarantee that the resulting steady state is stable. For this to occur we need the expression $\gamma(N - e)^\alpha - N/\rho$ to be decreasing at N°, which is true for the parameters $(\rho\gamma)^\circ$ in (10.33) if and only if

$$e/(1 - \alpha) < N^\circ \qquad (10.34)$$

When (10.33) and (10.34) both hold, the parameter values $(\rho\gamma)^\circ$ from (10.33) satisfy the condition in Lemma 10.9. The restriction in (10.34) is similar to A10.3 where we assumed $2e \leq N$ to ensure that the elite wanted positive taxation. We are not concerned with this question here. But we do observe that if $\alpha \geq 1/2$ then (10.34) implies A10.3. If $\alpha < 1/2$, then A10.3 implies (10.34).

Next we want to identify the productivity levels γ for which a purely agricultural steady state subject to the constraint $L \equiv 0$ is also a full LRE with elite optimization as in D10.5. This requires that $L^E = 0$ be optimal. Conversely, we want to know when this is not true, so any LRE with elite optimization must involve positive manufacturing. Lemma 10.10 addresses this issue using the results on elite optimality from Lemma 10.2.

Lemma 10.10

Consider some steady state population $N°$ supported by $(\rho\gamma)°$ with $L = 0$ as in (10.33), where $N°$ satisfies the stability condition in (10.34). The optimal elite labor allocation L^E has the following features.

(a) Suppose $(qr)° \leq \alpha(2-\alpha)/(N° - e)^{1-\alpha}$. This implies $L^E = 0$ for all $\theta \in [0, \theta_{max})$ or equivalently all $\gamma \in [1, \gamma_{max})$.

(b) Suppose $(qr)° > \alpha(2-\alpha)/(N° - e)^{1-\alpha}$. There is a unique $\theta_e > 0$ implicitly defined by

$$(qr)°(N°- e)^{1-\alpha} \equiv [\beta_e{}^{1-\alpha} + \beta_e{}^{-\alpha}(1-\alpha)\alpha^{1/(1-\alpha)}]$$

where $\beta_e \equiv \beta(\theta_e) \equiv \alpha^{1/(1-\alpha)} + Z\theta_e{}^{1/(1-\alpha)}$
such that
(i) $L^E > 0$ for $\theta \in [0, \theta_e)$ or equivalently $\gamma \in [1, \gamma_e)$
(ii) $L^E = 0$ for $\theta \in [\theta_e, \theta_{max})$ or equivalently $\gamma \in [\gamma_e, \gamma_{max})$

where $\gamma_e \equiv \gamma(\theta_e) \equiv [\alpha^{\alpha/(1-\alpha)} + Z\theta_e{}^{1/(1-\alpha)}]/\beta(\theta_e)^\alpha$.

We will use Lemmas 10.9 and 10.10 to construct a sequence of events consistent with a long-run transition from a purely agricultural economy to one with manufacturing. Our argument has the following steps.

(a) Start with a purely agricultural LRE where productivity is $\theta°$ and population is $N°$. Let this population be supported by $(\rho\gamma)°$ and let the initial value for $(qr)°$ satisfy part (b) of Lemma 10.10. Suppose case (b)(ii) applies, so $0 < \theta_e \leq \theta°$. This ensures that it is initially optimal for the elite to choose $L^E = 0$.

(b) Consider a decline in commons productivity to $\theta' \in [0, \theta_e)$ with $N°$ held constant. From part (b)(i) of Lemma 10.10, in the short run the productivity θ' leads to $L^E > 0$.

(c) At the new productivity θ' consider a purely agricultural steady state population N' with $L \equiv 0$. Suppose $L^E > 0$ at step (b) yields $r' > r°$ via learning by doing. In addition suppose that $(qr)'$ leads to case (b)(i) of Lemma 10.10 for θ' and N'. This implies that there is no LRE associated with θ' such that $L^E = 0$.

(d) Suppose in the scenario from step (c) that we do have an LRE with θ' and $(qr)'$ such that $L^E > 0$. If so, the productivity drop from $\theta°$ to θ' triggers a transition from an LRE having only agriculture to an LRE with positive manufacturing.

Proposition 10.6 addresses each step in the preceding argument. The proof, which is included with the proofs for the other formal propositions in the chapter, constructs a set of parameter values for which the claims in the proposition are true. The point is to show that there are conditions under which a long run transition to urban manufacturing would still occur despite the inclusion of Malthusian population dynamics in the model.

One major simplification is to consider the most severe possible climate shock, where productivity in the commons drops to $\theta' = 0$ or equivalently $\gamma' = 1$. This implies that after the shock hits, agricultural labor is used only on elite estates. A less extreme shock can generate qualitatively similar results.

Proposition 10.6 (long-run transition to manufacturing).

Assume climate change reduces the commons productivity from $\theta^\circ > 0$ to $\theta' = 0$, or equivalently from $\gamma^\circ > 1$ to $\gamma' = 1$. Further assume that learning by doing in response to $L^E > 0$ increases manufacturing productivity from r° to r'. The parameters (α, Z, e, q, ρ) are unaffected by climate change.

Fix (α, Z) arbitrarily. Conditions (a)–(d) below are satisfied for suitable choices of the remaining parameters $(e, q, \rho, \theta^\circ, r^\circ, r')$.

(a) Before the climate shock there is an LRE with $L^E = 0$.
(b) After the climate shock there is an SRE with $L^E > 0$.
(c) After the climate shock there is no LRE with $L^E = 0$.
(d) After the climate shock there is an LRE with $L^E > 0$.

10.7 EXPLANATIONS

This section summarizes the ways in which the theory from Sections 10.2–10.6 accounts for the facts in Chapter 9. We also identify some areas where the model makes predictions that are open to future empirical testing. It may not be entirely surprising that our model can explain certain facts about southern Mesopotamia. After all, we had these facts in mind when we constructed the model. Nonetheless it is reassuring to know that the theory is consistent with available archaeological evidence. We discuss the potential generality of our framework in relation to other regions of the world in Chapter 11.

Recall from Chapter 9 that the early Uruk period is poorly documented in general, and the city of Uruk emerges into the archaeological daylight around 5200 BP largely in its full form. Therefore, theoretical speculation on the origins of southern Mesopotamian city-states is not tightly constrained by empirical observations. This is a problem for us, but it is likewise a problem for other scholars seeking to explain the transition.

The model in Section 10.2 is meant to capture some central features of the 'Ubaid period. Most importantly we want an equilibrium in which some agents are members of the elite and the rest are commoners. For this purpose we assumed that an organized elite with a high enough density of agents per unit of land can prevent outsiders from entering a site. By controlling access to especially productive areas, such an elite can collect land rent by hiring commoners at a wage (or alternatively by renting land to commoners).

In equilibrium the commoners are indifferent between working for the elite and working on open-access land of lower quality. When the stratification constraints from Section 10.2 are satisfied the elite are better off than the commoners, and the density of the commoner population at open-access sites is too low to allow the formation of elites there. Thus rather than assuming the existence of elite and commoner classes a priori, we derive stratification as an equilibrium outcome even though all agents are identical.

Due to the relatively favorable climate of the 'Ubaid, the region as a whole would have had a relatively high population for the Malthusian reasons in Section 10.6. As long as commoners enjoyed access to areas beyond elite control with good productivity when rainfall was abundant (whether food was obtained by rain-fed farming, pastoralism, or foraging in wetlands), the standard of living for commoners could have been close to that of the elite. This is compatible with archaeological evidence suggesting that during the 'Ubaid period, inequality was relatively mild.

In Section 10.3 we extended the model to allow for manufacturing in urban areas controlled by elites. As long as climate remained favorable at locations outside southern Mesopotamia and the southern wetlands remained productive, the southern elite did not establish urban workshops because the wage required to attract commoner labor was too high. But archaeologists agree that the entire region was becoming more arid as the Uruk period began. This triggered migration from outlying areas into the southern alluvium, and from both outlying areas and the southern wetlands into elite-controlled areas where food production was less vulnerable to aridity due to irrigation opportunities. Our model is consistent with the views of most archaeologists about these migration patterns.

Section 10.3 showed that a sufficiently large climate shift could induce the elite to engage in urban manufacturing. Other things equal, a larger population inherited from the 'Ubaid period would have strengthened the incentive for manufacturing in the Uruk period. Our framework is consistent with the observation that a city-state had multiple workshops (not one big factory), although manufacturing had increasing returns to scale at the level of the city as a whole. The incentive to create workshops would have been strongest for industries where latent productivity (our parameter r) and latent consumer demand (our parameter q) were the highest. Textiles would seem to fit this description although pottery, metalwork, and other trades were also significant. Our assumption of increasing returns at the level of the city is consistent with the size distribution of early Mesopotamian cities, where Uruk was much larger than its rivals.

The model in Section 10.3 did not include taxation and the scale of manufacturing there was determined through a zero-profit condition. We assumed a competitive market for manufactured goods throughout the region, including those sites not under the control of the southern elites. This is consistent with the emphasis by Algaze on regional trade in manufactured goods during the Uruk period, as discussed in Chapter 9.

To explain the rise of city-states, in Section 10.4 we allowed the elite to levy taxes on manufacturing. There is a broad archaeological consensus that state institutions arose by 5200 BP, and coincided with increased urbanization. Because we define a state as an organized elite with the power to tax, we need to explain why taxation and urbanization arose together. Our hypothesis is that southern elites initially benefited from agriculture only through land rent, because food production was hard to tax. But urban workshops were highly visible and easy to tax, so taxation and urbanization went hand in hand.

As discussed in Chapter 9, several lines of evidence suggest taxation in the late Uruk period, including four-tier settlement hierarchies, monumental architecture, and a few vague written records. We regard the growing inequality from 5200 BP onward as further evidence that taxes were being collected. But there is no direct archaeological evidence on the subject so we are free to speculate about the form these taxes may have taken. One possibility is that they were analogous to modern religious tithing. The gods lived in temples in the cities, and protected against bad outcomes in the present as well as meting out rewards and punishments in the future. Perhaps tithing was a social norm within the elite, with both divine punishment and social shunning directed toward the members of the elite who did not pay.

In our theoretical argument we assumed taxation had no administrative cost, and identified conditions under which the elite would want to tax manufacturing. If the elite does not find taxation profitable with zero administrative cost, then clearly this is also true when administrative costs are positive. On the other hand, if taxation is profitable with a zero administrative cost, it will also be profitable at a sufficiently small positive cost.

One key theoretical result is that even when it is costless to collect taxes, the elite may tax manufacturing at a prohibitive level or simply ban it. The reason is that the elite faces a tradeoff between land rent and tax revenue from manufacturing. Shifting some labor into manufacturing may have too high an opportunity cost in foregone land rent.

Another theoretical point is that states can arise purely for reasons of private elite consumption. In our model, elite agents only care about food and manufactured goods. We could have used a more complex utility function where elite agents also care about public goods, and most economists who study early states assume that public goods must somehow play a role. However, we deliberately omitted public goods from our definition of the state in order to show that this is not a necessary condition. Empirically speaking, early states generally did allocate some tax revenue to public goods as well as the support of specialized personnel (including those who collected the taxes). Accordingly, it makes sense to use monumental architecture and administrative bureaucracy as markers for the existence of a state. But this does not alter our conclusion that state formation could be motivated primarily by a desire for greater private consumption on the part of the elite.

In Section 10.5 we addressed the welfare effects of city-state formation. Although data on inequality or commoner standards of living are unavailable for most of the Uruk period, by the end of this period inequality had clearly increased substantially relative to the 'Ubaid. Inequality increased further in the Jemdet Nasr and Early Dynastic periods. Our results in Section 10.5 predict that elites always become better off in the process of city-state formation, and that commoners always become worse off in the early stages of this process. We were unable to show that the latter trend continues indefinitely. But we did show that if the climate is favorable enough before urbanization, the commoners must be worse off after city-states have formed.

The theoretical results from Sections 10.2–10.5 treated the regional population as fixed. This is not an ideal assumption for studying a process that unfolded over several centuries, where population probably evolved in response to changing standards of living through Malthusian dynamics. For this reason we extended the theory in Section 10.6 to consider city-state formation when population adjusts according to a simple Malthusian model. We showed that for certain parameter values our earlier conclusion still stands: increasing aridity can lead to urban manufacturing and taxation.

The role of wetlands in southern Mesopotamia has been a controversial question among archaeologists, and it may be useful to elaborate on how this question is handled in our formal modeling. The model aggregates a heterogeneous array of sites involving rainfall agriculture, pastoralism, and wetlands foraging, and labels them collectively as "the commons" (see Section 10.2). These sites share the feature that they are not under elite control, in contrast to the elite lands in the south where irrigation is feasible.

In our theory labor mobility maintains approximate equality of living standards throughout the commons, despite the heterogeneity of natural resources and production techniques used at the individual sites. If food per person differed substantially among these sites, labor would move from sites where food per capita was low to sites where it was high, which would tend to erase any such differences. We are assuming that such migration was possible on a decadal time scale, within one human generation.

Because we aggregate sites involving rainfall farming with those involving the wetlands, our model does not explicitly address flows of population between such sites. We do rely implicitly on migration within the commons to maintain a uniform standard of living across sites, as described above. But none of our formal propositions address migration from areas of rainfall farming to areas with wetlands because in our modeling these population flows are all internal to the commons. Our model is designed instead to examine how climate deterioration leads to a flow of labor out of the commons, regarded as an aggregate, into elite-controlled agricultural lands and ultimately (assuming various conditions are met) into the urban manufacturing sector.

Archaeologists have differing views about the timing and extent of climate effects on southern wetlands. Take Nissen as an example (see Chapter 9). In his view growing aridity was already causing the wetland areas to dry out during the Uruk period. In fact, he believes this led to a major expansion in the availability of dry land, which could have been associated with urbanization. This scenario is consistent with our model. If rainfall farming, pastoralism, and wetlands foraging all suffered from a more or less simultaneous productivity decline due to greater aridity, it is reasonable to combine these diverse sites into a single sector called the commons and use a single productivity parameter for all of them. In this scenario we would not expect large migrations among the individual sites in the commons, because productivity would decrease in a parallel way at all of these sites. However, labor flows from the commons into elite-controlled agriculture and ultimately manufacturing would still be important.

Now suppose instead we adopt the view of Pournelle, who believes the wetlands remained highly productive as late as the Early Dynastic (see Chapter 9). In this scenario the urbanization in the Uruk period could not be explained by the drying of the wetlands many centuries later. Moreover, it would be reasonable to think that the initial impact of aridity would be to cause migration from areas reliant on rainfall farming to the southern wetlands, which would function as a refuge. If the wetlands had an infinite capacity to absorb climate refugees, it would be hard to use increasing aridity as an explanation for the Uruk urbanization process.

These issues can be easily addressed. Suppose we disaggregate the commons into rainfall farming sites and wetland sites. Further suppose the early stages of aridity reduce productivity at the former sites but not the latter. As long as the resources of the wetlands are finite, the wetlands will have diminishing returns to labor for standard reasons, even if these sites are not directly affected by aridity themselves. The flow of labor from rainfall farming to wetland foraging will therefore reduce food per person at the wetlands sites in a way that maintains an equal standard of living with those areas that are directly affected by the lower rainfall. As before a reduced standard of living at both types of open-access site will imply that the elite now pays less for labor, and will cause an expansion of elite-controlled agriculture. If the decline in the commoner wage is large enough, we will get urban manufacturing. These tendencies are simply reinforced when intensifying aridity finally starts to affect the wetlands directly, perhaps during the Early Dynastic period.

In the Pournelle scenario the wetlands do provide some cushion against aridity. The commoner standard of living falls by less than if the wetlands were directly affected by aridity from the outset. The wetlands also restrain the tendency for elite agriculture to expand in response to aridity and postpone the beginning of urbanization. But as long as the wetlands have a limited physical scale and display diminishing returns as commoners flow in, the central mechanisms of our model still operate. To be sure, if the migration of rainfall farmers to the wetlands is an empirically important phenomenon, one might want to disaggregate the commons to study this process in detail. However, for our purposes a delayed or absent effect of climate deterioration on the productivity of the wetlands only has a quantitative effect on the amount of aridity needed to trigger urbanization and state formation. As long as there are enough climate refugees fleeing from rainfall-dependent farming or pastoralism, our qualitative conclusions remain unchanged.

One issue we did not address involves changing land endowments. As mentioned above, Nissen and others believe that wetlands were vulnerable to increasing aridity over time, that these effects were important during the Uruk period, and that the drying out of the wetlands made more land available for elite agriculture and urbanization. While the irrigated land controlled by the elite was also negatively affected by regional aridity, the elite invested in an expansion of irrigation systems after the Uruk period to deal with this problem. Our model simplifies this process by holding productivity constant for the elite lands, without incorporating either increased land or new irrigation investments.

The conversion of some local land from wet to dry would increase the elite land endowment at site U, assuming the newly dry land could be irrigated at reasonable cost. This would increase the demand for farm labor on elite estates. On the other hand, the retreat of the wetlands would decrease the "demand" for labor in the commons. It is not obvious whether the net result is upward or downward pressure on wages. If the former, the transition to manufacturing would have been delayed, but if the latter, the transition would have been accelerated.

Dry land might also have been an important input to urban activities as Nissen suggests. These could include manufacturing itself or closely related activities such as the provision of commoner residences. For these reasons one might think that more dry land would stimulate manufacturing. A possible counterargument is that agriculture was more land-intensive than manufacturing so effects involving agriculture would have been stronger. In any case this is an interesting line of inquiry for archaeological research.

Our model generates a variety of predictions that could be subjected to future empirical testing. One example involves migration. Among sites outside elite control, those with the greatest reductions in rainfall or the most vulnerability to drought should have seen the largest migratory outflows. On the receiving end, those sites where food production was least vulnerable to drought should have seen the largest inflows.

Another example involves inequality. Assuming that climate conditions changed gradually, our model predicts rising inequality at stratified sites during the 'Ubaid as the climate began to deteriorate, with standards of living gradually improving for the elites in southern Mesopotamia and falling for commoners throughout the region. This tendency should be visible prior to the emergence of cities and it should continue at least through the early stages of urbanization and state formation.

A third example involves regional population. Our long-run model in Section 10.6 predicts a region-wide decline in population due to deteriorating climate in outlying areas dependent on rainfall. This may appear to conflict with evidence for population growth and increasing numbers of settlements during the 'Ubaid and early Uruk periods. But to the extent that such evidence involves elite-controlled sites not vulnerable to drought, it can be explained by migratory effects and need not conflict with a Malthusian decline in overall population when outlying areas are also taken into account.

During the Uruk period, technical innovations associated with learning by doing in the manufacturing sector could well have dominated climate effects, generating region-wide population growth and more urban agglomeration. Such productivity growth almost certainly occurred through experiments with the division of labor, supervisory practices, and record keeping (including written records). These innovations would have had two effects: (a) a scale effect involving Malthusian population growth, and (b) a substitution effect intensifying the agglomeration of the population in cities.

Urban growth would probably have promoted investment in canals, warehouses, and other infrastructure, which would have stimulated additional learning, productivity growth, and population growth. Such developments could have been augmented by the selective migration of individuals with skills that were especially useful in the city, such as metallurgy. For these reasons a trajectory beginning with climate deterioration and a lower population could ultimately have led to better technology and a higher population.

10.8 CONCLUSION

Our argument in this chapter resembles the argument we used in Chapter 5 for the origins of agriculture. In Chapter 5 a negative climate shock induced short-run migration to a few refuge sites, creating local population spikes and triggering cultivation. We also showed that if the productivity of cultivation had remained constant, long-run Malthusian adjustments resulting from the climate shock would have reduced population, causing the system to return to universal foraging. In reality, learning by doing kept cultivation going and restrained the decline in population that would otherwise have occurred. Along with the favorable Holocene climate, these technical innovations led to substantial population growth and the eventual spread of agriculture across the region.

In this chapter a negative climate shock stimulated short-run migration from the commons to elite lands, which functioned as the equivalent of refuge sites. At the same time the commoner wage fell, triggering urban manufacturing. But if the productivity of manufacturing had stayed constant, long-run Malthusian dynamics could have reduced the commoner population, pushed the wage back up, and restored universal agriculture. This was averted through learning by doing in manufacturing, which raised productivity and kept manufacturing going despite these Malthusian tendencies. The outcome was a trajectory of continued urbanism, permanent manufacturing, regional population growth, and the augmentation of elite land rents with income from urban tax revenue.

The use of taxes for cartel enforcement (in our model, driving down commoner wages and driving up the price of manufactured goods) is the simplest economic rationale for the rise of a state because it does not involve public goods. In principle this rationale might also apply to an agrarian state where food is the only consumption good, although we tend to think that the administrative costs of taxes might be too high in this case. But the point is that the emergence of archaic states can potentially be explained in a model that includes only private consumption. Of course elites may also have valued certain public goods and used tax revenue to finance them, but this factor is not essential.

The cartel enforcement story only works when the elite can collectively exercise significant monopoly power over prices in the labor market, the product market, or both. This is less likely in a setting with many competing city-states. But increasing returns at the level of the city implies that in the early stages of urbanization, a single dominant city is likely to emerge, and in fact this was true for southern Mesopotamia. The distribution of city sizes is not only evidence for the presence of increasing returns, but is consistent with the exercise of market power by the elite at Uruk.

After a number of city-states had evolved, the market power of Uruk would have diminished, though it could still have been substantial if Uruk had transportation or other advantages. As competing cities developed, over time the tax system was probably used more to accommodate elite demand for public goods such as temples, palaces, walls, and armies, and less to enforce monopolistic restrictions. In the end the rival city-states were incorporated into a unified regional empire, curtailing the ability of local elites to exploit whatever market power they still possessed.

10.9 POSTSCRIPT

The first draft of the material for this chapter was completed in the summer of 2018. While we were developing the formal model in this chapter, we were generally aware of the archaeological literature from Chapter 9 and we constrained our modeling efforts to maintain consistency with the facts described there. For acknowledgments of advice and financial support, see Section 11.14.

II

The Emergence of Cities and States

II.I INTRODUCTION

Chapter 9 presented a case study of pristine city-state formation in southern Mesopotamia, and Chapter 10 provided a formal model that captured key features of that case. Here we take a more panoramic view of urbanization and state formation. We want to ask broader questions: What do we mean by "cities" and "states"? Do these institutions usually develop together, or can we have one without the other? What theories of city and state formation have archaeologists and economists proposed? Is there any evidence that speaks to the merits of the competing theories?

We will undertake systematic regional comparisons to shed light on these matters. Of course it is impossible to consider all early cities or all early states. Instead we study six key regions: Mesopotamia, Egypt, the Indus Valley, China, Mesoamerica, and South America. These are the classic cases of pristine state formation.

Section 11.2 discusses an economic puzzle about the emergence of cities, as well as hypotheses archaeologists have advanced to explain urbanization. In Section 11.3 we review a number of definitions of the state from archaeologists, anthropologists, political scientists, and economists. In Section 11.4 we consider ideas about the origins of the state and survey the literature on the subject.

Section 11.5 introduces our agenda for regional comparisons. We then move to a set of examples that supplement our detailed study of Mesopotamia in Chapter 9. These cover Egypt (11.6), the Indus Valley (11.7), China (11.8), Mesoamerica (11.9), and South America (11.10). Section 11.11 distills several general patterns from these cases.

In Section 11.12 we present our theoretical framework for the evolution of cities and states. We suggest three pathways leading to a pristine state. The first is based on ideas about endogenous property rights from Chapter 6, the second is based on the theory of elite warfare in Chapter 8, and the third is based on exogenous environmental shifts of the kind studied in Chapter 10. In all three of these pathways, cities and states are closely linked. Section 11.13 applies our three hypotheses to the regional cases described earlier. Section 11.14 concludes the chapter and Part IV of the book. We add a short postscript in Section 11.15 to thank people and institutions for their support.

11.2 URBANIZATION

A highly influential discussion of ancient cities among archaeologists was Childe (1950), who constructed a list of ten traits such cities allegedly possessed. They included densely populated settlements; specialized workers in non-subsistence activities; monumental public buildings; stored surplus; stratification; writing; predictive sciences; representational art; trade over long distances; and political organization based on residence rather than kinship. For a review of Childe's ideas, see Smith (2009). For a history of archaeological research on early cities, see Yoffee with Terrenato (2015). Modern archaeologists tend to define early cities using criteria such as the permanence of a settlement, dense population nucleation, and heterogeneity in social roles (Jennings and Earle, 2016, 475).

We use the term *city* informally to mean any large permanent agglomeration of people living in a compact area. We do not use specific numerical thresholds and we do not include economic specialization among residents as part of the definition, although as an empirical matter this is almost always observed. We use the term *urbanization* when referring to a process through which a subset of the settlements in a region becomes more "city-like." This may occur either because for a fixed regional population the ratio of rural to urban population shifts toward the latter, or because regional population increases and some individual settlement sizes also increase, without any reduction in rural population.

A rough sense of the numbers and sizes of ancient cities can be gleaned from data compiled by Modelski (1999), who uses archaeological site measurements and a constant population density of 200 people per hectare to estimate population levels. At 5700 BP there were two cities in the world with an estimated population of 10,000 or more, which increased to 27 cities at 4300 BP before starting a gradual decline. At 5300 BP there was one city (Uruk) with an estimated population of 20,000 or more. The number in this size category remained in single digits until 3200 BP.

Many agricultural or pastoral societies lack cities, and it is not obvious why cities would ever emerge in such societies. Because food production is land-intensive, it makes sense for the population to spread out over the landscape in order to minimize travel time between residences and production locations. We would expect population density to be positively correlated with soil fertility, access to surface water, gentleness of terrain, and similar aspects of land quality, but without a large concentration of population in a single location. At most we might expect a few small villages for trading activities or religious ceremonies, and perhaps small elite settlements in places that are especially pleasant or administratively convenient. Aside from travel time in relation to production activities, early cities were likely centers for disease transmission with high mortality rates (Algaze, 2018, 26), providing another incentive for population dispersion.

Our reading of the archaeological literature reveals three main hypotheses about the process of urbanization (see Marcus and Sabloff, 2008, for an overview). First, there is the development of manufacturing for local or long-distance markets as in the example of southern Mesopotamia (see Chapter 9). Because manufacturing is less land-intensive than agriculture or pastoralism, it does not require that the workforce disperse across the landscape. Indeed, the opposite is true: productivity tends to be higher when workers are concentrated in a compact area because this facilitates the shipping of raw materials and finished goods, the pooling of skilled labor, supply chain coordination, and knowledge spillovers. For a review of economic benefits and costs of urban density in the modern world, see Duranton and Puga (2020).

Second, warfare or the threat of warfare can cause people to seek refuge in easily defended and highly fortified locations. There is a pervasive tradeoff between economic convenience, which in an agricultural context motivates the population to disperse, and a security imperative, which motivates the population to agglomerate. This tradeoff goes back to sedentary foraging groups and is also visible in small-scale agricultural societies (see Johnson and Earle, 2000, on the cases of the Yanomamo, the Tsembaga Maring, and the Central Enga). When a society already has relatively high population density for the familiar Malthusian reasons (favorable climate, geography, and technology), defensive motives may lead to agglomerations that most people would be willing to call cities. Gat (2006, 278–280) argues that virtually all early city-states arose from the need to defend against other nearby city-states, citing evidence that (a) most of the population of such cities consisted of peasants who walked to nearby fields, not craft workers engaged in non-agricultural pursuits, and that (b) such city-states have tended to arise in mutually antagonistic clusters, not in isolation.

Third, urbanization could be propelled by culture. For example, Ur (2012, 554) concludes that Bronze-Age Mesopotamian cities most likely grew for ideological reasons. This may have involved religion: the gods lived in temples and people lived in cities near temples in order to be close to the gods. Other cultural attractors to central places include entertainment, social life, and ethnic or linguistic enclaves. We will not have much to say about cultural explanations because they do not generally identify a clear triggering event or condition that sets the urbanization process in motion.

The manufacturing and warfare mechanisms for urbanization lead to differing predictions about the locations of cities. In the manufacturing story we would expect cities to be in places that are convenient for large-scale economic activities, especially those having cheap transportation, even if they are difficult to defend against attack. In the warfare story we would expect cities to be on hills, cliffs, or peninsulas, with large investments in walls, moats, and other defenses, even if such locations make economic activity more expensive. It should therefore be possible to distinguish between the two mechanisms through archaeological evidence.

11.3 DEFINITIONS OF THE STATE

The definition of the state is not a trivial matter. Different writers often adopt different definitions, either explicitly or implicitly, so when they attempt to explain the origins of the state they are explaining different things. In addition to presenting a clear definition, it is important to explain how the definition fits into a relevant body of theory and to describe the archaeological markers used to infer the existence of a state.

A common starting point in archaeology and anthropology is the classic typology of Service (1962) involving bands, tribes, chiefdoms, and states. This system has been adapted and modified by other authors (e.g., Earle, 1987; Johnson and Earle, 2000). The principal issue here is how to distinguish states from chiefdoms. Both have stratification involving elites and commoners, both treat class positions as hereditary, and both exhibit multi-settlement hierarchies where central authority is exercised from larger settlements.

One popular point of distinction is that the elites in chiefdoms are generalists. A chief might negotiate an alliance on Monday, collect tribute on Tuesday, celebrate the gods on Wednesday, and organize a war party on Thursday. This makes it difficult to arrange a partial delegation of power, while a full delegation of power creates political instability. In a state, by contrast, elite agents are specialists: some are political rulers, some are tax collectors, some are priests, some are warriors, and so on (Wright, 1977; Johnson and Earle, 2000). A state can delegate partial authority over particular tasks like public works or tax collection to local representatives, which makes it easier to control a large population or geographic area while limiting the risk that a subordinate might lead an insurrection (Spencer and Redmond, 2004; Spencer, 2010).

Another way to distinguish chiefdoms from states is that chiefdoms are organized through kinship ties while states use non-kin-based bureaucratic principles (Johnson and Earle, 2000). However, early states often continue to rely on kinship connections within the elite to some degree (Yoffee, 2005, 16–17). For this reason among others, we assign little weight to the kinship criterion.

A third approach is to define states as having more tiers in their settlement hierarchies than chiefdoms. In the Standard Cross Cultural Sample, a data set widely used for anthropological research (Murdock and White, 1969, 2006), states are defined as having four tiers rather than two or three (e.g., hamlets, small villages, large villages, and towns). Economists sometimes use similar definitions. For example, one prominent data set on state history going back to 3500 BP (Borcan et al., 2018, 5) draws a line between simple chiefdoms (non-states) and paramount chiefdoms including "multiple individually substantial chiefdoms" (incipient states). Most writers who adopt such criteria interpret multiple tiers in a distribution of settlement sizes as reflecting multiple tiers of authority within an elite administrative structure.

Some authors distinguish states from chiefdoms based on the greater scale of states measured by population or land area (see Diamond, 1997, ch. 14). There is little agreement on where such lines should be drawn, with some writers arguing that states may involve only a few thousand people, others preferring a boundary between ten and fifty thousand, and still others wanting to reserve the term for very large polities having hundreds of thousands of people. Arbitrary numerical cutoffs of this sort are not very useful, and we prefer a definition linked to an explicit theoretical framework.

Having discussed ideas from archaeology and anthropology, we move on to other social sciences. Political scientists emphasize the idea that a state has a monopoly on the use of force within a territory, while economists emphasize the idea that a state supplies public goods and collects taxes to pay for them. The former definition dates to Weber (1968, 54–6) and is endorsed by some anthropologists (Service, 1975, ch. 1). The latter is widespread in the economic literature (see our review of economic theories below).

Neither of these criteria corresponds to the distinctions between chiefdoms and states drawn by anthropologists. In many of the societies an anthropologist would call chiefdoms, the elite might have an effective monopoly on the use of force. A political scientist would then have to accept these societies as examples of states. Likewise, in societies an anthropologist would call chiefdoms, the elite might tax people to provide defense, insurance, infrastructure, or monuments. An economist would then have to accept these societies as states.

From this standpoint, the origin of the state is likely to remain shrouded in the mists of time because there is no practical way to determine when a chief first used force to collect a tax from a commoner. Clearly, something more is needed in order to draw a meaningful dividing line between societies like the Northwest Coast of North America (which no one thinks were states) and Mesopotamian city-states (which everyone thinks were states). There is no perfect solution to this definitional quandary, but we think the best approach is to use the term "state" when taxation is *institutionalized*, in the sense that (a) it is carried out on a regular basis by a permanent set of specialized functionaries, and (b) the resulting resources are aggregated and placed at the disposal of a central elite group for allocation. Institutionalization is a matter of degree and has fuzzy boundaries but we see no better way to draw a suitable line. This leads to the definition adopted in Section 9.1: *a state* is an organized elite that has significant powers of taxation in a well-defined geographic area, where taxation is institutionalized in the above sense.

As in Chapters 9 and 10, we require a centralized fiscal system because a state can only function as a collective actor if the elite is organized enough to appropriate resources through mandatory payments and allocate them according to coherent preferences. We continue to define taxation as including all cases where the elite collectively confiscates resources (food, craft outputs, labor, raw materials, and so on). As explained in Section 9.1, the underlying technology of confiscation influences the conditions under which a state is likely to emerge. The supply of public goods is not part of our definition of the state (elites could use taxation simply to enhance their private consumption), but as an empirical matter most early states do devote significant resources to public goods.

We end this section by emphasizing the distinction between our *definition* of the state and the empirical *indicators* that suggest the existence of a state. This is important because taxation plays a central role in our theory, and we therefore give it a central role in our definition. At the same time taxation is difficult to observe directly in the absence of written records. Reasonable archaeological indicators of a state include

(a) Monumental architecture, such as very large temples or palaces, which would likely have required large-scale taxation for construction and maintenance.

(b) A multi-tiered settlement hierarchy that was likely associated with administrative hierarchy involving functional specialization, where
  (i) Substantial tax revenue would likely have been needed to support elite personnel, and
  (ii) One of the specialized functions would likely have been tax collection.

(c) Evidence for routine coercive labor practices organized by the elite (recall that we include coerced labor as a form of taxation).

(d) Large central transportation and storage facilities that were likely used for the collection of taxes in kind (such as grain or animal herds).

(e) Other evidence of central control such as extensive city planning or standardized weights and measures.

(f) A level of inequality that would have required systematic taxation because it went beyond the norm for stratified societies based on land rent alone.

(g) A large total population or total land area controlled by a unified elite, which may suggest the existence of a large tax base or a scale of elite activity that could only have been supported through taxation.

Each indicator has its problems. For example, simple chiefdoms can sometimes organize monumental construction projects (Stanish, 2001). Also it is hard to be certain that an administrative hierarchy is supported by tax revenue rather than land rent alone. But a flexible combination of

such indicators is likely to be the best one can do. Few if any archaeological cases will have strong evidence for all seven markers, but we
would be willing to infer the presence of a state if three or more are
clearly present, especially for criteria appearing higher up on the list.

11.4 THEORIES OF THE STATE

There are at least as many theories of pristine state formation as there are
pristine states. In our experience archaeologists are frequently skeptical
about a research agenda involving generalizations across regions of the
world and instead prefer to emphasize the particularities of each individual case. Among those willing to engage in generalization, there is substantial debate about causal mechanisms. For example, Yoffee (2005,
ch. 3) maintains that most early states began as city-states. But Carneiro
(1970, 2012), Marcus (1998), and Flannery (1999) maintain that most
early states arose through warfare among competing chiefdoms, a mechanism seemingly having little to do with cities. For a useful assortment of
archaeological perspectives, see Feinman and Marcus (1998).

Before reviewing individual theories, we first consider how alternative
theories of state formation can be assessed. A good theory should explain
why early states emerged at particular times and places rather than other
times and places. Ideally a theory would specify a set of necessary conditions for state formation that are jointly sufficient. The causal trigger must
logically be the last of the necessary conditions to be satisfied.

Accordingly, one way to evaluate a theory of state formation is to ask
whether it clearly identifies a causal trigger of this kind and whether the
role of this alleged trigger is backed up by convincing archaeological
evidence. Of course, the proximate cause of state formation need not be
the ultimate cause. Popular candidates for the role of ultimate cause
include climate change, technological innovation, and population growth,
although we would argue that technology and population could be
endogenous, depending on the relevant time frame. But whatever the
proximate cause may be, a change in this variable should be linked closely
in time to the emergence of state institutions.

Another way to assess theories of state formation is through comparisons across regions. Theory A might claim that geographic feature X is
conducive to state formation while theory B claims that geographic
feature Y is more important. Two examples to be discussed below involve
geographical circumscription and characteristics of food crops. Diamond
(1997) and Litina (2014) provide further examples. Because hypotheses

of this sort are generally based on permanent geographic differences across regions, they do not identify temporal triggers and therefore do not by themselves explain the timing of state formation. But in principle one could examine whether particular geographical features are correlated with the frequency or antiquity of state formation.

Cultural explanations for the origins of the state tend to have problems similar to cultural explanations for the origins of cities (see Section 11.2): they do not generally pin down any specific temporal trigger for state formation or any geographic conditions that make state formation more likely. Moreover, we tend to be dissatisfied with theories that treat unobserved cultural mutations or unobserved strategic manipulation of social norms as exogenous variables. For these reasons we do not pursue the cultural approach taken by Flannery and Marcus (2012), despite their rich empirical descriptions of the processes through which particular chiefdoms, kingdoms, and empires arose.

A popular classification system for theories of state origins divides them into two groups: integration theories and conflict theories. Integration theory is based on the idea that states develop in response to managerial problems facing the society as a whole. The writers in this camp tend to argue that the state makes both elites and commoners better off (in the language of economists, the state is a Pareto improvement). Conflict theory is based on the idea that the state serves the interests of the elite and helps the elite profit at the expense of commoners. Such writers tend to argue that early states involved coercion rather than coordination or public goods supply. These rival views go back centuries.

The distinction between integration and conflict theories is slippery for at least two reasons. First, some authors emphasize self-interest and the use of force, but even so, conclude that the state made everyone better off. Such arguments sometimes appear in the economics literature, as we will illustrate in our discussion of Grossman (2002).

Second, some authors claim that elite authority was originally necessary in order to solve a collective social problem, but that this authority was subsequently abused in a self-interested and coercive way. Perhaps the most spectacular example of this approach is the oft-cited and now discredited "hydraulic" theory of Wittfogel (1957, chs. 1–2), who argued that the benefits of irrigation and flood control systems in arid regions with rivers could only be achieved through mass labor. This required subordination to an authority that could coordinate the construction and maintenance of such systems, which then led to political despotism.

A similar example is provided by Diamond (1997, ch. 14), who argues that large societies require more contact among non-kin and therefore have greater interpersonal conflict. The solution is to establish an authoritative leader who can restrain conflict. The problem is that such leaders tend to operate in self-interested ways and ultimately become kleptocrats who exploit commoners.

For both Wittfogel and Diamond, authority is initially used as a tool for solving an important social problem (integration theory), but is eventually converted into a tool for oppression (conflict theory). We cite these authors only as examples; arguments of this sort are quite common in archaeological or anthropological discussions of the state. Such theories are often more than a little vague about how authoritative leaders escape from the control of the majority, or why a majority irreversibly grants power to an elite despite the danger that this power could be abused at a later date. These issues feature prominently in the literature on the evolution of modern democracy (see Section 12.5).

Apart from physical infrastructure and the maintenance of law and order, other versions of integration theory emphasize state-run storage or insurance systems (Adams, 1981), facilitation of regional trade (Litina, 2014), and collective defense against bandits or attackers (Grossman, 2002; Baker, Bulte, and Weisdorf, 2010; Konrad and Skaperdas, 2012). Among economists the most popular of these ideas is the last, perhaps because defense is a quintessential public good and is generally financed through taxation. We start with a review of this strand within the economic literature.

Grossman (2002) assumes that individual agents can choose whether to produce output or steal output from others. Producers devote resources to guarding output. If the technology of predation is highly effective, banditry will be a serious threat. In this case everyone (including potential bandits) can be made better off by creating a state that taxes producers and deters banditry. Though the state maximizes elite consumption, excessive taxation is restrained by the possibility that producers could choose to become (untaxed) bandits. Although one might think from Grossman's emphasis on the use of force and the self-interest of the state that this story belongs in the conflict theory camp, the claim that the state yields a Pareto improvement relative to anarchy flags it as an integration theory. Indeed, one could imagine that such states arise through a voluntary social contract. The main empirical prediction from the model is that states tend to emerge when it is easy for bandits to appropriate the output generated by producers.

Baker et al. (2010) use a similar theoretical framework. They do not distinguish between chiefdoms and states, and assume there is a government only if food producers benefit from it. Thus the state is a response to the demand for law and order. Unlike Grossman (2002), technology and population are endogenous where the former evolves through learning by doing and the latter through Malthusian dynamics. An argument running through the paper is that as technology advances, storage becomes more important, output becomes easier to steal, and the demand for a state intensifies.

By contrast with Grossman (2002), who assumes that a king has a monopoly on the sale of protection, Konrad and Skaperdas (2012) allow free entry of rival lords who all sell protection and fight for control over peasants. Competition among the lords will dissipate the potential gains from the sale of protection, leaving people no better off (and possibly worse off) than under anarchy. They are also pessimistic about the viability of self-government, in the sense of small groups that provide their own security as a local public good, in a world where such groups must compete against predatory states.

Boix (2015) elaborates on the latter point. He argues that there are two pathways to the state: one where the predators organize against the producers, leading to a monarchy, and another where producers defend themselves against the predators, leading to a republic. Boix believes that the pathway to a republic is rare but argues that the outcome depends partly on the nature of military technology (see Section 12.5 for a further discussion).

Conflict theories come in numerous flavors. One highly influential article in this tradition is Carneiro (1970), who argues that wars among rival chiefdoms can potentially lead to state formation, but only when commoners are unable to flee from the state due to geographical circumscription involving deserts, mountains, oceans, and the like. A lucid summary of this approach is provided by Flannery (1999), who cites Carneiro's recipe for a pristine state: defeat neighboring villages by force, incorporate their territory into your political unit, use prisoners of war as slaves, use close supporters to administer conquered territory if the local leaders are rebellious, require payment of tribute from your subjects, and require them to provide fighters in times of war.

Flannery (1999) adds that chiefdoms often cycle between simple and complex forms, where complex chiefdoms tend to fragment for a variety of reasons, including factional competition and succession problems. While acknowledging that only a very small fraction of chiefdoms ever give rise to states, Flannery maintains that almost all pristine states were formed through warfare and territorial expansion among chiefdoms.

Gat (2006, 278–293) believes that city-states in many parts of the world emerged through warfare, or at least a perceived need for defense. He explains the apparent lack of fortifications, especially walls, in the early stages of city-state development by arguing that proto-state warfare consisted mainly of raids, and that the sizes of cities alone would have made them difficult targets for raiding. Gat grants that once cities arose they were rarely attacked. One implication is that deterrence through urbanization was frequently effective, which would tend to stabilize a system of small autonomous city-states. Note that this story differs from the emphasis of Flannery and others on territorial expansion.

Allen (1997) builds on the ideas of Carneiro (1970) to explain the early Egyptian state, arguing that circumscription of the Nile valley by deserts enabled the elite to extract output from the commoners. According to Allen the temporal trigger for state formation was the arrival of agricultural technology from southwest Asia, leading to storable grain surpluses. Agriculture also made labor more seasonal, leaving commoners available for elite public works such as pyramid construction (for further discussion, see Section 11.6).

According to Mayshar et al. (2017, 2022), early states were most likely to arise in regions where food stores were readily appropriable (e.g., cereals but not tubers; see also Scott, 2017), and where production technology was transparent in the sense that the elite could readily measure or estimate the food output produced by commoners. They reject assertions that early states required a technologically determined surplus or arose through population pressure. In each case their objection is based on Malthusian considerations: surpluses resulting from high agricultural productivity will be eroded through population growth in the long run, and population pressure will be self-correcting due to the long-run effects of low food per capita on fertility and mortality.

Economists have begun to develop an empirical literature on state formation. The data sets are often dominated by non-pristine states, but the origins of pristine states have also received attention. Borcan et al. (2021) emphasize the central role of agriculture and stratification as preconditions (see Section 9.1). Mayshar et al. (2022) stress the roles of transparency, durability, storage, and other features of crops that facilitate appropriation by an elite (see Sections 9.8 and 9.9). They find no effect of land productivity on state formation after controlling for reliance on cereal crops. Schönholzer (2020) finds that states emerge in places that are agriculturally productive but also circumscribed by low productivity land, making it difficult to evade taxation through migration. He finds no effect of land productivity on state formation after controlling for circumscription.

All economic theories of the early state, whether based on integration or conflict theory, need to specify some limits on the ability of the elite to collect taxes. We do this by allowing agents to flee to an open-access commons. Other constraints on elite power include the possibilities that commoners will reduce effort in response to high tax rates, hide food from tax collectors, choose banditry over farming, or engage in rebellion.

Although we will not go into details, we make some brief remarks on the potential role of rebellion. Our combat technology from Chapters 7 and 8 says that the probability of a group winning a war depends on that group's size relative to the size of the opposing group. Suppose now that commoners want to use such a combat technology to overthrow an oppressive elite. The difficulty is that if the rebel group is initially small, the elite can defeat it with virtual certainty. Even given parity with respect to the quality of weapons and leadership, a commoner rebellion can only succeed if it is concealed from the elite in its early stages and then rapidly grows into an organized group on a scale comparable to that of the elite itself. Moreover, an elite under serious threat can use financial resources to recruit a mercenary army and such an army can be used to crush a commoner rebellion (see Chapter 8). But extreme forms of elite oppression might be deterred by the prospect of a rapidly spreading rebellion that would be costly to extinguish.

Looking at the debate between integration theorists and conflict theorists from a broad perspective, the picture is probably more mixed than either approach alone would suggest. Early states did provide some public goods that would likely have been valued by commoners such as infrastructure projects, insurance, sacred temples, law and order, suppression of local warfare, and protection from raiders or invaders. At the same time these states exercised coercive power, used forced labor, and diverted substantial output to elite consumption. The net effect on the nutrition, health, and life expectancy of the commoners is an empirical question, and the answer could differ from case to case.

The question is also hard to answer because the counterfactual is poorly defined. For example, if one defines a state by the use of taxation, should we compare the actual welfare of commoners in early city-states with what it would have been with no taxes and free entry into manufacturing? Chapter 10 gives a theoretical framework for comparisons of this kind, but empirical research along these lines would clearly be challenging.

A related problem is to distinguish the welfare effects of the factors that triggered state formation from the welfare consequences of the state itself. In the model of Chapter 10, increasing aridity makes commoners worse off even in an agricultural society without a state. It also causes city-states to form. How much of the total reduction in commoner welfare was due to climate effects that would have occurred anyway, and how much was due to elite taxation of manufacturing activities that arose in response to climate change?

A third problem involves the nature of elite income. No one disputes that elites benefited from state formation but there is genuine debate about how they became better off. A conflict theorist would maintain that rising elite welfare reflects greater success in taking output or labor time from commoners by force, while an integration theorist might argue that elites (also?) obtain returns on human capital. For example, elites may possess specialized knowledge about water management systems. Archaeologists will probably find it difficult to distinguish categories of elite income in ways that map neatly onto the theoretical categories economists would typically use.

11.5 REGIONAL COMPARISONS

The traditional regional list for pristine states includes Mesopotamia, Egypt, the Indus River, China, Mesoamerica, and South America (Service, 1975; Adams, 2001, 346; Spencer and Redmond, 2004, 174). The literature is enormous and we cannot undertake a complete review here. In the next five sections we summarize archaeological evidence about state formation for regions on the above list other than Mesopotamia, which was discussed at length in Chapter 9.

For each society, we explain why scholars regard that society as having a state, and provide a chronological narrative of the events leading up to state formation. To the extent possible, each narrative centers on variables relevant for our theoretical approach, such as climate, geography, food technology, population, inequality, migration, warfare, cities, and manufacturing. In cases where our search of the literature uncovered specific causal hypotheses about state formation, we summarize them. However, in some cases we did not find any causal hypotheses, and in no case did we find a set of hypotheses as rich as those we discussed for

Mesopotamia in Section 9.8. We describe our own causal hypotheses in Section 11.12 and suggest applications to regional cases in Section 11.13.

Readers who want additional information can consult Renfrew and Bahn (2014), Yoffee (2015), and Yoffee (2019). These edited volumes include chapters on regions of the world beyond those we discuss, such as southern and western Africa, Southeast Asia, Europe, and North America. Renfrew and Bahn address many subjects in prehistory by region, Yoffee (2015) focuses on early cities, and Yoffee (2019) focuses on early states.

11.6 EGYPT

The Egyptian part of the Nile River valley is traditionally divided into two major population centers, Upper Egypt (in the south) and Lower Egypt (in the north, including the Nile delta). These were separated by Middle Egypt, where the valley is narrow and the prehistoric population density was low. The Dynastic period in which the pharaohs ruled began around 5000 BP and was associated with the start of written records. This was preceded by the pre-Dynastic period covering the millennium from 6000–5000 BP, when written records are absent. Two key questions about the formation of the Egyptian state are why a state arose in Upper Egypt (and probably also Lower Egypt), and how the political unification of Upper and Lower Egypt was achieved.

Hunting, gathering, and fishing were long used for food acquisition at the mouths of wadis and the edges of lakes (recall that in the early Holocene, between about 12000–7000 BP, the Sahara was much wetter than it is today). A period of aridity around 7000–6000 BP forced populations from the deserts to migrate into the Nile valley. The earliest evidence for Neolithic sites having domesticated species appears around 7000 BP, where agricultural technology was not pristine but instead was borrowed from southwest Asia. Hunting, gathering, and fishing remained important and people did not become sedentary immediately (information is from Midant-Reynes, 2000, except where indicated).

Early in the pre-Dynastic, soon after 6000 BP, metalworking appears in the south. The southern population continued to rely heavily on fishing and hunting but abandoned the edges of wadis, which became inhospitable due to climate change, and concentrated in the limited area of the floodplain. Pastoralism was abandoned in favor of agriculture and the population began to cluster together. Settlements in the south in the early part of the pre-Dynastic period had about 50–200 people (183–184).

During the course of this millennium, the number of bodies buried in small pits increased while a small number of individuals began to be buried in larger graves (170). Grave goods from larger tombs indicate a trend toward hierarchy with a dominant elite directing the work of craft manufacturers. There were probably specialized workshops for flint knappers, potters, stoneworkers, and metalworkers (193–198).

Along with a number of smaller towns, three main urban centers arose in Upper Egypt: Naqada, Hierakonpolis, and Abydos. Naqada existed for at least 500 years, with an average calibrated radiocarbon date of about 5400 BP. Hierakonpolis emerged during 5800–5100 BP due to several factors: degradation of fragile desert ecosystems, increasing aridity leading to migration into the river valley, defensive clustering, the adaptation of agricultural technology to the annual flooding of the river plain, the use of the river for trade, and the role of the city as a religious center. Eventually it became the capital of an early Upper Egyptian kingdom (200–201).

Midant-Reynes estimates that an urban center from this period generally had a few hundred craft workers and officials, and that each non-food-producer was supported by fifty agriculturalists (198). This implies urban cores in combination with agricultural hinterlands on the order of 10,000 people, likely ruled by "kinglets" who controlled trade and manufacturing (207). Local irrigation may have begun around this time and toward the end of the pre-Dynastic period artistic images of irrigation are found. Early rulers in the Dynastic period may have encouraged further irrigation (232–234).

During the pre-Dynastic millennium, Lower Egypt became a sedentary society of pastoralist-agriculturalists, where cultural influences spread from the south to the north. Several sites are well known including Maadi, Heliopolis, and Buto. Metal objects are common at Maadi, which may have been a commercial center. Heliopolis appears to be mainly a cemetery. Buto, at the northern end of the Delta, became the capital of an early Lower Egyptian kingdom, comparable to Hierakonpolis in the south (218). With regard to the unification of south and north at the start of the Dynastic period, Midant-Reynes mentions fortified cities (including Hierakonpolis, also known as Nekhen) and depictions of battle scenes and victorious rulers, but not any skeletal evidence for warfare. She sees warfare as a minor factor by comparison with politics and culture (237–246).

Wengrow (2006) provides a portrait similar to that of Midant-Reynes but with a few differences in emphasis. He points out that the bulk of the evidence on economic and other matters in Egyptian prehistory comes from cemeteries rather than settlements due in part to the accumulation of river silts. He agrees that domesticates arrived from southwest Asia between 7000 and 6000 BP and that a unified territorial state with a central monarch followed with a lag of about 1500 years. Wengrow emphasizes that for some time after domesticates arrived there is little sign of permanent villages, and argues that this reflects the dominance of pastoralism relative to cereal cultivation (26–31, 63–64).

Early in the pre-Dynastic proper (6000–5000 BP), food sources in both Upper and Lower Egypt included cultivated wheat and barley, flax, lentils, and peas, along with wild roots, figs, and berries. Domesticated animals included cattle, sheep, goats and often pigs (84). Around the time of the transition from the Naqada I (6000–5650 BP) to the Naqada II (5650–5300 BP) period, cereal farming began to play a "decisive role" in Upper Egypt, with mud-brick housing indicating greater sedentism (33).

Wengrow is not convinced by arguments for urbanism or distinct city-states in Upper Egypt during Naqada I–II (72–73). Hierakonpolis was the largest habitation center of this period. Wengrow estimates that burials at Hierakonpolis in Naqada I–II number in the thousands, with additional nearby cemeteries having similar scales, including Naqada itself. Smaller centers had 100–200 burials and the majority had 600–1000 (73–75).

Although he downplays claims for early city-states, Wengrow believes that towns in Naqada I–II had craft specialization, trade networks, and some political centralization (76–83). During Naqada II (5650–5300 BP), migration to the floodplain in Upper Egypt was associated with the emergence of specialized craft zones for stonework, pottery, baking, and brewing (95–98). At Hierakonpolis, for example, "the concentration of activity along the floodplain is associated with the earliest evidence for specialised manufacturing areas" (consisting of debitage from stonework), and grave goods provide more evidence for expanding craft output (38). Material culture became broadly uniform for Upper and Lower Egypt in the Naqada II period. Metallurgical knowledge is evident in the later part of this millennium.

Wengrow believes that a process of urbanization was occurring in Upper Egypt prior to the emergence of a politically unified state in the Naqada III period (82–83), and that this process involved ritual centers as foci for craft production and trade (265). He states that at this time the number of sites was increasing in Lower Egypt (89), and with Naqada III there was a shift toward mass production for pottery, baking, and brewing (159–164). The wares of Lower Egypt were "the products of specialised workshops, oriented increasingly towards large-scale production and utility of form" (163).

A unified state spanning Upper and Lower Egypt, with kingship, elite dependents, and writing, arose in the Naqada IIIA–C1 period, corresponding to 5300–5100 BP (137). The elite took control over metal and mineral resources and introduced capital-intensive production techniques from southwest Asia, leading to an increasingly polarized society (142). In the Nile delta new centrally governed estates provided for the everyday needs of their dependents (173–175).

The account of pre-Dynastic Egypt by Hendrickx and Huyge (2014) is generally consistent with those of Midant-Reynes and Wengrow. The former authors place greater emphasis on skeletal evidence of violence by early Naqada II (fractures of the braincase, cut marks on neck vertebrae, and the like). However, they link this to capital punishment or human sacrifice rather than warfare. They also emphasize stratification dating back to 5700 BP, with cemeteries indicating that, "the elite clearly showed fewer traces of work stress and were far better fed" (252).

Hendrickx (2014) traces "royal tombs" back to early Naqada II at Hierakonpolis. However, by early Naqada III (around 5300 BP), Abydos had taken over as the center of power in Upper Egypt. While granting the role of violence in iconography, Hendrickx does not believe there was war between these two cities. He argues that a collaboration or alliance between them was much more likely. He also points to the earliest attestation of writing at Abydos as a sign that this city played a pivotal role in state formation. The eventual unification of Egypt resulted in a transfer of governance from Abydos north to Memphis, largely for economic reasons.

Some authors believe that pre-Dynastic Egypt had fortified city-states (Trigger, 2003, 104; Yoffee, 2005, 47). However, the arguments for fortifications in the late pre-Dynastic often appear to rest on artistic depictions (Hendrickx, 2014, 272) and may not warrant much attention without greater tangible evidence. The earliest sites that clearly do have fortifications are in peripheral areas far to the south or far to the north (Moeller, 2016, 76–81). For Hierakonpolis, which has good data, there is no town enclosure wall before 5200 BP and possibly not until 5100 BP, which for Moeller (2016, 81–84) is the start of the Early Dynastic period. We note that such a town wall could have been used to regulate individual access and does not necessarily imply a threat of war.

Another uncertainty involves the activities of non-food-producers in urban areas. Some authors suggest that the pre-Dynastic Egyptian cities had mainly administrative and ceremonial purposes (Yoffee, 2005, 48; Kemp, 2006). But Midant-Reynes and Wengrow both emphasize craft manufacturing and trade in the towns and cities of the pre-Dynastic period, and Moeller (2016, ch. 4) takes a similar view.

Allen's (1997) argument that the Egyptian state arose rapidly after the arrival of agriculture is clearly incorrect. Evidence for the use of domesticated plants and animals can be found at least 2,000 years before the Dynastic period, and there is no debate about the economic centrality of agriculture in the millennium-long pre-Dynastic period. Thus agricultural technology by itself cannot be regarded as a trigger for state formation.

A more plausible argument is that Egypt was affected by similar climate changes to those in Mesopotamia at around the same time. In both cases a prolonged reduction in rainfall caused the populations of outlying areas to migrate toward river valleys, resulting in the development of urban populations within societies controlled by landowning elites. In our view this climate shift was the trigger for urbanization and state formation in both cases (see Brooks, 2006, 2013, for evidence that these regions were affected by the same global climate events).

11.7 THE INDUS VALLEY

The early society of the Indus valley is sometimes called the "Indus Tradition" or the "Indus Civilization." The term "Indus valley" can be misleading as a geographic label because this culture is defined by a set of archaeological markers that extend well beyond the river valley to include tributaries of the Indus River in the north, coastal settlements in the south, and many other sites quite far from the river itself. When we refer to the Indus valley, we mean the "greater Indus valley" in this broad sense.

Chronologies and terminology differ somewhat from one source to another. For simplicity we define the pre-urban period to be 3200–2600 BCE, the urban period to be 2600–1900 BCE, and the post-urban period to be 1900–1300 BCE. Dates in the literature are almost always given as BC or BCE rather than BP, so we follow this convention. As many as 2600 sites are associated with one or more of the three periods listed above. An Indus script existed but has not been deciphered, so practically speaking Indus society is in the realm of prehistory. Information here is from Kenoyer (2014) except where noted.

The river valley has a rich alluvial plain. A winter cyclonic pattern brings rain from the northwest and a summer monsoon brings rain from the southwest. Agricultural and pastoral communities date to at least

5500 BCE and probably earlier. Winter–spring crops included wheat, barley, peas, and lentils, while summer–autumn crops included beans and millets. Domesticated animals included sheep, goats, and cattle. There was also some reliance on hunting in the pre-urban period, as well as riverine, lacustrine, or marine resources depending on the location of a particular site.

In the pre-urban period there were various distinct cultural traditions, but toward the end of this period there was a notable tendency toward uniformity of pottery styles, technology, architecture, and settlement organization. Copper-melting crucibles indicate metallurgical sophistication and there is evidence for textile production. The wheel may have been invented for carts drawn by oxen about 3700–3300 BCE. By 2800–2600 BCE three- or four-tier settlement patterns had arisen, with walls around larger centers. These walls could have had various functions such as offering protection against flooding or raiders, or controlling access to the site for trade and other purposes.

The transition from the pre-urban to urban period involved a smooth evolution at some sites, but in other places the abandonment of old sites and creation of new settlements. A few sites have ash layers at the transition, but evidence for any conflict at larger sites is absent. Kenoyer believes this transition did not involve warfare or conquest. The major cities of Harappa in the north and Mohenjo-Daro in the south were much larger than any earlier settlements (about 150–250 ha). These two leading cities were 570 km apart. The city of Harappa could accommodate 40,000–60,000 people, but seasonally the population was probably quite a bit less.

Ratnagar (2016, 52) stresses the radical nature of the shift from the pre-urban to the urban period, pointing to the emergence of many new settlements, citadels, planned street layouts, standardized weights, and writing. But according to Sinopoli (2015), only four or five sites from the "urban" period would actually qualify as urban, and these were separated by hundreds of kilometers. Petrie (2019) believes the larger cities arose quite rapidly (within a century) but suggests that most of the Indus population remained rural rather than urban.

The major cities housed administrators, ritual specialists, craft specialists, and traders. These groups were supported by farmers and herders inside and outside the city, with a hinterland of small towns and villages. Kenoyer distinguishes four categories of manufacturing activity: basic crafts using locally available materials (wood, clay, and animal products) with simple technologies; crafts using materials not available locally such as stone, but again with simple technologies; crafts using local materials but more complex technology (textiles, furniture, and some ornaments); and crafts with both non-local materials and complex technology (seals, artifacts of copper or copper alloys, hard stone beads, precious metals, glazes, and shells). He believes that the last two categories were most closely controlled by elites in order to produce high-status items and for local or long-distance trade. Pottery and copper-working operations were often located at the edges of settlements. Other operations "took place in segregated areas of larger domestic structures or in the streets between structures." Concentration of activity in certain parts of the city made it "easier for elites to monitor specific crafts" (2014, 421).

By 2450 BCE, new suburbs were added to the cities and massive new walls were constructed around them. Kenoyer remarks that, "the rapid population growth during this period can be explained only through the migration of new communities to the cities" (415). He observes that the nearby rural settlements remained occupied, so migrants may have come from more distant regions.

Differences in housing sizes, construction materials used, and locations (inside or outside city walls) indicate clear stratification within the large cities. Only a few burials have been found, which have distinctive pottery and ornaments showing membership in the elite. Commoners were not buried, providing additional evidence for stratification.

There is no evidence that cities were ever attacked or destroyed through warfare. Ratnagar (2016) places much greater emphasis than Kenoyer on the military significance of walls, citadels, and caches of defensive projectiles. This subject is controversial, with Kenoyer (2019) arguing that the walls were used mainly to control access and trade, and would have been militarily useless (2020, personal communication). We cannot resolve this debate here. What matters for us is that warfare was absent, whether this was due to the absence of military threats or the effectiveness of defense in deterring attacks. In any event Indus society in the urban period remained stable for over 700 years. We will not discuss the post-urban period except to note that it involved localized cultures, an end to writing, and the abandonment of most large cities.

The existence and nature of a state in the urban period is controversial. Based mainly on the absence of palaces and temples, Possehl (1998) argues that the region was an example of cities without a state. Possehl also emphasizes the apparent absence of a supreme political authority, a state religion, or a bureaucracy. Kenoyer (2014, 416), by contrast, argues that certain elite residences at Mohenjo-Daro might qualify as palaces.

Based mainly on the evidence for systematic city planning and the construction of large walls, Kenoyer asserts that the Indus area was characterized by independent city-states, with the major settlements ruled by corporate bodies representing wealthy landowners, merchants, and religious leaders. He regards the use of uniform stone weights, most commonly found near gateways and workshop areas, as evidence for taxation of trade items. Based on the standardization of weights and other aspects of cultural uniformity, Ratnagar (2016, ch. 7) suggests a degree of political centralization across the region as a whole. However, it is hard to reconcile arguments for a regional state with Ratnagar's own stress on the importance of military defenses at the level of the individual cities.

There is a longstanding tradition of including the Indus Valley on lists of pristine states (Service, 1975; Adams, 2001). We certainly accept the city-state description given evidence for four-tiered settlement systems, massive construction projects, city planning, the likelihood of taxation for trade goods, and the use of writing. We are less persuaded that political unification extended beyond the level of individual urban centers and their nearby rural hinterlands, particularly given the large distances between major centers.

The key question from our standpoint is whether there is any identifiable trigger for the urbanization process. We found relatively little discussion of causal mechanisms for the origin of city-states in this region, but the leading contender appears to be climate change. Madella and Fuller (2006) argue that Indus urbanism occurred during a lengthy trend toward declining rainfall. Evidence for this view comes from the sediments in salt lakes, pollen sequences, and correlations with other regional and global climate events. Madella and Fuller suggest that relatively high rainfall during the mid-Holocene led to the spread of sedentism and agriculture in the Indus area, partly through increased flood levels that allowed more extensive cultivation as the floods receded. This would have supported demographic expansion. However, diminishing rainfall by 2900–2450 BCE contributed to a rising population near the Indus and Ghaggar-Hakra rivers in the urban period, as rain-fed cultivation became more difficult.

These ideas are elaborated by Giosan et al. (2012, E1688), who find that aridity intensified after about 3000 BCE and suggest "a gradual decrease in flood intensity that probably stimulated intensive agriculture initially and encouraged urbanization" around 2500 BCE. Giosan et al. (2012, E1693) assert that "river floods have always been far more important and reliable for agriculture than rainfall," that precipitation feeding the rivers decreased after 3000 BCE, and that it reached its lowest level after about 2000 BCE. They conclude, "This drying of the Indus region supports the hypothesis that adaptation to aridity contributed to social complexity and urbanization."

This argument is reinforced by archaeological evidence that Indus cities made major investments in water management. Ratnagar (2016, ch. 9) argues that cities had deep wells tapping into a region-wide aquifer for drinking water, and that reservoirs for the storage of flood water "required enormous community labour under direction and coordination" (192). Kenoyer agrees that "one of the outstanding features of the Indus cities is the technology of water management through the construction of wells and reservoirs" (2014, 418). However, he is skeptical about the relevance of climate change.

In a detailed survey of the literature Petrie et al. (2017) describe a wide range of views, from the belief that there was no change in annual rainfall patterns between 4000 BCE and the present to the belief that climate change was the main cause of the collapse of Indus civilization. Petrie et al. accept that monsoonal rainfall decreased during 4400–3760 BCE and 2200–2000 BCE, but these episodes do not coincide with the timing of the initial urbanization. They stress the diversity of microclimates and ecosystems, as well as numerous data problems, and believe it is unlikely that climate change would have led to uniform effects across the region. However, they do not directly criticize the arguments of Madella and Fuller (2006) or Giosan et al. (2012). Although the debate over the role of climate change is unresolved, our assessment is that increasing aridity is a prominent candidate as a trigger for the emergence of Indus city-states.

11.8 CHINA

The process of pristine state formation in China is complex. There is still active debate both about which site was the first to become a state and about the causal forces that led to this outcome. We will describe what we believe is the majority view on the subject, but we include a contrary view at the end of this section so readers will gain a sense of the issues at stake.

Cohen and Murowchick (2014) provide a detailed description of the Middle and Late Neolithic periods in northern China from about 3500–1800 BCE. These cultures are known as Yangshao and Longshan, and provide the background for state formation. This period reveals a trajectory starting from simple egalitarian societies and moving over time toward increasing site numbers; increasing population densities;

increasing stratification; greater craft specialization (jade, lithics, pottery, and metallurgy); multi-tiered settlement hierarchies with central places; some very large site areas; defensive walls; and warfare.

Elite warfare appears to have been common in the Late Neolithic. In a review of the Chinese archaeological literature on warfare for 5000–2000 BCE involving 85 sites, James Kai-sing Kung (personal communication, 2020) identified 30 sites with weapons including arrowheads, spears, axes, and bullets or balls; 27 sites with fortifications (four had trenches and the rest were walled towns); and 18 sites with unnatural deaths (largely confined to the Yellow River area, and with skeletons usually having scars from arrows). We note that some of this evidence is ambiguous. For example, weapons might be used for hunting and walls might be used to control individual access to a site. However, two sites had strong evidence for mass violence: Taosi, located near the Yellow River, with a mass grave for 40 people along with the destruction of a town and tombs; and Yuanmou-Dadunzi in Yunnan province, where most victims were young men hit by large stones or killed by arrows.

Recent research at Shimao, in modern Shaanxi province well north of the central plain of the Yellow River, has shed new light on the role of warfare in the late Neolithic. This settlement existed from 2300–1800 BCE, and with an area of more than 400 ha was the largest walled settlement in China at the time (information is from Jaang et al., 2018). The first construction project was a palace center probably meant as a residence for ruling elites, with a design suggesting desires both for defense and restrictions on access. Metal artifacts were manufactured in this center. Construction beyond this complex was "much more humble, both in terms of size and building techniques" (1013). An initial stone wall enclosed an area of 210 ha, and this was followed by an outer wall around 2100 BCE that was clearly designed for defense. The Shimao polity had a four-tier hierarchy with up to 4,000 settlements.

Jaang et al. believe that Shimao destroyed Taosi, a large Neolithic urban center to the south, around 2000–1900 BCE. This involved a breach of the outer wall at Taosi, the death of at least 50 people in the palatial center, destruction of the palace, and dragging of elite corpses out of tombs. Cultural evidence suggests that the region surrounding Taosi became a colony in the Shimao network.

Sun et al. (2017) assert that Shimao flourished during a relatively warm and wet climate, and declined during climate deterioration around 1800 BCE. They believe the period of favorable climate was associated with a very high population and that the rapid nature of the population growth was attributable at least in part to migration into the area by pastoralists. Their discussion suggests causality running from climate to population to warfare. Sun et al. also suggest that people from Shimao may have been responsible for the destruction of Taosi.

There is a reasonably broad consensus that the first Chinese state was centered at Erlitou in the Yiluo basin from 1900 to 1500 BCE (a dissenting opinion will be discussed later in this section). This interval is divided into four phases of about one century each based on a ceramic typology, but precise dates are difficult to determine. Our description follows Liu and Chen (2012, ch. 8) and is supplemented by Liu and Chen (2003) and Liu (2006). Liu and Chen (2012, 258) define a state as having a ruling class and commoner class, where the elite has centralized decision-making with functional specialization and the regional settlement hierarchy has at least four tiers. They argue that Erlitou satisfied these requirements while Late Neolithic societies did not.

The region is a large fertile alluvial basin surrounded by hills, mountain ranges, and the Yellow River to the north. Good land quality provided high yields for grains and domesticated animals, and permitted a high population density. After previous Neolithic occupation, the area was abandoned for 500–600 years. While most regions exhibited a decline in population density and social complexity around 2000 BCE, the Yiluo basin was an exception, developing a large urban center and a four-tiered settlement hierarchy. The broader Erlitou culture, classified as Bronze Age rather than Neolithic, includes more than 300 sites with similar material characteristics spread across the middle Yellow River valley. Over 200 of these sites were distributed on the alluvial plains and loess tablelands of the core Erlitou region. The site of Erlitou was probably chosen for the transportation advantages of the Yiluo River system and because surrounding mountains offered some protection. The central site was not fortified, although a few fortified sites in peripheral areas outside the Yiluo basin are known to have existed.

In Phase I the site measures more than 100 ha in area and seems to be the largest site in the Yiluo region and beyond. The population of the site is estimated at 3,500–5,800. "Such rapid population nucleation can be explained only by migration from surrounding areas" (2012, 266). It is unclear where the migrants came from, what led them to move to the site, or whether there was an amalgamation of existing villages in the region. But Rawson (2017) has suggested that migrants from Shimao may have moved to Taosi and then on to Erlitou, bringing bronze technology with them.

Liu (2004, 235) points out that the Yellow River changed its course around 2000 BCE, that this was a time of flooding in many parts of the Yellow River valley, and that the floods may have been caused by climatic fluctuation. Cohen and Murowchick (2014, 783) refer to "a major cold event at 2000 BCE that may have been one driving factor in the end of Longshan-related cultures and the emergence of early state-level Bronze Age societies." Wu et al. (2016) have argued that an earthquake caused a landslide damming the Yellow River, which then led to a massive outburst flood around 1920 BCE and may have triggered the formation of Erlitou. Thus a number of scholars cite environmental shifts that could have caused the rise of a state, but there is little agreement on details.

The tool assemblages from Phase I at Erlitou included agricultural and hunting-fishing implements. The population engaged in both food production and crafts, with workshops producing both utilitarian and elite goods. Craft specializations from Phase I included pottery, bone carving, and bronze casting. Elite items included white pottery, ivory and turquoise artifacts, and bronze tools.

By Phase II the site area had increased to its maximum extent of 300 ha and the population is estimated to have increased to 8,300–13,900. A complex of rammed-earth buildings (12 ha) emerged, where the buildings were comparable in size and complexity to the palaces of the later Shang period. Two groups of elite burials were unearthed from the courtyards of a palace. More generally, Liu and Chen emphasize the "sharp contrast between the commoners' small and semisubterranean houses and poor burials on the one hand, and the elite's large, rammed-earth palatial structures and rich tombs containing artifacts made of bronze, jade, turquoise, cowry shell, ivory, and kaolinic clay (white pottery), on the other" (2012, 263). A bronze-casting foundry was located close to the palace complex. This area was densely populated by craftsmen and their families. The production of prestige items appears to have been controlled by the state. Agricultural tools continued to make up the largest proportion of tool assemblages. The number of arrowheads grew at a rate similar to other tools, indicating that their primary function was hunting rather than warfare. This phase had a four-tier settlement hierarchy for the Yiluo region as a whole.

Phase III was the peak period for Erlitou, with a marked increase in the numbers of pits, houses, burials, and kilns. The urban center probably had around 18,000–30,000 people. The old palaces were abandoned and six new palaces were constructed in a more organized way, likely requiring large-scale earth moving. Water wells and storage pits were dramatically reduced in the palace precinct, suggesting a larger elite role and more functional specialization. Craft workshops became even more numerous and produced both utilitarian and elite goods, where the latter included greater emphasis on turquoise. While high-prestige goods continued to be produced near the palace complex, probably under state control, bone and ceramic workshops were spread more widely, indicating a continuation of independent craft production. Agricultural tools decreased in proportion to craft goods. The city population probably relied heavily on food from the hinterland, and the total population of the Yiluo region may have reached 54,000–82,000 people. It is unclear whether market systems had developed for utilitarian goods or to what degree the supply of agricultural output to the center reflected a tribute system. The number of arrowheads increased rapidly, suggesting military expansion motivated by a desire to control outlying sources of salt and metals.

In Phase IV the site area stayed the same as in Phase III and palatial structures remained in use, with Erlitou maintaining its position as the largest urban center in the region. Quantities of tools in all categories increased except for needles and awls used in domestic crafts. However, the population declined, with craft production becoming less important in relation to food output and residential construction. Arrowhead production grew dramatically. In the late part of Phase IV a large fortified city (200 ha) was built 6 km northeast of Erlitou. The material remains are characteristic of the Erligang (or early Shang) period. Although the issue is controversial, this may reflect a conquest of Erlitou by the Shang. Elite goods production at Erlitou stopped after Phase IV, and the site was reduced to the scale of an ordinary village. It was ultimately abandoned as people moved to settlements linked with the new and larger Shang state.

The role of "the earliest Chinese state" is most often assigned to Erlitou, but some dissenters award this honor to one or another Late Neolithic settlement prior to Erlitou, or to the Erligang/Early Shang state around 1600 BCE. Shelach-Lavi (2015, chs. 7–8) falls in the latter category. We review his arguments partly for the light they shed on Erlitou, and partly to illustrate larger problems surrounding the identification of pristine states.

Shelach-Lavi accepts the idea that flooding around 2000 BCE, perhaps due to a shift in the course of the river, could have led to the collapse of societies in the middle and lower Yellow River regions, which could account for the rise of Erlitou. He is also willing to entertain the argument that such flooding was caused by anomalous monsoon patterns, which simultaneously brought exceptional aridity to North China. Although he does not say so directly, these events could have triggered migration to the Yiluo region. However, Shelach-Lavi expresses reservations about the aridity scenario, noting that it is hard to reconcile with population growth in parts of northeastern China that should have been particularly vulnerable to drought.

Shelach-Lavi's general description of the Erlitou site does not differ much from that given above. However, he rejects it as the center of a state-level society for several reasons (184–190). First, he questions arguments based on the size of the site, saying that Late Neolithic settlements like Taosi and Shijiahe were of similar size. He also remarks that no state-level monumental architecture has been found at Erlitou. In particular, the so-called "palaces" are small in relation to the palaces of pristine states in other parts of the world and are comparable to a Late Neolithic site in China. The labor investments needed to build the "palaces" were not especially impressive. Similarly grave sizes and grave goods do not reflect anything qualitatively new. Although Erlitou had a substantial bronze industry, it can be regarded as a continuation of earlier ceramic works rather than a new departure, and was unimpressive relative to the bronze works of the Shang period.

Shelach-Lavi doubts the claimed role of Erlitou in a four-tier settlement hierarchy, maintaining that there is little evidence that the alleged second and third tier centers had any administrative functions. He also points to the absence of large centralized granaries that would have supported royal or elite households. Claims of military expansion in the Erlitou Phase III are rejected on the grounds that cultural boundaries need not correspond to political boundaries, and that some of the asserted military activities are unrealistic. In conclusion Shelach-Levi asserts, "This discussion does not preclude the possibility that a state-level society did emerge in the Yiluo basin during Erlitou phase III. It suggests, however, that there is currently no clear evidence in support of this hypothesis" (190). He argues that the Erligang (or Early Shang) society formed around the time of Erlitou Phase IV does pass this test.

For brevity we will not pursue a discussion of the Shang polity here, although we note that it also has some questionable features. For example, Shelach-Lavi suggests that the Shang lacked institutionalized methods for tax collection and may have financed their "state" through land rent (nominally the king owned all the land; 222). He also describes the Shang administrative system as "generalized" rather than "specialized," despite giving considerable weight to functional specialization as a defining feature of the state in his preceding chapter. No one seriously doubts that the Shang polity counts as a state, but we raise these points to show that defining a state and identifying archaeological criteria for the presence of a state are not straightforward matters. On balance, however, we do accept what we take to be the majority view, which is that Erlitou was a pristine state.

11.9 MESOAMERICA

The region of Mesoamerica encompasses central and southern Mexico, Belize, Guatemala, and parts of El Salvador and Honduras. The development of early cities and states was complex, involving several sub-regions. It is often difficult to assess whether events at a specific time and location should be called "pristine," given the prevalence of interactions across the region involving migration, trade, warfare, and ideology.

Background conditions include regional population growth and rising numbers of tiers in settlement hierarchies during the Middle Formative (1000–400 BCE). The urban status of Early and Middle Formative centers is debated, but processes of nucleation and centralization at nodes within regional networks were underway (Pool, 2012). Spencer and Redmond (2004) use markers for states including a four-tiered settlement hierarchy, royal palaces and specialized temples, and conquest or subjugation of distant territories. In their view the Olmec society of the Middle Formative period involved chiefdoms and hence we omit a discussion of this case. Spencer and Redmond regard Oaxaca, the Basin of Mexico, and the Lowland Maya area as locations for the emergence of primary states. However, we begin with a discussion of events along the Pacific coast.

On the Pacific coastal plain from Chiapas to El Salvador, horticulture and partial sedentism arose by the Late Archaic period (information in this paragraph and the next is from Love, 2012). Maize and other cultigens existed by 3500 BCE. Pottery appeared in the Early Formative period (1900–1000 BCE). Increasing sedentism and cultivation led to increasing population, as well as wealth inequality and two-tiered settlement systems by 1700 BCE, suggestive of simple chiefdoms. Soon after 1400 BCE new paramount settlements arose, which appear to be successive capitals of a larger regional polity. In the Middle Formative (1000–400 BCE) population growth continued, probably due in part to improvements in the characteristics of maize, leading to greater density and larger settlements. The largest political systems were complex chiefdoms, which had incipient urbanism, rigid social stratification, and structured regional hierarchies.

This trajectory climaxed with fully urban states throughout the coastal plain and in the highlands during the Late Formative (400 BCE–200 CE). The cities were larger than those of the Middle Formative and spread over a larger area. This "Southern City-State Culture" had numerous urban centers of over 4 sq km with hinterlands generally less than 1,000 sq km. Love refers to these polities, which were linked by local and long-distance trade, as "micro-states." Each had a core with massive public construction, and several were focal for settlement hierarchies that had four or more tiers. Love does not speculate about the causality behind this process of city-state formation. In particular he does not discuss the possible roles of craft manufacturing or warfare. He does, however, suggest that drought brought an end to this system by 200 CE.

The nearby area of Oaxaca is the center of a zone called the "southern highlands" (information is from Elson, 2012). The timing for the emergence of stratification and hereditary leadership in the southern highlands is debated but may date back to around 700 BCE. During the Middle Formative, chiefdoms had varying population sizes and degrees of social complexity.

The Oaxaca Valley is divided into three areas that together form a Y shape. In the period 700–500 BCE there is evidence for ranked societies that had three-tier settlement hierarchies. The Middle Formative is known for widespread warfare among chiefdoms, with raiding, temple burning, and taking of captives for sacrifice. An uninhabited buffer zone developed at the center of the valley where the three branches met. Between 500–100 BCE several sites in the region became urban centers, with state formation occurring by the end of this period.

The settlement of Monte Albán dates to 500 BCE and was located at the center of the Oaxaca Valley, on a mountain 1,400 m tall at the juncture of the valley's three arms. Ongoing warfare among the chiefdoms in the valley branches, as well as external threats, made this defensive location attractive. Some authors also emphasize the ceremonial and religious significance of the site. The initial population of 5,000 tripled over the next four centuries. Specialized state architecture is apparent around 100 BCE–200 CE but likely dates back to 300 BCE. State formation is agreed to have occurred by 300–100 BCE. Expansion outside the valley began before the rival polities within the valley had been defeated. By 150 BCE the capital of one rival polity had been burned and abandoned. The last holdouts within the Oaxaca Valley were incorporated by

200 CE. This led to Zapotec civilization, which lasted for five more centuries. At its peak Monte Albán had a population of 15,000–30,000.

Balkansky (2014) adds a few elements to this review. Craft specialization was an early development in Oaxaca, dating to 1000 BCE and correlated with rising inequality. Important products included shell jewelry, pottery, chipped stone, and textiles. Around the time of its urbanization process, Oaxaca was an important demographic center for Mesoamerica as a whole. Chiefly competition and warfare dates at least to 600 BCE, with evidence including depictions of slain captives, unoccupied buffer zones, burned public buildings, and trophy taking. Toward the end of the Middle Formative there were many sites where chiefdoms gave way to urbanism: "The movement of entire populations from valley floor to terraced hilltops characterized Oaxaca's urban revolution" (1032). Urbanism at Monte Albán was a defense against external threats. This city-state covered 6.5 sq km of rugged hilltops, and controlled multiple valleys and ethno-linguistic groups.

The Central Mexican Highlands have a rich natural environment with alluvial plains and lakes surrounded by volcanic mountain ranges. The climate is temperate due to an altitude about 2,000 m above sea level, and rainfall averages 450–900 mm annually (information in this paragraph is from Sugiyama, 2012). A wide variety of plants were domesticated by 5000 BCE. During the Formative and Early Classic periods, irrigation and terracing were applied to maize, beans, squash, and other crops. Raised agricultural fields sustained increasing populations. Dogs and turkeys were domesticated, with deer, peccaries, rabbits, and other species providing additional animal foods. By the Middle Formative improving technology had led to growing population and social complexity, with craft industries, market economies, and several populous villages.

In the Late Formative, by 250–100 BCE, the Basin of Mexico had one location with 20,000–40,000 people (Teotihuacan) and a second with about 20,000 (Cuicuilco); see Spencer and Redmond (2004). The latter was focal for a cluster of sites exhibiting a four-tiered hierarchy and had several monumental buildings. It is less certain whether Teotihuacan was focal for a four-tiered hierarchy during this period or had similar large structures. Some authors argue that the site locations in the Basin of Mexico reflected a concern with defense, but there is no evidence for fortifications, warfare, or extension of control to distant areas around this time. Cuicuilco was destroyed by a volcanic eruption between 1 CE and 400 CE, and the duration of its overlap with Teotihuacan is uncertain (Sugiyama, 2012). Volcanic activity may have resulted in large-scale migration into the Teotihuacan Valley but this is likewise unclear (Clayton, 2015, 282–283).

According to Sugiyama, Teotihuacan began as a regional ritual center. By about 200 CE, it had 60,000–80,000 inhabitants, and some of its neighborhoods were occupied by migrants from distant areas. Construction followed a master plan starting around 200 CE. Offerings of projectile points and other war-related objects at major temples, as well as human sacrifices of prisoners of war, suggest that military institutions were important to city governance. "Ample data" indicate craft specialization and stratification. Its peak population may have been 100,000–150,000. The city was eventually destroyed through warfare by unknown enemies at an unknown date.

Manzanilla (2014) adds the following. Population growth in the basin of Mexico was sustained and substantial during 900–250 BCE. This was accompanied by the rise of settlement hierarchies with regional centers, large villages, small villages, and hamlets. Clustering of settlements with empty buffer zones and the use of sites on mountaintops suggest some degree of political hostility. However, the subsequent population growth at Teotihuacan in the northeast part of the basin "should be seen not as a forceful act or the effect of conquest … but the natural consequence of a large population shift" (991), probably associated with groups fleeing from volcanic eruptions to the south. By 200–350 CE, Teotihuacan was exceptional for its size, urban planning, settlement pattern (a huge city surrounded by rural sites), corporate elite strategy (including co-rulership), and multiethnic composition. Craft production occurred on multiple scales: everyday needs in apartment compounds, extensive craft sectors in the periphery to produce items for the urban population, specialized identity markers produced in barrio sectors supervised by noble "houses," and specific crafts from workshops under the control of rulers.

We close this section with a discussion of the southern Maya lowlands, covering parts of Mexico, Belize, and Guatemala (information in this paragraph is from Chase and Chase, 2012). The first sedentary Maya lived in fully formed villages dated to 1200–900 BCE. By sometime after 600 BCE ceramics and architecture across the region became more standardized and recognizably "Maya." In the Late Preclassic period (300 BCE–250 CE) raised agricultural fields were in use, and in the Classic period (250–800 CE) there was extensive terracing of the landscape.

Freidel (2014) emphasizes the emergence of large urban centers like El Mirador during the later Preclassic. He calls these the capitals of "kingdoms." One rich tomb at Tikal, dating to 200 CE, may have been for the founder of the royal dynasty of this city. Terms like "royal" and "kingdoms" suggest the existence of states, but Freidel does not offer much further archaeological evidence for the existence of states in the usual sense. He argues that the boundary of the Preclassic and Classic periods, around 200–250 CE, was marked by catastrophe, with the collapse of several political capitals. The possible reasons include environmental degradation, deforestation, climate change, and drought.

By 250 CE, at the start of the Early Classic, developments included elite tombs, political control by elite families, and stone monuments with written texts (information is from Chase and Chase, 2012). The latter indicate founding dates for political dynasties ranging from 100 CE to 426 CE. Burial data reveal ranked societies, and in some places stratification, throughout the lowlands; "rulership was a prerogative of a small elite group at each site" (260). Architectural complexes described as palaces became widespread and state-level societies were "surely achieved" by this time. There were numerous small city-states, with Tikal being the preeminent site of the Early Classic period.

In the Late Classic (550–800 BCE), Maya cities reached their maximum size, with Caracol and Tikal each having landscapes of about 200 sq km containing about 100,000 occupants. Chase and Chase describe these as "low-density cities" comparable to other examples of tropical urbanism in Southeast Asia and Africa. Spatially distinct areas of public architecture were linked by causeways and continuous residential settlements. A market economy probably existed.

Chase and Chase do not suggest any causal explanation for state formation in the Maya lowlands. Based upon the existence of palaces, temples, and a four-tier hierarchy, Spencer and Redmond (2004) agree that states had formed by around 250–500 CE. They likewise refrain from causal explanations, although they do not cite evidence for warfare or conquest during this period.

11.10 SOUTH AMERICA

Burger (2014) offers an account of early Peruvian developments, both along the coast and in the highlands, up to about 50 BCE. The story is one of initially simple food technologies and egalitarian social systems, which over time evolved in the direction of more complex technology, larger settlements, monumental architecture, the formation of elites, and (toward the end) strong evidence for warfare. This trajectory is the backdrop for subsequent processes of urbanization and state formation.

Stanish (2001) surveys the archaeological evidence for pristine state formation in South America. The key areas are the Peruvian coast and the central Andean highlands. Stanish downplays monumental architecture as an indicator of early states, arguing that non-state societies like chiefdoms are capable of mobilizing the required labor. He dates the first fully sedentary and complex societies on the Pacific coast of Peru to 3000–2500 BCE, with the first stratified societies in South America arising soon after. Most scholars describe these as simple chiefdoms. More complex but non-urban chiefdoms emerged in the period leading up to 200 BCE. These societies lacked the socioeconomic hierarchies normally found in connection with states.

According to Stanish (2001), the first states were Moche, Tiwanaku, and Wari, which arose in the Andes during the first millennium CE. These three cases were largely independent of one another. Stanish remarks that Moche was "perhaps the first true city in the Andes" (53) and was the center of a multi-valley polity. The view that Moche had state-level organization is controversial (Quilter and Koons, 2012), but for the purposes of the following discussion we will accept the claim that all three societies had states. Tiwanaku and Wari had similar site sizes and arose more or less simultaneously, not long after Moche. For detailed descriptions of Tiwanaku and Wari, see Quilter (2014, ch. 8).

Again according to Stanish (2001), all three states had elites, palaces, large urban capitals, settlement hierarchies with at least four tiers, economic specialization, and total populations for each polity from 50,000 to 200,000. The capital cities resembled Uruk and Teotihuacan. State formation occurred in unusually productive environmental zones where it was possible to intensify agriculture fairly easily, including through irrigation. Direct elite control of irrigation was probably not a significant factor. There was some gradual population growth but not population pressure within circumscribed areas. All three states have strong evidence of warfare involving iconography, physical remains, and defensive architecture, as well as good evidence for colonization of distant locations.

Moore (2014, ch. 9) believes that Moche society developed from multiple origins along the Peruvian coast in the period 200–850 CE. The extension of agricultural fields through improved and reliable irrigation technologies led to a rich elite culture. Moore argues that a centralized state emerged in the southern valleys of the Moche culture area, although he acknowledges that this view is controversial. The capital city (also known as Moche) was centered around two complexes of temples and plazas, with densely packed workshops and dwellings covering about 100 ha on a flat plain between these complexes. Roads had a grid system and in each block there were workshops that produced ceramics, metal objects, semi-precious stone ornaments, and textiles. "Craft production was specialized and organized" (323). The elite mobilized commoner labor for public works projects such as irrigation canals. The Moche state was followed by secondary states in the same region that need not be discussed here.

According to Moore (2014, ch. 9), the Wari state arose in the Central Andes about 550–600 CE and lasted until about 1000 CE. It is unclear whether Wari was actually a pristine state or coalesced from earlier settlements that had already achieved state-level organization. The capital city of Huari was located in the Ayacucho Valley, which was agriculturally fertile and heavily reliant on maize. Its urban core covered 2.5 sq km and was surrounded by 15 sq km of less monumental buildings and residences. Elite culture was reflected in fine craft production. Infrastructure included compounds, storerooms, and roads. The Wari constructed local administrative centers elsewhere in their empire, which probably extended to sites in Peru more than 900 km from the capital. Outposts were often located on impregnable hilltops.

Moore (2014, ch. 9) dates the Tiwanaku society around the Lake Titicaca basin to about 400–1100 CE and describes it as a rival of Wari. The core of the capital city (also called Tiwanaku) was a large planned area of pyramids and plazas surrounded by 4–6 sq km of middens. Population estimates vary but Moore believes the capital had 15,000–25,000 inhabitants. The elite lived in a distinct residential area near sacred spaces, with elaborate architecture and rich burials. The remainder of the population lived in denser settlements stretching from the city core to Lake Titicaca. Raised fields were a crucial component of the agricultural economy. About 100,000 people in the lake basin could have been fed by these fields. The extent of the fields increased as the Tiwanaku empire coalesced and expanded. The empire displayed explosive growth during 725–1000 CE, when loosely integrated colonies were converted into a system of centrally governed provinces. Climate change led to prolonged droughts during 950–1100 CE that brought a massive reduction in population and an end to the empire.

11.11 GENERAL PATTERNS

In this section we attempt to distill some general patterns from the regional cases sketched above, as well as the case of southern Mesopotamia from Chapter 9. Patterns of this kind impose useful constraints on theory. Some causal mechanisms that can account for these patterns will be discussed in Section 11.12. Six regions do not constitute a large sample, so the ideas developed in these two sections should be regarded as hypotheses or conjectures to be tested through more research, both for the regions we have discussed as well as other regions not covered here.

Agricultural Productivity: Almost every account of pristine state formation in a given region includes a comment to the effect that fertile agricultural land was plentiful. Depending on the case this may involve alluvial plains, volcanic soil, or the like. We are unaware of pristine states based exclusively on hunting, gathering, and fishing, although the latter activities were often important supplements to agriculture. Indeed, it has been argued that in the early stages of urbanization at Uruk, food from wetlands was primary and agriculture was secondary (see our remarks on Algaze and Pournelle in Chapter 9).

Stratification: Every account of pristine state formation we have seen reports the existence of elite and commoner classes. Furthermore, these class divisions existed prior to state formation and were not simply a product of it. We have seen no account where a state arose in an egalitarian society. As with a highly productive food technology, pre-existing stratification appears to be a necessary condition.

Urbanization: As a conceptual matter we can imagine cities without states and states without cities. However, we are struck by the recurring role of cities in all of the regional cases we have investigated. From an empirical standpoint pristine cities and pristine states are closely intertwined. We are not quite ready to claim that cities are a necessary or sufficient condition for states, but pristine states assembled entirely by the political unification of rural territories appear to be rare.

We do want to acknowledge the possibility of counterexamples. Kirch (2010) asserts that Hawaii was an example of state formation and one could argue that cities had no role in this process, but the Hawaiian state was not pristine (Kamehameha I had access to European weapons and advisors). Other examples of state formation from historical or ethnographic accounts, such as those used by Flannery (1999) and Flannery and Marcus (2012), have similar difficulties. Hansen (2008, 69–70) suggests some examples of early states without cities and early cities without states that seem less problematic. We grant that such cases can be found, but believe that theories linking states with cities are likely to have greater explanatory power than theories that ignore the catalytic role of cities in the process of state formation.

Migration: In several (although not all) of the regional cases we studied, experts commented that the agglomeration of population in a compact area was too rapid to have occurred without migration from external sources. At least in these cases this means that urbanization probably had a short-run trigger and did not require Malthusian population growth over several generations. In some cases rural settlements located near emerging cities did not lose significant population, indicating that migrants must have come from farther afield. Of course, the importance of rapid migration in some cases does not rule out the potential relevance of slower migration flows extending over many generations, or long-run Malthusian dynamics, in other cases.

11.12 THREE PATHWAYS

Assuming the reader is willing to grant the existence of recurrent patterns across regions of the world, we take up the challenge of explaining these patterns. No theory will ever explain every particularity of every case, but there is no reason to believe that attempts to formulate general explanations are somehow intellectually illegitimate or doomed to failure. In our view there are three principal mechanisms that help to explain the patterns we have described. All build upon models we developed earlier in the book. We call them (a) the property rights hypothesis, (b) the elite warfare hypothesis, and (c) the environmental shift hypothesis. We will describe each of these causal mechanisms and discuss how it applies to regional cases. But first we make a few general points.

All three pathways to the state rest upon the theory of stratification from Chapter 6. This theory treated technological innovation in food production as exogenous, used Malthusian principles to derive an implication of long-run regional population growth, and showed that such population growth can eventually lead to the formation of elite and commoner classes at the best sites. Section 11.11 argued that stratification of this kind is a necessary condition for pristine state formation. Section 11.11 also argued that a good natural environment for food production is a necessary condition. The latter factor tends to support high regional population and makes it more likely that technological advances will eventually generate the population levels required to induce stratification.

We generally expect technological innovation and regional population growth to be observed prior to pristine state formation, because these factors drive stratification and the latter is a precondition for the state. Such innovations could include improvements in the characteristics of domesticated plant or animal species, or adaptation of these species to local conditions; improvements in sowing, plowing, and harvesting; or investments in irrigation and terracing systems. We expect technological developments of this kind to result in population growth that should become archaeologically visible through a higher settlement density and/ or larger settlements as measured by geographic size or number of inhabitants. Stratification should become visible in the usual ways: more inequality with respect to housing, burials, nutrition, health, access to exotic items, and so on. Although our model in Chapter 6 did not capture the idea of settlement hierarchies, as an empirical matter such stratification is usually associated with simple or complex chiefdoms having two or three-tiered hierarchies.

Another preliminary remark involves urbanization and craft manufacturing. Any causal mechanism that leads to urban agglomeration is likely to stimulate manufacturing. The reason is summed up in Adam Smith's adage that the division of labor is limited by the extent of the market. Because urbanization creates large local markets, it encourages craft specialization as long as food producers are willing to exchange some of their output for manufactured goods. Processes of learning by doing then tend to raise manufacturing productivity, reinforcing the trend toward urbanization. We have also argued that urban manufacturing can sometimes be easier to tax than rural agriculture, so these dynamics can lead to city-states.

The three hypotheses we will discuss below have these features in common, but differ with respect to the causal trigger that initiates the agglomeration process.

The Property Rights Hypothesis: We showed in Chapter 6 that technical progress and the resulting population growth make commoners worse off (see especially Section 6.8). The reason is that as technology improves and the regional population rises, more sites become closed. Due to the endogeneity of property rights, fewer sites remain in the commons, these sites are the least desirable ones, and the commoner standard of living falls. This drives down the wage offered to commoners by elites at stratified sites.

There are several implications. First, the declining wage means that elites want to hire more commoners, so the populations of the high-quality sites will grow. Second, we showed in Chapter 10 that a falling wage can trigger a shift toward urban manufacturing. In Chapter 10 the falling wage was the short-run result of a negative climate shock while here it is a long-run result of technological advance, population growth, and endogenous property rights. The result, however, is much the same. Elites eventually allocate some labor to craft manufacturing, this stimulates urbanization, and the visibility of inputs and outputs in the urban sector makes it easier to collect taxes there. This yields a city-state.

If there are several good sites of roughly equal quality within a region, we would expect the property rights mechanism to generate several small city-states, one for each local elite in control of a high-quality site. Because market power is less significant in a region with competing city-states, in this situation we expect taxation to be motivated less by exploitation of monopoly or monopsony positions in the markets for goods and labor, and more by the provision of local public goods of interest to the elite. These predictions could, however, be overturned if geography implies the existence of a single good site, or increasing returns to scale at the level of the city strongly outweigh transportation costs. In the latter situations, a single dominant city could arise. But in any event, because the property rights hypothesis relies upon Malthusian population growth we would expect city-state formation to be a gradual process extending over multiple generations, not an abrupt response to migration flows.

The Elite Warfare Hypothesis: In Chapter 8 we showed that stratified societies are prone to chronic conflict over land rents. This may either take the form of open warfare or credible threats to engage in such warfare. The key parameter in determining which of the two is more likely is the degree of stratification. We showed that if land rents are of moderate size relative to commoner wages (and thus relative to the cost of a hired army), there are equilibria where intimidation tactics can succeed without any need for open war. However, when land rents are large relative to the commoner wage, equilibria must have a positive probability of open warfare. In a region with many production sites the elites controlling the best sites are the most likely to engage in open warfare with one another, because these are the sites with the highest land rents relative to the region-wide wage.

Successful elites engage in territorial expansion. In principle this expansion can yield a geographically extensive agrarian state without cities. However, a region having serious threats of warfare can be expected to have some degree of urbanization due to the benefits of agglomeration at defensible locations, and the fact that the large size of a city in itself tends to deter attack. As with the environmental shift hypothesis to be discussed below (although for different reasons), the threat of warfare can generate an implosion of the regional population from the periphery to one or more centers. We do not expect any similar regional implosion under the property rights hypothesis.

Our analysis of elite warfare in Chapter 8 did not focus on the distinction between short-run and long-run equilibria because warfare was driven by wages and land rents, not directly by regional population. But if technological progress in agriculture and resulting Malthusian population growth leads to high land rents for the elite and low standards of living for commoners, as we expect from Chapter 6, in the long run this will exacerbate elite warfare, promote territorial expansion, and encourage city-state formation.

The primary factor restraining elite warfare (or intimidation) is defensive military technology, which can potentially deter attacks. Accordingly, it is crucial not to infer the prevalence of warfare from evidence of defensive locations or fortifications. When these preventive measures are effective, deterrence works, and elite warfare shuts down. Better indicators of active warfare include skeletal evidence for mass violence; settlements that were sacked, destroyed, or conquered despite defensive investments; and perhaps artistic images of conquest. Of course, these indicators may be absent in cases where territorial expansion and political unification occur through intimidation rather than open warfare. Although effective defensive technology does restrain territorial expansion through overt coercion or covert threats, it does not rule out the formation and stability of autonomous city-states, which may well arise in response to threats of warfare (Gat, 2006, 278–293).

Given the possibility that defensive military technology could stabilize a region with competing elites, we should consider some factors that might destabilize a peaceful equilibrium. One potential trigger for warfare is a climate shock, which could increase the temptation for one elite to attack another. A second potential trigger is a change in production technology rendering agricultural output a more tempting target for predation (perhaps involving more storage or more transparency in the production process), which could strengthen the incentive for elites to engage in violent competition over land rents. A third might be a change in military technology that favors attackers over defenders.

The Environmental Shift Hypothesis: We already discussed this causal mechanism at length in Chapter 10 and it is not necessary to repeat that discussion here. As with the property rights hypothesis, the key idea is that the commoner wage falls, triggering elite interest in urban manufacturing and the tax revenue obtainable from it.

These two hypotheses differ because the property rights mechanism requires long-run Malthusian population growth, while environmental shifts can operate as triggers for urbanization and state formation through short-run migration (recall that we held regional population constant for most of Chapter 10). A second difference is that in the property rights hypothesis, *falling* wages result from *rising* agricultural productivity. This is due to Malthusian population growth, endogenous property rights, and the contraction of the commons. But in the environmental shift hypothesis, *falling* wages result from *falling* agricultural productivity due to a deterioration in natural conditions, at least for a subset of vulnerable sites in the region. A third difference is that an environmental shift could lead to city-state formation even if property rights at individual sites do not change (it is unnecessary for additional sites to become closed and for the commons to contract).

We prefer the term "environmental shift" to "environmental shock" because while short-run shocks could be sufficient for city and state formation, a gradual deterioration in the natural environment unfolding over centuries can have similar long-run consequences. The most obvious kind of environmental shift is increasing aridity, which drives a wedge between the productivity of outlying areas in the commons (dependent on rainfall) and refuge areas controlled by elites (with access to rivers or irrigation systems). But similar effects could result from alterations in river courses, volcanic eruptions, changing disease conditions, exogenous ecological disruptions, or endogenous environmental degradation such as soil loss due to deforestation. Any of these factors could potentially change the relative productivities of the sites within a region, motivate migration from the commons to sites controlled by elites, and depress the commoner wage to a level that causes local elites to pursue urban manufacturing. These effects will be larger when the pre-existing regional population is larger, when the productivity wedge between the commons and the refuge sites is larger, and when there are few good refuge locations.

The environmental shift hypothesis makes different predictions from the previous two hypotheses. In contrast to the property rights hypothesis, it predicts agglomerations of population in refuge areas sheltered from the changing natural environment rather than a gradual proliferation of small city-states at sites with permanently high productivity for geographic reasons. In contrast to the warfare hypothesis, it predicts intensive growth in areas that are relatively immune to environmental decline, rather than formation of city-states in places that are relatively immune to attack, or extensive growth of a unified state over a broad geographic area.

We also point out that according to the environmental shift hypothesis, people are pushed from the periphery (commons) to the center (refuge area). We are doubtful that a magnetic pull emanating from the center can give similar results because the productivity of urban manufacturing is unlikely to rise without learning by doing. In turn, learning by doing is unlikely to occur when an urban manufacturing sector has not yet developed. An external trigger is therefore needed in order for the urbanization process to get underway. This is similar to the role of climate change in pushing Upper Paleolithic societies out of stagnation traps (see Chapter 3).

11.13 APPLICATIONS

The preceding section described three pathways leading to cities and states. In this section we discuss how our hypotheses might apply to the six regional cases we have surveyed. In every case there is strong evidence for stratification before state formation, so for brevity we omit any comments on this factor.

Mesopotamia: As discussed in Chapter 9, there is no evidence of warfare leading up to the formation of the Uruk city-state. The preceding 'Ubaid period had little or no warfare, and the first wall at Uruk was constructed only after the formation stage. In the ensuing centuries there was warfare among city-states, and after almost a millennium the region was unified politically through conquest, but all of this came much later. We do have reasonable evidence for an environmental shift story based on increasing aridity, a migratory response where some people moved to elite-controlled areas in the south, and resulting urbanization based on craft manufacturing and trade.

Egypt: The evidence for warfare in the period leading to state formation in Upper Egypt is a bit more pronounced than in Mesopotamia, with not only fortified city-states but also vivid artistic depictions of warfare.

However, we do not know of any evidence for warfare in the relevant time period based upon skeletal trauma or destroyed cities, and some experts emphasize politics and culture as key factors in the unification of Upper and Lower Egypt. Whatever the role of warfare may have been, Egypt clearly experienced a trend toward greater aridity (the same trend that affected Mesopotamia), migration away from the desert toward the elite-controlled Nile valley, and urbanization based upon craft manufacturing and some trade. Thus the emergence of early city-states was likely driven by environmental factors, even if their later unification required the use or threat of force.

In the early (pre-Dynastic) stages, both Egypt and Mesopotamia had urbanization and substantial craft manufacturing. But in Egypt independent city-states did not last for very long, while in southern Mesopotamia this stage lasted for almost a full millennium prior to political unification. One possible explanation involves differences in geography such as tighter circumscription in Egypt. Another involves the greater reliance on cereals in Egypt, with the Nile flood plain being ideally suited for cereal agriculture, while the floods in southern Mesopotamia were poorly timed and demanded more costly forms of irrigation. A third explanation is that in Egypt it was easy to infer cereal output from the height of the flood (Mayshar et al., 2017, 2022), so a centralized state could be based mainly on tax revenue derived from the agricultural sector. In Mesopotamia, by contrast, it may have been harder for elites to tax agricultural output, so at least in the early stages Mesopotamian elites were more dependent on the tax revenue from urban manufacturing. Such factors may have slowed political unification in southern Mesopotamia by limiting the incentive for a local elite at one city-state to attempt the conquest of a rival city-state.

The Indus Valley: The principal cities had walls but their purpose is controversial and it might not have been to deter attacks. There is no evidence of open warfare during the pre-urban period, and little evidence around the start of the urban period as city-states were forming, aside from ambiguous ash layers at a subset of sites. There is no evidence that one large city-state attacked another in the ensuing centuries, and little evidence that the region was a territorially unified state. Some researchers argue that increasing aridity contributed to city-state formation, but others disagree or maintain that adequate evidence is lacking. The jury clearly remains out on the environmental shift hypothesis, although this would be consistent with evidence for migration to elite-controlled areas near rivers. If the elite warfare and environmental shift theories are both rejected, we would have to fall back on the property rights hypothesis and argue that improving technology led to a gradual demographic expansion, closure of good sites, stratification, falling wages, and urban manufacturing. We leave it for the experts to evaluate the merits of this scenario.

China: There is little doubt that stratified societies engaged in considerable war during the millennia leading up to state formation at Erlitou. The evidence includes not only fortifications but also weapons and skeletal trauma. On the other hand, there seems to be no direct evidence of warfare from the first two centuries of Erlitou. In its third and fourth centuries Erlitou appears to have engaged in territorial expansion through military means, and may have been conquered by a more powerful rival. Most scholars agree that Erlitou arose largely through migration and that craft manufacturing played an important role. It seems possible that the initial migrants were fleeing from warfare. There are also suggestions that environmental shifts could account for the rise of Erlitou, such as colder conditions, changing monsoons, flooding, or drought, but better evidence is needed.

Mesoamerica: This region is complex and two or all three of our hypotheses may apply. The "Southern City-State Culture" along the Pacific coast resembles the cluster of microstates we would expect under the property rights hypothesis, and the same may be true for the initial set of small city-states in the Maya lowlands. In the absence of direct evidence for environmental shocks or warfare at the time these city-states were forming, we lean toward that interpretation. This does not contradict strong evidence for warfare and fortifications later in Maya history (Gat 2006, 282–284). On the other hand it is quite clear that the rise of Monte Albán in Oaxaca occurred in a context of warfare and that the city arose for defensive reasons. We also note the prominence of territorial expansion in this case. Finally, the story for the basin of Mexico is unclear, but some authors put little weight on warfare in the early phases of Teotihuacan, instead stressing volcanic eruptions and migration effects, which could be consistent with our environmental shift hypothesis. Military conflict clearly became important later, but more evidence would be needed to make a case that it played a significant role in the initial establishment of this city-state.

South America: Moche, which in the view of some scholars was the first pristine state along the Peruvian coast, seems to have arisen through warfare. Evidence includes not just fortifications but also extensive artistic depictions, weapons, and practices often associated with warfare such as human sacrifice of prisoners. Similar remarks apply to the later states in the Andean highlands, Wari and Tiwanaku. In all three cases territorial expansion was significant. The rapid growth of large capital cities rules out the property rights hypothesis, which predicts a gradual rise of city-states on a Malthusian time scale. We are not aware of any credible evidence for environmental factors, and conclude that the warfare hypothesis provides the best fit.

In sum, for all six examples of pristine state formation we find a close link with urbanization. The causal factors behind the development of city-states vary by region. Increasing aridity appears to have been the main driver for Mesopotamia and Egypt. It is possible that environmental factors played a role in the Indus valley and northern China, but the situation is unclear. Mesoamerica is complicated, with certain subregions where the property rights hypothesis may be a good fit, at least one subregion that supports the warfare hypothesis, and substantial uncertainty about state origins in the basin of Mexico. The three cases from South America all appear consistent with the warfare hypothesis. It would be of great interest to expand the data set to study the relative frequency of these causal mechanisms in other regions of the world such as Africa, Southeast Asia, Europe, and North America.

11.14 CONCLUSION

Our exploration of the institutional trajectories of prehistory has taken us from the origins of inequality (Chapter 6) and the emergence of warfare over land (Chapters 7–8) to the rise of cities and states (Chapters 9–11). With the last two developments we reach what is often called "civilization." In particular we reach the technological innovation of writing, which brings prehistory to an end.

We will not attempt to summarize everything that has gone before, but we remind the reader of a few general points. First, our theoretical approach throughout Parts III and IV of the book has been based on what we call "technologies of coercion." These come in three varieties: A technology of exclusion (Chapter 6), a technology of combat (Chapters 7–8), and a technology of confiscation (Chapter 10). We have shown that even relatively simple formalizations of these ideas can lead to rich modeling frameworks. We hope the reader has been persuaded that these exercises can enhance our understanding of the data.

Stepping back from the math, our argument is fundamentally about the manner in which elite groups arise and how they pursue their joint interests. This takes for granted that such elite groups are organized enough to overcome the coordination and free rider problems bedeviling all forms of collective action. Although we do not make universal claims about the organizational coherence of elites, they have several advantages: elites are relatively small numerically, they tend to arise in geographically compact places (at least initially), and their members are quite likely to engage in repeated interaction, with strong information flows within the group and the capacity to impose large penalties on noncooperators through ostracism (expulsion to the commoner class).

Commoners, in contrast, tend to be numerous and possibly mobile, perhaps with weaker information flows among members and less ability to impose large penalties via ostracism. Commoners may also have more heterogeneous objectives than elite agents, who are likely to share an interest in the maximization of land rent or profit. Moreover, once an elite class emerges, it has a strong incentive to discourage effective organization within the commoner class and to promote ideologies legitimizing its dominance. In this view, the pristine state represents the victory of the organized over the unorganized.

11.15 POSTSCRIPT

Chapter 11 was largely written in the summer of 2020. The formal models from Chapters 6, 8, and 10 were constructed before we read most of the literature on the five regional cases discussed in this chapter.

The following acknowledgments apply to all of Part IV (Chapters 9–11). In fall 2018 we visited Harvard University at the invitation of two members of the economics department, Nathan Nunn and Melissa Dell. During that semester we presented our work on southern Mesopotamia to the economic history group. We are grateful to the seminar participants, especially Claudia Goldin, for helpful comments. During the same semester we visited the Standing Committee of Archaeology at Harvard at the invitation of Rowan Flad, who provided valuable guidance on China. We attended a course offered by Jeffrey Quilter and Jason Ur called "Urban Revolutions," and both were generous in responding to our many questions. We thank Gojko Barjamovic for feedback on the Mesopotamian part of our research.

From January until March 2019 we visited the Institute of Advanced Studies at University College London, hosted by the director Tamar Garb. IAS was a friendly and stimulating research environment. We attended weekly meetings at IAS and presented our work on southern Mesopotamia in a seminar there. Stephen Shennan of the Institute of

Archaeology organized our overall visit to UCL and invited us to give two seminars at the Institute. We thank the audiences at both IAS and the Institute of Archaeology for the valuable comments and suggestions we received, and especially Stephen Shennan for his persistent attempts to educate us about archaeology.

Guillermo Algaze was highly generous in reading multiple drafts of Chapter 9 and responding with very extensive comments. Archaeological experts who provided helpful suggestions for Chapter 11 include Jonathan Mark Kenoyer, Li Liu, Jeff Quilter, David Wengrow, and Norman Yoffee. Among economists we thank Omer Moav for comments on Chapter 9 and Louis Putterman for comments on Chapters 9 and 11. Due to looming deadlines and page constraints, as well as our own intellectual idiosyncrasies, we did not follow every piece of advice we were offered, but we deeply appreciate all of it.

As mentioned in Section 11.8, James K.-S. Kung shared an unpublished literature review on warfare in Neolithic China. Huiqian Song assisted in our discussion of Kung's data and created the graphs in Chapter 10. Michael Straw was a research assistant in the early stages of our work on Part IV.

We also thank the Social Sciences and Humanities Research Council of Canada for generously funding our visits to Harvard and UCL. All of the chapters in this book, but especially Chapters 9–11, were substantially improved as a result. However, we are solely responsible for the content. None of the individuals or organizations listed in this postscript should be blamed for our interpretations or mistakes.

PART V

EPILOGUE

12

Bridges to the Present

12.1 TEN THOUSAND YEARS OF PREHISTORY

No one disputes that the city-states of southern Mesopotamia were states, or that dynastic Egypt was a state. Both arose shortly before 5000 years ago. At about the same time cuneiform writing developed in Mesopotamia and hieroglyphic writing developed in Egypt. Additional pristine states emerged in other parts of the world over subsequent millennia, and most had their own writing systems. However, from a global perspective the line between prehistory and history was crossed 5000 years before the present.

Some of the developments we have discussed in this book have unclear starting points. For example, there may have been occasional sedentism in the Upper Paleolithic at times and places where resource patches happened to be concentrated and predictable. Similarly, raiding among foraging groups may extend into the indefinite past, although warfare aimed at gaining permanent control of valuable land appears to be a more recent development. But in general, substantial and lasting transitions to sedentism, agriculture, inequality, warfare, cities, and states began between 15,000 BP and 5000 BP.

From the standpoint of an individual human life, 10,000 years is a very long time, about 500 generations. But in relation to the time *Homo sapiens* has been on the planet, perhaps 300,000 years, it is only 3% of the total. Of the time in which the biological genus *Homo* has been on the planet, perhaps 2.3 million years, it is only 0.4% of the total. On such time scales the 10,000 years of central concern in this book were a blink of an eye, and the six transitions we have studied were revolutionary in their speed and scope.

One cannot convincingly explain a set of transitions this dramatic and widespread by appealing to random local conditions or idiosyncratic cultures. Global revolutions are best explained by global causes. We believe the prime mover for the revolutionary social transformations of 15,000–5000 BP was climate change. We argued in Chapters 4 and 5 that the recovery from the Last Glacial Maximum, followed by the abrupt shock of the Younger Dryas and the arrival of the Holocene, were the triggers for sedentary lifestyles among foragers and later for village agriculture.

Domestication of plants and animals set off a process of technological innovation that has never ended. Over time this trajectory became increasingly decoupled from the natural environment and no longer required an external stimulus from climate shocks. For Malthusian reasons, rising agricultural productivities resulted in rising population densities. We argued in Chapters 6–8 that population growth led to class stratification between elites and commoners at particularly attractive sites, and that stratification laid the foundations for chronic warfare over land among rival elites.

Finally, we showed in Chapters 9–11 how these processes ultimately led to cities and states. We argued that there were at least three causal pathways in the intertwined development of cities and states: one based on property rights, involving gradual closure of the commons and falling living standards for commoners on Malthusian time scales; a second based on warfare among elites, leading to agglomeration in cities by the defenders and formation of large territorial states by aggressors; and a third based on environmental shifts during the Holocene, which sometimes pushed rural populations into refuge areas, often in river valleys, that evolved into city-states by way of urban manufacturing.

Although the resulting societies displayed kaleidoscopic institutional and cultural variation, we believe the underlying economic processes were relatively simple. The key exogenous variables were geography and climate. Geographical variations across regions of the world, and across the individual sites within regions, were largely permanent, but played a crucial role by determining the spatial distribution of natural resources. Climate varied from one decade, century, or millennium to another, as well as across regions, and accounted for the timing of several transitions through its interaction with geography.

Two other key variables, technology and population, were endogenous on long time scales. Technology largely evolved through learning by doing. This created both stagnation traps, where societies continued using

known techniques for long periods of time, and intervals of rapid technological innovation when external conditions such as climate shocks
pushed societies into the use of new resources or production techniques.
Population largely evolved according to Malthusian principles, where
regional densities rose when climate improved or technology became
more productive. Throughout the 10,000-year period with which we have
been concerned, the gains from technological innovation went almost
entirely into population growth rather than improvements in the average
standard of living.

In short-run settings where technology and population were largely
fixed, social responses to environmental shocks depended on other
factors. The most prominent were migration and warfare. We have
argued in a number of cases that migratory responses to environmental
shocks triggered cultivation and manufacturing. We have also argued that
large shocks to climate or technology changed the relative productivities
of sites, which sometimes led to warfare when individual migratory
responses were precluded by social barriers to physical mobility.

We have offered a number of hypotheses that are open to archaeological testing. We do not expect every hypothesis to hold up under
empirical scrutiny. Science is about taking risks, especially the risk of
being wrong. But even if the reader is skeptical about some (or all!) of
our hypotheses, we hope she or he has been persuaded that economics can
be a fruitful source of research ideas about prehistory.

The great advantage of economic reasoning is that it can explain many
seemingly disparate phenomena using a fairly small set of concepts and
assumptions. Accordingly, it facilitates theoretical unification. The price,
of course, is that many important details of individual cases must be
suppressed. For those who want to stress the unique features of each
society, this price will be too high. But for those who believe that the
evolution of human societies displays recurrent patterns that are open to
causal explanation, perhaps the price will be acceptable.

12.2 FIVE THOUSAND YEARS OF HISTORY

This has largely been a book about "firsts": the first sedentary foragers,
the first cultivators, the first states, and so on. If one wants to understand
major transitions of this kind, it makes sense to look for the earliest
instances of the phenomenon in question and explore the forces that
could have generated that phenomenon in its pristine form. But by
definition, pristine examples are not representative. While the residents

of Abu Hureyra were cultivating cereal crops, almost everyone else was gathering wild plants and hunting wild animals. While the Mesopotamian city-states were emerging, almost everyone else was living in societies where state-level institutions were absent.

A similar perspective is needed in thinking about the last 5,000 years. Until quite recently, foraging societies persisted in large parts of the Americas, Africa, and Asia, as well as all of Australia and the Arctic. Elsewhere agricultural villages of a few hundred people were the norm. In some places these villages were politically autonomous, while in other places they were components of two-tier or three-tier settlement hierarchies that anthropologists might call simple or complex chiefdoms.

As we have seen, over the last 5,000 years cities and states emerged in the Indus River region, China, Mesoamerica, and the Andes. Similar processes led to cities and states in the Sahel region of West Africa, Ethiopia, Zimbabwe, and on the east coast of Africa. Additional precocious developments occurred at Cahokia in North America and Angkor Wat in Southeast Asia. Within Europe, city-states emerged in Greece, while the village of Rome became a city, a state, and eventually the capital of an empire.

Much of world history over the last few millennia is a dreary and repetitive story about kings (and a few queens) who fought wars and built empires. Often these empires remained intact for a few generations or a few centuries, collapsed, and were replaced by new empires assembled by new rulers. Despite these micro-level instabilities, at a macro level this system of rising and falling empires superficially exhibited a kind of structural stasis. But gradually the fraction of the globe subject to state control grew (Borcan et al., 2018) and the number of autonomous political units declined (Bowles, 2012).

This process culminated with the conquest of the Americas and Australia by the European powers, which also colonized large areas of Africa and Asia. Perhaps 50–80% of the indigenous population of the Americas was lost to virulent diseases like smallpox and measles. Others were lost to genocide, enslavement, and forced assimilation. The Atlantic slave trade added further horrors, as did other slave trades in the Arab world and around the Indian Ocean. The settler populations of the Americas gained independence from Europe by about 1820, and decolonization movements in Africa and Asia led to the formation of many independent nations after World War II.

Three more developments had massive effects on the modern world: the Industrial Revolution, the Demographic Transition, and political democracy. Together these events provided billions of people with rising incomes and protection from abusive elites. They represent a seventh transition in world history, and we will discuss them in this chapter.

In the process we will undertake a deeper exploration of the causal connections between prehistory and contemporary global civilization. It would be natural to assume that prehistory is dead and buried, but this belief is incorrect. The ghosts of prehistory continue to stalk the modern world. Three provocative lines of research show how.

The first, pioneered by Louis Putterman, Ola Olsson, and their co-authors, argues that early agriculture and early state formation conferred persistent advantages on some modern nations. Specifically, nations that had earlier agricultural transitions and earlier state institutions on average enjoy higher incomes or rates of economic growth today. A large number of caveats must be attached to this summary statement, but the correlations are striking. The possibility that prehistoric events exerted causal influences extending over millennia, and continue to shape economic growth today, is highly intriguing. We discuss this research in Section 12.3.

Oded Galor and his co-authors approach related questions from a more theoretical point of view. Their goal is to develop a causal framework that can explain the complete sweep of economic development from Neolithic agriculture to modern industrialization. This ambitious research program, called "unified growth theory," incorporates technology, population, and other variables that have been central to this book. We will describe this theoretical framework and the facts it can explain in Section 12.4.

Carles Boix is a political economist who adopts an equally long time frame, ranging from prehistoric foraging to modern democracies. He emphasizes the development of military technology, a subject we have not highlighted, and argues that the emergence of political democracy was tied to an unusual constellation of economic and military conditions that prevailed in early modern Europe. We review his arguments in Section 12.5, along with related arguments about the origins of political democracy from Douglass North and his co-authors, as well as Daron Acemoglu and James Robinson.

These ambitious efforts to understand social, political, and economic change in the very long run provide foundations for a further inquiry. What, if anything, can one say about trends in human welfare over the last 15,000 years? Has life gotten better for the majority of people, has it gotten worse, or is the picture more complicated? Given data limitations, we focus on basic indicators such as diet, health, and life expectancy. For the majority of the world's population, we believe the trajectory of human welfare has followed a U shape: reasonably good for mobile hunter-gatherers, worse for commoners in agricultural societies and ancient cities, and improving drastically since the Industrial Revolution. The theory and evidence behind these claims are described in Section 12.6.

We close this chapter by returning to our key exogenous variable: climate. We have argued that climate change from the late Pleistocene through the Holocene was the principal driving force, either directly or indirectly, behind the six transitions examined in this book. Given the existential threat our own civilization faces from global warming, it is appropriate to conclude by asking whether prehistory offers any lessons for our current predicament. We hazard a few remarks on this topic in Section 12.7, followed by a brief postscript in Section 12.8.

12.3 THE SHADOW OF THE PAST

Economists interested in very-long-run economic growth have been intrigued by the arguments of Diamond (1997), who asserts that differing biogeographic endowments across regions of the world (in particular, the supply of domesticable plants and animals) led to differences in the timing of pristine agriculture. In turn, regions that developed an early agricultural economy tended to have a high early population density as well as an early transition to state institutions. According to Diamond these developments led to permanent technological, military, and institutional advantages that explain why Spain conquered the Incan Empire rather than vice versa, and more generally why European nations were able to colonize large parts of the world during the last 500 years.

Diamond's arguments inspired Louis Putterman, Ola Olsson, and their co-authors to study a related question: Do countries with a longer history of agriculture or state-level institutions have advantages with respect to modern economic performance? If so, why? This agenda was pioneered by Bockstette et al. (2002) and Hibbs and Olsson (2004). The literature has grown enormously in recent years and we cannot provide a comprehensive review, but we will discuss several key findings and interpretive issues.

Economists have long understood that "good" institutions contribute to economic growth while "bad" institutions restrain it (for a highly readable series of case studies, see Acemoglu and Robinson, 2012). Institutional quality has been measured in a number of ways, including indexes for social development, social infrastructure, social capital, and the rule of law. Bockstette et al. (2002) added something new: the sheer antiquity of state institutions has apparently had a powerful influence on modern economic growth.

Bockstette et al. carried out the following empirical exercise. For each of the 119 modern countries having the necessary data, they divided the interval from 1 CE to 1950 CE into 39 periods of 50 years each. For each half-century they determined whether the country had a government above the tribal level, whether this government was local or foreign, and how much of the territory of the modern country it controlled. After giving points on each criterion, they calculated a measure of state antiquity for the country. To put less weight on events in the distant past, they discounted the scores by 5% for each half century, although the results were not sensitive to the details of this procedure.

The resulting index, called "statehist5," was positively correlated with measures of political and institutional quality such as stability, lack of corruption, lack of government contract repudiation, lack of expropriative risk, the rule of law, and bureaucratic quality; negatively correlated with ethnic fragmentation; positively correlated with the population density in 1960, social development, and civic norms; and positively correlated with GDP per capita in 1960, 1970, 1980, 1990, and 1995, as well as GDP growth during the period 1960–1995. Of course, simple correlations do not imply causality, an issue to which we will return below.

The next step was to include statehist5 in conventional cross-country regression equations used to explain economic growth. The dependent variable was GDP growth during 1960–1995 and the control variables included the level of GDP in 1960, schooling, population growth, and the investment rate. When statehist5 was added, it had a positive sign and was consistently significant at the 0.01 level. This continued to be true, and the magnitude of the coefficient remained stable, when more controls were added, including measures of institutional quality, population density in 1960, ethnic fragmentation, and dummy variables for region of the world (East-Asia Pacific, Latin America, and so on). Furthermore, the effect was large: the difference in statehist5 between China (the oldest state) and Mauritania (one of the newest) accounted for about half of the total difference in growth rates between the two countries. Similar results were obtained for a subsample excluding the OECD (Organization for Economic Co-operation and Development) countries, so the findings were not driven by the presence of richer countries in the sample.

We now return to the question of causality. Given the way in which statehist5 is defined, reverse causality can be ruled out: high economic growth today does not cause state formation centuries ago. However, it is possible that this variable simply proxies for institutional quality without having any further effects of its own. Bockstette et al. tested this possibility by including both statehist5 and a commonly used measure of institutional quality in their regressions. Both variables were significant, showing that statehist5 adds predictive power. The same was true when population density was included. Therefore statehist5 is not merely proxying for these variables. Moreover, ethnic fragmentation was no longer significant when statehist5 was also included. Statehist5 remained significant and quantitatively strong when regional dummy variables were added, showing that it helps explain differences in economic growth even among countries in the same region.

These results suggest that processes of state formation over the last two millennia have had powerful effects on modern economic growth. Bockstette et al. suggest that the effects of the Industrial Revolution diffused slowly at first, but that in the second half of the twentieth century countries having greater antiquity of state institutions were better able to catch up with the industrial leaders, and that this linkage became stronger as the effects of colonialism waned. The nature of the causal linkage is not entirely clear, but Bockstette et al. propose several possibilities: (a) countries with a longer history of state institutions have had more time to benefit from learning by doing in public administration; (b) the populations in such countries may have more positive attitudes toward state bureaucracy; and (c) state antiquity promotes linguistic unity, which may encourage a sense of shared identity and social trust, while discouraging civil wars and political instability.

Deeper causal issues remain. For example, one might argue that some geographic factor X (such as having many domesticable species, or fertile soil for agriculture) led to both early state formation and high economic growth, so the correlation of statehist5 with modern growth rates is spurious. Bockstette et al. (2002) were aware of this issue but did not address it directly. However, research on migration discussed below tends to counter these concerns by suggesting that the causal links involve human capital rather than fixed characteristics of geographic locations.

Hibbs and Olsson (2004) and Olsson and Hibbs (2005) address the influence of an early pristine transition to agriculture on modern incomes. We base our discussion on the first of these articles. The authors build upon Diamond's (1997) insight that some regions of the world had more wild plant and animal species that could be domesticated, and that an early agricultural transition gave such regions a persistent head start with respect to the broader process of economic development. Causality for Hibbs and Olsson runs from the geographic features of a region (climate, latitude, and the degree of east–west orientation of the continental axes) and its biological endowment of domesticable plants and animals, to its predicted date for a pristine transition to agriculture, and finally to the level of GDP per capita in 1997. Modern countries were assigned to eight regional groups based upon the distinct biological endowments of their regions (the sample includes 112 countries).

Hibbs and Olsson (2004) use six pristine agricultural transitions (southwest Asia, China, west Africa, the Andes, Mesoamerica, and the eastern United States) to estimate a relationship between biological endowments and the timing of the agricultural transition. The predicted timing of this transition is then used in cross-country regressions to explain modern incomes. They find that geography, predicted agricultural timing, and the square of predicted agricultural timing together account for 57% of the variance across countries in the log of 1997 per capita income. All three variables are significant at the 0.01 level and the effects are quantitatively substantial. When the authors add a standard index of institutional quality (an average of bureaucratic quality, rule of law, low corruption, low expropriation risk, and low risk of government contract repudiation), this increases the explanatory power of the equation to 80%.

A large part of the variance across countries in modern institutional quality (43%) is explained by the time since a pristine agricultural transition in the region. Furthermore, geography and time since the agricultural transition remain significant when institutional quality is included. Thus an early agricultural transition probably confers some benefit through the presence of good institutions, but it also makes an independent contribution.

A byproduct of this research is the finding that regions with better geographical and biological characteristics had earlier pristine agricultural transitions. The sample size is small, but this finding provides support for the perspective of Diamond (1997). As we argued in Section 5.12, Diamond proposes a theory about the supply side of the Neolithic transition, and Hibbs and Olsson provide evidence that these supply-side factors matter. However, the timing of a given pristine transition also depends on demand-side factors, including climate change. The geographic index used by Hibbs and Olsson incorporates a static climate variable associated with the suitability of a region for agriculture, but not a variable describing changes in climate over time. Thus they do not test the hypothesis we developed in Chapter 5.

We are impressed that a large fraction of the variation in incomes across modern countries can be explained by variables that are undeniably exogenous and prehistoric in nature (geography, biology, and years since the origin of pristine agriculture in a region). The main causal issue is that these variables could be proxies for other factors that affect incomes today (such as latitude or climatic suitability of a region for agriculture), so that it is not the elapsed time since the advent of agriculture that is driving the results.

Putterman (2008) builds upon the work of Hibbs and Olsson (2004) by gathering country-specific information on the timing of initial agriculture in 112 nations. He shows that nations having early Neolithic transitions have higher income levels in the year 1997 after controlling for geography, and that this effect is already visible in income data as far back as 1500 AD. When "years since transition" is measured using the methods of Hibbs and Olsson, agricultural timing remains significant as a determinant of modern income after controlling for institutional quality, but is insignificant when agricultural timing is measured using the Putterman country-specific approach.

One important difference between Hibbs and Olsson (2004) and Putterman (2008) is that the former use information about pristine agricultural transitions in eight regions of the world, while the latter mainly relies on information about the diffusion of agriculture. Putterman's results should be interpreted as showing the effects from an early arrival of farming in a particular nation, not the effects of an early pristine transition (although the sample does include a few pristine cases). Nevertheless, Putterman confirms the finding from Hibbs and Olsson (2004) that geographic factors (climate, latitude, east–west versus north–south continental axes) are a powerful determinant of the timing of the agricultural transition. For more on the diffusion process, see Ashraf and Michalopoulos (2015).

Probably the most important finding of Putterman (2008) is that the advantages from lengthy experience with agriculture and states can be transferred from one region of the world to another through migration. To show this, Putterman calculates a measure of "years since transition" that is a weighted average based on the years since transition for the source countries of immigrants, with weights based on the fraction of migrants from each source country. This calculation is based on migration flows over the last 500 years (including, but not limited to, the migration of Europeans to the USA, Canada, Australia, and New Zealand). Putterman shows that the fit of the model for the 1997 income data is substantially better when "years since transition" is adjusted for migration in this way. For further results along these lines, see Putterman and Weil (2010).

This tends to blunt any critique that correlations between prehistoric events and modern growth are driven by some geographic factor that influences both. Apparently individuals can carry the benefits of lengthy experience with agriculture and states when they move, suggesting that the crucial causal links involve human capabilities rather than geographic conditions. These capabilities may include technical knowledge, institutional experience, cultural norms, or similar factors.

Putterman finds that the antiquity of agricultural technology is highly correlated with the antiquity of state institutions (a bivariate correlation of 0.649, significant at the .001 level), where state antiquity is measured as in Bockstette et al. (2002). Moreover, the state antiquity variable again helps to predict 1997 incomes, and the fit of the model improves substantially after correcting the state antiquity variable for post-1500 CE migration flows. With this adjustment, state history explains about 25% of the variance in national income per capita for 1997. Borcan et al. (2021) have confirmed the close connection between early agriculture and early states.

The data set for the history of state institutions used by Bockstette et al. (2002) has been extended back to 3500 BCE by Borcan et al. (2018), so it now covers all of the episodes of pristine state formation discussed in this book, including Mesopotamia and Egypt. Data are available for 159 modern nations. Borcan et al. discount the past using a lower rate than Bockstette et al. (1% per 50-year period rather than 5%) but their results are not highly sensitive to small changes in the discount rate.

Borcan et al. report two major empirical findings. First, a relationship between a long history of state institutions and productivity is already visible in 1500 CE. A linkage of this kind is found for various measures of productivity including technology adoption, population density, and urbanization. Interestingly, quadratic terms for state history are large and significant even with numerous control variables for geography and climate (but not if continental fixed effects are included). This yields an increasing and concave relationship between the antiquity of the state and productivity in the year 1500. Also, a variable for the antiquity of agriculture adds explanatory power for technology adoption and population density (but not urbanization).

Second, there is a similar quadratic relationship between state history and GDP per capita in the year 2000, again with numerous geographic controls. The coefficient on the quadratic term is negative enough that the overall relationship is hump-shaped, with states of intermediate age having higher income per capita than those that are either older or younger. The antiquity of agriculture is insignificant, suggesting that in modern data it makes no additional contribution to income levels beyond what state institutions provide. The hump-shaped relationship is only visible for regressions using the entire state history going back to 3500 BCE (or 5500 BP), and disappears when the state history variable is defined using the data since 1 CE. Thus the early millennia in the dataset are crucial for this result. Explanatory power is greatly improved by the use of state history measures adjusted for migration flows (the latter explain 23% of the variance in modern incomes rather than just 5%). The qualitative results described in this paragraph are also obtained when the dependent variable of GDP per capita is replaced by technology adoption.

Borcan et al. suggest that a simple theoretical model can account for these results. Suppose (a) individual states tend to have rising productivity over time due to increasing fiscal and institutional capacities; (b) this process has diminishing returns because elites eventually divert tax revenue to unproductive activities; and (c) newer states learn from the experience of older states, so their peak productivity level exceeds that of the earlier states. At a given moment in time there will be a mix of old states that have become too centralized and have relatively low productivity, states of middling age that have learned from their predecessors and achieved higher productivity, and young states that have low but increasing productivity. This pattern gives a hump-shaped relationship between state antiquity and economic performance in modern cross-sectional data.

We close this section with some fascinating recent findings about the relationship between early agricultural transitions and modern economic performance. Although at a global level, early transitions are positively correlated with contemporary incomes across nations, this relationship appears to be driven by differences across regions with distinct pristine agricultural transitions (specifically western Eurasia, East Asia, and sub-Saharan Africa). Within each of these regions, Olsson and Paik (2020) find that there is actually a *negative* relationship between an early agricultural transition and GDP per capita in 2005. For example, in western

Eurasia countries like Iraq and Syria are currently poor, while countries like the Netherlands and Sweden are currently rich, despite the late arrival of agriculture in northwestern Europe from the core area of southwestern Asia. It appears that similar reversals occurred in East Asia and sub-Saharan Africa, and that the western reversal was visible by 1500 CE, prior to European colonization and industrialization.

Olsson and Paik suggest two possible explanations. First, there is the institutional explanation of Borcan et al. (2018), where early agriculture led to early states. The elites in early states tended to restrain economic growth, while elites in later states were able to learn from earlier states and have not (yet?) reached the point where they limit growth to the same degree. A second explanation is cultural. In this view early farmers in the core area of southwestern Asia had a strongly collectivist orientation for various reasons, and agriculture was carried into Europe through the migration of more individualistic farmers. Repeated self-selection of this kind led to more individualistic cultures in northwestern Europe, which were conducive to economic growth. Olsson and Paik (2016) document the existence of a cultural gradient in collectivism versus individualism that is correlated with the timing of agricultural adoption in western Eurasia.

12.4 UNIFIED GROWTH THEORY

Most readers have no doubt heard of the Industrial Revolution, have a general awareness that it occurred in the last few centuries, and believe it contributed to rising standards of living for people around the world. A less well-known revolution, but as important for living standards, is the so-called Demographic Transition, which followed in the wake of the Industrial Revolution. We begin with an explanation of this concept.

Throughout this book we have worked with Malthusian population dynamics. Briefly put, the Malthusian framework says that if living standards rise in the short run (perhaps due to climate improvement, technological advance, or the availability of new land), population will rise in the long run, and the resulting population growth takes the standard of living per person back to its previous level. In the long run any productivity benefits from technological progress are absorbed through population growth rather than higher income per capita. We argued in Chapter 2 that this was an appropriate way to think about population dynamics in prehistory, and drove the point home theoretically and empirically throughout the book.

The Demographic Transition of the last century and a half turned all of this on its head. As industrialization spread around the world, societies shifted from a regime where people have more children when they become richer to a regime where people have fewer children when they become richer. This trend is visible in several ways: (a) in individual countries, the rate of population growth tends to slow down as GDP per person increases; (b) in cross-sectional samples, the richer countries tend to have slower population growth than the poorer countries; and (c) within a specific country, the richer people tend to have fewer children than the poorer people.

The consequences have been enormous. For the first time in history or prehistory, productivity growth has persistently outpaced population growth, generating a sustained rise in living standards for the majority of the world's population. These gains have been very uneven. Some countries had an earlier demographic transition and an earlier start to modern growth, while others had a later transition (or no transition) and a later start to modern growth. This has created a "great divergence" of income levels across countries, which development economists have tried to understand and ameliorate.

A key question is how the modern world broke out of the Malthusian trap. Many economists have worked on this question, and the related question of why the Industrial Revolution happened at all. Space limitations preclude a comprehensive treatment here. Instead we focus on the contributions of Oded Galor, an economist who has attempted to create a unified theory that accounts for the trajectory of economic growth from Neolithic agriculture to the present day. Some of Galor's ideas are controversial and we indicate a number of subjects for debate. But Galor's ambitious attempt to bridge the gap between prehistory and modernity deserves attention.

In this section we treat Galor (2011) as the definitive statement of unified growth theory, but Galor (2005) supplies another useful summary. Interested readers can explore the reference lists in these two sources, as well as Galor's journal articles with various co-authors. Galor (2011, 4–5) wants to explain the following features of the development process: (a) Malthusian stagnation, (b) the escape from the Malthusian trap, (c) human capital formation, (d) the Demographic Transition, (e) contemporary sustained growth, and (f) the modern divergence of income per capita across countries.

For this purpose Galor divides economic development into a Malthusian epoch, a post-Malthusian regime, and a modern growth regime. The Malthusian epoch covers the entire period from early agriculture until recent centuries. It is characterized by gradual technological advance, gradual population growth, and stagnation of income per capita. Growth theorists frequently emphasize a positive feedback loop between technology and population under such conditions, where better technology leads to higher population for the normal Malthusian reasons, and higher population leads to more rapid technological advance due to a larger number of innovators, more learning by doing, greater gains from specialization, and the like (see Kremer, 1993, for an early model). When Galor refers to "stagnation" in the Malthusian epoch, he is referring to income per capita, while accepting the underlying dynamism of technology and population.

The post-Malthusian regime exhibits simultaneous growth in all three variables: technology, population, and income. The Malthusian causal channel going from income to population still exists. However, productivity growth from technological innovation and capital accumulation begins to outpace population growth so that income per capita starts to rise. There is not yet a demographic transition, and income growth leads to an acceleration of population growth.

Finally, development moves into the modern growth regime, where technology and income continue to grow, but the population growth rate slows and the Demographic Transition becomes visible. Productivity continues to rise due to technical innovation and investment in both physical and human capital. This and the declining population growth rate lead to sustained expansion of income per capita.

Most growth theorists, development economists, and economic historians would probably agree that this sequence of events is a reasonable description of reality. Galor documents the sequence using an array of facts, statistics, graphs, and regressions, which we need not review here. The transitions from one growth regime to another unfolded at different times in different parts of the world, with the earliest transitions generally taking place in the UK, western Europe, North America, Australia, and New Zealand, and later transitions occurring in Asia and Latin America. The modern growth regime does not yet prevail everywhere, and is most notably absent in some parts of Africa. The key issues of interest here are the reasons for the transitions from one growth regime to another.

First, however, we comment briefly on some empirical findings. Galor (2011, ch. 3) goes to considerable lengths to show that the Malthusian epoch was in fact Malthusian. He estimates cross-country regressions for the pre-industrial world where technology and land productivity have large significant effects on population, but insignificant effects on income per capita (see also Ashraf and Galor, 2011). These results are obtained whether population and income are measured in 1 CE, 1000 CE, or 1500 CE. All of the results are robust to the inclusion of numerous geographic controls.

For most regressions, technology is proxied by the elapsed years since the start of agriculture and instrumented by endowments of domesticable plants and animals. Galor's results are consistent with other findings that the Neolithic transition has had long-lasting consequences for subsequent economic development (see Section 12.3). In particular, the time elapsed since the beginning of agriculture in a country is strongly associated with that country's non-agricultural technology (communication, transportation, and industry) in the years 1 CE and 1000 CE. The Neolithic transition clearly touched off a process of productivity growth that played out for many millennia afterward.

We turn next to Galor's (2011, ch. 4) explanation for the Demographic Transition. The main question is why fertility and population growth rates dropped in the wake of the Industrial Revolution. Galor argues on theoretical and empirical grounds that fertility fell mainly because the second phase of the Industrial Revolution, starting around 1870 in the advanced countries, increased the demand for human capital. This demand resulted from the increasing complexity of industrial production and associated organizational activities like management, accounting, and marketing. One consequence was a major expansion in public education, promoted to a large degree by industrialists.

At the level of the individual household the increasing demand for human capital caused substitution from the quantity of children to the quality of children, especially the resources families invested in education. Galor argues that education was beneficial in an economic environment where technology was changing rapidly and existing skills tended to become obsolete. Due to this shift from quantity to quality, fertility declined.

A supporting factor was a shrinking gender wage gap due to greater demand for cognitive work in relation to physical labor. Because most child-raising burdens were placed on women, the increasing opportunity cost for women of having children tended to reduce fertility. Another factor was a growing wage gap between adults and children, which reduced the incentive for parents to treat their children as sources of income.

Galor rejects or minimizes the importance of various alternative hypotheses. He considers the idea that higher incomes led directly to reduced fertility, but argues that the data do not support this idea. Although the northwestern European countries had roughly simultaneous demographic transitions around the start of the twentieth century, levels of income per capita were quite different across countries. He argues that the fertility drop was more closely linked to rates of income growth than to levels of income, supporting the view that the process was driven by rapid technological innovation.

He also rejects the claim that the reduction in fertility was a response to a decline in infant and child mortality, arguing that mortality had been declining in western Europe for about a century before the reduction in fertility, and that in some countries lower child mortality was initially associated with rising fertility. Finally, Galor sees improvement in old-age security as a minor component of the Demographic Transition because the timing of the relevant institutional changes does not closely coincide with fertility trends.

Without going into the mathematics, we sketch the framework of Galor's formal model in order to show how he explains the transition from the Malthusian epoch to the post-Malthusian regime, and from the latter to modern economic growth. There are four key endogenous variables: the rate of technological growth, the level of population, the level of parental investment in education (broadly defined), and resources per worker (in effect, income per capita).

Output is obtained from a Cobb–Douglas production function with inputs of labor and land (the latter does not change over time), with a coefficient indicating the level of technology. Consumers have Cobb–Douglas utility functions depending on consumption and the aggregate human capital of their surviving children. A crucial wrinkle is that the consumers have a positive lower bound on consumption due to subsistence requirements. Parents choose the quantity and quality of their children, as well as their consumption, where quality depends on educational investments. The human capital of a child is an increasing function of education and a decreasing function of the rate of technological change (due to the obsolescence of skills). There are two key thresholds in the model: the rate of technological progress at which parents start to invest in education, and the income level at which the subsistence consumption constraint no longer binds.

At low levels of population, the difference equations describing the model have a unique stable equilibrium where parents invest nothing in education. There is a feedback loop between technology and population but both grow slowly. Due to Malthusian forces growth in per capita income is zero or tiny. But eventually population growth generates a qualitative shift in the dynamics, where two stable equilibria are separated by an unstable equilibrium. The first stable equilibrium has Malthusian features while the second has high levels of education and technological innovation. The Malthusian equilibrium is locally stable so the system remains in this vicinity.

Another qualitative shift occurs at higher population levels, where the Malthusian equilibrium vanishes and the only stable equilibrium is the one having high education and rapid innovation. At this point the economy moves into the post-Malthusian regime. The subsistence constraint on household consumption continues to bind, but incomes increase and some resources are devoted to education. However, the demand for human capital is initially limited, so the relaxation of the budget constraint leads to increased family sizes.

Eventually a virtuous circle involving a positive feedback loop between education and innovation takes the economy into the modern growth regime. Parental substitution from quantity to quality of children gives declining fertility and a demographic transition where the rate of population growth drops. A larger share of the productivity gains from technological progress is therefore devoted to growth in income per capita.

We pause at this point to compare Galor's agenda with our own. There are areas of overlap with respect to key variables (especially technology and population) and time frame (a shared interest in events during the Neolithic). However, the two projects have different goals. Galor's ambition is to construct a mathematically unified theory in which his four endogenous variables mimic the transition from Malthusian stagnation to modern growth. His formal model is not designed to explain why the Industrial Revolution began in England rather than France or China, or why it began around 1750–1820 rather than a few centuries earlier or later.

Our ambition has been to explain a series of prehistoric transitions using a family of related models, which are unified by consistent assumptions about certain core factors, especially time allocation, population dynamics, and technological dynamics. We have frequently extended our framework in order to accommodate the facts about a particular transition, for example by including migration, warfare, or manufacturing. Our quest has been to explain the details of place and time: why did a transition occur within a specific region at a specific date?

Economic historians have an enormous literature that attempts to answer precisely these questions in the case of the Industrial Revolution.

Galor's theoretical approach has been criticized for operating at a level of abstraction that is too high to address questions of this kind (Temin, 2012). We also note that Crafts and Mills (2009) found empirical difficulties with the causal channel running from population to innovation, which plays a central role not only in Galor's approach but in many other models of economic growth. Alternative hypotheses about the sources of technological innovation in the Industrial Revolution emphasize knowledge networks (Mokyr, 2002), mechanistic science (Lipsey et al. 2005), institutional innovation (North, 1981; Acemoglu et al. 2005; Greif, 2006), and reproductive success (Clark, 2007). For a review of what is currently known and unknown about the Industrial Revolution, see Clark (2014).

We note a few other important differences between unified growth theory and our own approach. Galor's theory has no explicit role for climate, or the natural environment more broadly, and he does not explain the transitions from mobile to sedentary foraging, or from sedentary foraging to agriculture. We have argued that climate change drove the evolution of technology and population during the Upper Paleolithic (Chapter 3) and that it triggered the transitions to sedentism and agriculture (Chapters 4 and 5). In effect, we add a climate-based economic regime at the beginning of Galor's sequence.

The amount of progress generated via endogenous growth mechanisms depends on the degree to which production is isolated from environmental shocks. In a foraging society technological advance is almost entirely driven by shocks from nature, if it occurs at all. Feedbacks from population or human capital to technology have little quantitative impact except when climate shifts prompt experimentation with latent resources, as we discussed in Chapter 3.

The spread of agriculture during the Holocene was conducive to technological progress in several ways. First, agriculture created large opportunities for productivity growth through social learning and domestication. Second, the accumulation of technical knowledge was less often disrupted by large climate shocks. Third, agricultural societies were less directly dependent upon nature than foraging societies, although they were still vulnerable to droughts and floods. Eventually manufacturing and service sectors arose that were even further removed from the influence of nature. All of this strengthened the feedback loop between population and technology emphasized in long-run growth theory.

In our view climate change remained important in shaping agricultural societies during the Holocene. For example, it led to city-state formation in certain regions of the world (Chapters 9–11). Galor's theory avoids reliance on exogeneous shocks of this sort in favor of dynamics that are entirely internal to the system. As a result, Galor sees the transition to modern economic growth as inevitable. We do not regard our prehistoric transitions as having been inevitable, because they were often triggered either directly by exogenous climate shifts or indirectly by the technological and demographic fallout from these shifts. With a different climate history, modern civilization might not exist at all.

Relatedly, Galor has a fixed set of stages through which an economy develops. This is reminiscent of the unilinear theories of social evolution that were once popular among anthropologists and archaeologists (see Chapter 1). Our approach is multilinear because developments in a particular region are conditional on the details of climate and geography for that region, as well as the technological, demographic, and institutional history of the region.

Our agenda differs from that of Galor in other ways. For example, the transitions we want to explain are often institutional in nature. Unified growth theory is not intended to explain property rights, stratification, warfare, urbanization, or taxation. Galor devotes much attention to the sources of inequality across countries in the modern world (2011, ch. 6), and in that context he stresses that country-specific growth trajectories have been shaped by differences in institutions and culture. However, he does not treat institutions as endogenous in his formal modeling.

Galor has a sophisticated treatment of human capital, which in his theory results from educational investments by parents. These investments need not involve formal schooling and could occur through direct parental teaching, where parents face tradeoffs involving the quality and quantity of children as well as parental consumption levels. By contrast, we model "education" as a process in which children learn by imitating all of the adults in a community. This learning process does not have any opportunity cost.

We do not doubt that education played an increasing role in later stages of the Industrial Revolution, or that the substitution from quantity to quality contributed to the Demographic Transition. But we emphasize that foraging societies also make very large investments in human capital as practical knowledge is passed on from one generation to the next (Robson and Kaplan, 2006). Even so, technological progress is largely absent in these societies, in contrast to societies following a modern growth path. Our concept of stagnation traps in foraging societies provides an explanation (see Chapter 3).

A final point of contrast is the treatment of consumption. Galor assumes that a parent's consumption cannot fall below a biological subsistence constraint. His analysis implies that this constraint binds not only throughout the Malthusian epoch but also in the post-Malthusian regime, and only becomes non-binding with modern growth (roughly the last century among the advanced economies). We impose no such subsistence minimum, so we are free to address questions about whether living standards fell in the transitions to sedentism and agriculture, whether commoners became worse off due to stratification, or whether commoners became better off or worse off in early states. This matters because archaeologists have evidence about diet, health, life expectancy, and other indicators of living standards, and a theory of prehistoric economic development should address this evidence. We will return to this topic in Section 12.6 when we discuss the trajectory of human welfare.

12.5 DEMOCRATIC INSTITUTIONS

The empirical research reviewed in Section 12.3 indicates that early transitions to state-level organization have had persistent effects on modern economic growth. Borcan et al. (2018) suggest that early states encountered diminishing returns because elites used central power to maintain their own privileges at the expense of wider economic growth. This raises a key question: why have some contemporary states evolved in a democratic direction, encouraging sustained economic growth and spreading the gains across much of the population?

Carles Boix (2015) offers one approach to this question. We previously discussed Boix's views on inequality, warfare, and state formation (see Chapters 6–9 and 11). Here we consider the explanation he proposes for the rise of political democracy in Europe over the last millennium.

From a broad perspective, Boix advances arguments that are consistent with the ideas of other researchers in economic prehistory. He asserts that favorable climate and geography, along with good biological endowments of domesticable plants and animals, caused some regions to have unusually high agricultural productivity. This supported unusually high population densities. Regions of this kind had more towns and cities, which were centers of technological innovation, especially in textiles and metallurgy.

The rise of these proto-industrial centers, although necessary, was not sufficient for sustained growth. Many such places arose in non-European regions. Indeed we note that this description could be applied to some of the early cities described in Chapters 9–11, including Uruk, Mohenjo-Daro, Erlitou, and Teotihuacan. It could also be applied to cities around the year 1500 CE in China (Pomeranz, 2000). Hence Boix argues for the importance of other necessary conditions. Our discussion in the next several paragraphs follows Boix (2015, ch. 6).

Boix agrees with Borcan et al. (2018) that pre-industrial elites used state power in ways that preserved high levels of inequality and thwarted economic growth. Although republican polities could have encouraged growth, they suffered military disadvantages relative to their larger monarchical neighbors and tended to be short-lived. He attributes the escape from this situation in western Europe to an unprecedented confluence of three factors: emergence of proto-industrial cities, political fragmentation of the continent, and military innovations favoring urban and commercial interests. This enabled commercial centers to capture or partially control the state, yielding parliamentary institutions (204). In Britain and elsewhere, the industrial class was eventually able to buy off the landed elite and implement a liberal political order.

Boix begins his story with the Carolingian dynasty, which relied upon a highly decentralized military system where local overlords were given territory in exchange for rents and military assistance to the emperor. European feudalism continued to evolve in a fragmented way, with many political units exercising varying degrees of sovereignty. Noble and religious authorities often allowed towns to attract population around castles and cathedrals. By the thirteenth century these towns began to assert their autonomy, demolishing castles and establishing institutions of urban governance (222–223).

This trajectory was made possible by the rising military power of urban centers. Urban militias marched in closed columns and used long pikes to defend against cavalry charges. Prosperous cities could support armies of a few thousand foot-soldiers armed with expensive military gear, while the landed aristocracy could not match this power through cavalry. "By the turn of the fourteenth century, town dwellers had succeeded in defeating the aristocracy everywhere in the urban core of Europe" (223).

Boix grants that other parts of the world had proto-industrial cities with clusters of merchants and artisans. However, he argues that these cities were generally seats of state power governed by elite rent-seekers, who were mainly concerned with the extraction of surpluses from agricultural hinterlands. He provides data to show that during 1000–1500 CE the fraction of the total population living in cities grew rapidly in western Europe but did not change in non-European regions.

Within Europe, in areas where agriculture was unusually productive the urban population in 1200 CE was unusually high. Moreover, in areas where urban population was predicted to be high in 1200 CE, there was more proto-industrialization in the form of textile manufacturing (wool, linen, silk) and metallurgy (iron forges) during the period 1200–1500 CE (213–218). The resulting distribution of city sizes in Europe differed from other regions of the world. On the eve of the Industrial Revolution, Europe had a roughly log normal distribution while East Asia, South Asia, and the Middle East tended to have bimodal distributions with a few very large cities and a collection of lesser centers with substantially smaller populations (222–228).

Subsequent military innovations reinforced the power of urban centers in Europe. While the horse had supported mounted knights and the pike helped defend urban areas, firearms were more capital intensive and the side with more economic resources enjoyed an advantage. This forced the existing monarchies to grow in scale or disappear, leading to a drop in the number of independent states. At the same time prosperous commercial areas could survive militarily and resist monarchies. The Dutch cities formed a military alliance that defeated Spain. In England parliamentary forces defeated royal forces in 1640 and 1688. Urban centers could not only finance firearms but also benefited from the close complementarity between trading activities and naval power (228–229). Boix argues that these developments established political institutions in northwestern Europe that were hospitable to economic growth and set the stage for the Industrial Revolution. Ultimately the landed aristocracy began investing in the rising industrial sector and no longer opposed political liberalization.

Like the authors discussed in Sections 12.3 and 12.4, Boix has a highly ambitious intellectual agenda. He seeks to explain the evolution of political institutions from small foraging bands to contemporary states, and provides extensive supporting evidence from archaeology, anthropology, and history. While he is often persuasive empirically, there are important gaps in his theoretical framework.

One limitation is that Boix lacks a clear story about how agriculture began. We provide such a story in Chapter 5. Boix also has an incomplete explanation of why rising productivity in agriculture would lead to an urban non-agricultural sector. There is more to urbanization than having a high population density or a food surplus that can support manufacturing. As we stressed in Chapters 9–11, even if we grant that favorable regions had higher densities for Malthusian reasons, it is necessary to explain why the people in a largely agricultural society would start to agglomerate in urban centers. Possible answers include endogenous property rights that caused wages to fall as agricultural technology improved, and thus made manufacturing profitable; warfare that pushed people to easily defensible locations; or environmental shifts that pushed people toward natural refuges. Nevertheless, Boix contributes valuable insights about the role of innovations in military technology as a determinant of political institutions. In particular he provides a coherent explanation for the triumph of industrial and trading interests over landed interests.

There are, of course, other theories connecting political institutions with economic growth. Many economists argue that the main factor behind economic growth in Europe was the quality of political institutions. This included constitutional checks on the state, the rule of law, and protection of private property, which supported investment and trade. We limit our remarks on this topic to two influential schools of thought: that of Douglass North and his co-authors, and that of Daron Acemoglu and James Robinson.

Douglass North has written extensively on the relationship between institutions and economic performance. This culminated in the book *Violence and Social Orders* by Douglass C. North, John Joseph Wallis, and Barry R. Weingast (2009; hereafter NWW). These writers distinguish three types of political/economic institutions.

The first type is the "foraging order" exemplified by egalitarian hunter-gatherers, although NWW also include "big man" societies and chiefdoms. We have already said a good deal about this subject and will not linger on it here.

The second category is the "limited access order" or "natural state." Such states are governed by a dominant coalition consisting of elites who agree to respect each other's privileges, including property rights over resources and activities. Limiting access to these privileges creates rents (returns to holding economic assets that are greater than what the assets could earn in their next best alternative use), which would otherwise be dissipated through competition. The rents accrue to the elite and are allocated in a way that restrains violence among elite groups or factions.

Mature natural states specify legal procedures that constrain interactions between elite groups. Perpetually lived organizations, able to commit credibly to future behavior, expand the possibilities for impersonal relationships and exchanges. Although mature natural states attempt to acquire a monopoly over violence through consolidated control of military resources, they rarely succeed completely. The threat of violence motivates the allocation of rents among elite groups in proportion to their capacities for violence. While violence is therefore limited, so is the potential for economic growth.

The third broad category of political/economic institutions consists of "open access orders." These states are perpetually lived, combine a monopoly over violence with democratic control over the military, and impartially enforce the rule of law. All citizens can participate in political, economic, educational, and religious organizations, fostering competition in politics and the economy. There are widely held beliefs relating to inclusion and equality for all citizens. Impersonal exchange is common, and political and economic competition discipline the use of state power. Such institutions, in contrast to natural states, promote economic growth through efficient resource allocation, flexible responses to external shocks, and incentives to develop new technologies.

According to NWW, the first natural states emerged around 5000 years ago, with inequality and stratification predating state formation by thousands of years (see Chapters 6 and 9–11 in this volume). They see the transition from a "foraging order" to a "limited access order" as being driven by a number of factors: the development of agriculture, the rise of elites, the increased need to control violence in larger societies, and the integration of economic, military, and ideological sources of power. However, they do not provide a detailed analysis of these processes.

The main focus of NWW is to explain the transition, within the last few hundred years, from natural states to a small number of states characterized by open-access orders. They propose three necessary conditions (called "doorstep conditions") for the transition: the rule of law for elites, perpetually lived organizations, and consolidated control of the military. However, they do not regard these as jointly sufficient. The principal historical examples they use to illuminate this transition are Britain, France, and the United States.

NWW depart from our treatment of elites in early states as unitary actors. Their emphasis on the potential for violence among elite groups resembles Boix's emphasis on the conflict between landed and urban/commercial interests. However, Boix regards the transition to political democracy as resulting from a clear victory by urban interests rather than from a balanced accommodation among elite factions.

Another influential approach to the relationship between political institutions and economic growth is that of Daron Acemoglu and James A. Robinson. Here we focus on Acemoglu and Robinson (2016, 2017, 2019; hereafter AR). These authors are concerned with the origins of "the inclusive state," or more dramatically, "the shackled Leviathan." For both NWW and AR, the fundamental question is how one can have a powerful state where power is ultimately in the hands of citizens rather than an elite.

AR consider a polity consisting of a smaller elite group and a larger non-elite group (civil society or citizens). These two groups compete for power. The distribution of power is determined by competitive investments made by both groups in determining the capacity of the state to enforce laws, provide public services, and tax and regulate economic activities. Depending on initial conditions, and assuming scale economies in political investments, three steady-state outcomes can arise: a weak state (Absent Leviathan), in which the state has little power to regulate economic or social activities; a despotic state (Despotic Leviathan), in which elites impose order through oppression; or an inclusive state (Shackled Leviathan), in which states have immense powers but are constrained by their citizens through a broad distribution of political power, as in modern democracies. The concept of a despotic state overlaps with a natural state in NWW, and the concept of an inclusive state overlaps with open access orders in NWW.

The pathway to an inclusive state requires a rough balance of power between elites and non-elites that must be maintained through continuous investment on each side. If power is approximately balanced, citizens will allow the state greater scope because they expect to retain some control over it. But if both groups have only modest power, even small initial differences can result in convergence to one of the other steady states. This leads to the imagery of a "narrow corridor" in navigating to an inclusive state.

While initial conditions are exogenous, the outcome is not predetermined. AR (2019, 435–438) provide examples where changes in initial conditions redirected state trajectories. A particularly clear case is that of Japan after World War II, where the previous despotic state was disbanded after its military defeat. To alter initial conditions that gave rise to despotism, the United States imposed total demilitarization, demanded that the emperor publicly renounce claims to divinity, and worked with senior members of the military and bureaucracy to transform the structure of the government and society. This allowed an inclusive state to emerge.

Perhaps the most fundamental difference between NWW and AR is that NWW start with a society characterized by a non-homogeneous elite, where elite factions are continuously interacting and often in conflict. AR assume the elite is a unified wealth-maximizing group.

What can prehistory add to this discussion? First, it provides the building blocks underlying these analyses: e.g., our explanations for the transitions to sedentism, agriculture, inequality, warfare, cities, and states. Second, we (and many others) view the process of early state formation through the lens of public finance. Our key question is how elites gained the power to tax, which is central to the formation of powerful states like those described by Boix, NWW, and AR.

How such states came under democratic control is a different but related question. We are sympathetic to the view of Boix that specific military technologies, along with other background conditions, played a key role in strengthening urban and commercial interests. However, it is not entirely obvious why the economic elites in industrializing societies would grant broader control over state decisions to citizens in general, and there are examples like Japan where this did not occur. We are also sympathetic to the view of NWW that elites are often internally factionalized, and the view of AR that democracy results from investments by non-elites in the development of political power. However, these arguments strike us as incomplete.

What appears to be needed is an explanation of how non-elites can (sometimes) overcome the collective action problems they face in contests against entrenched elites. As we observed in Chapter 11, elites typically have advantages of organization, wealth, leadership, and coercive power that more than compensate for their smaller numbers. In such regimes, incipient rebellions or subversive movements are easily suppressed and the ringleaders usually pay a heavy price. Under these conditions few leaders step forward.

However, technological and institutional innovations may present commoners with opportunities to organize while avoiding immediate suppression. This can include novel developments with respect to communication, transportation, weaponry, urbanization, or education, for example. As collective action problems dissipate and commoners become more capable of making demands on elites, backed up by threats to do serious physical or economic damage to elite interests, the elite (or a subset of it) may find that compromise is cheaper than violence. When this occurs, institutions must be negotiated to ensure the credibility of commitments to share power. Political democracy is one such institution (Acemoglu and Robinson, 2006).

In a heavily agricultural economy, taxes on land and output may be sufficient to finance the state. Taxes are collected through confiscation and policies are imposed by edict. There is no need to include peasant farmers in the governing process (e.g., ancient Egypt). Economic growth, however, can result in the accumulation of wealth in urban areas through trade, manufacturing, and services. At the same time large administrative and military expenses may be required for state survival, especially in competitive state environments. Under such conditions, offering property rights, open access to markets, and voting rights in return for tax revenue and acceptance of state policies can become a preferred option for elites (see North and Thomas, 1973, for an early analysis of the transactional state). In our view factors of this kind help explain why industrialization was accompanied by democratization in Western Europe.

Voting rights are particularly important when a credible commitment on the part of the state is required. This is widely accepted for zero-sum games involving income redistribution. But NWW and AR move beyond a zero-sum setting by pointing out that democratic constraints shift state priorities toward the provision of public goods. NWW (2009, 142–143) emphasize that open-access orders encourage state investments in mass education, infrastructure, and social insurance programs that facilitate economic growth while lowering individual risks. AR (2019, 72–73) make the related point that when citizens gain some control over the state, the state can be given a long leash and can become an instrument for the political, economic, and social development of the society as a whole. These are lofty hopes. On the other hand, NWW and AR agree that "open-access orders" and "inclusive states" are rare and fragile.

12.6 THE TRAJECTORY OF HUMAN WELFARE

People in rich countries today have enjoyed a century or two of exponential growth in per capita income. This trend has occasionally been interrupted by wars, pandemics, or recessions, and the benefits have been distributed very unequally. But averaging over the decades, economic growth has prevailed.

For this reason it is tempting to extrapolate backward and assume that those who lived hundreds or thousands of years ago were much worse off. In this way of thinking, the mobile foragers of the Upper Paleolithic must have been the least well-off people of all, because they are the furthest in the past. One needs to avoid such thinking. The last two centuries have no precedent in human history or prehistory, and the contours of human welfare were very different in the pre-industrial world.

However, if one wants to say something more nuanced about the path of human welfare over thousands of years, there are some obvious pitfalls.

First, it is unclear how one should even think about welfare comparisons over such long time spans. Second, if we can agree on what welfare means, where can we find data about it? And third, how should we deal with inequalities across the individuals or classes making up a society?

We will address each of these issues below. Welfare comparisons across spans of millennia, and across enormously different societies, are quite difficult and must be made cautiously. Nevertheless, relevant data do exist, and the theory we have developed in this book provides some guidance. To cut to the chase, we think human welfare has generally followed a U-shaped curve for the last 15,000 years. Taking mobile hunter-gatherers as a starting point, life appears to have become worse in the transition to sedentism and again in the transition to agriculture. For the majority of the population, the standard of living probably bottomed out in early states (e.g., ancient Egypt), and did not begin to recover in any substantial way until the last two centuries.

The first question involves what we mean by the concept of human welfare. It is clear that if we define welfare in terms of subjective happiness, we will not get very far. Harari (2014, 376) asks, "Was the late Neil Armstrong, whose footprint remains intact on the windless moon, happier than the nameless hunter-gatherer who 30,000 years ago left her handprint on a wall in Chauvet Cave? If not, what was the point of developing agriculture, cities, writing, coinage, empires, science and industry?" This is a rhetorical question and we cannot know the answer.

Modern populations are frequently asked questions like whether they agree that "life is good" on a scale from zero to ten. The main findings are that happiness is linked with income or wealth only for people at the low end of the economic scale. Illness can cause short-term distress, but this does not generally extend to the long term unless the person is in constant pain. Family and community matter more, and happiness may be affected mostly by conditions relative to one's expectations (Harari, 2014, 380–384).

Another way to think about happiness involves biology and chemistry. From this perspective a sense of happiness is generated by neurotransmitters: serotonin, dopamine, and oxytocin. The average levels of these brain chemicals have probably changed little in recent millennia because they are biologically programmed. Levels may differ across individuals, but it seems unlikely that happiness in this sense would rise or fall for entire societies (Harari, 2014, 385–390).

Perhaps what matters the most is a long-term sense of meaning or significance in one's life, rather than the day-to-day ups and downs of happiness (Harari, 2014, 390–396). Harari also points to the view taken by Stoics and Buddhists that unhappiness, suffering, and pain are caused by the fact that people want things, and that if they stopped wanting things, this pain would disappear. Maybe so, but physical and mental constraints appear to be important for the vast majority of people.

Whatever one believes about these proposals for conceptualizing human welfare, they all pose a fundamental problem for the economic prehistorian: lack of data. We do not have questionnaire results, neurotransmitter readings, or estimates of meaningfulness for people who lived thousands of years ago. We cannot know whether a laborer under the hot sun in the agricultural fields around Uruk had a deeply meaningful life due to the proximity of a temple, or was deeply depressed by the authoritarianism of the local elite.

Archaeologists do have data on factors that almost everyone today would consider relevant for human welfare, including nutrition, health, security, and life expectancy. The United Nations and similar bodies often base international comparisons of the quality of life on measures of this kind, although people can and do disagree about the weight that should be attached to each factor. Even if these welfare measures only reflect the preferences of contemporary people, we might want to use archaeological data to assess the quality of life in the past from the standpoint of our present values.

Furthermore, although we cannot read the minds of people from the distant past, it would be strange to argue that people 15,000 years ago did not care about such things. Evolutionary logic suggests that nature would long ago have programmed the members of our species to care about exactly these things. People who are indifferent toward nutrition, health, and security are unlikely to live very long and are unlikely to raise children to adulthood.

In principle, criteria like these can be used for welfare comparisons across diverse societies and over long time intervals. But one might still ask, what is the point? Why make welfare comparisons over 15,000 years? One answer is simple curiosity. Another is that this exercise may lead us to rethink casual assumptions about the inevitability of human progress. A third motive is to better understand social evolution. For example, if important prehistoric transitions made people worse off, how is this consistent with the usual view (at least in economics) that people try to make themselves better off whenever they can?

A complicating factor involves the role of inequality. As we discussed in earlier chapters, mobile foragers are usually quite egalitarian, apart from minor distinctions involving gender and age. Sedentary foragers often have significant inequality, and this increases with the transition to agriculture. When there are both privileged elites and impoverished commoners, how can we aggregate individual welfare to obtain an index of social welfare? Should we even try?

The political philosopher John Rawls (1971) suggested that social welfare should be evaluated based on the condition of the least well off members of society. We will not give any detailed philosophical justification for this view, but it is a useful way to address the issue. When a society has elite and commoner classes, we will concern ourselves with the welfare of the commoners. This is partly because commoners will typically be the overwhelming majority of the population (probably 80–90%, even if one defines the elite to include skilled artisans and warriors). Also, commoner living standards are more problematic (no one seems very concerned about whether living standards for the elite rose or fell). If suitable data existed, we might want to study heterogeneity within the commoner class, but drawing fine distinctions of this sort is usually infeasible. For agricultural societies, in effect we will be tracking the welfare of agricultural laborers.

Of course, if there are both free commoners and slaves, the Rawlsian framework implies a focus on the welfare of the slaves. However, for many societies in prehistory it is unclear whether or not slavery existed. Even when it clearly did, we cannot necessarily obtain data that quantify the differences in living standards between these two classes.

Another complicating factor is population. In a Malthusian world, technological progress is channeled toward population growth rather than improved standards of living per person. One could conceivably argue that population growth is desirable for its own sake. However, our concern is with the living standards of individuals (both the average and the distribution). We are not Benthamites who want to maximize the sum total of human happiness. Thus we do not award a society more points for having a larger population.

In the rest of this section we review what our theory says about human welfare and then discuss some evidence. We start with the simplest case: an egalitarian society using a fixed technology and fixed natural resources to produce food. Due to diminishing returns the average product of labor (y) decreases as aggregate population (N) increases. The average product is equivalent to food per capita, an obvious candidate for a welfare index. Alternatively one could use surviving children per adult as a welfare index. This is correlated with food per capita and can be regarded as a biological objective function.

If we compare (y, N) points along the average product curve, our unwillingness to assign social value to population implies a preference for points having higher levels of y and lower levels of N. Perhaps counter-intuitively, this implies that N should ideally be the smallest number exceeding zero. But in reality there may be reasons to want a larger group size that are omitted from simple versions of the model. Starting from a low initial level, higher population may result in higher food per person due to scale economies with respect to labor specialization or insurance, the supply of public goods such as defense, or other positive externalities among group members.

Malthusian theory says that over multiple generations food per capita will settle at a constant level y^* (see Chapter 2). This long-run standard of living will not normally be affected by changes in climate or technology. Recall that we do not interpret this level of food as a biological subsistence minimum, or a point below which starvation occurs. It is simply the level at which population is stationary, neither rising nor falling, because fertility and mortality rates are in balance. Whether the standard of living happens to be high or low in such a steady state is a separate question.

Our principle that aggregate population is irrelevant for social welfare means that we are not concerned with the particular population level occurring in a steady state. But such a population could be supported either by high fertility and high mortality or by low fertility and low mortality. Other things being equal, most people would probably prefer the latter. For the moment we ignore this issue and focus on another theoretical problem.

If we embrace food per capita as a welfare measure, if the world was Malthusian before the Industrial Revolution, and if food per capita (y^*) was therefore constant in the long run, this implies that social welfare was likewise constant. A similar problem arises if we treat surviving children per adult as a welfare measure. In long-run equilibrium this must be unity (on average, one adult is replaced by one surviving child). Again we get a constant.

However, y^* can change when large transformations in technology alter the fertility and mortality rates associated with a given level of food per person. In Chapter 4 we argued that the transition from mobile to sedentary foraging decreased y^*. We constructed a simple model in Section 4.10 where parents maximized their expected number of surviving offspring, a reasonable objective from the standpoint of biological evolution, and confronted tradeoffs between the quantity and quality of children. We defined "quality" to be the probability that a child survived to adulthood.

There is a consensus among anthropologists that sedentism lowered the cost of a child because mothers had to spend less time carrying young children. We showed that as a result parents would substitute toward quantity rather than quality among children. This decreases y* in equilibrium. Higher quantity implies more births over a woman's reproductive career while lower quality reduces childhood survival rates. The resulting equilibrium is supported by higher fertility and higher mortality.

Our model assumed that adults live for one period but a more sophisticated model could have mortality increasing for adults due to the lower food per capita. Even so, it is likely that in reality most of the increased mortality would fall upon children. One must therefore be cautious about estimates of life expectancy. Sedentism could cause a lower life expectancy at birth due to higher child mortality, while having little effect on adult life expectancy (for example, conditional on survival to the age of 15).

We used the same general reasoning in Chapter 5 to argue that the transition from sedentary foraging to agriculture likely decreased y* further. It is generally believed that agricultural technology makes children more productive relative to foraging technology. This reduces the economic cost of children and again tends to lower the equilibrium level of y* in the long run, as well as childhood survival and life expectancy from birth. Thus, our theory leads us to believe that both sedentism and agriculture had negative effects on social welfare, even when societies remained egalitarian.

As these arguments show, it is overly simplistic to assume that Malthusian forces always imply a constant standard of living in the long run. This is true, or at least a good first approximation, when climate fluctuations or technological innovations do not disturb the underlying relationship between food and demography. However, large technological transformations can shift this relationship through the quantity/quality channel, much as the Industrial Revolution led to the Demographic Transition (see Section 12.4).

Another complication for the Malthusian approach involves inequality. The idea that aggregate population must be stationary in the long run implies some equilibrium y*. But this is only the food per capita for the population as a whole. In stratified societies the elite's food consumption will be above y* and the commoners' food consumption will be below it. Because we do not employ the notion of a biological subsistence minimum, this need not imply that the commoners will starve to death. However, it does imply that commoners fail to replace themselves demographically (on average, each commoner has less than one surviving adult child). This means that in each generation the commoner population must be replenished by downward mobility where some children of the elite become commoners. This flow of surplus elite children into the commoner class is just enough to compensate for the rate of natural decrease among commoners themselves.

Chapter 6 showed that when property rights to land are endogenous, technological progress tends to impoverish commoners by raising the regional population and enabling insiders to close more sites to outsiders. At the same time elites at the best sites become better off because they enjoy larger land rents. In our model those who remain behind in the (shrinking) commons and those hired by elites have the same food consumption, and are worse off than insiders or elites. By our Rawlsian criterion, social welfare continues to decline as agricultural technology improves.

Chapter 10 complicated the story by adding an urban manufacturing sector, which became active when the commoner standard of living became low enough. We showed that with a fixed regional population, commoners became worse off in the early stages of city-state formation. However, it was uncertain whether this trend would continue. For example, commoners might eventually benefit from consumer surplus associated with manufacturing, from higher wages as manufacturing expanded, or from public goods provided by elites.

Further complications arise from the endogeneity of population in the long run. In previous settings this led to an equilibrium food per capita y^*. When both food production and craft production occur, the model has to be generalized to yield a long-run equilibrium utility u^*. As with y^*, this is only an equilibrium in an aggregate sense, and inequality implies that elites get more utility per person than u^* while commoners get less. We therefore need to know how the evolution of manufacturing and taxation affect elite–commoner inequality before reaching any judgment about commoner welfare and (via Rawls) a judgment about social welfare. The issue is complex, but commoner standards of living may have finally stabilized as the early city-states matured.

Much has been made of the possibility that commoners can benefit from state provision of security, insurance, infrastructure, and other public goods. However, in the long run average utility is likely to remain close to the level u^* consistent with a stationary aggregate population. Malthusian dynamics will guarantee a zero-sum game where the commoner class only becomes better off when the elite class becomes worse off. Thus, commoner welfare in early states depends on whatever social, economic, political, and military forces determine the overall degree of inequality within the society.

Given the difficulty of measuring utility, we suggest using the average number of surviving offspring per commoner as an index of commoner welfare. Surviving children per adult is only required to equal unity at an aggregate level when elites and commoners are averaged together. This figure will be below unity among the commoners, and when it is closer to unity commoners have a higher standard of living. Such a welfare measure is attractive because it captures various factors such as child mortality, nutrition for adults and children, health status, physical security, and so on, insofar as these contribute to the reproductive success of commoners. One need not worry about how to assign weights to each factor because nature weights them automatically. Of course it may be difficult to obtain demographic data of this kind through archaeological methods. If so, it will be necessary to rely on narrower measures like nutrition, health, and life expectancy.

In the rest of this section we briefly review evidence about the welfare trajectory suggested by our theory. Systematic archaeological research on prehistoric standards of living developed in the 1970s and 1980s, motivated by a then-popular hypothesis about the origins of agriculture. According to this hypothesis, exogenous population pressure among Upper Paleolithic foraging societies led to declining living standards, triggering a transition to agriculture (Cohen, 1977). We hasten to add that this view is not consistent with the Malthusian framework used in this book. Instead we would expect a decline in living standards to generate feedback effects that lower fertility and raise mortality until foraging societies reach a stationary demographic equilibrium (see Chapters 2 and 3).

It soon became clear that there was little or no evidence for a food crisis among foragers in the Upper Paleolithic or Epi-Paleolithic, but there was strong evidence that nutrition and health declined among early farmers (Cohen and Armelagos, 1984, 2013). There is now a consensus that relative to their foraging ancestors, early farmers had less varied and nutritious diets, shorter adult stature (a common proxy for a poor diet early in life), more infectious disease, more repetitive work, and shorter life spans (see Cohen, 1991, 2009; Lambert, 2009; Scott, 2017, 96–113; and the references cited there).

We do not want to romanticize the small foraging bands of the Upper Paleolithic. People in these bands probably had relatively short lives, faced occasional starvation, and had frequent individual homicides. However, it seems clear that early farmers had living standards that were measurably worse according to standard archaeological indicators.

The archaeological literature does not always distinguish between effects of the transition from mobile to sedentary foraging (Chapter 4) and effects of the transition from sedentary foraging to agriculture (Chapter 5). There is good evidence that infectious disease was more prevalent in larger settlements, a problem that would have affected both sedentary foragers and farmers, although with greater impact on the latter. There is also strong evidence that proximity to domesticated animals promoted infectious disease (Diamond, 1997), a problem limited to farmers and pastoralists as opposed to foragers.

Another area of ambiguity involves the causal channels leading to disease. A poorer diet tends to reduce immune function, weakening the body's defenses against infectious disease. At the same time sedentary foragers and early farmers had greater exposure to pathogens from living in larger communities and (in the case of farmers) having domestic animals. It is frequently unclear to what extent the skeletal evidence for disease reflects poor diet and to what extent it reflects high pathogen exposure.

We have already documented the increasing inequality that arose in agricultural societies with the onset of stratification between elites and commoners (see Chapter 6). In a Malthusian world this almost certainly implied a further decline in living standards for commoners (Cohen, 1991, ch. 7). Although raiding among foraging bands probably has deep roots, we provided evidence in Chapters 7 and 8 that warfare over land became more common in sedentary foraging societies and chronic in agricultural societies with stratification. Our formal model in Chapter 8 omitted any costs of elite warfare for the commoner population, but in practice it appears likely that increasing stratification and increasing warfare would both have made commoners increasingly miserable.

Early cities like Uruk and Teotihuacan had high mortality rates (Cohen, 1991, ch. 7; Algaze, 2018, 26), and this likely remained true for most cities until clean water supplies and modern sanitation systems became available in the nineteenth century. On the other hand, urban populations were continually replenished through migration from the countryside, suggesting that rural life may have been even worse, or at least that migrants to the city were less risk averse than those who stayed behind.

We have discussed the possible effects of state formation on commoner welfare in Chapters 9–11 and will not repeat those remarks here. Empirical research by Ashraf and Galor (2011) confirms the Malthusian expectation that technological innovation and land productivity had no significant effect on per capita incomes in the years 1 CE, 1000 CE, and 1500 CE (see Section 12.4), so commoners would probably not have benefited from aggregate economic growth in the state societies of the time.

Commoners did occasionally benefit from changes in economic conditions. For example, real wages rose for a century after the Black Death epidemic of 1347–1351 in England (Clark, 2005). But putting this exception aside, economic historians find that inequality of income and wealth tended to grow monotonically from 1450/1500 CE until 1800 CE in almost all of Europe (Alfani, 2021). Possible explanations include economic growth, population growth, proletarianization, urbanization, and inheritance systems. However, Alfani (2021) puts special emphasis on state building, warfare, the resulting heavy fiscal burden per capita, and regressive taxation.

The Industrial Revolution and the Demographic Transition changed the picture drastically. For the advanced economies, Boix (2015, 202) cites evidence that between 1820 and 2008, per capita income rose by a factor of 20, average height increased by 10–12 centimeters, and life expectancy almost doubled due largely to reduced infant mortality and the elimination of infectious diseases. Rates of childhood mortality (death by the age of 15) dropped from nearly 50% in pre-industrial societies to 1% or less in modern developed countries (Volk and Atkinson, 2013).

This has also been a period of rapidly expanding education and, at least during 1900–1970, declining inequality. Using data on sovereign countries at 10-year intervals since 1820, Boix (2015, 232–242) finds that the growth of per capita income was strongly correlated with greater democracy, and that the causality ran from income to democracy. He also argues that greater democracy led to greater equality through public education, health expenditures, public pensions, and unemployment benefits.

We believe that the Industrial Revolution, the Demographic Transition, and the expansion of political democracy were each necessary for welfare to improve. Without the Industrial Revolution, there would have been no technological basis for a substantial welfare gain. Without the Demographic Transition, the productivity boost derived from industrialization would have been absorbed by Malthusian population growth rather than translating into higher income per capita. Without political democracy, elites would have captured a disproportionate share of the higher average income.

These three necessary conditions were almost certainly linked. For example, one could argue that although uneducated workers were employed in the early stages of the Industrial Revolution, subsequent stages stimulated a demand for education (see Section 12.4), which led to a demographic transition as well as pressure for political democracy. Alternatively, one could attribute the spread of political democracy to other features of industrialization such as the decreased cost of communication and transportation, which facilitated the formation of labor unions, civic organizations, and mass political parties. But in any event these three factors together were sufficient to bring about an enormous gain in the quality of life for most people in developed nations.

In sum, the evidence supports our view that material welfare for the majority of the population has followed a long U-shaped curve, with living standards deteriorating in the transition from foraging to agriculture, staying low for millennia due to stratification and Malthusian population dynamics, and then exhibiting an extraordinary jump during the last two centuries due to the combined effects of the Industrial Revolution, the Demographic Transition, and the expansion of political democracy.

We close this section where we began: it is very difficult to make meaningful welfare comparisons between societies separated by vast gulfs of time and space. We don't really know much about the quality of life for the foragers of the Upper Paleolithic. Even within the modern world it is difficult to compare the welfare of the few remaining foragers with the welfare of people who live in cities and work in offices. Mobile hunter-gatherers who make peaceful contact with the modern economy seem to like metal tools, radios, firearms, running water, modern clothing, and modern medicine. On the other hand, very few people living in industrial societies have the technical or social skills to join hunter-gatherer societies (only rare anthropologists can do this), and we don't know how many modern people would want to become foragers if they could. Perhaps many among us would be happier and healthier as foragers. In the opinion of the authors, the two best places to be born were probably (a) in a foraging group that had just discovered a new continent or (b) in a middle- or upper-class community located in North America in the mid-twentieth century. Most of the other options seem less attractive.

12.7 CLIMATE: PAST, PRESENT, AND FUTURE

Whether the exponential income growth of the last two centuries will prove to be sustainable over the next two is an open question. Technological advances continue, but there are warning signs. Some poor countries remain very poor, inequality is growing in the rich countries, and democracy looks more fragile than it did a few decades ago. There are justified worries about overpopulation, resource depletion, and pandemics. But almost certainly the greatest threat to our global civilization is climate change.

Most readers are probably well aware of the climate change problem, but we will summarize a few basic points. Several gases in the Earth's atmosphere, including carbon dioxide, methane, and water vapor, allow light from the sun to pass through but trap heat that would otherwise radiate away into space. These so-called greenhouse gases have natural sources such as volcanoes and are needed to keep the planet warm enough for life to exist. But human activities since the Industrial Revolution, especially the burning of fossil fuels (coal, oil, and natural gas), have increased the concentration of carbon dioxide and other greenhouse gases in the atmosphere. Deforestation has also played a role.

Carbon dioxide (CO_2) emissions are the largest single driver of global warming. The pre-industrial atmospheric concentration of carbon dioxide in the year 1820 was 280 parts per million (ppm). At this writing it has risen above 410 ppm for a 46% increase in two centuries. The last time the CO_2 concentration exceeded 400 ppm was during the Pliocene, 3–5 million years ago (NASA, 2020). At that time global temperatures were 3–4 °C warmer and the sea level was 5–40 meters higher. No member of the genus *Homo* had yet walked the Earth.

The planet is now far from an equilibrium state, and substantial temperature rises will occur as oceanic and atmospheric systems catch up with the new CO_2 concentration. We lack a technology for removing large quantities of CO_2 from the atmosphere, and the natural processes that do so operate on time scales of thousands of years. Therefore any human-produced increment in the CO_2 concentration is essentially permanent.

The Intergovernmental Panel on Climate Change (IPCC) produces the most authoritative forecasts of the effects of climate change. At this writing the most recent synthesis report is IPCC (2014) and the next synthesis report is scheduled for late 2022 or early 2023. More specialized reports are published at more frequent intervals. The current and foreseeable consequences of global warming include more intense heat waves, droughts, floods, and storms, and higher sea levels. The severity of these consequences will depend on the future emissions path for greenhouse gases, which can be affected by technological innovation and public policy. For example, innovations that bring down the cost of renewable energy sources (such as solar, wind, and hydroelectric) would help, as would economic incentives for people to substitute away from fossil fuels (such as carbon taxes and cap-and-trade systems). It would also help to have policies that prevent and reverse deforestation, because trees are an important mechanism for removing carbon from the atmosphere. But these measures will only limit the scale of the damage. Past emissions guarantee that future warming is inevitable, and large investments will be needed to adapt to new climate conditions.

Global mean temperature has already increased by about 1 °C relative to the level prevailing prior to the Industrial Revolution. The Paris climate accord (UNFCCC, 2015) set the goal of keeping the global temperature rise during this century to no more than 2 °C (that is, one additional degree) relative to the pre-industrial level. This limit was set in part because many scientists believe that the world climate system could pass a series of irreversible tipping points beyond that. The accord also commits signatories to make an attempt to keep the rise to 1.5° (one half of a degree beyond what has already occurred). Because CO_2 emissions are permanent, this implies a "carbon budget" for the world that puts an upper bound on the additional emissions that can be tolerated without exceeding these temperature targets.

Most climate researchers believe that the existing national commitments to limit greenhouse gas emissions under the Paris accord are inadequate to hold the line at 2 °C even if they are honored, and there is much room for doubt about whether they will be honored. Accordingly, modelers often study scenarios involving increases of 3–4 °C by the end of this century relative to the pre-industrial baseline. For example, Raftery et al. (2017) suggest that the likely range is 2.0–4.9 °C with a median of 3.2 °C. They find a 5% chance of remaining below 2 °C and a 1% chance of remaining below 1.5 °C, taking into account uncertainties in future population growth, economic growth, carbon intensity per dollar of GDP, and climate sensitivity to carbon emissions. They do not account for the possibilities of dramatic technological breakthroughs or unforeseen natural disasters. Although the baseline is determined by pre-industrial conditions, most of the temperature increase will occur in the twenty-first century.

Aside from uncertainty about the effect of a given emissions trajectory on global mean temperature, it is difficult to forecast the effects of global mean temperature on sea level, agricultural productivity, and other crucial outcomes. It is also difficult to predict how carbon emissions will influence temperature, precipitation, and similar variables at the regional level (except for very large-scale generalizations, such as the fact that polar regions are warming much more rapidly than lower latitudes and will continue to do so). The regional effects will almost certainly be distributed in a very uneven manner.

Climate history provides a sense of scale. During the Last Glacial Maximum of 21,000 years ago, ice sheets spread as far south as London and New York, and sea level was 125 meters lower than at present. People could walk from Siberia to Alaska. The rise in global temperature to Holocene levels shifted the planet from an intense Ice Age with very cold, very dry, and highly variable conditions to the warm, wet, and relatively stable conditions of the last 11,600 years.

According to Antarctic ice core data from Petit et al. (1999), at the Last Glacial Maximum the temperature was about 8 °C below modern levels (see Figure 3.1). But the polar regions were subject to greater cooling, and one estimate of global mean surface air temperature places the LGM at about 6 °C below the pre-industrial level (Schneider von Deimling et al., 2006). More recent work has produced a similar estimate of 6.1 °C with a 95% confidence interval of 5.7–6.5 (Tierney et al., 2020).

If we regard an increase of 2 °C by the year 2100 relative to pre-industrial levels as the best reasonably plausible scenario, and we believe that the recovery from the LGM involved an increase of 6 °C, then we are looking at an increase roughly 33% of the size of the jump from the Last Glacial Maximum to the present. The situation could easily be worse. If the true extent of global warming will be 4 °C, the change we are confronting will be about 66% of the transition from the worst conditions of the last glacial period to our present interglacial period. The jump from the LGM to the Holocene required 10,000 years while we are facing a substantial fraction of such a jump within a single century.

Much effort has been devoted to examining the effects of weather on economic variables (for a thorough survey, see Dell et al., 2014). This literature studies impacts on agricultural output, industrial output, labor productivity, energy demand, health, conflict, and economic growth. Others have investigated the effects of climate on individual and group violence (Burke et al., 2015). Although the effects in such studies are sometimes statistically significant and quantitatively large, the datasets (with a few exceptions) are mostly based on information since 1900 or 1950. We are currently facing rapid climate changes far outside this historical range.

Other researchers have explored the social effects of weather on millennial time scales. We mentioned a few examples in Chapter 7. Zhang et al. (2006, 2007) found a correlation between abnormal cold and domestic rebellions in China during 1000–1911 CE. Bai and Kung (2011) found a correlation between droughts and nomadic invasions of China during 220 BCE–1839 CE. Tol and Wagner (2010) discovered a correlation between cold periods and violent conflict in Europe during 1000–1990 CE. In each case, the violence almost certainly resulted from large reductions in food supplies. At a more impressionistic level it has been argued that the Little Ice Age of 1600–1700 CE, which may have involved a decline in global mean temperature of about 1.0 °C, led to warfare, rebellions, and social collapse in many parts of the world (Parker, 2013). But again the climate shifts of our century will be substantially larger.

If we want to grasp the social effects of truly massive climate change, we need to study prehistory. We have argued that climate change was a driving force behind several major economic transformations. The recovery from the Last Glacial Maximum and the onset of the Holocene led to a transition from mobile to sedentary foraging in many parts of the world (Chapter 4). The large negative shock of the Younger Dryas resulted in a transition from sedentary foraging to cultivation in southwest Asia and perhaps in China, with later climate shifts probably playing a role in Africa and elsewhere (Chapter 5). A shift toward increased aridity around 6000–5000 BP is thought to have triggered the rise of cities and states in Mesopotamia and Egypt, and similar mechanisms may have led to later city-states in the Indus Valley and northern China (Chapters 9–11).

Some of these events may not seem very dramatic from our own vantage point. For example, communities of sedentary foragers or early farmers typically had at most a few hundred people. But village life was a radical change from life in mobile foraging bands. It involved a commitment to use resources within walking distance of a central place, a vulnerability to natural shocks that could temporarily take away these resources, investments in stationary tools and housing, more reliance on storage to manage risks, a greater tendency to marry within one's own community rather than outside it, stronger barriers to migration across communities, and new types of property rights. Inequality and warfare over land were not far behind.

Most of us would probably recognize the formation of early city-states as a more dramatic transition. Such cities, often with as many as 50–100,000 residents, had diverse craft manufacturing activities, monumental architecture, and elites wielding state power. The rulers taxed their citizens, frequently fought wars against rivals, and eventually built regional empires. Most early states developed systems of writing.

We are not trying to portray these developments as part of a rising tide of human progress. As we argued in Section 12.6, these transitions generally had negative impacts on human welfare, at least for the vast majority. Our point here is simply that exogenous climate shifts have had revolutionary consequences for social, economic, and political life. It is reasonable to ask whether equally large consequences should be expected now that climate has become endogenous.

First, however, we need to recognize some key differences between the world of prehistory and the world of today. Most obviously the modern world has vast technological capabilities, can generate new knowledge rapidly, and can easily transfer knowledge across space and time. Another contrast is the absence of a Malthusian population trap. In the modern world, when people become better off they generally have fewer children rather than more. Thus our long-run models of technology and population have little relevance.

On the other hand, one can argue that these differences do not matter much. Our models of technological innovation and population dynamics were designed for societies evolving over many human generations. For most of the applications we had in mind, a century was a short interval, often within the margin of error for archaeological dating. But modern climate changes will have large impacts over decades. From our modeling perspective this is the short run.

In our view the two main prehistoric analogies to the present are the rapid onset of the Younger Dryas, which may have triggered cultivation in southwest Asia on a scale of decades, and the emergence of early city-states, which in some regions may have taken less than a century (although for southern Mesopotamia and other cases, dates are highly uncertain). For these transitions we argued that the short-run effects of climate change largely involved migration.

In the Younger Dryas some previously sedentary foragers reverted to a nomadic lifestyle while others moved to a few refuge locations like Abu Hureya. The resulting local population spikes at these climate sanctuaries depressed the marginal product of labor in foraging and made cultivation attractive. We do not see cultivation as a technological breakthrough. Instead it involved a resort to a known backstop technology, previously regarded as unattractive, under difficult natural conditions. Thousands of years later, cultivation led to domestication and sustained technological progress, but this provided no comfort to the inhabitants of Abu Hureyra during the centuries of the Younger Dryas.

Similarly we believe increasing aridity during 6000–5000 BP caused migration away from areas of southwest Asia and North Africa dependent on rainfall agriculture. Again people looked for environmental refuges and found them near river valleys. The short-run effect of this climate shift, according to the model in Chapter 10, was to drive down wages and re-allocate commoner labor toward elite agricultural estates in southern Mesopotamia and the Nile Valley. Once wages had declined enough, manufacturing and taxation became profitable for the elites. These developments had enormous technological and institutional consequences in later millennia, but if the commoners of the time had somehow known this, it would have offered them little solace.

Another short-run effect from climate change involves warfare. In Chapter 7 we argued that even in societies that are internally egalitarian, climate shocks can destabilize relationships between population and productivity across sites and trigger group conflict. This is particularly likely when social barriers make it difficult for individuals to move in response to these shocks. Similar mechanisms are likely to trigger warfare in stratified societies where elites compete over the rents from land and other natural resources. Such societies are prone to military conflict, and climate shocks could shift resources in ways that make aggression more tempting, despite defensive technology or institutional restraints on war.

This, then, may be our future. Climate change will redistribute natural resources around the world, making many places poorer and a few places richer. Individuals will flee from areas that become hotter, drier, stormier, or flooded by seawater. They will look for refuge in places with milder temperatures, reliable rainfall, usable farmland, and higher elevations. Insiders who already occupy these places will try to exclude the refugees, put them to work for low wages, charge high entry fees, or screen out those who lack special skills. Inequality and warfare will increase and elites who can keep control over valuable territories will prosper. People will adopt available technologies that were not previously attractive but become necessary for survival. Political and social institutions, and technological systems requiring the support of these institutions, could crumble under the weight of migration, poverty, and violence.

People who have not read this book might make similar forecasts. We do not claim any special ability to predict the future. But economic prehistory has value in thinking about the fate of the modern world. It provides perspective on the scale and urgency of the problem, helps to identify relevant precedents, and corroborates intuitions about how people respond to environmental upheavals.

Most fundamentally, economic prehistory reveals that the technological and institutional consequences of climate change are likely to play out in ways we cannot really imagine, any more than the residents of Abu Hureyra could have imagined agricultural societies, or the residents of Mesopotamian villages could have imagined the conquests of Sargon. The only certainty is that the way of life many of us presently enjoy will eventually become a distant memory.

Meanwhile, there is always hope. Perhaps the governments of the world will impose high prices on carbon emissions. Perhaps renewable energy will become so cheap that fossil fuels will be abandoned. Perhaps researchers will find ways to remove carbon dioxide from the atmosphere more efficiently than trees do. But the clock is ticking loudly.

12.8 POSTSCRIPT

We thank Carles Boix, Richard Lipsey, Ola Olsson, Louis Putterman, Robert Springborg, and John Wallis for comments on earlier drafts of this chapter. They are not responsible for our errors, omissions, or opinions.

References

Acemoglu, Daron, Mikhail Golosov, Aleh Tsyvinski, and Pierre Yared, 2012, A dynamic theory of resource wars, *Quarterly Journal of Economics* 127(1), February, 283–331.

Acemoglu, Daron, Simon Johnson, and James A. Robinson, 2005, Institutions as the fundamental cause of long-run growth, in Philippe Aghion and Steven Durlauf, eds., *Handbook of Economic Growth*, North-Holland, New York, 385–472.

Acemoglu, Daron and James A. Robinson, 2006, *Economic Origins of Dictatorship and Democracy*, Cambridge University Press, New York.

2012, *Why Nations Fail: The Origins of Power, Prosperity, and Poverty*, Random House, New York.

2016, Paths to inclusive political institutions, in J. Eloranta, E. Golson, A. Markevich, and N. Wolf, eds., *Economic History of Warfare and State Formation*, Studies in Economic History, Springer, Berlin/ Heidelberg, 3–50.

2017, The emergence of weak, despotic, and inclusive states, NBER Working Paper No. 23657, www.nber.org/papers/w23657

2019, *The Narrow Corridor: States, Societies, and the Fate of Liberty*, Penguin Books, New York.

Adams, Robert McC., 1981, *Heartland of Cities: Surveys of Ancient Settlement and Land Use on the Central Floodplain of the Euphrates*, University of Chicago Press, Chicago.

2001, Complexity in archaic states, *Journal of Anthropological Archaeology* 20 (3), September, 345–360.

Aikens, C. Melvin and Takeru Akazawa, 1996, The Pleistocene–Holocene transition in Japan and adjacent northeast Asia: Climate and biotic change, broad-spectrum diet, pottery, and sedentism, ch. 11 in L. G. Straus, B. B. Ericksen, J. M. Erlandson, and D. R. Yesner, eds., *Humans at the End of the Ice Age: The Archaeology of the Pleistocene–Holocene Transition*, Plenum Press, New York, 215–227.

Aiyar, Shekhar, Carl-Johan Dalgaard, and Omer Moav, 2008, Technological progress and regress in pre-industrial times, *Journal of Economic Growth* 13(2), June, 125–144.

Alfani, Guido, 2021, Economic inequality in preindustrial times: Europe and beyond, *Journal of Economic Literature* 59(1), 3–44.

Algaze, Guillermo, 2001, Initial social complexity in southwestern Asia: The Mesopotamian advantage, *Current Anthropology* 42(2), April, 199–233.

2008, *Ancient Mesopotamia at the Dawn of Civilization: The Evolution of an Urban Landscape*, University of Chicago Press, Chicago.

2013, The end of prehistory and the Uruk period, in Harriet Crawford, ed., *The Sumerian World*, Routledge, New York, 68–94.

2018, Entropic cities: The paradox of urbanism in ancient Mesopotamia, *Current Anthropology* 59(1), February, 23–54.

Allen, Mark W., Robert Lawrence Bettinger, Brian F. Codding, Terry L. Jones, and Al W. Schwitalla, 2016, Resource scarcity drives lethal aggression among prehistoric hunter-gatherers in central California, *Proceedings of the National Academy of Sciences USA* 113(43), October 25, 12120–12125.

Allen, Robert C., 1997, Agriculture and the origins of the state in ancient Egypt, *Explorations in Economic History* 34(2), April, 135–154.

Allen, Robert C., Mattia C. Berazzini, and Leander Heldring, 2020, The economic origins of government, working paper, https://www.leanderheldring.com/.

Ames, Kenneth M., 1995, Chiefly power and household production on the northwest coast, ch. 6 in T. Douglas Price and Gary M. Feinman, eds., *Foundations of Social Inequality*, Plenum Press, New York, 155–187.

Ames, Kenneth M. and Herbert D. G. Maschner, 1999, *Peoples of the Northwest Coast: Their Archaeology and Prehistory*, Thames & Hudson, London.

Anderson, David G., Albert C. Goodyear, James Kennett, and Allen West, 2011, Multiple lines of evidence for possible human population decline/settlement reorganization during the early Younger Dryas, *Quaternary International* 242, 570–583.

Arnold, Jeanne E., 1993, Labor and the rise of complex hunter-gatherers, *Journal of Anthropological Archaeology* 12, 75–119.

1995, Social inequality, marginalization, and economic process, in T. Douglas Price and Gary M. Feinman, eds., *Foundations of Social Inequality*, Plenum Press, New York, 87–103.

Ashraf, Quamrul and Oded Galor, 2011, Dynamics and stagnation in the Malthusian epoch, *American Economic Review* 101(5), August, 2003–2041.

2013, The "out of Africa" hypothesis, human genetic diversity, and comparative economic development, *American Economic Review* 103(1), February, 1–46.

Ashraf, Quamrul and Stelios Michalopoulos, 2011, The climatic origins of the Neolithic Revolution: Theory and evidence, Working Paper No. 2010-2, Department of Economics, Williams College.

2015, Climatic fluctuations and the diffusion of agriculture, *Review of Economics and Statistics* 97(3), July, 589–609.

Asouti, Eleni and Dorian Q. Fuller, 2013, A contextual approach to the emergence of agriculture in Southwest Asia: Reconstructing early Neolithic plant-food production, *Current Anthropology* 54(3), June, 299–345.

Bae, Christopher J., Katerina Douka, and Michael D. Petraglia, 2017, On the origin of modern humans: Asian perspectives, *Science* 358(6368), December 8, 1269.

Bai, Ying and James Kai-sing Kung, 2011, Climate shocks and Sino-nomadic conflict, *Review of Economics and Statistics* 93(3), August, 970–981.

Baker, Matthew J., 2003, An equilibrium conflict model of land tenure in hunter-gatherer societies, *Journal of Political Economy* 111(1), February, 124–173.

2008, A structural model of the transition to agriculture, *Journal of Economic Growth* 13(4), December, 257–292.

Baker, Matthew J. and Erwin H. Bulte, 2010, Kings and Vikings: On the dynamics of competitive agglomeration, *Economics of Governance* 11(3), 207–227.

Baker, Matthew J., Erwin H. Bulte, and Jacob Weisdorf, 2010, The origins of governments: From anarchy to hierarchy, *Journal of Institutional Economics* 6(2), June, 215–242.

Balkansky, Andrew, 2014, Oaxaca, ch. 2.21 in Colin Renfrew and Paul G. Bahn, eds., *Cambridge World Prehistory*, Cambridge University Press, New York, 1026–1042.

Balme, Jane and Alistair Paterson, eds., 2006, *Archaeology in Practice: A Student Guide to Archaeological Analyses*, Blackwell, Oxford.

Balter, Michael, 2007, Seeking agriculture's ancient roots, *Science* 316, June 29, 1830–1835.

Barham, Lawrence and Peter Mitchell, 2008, *The First Africans: African Archaeology from the Earliest Toolmakers to Most Recent Foragers*, Cambridge University Press, New York.

Bar-Yosef, Ofer, 2002a, The Upper Paleolithic revolution, *Annual Review of Anthropology* 31, 363–393.

2002b, The Natufian culture and the early Neolithic: Social and economic trends in Southwestern Asia, in Peter Bellwood and A. Colin Renfrew, eds., *Examining the Farming/Language Dispersal Hypothesis*, McDonald Institute Monographs, University of Cambridge, Cambridge, 113–126.

2002c, Natufian, in Ben Fitzhugh and Junko Habu, eds., *Beyond Foraging and Collecting: Evolutionary Change in Hunter-Gatherer Settlement Systems*, Kluwer Academic/Plenum, New York, 91–149.

2011, Climatic fluctuations and early farming in West and East Asia, *Current Anthropology* 52 (Supplement 4), October, S175–S193.

Bar-Yosef, Ofer and Richard H. Meadow, 1995, The origins of agriculture in the near east, ch. 3 in T. Douglas Price and Anne Birgitte Gebauer, eds., *Last Hunters, First Farmers: New Perspectives on the Prehistoric Transition to Agriculture*, School of American Research Press, Santa Fe, NM, 39–94.

Becker, Gary S., Edward L. Glaeser, and Kevin M. Murphy, 1999, Population and economic growth, *American Economic Review* 89(2), May, 145–149.

Bellwood, Peter, 2005, *First Farmers: The Origins of Agricultural Societies*, Blackwell, Oxford.

Bennett, Matthew R., et al., 2021, Evidence of humans in North America during the Last Glacial Maximum, *Science* 373(6562), September 24, 1528–1531, DOI: 10.1126/science.abg7586

Bentley, R. Alexander, Matthew W. Hahn, and Stephen J. Shennan, 2004, Random drift and culture change, *Proceedings of the Royal Society of London: Biological Sciences* 271(1547), July 22, 1443–1450.

Bettinger, Robert L., 2009, *Hunter-Gatherer Foraging: Five Simple Models*, Eliot Werner, Clinton Corners, NY.

    2016, Prehistoric hunter-gatherer population growth rates rival those of agriculturalists, *Proceedings of the National Academy of Sciences USA* 113(4), January 26, 812–814.

Bettinger, Robert L. et al., 2010a, The transition to agriculture at Dadiwan, People's Republic of China, *Current Anthropology* 51(5), October, 703–714.

Bettinger, Robert L., Loukas Barton, and Christopher Morgan, 2010b, The origins of food production in North China: A different kind of agricultural revolution, *Evolutionary Anthropology* 19, 9–21.

Bhattacharya, Sourav, Joyee Deb, and Tapas Kundu, 2015, Mobility and conflict, *American Economic Journal: Microeconomics* 7(1), February, 281–319.

Binmore, Ken, 2007, *Game Theory: A Very Short Introduction*, Oxford University Press, New York.

Bird, Douglas W. and James F. O'Connell, 2012, Human behavioral ecology, ch. 3 in Ian Hodder, ed., *Archaeological Theory Today*, 2nd ed., Polity, Malden, MA, 37–61.

Bleaney, Michael and Arcangelo Dimico, 2011, Biogeographical conditions, the transition to agriculture and long-run growth, *European Economic Review* 55(7), October, 943–954.

Bockstette, Valerie, Areendam Chanda, and Louis Putterman, 2002, States and markets: The advantage of an early start, *Journal of Economic Growth* 7(4), December, 347–369.

Bocquet-Appel, Jean-Pierre, 2008a, The Neolithic demographic transition, population pressure and cultural change, *Comparative Civilizations Review* 58, Spring, 36–49.

    2008b, Explaining the Neolithic demographic transition, in Jean-Pierre Bocquet-Appel and Ofer Bar-Yosef, eds., *The Neolithic Demographic Transition and Its Consequences*, Springer Science+Business Media B.V., Berlin/Heidelberg, 35–55.

    2009, The demographic impact of the agricultural system in human history, *Current Anthropology* 50(5), October, 657–660.

    2011, When the world's population took off: The springboard of the Neolithic demographic transition, *Science* 333, July 29, 560–561.

Bocquet-Appel, Jean-Pierre and Ofer Bar-Yosef, 2008, Prehistoric demography in a time of globalization, in Jean-Pierre Bocquet-Appel and Ofer Bar-Yosef, eds., *The Neolithic Demographic Transition and Its Consequences*, Springer Science+Business Media B.V., Berlin/Heidelberg, 1–10.

Bocquet-Appel, Jean-Pierre and Stephan Naji, 2006, Testing the hypothesis of a worldwide Neolithic demographic transition: Corroboration from American cemeteries (with replies), *Current Anthropology* 47(2), April, 341–365.

Bogaard, Amy, Mattia Fochesato, and Samuel Bowles, 2019, The farming-inequality nexus: New insights from ancient Western Eurasia, *Antiquity* 93 (371), October, 1129–1143.

Boix, Carles, 2015, *Political Order and Inequality: Their Foundations and Their Consequences for Human Welfare*, Cambridge University Press, New York.

Boix, Carles and Frances Rosenbluth, 2014, Bones of contention: The political economy of height inequality, *American Political Science Review* 108(1), February, 1–21.

Borcan, Oana, Ola Olsson, and Louis Putterman, 2018, State history and economic development: Evidence from six millennia, *Journal of Economic Growth* 23(1), March, 1–40.

2021, Transition to agriculture and first state presence: A global analysis, *Explorations in Economic History* 82(2), 101404, 1–19, DOI: 10.1016/j.eeh.2021.101404

Borgerhoff Mulder, M., et al., 2009, Intergenerational wealth transmission and the dynamics of inequality in small-scale societies, *Science* 326(5953), October 30, 682–688.

Boserup, Ester, 1965, *The Conditions of Agricultural Growth: The Economics of Agrarian Change Under Population Pressure*, Earthscan, London.

Bowles, Samuel, 2006, Group competition, reproductive leveling, and the evolution of human altruism, *Science* 314(5805), December 8, 1569–1572.

2009, Did warfare among ancestral hunter-gatherers affect the evolution of human social behaviors? *Science* 324(5932), 5 June, 1293–1298.

2011, The cultivation of cereals by the first farmers was not more productive than foraging, *Proceedings of the National Academy of Sciences USA* 108 (12), March 22, 4760–4765.

2012, Warriors, levelers, and the role of conflict in human social evolution, *Science* 336(6083), 18 May, 876–879.

Bowles, Samuel and Jung-Kyoo Choi, 2013, Coevolution of farming and private property during the early Holocene, *Proceedings of the National Academy of Sciences USA* 110(22), May 28, 8830–8835.

2019, The Neolithic agricultural revolution and the origins of private property, *Journal of Political Economy* 127(5), October, 2186–2228.

Bowles, Samuel and Herbert Gintis, 2011, *A Cooperative Species: Human Reciprocity and Its Evolution*, Princeton University Press, Princeton.

Boyd, Brian, 2006, On "sedentism" in the Later Epipalaeolithic (Natufian) Levant, *World Archaeology* 38(2), June, 164–178.

Boyd, Robert and Peter J. Richerson, 1985, *Culture and the Evolutionary Process*, University of Chicago Press, Chicago.

Boyd, Robert, Peter J. Richerson, and Joseph Henrich, 2011, The cultural niche: Why social learning is essential for human adaptation, *Proceedings of the National Academy of Sciences USA* 108(suppl. 2), June 28, 10918–10925.

Brander, James and Scott Taylor, 1998, The simple economics of Easter Island: A Ricardo–Malthus model of renewable resource use, *American Economic Review* 88(1), March, 119–138.

Brantingham, P. Jeffrey, Andrei I. Krivoshapkin, Li Jinzeng, and Ya. Tserendagva, 2001, The initial Upper Paleolithic in Northeast Asia, *Current Anthropology* 42(5), December, 735–746.

Brantingham, P. Jeffrey, Kristopher W. Kerry, Andrei I. Krivoshapkin, and Yaroslav V. Kuzmin, 2004, Time–space dynamics in the Early Upper Paleolithic of Northeast Asia, chapter 9 in David B. Madsen, ed., *Entering America: Northeast Asia and Beringia Before the Last Glacial Maximum*, University of Utah Press, Salt Lake City, UT, 255–283.

Brisch, Nicole, 2013, History and chronology, in Harriet Crawford, ed., *The Sumerian World*, Routledge, New York, 111–127.

Brooks, Nick, 2006, Cultural responses to aridity in the Middle Holocene and increased social complexity, *Quaternary International*, 151(1), July, 29–49.

2013, Beyond collapse: Climate change and causality during the Middle Holocene Climatic Transition, 6400–5000 years before present, *Geografisk Tidsskrift – Danish Journal of Geography*, 112(2), 14 Jan, 93–104.

Burger, Richard L., 2014, The development of early Peruvian civilisation (2600–300 BCE), ch. 2.24 in Colin Renfrew and Paul G. Bahn, eds., *Cambridge World Prehistory*, Cambridge University Press, New York, 1075–1097.

Burke, Marshall, Solomon M. Hsiang, and Edward Miguel, 2015, Climate and conflict, *Annual Review of Economics* 7, August, 577–617, DOI 10.1146/annurev-economics-080614-115430.

Burley, David V., 2007, Archaeological demography and population growth in the Kingdom of Tonga, in Patrick V. Kirch and Jean-Louis Rallu, eds., *The Growth and Collapse of Pacific Island Societies: Archaeological and Demographic Perspectives*, University of Hawai'i Press, Honolulu, 177–202.

Byrd, Brian F., 2005, Reassessing the emergence of village life in the Near East, *Journal of Archaeological Research* 13(3), September, 231–290.

Caldwell, John C. and Bruce K. Caldwell, 2003, Pretransitional population control and equilibrium, *Population Studies* 57(2), July, 199–215.

Carneiro, Robert L., 1970, A theory of the origin of the state, *Science*, 169(3947), 21 August, 733–738.

2003, *Evolutionism in Cultural Anthropology: A Critical History*, Westview, Boulder, CO.

2012, The circumscription theory: A clarification, amplification, and reformulation, *Social Evolution and History* 11(2), September, 5–30.

Chase, Arlen F. and Diane Z. Chase, 2012, Complex societies in the southern Maya lowlands: Their development and florescence in the archaeological record, ch. 18 in Deborah L. Nichols and Christopher A. Pool, eds., *The Oxford Handbook of Mesoamerican Archaeology*, Oxford University Press, New York, 255–267.

Chassang, Sylvain and Gerard Padró i Miquel, 2009, Economic shocks and civil war, *Quarterly Journal of Political Science* 4(3), October, 211–228.

Chiaroni, Jacques, Peter A. Underhill, and Luca L. Cavalli-Sforza, 2009, Y chromosome diversity, human expansion, drift, and cultural evolution, *Proceedings of the National Academy of Sciences USA* 106(48), December 1, 20174–20179.

Childe, V. Gordon, 1950, The urban revolution, *Town Planning Review* 21, 3–17.

1951, *Man Makes Himself*, New American Library, New York.

Choi, Jung-Kyoo and Samuel Bowles, 2007, The coevolution of parochial altruism and war, *Science* 318(5850), 26 October, 636–640.

Clark, Gregory, 2005, The condition of the working class in England, 1209–2004, *Journal of Political Economy* 113(6) December, 1307–1340.

2007, *A Farewell to Alms: A Brief Economic History of the World*, Princeton University Press, Princeton.

2014, The Industrial Revolution, in Philippe Aghion and Steven Durlauf, eds., chapter 5 in *Handbook of Economic Growth*, volume 2, Elsevier, 217–262.

Clarkson, Chris, et al., 2017, Human occupation of northern Australia by 65,000 years ago, *Nature* 547(7663), 20 July, 306–310.

Clayton, Sarah C., 2015, Teotihuacan: An early urban center in its regional context, ch. 13 in Norman Yoffee, ed., *The Cambridge World History Volume III: Early Cities in Comparative Perspective, 4000 BCE–1200 CE*, Cambridge University Press, Cambridge, UK, 279–299.

Coase, Ronald H., 1937, The nature of the firm, *Economica* 4, November, 386–405.

1960, The problem of social cost, *Journal of Law and Economics* 3, October, 1–44.

Cohen, David Joel, 2011, The beginnings of agriculture in China: A multiregional view, *Current Anthropology* 52(S4), October, S273–S293.

Cohen, David J. and Robert E. Murowchick, 2014, Early complex societies in northern China, ch. 2.7 in Colin Renfrew and Paul G. Bahn, eds., *Cambridge World Prehistory*, Cambridge University Press, New York, 782–806.

Cohen, Mark Nathan, 1977, *The Food Crisis in Prehistory: Overpopulation and the Origins of Agriculture*, Yale University Press, New Haven, CT.

1991, *Health and the Rise of Civilization*, Yale University Press, New Haven, CT.

2009, Introduction: Rethinking the origins of agriculture, *Current Anthropology* 50(5), October, 591–595.

Cohen, Mark N. and George J. Armelagos, 1984, 2013, *Paleopathology at the Origins of Agriculture*, Academic Press, New York. Reprinted in paperback by University Press of Florida in 2013.

Collard, Mark, Briggs Buchanan, and Michael J. O'Brien, 2013, Population size as an explanation for patterns in the paleolithic archaeological record: More caution is needed, *Current Anthropology* 54(S8), December, S388–S396.

Colledge, Sue and James Conolly, 2010, Reassessing the evidence for the cultivation of wild crops during the Younger Dryas at Tell Abu Hureyra, Syria, *Environmental Archaeology* 15(2), 124–138. DOI 10.1179/146141010X12640787648504

Comin, Diego, William Easterly, and Erick Gong, 2010, Was the wealth of nations determined in 1000 BC? *American Economic Journal: Macroeconomics* 2(3), 65–97.

Crafts, Nicholas and Terence C. Mills, 2009, From Malthus to Solow: How did the Malthusian economy really evolve? *Journal of Macroeconomics* 31(1), March, 68–93.

Crawford, Gary W., 2009, Agricultural origins in North China pushed back to the Pleistocene–Holocene boundary, *Proceedings of the National Academy of Sciences USA* 106(18), May 5, 7271–7272.

References   537

Crawford, Harriet, 2004, *Sumer and the Sumerians*, 2nd ed., Cambridge University Press, Cambridge, UK.

2013, Trade in the Sumerian world, in Harriet Crawford, ed., *The Sumerian World*, Routledge, New York, 447–461.

Creative Commons, 2019, https://creativecommons.org/ https://en.wikipedia.org/wiki/List_of_periods_and_events_in_climate_history#/media/File:Vostok_Petit_data.svg

Crema, Enrico R., Junko Habu, Kenichi Kobayashi, and Marco Madella, 2016, Summed probability distribution of 14C dates suggests regional divergences in the population dynamics of the Jomon period in eastern Japan, *PLOS One*, April 29.

Crema, Enrico Ryunosuke and Mark W. Lake, 2015, Cultural incubators and the spread of innovation, *Human Biology* 87(3), 151–168.

Crevecoeur, Isabelle, Marie-Hélène Dias-Meirinho, Antoine Zazzo, Daniel Antoine, and François Bon, 2021, New insights on interpersonal violence in the Late Pleistocene based on the Nile valley cemetery of Jebel Sahaba, *Scientific Reports* 11, 9991, 27 May, https://doi.org/10.1038/s41598-021-89386-y

Cronin, Thomas M., 1999, *Principles of Paleoclimatology*, Columbia University Press, New York.

Dell, Melissa, Benjamin F. Jones, and Benjamin A. Olken, 2014, What do we learn from the weather? The new climate-economy literature, *Journal of Economic Literature* 52(3), September, 740–798.

De Meza, David and J. R. Gould, 1992, The social efficiency of private decisions to enforce property rights, *Journal of Political Economy* 100(3), June, 561–580.

Denham, Tim, 2011, Early agriculture and plant domestication in New Guinea and Island Southeast Asia, *Current Anthropology* 52(S4), October, S379–S395.

Deur, Douglas, 1999, Salmon, sedentism, and cultivation: Toward an environmental prehistory of the northwest coast, ch. 7 in P. Hirt and D. Goble, eds., *Northwest Lands and Peoples: An Environmental History Anthology*, University of Washington Press, Seattle, 119–144.

2002, Plant cultivation on the northwest coast: A reconsideration, *Journal of Cultural Geography* 19(2), Spring/Summer, 9–35.

Diamond, Jared, 1997, *Guns, Germs, and Steel: The Fates of Human Societies*, Norton, New York.

Dillehay, Tom, Jack Rossen, Thomas Andres, and David Williams, 2007, Preceramic adoption of peanut, squash, and cotton in northern Peru, *Science* 316, June 29, 1890–1893.

Dolukhanov, Pavel M., 1996, The Pleistocene-Holocene transition on the east European plain, ch. 8 in L. G. Straus, B. B. Ericksen, J. M. Erlandson, and D. R. Yesner, eds., *Humans at the End of the Ice Age: The Archaeology of the Pleistocene-Holocene Transition*, Plenum, New York, 159–169.

Dow, Gregory K., 1987, The function of authority in transaction cost economics, *Journal of Economic Behavior and Organization* 8(1), March, 13–38.

Dow, Gregory K., Leanna Mitchell, and Clyde G. Reed, 2017, The economics of early warfare over land, *Journal of Development Economics* 127, July, 297–305.

Dow, Gregory K. and Clyde G. Reed, 2011, Stagnation and innovation before agriculture, *Journal of Economic Behavior and Organization* 77(3), March, 339–350.

2013, The origins of inequality: Insiders, outsiders, elites, and commoners, *Journal of Political Economy* 121(3), June, 609–641.

2015, The origins of sedentism: Climate, population, and technology, *Journal of Economic Behavior and Organization* 119, November, 56–71.

Dow, Gregory K., Clyde G. Reed, and Nancy Olewiler, 2009, Climate reversals and the transition to agriculture, *Journal of Economic Growth* 14(1), March, 27–53.

Dow, Gregory K., Clyde G. Reed, and Simon Woodcock, 2016, The economics of exogamous marriage in small-scale societies, *Economic Inquiry* 54(4), October, 1805–1823, DOI 10.1111/ecin/12321.

Duranton, Gilles and Diego Puga, 2020, The economics of urban density, *Journal of Economic Perspectives*, 34(3), Summer, 3–26.

Earle, Timothy K., 1987, Chiefdoms in archaeological and ethnohistorical perspective, *Annual Review of Anthropology* 16, 279–308.

1997, *How Chiefs Come to Power*, Stanford University Press, Stanford, 33–46, 75–89.

Ellickson, Robert C., 1994, *Order Without Law: How Neighbors Settle Disputes*, Harvard University Press, Cambridge, MA.

Elson, Christina, 2012, Cultural evolution in the southern highlands of Mexico: From the emergence of social inequality and urban society to the decline of classic-period states, ch. 16 in Deborah L. Nichols and Christopher A. Pool, eds., *The Oxford Handbook of Mesoamerican Archaeology*, Oxford University Press, New York, 230–244.

Ember, Carol R. and Melvin Ember, 1992, Resource unpredictability, mistrust, and war: A cross-cultural study, *The Journal of Conflict Resolution* 36(2), June, 242–262.

Endicott, Karen L., 1999, Gender relations in hunter-gatherer societies, in Richard B. Lee and Richard Daly, eds., *The Cambridge Encyclopedia of Hunters and Gatherers*, Cambridge University Press, New York, 411–418.

Englund, Robert K., 2009, The smell of the cage, *Cuneiform Digital Library Journal* 4, 21 August, 1–27.

EPICA community members, 2004, Eight glacial cycles from an Antarctic ice core, *Nature* 429(6992), June 10, 623–628.

Fagan, Brian M. and Nadia Durrani, 2016, *A Brief History of Archaeology: Classical Times to the Twenty-First Century*, 2nd ed., Routledge, London and New York.

2019, *People of the Earth: An Introduction to World Prehistory*, 15th ed., Routledge, New York.

Fassbinder, Jörg W. E., Sandra Hahn, Marion Scheiblecker, and Margarete van Ess, 2018, Uruk (Iraq) magnetometry in the first megacity of Mesopotamia,

Conference paper on Recent Work in Archaeological Geophysics, The Geological Society, December, Burlington House, London.

Fearon, James D., 1995, Rationalist explanations for war, *International Organization* 49(3), July, 379–414.

Feder, Kenneth L., 2019, *The Past in Perspective: An Introduction to Human Prehistory*, 8th ed., Oxford University Press, New York.

Feinman, Gary M. and Joyce Marcus, eds., 1998, *Archaic States*, School of American Research Press, Santa Fe, NM.

Ferguson, R. Brian, 2013a, Pinker's list, in Douglas P. Fry, ed., *War, Peace, and Human Nature: The Convergence of Evolutionary and Cultural Views*, Oxford University Press, New York, 112–131.

2013b, The prehistory of war and peace in Europe and the Near East, in Douglas P. Fry, ed., *War, Peace, and Human Nature: The Convergence of Evolutionary and Cultural Views*, Oxford University Press, New York, 191–230.

2018, Why we fight, *Scientific American* 319(3), September, 76–81.

Fernández-López de Pablo, Javier, Mario Gutiérrez-Roig, Madalena Gómez-Puche, Rowan McLaughlin, Fabio Silva, and Sergi Lozano, 2019, Paleodemographic modelling supports a population bottleneck during the Pleistocene-Holocene transition in Iberia, *Nature Communications* 10, 1872, https://doi.org/10.1038/s41467-019-09833-3

Flannery, Kent V., 1969, Origins and ecological effects of early domestication in Iran and the Near East, in Peter J. Ucko and G. W. Dimbleby, eds., *The Domestication and Exploitation of Plants and Animals*, Aldine, Chicago, 73–100.

1986, *Guila Naquitz*, Academic Press, New York.

1999, Process and agency in early state formation, *Cambridge Archaeological Journal* 9(1), 3–21.

Flannery, Kent and Joyce Marcus, 2012, *The Creation of Inequality: How Our Prehistoric Ancestors Set the Stage for Monarchy, Slavery, and Empire*, Harvard University Press, Cambridge, MA.

Fochesato, Mattia and Samuel Bowles, 2017, Technology, institutions, and wealth inequality over eleven millennia, SFI Working Paper 2017–08–032, https://sfi-edu.s3.amazonaws.com/sfi-edu/production/uploads/working_paper/pdf/2017-08-032_11569f.pdf

Fochesato, Mattia, Amy Bogaard, and Samuel Bowles, 2019, Comparing ancient inequalities: The challenges of comparability, bias, and precision, *Antiquity* 39(370), 853–869.

Freidel, David, 2014, The origins and development of lowland Maya civilisation, ch. 2.22 in Colin Renfrew and Paul G. Bahn, eds., *Cambridge World Prehistory*, Cambridge University Press, New York, 1043–1057.

French, Jennifer C., 2016, Demography and the Palaeolithic archaeological record, *Journal of Archaeological Method and Theory* 23(1), March, 150–199.

Fry, Douglas P., 2006, *The Human Potential for Peace: An Anthropologic Challenge to Assumptions about War and Violence*, Oxford University Press, New York.

2012, Life without war, *Science* 336(6083), May 18, 879–884.

Fry, Douglas P., ed., 2013, *War, Peace, and Human Nature: The Convergence of Evolutionary and Cultural Views*, Oxford University Press, New York.

Fry, Douglas P. and Patrick Soderberg, 2013, Lethal aggression in mobile forager bands and implications for the origins of war, *Science* 341(6143), July 19, 270–273.

Fuller, Dorian Q., 2011, Finding plant domestication in the Indian subcontinent, *Current Anthropology* 52(S4), October, S347–S362.

Fuller, Dorian Q. and Elisabeth Hildebrand, 2013, Domesticating plants in Africa, in Peter Mitchell and Paul J. Lane, eds., *The Oxford Handbook of African Archaeology*, Oxford University Press, New York.

Fuller, Dorian Q. and Chris J. Stevens, 2018, Sorghum domestication and diversification: A current archaeobotanical perspective, in Anna Maria Mercuri, A. Catherine D'Andrea, Rita Fornaciari and Alexa Hohn, eds., *Plants and People in the African Past: Progress in African Archaeobotany*, Springer, Berlin/Heidelberg, 427–452.

Gallagher, Elizabeth, Stephen Shennan, and Mark G. Thomas, 2019, Food income and the evolution of forager mobility, *Scientific Reports* 9, 5438.

Galor, Oded, 2005, From stagnation to growth: Unified growth theory, ch. 4 in Philippe Aghion and Steven Durlauf, eds., *Handbook of Economic Growth*, volume 1, Elsevier, Amsterdam, 171–293, available at http://econpapers .repec.org/bookchap/eeegrochp/

2011, *Unified Growth Theory*, Princeton University Press, Princeton and Oxford.

Galor, Oded and David Weil, 2000, Population, technology, and growth: From Malthusian stagnation to the demographic transition and beyond, *American Economic Review* 90(4), September, 806–828.

Galor, Oded and Stelios Michalopoulos, 2012, Evolution and the growth process: Natural selection of entrepreneurial traits, *Journal of Economic Theory* 147 (2), March, 759–780.

Galor, Oded and Omer Moav, 2002, Natural selection and the origin of economic growth, *Quarterly Journal of Economics* 117(4), November, 1133–1191.

Gamble, Clive, William Davies, Paul Pettitt, Lee Hazelwood, and Martin Richards, 2005, The archaeological and genetic foundations of the European population during the Late Glacial: Implications for "agricultural thinking," *Cambridge Archaeological Journal* 15(2), 193–223.

Gamble, Clive and Olga Soffer, eds., 1990, *The World at 18000* BP, Volume Two: Low Latitudes, Unwin Hyman, London.

Garcea, Elena A. A., 2006, Semi-permanent foragers in semi-arid environments of North Africa, *World Archaeology* 38(2), June, 197–219.

Garfinkel, Michelle R. and Stergios Skaperdas, 2007, Economics of conflict: An overview, ch. 22 in Keith Hartley and Todd Sandler, eds., *Handbook of Defense Economics*, vol. 2, Elsevier, New York, 649–709. Available for download at www.sciencedirect.com/science/article/B7RKP-4N6Y69H-5/2/6ef71983a9657a41c6a24804d8c6c49d

Gat, Azar, 2006, *War in Human Civilization*, Oxford University Press, Oxford, UK.

Gibson, Jon L., 2006, Navels of the Earth: Sedentism in early mound-building cultures in the Lower Mississippi Valley, *World Archaeology* 38(2), June, 311–329.

Gibson, McGuire, 2014, Summary comments, in Augusta McMahon and Harriet Crawford, eds., *Preludes to Urbanism: The Late Chalcolithic of Mesopotamia in Honour of Joan Oates*, McDonald Institute for Archaeological Research, Cambridge, UK, 189–192.

Gilman, Antonio, 1981, The development of social stratification in Bronze Age Europe, *Current Anthropology* 22(1), 1–23.

Giosan, Liviu, et al., 2012, Fluvial landscapes of the Harappan civilization, *Proceedings of the National Academy of Sciences USA*, published online May 29, E1688–E1694, www.pnas.org/cgi/doi/10.1073/pnas.1112743109

Giuliano, Paola and Nathan Nunn, 2021, Understanding cultural persistence and change, *Review of Economic Studies* 88(4), July, 1541–1581.

Goebel, Ted, Michael R. Waters, and Dennis H. O'Rourke, 2008, The late Pleistocene dispersal of modern humans in the Americas, *Science*, New Series, 319(5869), March 14, 1497–1502.

Goldberg, Amy, Alexis M. Mychajliw, and Elizabeth A. Hadly, 2016, Post-invasion demography of prehistoric humans in South America, *Nature* 532, April 14, 232–235.

Goldewijk, Kees Klein, Arthur Beusen, and Peter Janssen, 2010, Long-term dynamic modeling of global population and built-up area in a spatially explicit way: HYDE 3.1, *The Holocene* 20(4), 565–573.

Goldman, Irving, 1970, *Ancient Polynesian Society*, University of Chicago Press, Chicago.

Graeber, David and David Wengrow, 2021, *The Dawn of Everything: A New History of Humanity*, Farrar, Straus and Giroux, New York.

Greif, Avner, 2006, *Institutions and the Path to the Modern Economy*, Cambridge University Press, New York.

Grosman, Leore and Natalie D. Munro, 2017, The Natufian culture: The harbinger of food-producing societies, ch. 77 in Yehouda Enzel and Ofer Bar-Yosef, eds., *Quaternary of the Levant: Environments, Climate Change, and Humans*, online at www.cambridge.org/core, 699–707.

Grossman, Herschel I., 2002, "Make us a king": Anarchy, predation, and the state, *European Journal of Political Economy* 18(1), March, 31–46.

Gurven, Michael, et al., 2010, Domestication alone does not lead to inequality: Intergenerational wealth transmission among horticulturalists, *Current Anthropology* 51(1), February, 49–64.

Guzmán, Ricardo Andrés and Jacob Weisdorf, 2011, The Neolithic Revolution from a price-theoretic perspective, *Journal of Development Economics* 96(2), November, 209–219.

Haas, Jonathan and Matthew Piscitelli, 2013, The prehistory of warfare: Misled by ethnography, in Douglas P. Fry, ed., *War, Peace, and Human Nature: The Convergence of Evolutionary and Cultural Views*, Oxford University Press, New York, 168–190.

Habu, Junko, 2004, *Ancient Jomon of Japan*, Cambridge University Press, New York.

Hallpike, C. R., 1988, *The Principles of Social Evolution*, Clarendon, Oxford.

Hansen, Mogens Herman, 2008, Analyzing cities, ch. 4 in Joyce Marcus and Jeremy A. Sabloff, eds., *The Ancient City: New Perspectives on Urbanism in the Old and New Worlds*, School for Advanced Research Press, Santa Fe, NM, 67–76.

Harari, Yuval Noah, 2014, *Sapiens: A Brief History of Humankind*, Penguin, Random House.

Harlan, Jack R., 1995, *The Living Fields: Our Agricultural Heritage*, Cambridge University Press, Cambridge.

Harris, Marvin, 1977, *Cannibals and Kings: The Origins of Cultures*, Vintage, New York.

2001, *The Rise of Anthropological Theory*, updated ed., Rowman & Littlefield, New York.

Harris, Marvin and Eric B. Ross, 1987, *Death, Sex, and Fertility: Population Regulation in Preindustrial and Developing Societies*, Columbia University Press, New York, chapter 1, 21–35.

Hayden, Brian, 1995, Pathways to power: Principles for creating socioeconomic inequalities, in T. Douglas Price and Gary M. Feinman, eds., *Foundations of Social Inequality*, Plenum, New York, 15–85.

Hendrickx, Stan, 2014, The emergence of the Egyptian state, ch. 1.16 in Colin Renfrew and Paul G. Bahn, eds., *The Cambridge World Prehistory*, Cambridge University Press, New York, 259–278.

Hendrickx, Stan, and Dirk Huyge, 2014, Neolithic and predynastic Egypt, ch. 1.15 in Colin Renfrew and Paul G. Bahn, eds., *The Cambridge World Prehistory*, Cambridge University Press, New York, 240–258.

Henrich, Joseph, 2004, Demography and cultural evolution: How adaptive cultural processes can produce maladaptive losses: The Tasmanian case, *American Antiquity* 69(2), April, 197–214.

2016, *The Secret of Our Success*, Princeton University Press, Princeton.

Henrich, Joseph and Robert Boyd, 2008, Division of labor, economic specialization, and the evolution of social stratification, *Current Anthropology* 49(4), August, 715–724.

Henry, Donald O., 2013, The Natufian and the Younger Dryas, in Ofer Bar-Yosef and François R. Valla, eds., *Natufian Foragers in the Levant: Terminal Pleistocene Social Changes in Western Asia*, International Monographs in Prehistory, Archaeological Series 19, Ann Arbor, MI, 584–610.

Hershkovitz, Israel et al., 2018, The earliest modern humans outside Africa, *Science* 359(6374), 26 January, 456–459.

Hibbs, Douglas A., Jr. and Ola Olsson, 2004, Geography, biogeography, and why some countries are rich and others are poor, *Proceedings of the National Academy of Sciences USA* 101(10), March 9, 3715–3720.

Higham, Charles, 1995, The transition to rice cultivation in southeast Asia, ch. 5 in T. Douglas Price and Anne Birgitte Gebauer, eds., *Last Hunters, First Farmers: New Perspectives on the Prehistoric Transition to Agriculture*, School of American Research Press, Santa Fe, NM, 127–155.

Hill, Kim and A. Magdalena Hurtado, 1996, *Ache Life History: The Ecology and Demography of a Foraging People*, Aldine de Gruyter, New York.

Hillman, Gordon C. and M. Stuart Davies, 1990, Measured domestication rates in wild wheats and barley under primitive cultivation, and their archaeological implications, *Journal of World Prehistory* 4(2), 157–222.

Hillman, Gordon, Robert Hedges, Andrew Moore, Susan Colledge, and Paul Pettitt, 2001, New evidence of lateglacial cereal cultivation at Abu Hureyra on the Euphrates, *The Holocene* 11(4), July, 383–393.

Hiscock, Peter, 2008, *Archaeology of Ancient Australia*, Routledge, New York.

Hoffecker, John F., 2009, The spread of modern humans in Europe, *Proceedings of the National Academy of Sciences USA* 106(38), September 22, 16040–16045.

Hublin, Jean-Jacques et al., 2017, New fossils from Jebel Irhoud, Morocco and the pan-African origin of *Homo sapiens*, *Nature* 546, 8 June, 289–292.

Ibáñez, Juan José, Jesús González–Urquijo, and Xavier Terradas, 2017, The Natufian period in Syria, ch. 78 in Yehouda Enzel and Ofer Bar-Yosef, eds., *Quaternary of the Levant: Environments, Climate Change, and Humans*, online at www.cambridge.org/core, 709–714.

IPCC, 2014, *Climate Change 2014: Synthesis Report*, Core Writing Team, Rajendra K. Pachauri, and Leo A. Meyer, eds., IPCC, Geneva, Switzerland.

Jaang, Li, Zhouyong Sun, Jing Shao, and Min Li, 2018, When peripheries were centres: A preliminary study of the Shimao-centred polity in the loess highland, China, *Antiquity* 92(364), 1008–1022.

Jacobsen, Thorkild, 1976, *The Treasures of Darkness: A History of Mesopotamian Religion*, Yale University Press, New Haven, CT.

Jennings, Justin and Timothy Earle, 2016, Urbanization, state formation, and cooperation: A reappraisal, *Current Anthropology* 57(4), August, 474–493.

Johnson, Allen W. and Timothy Earle, 2000, *The Evolution of Human Societies: From Foraging Group to Agrarian State*, 2nd ed., Stanford University Press, Stanford, CA.

Johnson, Matthew, 2010, *Archaeological Theory: An Introduction*, 2nd ed., Wiley-Blackwell, Oxford.

Jones, Charles I., 2001, Was an industrial revolution inevitable? Economic growth over the very long run, *Advances in Macroeconomics* 1(2), 1–43.

Keeley, Lawrence H., 1988, Hunter-gatherer economic complexity and "population pressure": A cross-cultural analysis, *Journal of Anthropological Archaeology* 7, 373–411.

1991, Ethnographic models for late glacial hunter-gatherers, in N. Barton, A.J. Roberts, and D.A. Roe, eds., *The Late Glacial in Northwest Europe*, Council for British Archaeology, London, 179–190.

1996, *War Before Civilization*, Oxford University Press, New York.

Kelly, Raymond, 2000, *Warless Societies and the Origin Of War*, The University of Michigan Press, Ann Arbor.

Kelly, Robert L., 1992, Mobility/sedentism: Concepts, archaeological measures, and effects, *Annual Review of Anthropology* 21, 43–66.

1995, *The Foraging Spectrum: Diversity in Hunter-Gatherer Lifeways*, Smithsonian Institution, Washington, DC.

2007, *The Foraging Spectrum: Diversity in Hunter-Gatherer Lifeways*, reprinted by Percheron Press, previously published in 1995, Smithsonian Institution Press, Washington, DC.

2013a, *The Lifeways of Hunter-Gatherers: The Foraging Spectrum*, Cambridge University Press, New York.

2013b, From the peaceful to the warlike: Ethnographic and archaeological insight into hunter-gatherer warfare and homicide, in Douglas P. Fry, ed., *War, Peace, and Human Nature: The Convergence of Evolutionary and Cultural Views*, Oxford University Press, New York.

Kelly, Robert L., Todd A. Surovell, Bryan N. Shuman, and Geoffrey M. Smith, 2013, A continuous climatic impact on Holocene human population in the Rocky Mountains, *Proceedings of the National Academy of Sciences USA* 110(2), January 8, 443–447.

Kemp, Barry J., 2006, *Ancient Egypt: Anatomy of a Civilization*, 2nd ed., Routledge, London and New York.

Kennett, Douglas J., 2005, *The Island Chumash: Behavioral Ecology of a Maritime Society*, University of California Press, Berkeley.

2012, Archaic-period foragers and farmers in Mesoamerica, ch. 10 in Deborah L. Nichols and Christopher A. Pool, eds., *The Oxford Handbook of Mesoamerican Archaeology*, Oxford University Press, New York, 141–150.

Kennett, Douglas J. and James P. Kennett, 2006, Early state formation in southern Mesopotamia: Sea levels, shorelines, and climate change, *Journal of Island and Coastal Archaeology* 1(1), 19 August, 67–99.

Kennett, Douglas J., Bruce Winterhalder, Jacob Bartruff, and Jon M. Erlandson, 2009, An ecological model for the emergence of institutionalized social hierarchies on California's Northern Channel Islands, in Stephen Shennan, ed., *Pattern and Process in Cultural Evolution*, University of California Press, Berkeley, 297–314.

Kenoyer, Jonathan Mark, 2014, The Indus civilization, ch. 1.25 in Colin Renfrew and Paul G. Bahn, eds., *The Cambridge World Prehistory*, Cambridge University Press, New York, 407–432.

2019, The Indus tradition: The integration and diversity of Indus cities, keynote address, 52nd Annual Conference of the Indian Archaeological Society, University of Kerala, Thiruvananthapuram, November 7.

Kirch, Patrick V., 1984, *The Evolution of the Polynesian Chiefdoms*, Cambridge University Press, New York.

2010, *How Chiefs Became Kings: Divine Kingship and the Rise of Archaic States in Ancient Hawai'i*, University of California Press, Berkeley, Los Angeles, and London.

Kohler, Timothy A. et al., 2017, Greater post-Neolithic wealth disparities in Eurasia than in North America and Mesoamerica, *Nature* 551, 30 November, 619–623.

2018, Deep inequality: Summary and conclusions, ch. 11 in Timothy A. Kohler and Michael E. Smith, eds., *Ten Thousand Years of Inequality: The*

Archaeology of Wealth Differences, Amerind Studies in Anthropology, University of Arizona Press, Tucson, 289–317.

Kohler, Timothy A. and Michael E. Smith, eds., 2018, *Ten Thousand Years of Inequality: The Archaeology of Wealth Differences*, Amerind Studies in Anthropology, University of Arizona Press, Tucson.

Konrad, Kai A. and Stergios Skaperdas, 2012, The market for protection and the origin of the state, *Economic Theory* 50(2), June, 417–443.

Kouchoukos, Nicholas and Tony J. Wilkinson, 2007, Landscape archaeology in Mesopotamia: Past, present, and future, in Elizabeth C. Stone, ed., *Settlement and Society: Essays Dedicated to Robert McCormick Adams*, Cotsen Institute of Archaeology, University of California-Los Angeles, and The Oriental Institute of the University of Chicago, 1–18.

Kremer, Michael, 1993, Population growth and technological change: One million B.C. to 1990, *Quarterly Journal of Economics* 108(3), August, 681–716.

Kröpelin, S., et al., 2008, Climate-driven ecosystem succession in the Sahara: The past 6000 years, *Science*, new series, 320 (5877), May 9, 765–768.

Krugman, Paul, 1991, *Geography and Trade*, MIT, Cambridge, MA.

Kuijt, Ian and Nigel Goring–Morris, 2002, Foraging, farming, and social complexity in the Pre-Pottery Neolithic of the southern Levant: A review and synthesis, *Journal of World Prehistory* 16(4), 361–440.

Kuijt, Ian and Anna Marie Prentiss, 2009, Niche construction, macroevolution, and the Late Epipaleolithic of the Near East, in Anna Marie Prentiss, Ian Kuijt, and James Chatters, eds., *Macroevolution in Human Prehistory: Evolutionary Theory and Processual Archaeology*, Springer, New York, 253–271.

Kuzmin, Yaroslav V. and Susan G. Keates, 2005, Dates are not just data: Paleolithic settlement patterns in Siberia derived from radiocarbon records, *American Antiquity* 70(4), October, 773–789.

Kyriacou, Andreas P., 2020, *Inequality and Governance*, Routledge, New York.

Lahr, M. Mirazón et al., 2016, Inter-group violence among early Holocene hunter-gatherers of West Turkana, Kenya, *Nature* 529(7586), 21 January, 394–398.

Lambert, Patricia M., 2009, Health versus fitness: Competing themes in the origins and spread of agriculture? *Current Anthropology* 50(5), October, 603–608.

Lambert, Patricia M. and Phillip L. Walker, 1991, Physical anthropological evidence for the evolution of social complexity in coastal Southern California, *Antiquity* 65, 963–973.

LaMotta, Vincent M., 2012, Behavioral archaeology, ch. 4 in Ian Hodder, ed., *Archaeological Theory Today*, 2nd ed., Polity, Malden, MA, 62–92.

Larson, Greger, et al., 2014, Current perspectives and the future of domestication studies, *Proceedings of the National Academy of Sciences USA* 111(17), April 29, 6139–6146.

Leacock, Eleanor, 1992, Women's status in egalitarian society: Implications for social evolution, *Current Anthropology* 33(1), Supplement, February, 225–259.

LeBlanc, Steven A., 1999, *Prehistoric Warfare in the American Southwest*, University of Utah Press, Salt Lake City.

2007, Why warfare? Lessons from the past, *Daedalus* 136(1), Winter, 13–21.

2020, The origins of warfare and violence, in Garrett Fagan, Linda Fibiger, Mark Hudson, and Matthew Trundle, eds., *The Cambridge World History of Violence*, vol. 1, Cambridge University Press, New York, 39–57. DOI: https://doi.org/10.1017/9781316341247.003.

LeBlanc, Steven A. with Katherine E. Register, 2003, *Constant Battles: Why We Fight*, St. Martin's, New York.

Lee, Richard B. and Richard Daly, eds., 1999, *The Cambridge Encyclopedia of Hunters and Gatherers*, Cambridge University Press, New York.

Lipsey, Richard G., Kenneth I. Carlaw, and Clifford T. Bekar, 2005, *Economic Transformations: General Purpose Technologies and Long Term Economic Growth*, Oxford University Press, New York.

Litina, Anastasia, 2014, The geographical origins of early state formation, working paper, Faculty of Law, Economics and Finance, University of Luxembourg.

Liu, Li, 2004, *The Chinese Neolithic: Trajectories to Early States*, Cambridge University Press, New York, ch. 8, 223–238.

2006, Urbanization in China: Erlitou and its hinterland, ch. 9 in Glenn R. Storey, ed., *Urbanism in the Preindustrial World: Cross-Cultural Approaches*, University of Alabama Press, Tuscaloosa, 161–189.

Liu, Li and Xingcan Chen, 2003, *State Formation in Early China*, Duckworth, London.

2012, *The Archaeology of China: From the Late Paleolithic to the Early Bronze Age*, Cambridge University Press, New York.

Liverani, Mario, 2006, *Uruk: The First City*, ed. and trans. Zinab Bahrani and Marc Van de Mieroop, Equinox Publishing, Jakarta, Indonesia.

Locay, Luis, 1989, From hunting and gathering to agriculture, *Economic Development and Cultural Change*, 37(4), July, 737–756.

1997, Population equilibrium in primitive societies, *Quarterly Review of Economics and Finance* 37(4), September, 747–767.

Love, Michael, 2012, The development of complex societies in formative-period Pacific Guatemala and Chiapas, ch. 14 in Deborah L. Nichols and Christopher A. Pool, eds., *The Oxford Handbook of Mesoamerican Archaeology*, Oxford University Press, New York, 200–214.

Lu, Houyuan et al., 2009, Earliest domestication of common millet (Panicum miliaceum) in East Asia extended to 10,000 years ago, *Proceedings of the National Academy of Sciences USA* 106(18), May 5, 7367–7372.

Madella, Marco, and Dorian Q. Fuller, 2006, Palaeoecology and the Harappan civilization of South Asia: A reconsideration, *Quaternary Science Reviews* 25, 1283–1301.

Madeyska, Teresa, 1990, The distribution of human settlement in the extra-tropical Old World 24000–15000 BP, ch. 1 in Clive Gamble and Olga Soffer, eds., *The World at 18000 BP Volume Two: Low Latitudes*, Unwin Hyman, London, 24–37.

Maher, Lisa A., E. B. Banning, and Michael Chazan, 2011, Oasis or mirage? Assessing the role of abrupt climate change in the prehistory of the southern Levant, *Cambridge Archaeological Journal* 21(1), February, 1–29.

Maher, Lisa A., Tobias Richter, and Jay T. Stock, 2012, The Pre-Natufian Epipaleolithic: Long-term behavioral trends in the Levant, *Evolutionary Anthropology* 21, 69–81.

Malthus, Thomas R., 1798 [2004], *An Essay on the Principle of Population*, edited by Philip Appleman, 2nd ed., Norton, New York.

Manning, Katie and Dorian Q. Fuller, 2014, Early millet farmers in the lower Tilemsi Valley, Northeastern Mali, ch. 6 in Chris J. Stevens, Sam Nixon, Mary Anne Murray, and Dorian Q. Fuller, eds., *Archaeology of African Plant Use*, Left Coast Press, Inc., Routledge, Abingdon on Thames, 73–81.

Manning, Katie and Adrian Timpson, 2014, The demographic response to Holocene climate change in the Sahara, *Quaternary Science Reviews* 101, 28–35.

Manzanilla, Linda R., 2014, The basin of Mexico, ch. 2.19 in Colin Renfrew and Paul G. Bahn, eds., *Cambridge World Prehistory*, Cambridge University Press, New York, 986–1004.

Marceau, Nicolas and Gordon Myers, 2006, On the early Holocene: Foraging to early agriculture, *Economic Journal* 116(513), July, 751–772.

Marcus, Joyce, 1998, The peaks and valleys of ancient states: An extension of the dynamic model, ch. 3 in Gary M. Feinman and Joyce Marcus, eds., *Archaic States*, School of American Research Press, Santa Fe, NM, 59–94.

Marcus, Joyce and Kent V. Flannery, 1996, *Zapotec Civilization: How Urban Society Evolved in Mexico's Oaxaca Valley*, Thames & Hudson, London.

Marcus, Joyce and Jeremy A. Sabloff, 2008, Introduction, ch. 1 in Joyce Marcus and Jeremy A. Sabloff, eds., *The Ancient City: New Perspectives on Urbanism in the Old and New World*, School for Advanced Research Press, Santa Fe, NM, 3–26.

Marshall, Yvonne, 2006, Introduction: Adopting a sedentary lifeway, *World Archaeology* 38(2), June, 153–163.

Mas-Colell, Andreu, Michael D. Whinston, and Jerry R. Green, 1995, *Microeconomic Theory*, Oxford University Press, New York.

Matranga, Andrea, 2017, The ant and the grasshopper: Seasonality and the invention of agriculture, Munich Personal RePEc Archive, MPRA Paper No 76626, posted 6 February.

Matsuoka, Yoshihiro, Yves Vigouroux, Major M. Goodman, Jesus Sanchez, Edward Buckler, and John Doebley, 2002, A single domestication for maize shown by multilocus microsatellite genotyping, *Proceedings of the National Academy of Sciences USA* 99(9), 6080–6084.

Mattison, Siobhan M., Eric A. Smith, Mary K. Shenk, and Ethan E. Cochrane, 2016, The evolution of inequality, *Evolutionary Anthropology* 25, 184–199.

Mayewski, Paul A. et al., 2004, Holocene climate variability, *Quaternary Research* 62(3), November, 243–255.

Mayshar, Joram, Omer Moav, and Zvika Neeman, 2017, Geography, transparency, and institutions, *American Political Science Review* 111(3), August, 622–636.

Mayshar, Joram, Omer Moav, and Luigi Pascali, 2022, The origin of the state: Productivity or appropriability? *Journal of Political Economy* 130(4), April, 1091–1144, https://doi.org/10.1086/718372

McCorriston, Joy, 1997, Textile extensification, alienation, and social stratification in Ancient Mesopotamia, *Current Anthropology* 38(4), August/October, 517–535.

McDougall, I., F. H. Brown, and J. G. Fleagle, 2005, Stratigraphic placement and age of modern humans from Kibish, Ethiopia, *Nature* 433(7027), February 17, 733–736.

McManus, Jerry F., 2004, A great grand-daddy of ice cores, *Nature* 429(6992), June 10, 611–612.

Mellars, Paul, 2007, Rethinking the human revolution: Eurasian and African perspectives, in Paul Mellars, Katie Boyle, Ofer Bar-Yosef, and Chris Stringer, eds., *Rethinking the Human Revolution*, McDonald Institute for Archaeological Research, University of Cambridge, UK, 1–11.

Midant-Reynes, Béatrix, 2000, *The Prehistory of Egypt: From the First Egyptians to the First Pharaohs*, Blackwell, Oxford, UK.

Milanovic, Branko, Peter H. Lindert, and Jeffrey G. Williamson, 2011, Pre-industrial inequality, *Economic Journal* 121(551), March, 255–272.

Mithen, Steven, 2003, *After the Ice: A Global Human History, 20,000–5000 BC*, Weidenfeld & Nicolson, London.

Modelski, George, 1999, Ancient world cities 4000–1000 BC: Centre/hinterland in the world system, *Global Society* 13(4), 383–392.

Moeller, Nadine, 2016, *The Archaeology of Urbanism in Ancient Egypt: From the Predynastic Period to the End of the Middle Kingdom*, Cambridge University Press, New York.

Mokyr, Joel, 2002, *The Gifts of Athena: The Historical Origins of the Knowledge Economy*, Princeton University Press, Princeton.

2018, *A Culture of Growth: The Origins of the Modern Economy*, Princeton University Press, Princeton.

Molleson, T. L., 2000, The people of Abu Hureyra, in A. M. T. Moore, G. C. Hillman, and A. J. Legge, 2000, *Village on the Euphrates: From Foraging to Farming at Abu Hureyra*, Oxford University Press, Oxford, 301–324.

Moore, A. M. T., G. C. Hillman, and A. J. Legge, 2000, *Village on the Euphrates: From Foraging to Farming at Abu Hureyra*, Oxford University Press, Oxford.

Moore, Jerry D., 2014, *A Prehistory of South America: Ancient Cultural Diversity on the Least Known Continent*, University Press of Colorado, Boulder.

Moreno-Mayar, J. Victor et al., 2018, Terminal Pleistocene Alaskan genome reveals first founding population of Native Americans, *Nature* 553(7687), 11 January, 203–208.

Mourre, Vincent, Paola Villa, and Christopher S. Henshilwood, 2010, Early use of pressure flaking on lithic artifacts at Blombos Cave, South Africa, *Science*, New Series, 330(6004), October 29, 659–662.

Mundell, Robert, 1968, *Man and Economics: The Science of Choice*, McGraw-Hill, New York.

Murdock, George P. and Douglas R. White, 1969, Standard cross-cultural sample, *Ethnology* 8(4), October, 329–369.

2006, Standard cross-cultural sample: online edition, Social Dynamics and Complexity Working Papers Series, University of California-Irvine, http://escholarship.org/uc/item/62c5co2n

NASA, 2020, Graphic: Carbon dioxide hits new high, https://climate.nasa.gov/climate.../7/graphic-carbon-dioxide-hits-new-high/

Nesbitt, Mark, 2002, When and where did domesticated cereals first occur in southwest Asia?, in R. Cappers, S. Bottema, and U. Baruch, eds., *The Transition from Foraging to Farming in Southwest Asia*, Berlin, ex oriente. 113–132.

Nissen, Hans J., 1988, *The Early History of the Ancient Near East, 9000–2000 BC*, University of Chicago Press, Chicago.

2015, Urbanization and the techniques of communication: The Mesopotamian city of Uruk during the fourth millennium BCE, ch. 6 in Norman Yoffee, ed., *The Cambridge World History vol. III: Early Cities in Comparative Perspective, 4000 BCE–1200 CE* Cambridge University Press, New York, 113–130.

Nissen, Hans J. and Peter Heine, 2009, *From Mesopotamia to Iraq: A Concise History*, translated by Hans J. Nissen, University of Chicago Press, Chicago.

North, Douglass C., 1971, Institutional change and economic growth, *Journal of Economic History* 31(1), March, 118–125.

1978, Structure and performance: The task of economic history, *Journal of Economic Literature* 16(3), September, 963–978.

1981, *Structure and Change in Economic History*, Cambridge University Press, New York.

1990, *Institutions, Institutional Change, and Economic Performance*, Cambridge University Press, New York.

1994, Economic performance through time, *American Economic Review* 84(3), June, 359–368.

2005, *Understanding the Process of Economic Change*, Princeton University Press, Princeton.

North, Douglass C. and Robert Paul Thomas, 1973, *The Rise of the Western World: A New Economic History*, Cambridge University Press, New York.

1977, The first economic revolution, *Economic History Review*, Second Series, 30(2), May, 229–241.

North, Douglass C., John Joseph Wallis, and Barry R. Weingast, 2009, *Violence and Social Orders: A Conceptual Framework for Interpreting Recorded Human History*, Cambridge University Press, New York.

North, Douglass C., John Joseph Wallis, Steven B. Webb, and Barry R. Weingast, eds., 2013, *In the Shadow of Violence: The Problem of Development in Limited Access Societies*, Cambridge University Press, New York.

Nowell, April, 2010, Defining behavioral modernity in the context of Neandertal and anatomically modern human populations, *Annual Review of Anthropology* 39, August 20, 437–452.

Nunn, Nathan, 2021, History as evolution, in Alberto Bisin and Giovanni Federico, eds., *Handbook of Historical Economics*, North-Holland, New York, 41–91.

Oates, Joan, 2014, Prehistory and the rise of cities in Mesopotamia and Iran, ch. 3.7 in Colin Renfrew and Paul G. Bahn, eds., *Cambridge World Prehistory*, Cambridge University Press, New York, 1474–1497.

Olsson, Ola, 2001, The rise of Neolithic agriculture, Working Papers in Economics 57, Department of Economics, University of Gothenburg, September, available at http://ideas.repec.org/p/hhs/gunwpe/0057.html

2005, Geography and institutions: A review of plausible and implausible linkages, *Journal of Economics* 10(1), supplement, 167–194.

Olsson, Ola and Douglas A. Hibbs, Jr., 2005, Biogeography and long-run economic development, *European Economic Review* 49(4), May, 909–938.

Olsson, Ola and Christopher Paik, 2016, Long-run cultural divergence: Evidence from the Neolithic Revolution, *Journal of Development Economics* 122, September, 197–213.

2020, A Western reversal since the Neolithic? The long-run impact of early agriculture, *Journal of Economic History* 80(1), March, 100–135.

Ostrom, Elinor, 1990, *Governing the Commons: The Evolution of Institutions for Collective Action*, Cambridge University Press, New York.

Pandit, Sagar, Gauri Pradhan, and Carel van Schaik, 2017, A model for warfare in stratified small-scale societies: The effect of within-group inequality, *PLoS ONE* 12(12), December 11.

Parker, Geoffrey, 2013, *Global Crisis: War, Climate Change and Catastrophe in the Seventeenth Century*, Yale University Press, New Haven and London.

Peros, Matthew C., Samuel E. Munoz, Konrad Gajewski, and André E. Viau, 2010, Prehistoric demography of North America inferred from radiocarbon data, *Journal of Archaeological Science* 37, 656–664.

Petit J. R., et al., 1999, Climate and atmospheric history of the past 420,000 years from the Vostok ice core, Antarctica, *Nature* 399(6735), June 3, 429–436.

Petrie, Cameron A., et al., 2017, Adaptation to variable environments, resilience to climate change: Investigating land, water and settlement in Indus Northwest India, *Current Anthropology* 58(1), February, 1–30.

2019, Diversity, variability, adaptation and "fragility" in the Indus Civilization, ch. 7 in Norman Yoffee, ed., *The Evolution of Fragility: Setting the Terms*, McDonald Institute for Archaeological Research, University of Cambridge, Cambridge, UK, 109–133.

Pinker, Steven, 2011, *The Better Angels of Our Nature: Why Violence Has Declined*, Viking, New York.

Piperno, Dolores R., 2011, The origins of plant cultivation in the New World tropics: Patterns, process, and new developments, *Current Anthropology* 52 (S4), October, S453–S470.

Piperno, Dolores R. and Bruce D. Smith, 2012, The origins of food production in Mesoamerica, ch. 11 in Deborah L. Nichols and Christopher A. Pool, eds., *The Oxford Handbook of Mesoamerican Archaeology*, Oxford University Press, New York, 151–164.

Polanyi, Karl, 1957, *The Great Transformation: The Political and Economic Origins of Our Time*, Beacon, Boston.

Pollock, Susan, 1999, *Ancient Mesopotamia: The Eden That Never Was*, Cambridge University Press, New York.

2001, The Uruk period in southern Mesopotamia, ch. 6 in Mitchell S. Rothman, ed., *Uruk Mesopotamia and its Neighbors: Cross-Cultural Interactions in the Era of State Formation*, School of American Research Press, Santa Fe, NM, 181–231.

Pomeranz, Kenneth, 2000, *The Great Divergence: Europe, China and the Making of the Modern World Economy*, Princeton University Press, Princeton.

Pool, Christopher A., 2012, The formation of complex societies in Mesoamerica, ch. 12 in Deborah L. Nichols and Christopher A. Pool, eds., *The Oxford Handbook of Mesoamerican Archaeology*, Oxford University Press, New York, 169–187.

Possehl, Gregory L., 1998, Sociocultural complexity without the state: The Indus civilization, ch. 8 in Gary M. Feinman and Joyce Marcus, eds., *Archaic States*, School of American Research Press, Santa Fe, NM, 261–291.

Postgate, Nicholas, 1994, How many Sumerians per hectare? Probing the anatomy of an early city, *Cambridge Archaeological Journal* 4(1), April, 47–65.

Pournelle, Jennifer R., 2007, KLM to CORONA: A bird's-eye view of cultural ecology and early Mesopotamian urbanization, in Elizabeth C. Stone, ed., *Settlement and Society: Essays Dedicated to Robert McCormick Adams*, Cotsen Institute of Archaeology, University of California-Los Angeles, and The Oriental Institute of the University of Chicago, 29–62.

2013, Physical geography, in Harriet Crawford, ed., *The Sumerian World*, Routledge, New York, 13–32.

Pournelle, Jennifer R. and Guillermo Algaze, 2014, Travels in Edin: Deltaic resilience and early urbanism in Greater Mesopotamia, in Augusta McMahon and Harriet Crawford, eds., *Preludes to Urbanism: The Late Chalcolithic of Mesopotamia in Honour of Joan Oates*, McDonald Institute for Archaeological Research, Cambridge, UK, 7–34.

Powell, Adam, Stephen Shennan, and Mark G. Thomas, 2009, Late Pleistocene demography and the appearance of modern human behavior, *Science*, New Series, 324(5932), June 5, 1298–1301.

2010, Demography and variation in the accumulation of culturally inherited skills, in Michael J. O'Brien and Stephen J. Shennan, eds., *Innovation in Cultural Systems: Contributions from Evolutionary Anthropology*, MIT, Cambridge, MA, 137–160.

Powell, Robert, 1996, Stability and the distribution of power, *World Politics* 48 (2), January, 239–267.

2006, War as a commitment problem, *International Organization* 60(1), January, 169–203.

Price, T. Douglas and Ofer Bar-Yosef, 2011, The origins of agriculture: New data, new ideas, *Current Anthropology* 52, Supplement 4, October, S163–S174.

2012, Traces of inequality at the origins of agriculture in the ancient Near East, in T. Douglas Price and Gary M. Feinman, eds., *Pathways to Power: New Perspectives on the Emergence of Social Inequality*, Springer Science +Business Media B.V., Berlin/Heidelberg, 147–168.

Price, T. Douglas and J. A. Brown, eds., 1985, *Prehistoric Hunter-Gatherers: The Emergence of Cultural Complexity*, Academic Publishers, New York, 3–20.

Price, T. Douglas and Gary M. Feinman, eds., 1995, *Foundations of Social Inequality*, Plenum, New York.

eds., 2012, *Pathways to Power: New Perspectives on the Emergence of Social Inequality*, Springer Science+Business Media B.V., Berlin/Heidelberg.

Pryor, Frederic, 1983, Causal theories about the origins of agriculture, *Research in Economic History* 8, 93–124.

1986, The adoption of agriculture: Some theoretical and empirical evidence, *American Anthropologist* 88(4), December, 879–897.

2004, From foraging to farming: The so-called "Neolithic Revolution", in Alexander J. Field, Gregory Clark, and William A. Sundstrom, eds., *Research in Economic History* 22, Elsevier, JAI, August, 1–41.

Purugganan, Michael D. and Dorian Q. Fuller, 2009, The nature of selection during plant domestication, *Nature* 457, 12 February, 843–848.

Putterman, Louis, 2008, Agriculture, diffusion and development: Ripple effects of the Neolithic revolution, *Economica* 75(300), November, 729–748.

2012, *The Good, the Bad, and the Economy: Does Human Nature Rule Out a Better World?* Langdon Street, Minneapolis, MN.

Putterman, Louis and David N. Weil, 2010, Post-1500 population flows and the long-run determinants of economic growth and inequality, *Quarterly Journal of Economics* 125(4), 1627–1682.

Quilter, Jeffrey, 2014, *The Ancient Central Andes*, Routledge, London and New York.

Quilter, Jeffrey and M. Koons, 2012, The fall of the Moche: A critique of claims for South America's first state, *Latin American Antiquity* 23(2), 127–143.

Raftery, Adrian E., Alec Zimmer, Dargan M. W. Frierson, Richard Startz, and Peiran Liu, 2017, Less than 2 °C warming by 2100 unlikely, *Nature Climate Change* 7(9), September, 637–643.

Ratnagar, Shereen, 2016, *Harappan Archaeology: Early State Perspectives*, Primus, Delhi.

Rawls, John, 1971, *A Theory of Justice*, Belknap Press of Harvard University Press, Cambridge, MA.

Rawson, J., 2017, Shimao and Erlitou: New perspectives on the origins of the bronze industry in central China, *Antiquity* 91(355), e5, 1–5.

Reich, David, 2018, *Who We Are and How We Got Here: Ancient DNA and the New Science of the Human Past*, Vintage, New York.

Renfrew, Colin and Paul G. Bahn, eds., 2014, *Cambridge World Prehistory*, Cambridge University Press, New York.

Riahi, Ideen, 2020, How hominin dispersals and megafaunal extinctions influenced the birth of agriculture, *Journal of Economic Behavior and Organization* 175, 227–250.

2021a, Why Eurasia? A probe into the origins of global inequalities, *Cliometrica*, https://doi.org/10.1007/s11698-021-00222-9.

2021b, Animals and the prehistoric origins of comparative development, *European Review of Economic History*, heaao16, https://doi.org/10.1093/ereh/heaao16.

Richards, Michael P., Paul B. Pettitt, Mary C. Stiner, and Erik Trinkaus, 2001, Stable isotope evidence for increasing dietary breadth in the European mid-upper Paleolithic, *Proceedings of the National Academy of Sciences USA* 98 (11), May 22, 6528–6532.

Richerson, Peter, 2013, Human evolution: Group size determines cultural complexity, *Nature* 503, November 21, 351–352.

Richerson, Peter J., Robert Boyd, and Robert L. Bettinger, 2001, Was agriculture impossible during the Pleistocene but mandatory during the Holocene? A climate change hypothesis, *American Antiquity* 66(3), July, 387–411.

Riehl, Simone, Konstantin E. Pustovoytov, Heike Weippert, Stefan Klett, and Frank Hole, 2014, Drought stress variability in ancient Near Eastern agricultural systems evidenced by δ13C in barley grain, *Proceedings of the National Academy of Sciences USA* 111(34), August 26, 12348–12353.

Roberts, Neil, Jessie Woodbridge, Andrew Bevan, Alessio Palmisano, Stephen Shennan, and Eleni Asouti, 2018, Human responses and non-responses to climatic variations during the last Glacial-Interglacial transition in the eastern Mediterranean, *Quaternary Science Reviews* 184, 47–67.

Robinson, Stuart A., Stuart Black, Bruce W. Sellwood, and Paul J. Valdes, 2006, A review of palaeoclimates and palaeoenvironments in the Levant and Eastern Mediterranean from 25,000 to 5000 years BP: Setting the environmental background for the evolution of human civilisation, *Quaternary Science Reviews* 25, 1517–1541.

Robson, Arthur J., 2001, The biological basis of economic behavior, *Journal of Economic Literature* 39(1), March, 11–33.

2010, A bioeconomic view of the Neolithic transition, *Canadian Journal of Economics* 43(1), February, 280–300.

Robson, Arthur J. and Hillard Kaplan, 2006, The economics of hunter-gatherer societies and the evolution of human characteristics, *Canadian Journal of Economics* 39(2), May, 375–398.

Roche, Kevin R., Michèle Müller–Itten, David N. Dralle, Diogo Bolster, and Marc F. Müller, 2020, Climate change and the opportunity cost of conflict, *Proceedings of the National Academy of Sciences USA*, 117(4), January 28, 1935–1940.

Rohling, Eelco J. et al., 2002, Rapid Holocene climate changes in the eastern Mediterranean, in Fekri A. Hassan, ed., *Droughts, Food and Culture: Ecological Change and Food Security in Africa's Later Prehistory*, Kluwer Academic/Plenum, New York, 35–46.

Roland, T. P., et al., 2015, The 5.2 ka climate event: Evidence from stable isotope and multi-proxy palaeoecological peatland records in Ireland, *Quaternary Science Reviews* 124, September 15, 209–223.

Rowley-Conwy, Peter, 2001, Time, change and the archaeology of hunter-gatherers: How original is the 'Original Affluent Society'? ch. 3 in Catherine Panter-Brick, Robert H. Layton, and Peter Rowley-Conwy, eds., *Hunter-Gatherers: An Interdisciplinary Perspective*, Cambridge University Press, Cambridge, 39–72.

Rowthorn, Robert, Ricardo Andrés Guzmán, and Carlos Rodríguez–Sickert, 2014, The economics of social stratification in premodern societies, *Journal of Mathematical Sociology* 38(3), 19 June, 175–202.

Rowthorn, Robert and Paul Seabright, 2010, Property rights, warfare, and the Neolithic transition, Ecole d'économie de Toulouse, working paper 10-207, November; also IDEI working paper no. 654, November.

Sahlins, Marshall, 1958, *Social Stratification in Polynesia*, University of Washington Press, Seattle.

1972, *Stone Age Economics*, Aldine de Gruyter, New York.

Sahlins, Marshall and Elman R. Service, eds., 1960, *Evolution and Culture*, University of Michigan Press, Ann Arbor.

Sanderson, Stephen K., 1990, *Social Evolutionism: A Critical History*, Basil Blackwell, Oxford.

1999, *Social Transformations: A General Theory of Historical Development*, expanded ed., Rowman & Littlefield, Boulder, CO.

Sandweiss, D. H., K. A. Maasch, and D. G. Anderson, 1999, Transitions in the mid-Holocene, *Science* 283, January 22, 499–500.

Savard, Manon, Mark Nesbitt, and Martin K. Jones, 2006, The role of wild grasses in subsistence and sedentism: New evidence from the northern Fertile Crescent, *World Archaeology* 38(2), June, 179–196.

Schneider von Deimling, Thomas, Andrey Ganopolski, Hermann Held, and Stefan Rahmstorf, 2006, How cold was the Last Glacial Maximum? *Geophysical Research Letters* 33(14), July.

Schönholzer, David, 2020, The origin of the incentive compatible state: Environmental circumscription, working paper, Institute for International Economic Studies, Stockholm Univeristy, February 12.

Schulz, Jonathan F., Duman Bahrami–Rad, Jonathan P. Beauchamp, and Joseph Henrich, 2019, The Church, intensive kinship, and global psychological variation, *Science* 366(6466), November 8, eaau5141.

Scott, James C., 2017, *Against the Grain: A Deep History of the Earliest States*, Yale University Press, New Haven and London.

Service, Elman R., 1962, *Primitive Social Organization: An Evolutionary Perspective*, 1st ed., Random House, New York.

1971, *Primitive Social Organization: An Evolutionary Perspective*, 2nd ed., Random House, New York.

1975, *Origins of the State and Civilization: The Process of Cultural Evolution*, Norton, New York.

Shelach-Lavi, Gideon, 2015, *The Archaeology of Early China: From Prehistory to the Han Dynasty*, Cambridge University Press, New York.

Shennan, Stephen, 2001, Demography and cultural innovation: A model and its implications for the emergence of modern human culture, *Cambridge Archaeological Journal* 11(1), 5–16.

2008, Population processes and their consequences in early Neolithic Central Europe, in Jean-Pierre Bocquet-Appel and Ofer Bar-Yosef, eds., *The Neolithic Demographic Transition and Its Consequences*, Springer Science +Business Media B.V., Berlin/Heidelberg, 315–329.

2012, Darwinian cultural evolution, ch. 2 in Ian Hodder, ed., *Archaeological Theory Today*, 2nd ed., Polity, Malden, MA, 15–36.

2018, *The First Farmers of Europe: An Evolutionary Perspective*, Cambridge University Press, New York.

Sima, Adriana, Andre Paul, and Michael Schulz, 2004, The Younger Dryas: An intrinsic feature of the Late Pleistocene climate change at millennial time-scales, *Earth and Planetary Science Letters* 222(3–4), 741–750.

Sinopoli, Carla M., 2015, Ancient South Asia cities in their regions, ch. 15 in Norman Yoffee, ed., *The Cambridge World History Volume III: Early Cities in Comparative Perspective*, 4000 BCE–1200 CE Cambridge University Press, Cambridge, UK, 319–342.

Smith, Bruce D., 1998, *The Emergence of Agriculture*, Scientific American Library, New York.

    2001, Documenting plant domestication: The consilience of biological and archaeological approaches, *Proceedings of the National Academy of Sciences USA* 98(4), February 13, 1324–1326.

    2011, The cultural context of plant domestication in eastern North America, *Current Anthropology* 52(S4), October, S471–S484.

Smith, Michael E., 2009, V. Gordon Childe and the urban revolution: A historical perspective on a revolution in urban studies, *Town Planning Review* 80(1), 3–29.

Smith, P., 1991, Dental evidence for nutritional status in the Natufians, in O. Bar-Yosef and F. R. Valla, eds., *The Natufian Culture in the Levant*, International Monographs in Prehistory, Ann Arbor, MI, 425–433.

Smith, Patricia and Liora Kolska Horwitz, 2007, Ancestors and inheritors: A bioanthropological perspective on the transition to agropastoralism in the southern Levant, ch. 14 in Mark N. Cohen and Gillian M. M. Crane-Kramer, eds., *Ancient Health: Skeletal Indicators of Agricultural and Economic Intensification*, University Press of Florida, Gainesville, 207–222.

Smith, Vernon L., 1975, The primitive hunter culture, Pleistocene extinction, and the rise of agriculture, *Journal of Political Economy* 83(4), August, 727–756.

Soffer, Olga and Clive Gamble, eds., 1990, *The World at 18000 BP*, Volume One: High Latitudes, Unwin Hyman, London.

Spencer, Charles S., 2010, Territorial expansion and primary state formation, *Proceedings of the National Academy of Sciences USA*, 107(16), April 20, 7119–7126.

Spencer, Charles S. and Elsa M. Redmond, 2004, Primary state formation in Mesoamerica, *Annual Review of Anthropology* 33, 173–199.

Stanish, Charles, 2001, The origin of state societies in South America, *Annual Review of Anthropology* 30, 41–64.

Steckel, Richard H., 2010, Inequality amidst nutritional abundance: Native Americans on the Great Plains, *Journal of Economic History* 70(2), June, 265–286.

Stein, Gil, 1994, Economy, ritual, and power in 'Ubaid Mesopotamia, ch. 3 in Gil Stein and Mitchell S. Rothman, eds., *Chiefdoms and Early States in the Near East: The Organizational Dynamics of Complexity*, Monographs in World Archaeology No. 18, Prehistory Press, Madison, WI, 35–46.

Steinkeller, Piotr, 2015a, Labor in the early states: An early Mesopotamian perspective, in Piotr Steinkeller and Michael Hudson, eds., *Labor in the Ancient World*, The International Scholars Conference on Ancient Near Eastern Economics 5, Dresden, ISLET, 1–36.

    2015b, The employment of labor on national building projects in the Ur III period, in Piotr Steinkeller and Michael Hudson, eds., *Labor in the Ancient*

World, The International Scholars Conference on Ancient Near Eastern Economics 5, ISLET, Dresden, 137–236.

2018, Comments on Guillermo Algaze, Entropic cities: The paradox of urbanism in Ancient Mesopotamia, *Current Anthropology* 59(1), February, 46–47.

Steward, Julian H., 1955, *Theory of Culture Change: The Methodology of Multilinear Evolution*, University of Illinois Press, Urbana, IL.

Stiner, Mary C., 2001, Thirty years on the 'broad spectrum revolution' and Paleolithic demography, *Proceedings of the National Academy of Sciences USA* 98(13), June 19, 6993–6996.

Stiner, Mary C., Natalie D. Munro, and Todd A. Surovell, 2000, The tortoise and the hare: Small-game use, the broad-spectrum revolution, and Paleolithic demography, *Current Anthropology* 41(1), February, 39–73.

Stiner, Mary C., Natalie D. Munro, Todd A. Surovell, Eitan Tchernov, and Ofer Bar-Yosef, 1999, Paleolithic population growth pulses evidenced by small animal exploitation, *Science*, New Series, 283(5399), January 8, 190–194.

Stone, Elizabeth C., 2017, How many Mesopotamians per hectare? in Yağmur Heffron, Adam Stone, and Martin Worthington, eds., *At the Dawn of History: Ancient Near Eastern Studies in Honour of J. N. Postgate*, volume 2, Eisenbrauns, Winona Lake, IN, 567–582.

2018, The trajectory of social inequality in ancient Mesopotamia, ch. 9 in Timothy A. Kohler and Michael E. Smith, *Ten Thousand Years of Inequality: The Archaeology of Wealth Differences*, University of Arizona Press, Tucson, 230–261.

Straus, Lawrence Guy, 1996, The archaeology of the Pleistocene-Holocene transition in southwest Europe, ch. 5 in L. G. Straus, B. B. Ericksen, J. M. Erlandson, and D. R. Yesner, eds., *Humans at the End of the Ice Age: The Archaeology of the Pleistocene-Holocene Transition*, Plenum Press, New York, 83–99.

Sugiyama, Saburo, 2012, Ideology, policy, and social history of the Teotihuacan state, ch. 15 in Deborah L. Nichols and Christopher A. Pool, eds., *The Oxford Handbook of Mesoamerican Archaeology*, Oxford University Press, New York, 215–229.

Sun, Zhouyong, et al., 2017, The first Neolithic urban center on China's north Loess Plateau: The rise and fall of Shimao, *Archaeological Research in Asia* 14, 33–45.

Symposium on intergenerational wealth transmission and inequality in premodern societies, 2010, various authors, *Current Anthropology* 51(1), February, 1–126.

Tallavaara, Miikka, Miska Luoto, Natalia Korhonen, Heikki Järvinen and Heikki Seppä, 2015, Human population dynamics in Europe over the Last Glacial Maximum, *Proceedings of the National Academy of Sciences USA* 112(27), July 7, 8232–8237.

Tanno, Ken-ichi and George Willcox, 2006, How fast was wild wheat domesticated? *Science* 311, March 31, 1886.

Temin, Peter, 2012, *Unified Growth Theory* by Oded Galor, *Journal of Interdisciplinary History* 43(1), Summer, 78–79.

Tierney, Jessica E., Jiang Zhu, Jonathan King, Steven B. Malevich, Gregory J. Hakim, and Christopher J. Poulsen, 2020, Glacial cooling and climate sensitivity revisited, *Nature* 584(7822), August 26.

Tol, Richard S. J. and Sebastian Wagner, 2010, Climate change and violent conflict in Europe over the last millennium, *Climatic Change* 99(1–2), March, 65–79.

Trigger, Bruce G., 1998, *Sociocultural Evolution*, Blackwell, Oxford.

2003, *Understanding Early Civilizations*, Cambridge University Press, New York.

2006, *A History of Archaeological Thought*, 2nd ed., Cambridge University Press, New York.

Umbeck, John R., 1981, *A Theory of Property Rights with Application to the California Gold Rush*, The Iowa State University Press, Ames.

UNFCCC (United Nations Framework Convention on Climate Change), 2015, Paris agreement, https://unfccc.int/process-and-meetings/the-paris-agreement/the-paris-agreement

Ur, Jason, 2012, Southern Mesopotamia, ch. 28 in D. T. Potts, ed., *A Companion to the Archaeology of the Ancient Near East*, Blackwell, Hoboken, NJ, 533–555.

2013, Patterns of settlement in Sumer and Akkad, in Harriet Crawford, ed., *The Sumerian World*, Routledge, New York, 131–155.

2014, Households and the emergence of cities in ancient Mesopotamia, *Cambridge Archaeological Journal* 24(2), June, 249–268.

Ur, Jason, Philip Karsgaard, and Joan Oates, 2007, Early urban development in the Near East, *Science* 317(5842), August 31, 1188.

Valla, François R., H. Khalaily, N. Samuelian, F. Bocquentin, A. Bridault, and R. Rabinovich, 2017, Eynan (Ain Mallaha), ch. 34 in Yehouda Enzel and Ofer Bar-Yosef, eds., *Quaternary of the Levant: Environments, Climate Change, and Humans*, online at www.cambridge.org/core, 295–301.

Van de Mieroop, Marc, 1997, *The Ancient Mesopotamian City*, Oxford University Press, Oxford.

Varian, Hal R., 1992, *Microeconomic Analysis*, 3rd ed., Norton, New York.

2019, *Intermediate Microeconomics: A Modern Approach*, 9th ed., Norton, New York.

Vitzthum, Virginia J., 2008, Evolutionary models of women's reproductive functioning, *Annual Review of Anthropology* 37, 53–73.

Volk, Anthony A. and Jeremy A. Atkinson, 2013, Infant and child death in the human environment of evolutionary adaptation, *Evolution and Human Behavior* 34, 182–192.

Weber, Max, 1968, *Economy and Society: An Outline of Interpretive Sociology*, vol. I, edited by Guenther Roth and Claus Wittich, University of California Press, Berkeley, Los Angeles, and London, 54–56.

Webster, Gary S., 1990, Labor control and emergent stratification in prehistoric Europe, *Current Anthropology* 31(4), August–October, 337–366.

Weide, Alexander, et al., 2021, The association of arable weeds with modern cereal habitats: Implications for reconstructing the origins of plant cultivation in the Levant, *Environmental Archaeology*, published online February 18. www.tandfonline.com/doi/abs/10.1080/14614103.2021.1882715?journalCode=yenv20

Weisdorf, Jacob L., 2003, Stone age economics: The origins of agriculture and the emergence of non-food specialists, Discussion Paper 03-34, Institute of Economics, University of Copenhagen, available at www.econ.ku.dk/okojwe/
　2005, From foraging to farming: Explaining the Neolithic revolution, *Journal of Economic Surveys* 19(4), September, 561–586.
　2009, Why did the first farmers toil? Human metabolism and the origins of agriculture, *European Review of Economic History* 13(2), August, 157–172.
Weiss, Ehud, Mordechai E. Kislev, and Anat Harmann, 2006, Autonomous cultivation before domestication, *Science* 312, June 16, 1608–1610.
Weiss, Ehud, Wilma Wetterstrom, Dani Nadel, Ofer Bar–Yosef, and Bruce D. Smith, 2004, The broad spectrum revisited: Evidence from plant remains, *Proceedings of the National Academy of Sciences USA* 101(26), June 29, 9551–9555.
Wengrow, David, 2006, *The Archaeology of Early Egypt: Social Transformations in North–East Africa, 10,000 to 2650 BC*, Cambridge University Press, New York.
Wiessner, Polly and Akii Tumu, 1998, *Historical Vines: Enga Networks of Exchange, Ritual, and Warfare*, Smithsonian Institution Press, Washington, DC.
Wilkinson, Tony J., 2013, Hydraulic landscapes and irrigation systems of Sumer, in Harriet Crawford, ed., *The Sumerian World*, Routledge, New York, 33–54.
Willcox, George, 2012, Searching for the origins of arable weeds in the Near East, *Vegetation History and Archaeobotany* 21(2), March, 163–167. DOI 10 .1007/s00334-011-0307-1
Williams, Alan N., 2013, A new population curve for prehistoric Australia, *Proceedings of the Royal Society: Biological Sciences* 280(1761), June 22, 1–9.
Williamson, Oliver E., 1985, *The Economic Institutions of Capitalism*, Free Press, New York.
Wills, W. H., 1988, Early agriculture and sedentism in the American Southwest: Evidence and interpretations, *Journal of World Prehistory* 2(4), December, 445–488.
Winchell, Frank, et al., 2018, On the origins and dissemination of domesticated sorghum and pearl millet across Africa and into India: A view from the Butana Group of the far eastern Sahel, *African Archaeological Review* 35, 483–505.
Winterhalder, Bruce and Douglas J. Kennett, 2006, Behavioral ecology and the transition from hunting and gathering to agriculture, ch. 1 in Douglas J. Kennett and Bruce Winterhalder, eds., *Behavioral Ecology and the Transition to Agriculture*, University of California Press, Berkeley, 1–21.
　2009, Four neglected concepts with a role to play in explaining the origins of agriculture, *Current Anthropology* 50(5), October, 645–648.
Winterhalder, Bruce, Douglas Kennett, Mark Grote, and Jacob Bartuff, 2010, Ideal free settlement of California's Northern Channel Islands, *Journal of Anthropological Archaeology* 29, 469–490.

Wittfogel, Karl A., 1957, *Oriental Despotism: A Comparative Study of Total Power*, Yale University Press, New Haven, CT.

Wood, James W., 1998, A theory of preindustrial population dynamics: Demography, economy, and well-being in Malthusian systems, *Current Anthropology* 39(1), 99–135.

Woodward, Jamie, 2014, *The Ice Age: A Very Short Introduction*, Oxford University Press, New York.

Wright, Henry T., 1977, Recent research on the origin of the state, *Annual Review of Anthropology* 6, 379–397.

   1981, The southern margins of Sumer: Archaeological survey of the area of Eridu and Ur, in Adams, Robert McC., ed., *Heartland of Cities: Surveys of Ancient Settlement and Land Use on the Central Floodplain of the Euphrates*, University of Chicago Press, Chicago, 295–338.

Wright, Rita P., 2013, Sumerian and Akkadian industries: Crafting textiles, in Harriet Crawford, ed., *The Sumerian World*, Routledge, New York, 395–418.

Wu, Qinglong, et al., 2016, Outburst flood at 1920 BCE supports historicity of China's Great Flood and the Xia dynasty, *Science* 353(6299), 5 August, 579–582.

Yang, Xiaoyan et al., 2012, Early millet use in northern China, *Proceedings of the National Academy of Sciences USA* 109(10), March 6, 3726–3730.

Yoffee, Norman, 2005, *Myths of the Archaic State: Evolution of the Earliest Cities, States, and Civilizations*, Cambridge University Press, New York.

Yoffee, Norman, ed., 2015, *The Cambridge World History Volume III: Early Cities in Comparative Perspective, 4000 BCE–1200 CE*, Cambridge University Press, Cambridge, UK.

   ed., 2019, *The Evolution of Fragility: Setting the Terms*, McDonald Institute for Archaeological Research, University of Cambridge, UK.

Yoffee, Norman with Nicola Terrenato, 2015, Introduction: A history of the study of early cities, ch. 1 in Norman Yoffee, ed., *The Cambridge World History vol. III: Early Cities in Comparative Perspective, 4000 BCE–1200 CE*, Cambridge University Press, New York, 1–24.

Younger, Stephen M., 2008, Conditions and mechanisms for peace in precontact Polynesia, *Current Anthropology* 49(5), 927–934.

Yu, Shi-Yong, Xue-Xiang Chen, and Hui Fang, 2019, Inferring inequality in prehistoric societies from grave sizes: A methodological framework, *Archaeological and Anthropological Sciences* 11, 4947–4958.

Zahid, Jabran H., Erick Robinson, and Robert L. Kelly, 2016, Agriculture, population growth, and statistical analysis of the radiocarbon record, *Proceedings of the National Academy of Sciences USA*, 113(4), January 26, 931–935.

Zeder, Melinda A. and Bruce D. Smith, 2009, A conversation on agricultural origins: Talking past each other in a crowded room, *Current Anthropology* 50(5), October, 681–691.

Zhang, David D., C. Y. Jim, George C-S Lin, Yuan-Qing He, James J. Wang, and Harry F. Lee, Climatic change, wars and dynastic cycles in China over the last millennium, *Climatic Change* 76(3–4), June, 459–477.

Zhang, David D., Jane Zhang, Harry F. Lee, and Yuan-Qing He, 2007, Climate change and war frequency in eastern China over the last millennium, *Human Ecology* 35, 403–414.

Zhao, Zhijun, 2011, New archaeobotanic data for the study of the origins of agriculture in China, *Current Anthropology* 52(S4), October, S295–S306.

Zuo, Xinxin et al., 2017, Dating rice remains through phytolith carbon-14 study reveals domestication at the beginning of the Holocene, *Proceedings of the National Academy of Sciences USA* 114(25), June 20, 6486–6491.

Author Index (Abridged)

Subject Index

Abu Hureyra settlement,
    169–172, 174
    Abu Hureyra 2 site, 262–263
Ache society, 62–63
Africa
    agricultural development, in sub-Saharan
        region, 161, 202–204
    African Humid Period, 202
    domestication of plants, 202–203
    of sorghum, 203
    sedentism in, archaeological evidence of,
        150–151
African Humid Period (AHP), 202
agents, in methodological approaches to
        economic prehistory, 25
    classification of agents, 29
    heterogeneity of agents, 29
aggregate production function, inequality
        and, 246–249
    propositions for, 247
agricultural heterogeneity, 211–212
agriculture, development of, 3–4. *See also*
        climate change; cultivation
    agricultural heterogeneity, 211–212
    biological endowments, by region,
        209–211
    in China, 161, 197–199
        in North China, 197–198
        in South China, 198–199
    city-states and, 38
        agricultural productivity, 470
        in theoretical approaches, 446–447
    conceptual approach to, 157–162

cultivation, 35–36, 105, 112, 118,
        120–121, 124, 148, 158–175
    of cereal, 373, 383–384, 450–451
    climate change and, 211
    demography and, 190–195
    during Holocene, 190
    during Ice Age, 184
    India, 204–206
    Japan, 207–208
    New Guinea, 201–202
    North America, 204, 207–208
    North China, 197–199
    at production site, 175–178
    South America, 200–201
    Sub-Saharan Africa, 202–204
    during Younger Dryas, 185–190,
        259–260, 526–527
domestication of animals, 165
domestication of plants, in sub-Saharan
        Africa, 202–203
economic growth and, 4, 496–497
    in economic literature, 39
food production sites, 175–178
    climate changes as influence on,
        177–178
    site quality, 176
in foraging societies, 164–167
in *Guns, Germs, and Steel*, 47–49
Holocene period and, 70–71, 190
during Ice Age, 7, 184, 206–207
in India, 204–206
inequality and, 231
    labor-limited farming, 236

565

sedentism and, 111
in Southern Mesopotamia city-states
constraints on, 399
food production and, 394–399
during Uruk period, 377–378
welfare measures and, 520–521
South America
agricultural development in, 200–201
in Andes region, 201
domestication of plants, 200
city-states in, 467–469
archaeological evidence of, 468
early settlements, 468
Moche state, 468–469, 478–479
Tiwanaku state, 469
Wari state, 469
sedentism in, archaeological evidence of, 151
Upper Paleolithic period, 78
Southern Mesopotamia, city-states in, 366–391. *See also* 'Ubaid period; Uruk period
archaeological background of, 368–369
through radiocarbon dating, 369
causal hypotheses for, 380–390
climate change, 381–382
food supply, 381
manufacturing and trade, 376–377, 387–390
migration patterns, 381–382
religious practices, 385
taxation, of cereals, 382–384, 389–390
warfare, 385
climate change in, 368
causal hypotheses for, 381–382
conceptual approach to, 392–394
historical development of, 367
inequality in, 431–432
during 'Ubaid period, 371
land endowments in, 431
manufacturing and trade in, 426–427
causal hypotheses for, 376–377, 387–390
as function of commons productivity, 413
labor allocation in zero-profit equilibrium, 403–404
population dynamics influenced by, in transition from agriculture, 424–425
scale economies and, 400
taxation of, 406–407

during 'Ubaid period, 371–372
urbanization as influence on, 400
during Uruk period, 376–377
methodological approach to, 366–368
migration between, 431–432
causal hypotheses for, 381–382
during Uruk period, 375
overview of, 366–369
population dynamics, 420–425, 431–432
long run equilibrium, 420–422
Malthusian population model, 420
short run equilibrium, 422
transition from agriculture to manufacturing, 424–425
during 'Ubaid period, 370–371
post-Uruk period (5100–4350 BP), 379–380
Early Dynastic period (4900–4350 BP), 379–380
Jemdet Nasr period (5100–4900 BP), 377–379
warfare during, 380
pre-'Ubaid period (before 8000 BP), 369–370
agricultural development during, 369
social stratification in
constraints on, 399
food production and, 394–399
during Uruk period, 377–378
taxation in, 405–413, 427–428
cartel enforcement and, 433
causal hypotheses for, 382–384, 389–390
commons productivity, 413
elite taxation equilibrium, 408
of manufacturing labor, 406–407
during Uruk period, 377
topography, 369–370
wetlands, 372–373, 429–431
urbanization in, 399–405
manufacturing influenced by, 400
during Uruk period, 367–368
warfare and, 476
causal hypotheses for, 385
during post-Uruk period, 380
during Uruk period, 378–379
welfare implications in, 414–419, 428
decreased commons productivity, 414
envelope theorem, 415–416
global effects, 417
local effects, 417
urbanization as influence on, 414–415

wealth. *See also* economic inequality;
    inequality
  embodied, 230
  material, 230
  relational, 230
welfare dynamics, 512–522
  biological factors, 513–514
  definition of welfare, 513
  inequality and, 514–515, 517–518
  sedentism and, 517, 520
  social stratification factors, 520–521
  in Southern Mesopotamia city-states,
    414–419, 428
    decreased commons productivity, 414
    envelope theorem, 415–416
    global effects, 417
    local effects, 417
    urbanization as influence on, 414–415
  standards of living and, 517–519

wetlands, in Southern Mesopotamia,
    372–373, 429–431
winning through intimidation, in elite
    warfare, 308

Younger Dryas period,
    35–36, 526–527
  agricultural development during,
    159–161, 163, 185–190
  demography in,
    192–195
    in Southwest Asia, 168–172, 174–175
  climate change during,
    185–190
  inequality during, 259–262
  sedentism during, 120–123

zero-profit equilibrium,
    403–404